THE FOREIGN POLICY OF VICTORIAN E

1830-1902

THE
FOREIGN POLICY
OF VICTORIAN
ENGLAND

1830-1902

KENNETH BOURNE

READER IN INTERNATIONAL HISTORY, UNIVERSITY OF LONDON

CLARENDON PRESS · OXFORD

1970

Oxford University Press, Ely House, London W.1

GLASGOW NEW YORK TORONTO MELBOURNE WELLINGTON
CAPE TOWN SALISBURY IBADAN NAIROBI DAR ES SALAAM LUSAKA ADDIS ABABA
BOMBAY CALCUTTA MADRAS KARACHI LAHORE DACCA
KUALA LUMPUR SINGAPORE HONG KONG TOKYO

LC 75-543411

Rpr. p. 162-
1971

MADE AND PRINTED IN GREAT BRITAIN
BY WILLIAM CLOWES AND SONS, LIMITED
LONDON AND BECCLES

ACKNOWLEDGEMENTS

I HAVE had most valuable help in the preparation of this book. My friends and colleagues, Dr. F. R. Bridge, Mr. R. J. Bullen, and Mr. Gareth Davies read some or all of the chapters and saved me from many errors of fact and interpretation. Mr. Bullen also suggested to me several of the more interesting documents.

I have also to acknowledge the gracious permission of Her Majesty the Queen to make use of material from the Royal Archives at Windsor. Crown copyright material from the Public Record Office in London appears by permission of the Controller of Her Majesty's Stationery Office. For permission to examine papers and to print items I have also to thank:

The Marquess of Salisbury and Christ Church, Oxford
The Earl of Clarendon and the Bodleian Library, Oxford
The Broadlands Trustees
The Times
Lord Primrose and the Trustees of the National Library of Scotland
The National Trust
The Trustees of the British Museum
Birmingham University Library

CONTENTS

PART I: THE FOREIGN POLICY OF VICTORIAN ENGLAND

PART II: SELECTED DOCUMENTS
(The page numbers in parentheses indicate references in Part I)

viii   *Contents*

x   *Contents*

Part I

THE FOREIGN POLICY
OF VICTORIAN ENGLAND

I

INTRODUCTION: THE PRAGMATIC FOUNDATIONS OF BRITISH FOREIGN POLICY, 1815-1830

'BRITISH Foreign Ministers', wrote Sir Edward Grey, 'have been guided by what seemed to them to be the immediate interest of this Country without making elaborate calculations for the future.'[1] Even so, the historian has been able to point to 'that remarkable continuity of ideas which runs through our foreign policy during the nineteenth century'.[2] The explanation is obvious. Britain's interests, and therefore British foreign policy, were conditioned by circumstances and attitudes which changed only very gradually in the course of the century.

History and geography had determined that by the beginning of the nineteenth century Great Britain should have acquired the greatest commercial empire the world had ever seen. Politically she was a satiated power. So far as Britain was concerned the Congress of Vienna in 1814-15 had amply confirmed the limits of her ambitions as indeed the measure of her power. Her political objectives were largely, perhaps exclusively, defensive: to maintain the material bases of her success. But her commercial appetite *was* insatiable, and the attempt to feed it thereafter forced an ever enlarging, though usually reluctant, commitment to political control over large areas of the world. Few Englishmen would have denied that their country's pursuit of trade was vigorous; to most foreigners it was downright aggressive. Yet when, in the 1820s, Spanish-American Governments defaulted on their loans and their British creditors complained to the Foreign Office, they were told quite bluntly that such risks were the price of high interest rates. Later

[1] Viscount Grey of Fallodon, *Twenty-Five Years* (London, 1925), i. 6.
[2] E. Jones Parry, 'British Foreign Policy in the Nineteenth Century', *History*, xxiii (1938-9), 323.

foreign secretaries like Palmerston were not quite so rigidly unsympathetic but fundamentally their attitude remained the same throughout the century. The Foreign Office must reserve some discretion to intervene, especially where legal rights had been infringed. But it was their business, the Foreign Office believed, to promote and ensure reasonable conditions of international trade, not to give unreserved support to the speculative or unscrupulous among their nationals (Doc. 46).[3]

This policy was never quite consistently applied. The impossibility of subjecting to it all her far-flung, and, at the lower levels, often rather seedy agents and representatives was but one disadvantage of an empire that spanned the world. But British statesmen throughout the nineteenth century considered it to be their duty to protect and expand international trade for the benefit of others as well as for themselves. The adoption of Free Trade principles, indeed, became for governments and people alike virtually an article of faith (Docs. 29 and 38). Yet this policy had some pretty odd results. In spite of all their admirable reservations about supporting direct trading or financial ventures, British governments genuinely tended to believe that the expansion of Free Trade was positively beneficial, not only to the economy of Great Britain and similar western nations, but also to the welfare of barbarians like the Chinese or the Egyptians (Doc. 64). Hence they persisted in imposing upon such backward peoples the so-called 'unequal treaties', exercising through them a degree of interference in commercial and judicial matters which they would have regarded as utterly intolerable if anyone had attempted to impose them on their own country.[4]

To the Chinese this 'economic imperialism' remains an historic wrong which seems to merit permanent hostility. At the time, however, the British did not hesitate in their conviction that such areas must be opened up to trade and the manner in which it was done seemed to them far preferable to actual colonial acquisition. It was less costly and less likely to stimulate political rivalry with the other Great Powers (Doc. 64). In India, by contrast, the chronic instability of the British frontier and the persistent approach, or en-

[3] Leland Hamilton Jenks, *The Migration of British Capital to 1875* (London, 1963), pp. 117–18; D. C. M. Platt, *Finance, Trade, and Politics in British Foreign Policy, 1815–1914* (Oxford, 1968), pp. 34–53.

[4] See below, pp. 44–5, 47, and 81–3.

croachment as the British regarded it, of another Great Power, Russia, obliged them, however reluctantly, to protect what they had by territorial conquest rather than by diplomatic influence. But the virtually complete subjugation of the Indian sub-continent was the exception, however glaring. The ideal pattern of British expansion, of which the Chinese policy was one of the most successful examples and which also embraced Africa and Latin America, was what has come to be known as 'informal empire'.[5]

'Informal empire' meant quite simply the expansion of trade and influence so far as possible without incurring the expense and responsibility of colonial sovereignty. Great Britain's ability to profit from this policy depended fundamentally upon her generally unrivalled commercial power and her world-wide naval superiority. Her leading position as a manufacturing nation and in the carrying trade, and not least her system of financial credit, made Free Trade especially convenient to her, and colonial markets and sources of supply, in the formal sense, almost totally unnecessary. The principal exception was the possession of strategic bases like Hong Kong. But these bases allowed Great Britain to rely heavily upon naval power for the promotion and the defence of her interests without having to acquire large hinterlands. Gunboat diplomacy could compel reluctant countries and peoples to open their doors to western trade, while vast battlefleets warned off would-be rivals among the Great Powers from making intolerable political threats.

It was this 'policing' role that was implied in the rather extravagant term *Pax Britannica*. Its most effective and beneficial achievement was undoubtedly the suppression of the slave trade. Yet to the primitive and more unruly peoples of the overseas world the British peace seemed very heavy-handed and arbitrarily imposed. It was also a very uneasy one so far as concerned the other Great Powers. Before the century was out the progress of the industrial revolution among the Western Powers—in America as well as in Europe—had utterly undermined the foundations of Britain's policy, confronted her with serious commercial and naval rivals, and helped persuade her to abandon her informal empire in favour of more jingoistic imperialism.

It would in any case be highly misleading to suggest that the

[5] See especially the chapter on 'The Spirit of Victorian Expansion', in Ronald Robinson and John Gallagher, with Alice Denny, *Africa and the Victorians: The Official Mind of Imperialism* (London, 1961), pp. 1–26.

British had ever felt quite invulnerable. The end of the wars in Europe and America in 1814–15 had left their rivals—enemy or ally —with little or no force at sea and themselves with a fleet far larger than even their riches could maintain in peacetime. But the advance of technology and invention—steam propulsion, iron hulls, and shell guns—though strongly resisted by the British Admiralty, inexorably out-dated their accumulated battlefleets and offered an opportunity for old rivals, and in particular France, to renew their challenge. For most of the century that challenge was much less serious than nervous Englishmen professed to fear. Britain's resources, of wealth and ship-building, always made it possible for her to out-run her rivals when she wished. But she did not believe that she could spend so freely upon both naval and land forces. Contrary to popular belief, Great Britain was by no means a contemptible power on land. In the years of peace she maintained an active army of between 123,000 (1819) and 187,000 (1880). And during the Crimean War her total force of actives and reserves reached over half a million—much more than Prussia's and nearly as many as those of France and Austria, though of course only about a third of Russia's. But after 1870 all the Continental powers rapidly out-stripped the British Army. By the end of the century the Boer War had brought the total British force of actives and reserves to about a million. But in 1900 Austria's was over two million, France's and Russia's about three, and Germany's nearly four. Moreover, in the first half of the nineteenth century, the vast extent and scattered nature of Britain's possessions and responsibilities had stretched her military resources beyond the limit. Unable to duplicate the Indian Army elsewhere and with a large part of her regular army tied down in Ireland, Great Britain found it impracticable from the very first to maintain satisfactory garrisons even in the scattered bases along her global lifeline, let alone on the mainland of North America. In 1841 there were seventy-eight battalions in India and the colonies, six in passage, and, household troops apart, a mere nineteen in the British Isles. At the outbreak of the Crimean War just over half the active army was still tied down overseas. This difficulty amply confirmed the wisdom of the policy of informal empire; to increasing numbers of people it even suggested that they would do well to shed the vast, unprofitable, and barely defensible dominions like Canada. But here the practical statesmen of Great Britain faced a real dilemma. Just as they were forced to expand their control in

India partly out of fear of Russia's opportunism, so they believed too that they were compelled to retain comparatively worthless possessions like Canada, partly out of fear that its annexation to the American Union would dangerously boost the power of an already troublesome rival.

Thus, however limited Great Britain's territorial objectives were for most of the century, she was generally opposed to the expansion of other powers. Partly this followed from the desire to keep open against exclusive colonialism the trading door which she had so often and so expensively unlocked. Partly too it was designed to check the growth of any potential rival. But the constant watchfulness that this demanded also put an increasingly heavy strain upon the apparently overwhelming power of the Royal Navy. And the cost of Britain's continuing commercial success was an increasing dependence on vast imports of such things as cotton and wheat to feed the appetites of her factories and her manpower. Even so Britain generally remained in a better position to fend off any challenge, than others were to present it. The one great exception, the one great fear of government after government, was that of a coalition of her enemies, and especially one of Europe and America.

Britain's circumstances dictated a particular attitude towards the continent of Europe. Her special position was her island security. But this only sheltered her from the Continent, it did not *isolate* her. What she lacked in Europe were aggressive ambitions, not substantial interests. Her empire—formal or informal—did not eliminate or even depreciate the importance of her European connections. Rather it stressed the inter-dependence of her global and her European policies. Europe remained for the whole of the century one of Britain's biggest markets and the greatest threat to her security.

Great Britain could bring her special power to bear at many of the points which were of particular strategic importance to her. The Royal Navy could generally expect to command or at least neutralize such vital positions as the Channel ports, the Dardanelles, the Mediterranean, and even the Baltic. It could also counter pretty effectively the imperial and naval rivalries offered by France and Russia. But against the greatest danger of all the navy was quite insufficient. The consolidation of Europe under one potentially hostile régime was rightly considered fatal to Britain's political, economic, and strategic security. In that event she would risk being shut out of one of her richest markets, faced with an antagonistic political system, and menaced simultaneously from an overwhelming number of offensive bases. To counter this awful possibility it was essential for Britain to have an auxiliary on the mainland to complement the offshore strength of the Royal Navy. But a permanent ally was constitutionally and practically inconvenient. Only very special and very temporary circumstances, such as actual war, could justify such binding obligations.

The obstinacy with which British foreign secretaries resisted supposedly tempting offers of understanding and alliance, marked them off from their colleagues overseas perhaps more strikingly than anything else. One of the arguments they used—that permanent undertakings might ultimately conflict with overwhelming interest and in particular that an advance undertaking to go to war might be opposed by parliament when the occasion arose—obviously had a great deal of force in it. Foreign ambassadors often suspected, however, that the difficulties which England's parliamentary institutions and popular elections were supposed to present were grossly exaggerated. Even Tsarist Russia, after all, had to adjust its foreign policy to the mood of public opinion. But no other European Power had its policy so systematically scrutinized. The principal feature in this scrutiny was the production and use made of printed documents, especially the collections of diplomatic correspondence misleadingly known as Blue Books. Until the early nineteenth century these were intended, with the exception of such things as texts of treaties which the government was constitutionally bound to produce, to persuade parliament to meet some specific government request, such as a vote of supply. But they soon became a major part of the government's publicity apparatus. George Canning is usually credited with beginning this game and Palmerston with bringing it to its Golden Age. But some doubt has been cast on the accuracy of describing Canning as an innovator.[6] The differences between Castlereagh and Canning, in this respect as in others, were probably those of manner rather than of intention. Castlereagh tended to be cautious and apologetic; Canning more confident in appealing to the country over the heads of his enemies.

It was not customary to produce diplomatic correspondence while the negotiations were still in progress, and, of course, Blue Books could always be edited by the government of the day. But the enor-

---

[6] See Sheila Lambert's review article, 'A Century of Diplomatic Blue Books', *Historical Journal*, x (1967), 125-31.

mous amount of detailed information they contained provided the basis for *post facto* criticism on a wide scale. Gladstone once complained during a debate on foreign affairs in 1856: 'there are many things that the English people will do. They will sign petitions; they will attend meetings; they will get up agitations; they will pay taxes, and double taxes if need be. But Blue Books they will not read.'[7] Nevertheless, with all their limitations, the Blue Books systematically exposed the conduct of British foreign policy to public criticism to a degree that had no parallel among the other Powers of the nineteenth century. The Blue Books themselves were publicly for sale at reasonable prices and the parliamentary debates were not only public but their record too was easily available in print. The Blue Books may or may not have been read, but there were plenty of political publicists, like Gladstone himself, ready to circulate their revelations through the newspaper, journal, and pamphlet presses and governments themselves often used the Press, at home and abroad, to fend off or counter domestic and foreign criticism. Palmerston in particular excelled at influencing newspapers, not only to support government policy, but also to answer the hostile criticisms of his colleagues. By 1815 commercial success had made the Press in general much less prone to direct financial subsidy. It was commonly recognized that good newspapers, with an established sale, would not squander public confidence by accepting money, and bad papers were not worth buying. Even so, their opinions could still be influenced to an important degree by supplying them not only with privileged information but also with leading articles. Palmerston certainly provided both of these services for the evening paper, the *Globe*, and, until it changed allegiance in 1848, for the *Morning Chronicle* too (Doc. 11). But Palmerston had no monopoly of influence over even the ministerial journals, and in the 1840s they served, to some extent, to air the dissatisfaction of his Cabinet colleagues as much as his own point of view. And the most powerful newspaper in the country, *The Times*, quarrelled with the Whig Government in 1834 and thereafter was generally hostile to Palmerston and inclined to favour Aberdeen.

The Golden Age of Palmerstonian publicity came after the 1832 Reform Act, which more than doubled the electorate by adding half a million voters and greatly increased party interest in newspapers. From the late 1880s, however, the pattern of publicity

[7] *Hansard's Parliamentary Debates*, 3rd series, cxliii. 146.

changed rapidly. The much greater enfranchisement accomplished by the second and third Reform Acts of 1867 and 1885 forced procedural changes and more effective control of parties in Parliament which made Blue Books on such a scale as they had achieved in Palmerston's day much less important. Considerably less diplomatic correspondence was therefore produced in the period down to 1914. In any case the new Yellow Press, in part the consequence of the removal of the last 'tax on knowledge', the paper duty, in 1861, and the passage of the Education Act of 1870, would probably have been too impatient to digest much more.

Whatever the effects of parliamentary and public opinion, all British governments found it inconvenient and objectionable to seek an ally. It was more flexible and more valuable to support a Balance of Power policy in Europe; that is to say, to participate actively in that acknowledged system by which the European Powers constantly regrouped themselves and intervened to check the actual or potential aggressor among their own number. Carried in the eighteenth century to the extreme of almost mechanical adjustment to every petty alteration in the *status quo*, this system became a distinctly warlike and uneconomic one for Britain, involving her in almost every continental contest at considerable financial expense. Worse still, it failed to fend off the gravest danger which Britain had faced since the Armada—the wars of the French Revolution and Napoleon. For more than a generation Britain faced, and barely survived, the occupation by an enemy of the areas in Europe of most vital importance to her and her political and economic exclusion from Napoleon's great 'Continental System'.

The cataclysm of the French wars, however, did not induce British governments to abandon the Balance of Power policy. They sought rather to rid it of its qualities of continual meddling and ultimate ineffectiveness. The keynote here was set by William Pitt the Younger, not in his rather unsuccessful war policy, but in the plans he made for peace. What he envisaged in those plans was the establishment of a concert among the Powers in order to provide Europe with a system of international security, the reassertion of a new and more effective distribution of power in Europe in order to contain future French aggression, and a guarantee between the Powers to maintain it (Doc. 1). Since he did not live to see Napoleon's final defeat, this 'legacy' of Pitt's fell to Lord Castlereagh to apply to the great peace settlement which was made at Paris and

Vienna in 1814–15 after Napoleon's defeat. The Vienna Settlement brought Great Britain extraordinarily few territorial gains for a victor. But their location emphasized Britain's major pre-occupations: the Cape of Good Hope, Heligoland, Malta, Mauritius, St. Lucia, Trinidad, Tobago, and, as a protectorate, the Ionian Islands. The benefit of the European provisions was also considerable. Britain's special interests in the Low Countries, which were her vestibule to the trade of Europe and the potential base for the invasion of England, were specifically safeguarded; a sort of territorial *cordon sanitaire* was erected around France by consolidating and strengthening the states of the Netherlands, Switzerland, and Piedmont, and the position of Prussia on the Rhine. At the same time particular care was taken to curb the jealous vengeance of such allies as Prussia and to preserve the Balance of Power more genuinely by maintaining France as a Great Power and by guarding against the advance into Europe of the new colossus, Russia. In addition, therefore, the centre of Europe was strengthened against aggression from both east and west by consolidating the power of Austria in Germany and in Italy. But what would have most impressed Pitt and what gave the Settlement its special character was that the whole complex treaty system was endowed with the quality of a sort of higher international law and that the Concert of the Powers agreed to maintain it not only by their promises but also by holding further special congresses and conferences from time to time.

Unfortunately what was achieved at Vienna was by no means a perfect settlement of Europe's political problems and the Congress System which followed failed to provide proper means of making to it the changes and improvements which the passage of time revealed to be necessary. The fatal flaw in the Vienna Settlement was its constricting effect on the internal systems of individual states rather than its direct effect on the relations between states. But this weakness in turn put an intolerable strain upon those relations, undermined the Concert of Europe, and eventually destroyed the Settlement itself. The Settlement was by no means as reactionary as it is often depicted—though it did sponsor the restoration of rulers or systems which were, or were soon to become, reactionary. But the Concert's concept of the 'repose' which it wished to maintain by the Congress System was essentially a static one. The dynamic forces of the age—liberalism and nationalism—too often found themselves thwarted or repressed and therefore sought fulfilment in more violent ways. The Congresses, which might have been used to adjust the Vienna Settlement to the needs which these movements had exposed, were devoted instead to reinforcing the system of international repression. At Troppau in 1820 the Eastern Powers of Austria, Prussia, and Russia formally adopted the policy of interference against revolutions which they deemed might disturb international peace; at Laibach in 1821 Austria was empowered so to intervene in the Italian peninsula; and at Verona in 1822 France was authorized to intervene against revolution in Spain. These decisions were all taken in spite of objections from Great Britain. It was not that Castlereagh or his Government favoured liberalism or nationalism, least of all in the earlier years of Lord Liverpool's Administration (1812–27). They too were addicted to 'repose'. But neither had they intended to tie their country to a conservative alliance and to lose the flexibility and relative independence which were supposed to be the great merits of their new Balance of Power policy.

Castlereagh had made known his country's reservations about the way things were going in a famous State Paper of 5 May 1820 (Doc. 2). But he was very unwilling to take any step which would break up the Concert which he had played so large a part in setting up. What followed, therefore, was a process of slow, reluctant, and piecemeal disengagement from the Congress System. He cautiously absented himself from Troppau and sent instead his half-brother, the Ambassador in Vienna. It was only the fear that Russia might seize the opportunity of a Greek revolt against the Turks to threaten British interests in the Near East, that obliged him to envisage attending in person at the next congress in Verona. But shortly before it was due to meet the strain of his responsibilities finally overcame him and on the morning of 12 August 1822 he cut his throat.

Castlereagh's successor at the Foreign Office was his old rival, George Canning. Canning's objectives were pretty much the same as his predecessor's, but his character and his circumstances were very different. Castlereagh was shy and clumsy; Canning was bold and eloquent. Castlereagh had been popular at court and unpopular in the country (as Leader of the House of Commons he had had to defend the Administration's repressive domestic policy); Canning was disliked by the King and by many of his Cabinet colleagues, but was immensely popular among the people at large. Castlereagh had been pushed into disagreements with Britain's allies reluctantly by the pressure of public opinion and to some extent by his appreciation of Britain's basic interests; Canning set himself vigorously in the van of that opinion and ruthlessly pursued the interests of his country. Thus, while Castlereagh was regarded to the last by the statesmen of Europe as truly one of them, Canning soon came to be regarded by the Austrian Chancellor, Metternich, as the devil incarnate and the evil genius of revolution.

So far as revolution was concerned Metternich plainly exaggerated Canning's purposes. He was, after all, a Tory, however 'liberal' a one. But it was certainly true that he had no liking for what he called the 'predominating areopagitical spirit' which sought to bend all Europe to the selfish and short-sighted ends of the legitimist *status quo*.[8] According to a colleague he had long since in 1818 declaimed against the periodical meetings which would 'necessarily involve us deeply in all the politics of the Continent'.[9] Once in office therefore Canning set out to regain that freedom of action which he thought alone would permit England to pursue her proper interests. He declined to go to Verona and the Duke of Wellington, who went in his stead, was soon withdrawn. 'So things are getting back to a wholesome state again', Canning concluded. 'Every nation for itself, and God for us all.'[10] But Canning exaggerated his achievement. Britain's participation in the Congress System had come to an abrupt end. But that alone did not defeat its reactionary purposes. Doubts on the Tsar's own part, reinforced by the arguments of Metternich, prevented Russia from intervening on behalf of revolution in Greece or against it in Spain. Spain instead was left open to the intervention of France whose policies were now falling more and more into the hands of conservatives and out of alignment with England. In January 1823 Louis XVIII announced his intention of rescuing his fellow Bourbon monarch with an army of one hundred thousand men.

Canning, and many in England who thought as he did, were at once reminded of the years of war which England had waged in the seventeenth and eighteenth centuries to prevent the union of French and Spanish power under the Bourbons. They also feared the

---

[8] R. Therry, ed., *The Speeches of George Canning* (London, 1836), v. 63.

[9] C. W. Vane, *Correspondence, Despatches and other Papers of Viscount Castlereagh* (London, 1853), 3rd series, iv. 57.

[10] Augustus George Stapleton, *George Canning and his Times* (London, 1859), p. 370.

extension of French intervention to Portugal and Spanish America, in both of which Britain had important commercial interests. Britain was powerless to prevent the French advance across the Pyrenees in April 1823. In any case the French gave reasonably satisfactory assurances about their future behaviour with regard to both Spain and Portugal. On the question of the Spanish colonies, however, they remained ominously silent.

For centuries the British had eyed with jealousy the restricted markets of the Spanish colonial empire. Large inroads were opened up illegally, but the legal opportunities remained very sparse indeed until Napoleon provoked Spain into war against him and obliged her to accommodate an unfamiliar ally. Quite possibly it was this new trade alone which saved Great Britain from disaster when Bonaparte's Continental System cut her off from European markets. It is not at all surprising, then, that the British should have deplored the prospect of the old Spanish barriers being set up again on the restoration of peace and just when Britain's industry would need more, not fewer, outlets for her goods now that the demands of war were past. Castlereagh had been anxious enough about this. Still more so was Canning, who spoke for England's commercial interests and was for a time Member of Parliament for the great Atlantic port of Liverpool. What saved the British from this unhappy prospect was not the gratitude or loyalty of their Spanish ally, but rebellion in Latin America and the rebels' reliance on supplies and sympathy from England.

Faced with this situation Lord Liverpool's Government had all along urged upon Spain and upon the rebels the wisdom of a compromise settlement which would preserve the semblance of Spanish sovereignty and guarantee at the same time the continuation of Britain's trade. But Spain remained intransigent. The British, on their side, were most reluctant to resolve the issue unilaterally by recognizing revolutionary and particularly republican régimes. Indeed, contrary to Metternich's belief, not even Canning approved of what he, too, called 'Jacobin democracy'. But England could not afford to wait for ever upon the faint prospect of Spain's conversion to good sense. Shortly before his death Castlereagh himself seems to have decided that time was running out. For England to wait much longer would risk losing the favour of Latin America to a dangerous political or commercial rival without gaining the gratitude of Spain. Spain, rather, was already looking to the reactionary camp in Europe for political and even military assistance against her rebellious colonies. By 1823 all these dangers had been brought into the foreground by a series of rebel victories which demonstrated the hopelessness of any reconquest by Spain alone. In March 1822 President Monroe of the United States announced his decision to recognize the rebel Governments and by the end of January the following year American recognition had been extended to Mexico, Colombia, Chile, and the Rio de la Plata. Then, after some inconclusive Russian meddling, France's intervention in Spain in the summer of 1823 opened up a serious prospect that she might extend her assistance to the New World.

Britain's overwhelming seapower could have been interposed very effectively against this threat in the Atlantic. But Canning soon revealed himself as very unwilling to face the threat alone. Instead he turned for support to Britain's old enemy and present rival, the United States of America. It was plainly true that in contrast to the other Powers of Europe, Britain and the United States had relatively liberal systems of government and a common economic and political interest in safeguarding Latin America from the exclusive and repressive control of the conservative Powers. On the other hand they were very uneasy neighbours in North America, where they had fought a bitter but inconclusive war in 1812–14, and in Latin America they regarded each other as the ultimate rivals for political and commercial ascendancy. The American Secretary of State, John Quincy Adams, who was certainly no friend of Britain's, suspected that the real object of Canning's approach was to pull back the lead the Americans had taken with their recognition policy and to score a propaganda victory in Latin America by bringing in the United States as a 'cockboat in the wake of a British man-of-war'. It was very much this suspicion which checked any firm response on the part of the American Government. Britain refused to follow in the wake of the United States by first conceding recognition as the Americans demanded they should; and the United States refused to come in Britain's wake by making any agreement without that concession. Instead the Americans substituted for co-operation with Great Britain a unilateral assertion by President Monroe in his famous Message of 2 December 1823, which prohibited European assistance to Spain in her struggle against the rebels and, indeed, any transfer or extension of European possessions in the New World.

Probably Monroe's declaration was as ill-suited to Canning's real motives as it was to the power of the United States to enforce it. The motives which Adams suspected were certainly present and Canning's pose as a true friend of the American republic was not convincing. But the manner of his approaches and the haphazard way in which he followed them up suggest that he had nothing very subtle in mind. It is important to remember that in the summer of 1823 he was isolated, not only in European councils, but very largely also at the English Court. The noisy threats he was making against France met with a good deal of criticism at home, and certainly he could not have made them good in the face of the King's opposition. One authority has therefore suggested that in his approach to the United States he was turning 'instinctively to the one country where his actions had been viewed with approval'.[11] Quite probably Canning was searching around for some means of drumming up popular support against the reactionaries in England and quite possibly too, since his approach was secret and informal, even to present them with a *fait accompli*. Naturally he lost enthusiasm when he met only with a cautious and even suspicious response from the United States. He was saved instead by the French desire not to call his bluff, if bluff it really was. Early in October, Polignac, the French Ambassador in London, attached his signature to a memorandum giving all the undertakings that Canning required with respect to Portugal and Spain, and to the Spanish colonies.

By the end of 1823 Great Britain and the United States had completed their contribution to the accomplishment of Latin American independence and had also verbally committed themselves to the active maintenance of that independence. But the opportunity for positive and friendly co-operation between them was now lost in an atmosphere of mutual suspicion, and the checking of the conservative alliance in the New World left the field free for Anglo-American rivalry to flourish. Here the advantages lay very largely with Britain. She alone had the goods the Latin Americans wanted and the credit terms which were a necessary condition for international trade in that part of the world. The Polignac Memorandum, moreover, was backed by an awe-inspiring array of naval force; while the Monroe Doctrine, as the United States' neglect of other European intrusions soon made apparent, was merely so much paper. Britain's only major disadvantage was her failure to recognize the

[11] Charles Kingsley Webster, *Britain and the Independence of Latin-America, 1812–1830* (London, 1938), i. 47.

new states. Her interests had obliged Castlereagh to extend a commercial recognition in May 1822, but a lingering reluctance to make a final break with Spain or to encourage republicanism anywhere held him back from any further step. Canning, too, undoubtedly felt much the same about international Jacobinism, but he was realist enough not to get too optimistically involved in the many monarchical plots and schemes which men like San Martin and Simon Bolivar put up in that part of the world. In a little more than a year after Monroe's Message Canning and his Prime Minister, with arguments about the danger of a 'Trans-Atlantic League' led by the United States, had extracted from their Tory colleagues and from the King their reluctant assent to a policy of formal recognition. Within a few years more, certainly by 1830, Britain had largely won the battle for commerce and influence in Latin America and the unpleasant prospect of the Trans-Atlantic League had quite disappeared from view. In reality it had never been a serious possibility. Doubts about their Latin American neighbours, as well as the local preoccupations which more than absorbed their tiny military strength, made the United States Government singularly unenthusiastic about such schemes. Nonetheless the misunderstandings of the period between the two English-speaking nations were very unfortunate, especially in the legacy of mutual suspicion which they contributed to the history of Anglo-American relations.

In Europe Canning was soon claiming to have 'called the New World into existence, to redress the balance of the Old' (Doc. 3). He had undoubtedly checked the 'AREOPAGITICAL SPIRIT' of the conservative Powers in the New World. The Royal Navy had also enabled Britain's strength to be felt in Portugal. Here too revolutionaries and reactionaries had struggled for the ascendancy and England and France for the predominant influence at court. In Lisbon Canning only just managed to maintain British predominance and to support King John under a compromise constitution. With Brazil he was rather more successful, helping to arrange the peaceful separation of the former colony and incidentally preserving monarchical institutions there and opening up the way for an attack on the slave trade. In both cases the presence of the British fleet in the Tagus was of vital importance. In the first it provided a refuge for the King and a base from which he could recover his position. In the second, the threat of its withdrawal helped bring the Portuguese to reason. But when King John died in March 1826 and his son, Pedro, preferred to become Emperor of Brazil, this left the Portuguese throne to Pedro's eight-year-old daughter, surrounded by reactionary relatives and under yet another constitution. French intrigues this time were more easily overcome. They had already openly admitted the priority of British interest in the Polignac Memorandum and the suicidal reaction of the Spanish legitimists had made them regret even their intervention in Madrid. But Ferdinand of Spain was soon forcibly interfering in Portuguese affairs by helping the reactionaries to organize armed raids across the border. When Portugal appealed for help therefore, Canning rushed out a force of 4,000 troops and threatened Spain with war (Doc. 3). This operation was made possible by the presence of the British warships in the Tagus, and a respectable force was usually kept there, to preserve British influence in Lisbon, until the middle of the century. Occasionally, as in 1846 and 1847, the British would threaten to withdraw the squadron and leave the Portuguese Government at the mercy of their opponents. In this way the Portuguese were sometimes persuaded to act as they would not otherwise have done (Doc. 42). But British seapower could operate in this manner only on the periphery of Europe. Elsewhere the conservative alliance kept Europe firmly in its grip and made Canning's boast seem idle and extravagant.

The position into which Canning's exit from the Congress System had led Great Britain well illustrated the fundamental strengths and weaknesses of her general circumstances. Her insular separation and her naval power allowed her to operate effectively in isolation only where water dominated communications—overseas in America or on the periphery of Europe. Beyond this, Canning realized, Britain could issue little more than defiance while she was isolated and the conservative alliance remained intact. Fortunately for him the Austrians and the Russians were already falling out and over a question in which England had a considerable interest—the Greek revolt against the Turks.

Stimulated over a long period by the example of the French Revolution and more immediately by disturbances in the Danubian provinces of Moldavia and Wallachia, revolt broke out in March 1821 against the Turks in the Greek Morea. Outraged by the ruthless slaughter of Turkish minorities, the Turkish Government in Constantinople retaliated by hanging the Greek Patriarch and massacring the Greek community in the city. In January 1822 the

Greeks proclaimed their independence and for a time continued to score successes against the Turks. But the tide turned in 1823-5 with the outbreak of civil war among the rebels and the intervention of the Sultan's powerful vassal in Egypt, Mehemet Ali. From this point it was clear that without the intervention of the Powers the Greek cause would be lost.

Britain's main interests in the Near East were clear enough: to check the expansion of Russia, to protect the Mediterranean and its communications with the Near and Middle East against the intrusion of Russian naval power, and to preserve the security of a large area susceptible to British economic penetration. The maintenance of the Turkish Empire, with its axis at Constantinople and the Straits, was therefore of vital importance to England. Unfortunately the Turk's cause was a difficult one to make popular, especially when he dealt so ferociously and at the same time so ineffectively with the rebellious Christians and when the Russian bogey was disguised by the Tsar's pose as the would-be liberator of the Greeks. At Verona in 1822 the British representatives, while on the brink of breaking with Austria over Italy and Spain, had nonetheless supported Metternich in his refusal to listen to the Greeks. In March the following year Canning recognized the Greeks as belligerents, but only in order to make it easier to defend British shipping in the vicinity.

Canning would no doubt have agreed with Castlereagh that 'barbarous as it is, Turkey forms in the system of Europe a necessary evil.'[12] But to Canning it must also have seemed tragic that substantial interests and considerable popular sympathy should have appeared to be at such odds. Somehow a solution to this dilemma had to be found, and found without risking war with Russia. Here Canning undoubtedly enjoyed great good fortune, but it was another evidence of his genius that when presented with the opportunity he both recognized and successfully seized it.

While Turkey's obstinate resistance to all compromise and a simultaneous growth of popular philhellenism in Britain was threatening to undermine British policy in the Near East, the alignment between Austria and Russia against revolution was also breaking on the rocks of Alexander's sympathy for the Greeks and of Russia's material interest in eroding the frontiers of the Turkish

---

[12] Quoted in R. W. Seton-Watson, *Britain in Europe, 1789-1914* (Cambridge, 1937), p. 61.

Empire. At Laibach and Verona Alexander had been persuaded by Metternich that the Greek revolt was merely an extension of the Jacobin infection in Europe. The Tsar continued to quarrel with the Sultan over the treatment of his Christian subjects and his patience was severely strained, too, by Britain's unwillingness to co-operate in putting pressure on the Turks. At the end of 1824 he decided to abandon all attempts to reach an agreement with the British Government. But at this stage he had no intention of going to war with Turkey since he still agreed with Metternich that this would open the floodtide of revolution. However, with Mehemet Ali's intervention in 1824, popular sympathy for the Greeks spread rapidly both in Russia and in the western countries of Britain and France. The conservative alliance convened an ambassadorial conference at St. Petersburg (1824–5), but could still find no solution for the Tsar's dilemma, even though both he and Metternich were now prepared to compromise. Then, most ominously for Russia's Byzantine and Orthodox pretensions, the Greeks formally appealed for protection and mediation in July 1825 not to Russia or the Powers, but directly to Great Britain.

The signs are that Alexander was becoming restive about losing face in the Balkans and irritated by the patronizing advice that came so monotonously from Vienna. His ambassador in London—or rather the ambassador's more famous wife, Princess Lieven—was already speculating upon the possibility of a *détente* with the mercurial Canning. The Tories naturally continued to stress the importance of supporting Turkey against Russia, but it was not unreasonable to suppose that Canning might respond more positively to the growing philhellenism of the British people. But Canning had now at last been reconciled to the King and he did not leap at the opportunity which came from Russia. What finally converted him was the death of Alexander and, after the brief interval of the Decembrist revolt, the succession of Nicholas I as Tsar in December 1825. Urged on by the Lievens in London, Canning cleverly despatched the Duke of Wellington to St. Petersburg in February 1826 in order to convey his country's congratulations and to concert a policy over the Greek Question.

Canning's immediate objective was to avert a Russo-Turkish war which would open up dangerous opportunities for Russia to pursue her expansionist ambitions just when opinion in Great Britain would make resistance difficult if not impossible. By an alignment with Russia Canning might expect both to restrain her and to demonstrate to the Porte (the Turkish Government) the wisdom of making concessions. The St. Petersburg Protocol of 4 April 1826 gave him the essence of what he wanted. Nicholas and Wellington agreed that Greece should form an autonomous state, only nominally under the sovereignty of the Sultan, and that Russia should support Britain's mediation for this purpose at Constantinople. Both Powers renounced any territorial or commercial advantages in the prospective settlement, though the precise territorial boundaries were to be left open for further negotiation. The lack of any agreement over this last point in particular left an air of dangerous uncertainty. More serious, in view of Canning's main purpose, was that the agreement did not exclude the possibility of a war between Russia and Turkey, but specifically provided for intervention in the Greek Question 'jointly or separately'. Still, the omission gave the best chance of bringing the Sultan to his senses and making force unnecessary. In any case there was no mistaking the general importance of what had been done. Canning had broken the unity of the conservative alliance by separating Russia from Austria, and in place of the isolation of Great Britain he had substituted the near isolation of Metternich and Austria. Given that the conservative alliance was inimical to Britain's interests and that a freedom of action suited her better, he had better reason to exclaim in triumph now than early in 1823 after the withdrawal from Verona. It was, moreover, hardly his fault that Wellington had gone further to meet Nicholas than had ever been intended and that in the Greek Question an important tactical advantage had been surrendered to the Russians.

Shortly before he reached the agreement with Wellington Nicholas had prepared the ground for exploiting his initiative by sending to Turkey a new and separate ultimatum which carefully avoided any mention of the Greeks. He demanded the restoration of the privileges formerly enjoyed by the Danubian provinces; recognition of the autonomy of Serbia (which Russia had hitherto neglected to support); and immediate negotiations about various other Russian claims. The Turks quickly accepted this ultimatum and all Russian demands were eventually conceded by the Convention of Akkerman of 7 October 1826. But the convention made no mention of the Greek Question; in that affair, it was clear, the Sultan's objective was merely to gain time. In June he had ordered

2—F.P.V.E.

the massacre of his tyrannous palace guard, the Janissaries, as a necessary preliminary to the military reform of his Empire and the successful repression of the Greek revolt.

Canning was quite well aware that through the ineptitude of Wellington and the obstinacy of the Turks his scheme to curb Russia by British co-operation was being ruined and that Britain rather was being forced more and more into a position where she would be obliged to support Russia. Canning's answer to the problem was to attempt to reinforce the original idea behind Wellington's mission by extending the invitation at the end of 1826 to the other Powers to join the St. Petersburg Protocol. Metternich, as Canning expected, refused to contemplate the coercion implied in that Protocol and Prussia followed Austria's lead. But in France, where popular philhellenism was also running high, even the reactionary Charles X fell in with it, and at his insistence the Protocol was cemented into a treaty in London on 6 July 1827. Unfortunately there was no checking the drift into active intervention against the Turks. The Greeks were making no headway in their fight and Turkish obstinacy was flourishing on unaccustomed military successes. In August the Turks refused the promises demanded by the Powers and at Russia's insistence the allied fleets mounted a blockade in order to coerce them without actually engaging in hostilities. A direct clash followed almost inevitably from these incompatible objectives. On 20 October 1827 Turkish irritation broke out into actual firing and within a few hours the Turkish and Egyptian fleets had both been annihilated in the harbour of Navarino by the combined squadrons of Britain, France, and Russia. On 31 November the Porte repudiated the Convention of Akkerman; on 18 December the Sultan pronounced a Holy War against Russia; and at length, on 26 April 1828, Russia declared war.

Canning did not live to witness this unhappy course of events. In April 1827 Liverpool had retired and Canning had succeeded as Prime Minister. He by no means relaxed his control of foreign affairs—he was succeeded at the Foreign Office by a cypher, Lord Dudley—and his assumption of the premiership became all the more burdensome since it further strained his relations with the extreme Tories and led them to quit the Government. Canning's health was undermined by the strain and by overwork, and on 8 August 1827 he died. His successor, after the brief interlude of the Goderich Government, was Wellington. Wellington now pronounced Navarino to be 'an untoward event'. Certainly Canning would not have wished such a battle; and the outbreak of the Russo-Turkish War was undoubtedly a sharp setback to the policy he had conceived on the eve of Wellington's mission to St. Petersburg. But for him the setback would have been merely a tactical one and probably therefore temporary in its effects. Under Wellington's leadership, however, Britain's Greek policy merely drifted. The British and French Ambassadors were withdrawn from Constantinople in December 1827, but before long Wellington was not only publicly regretting Navarino, he was also talking in menacing terms about Britain's obligations to her 'ancient ally', Turkey. Distracted too by the question of Catholic emancipation, the Government was now reduced almost to the role of a spectator in the Eastern Question. 'All I want', the Prime Minister wrote in October 1829, 'is to get out of the Greek affair without loss of honour and without inconvenient risk to the safety of the Ionian Islands.'[13] He joined with France in extracting Mehemet Ali's promise to withdraw Egyptian troops, but it was the French army alone who saw to the evacuation and protected that achievement by temporarily occupying the Morea. Meanwhile Russia was allowed to press on with the war until Turkish resistance collapsed in the autumn of 1829. Wellington was now resigned to the prospect of some sort of autonomous Greek state, but both he and even the philhellene Earl of Aberdeen, who had succeeded to the Foreign Office in June 1828, believed it would fall under Russian influence and therefore wished to restrict its boundaries as much as possible. In fact the Russians had already secretly concluded that they were not yet strong enough, diplomatically or militarily, to secure to themselves the exclusive benefits of the collapse of the Turkish Empire and that they too must therefore proceed very cautiously. It was for this reason that they had consented to the London Protocol of 22 March 1829 which envisaged a new Greek state under a European prince but one who was still to be a vassal of the Sultan and whose territory was to be severely limited. The Russians therefore made a relatively moderate peace with the Turks at the end of the war. The Treaty of Adrianople (14 September 1829) gave Russia substantial concessions in the Caucasus, but only a small gain in Europe at the mouth of the Danube. She considerably extended her influence in

[13] C. W. Crawley, *The Question of Greek Independence; a Study of British Policy in the Near East, 1821–1833* (Cambridge, 1930), p. 168.

the Balkans by enlarging and acquiring rights of supervision in the privileges which were to be conceded to Serbia and the Danubian provinces (Doc. 4). But, so far as Greece was concerned, the settlement was to follow the lines indicated by the London Protocol. Ultimately, and in spite of the original calculations of the Powers, Greece got first her independence and then more territory. It gradually dawned on Austrians and British alike that only then would the new state have some chance of survival and some chance of resisting Russian influence. A new conference in London therefore produced a new protocol (3 February 1830), which agreed that Greece would after all have independence but, to offset that, frontiers which were even more restricted. Then, when no prince could be found willing to accept such a miserable patrimony, a further protocol, of 21 July 1832, considerably enlarged the kingdom for Otto of Bavaria.

Something, then, was saved from the wreck of Canning's Near Eastern policy. Russia made very considerable gains, though the worst of them, her usurpation of a predominant influence at Constantinople itself, was not yet apparent. But Greece was not pushed into her arms, nor was the Turkish Empire yet destroyed. Still this was little thanks to the Wellington Government which came near to ruining Canning's work all along the line. The one bright spot was in relation to the United States. Congratulating each other upon the superior wisdom of the generals over diplomats, Wellington and President Jackson extricated Anglo-American relations from a minor but dangerous quarrel over the conditions of American trade with the British West Indies and smoothed over the boundary disputes in the north-west and north-east by extending a temporary arrangement about the first and submitting the other to arbitration. The recourse to arbitration eventually failed but that was hardly the fault of the British. Elsewhere, however, things were far from healthy. The Wellington Government badly bungled the situation in Portugal where they weakened British influence and allowed the reactionaries to regain their hold by withdrawing the expeditionary force and the naval squadron that had been there since 1822. Across the Mediterranean, in North Africa, they had too to watch in frustrated fury while the French mounted an expedition against Algiers in July 1830. But worst of all perhaps was the way in which they squandered Canning's victory over the conservative alliance and, in the Greek Question in particular, came near instead to restoring

Britain's isolation. Fortunately, when revolution came again to France late in July 1830, and revived the alliance of the Eastern Courts against the contagion, the days of the Wellington Government were already numbered and a fitter heir to Canning was about to claim his place.

PALMERSTON, 1830–1841

CANNING'S death was welcomed by reactionaries at home and abroad. Metternich thanked a merciful Providence for delivering Europe and the world from this 'malevolent meteor' and 'scourge'.[1] But the relief, in the shape of the Goderich and Wellington Ministries of 1827 and 1828–30, was merely temporary. The leadership among Canning's followers passed at his death to William Huskisson. The mantle of his foreign policy, at first, fell very awkwardly on the shoulders of the feeble and erratic Dudley but it passed before long to Henry John Temple, third Viscount Palmerston. An Irish peer who never sat in the House of Lords, Palmerston was to have an unrivalled career in British foreign policy. He was to occupy the Foreign Office (with only a brief interval of four months in 1834–5) from 1830 to 1841, and again from 1846 to 1851; he was Home Secretary from 1852 to 1855; and Prime Minister from 1855 to 1858 and from 1859 to his death in 1865 at the age of almost eighty-one. Yet in 1830 his selection for the Foreign Office by Grey was certainly not expected. He had entered the Portland Administration as long ago as 1808 and when he took over the Secretaryship at War the following year he had even had the opportunity of a seat in the Cabinet. Then for twenty years, he stuck where he was, a relatively minor figure, uncertain of his future and largely ignored in the political infighting that went on around him. None the less he was one of Canning's men and, but for the King's objections, he would have had the Treasury in 1827. In the awkward days that followed Canning's death, he had stayed on with Huskisson in the Goderich and Wellington Administrations and he had even found it necessary to join the Duke in publicly regretting Navarino. But he soon reclaimed his independence and he followed Huskisson in

[1] Harold Temperley, *The Foreign Policy of Canning 1822–1827* (London, 1925), p. 446.

the Canningite exodus which took place in May and June 1828. In June 1830 the death of George IV removed a baneful influence from British politics and produced a general election. In that election Wellington lost his majority and his defeat in parliament in November 1830 brought in a coalition government of Whigs and Tories under Lord Grey, and with Lord Palmerston at the Foreign Office.

Britain's foreign policy in 1830 was dominated, as was the Reform Question in domestic politics, by the revolution which had brought down the Restoration Monarchy in France. From France the revolution spread to the Low Countries, to Poland, and to Italy. Success, however, was limited to the western periphery of Europe where French and British power and influence could prevail. In the east the Polish rebellion was savagely repressed by Nicholas and in Italy Metternich was eventually able to restore the *status quo*. Europe, it appeared, was once more divided under the influence of the revolution into two armed camps, with the Western, liberal Powers on the one hand and the conservative alliance on the other.

There was even an apparent reconciliation between Austria and Russia over the Near Eastern Question. The Turks had barely reconciled themselves to their loss of Greece when they found their empire under even more serious attack from the south. Mehemet Ali, the Pasha of Egypt, had been just as ruthless and still more successful in reforming his country than his master, the Sultan. Before long he was busily consolidating his frontiers by advancing, and not by retreating like the Turk. The Sultan's refusal to reward him with Syria as well as Crete for his intervention against the Greeks, on the grounds that it had all been unsuccessful, gave Mehemet Ali every excuse for attempting to improve his frontier at his master's expense. In 1831 he forced a quarrel over the Lebanon and sent his son Ibrahim to seize Acre. In 1832 Ibrahim took that city and routed all the Turkish armies sent against him. With the prospect of a land advance upon Constantinople so unexpectedly opened up from the south, the Sultan naturally appealed to Britain for help. But British naval forces were pretty well occupied in western Europe, and Palmerston, who feared the Turkish Empire was 'rapidly falling to pieces' and would have preferred to act promptly, was overruled by the Cabinet.[2] Resisting the French suggestions of

[2] Sir Charles Webster, *The Foreign Policy of Palmerston 1830–1841* (London, 1951), i. 281–3.

joint intervention, the British Government rejected the Sultan's request and forced him in desperation to turn instead to his old enemy Russia. February 1833 therefore found a Russian squadron anchored with Austrian and Prussian approval off the Golden Horn and April a force of Russian troops established a few miles to the north. With Constantinople thus guarded against their advance and with the worried British and French pressing them to compromise, the Egyptians then accepted the Peace of Kutahiya of 6 May 1833 which gave them pretty well what they wanted in Syria.

This settlement eventually permitted the withdrawal of the Russian force from Constantinople and therefore greatly relieved the anxieties of the two Western Powers. But in spite of a great deal of pressure from the French in particular, they did not succeed in checking the growth of Russian influence at Constantinople. For Nicholas followed up his advantage before withdrawing his force altogether by sending a special mission to the Sultan to assure him that Russia would defend him against the passage of the Dardanelles by French or British naval forces as well as against the armies of Ibrahim. And on 8 July 1833 the Russians consolidated their advantage by signing the Treaty of Unkiar Skelessi with the Turks. This treaty provided for mutual aid in case of attack, but by a secret clause the Sultan was released from his obligation to Russia in return for agreeing in the event of an attack on Russia to close the Dardanelles to all foreign warships, including Russia's. Then, at a meeting with the Austrian Emperor and Chancellor in September, Nicholas followed up this treaty with the Convention of Munchengrätz to which Prussia adhered the following month in the separate Berlin Convention. By these arrangements the three Eastern Powers agreed in the published articles to maintain the integrity of the Sultan's dominions and in secret clauses to oppose any further advances by Mehemet Ali. They also agreed to act in co-operation should the Turkish Empire collapse in spite of their support. It was further decided to revive and consolidate the conservative alliance by affirming the right of any ruler to call for help against revolution and by arranging for mutual aid in the event of another Power intervening against the suppression of revolution.

When the news of these arrangements reached him, Palmerston at last became as alarmed as the French. In part this was due to his very imperfect knowledge of the secret clauses of Unkiar Skelessi and of what had passed at Munchengrätz. He wrongly believed that

Unkiar Skelessi had given Russia the right of passing her warships through the Dardanelles (though it was true that the Sultan could ask the Russians to send ships to his aid), and he also mistakenly believed that there had been some kind of secret agreement at Munchengrätz for the partition of the Turkish Empire. Still, the patent facts that Russia had established her superior influence at Constantinople and that the conservative alliance had been revived were sufficient justification for his alarm and for the fruitless protests he addressed to St. Petersburg and to the Porte (Doc. 12). He was not so far from the truth when he asserted in March 1834 that 'Russia . . . perhaps thinks it better to take the place by sap than by storm.'[3] It was the Eastern Question moreover which loomed largest in his antagonism to the Neo-Holy Alliance. Palmerston, indeed, was no more in favour of revolution than had been Canning. What he wanted rather was an amalgam of progress and stability; that was what he and most Englishmen of his class meant when they talked of the virtues of moderate, *liberal* régimes. Britain's interests and sentiments were offended by both revolution and despotism.

Just as the interaction of the Eastern Question and the monarchical resistance to revolution revived the Holy Alliance, so it stimulated in turn the formation of a western liberal alliance. The Bourgeois Monarchy of Louis Philippe, to which the Paris revolution of 1830 had given birth, seemed to present Great Britain with an ideal partner. Even the Wellington Government had found it convenient to accept the new régime, rather than see the Powers of Europe involved in a potentially dangerous attempt at a second Bourbon restoration (Doc. 5). Palmerston was more positively enthusiastic. He had greeted the news from Paris in 1830:

We shall drink the cause of Liberalism all over the world. Let Spain & Austria look to themselves; this reaction cannot end where it began, & Spain & Italy & parts of Germany will sooner or later be affected. This event is decisive of the ascendancy of Liberal Principles throughout Europe; the evil spirit has been put down and will be trodden under foot. The reign of Metternich is over. . . .[4]

Once back in office Palmerston was not quite such a Jacobin. Nevertheless he was among the first to use the term 'entente cor-

[3] Henry Lytton Bulwer, *The Life of Henry John Temple, Viscount Palmerston* (London, 1870), ii. 179.
[4] Mabell, Countess of Airlie, *Lady Palmerston and her Times* (London, 1922), i. 173.

diale' to describe Britain's relations with the new régime in France, and by 1834 he had converted the entente into an alliance which he could flourish in the face of the Neo-Holy Alliance.

The 1830 revolution in France had at once inflamed the long-standing dissatisfaction of the Belgians at their incorporation by the Treaty of Vienna in the Kingdom of the Netherlands. Before the year was out a separate provisional government had been formed in Brussels and Belgium's independence had been proclaimed. The conservative Powers, who had acquiesced only reluctantly in the establishment of the Bourgeois Monarchy in France, were distinctly unhappy that the contagion should be spreading so quickly and they would have preferred to maintain the Vienna Settlement by force if necessary. But in November revolt also broke out in Poland and this kept the Russians fully occupied well into the following year. Austria would not act without Russia; nor Prussia in the face of British disapproval. All three rested their hopes instead on the liberal alignment of Britain and France foundering on the rock of the Belgian Question.

The hope was not by any means a blind one and it came close to realization. The French, almost in spite of themselves, found it impossible to resist such an opportunity for aggrandizement and the redress of old wrongs. On the other hand the British were, of course, deeply suspicious of French designs in an area of such vital importance to the strategic defence of the Channel and of the United Kingdom itself. At first the French were scrupulously careful to avoid giving cause for concern and the shrewd old French Minister, Talleyrand, who had been specially appointed to the Embassy in London, soothed the fears of first Wellington and then Palmerston. With Wellington he arranged to follow up the London ambassa-dorial conference on the Greek Question with a larger one on Belgium, and with Palmerston he co-operated in cajoling the other Powers to restrict Holland to her former boundaries of 1790 and to accept the principle of independence for Belgium under the per-manent guarantee of its neutrality. Unfortunately, with the main question won, the latent rivalry between Britain and France now found plenty of scope for growth in subordinate questions like the fate of Luxemburg and of the old barrier fortresses on the French border, and, above all, the candidacy for the new throne. Talleyrand immediately alerted Palmerston's suspicions and provoked some of the very first of what were to become that Minister's famously blunt warnings by asking that France should have Luxemburg (Doc. 6). And the Foreign Secretary's worst suspicions seemed realized when in February 1831 the Belgian Congress voted for Louis Philippe's second son, the Duke de Nemours, as their king. When Talleyrand informed him this would mean immediate war with Britain, Louis Philippe repudiated the offer in his son's name. The favourite candidate of the British was the Prince of Orange, but the Belgians would not have him. Fortunately they turned now to Prince Leopold of Saxe Coburg, the widower of Princess Charlotte and the uncle of the future Queen Victoria. The British, and even the French, readily agreed; unfortunately the King of Holland did not. On 26 June 1831 the London Conference finally arranged the terms of the proposed settlement; on 9 July it was accepted by the Belgians; and on 2 August King William denounced it and marched his troops once more into Belgium. Leopold then appealed to Britain and France and, with the approval of the conference, a French army and a British squadron intervened to compel the retreat of the Dutch. But William had succeeded very well in muddying troubled waters. With an army of 50,000 men actively installed in Belgium, the French began to dream again of territorial improvements. Palmerston had to rebuff Talleyrand's renewed proposals for partition with one of his bluntest warnings ever: 'One thing is certain—the French must go out of Belgium or we have a general war, and war in a given number of days' (Doc. 10). But, in the end, Leopold had to promise to hand over five of the barrier fortresses to France before Louis Philippe would order the withdrawal of his troops. Then, on 14 October 1831, the London Conference agreed on some further small concessions to Holland and on 15 November Belgium accepted these in a final treaty. Yet still the affair would not come to a satisfactory end. There was a brief but nasty quarrel between France and Belgium over the particular fortresses to be handed over. Worse, King William was still banking on help from the Eastern Powers, and though they were in no position to give it and reluctantly ratified the treaty in April and May 1832, their sympathies lay plainly with him, and by making their acceptance dependent upon his, they encouraged him in his obstinacy for the better part of the year. 'Metternich has made April fools of us', wrote Palmerston.[5] At length the Western

[5] C. K. Webster, 'Palmerston, Metternich, and the European System 1830–1841,' *Proceedings of the British Academy*, x (1934), 132.

Powers had to conclude that William must be coerced again and on 22 October 1832 Palmerston and Talleyrand signed a convention to that effect. In December a French army forced his troops out of Antwerp and together French and British squadrons kept up the pressure on him by a blockade of the Scheldt. The Austrians and Russians were furious but they could hardly deny that the Dutch were being unreasonably difficult. However much they sympathized with William and however much they disapproved of the 'revolutionary' liberal alliance of Britain and France they knew that William's purpose was to save something for himself by provoking a general European war between East and West and this they were not prepared to undertake. In May 1833, therefore, William, reluctantly and with bad grace, agreed to accept an indefinite armistice with the Belgians. The Belgian crisis was over, though William did not finally accept the settlement agreed by the Powers in 1831 until April 1839. The Belgians then had their perpetual neutrality guaranteed by the five Powers, but they got only part of Luxemburg leaving the rest, as a personal duchy of the King of Holland, to provide the fuel for yet another crisis in Bismarck's day.

In very trying circumstances, Palmerston had kept Britain and France together in the Belgian Question and in March 1832 he was boasting that: 'There never was a period when England was more respected than at present in her foreign relations, in consequence of her good faith, moderation, and firmness.' 'The interest of England', he went on, 'was the maintenance of general peace throughout Europe, and this object was . . . most easily, most safely, and most securely to be attained, by the maintenance of a firm and strict alliance between France and this country.'[6] Palmerston well knew, however, that only his firmness had kept the Anglo-French front together. Whether such bluntness was a good foundation for a permanent alignment only time could tell. The questions provoked by the revolutions in Poland and Italy further emphasized the rift between the Eastern and Western blocs, but they gave no opportunity to the British to concert their alliance in action. In both questions it was France who led. While Austria prepared to march her troops to restore order in central Italy, Louis Philippe retorted with a declaration in favour of non-intervention; when Austrian troops entered the Papal States, the French occupied Ancona. But

6 *Hansard's Parliamentary Debates*, 3rd series, xi. 881–2.

neither side really wanted a showdown and the Austrians went half way to meet French sensibilities by withdrawing as soon as they conveniently could. Palmerston, for his part, was frightened by the possibility of a war between Austria and France and at the same time suspicious about French ambitions in the Italian peninsula. He even warned the French that their tolerance of Italian refugees was hardly consistent with their declaration of non-intervention. Indeed, although Palmerston supported France in her demands for Austria's withdrawal, he also pressed for France's evacuation of Ancona and he made it clear that in general he preferred Austrian to French influence in Italy and, in the individual states, peaceful progress from above rather than violent revolution from below. Palmerston therefore at an early stage underlined the complexity of British interests in the Italian Question and the equivocal nature of Whig policy (Doc. 7). And Metternich, for his part, signified at the same time how well he appreciated Palmerston's dilemma by asking, in April 1831, for the reinforcement of the British squadron in the Mediterranean![7]

Britain's naval power, however, did not need yet to be brought to bear directly on the Italian Question. Rather France and Austria both retreated from their extreme positions and the Pope's refusal of Palmerston's reform suggestions postponed the crisis to a later day. But British naval power was there in the Mediterranean to be called upon if necessary. In the Polish Question things were very different and Palmerston well knew it. 'We cannot send an army to Poland', he told a Polish revolutionary leader, 'and the burning of the Russian fleet would be about as effectual as the burning of Moscow.'[8] Thus on this occasion he firmly resisted the pressure of an outraged public opinion at home and of French diplomacy from across the Channel. He rejected French proposals for joint mediation and even for intervention, and he insisted that he would remonstrate only if the Russians departed from the Treaty of Vienna (Docs. 8 and 9). He did therefore protest against the end of the Polish constitution and he could not entirely stop something of that new hectoring tone of his coming out in imprecations to Russia to temper the barbarity of her repression.

It was in the Iberian peninsula rather that Britain and France found an apparently better opportunity to consolidate their alliance.

[7] Webster, *Foreign Policy of Palmerston*, i. 207.
[8] R. W. Seton-Watson, *Britain in Europe 1789–1914* (Cambridge, 1937), p. 179.

The tortuous nature of politics in that part of the world did not prevent the Western Powers seeing in the young Queens of Portugal and Spain the last defence of constitutionalism, and the Eastern Powers seeing in the reactionary pretenders, Miguel of Portugal and Carlos of Spain, the best hopes of absolute monarchy. The British and French Governments, throwing consistency to the winds, were soon actively interfering, while denying the right of intervention to the conservative Powers. In the winter of 1831 they helped rally the cause of the Queen of Portugal by secretly encouraging private aid and assistance, at the same time warning off the other Powers with undisguised threats. Then, in 1834, Palmerston answered Munchengrätz by suggesting to France that they concert their co-operation in Portugal and Spain into an actual alliance. The terms of the alliance, to which Talleyrand readily agreed, were aimed at the expulsion of Miguel. But Palmerston— who boasted that it was 'a capital hit, and all my own doing'9—also flourished it as a challenge to Metternich. It would not only settle affairs in Portugal and possibly also in Spain; 'what is of more permanent and extensive importance, it establishes a quadruple alliance among the constitutional states of the west, which will serve as a powerful counterpoise to the Holy Alliance of the east' (Doc. 13).

What so worried Palmerston in the east was the threat to India and India's communications with the Mediterranean which it was believed had grown from Russia's victories in wars with Persia and Turkey in 1826–8 and 1828–9. These victories had given Russia such acquisitions of territory and influence that even Lord Aberdeen was compelled to conclude about the cession of the Asiatic fortresses in the Treaty of Adrianople that, 'Russia holds the keys both of the Persian and the Turkish provinces; and whether she may be disposed to extend her conquests to the East or to the West, to Teheran or to Constantinople, no serious obstacle can arrest her progress' (Doc. 4).

In Persia British policy was concerned with Russia's advance both upon her lines of communication with India and upon the frontiers of India itself.10 To counter the effects in this area of the Napoleonic alliance with Russia, Britain had in 1809 secured treaties with Persia, Afghanistan, and Sind which were designed to hold off the Russian

---

9 Bulwer, ii. 186.
10 For an important analysis of this question see J. A. Norris, *The First Afghan War, 1838–1842* (Cambridge, 1967).

advance. But this policy was totally upset by Russia's victory over
Persia in 1828 and the predominance of Russian influence which
followed at Teheran and which encouraged the Persians to press on
India's buffer in Afghanistan and particularly upon the strategic
fortress of Herat. In October 1829 the publication of Colonel de
Lacy Evans's *Practicability of an Invasion of British India* awakened
the Wellington Government to the potential dangers on the north-
west frontier and although it was its successors under Grey and
Melbourne which earned all the blame later, it was that Government which consciously initiated the policy of the counter-pene-
tration of Central Asia which led to the first unhappy Afghan War
(1838–42) and the uneasy annexation of Sind. The general idea was
to open up the Indus to British trade and influence as a counter to
Russia's direct advance on the Oxus and to her indirect advance in
the guise of Persian pressure upon Afghanistan. This general policy
was pursued consistently by Whig and Tory administrations alike,
but Palmerston was undoubtedly very vigorous in prosecuting it.
In 1833 Persia's advance was temporarily checked by the death of
the heir-apparent and the retreat of the commander of her forces to
Teheran in order to claim the succession. The following year the
Russians agreed with the British to co-operate in the Persian succession question. But Palmerston remained very suspicious of the Russians (Doc. 14) and he rightly believed that their representatives,
authorized or not, were still pressing the Persians to renew the attack
on Herat, which indeed they did in July 1837.

In 1836 Palmerston had wanted to retaliate against Russian policy
by helping the Circassians in their resistance to Russia's pacification
of the Caucasian route into Central Asia. But Melbourne had resisted
this proposal with the sensible observation that he was 'against
exciting people to commit themselves to a warfare in which you
cannot give them effectual support'.[11] Palmerston in fact was not
responsible for the unpleasant incident with Russia which the sloop
Vixen provoked in an attempt to run the blockade of the coast of
Circassia.[12] More sensibly Palmerston concentrated his efforts in
the Persian problem on the Indus where Britain was stronger. The
main difficulty here was the internal chaos of Afghanistan. This not
only weakened her resistance against Persia in the west, it also gave
the Russians the opportunity to get a foothold in the country itself.

[11] Philip Guedalla, *Palmerston* (London, 1926), p. 198.
[12] Webster, *Foreign Policy of Palmerston*, ii. 570–5.

In turn the Russians encouraged Afghanistan to look to the east for compensation for the prospective loss of Herat and to quarrel with the other neighbours of British India and in particular with the Punjab. The Central Asian problem was therefore one of extraordinary complexity for the British and they were not helped by the difficulty, at such a distance, and with two Governments, British and Indian, so involved, of keeping up with events and controlling and reconciling the actions of often egocentric agents on the spot. In the end it was decided that the only possible solution was for the British, in concert with the Punjab, to intervene directly in Afghanistan. By this means they would consolidate the country under one ruler, resolve the disputes on the eastern frontier, and strengthen the resistance to Persia in the west.

This decision followed logically from the earlier one of the Wellington Government, but it was none the less loudly criticized in the light of the later disasters of the Afghan War for involving the British in the distant and insoluble politics of semi-barbaric states. And this criticism seemed all the more valid in that, after the necessary arrangements had been made but before it was too late to stop the expedition, it was learned that in June 1838 Herat had surprisingly beaten off the Persian attack. It is significant, however, that Melbourne, who was so often the restraining hand upon Palmerston and whose constant advice to him was characterized in the famous words, 'for God's sake don't',[13] this time agreed with Palmerston that 'Afghanistan must be ours or Russia's'.[14] With this view the most recent historian of British Central Asian policy fully agrees. Although Persia had failed and Russia now backed down before British protests, if the expedition had not gone ahead British influence in Afghanistan would not have been restored and the opportunity would have remained open to Russia to resume her pressure in the near future. How important it was to have avoided this was soon illustrated from a different direction. Checked in their Persian schemes, the Russians in the autumn of 1839 mounted a new campaign against Khiva and Bokhara. They insisted that their object was simply to pacify the caravan route, but Palmerston rightly suspected that their aims were rather more ambitious. The expedition failed, but not before it had compelled the British to extend the objectives of their own expedition and for the time being to keep garrisons in the key cities of Afghanistan. It was these garrisons whose ugly fate in 1841-2 exposed the whole affair to criticism. It was true that Palmerston was over-enthusiastic about such schemes; he even proposed a further expedition to bind Herat more securely to Afghanistan.[15] But the real mistake was not the policy of intervention itself, but the too casual assumption that it had succeeded and that the garrisons were safe. The decision to keep the garrisons was the direct consequence of the renewed threat from Russia. Moreover, although the expedition was ultimately disastrous to the force itself, it was immediately successful inasmuch as it obviated any need on the part of the British Empire to concentrate all resources on the defence of India at a time when those resources were about to be required in the Near East.[16]

At Constantinople it was, of course, the 'disguised aggression' of Unkiar Skelessi which Palmerston felt he had to combat. He soon dropped his scepticism about Turkish reform and insisted instead that all talk about the Empire's decay was 'pure and unadulterated nonsense' (Docs. 19 and 20). His offers of assistance to improve the Sultan's naval and military forces were, however, of very little practical benefit. He did secure a major success in the signature of the Anglo-Turkish Commercial Convention of 1838, but he was not able to displace Russian influence since he believed that the Empire needed a period of peace in which to recover and he would not therefore agree to give Mahmoud the one thing he really wanted—active help against Mehemet Ali.

After the compromise forced upon them by the Powers in 1833 neither Mahmoud nor Mehemet Ali was content to leave things as they were. The Sultan was thirsting for revenge against his ambitious vassal; the Pasha, on his part, continued to press hard upon the southern provinces of the Empire and to look, if not for complete independence, at least for an hereditary possession under the merely nominal suzerainty of the Turk. For a time the pressure of the Powers managed to hold back both, but finally, in April 1839, after Palmerston had categorically refused his offer of an offensive/ defensive alliance, Mahmoud lost patience and sent his army to drive the Egyptians out of Syria. But towards the end of June his forces were utterly defeated, and on 1 July his navy too went over to

[15] Norris, pp. 351-2.
[16] Ibid., pp. 321-2.

the Egyptians. Once again the Turkish Empire seemed on the point of total collapse.

Although Palmerston had done his best to fend off this crisis because he saw that it would offer Russia still another opportunity of strengthening her position at Constantinople (Doc. 17), once it had arisen there was no question of his taking the opposite side to Russia. Neither Power wished the Sultan to be overthrown by the Egyptians. After all the Russians' strength in Constantinople depended upon the weakness of the Moslems and they wanted consequently neither the Sultan nor Mehemet Ali to win a great victory. The British had an additional and a direct interest in resisting the ambitions of Mehemet Ali, and this interest had greatly increased since 1833. This was the protection of their trade and their Mediterranean routes to India, which Captain Francis Chesney's exploring expedition had emphasized in 1835. Mehemet Ali's ambitions in Syria directly threatened the routes to the Euphrates and to the Persian Gulf, which his forces had actually reached by 1838. At the same time the Egyptians were also threatening the Red Sea route to the Indian Ocean. As long ago as 1820 the British had had to warn them off meddling in Abyssinia, and in January 1839 had countered by occupying the important strategic position of Aden.[17]

Although the British were extremely worried about the Russian penetration at Constantinople, their immediate commercial interests in the Near East tended to fend off any direct quarrel with Russia. It was rather relations with France which were to be strained to breaking point. The cordiality of the *entente* had been in doubt almost from the beginning. By February 1831 Palmerston was already inclined to suspect that the 'policy of France is like an infection clinging to the walls of the dwelling, and breaking out in every successive occupant who comes within their influence'.[18] Belgium and Spain, over which Britain and France had first been brought together, were in fact just as much inclined to separate them. They had held together over the Belgian Question only with the greatest difficulty and in an atmosphere of mutual suspicion rivalled only by their conflict with the Eastern Powers. In Spain that suspicion spread rapidly after the signature of the Quadruple Alliance of 1834 and was eventually to force them completely apart. The same was true of the Near Eastern Question.

17 Webster, *Foreign Policy of Palmerston*, i. 276.
18 Bulwer, ii. 36.

Although the French had so far co-operated with the British and the other Powers in the Egyptian Question, they were already deeply involved, emotionally and materially, on Mehemet Ali's side. The French had long since established a special connection with Egypt, founded on Catholic missionary activity and dramatized by Napoleon's invasion in 1798. Under Mehemet Ali French officers were employed in considerable numbers in the Egyptian Army and French trade had grown rapidly. By the mid 1830s France and Britain were involved in a considerable commercial rivalry in the eastern Mediterranean, and wherever the British found their progress impeded by the Egyptians they found also the French behind the Egyptians. The Mehemet Ali Question therefore also involved the direct conflict of Britain and France for trade and in particular for the control of communications with the Indian Ocean.

The means of defending Britain's interests in the Near East and of resolving the contest for supremacy at Constantinople were not therefore to be found in the Western Alliance (Docs. 17 and 18). Fortunately the division of Europe into two alliance systems was by no means rigid and Palmerston, with some help, had the wit to discover a solution for his problems and to make a triumphant success out of his difficulties. The combination of the Peninsular and the Eastern Questions, far from consolidating the alliance system, in fact proved its undoing. Indeed the division of Europe into two hostile camps was itself unstable from the first. There was, in the first place, a deep distrust between Austria and Russia. Metternich had been as alarmed as Palmerston at the Treaty of Unkiar Skelessi and Munchengrätz had not entirely relieved his anxieties. Nicholas and Metternich, moreover, were not on very friendly terms. Nicholas seems to have suspected that Metternich had intrigued against him during the Decembrist troubles and he continued to resent Metternich's constant attempts to lecture and to lead him in matters of policy. Metternich, the Tsar was later to confirm, 'had become aged, and had now a mania for writing papers upon all subjects', imagining that he could 'advise upon every subject', and from his closet 'direct and instruct all the world'.[19] The two Eastern statesmen were also separated by their attitude towards France. Nicholas carried his disapproval of revolution to an almost pathological hatred of the Bourgeois Monarchy and of Louis

---

[19] Frederick Stanley Rodkey, 'Anglo-Russian Negotiations about a "Permanent" Quadruple Alliance, 1840–1841', *American Historical Review*, xxxvi (1930–1), 347.

Philippe personally. Metternich, on the other hand, appreciated how fundamentally conservative that monarchy was and he therefore invited, though he never firmly accepted, continual French offers of co-operation and *rapprochement* in European affairs. These exchanges—there was even a French scheme for a marriage between the Houses of Habsburg and Orléans—naturally further eroded the *entente* between Britain and France.

In these circumstances even the British appeared to favour the reassertion of the European Concert rather than be left in isolation once again. When a new quarrel loomed up over Cracow early in 1836 Palmerston simply got annoyed at another blatant attempt of Metternich's to separate France from England, but Melbourne complained along with the Eastern Powers that he too did not like the division of Europe into two armed camps. In 1815 Cracow had been made into a free city under the protection of the Eastern Powers. The Powers were expressly forbidden to send military forces into the city, but at the same time Cracow was not to give refuge to fugitives from her neighbours' territories. The aftermath of the abortive Polish revolt of 1830–1, however, gave Russia all the excuse she needed, and in February 1836 she at last persuaded her partners that the city must be occupied. At the same time Metternich gave formal notice of the decision to France, but deliberately omitted to do so in London on the grounds of the habitual enmity which had been displayed by the British Foreign Secretary. Metternich's tactics did him no good in Paris, and they could hardly have improved matters in London. In particular they probably helped the Foreign Secretary demonstrate to Melbourne that the two groups 'think differently, and therefore they act differently' (Doc. 15). But, while making the most of the opportunity to give free rein to his feelings about the Austrian Chancellor, Palmerston really had none of Canning's aversion to international congresses and it seems that he wanted something like a new Congress System, though one which would be dominated by him rather than by Metternich. The crises of the 1830s had therefore been marked by a tug-of-war for conferences at London and Vienna, which Palmerston who had begun with the advantage of the Belgian Conference inherited from Wellington, carried in the Near Eastern crisis to a triumphant victory over Metternich.[20] That victory was made

---

[20] This is the subject of Sir Charles Webster's famous Raleigh Lecture, 'Palmerston, Metternich, and the European System'.

possible, however, only by a reappraisal of British policy. By the late 1830s Palmerston was becoming not only increasingly annoyed with France's failure to co-operate but also less convinced of the inevitability of war with Russia. In Central Asia, where he felt there was no alternative, he kept up a firm front against the Russians. But in the Near East the effects of the Mehemet Ali Question made him doubt both the necessity and the wisdom of attempting to confront the Russians alone. The objective he therefore pursued in the Near Eastern crisis of 1839–41 was 'to merge the Treaty of Unkiar Skelessi into some more general compact'[21] (Docs. 17 and 18).

Since Russia as well as Britain wished to avoid a showdown, they both found it convenient to acquiesce in Austro-French pressure for a new conference about the Mehemet Ali Question at Vienna. On 27 July 1839, therefore, there came from Vienna the five Powers' collective note to the Sultan, reserving to themselves the right to settle the Turco-Egyptian Question. The restoration of the old Concert, however, was superficial and therefore temporary. The process of deterioration at work upon both the eastern, conservative, and the western, liberal, alliances, which had permitted the revival of the Concert, was already working more strongly for its destruction. The key to this process was the rapid deterioration in Anglo-French relations. Metternich's success had depended upon a strictly limited and controlled disagreement between Britain and France. But at Vienna that disagreement rapidly developed into downright hostility as Britain demanded and France resisted Mehemet Ali's expulsion from Syria.

The real opportunity to exploit the differences between the Powers fell not to Metternich but to Nicholas. Metternich had used them to lead first France and then Britain back into a Concert dominated by himself. Nicholas now saw how those differences had reached a point where he could use them to separate Britain from France and, in doing so, also snub Metternich. To achieve this and to overcome the obstacles created by Anglo-Russian rivalry and popular ill-feeling, he was prepared to offer a good deal. Russia's finances left him in no position to seek a showdown with Britain. And it is very probable that he was encouraged to consider the expediency of a *rapprochement* with Britain by the firmness and apparent success of

Palmerston's policy in Central Asia.[22] Certainly Palmerston himself thought that this was the case and the inter-relationship of the two main areas of the Eastern Question was an additional vindication of the wisdom of his controversial policy in Central Asia. In any event the Russians had backed down in Afghanistan and Persia in March 1839, only a short while before the Turks attacked the Egyptians. Now Nicholas made it clear that he thought it best to co-operate with Britain against Mehemet Ali, rather than exploit the crisis in the pursuit of Russia's predominance at Constantinople. In September and December 1839 he sent his confidant, Baron Brunnow, on two special missions to London to relieve Palmerston's suspicions and to concert Anglo-Russian action against Egypt. Russia promised not to renew the Treaty of Unkiar Skelessi, provided that the principle of the closure of the Straits was accepted by the Powers. Britain and Russia would then lead the Powers in checking the advance of Mehemet Ali.

Palmerston was by no means slow to appreciate the merits of the Tsar's proposals (Doc. 21). Not only would they secure Britain's principal objectives at Constantinople and in Syria; they would also revive and consolidate the substitution of a London conference system for that of Metternich at Vienna. At first he could make no headway against his colleagues' opposition to the Russians' insistence on the closure of the Straits, and in October the French were informed that the Cabinet had rejected Brunnow's offer out of deference to their wishes. But Brunnow returned in December with the Tsar's agreement that if the Sultan called for help the Russian and British fleets might enter the Sea of Marmora together. At length, therefore, Palmerston, with the threat of resignation, carried through the agreement with Russia against the opposition in the country and in the Cabinet of Russophobes and Francophiles alike (Docs. 22, 23, and 24). In this he was helped by the unreasonable obstinacy of the French themselves. In March 1840 a change of ministry in France brought Thiers to the premiership and France's defence of Mehemet Ali now became more open and downright. The battle between Palmerston and Thiers, however, was a very unequal one. At the end of June Thiers refused all compromise short of the hereditary possession of both Egypt and Syria for Mehemet Ali; early in July Palmerston got the approval of the majority of the Cabinet to counter by ignoring France and signing a new treaty in London with

[22] Norris, pp. 318–19.

Austria, Russia, and Prussia. The Treaty of London (15 July 1840) provided for the closing of the Straits and for the settlement of the Egyptian Question. Mehemet Ali was to be offered the hereditary possession of Egypt and the possession of Syria only during his lifetime. If he did not accept in ten days, he was to get only Egypt; if he did not accept in twenty days, even that offer was to be withdrawn. When the Egyptians failed to respond to this generosity, Palmerston did not hesitate to press on. In Paris there was talk of war and in London many of Palmerston's colleagues were uneasy (Doc. 25). But Palmerston calculated that it was no more than talk and it tended to encourage rather than to deter him (Doc. 26). On 11 September a British naval force bombarded Beirut and helped land Turkish troops; on 4 November they bombarded and captured Acre; before the end of February 1841 Ibrahim's force had been compelled to retire to Egypt. In the meantime, his bluff called, Thiers had been replaced and the more circumspect Guizot had been made Foreign Minister, while Mehemet Ali had agreed to return the Sultan's fleet and to accept the hereditary possession of Egypt alone. Palmerston was less generous to France and Guizot had to come back into the Concert cap in hand. On 13 July 1841 the triumph of Palmerston's Concert in London over Metternich's Vienna System was completed by new agreements in which France joined the other Powers in confirming the Egyptian settlement and the closure of the Straits.

Palmerston has been heavily criticized by historians as much as by his contemporaries for the merciless and threatening manner in which he treated the French. For all his professions of devotion to the *entente*, Thiers's behaviour justified Palmerston to a considerable extent. Thiers's policy in Egypt was both defiant and deceitful, and his manner towards the British was also menacing. But Palmerston certainly did neglect the opportunity of Thiers's fall to offer the French an escape from their humiliation (Doc. 26). Instead he insisted on finishing off the Egyptian crisis without even the co-operation which the French then offered. Only when Mehemet Ali had finally submitted was France allowed to rejoin the Concert. On the other hand he firmly resisted the Tsar's attempts to make the rift between France and England lasting by the offer of a secret formal alliance, incidentally spelling out some fundamental principles of British foreign policy (Doc. 27).[23]

[23] The approach is discussed in Rodkey, pp. 343–9.

The new assertiveness which Palmerston displayed was not confined to his dealings with France in the Near East and with Russia in Central Asia. While the Government of India had been preparing itself to cope with problems on the north-western frontier, it was also called upon to dispatch a force to the aid of Britain's representatives in China. Trade with China had always been difficult, but the East India Company, who had the monopoly of that trade, felt that it was worth it. However, when that monopoly was abolished in 1833, the task of protecting British trade and British lives passed to government officials and they were not prepared to tolerate the contempt and harassment meted out by the Chinese authorities. The occasion of the eventual explosion was the vigorous attempt by Chinese officials in 1839 to eradicate the supply of opium from India. The opium trade had long been illegal but British officials saw no good reason why they should interfere with what local Chinese officials usually connived at. Even now the Chinese Emperor's chief object was not a moral crusade against the drug, but the checking of the drain of silver which was used to pay for its importation. In the first instance the British merchants were compliant and their opium was surrendered to the Chinese officials. But the British Superintendent at Canton, Captain Elliot, had not received his Government's instructions not to protect British merchants who had broken Chinese law and he refused to leave any of them to the mercy of the barbaric Chinese courts. To press their point the Chinese then attacked a British warship and ordered the suspension of all trade with Great Britain. To the British, in London as well as in the East, it now seemed fatal to back down and, however unwillingly, they found themselves proceeding to war, apparently, though not intentionally, in defence of the opium trade.

Although opinion, at the time and ever since, has been severely critical of Palmerston's Chinese policy, there is really little doubt that much of that criticism has been unfair. Elliot, accidentally or not, did not serve his master very well and the Superintendent's behaviour should not be allowed to obscure the fact that the quarrel was certainly not a simple matter of the opium trade and that the Chinese had committed intolerable atrocities upon Europeans. Palmerston in fact demolished his complacent critics in the House of Commons: 'Why did they [the Chinese] not prohibit the growth of the poppy in their own country?', he asked.[24] The British, and

---

[24] Guedalla, p. 221.

Elliot in particular, spoiled their case by allowing the Chinese to manoeuvre them into a defence of the opium trade. But the real issue, as Palmerston recognized, was that of equal and civilized treatment of British traders and British representatives by the Chinese authorities (Doc. 41).

Unfortunately Palmerston himself certainly adopted an 'unequal' attitude to the European diplomats with whom he happened to disagree. The bluntness with which he delivered warnings and advice alike earned him the sobriquet of 'Lord Pumicestone', and he was certainly rather harsh in his treatment of France after he had won his battle over Mehemet Ali (though he had a good deal of personal, if not political, justification in the intrigues he knew the French had carried on in England in their vain attempts to oust him from the Cabinet). In this respect he had carried Canning's habit of 'lecturing' to what his critics called 'bullying' or 'bluster' according to their estimate of the force and resolution which lay behind his words. He also went further than Canning in his use of, and response to, public opinion. Given that there was no question of effective interference, he was certainly indiscreet in conveying so bluntly his country's disapproval of what Russia was doing in Poland. And in going out of his way to build up opinion against Russia and France he was making trouble for the future.

Ironically enough he was himself the victim of what he had encouraged. David Urquhart was a violent Russophobe whom Palmerston had deliberately placed at the Constantinople Embassy and whose wild fulminations in the *Portfolio* he at first strongly approved. But Urquhart, outraged by the Foreign Secretary's arrangement of the Near Eastern Question with Nicholas in 1839–1841, literally accused Palmerston of high treason and devoted the rest of his colourful career to the unmasking and defeat of this supposed Russian agent. More important than these fantasies of a half-mad fanatic, was the straitjacket which public prejudice, once so effectively developed, tended to put upon the conduct of foreign policy. In the Central Asian Question, for example, Palmerston deliberately whipped up anti-Russian opinion in order to forestall criticism of his policy in parliament and to unite his Cabinet colleagues behind him. But when the time came to take advantage of Nicholas's approaches over the Near Eastern Question, he had to go into reverse and play down the anti-Russian publicity over Central Asia. 'The objection to giving Papers', he said when considering what might be revealed to parliament and to the country, 'is that our case against Russia is *too good* a one to be made out against a dear ally. It would be a terrible shewing up for Nicholas; but not that he richly deserves it.'[25] Palmerston therefore deliberately neglected to make as strong a defence of his policy in Afghanistan as he might have done. His neglect to underline the danger from Russia and to reveal the continuity of Whig and Tory policy against it left him open to a great deal of criticism at the time and since. That he was prepared to pay this price in order to achieve his triumph at Constantinople is greatly to his credit. His record of substantial achievement during the 1830s was a triumphant application of what he considered to be the true principles of British foreign policy, principles which he had consciously adopted from Canning and which he later defended against the attack by Urquhart's friends in these words:

...it is a narrow policy to suppose that this country or that is to be marked out as the eternal ally or the perpetual enemy of England. We have no eternal allies, and we have no perpetual enemies. Our interests are eternal and perpetual, and those interests it is our duty to follow (Doc. 49).

[25] Norris, p. 221.

3

APPEASEMENT, REVOLUTION, AND WAR, 1841–1856

AT THE height of Palmerston's success the tottering Melbourne Government fell in the summer of 1841 and the foreign secretaryship in Peel's Tory Administration passed again into the hands of the Earl of Aberdeen. Aberdeen was one of a growing number in all parties who had grave doubts about the wisdom of Palmerston's policy, and more especially of his manner and methods. Aberdeen could not deny the value and importance of Palmerston's triumph at Constantinople; but he could and did condemn the price which Britain had to pay for it. For Palmerston's assertiveness had not only upset the *entente* with France, it had also left him a war with China, the chance of another with the United States, and, though no one knew it yet, an imminent disaster and a new campaign in Afghanistan.

About China and Afghanistan, Aberdeen could do little but make the best of a bad job—just as Palmerston himself would have done. Once committed to war Palmerston insisted it be continued until the Chinese made really valuable concessions. These were obtained with the Treaty of Nanking in August 1842. Five ports were opened up to foreign trade, and not merely to the British, though they did get a special grip on China by the cession of Hong Kong. Nothing at all was said about opium. The consequences of the Whigs' policy in Afghanistan were much less profitable. The insecurity of the British position in Afghanistan became apparent with the murders of British officials in November 1841 and in the following January the famous retreat began from Kabul. In India it was decided that the same mistake must not be made twice and that after a punitive expedition, there must be a new withdrawal from Afghanistan and a consolidation of Britain's hold on the Indus instead. Peel's Government did not enthusiastically endorse this decision, but it had no alternative. It encouraged Russia to co-operate with Britain in preventing a new Persian attack on Herat in 1842. But at the same time it allowed the Russians to consolidate their gains in Central Asia. Untroubled by any British threat from Afghanistan, they obtained a new treaty with Khiva and in 1844 successfully established themselves on the Aral Sea.[1]

Where Aberdeen thought he had a more positive alternative was in his French and American policies. To assist him in the reconstruction of the *entente* with France Aberdeen had powerful allies in both Paris and London. He had already established good personal relations with the leading French minister, Guizot, and on his side too was Guizot's mistress and Aberdeen's old friend, Princess Lieven. In London Aberdeen could count on a very substantial number of important persons who agreed with him in condemning Palmerston's truculence. Among these were the young Queen Victoria and her consort, Albert, who made a special visit to Louis Philippe in September 1843 and who exchanged further visits with him in 1845.

Eventually Aberdeen was to find that the clash of interests was too much for the *entente*. But of the mutual ill-will among French and British public opinion he had a strong warning almost at the very beginning. In December 1841, thanks very largely to the efforts of his predecessor at the Foreign Office, Britain at last secured by treaty from Prussia, Russia, Austria, and France much better provision for the suppression of the slave trade which all had piously condemned at Vienna in 1815, but which they had all permitted to survive out of a jealous resistance to the Royal Navy's claims to the right of search on the high seas. Unfortunately the French Chamber decided to mark their disapproval of Guizot and their resentment of England by refusing to ratify the treaty and Aberdeen did not manage to get a new arrangement until 1845, and even then he had to make substantial concessions for it.

One special factor which had worked against the French ratification of the Quintuple Treaty was the influence of the United States, the only Great Power to refuse to sign it in the first instance. The most active elements in the American attitude were naturally the slavery interests of the South, but there was too the presence of a general animus against Great Britain which threatened to confront

[1] J. A. Norris, *The First Afghan War, 1838–1842* (Cambridge, 1967), pp. 434–5.

Aberdeen with the most awful prospect of a hostile combination between France and the United States.

Palmerston, by a not uncharacteristic mixture of long neglect with moments of fitful energy, had kept relations with the United States in an even worse state than relations with France. Since the excitements of Canning's day, Anglo-American relations had subsided into a relatively quiet period of mutually profitable expansion of commerce, but nagging away all the time were the questions of the various unsettled parts of the boundary with Britain's North American provinces and in particular the north-eastern or Maine Boundary Question. The principal factor here was strategic. The American claim threatened the British army's winter route by land from the maritime seaports into Canada; the British claim threatened the chief American invasion route towards Quebec and Montreal. And beyond these considerations lay the questions of local interests, particularly Maine's, and the larger question of prestige on both sides of the Atlantic. The Treaty of Ghent which had ended the war with the United States on Christmas Eve, 1814 had provided for the independent arbitration of these boundary disputes in the event of deadlock and, accordingly, in 1827 recourse was had to the opinion of the King of the Netherlands. He, too, however, was perplexed by the mysteries of the evidence and in 1831 he arbitrarily divided the disputed territory between the two claimants. Dissatisfied with what they were offered, the Americans asked to be released, and Palmerston, who expected to do better on some later occasion, unwisely agreed. He was not to enjoy any more favourable opportunity. In 1837 Canada flared into rebellion, stirring up anti-British sentiment in the United States and embroiling Anglo-American relations in a series of incidents on the frontier. The defeated rebels found a safe refuge across the border and from here they continued to make their assaults upon British rule. Coincidentally, in the north-east, British and American settlers and trappers clashed violently over the disputed frontier. For some time a major crisis was avoided, thanks very largely to the pacific efforts which a rather pusillanimous American Government was able to make in spite of the state of public opinion, and thanks also to Palmerston's preoccupations with the Near Eastern crisis in spite of some of his colleagues' efforts to divert his warlike attentions from France to the United States. Palmerston's diversions and his delaying tactics over the boundary question were not, however, proof against fate. In December 1837 a party of Canadian volunteers had crossed into American territory and destroyed the *Caroline*, an American vessel being used to ferry supplies for the Canadian rebels. The whole affair aroused a good deal of ill-feeling; it also provoked a retaliatory attack upon a Canadian vessel. Far worse, in November 1840, a British citizen, Alexander McLeod, who was supposed to have boasted a part in the *Caroline* operation, was arrested by the New York State authorities and charged with the murder of an American citizen who had died when the ship was destroyed. Nothing was more likely to awaken Palmerston's serious attention, especially as the Near Eastern crisis was now past its climax, and he soon made it clear that he would regard McLeod's execution as an occasion for war (Doc. 28).

Although the United States Government was anxious to placate the British they could do nothing in the face of American opinion and the independence of the New York law courts. Matters therefore remained in an extremely dangerous condition and were still in this state when Palmerston gave way to Aberdeen late in the summer of 1841. Indeed, with Wellington now back in Peel's Cabinet, the pressure for serious war preparations against the United States, as well as against France, was kept up. Fortunately McLeod was able to prove an alibi, and in November 1841 he arrived in England to announce his release. Characteristically Aberdeen now decided to seize the peace initiative and to separate the United States from Britain's catalogue of enemies by sending out a special representative to settle, if he could, all outstanding issues. Lord Ashburton, who had an American wife and was a member of the Baring family of bankers, was chosen specifically because he represented pacifying factors of Anglo-American trade which men like Aberdeen and Peel, though not Palmerston, believed was already so much more important than squabbles over frontiers or even national honour. With a similar sense of moderation on the American side, agreement on the Maine frontier was not too difficult to achieve. Ashburton and Aberdeen accepted substantially less than what had been offered by the earlier Dutch award. But they were able to display to their military experts and to British opinion at large the gains made by fending off the American claim from the heights supposedly commanding the approaches to Quebec and by the retention of an intercolonial route entirely within British territory. Palmerston, who savagely attacked the Ashburton settlement, did not fail to point out that the price included the surrender of Rouse's Point, the Americans' forward base on the invasion route to Quebec and Montreal, which, to their consternation, the Americans had earlier found to lie within British territory. The road, moreover, though certainly now within British territory, was perilously close to the American frontier and exposed to being cut by them in the event of war. Palmerston's view of the settlement, then, was that it was not only an 'humiliation and sacrifice of real interests and established rights', but, by strengthening the Americans' position, a positive encouragement to them to attack [2] (Doc. 31). Aberdeen, for his part, stressed the incalculable value of appeasing the United States (Doc. 30), who though not yet a Great Power in the European sense, had the resources of the American continent to harass, if not overwhelm, Great Britain at an extremely vulnerable point. Undoubtedly a nasty quarrel over a not particularly vital issue had been safely disposed of. But whatever the abstract merits of appeasement, Aberdeen well knew that his case would have been more convincing if Ashburton had completed his task of 'healing all old sores'. As it was Ashburton and the American Secretary of State, Daniel Webster, managed to dispose only of comparatively minor matters beyond the Maine Boundary Question. In particular there remained unsettled, not only the Oregon Boundary Question in the northwest, but also the resolution of Anglo-American difficulties over the fate of Mexico's northern provinces from Texas to California.

The Oregon Question was another leftover from the inadequate Treaty of Ghent. Complicated at first by the existence of Russian and Spanish claims, the British and the Americans had been able to agree only on a temporary arrangement between themselves. By an agreement first made in 1818 and renewed in 1827 it was arranged to leave the disputed area open to settlement by both sides. Although the area concerned was very large, comprising about half of what is now British Columbia and all of the existing states of Washington, Oregon, and Idaho, and a good part of Montana and Wyoming, its immediate value stemmed mainly from the fur trade and this, in a period of increasing settlement, was a patently declining asset. But the real issue was the implications that possession of the lion's share would have, not only for the future mastery of the North American continent, but also for the trade of the Pacific. By the early 1840s

---

[2] Kenneth Bourne, *Britain and the Balance of Power in North America 1815–1908* (London, 1967), pp. 110–11.

significant elements in American public opinion were no longer prepared to wait for what they considered to be part of their Manifest Destiny.

Other elements in American opinion looked rather to the west and to the south, in particular to California and to Texas. There was nothing new about American ambitions in the borderlands of Mexico, but these had now been brought to a climax by the revolt of the largely American inhabitants of Texas in 1836. However, Texan approaches for admission into the Union, following the successful defence of their new independence, were frustrated by internal dissensions between the northern and southern states. Ultimately the problem was to be solved by a domestic political compromise, but the task of reconciling and combining the various expansionist elements in American opinion was made much easier by emphasizing the role of Great Britain as a common enemy to their ambitions in Texas and California as well as in Oregon.

Aberdeen was not very interested in Oregon any more than he had been in Maine. Both areas he considered to be miserable pieces of swamp. But in both cases he was well aware how important it was to secure for public opinion on both sides what could be presented to them as an honourable compromise. This was particularly important in Britain after Palmerston's savage criticism of the Maine settlement and now that the Peel Government was in such trouble over domestic policy. It seemed to him that there was plenty of scope for compromise or arbitration on the lines of the various proposals made over the years. Unfortunately the linking of the Oregon with the Texan and Californian questions so worked up the feelings on both sides that it made compromise even more difficult than before.

Up to 1842 there was not much justification for American suspicions about British designs on California and Texas. It was rather the suspicion which provoked the design. The strategic and commercial value of the great harbour of San Francisco was well understood in Britain and various proposals had been put up to gain control of it. But, although the Royal Navy did not have an adequate base at any point on the entire Pacific coastline of North and South America, no British government was ever persuaded to take up a scheme to acquire San Francisco. Each accepted, however, regretfully, that it was quite unrealistic to suppose that San Francisco could be saved from the United States in the long run. The establishment of Texan independence confirmed British suspicions about the weakness of Mexico as a barrier to American expansion. But the rejection of annexation by the United States and the Texans' flirtation with Europe which followed did suggest an alternative possibility for strengthening resistance to the expansion of the United States in North America. Peopled by Anglo-Saxons and backed by powerful friends in Europe, an independent Texas might provide a more effective counter to the United States, a back door through the tariff barriers of the Union, and even a nucleus about which disgruntled break-away states from the Union might cluster. No British government ever adopted such a fanciful scheme. Even Palmerston was lukewarm[3] (Doc. 16). Seeing that continued strife must sooner or later involve the United States and imperil still more of Mexico's territory, the British Government sought rather to arrange some kind of settlement between Mexico and her rebellious province. Beyond this the main British interest in Texas was to persuade the new state to abandon slavery.

British meddling in the slave question in Texas was regarded as quite sinister by the annexationists in the southern United States, and it was Aberdeen who had to bear the brunt of their accusations when, in June 1842, he completed the policy initiated by Palmerston of exchanging with Texas the ratification of treaties providing for political recognition on the one hand and the abolition of the slave trade on the other. The hostility which this 'interference' aroused in American opinion and continued American intransigence over the compromise in Oregon at length strained even Aberdeen's patience. No further progress was made in his design of improving Anglo-American relations; rather he found it increasingly difficult to counter suggestions of his colleagues that they must think again in terms of war rather than peace.

The crucial question was, as always, the state of British relations with France. Although the departure of Palmerston had brought a better atmosphere, no-one, not even Aberdeen, felt that the *entente* was really restored. The rejection of the slave trade treaty had been an unpleasant shock and differences in Greece, Spain, and North Africa were further aggravating relations. Aberdeen himself never completely lost his personal faith in Guizot; what really worried him was the increasing difficulty of checking a hostile response within his own Government. By the summer of 1842 some of his

[3] Bourne, pp. 76–8, and E. D. Adams, *British Interests and Activities in Texas, 1838–1846* (Baltimore, 1910), pp. 16–17.

colleagues were already harking back again to the dread theme of a war against the United States and France combined. This phase of Aberdeen's American policy is still clouded in obscurity, but it seems very likely that, with the improvement of Anglo-American relations checked and his American policy threatening to go into reverse, he had decided before the end of 1843 to make the best of a bad job and, setting aside for the moment all prospect of pacifying American opinion, to turn American hostility in Texas and California to good account in Anglo-French relations. Possibly in the hope of compromising relations between France and the United States and so removing the danger of their alliance in war against Great Britain, but still more likely in order to reassure his more bellicose colleagues about Anglo-French relations, Aberdeen in 1844 began to develop in Texas a common front with France against the United States. Guizot, who was as much inclined to resent the growth of American influence as he was to exploit Anglo-Saxon differences, was by no means disobliging, and by the summer of 1844 Aberdeen had apparently concerted a policy of almost Palmerstonian scope in the Texan Question. In May and June it was arranged that if Mexico and Texas could settle their differences, France and Britain would guarantee Texan independence and Mexico's territorial integrity.

The policy of the Diplomatic Act, as the arrangement was called, foundered almost at once on the rock which was supposed to have been its foundation—relations with France. Indeed within a few weeks those relations seemed as bad as Palmerston had ever left them. What worried the Government most was another burst of French activity in North Africa. In 1840–1 the French had at last turned the tide against the Algerians and, then, in spite of constant assurances to Aberdeen, they followed it up with an attack on Morocco in August 1844. And what underlined British concern was that the command of the naval expedition to Tangiers was given to Louis Philippe's third son, the Duke de Joinville, who shortly before had published an alarming pamphlet about the possibilities of challenging British naval power and of breaching the defences of the island. Then, in September, there arrived news of a less important but much more direct French outrage upon Britain. Public opinion in both countries had already been alerted to rivalry in Tahiti when the French attempted to annex the island in September 1842. British protests had forced them to back down but they maintained their protectorate in a spirit which was bound to lead to clashes with British Protestant missionaries. During the summer of 1844 the French imprisoned George Pritchard, a Protestant missionary who also happened to be British Consul. Pritchard was soon released but when he returned to England in August his woeful tales aroused a storm of protest against France.

This deterioration in relations with France was too rapid and too sharp to be checked by the contrived co-operation over Texas. Instead it made that co-operation quite unworkable. As early as July 1844 Aberdeen had already decided that he must postpone the implementation of the Diplomatic Act; by the end of October he had indicated to Guizot that he had abandoned it altogether. At the same time the temperature of public feeling in America had been rising to new heights of Anglophobia under the stimulus of rumours about these foreign 'plots' and the coincidence of a presidential election campaign later in the year. Polk, the successful candidate, owed his election in large part to his promises to pursue the most extreme claims of both the Texan and the Oregon expansionists. The outgoing President stole some of Polk's thunder by getting Texan annexation through at the last moment, but this only made Polk all the more determined, as he put it, 'to look John Bull straight in the eye' over Oregon and to exploit the quarrel which Texan annexation inevitably produced in relations with Mexico to get California as well.

1844–5, then, saw Aberdeen's French and American policies both in ruins. In the late summer of 1844 opinion at home and abroad even thought that war with France was virtually inevitable. Aberdeen was then able to restrain his colleagues until Guizot had offered compensation to Pritchard and France had made a reassuring peace with Morocco in September. But the tension and the tendency towards an arms race continued throughout the following year and before the end of 1845 Aberdeen found himself so at odds with his Prime Minister and so isolated in the Cabinet that he threatened resignation (Docs. 36 and 37). In the end the Foreign Secretary decided to stay with the administration during the few short months which remained to it. The *entente cordiale*, however, was clearly a hopeless dream. On the other hand, Aberdeen was now able to work successfully towards a new agreement with the United States by a combination of customary concession with uncharacteristic toughness. The failure of the Diplomatic Act left Aberdeen with no alternative but headlong retreat out of the Texan Question. When the United States at last agreed to admit Texas in March 1845 he made no objection and as relations between Mexico and the United States rapidly deteriorated he felt able to offer only sympathy. By implication therefore Aberdeen was conceding to the expanding empire of the United States not only Texas, but also the rich prize of California which, with much else besides, war with Mexico was to bring her in 1848. In the Oregon Question, however, the American refusal to arbitrate, Congress's threats to terminate the provisional occupation agreement of 1827, and, increasingly, Polk's loud and offensive language, all inclined Peel to urge serious preparation for war, Wellington once again to raise his cry of universal war, and even Aberdeen to talk publicly of maintaining British honour (Docs. 33, 34, and 35). But Aberdeen had never abandoned his search for compromise and he worked hard during the winter of 1845–6 on conditioning British opinion to getting less than they had expected and in keeping up the pressure on the United States for a negotiated agreement. Getting agreement from the United States now was his compensation for surrender in Texas. Polk could not really afford the simultaneous showdown with Mexico and Great Britain which Aberdeen hinted at while offering his compromise, but he remained very difficult right to the end. Perhaps what finally secured his consent in June 1846 to carrying the 49th parallel to the sea, leaving only Vancouver Island beyond this line to the British, was the prospect of Palmerston's imminent return to the Foreign Office.

Palmerston had been denied an earlier chance of returning to the Foreign Office in December 1845 when the Peel Cabinet collapsed and Lord John Russell was given the chance of forming a government. But Russell's attempt failed because Lord Grey was unwilling to serve with Palmerston back as Foreign Secretary. However, when Peel's Government finally fell in June 1846, the crises with France and the United States seemed to have passed, and Russell assured his colleagues and the Court that he would exercise control over the Foreign Office and so guard against any 'imprudence' on Palmerston's part. So far as the United States was concerned Palmerston did seem to have decided on prudence. He did not attempt to interfere in the Mexican War or to deny the United States the full fruits of her victory in 1848. He knew quite well that the Oregon settlement and the acquisition of Texas, California, and the whole of the territory between meant that, the internal collapse of the Union apart, all chance of establishing an effective Balance of Power on the North American Continent had passed and that the best Britain could now do was very cautiously to contain the expansion of the United States into Central America and the Caribbean.

In both these areas Britain, for once, appeared to have the advantage. In the Caribbean she had numerous colonial island bases; in Central America she had a variety of footholds—a colony in British Honduras, some more settlements on the Bay Islands, and a protectorate over the Mosquito Indians of the eastern coast. But even Palmerston recognized that the advantage in Central America was not a basis for downright opposition to the United States, but rather a means of extracting from her a valuable compromise. When the Americans' acquisition of California, following the discovery of gold there in 1847, awakened their anxiety for an interoceanic communication across Central America and alerted their antagonism to Britain's presence, Palmerston displayed a very sensible attitude and before long secured what seemed to be a useful bargain. By the Clayton-Bulwer Treaty of April 1850 the two Powers agreed not to colonize in Central America and to work together to encourage the construction of a neutral canal. Unfortunately the arrangement was reached only by glossing over some basic disagreements and these surfaced almost at once. The Americans professed to believe that the treaty obliged Great Britain to withdraw from all her positions in Central America save British Honduras. For their part, the British, including Palmerston, were inclined to agree, but not without finding first an honourable way out of their obligations to the Indian and other inhabitants under British protection. But no satisfactory formula could be found, and as American impatience grew, so too did British irritation in response. And while no progress was made with any canal scheme, a very unpleasant difference remained to bedevil Anglo-American relations throughout the 1850s.

In the meantime affairs in Europe and the Near East had reasserted their pre-eminence in British foreign policy. Before returning to office Palmerston had made some show of patching up his personal relations with the French by making a special visit to Paris. But hardly had he returned to office than relations with France were once more enveloped in furious hostility. The scene this time was Spain.

The chaotic and unhappy affairs of Spain had appeared to be improving during the early 1840s. But the marriages of Queen Isabella and her sister, the Infanta, remained an important political problem to be settled, the British being especially concerned lest a French prince should become the Queen's consort. Aberdeen had talked over this problem with the French when he accompanied Queen Victoria on her second visit to Louis Philippe in September 1845. He came away thinking that it was clearly agreed between England and France that the Infanta would not be allowed to marry Louis Philippe's youngest son, the Duke de Montpensier, until Isabella had married a Spanish cousin and produced some heirs to keep the inheritance of the Spanish throne safely out of French hands. Unfortunately mutual suspicion persisted in spite of this apparent agreement. One constantly recurring suggestion was that Isabella might marry Prince Leopold of Saxe-Coburg. Since Leopold was Queen Victoria's and Prince Albert's first cousin the French suspected that this was a British plot. Since Leopold happened also to be closely related to the Orléans by marriage, the British suspected that it was another French intrigue. At the same time the dabbling of British and French agents in Madrid certainly did not improve the atmosphere either there or in their own capitals. Aberdeen sternly discouraged both the Coburg candidacy and the atmosphere of intrigue, but even he did not manage to clear the air. Matters did not come to a head, however, until Palmerston wrote a dispatch to his Minister in Madrid on 19 July 1846 in which he mentioned Leopold, as well as Isabella's two Spanish cousins, the Dukes of Seville and Cadiz, as being the only possible candidates for her hand. The French had long ago insisted to Aberdeen that Leopold's candidacy would be regarded as releasing them from their earlier undertakings with regard to Montpensier. Now they violently denounced Palmerston and vigorously took up the French and anti-British cause in Spain, pressing the marriages of the Queen with the Duke of Cadiz and her sister with the Duke de Montpensier.

Palmerston's personal involvement in provoking the French and the speed with which his second great quarrel with France broke out after his return to office have always suggested that he deserved a good deal of blame for the crisis and that matters would have proceeded very differently had Aberdeen remained at the Foreign Office. But Aberdeen never seemed to be quite so sure himself. Rather he denied that he had ever accepted the conditions now put forward by France. In any case Palmerston had not avowedly supported Leopold's candidacy at first, merely mentioning his name among the known candidates, and taking up his claim only after the quarrel with France had begun. Aberdeen therefore appeared to agree with many others who did not habitually side with Palmerston, like the Queen, Prince Albert, Peel, and the diarist Greville, that the French seemed all too anxious to pick a quarrel. But so did Palmerston, and it is difficult to believe that he could ever be so innocent. Aberdeen, in fact, was not on this occasion in a good position to criticize Palmerston's dispatch publicly, since the Foreign Secretary knew that his predecessor had gone on record with a similar statement about the ultimate choice of husbands being Spain's own affair. Palmerston, moreover, had made his opposition to the Montpensier marriage well known long since. He must too have heard about the pressure being put upon Louis Philippe to go ahead with the French marriage schemes. The likelihood is, then, that he did write his dispatch with a view to provoking the French into some action which would release Britain from the agreements made by Aberdeen. What especially worried him was the rumour that the Duke of Cadiz was impotent and that Queen Isabella would never have an heir. The mention of Leopold was probably intended to frighten the French and perhaps to persuade them to accept Cadiz's younger brother, the Duke of Seville. Seville had the additional merit that he was a patron of the progressive party in Spain whose influence with Isabella and her Government Palmerston was anxious to reinforce. No doubt, then, the French were right to be suspicious of Palmerston, just as he was right to be suspicious of them. But he certainly exaggerated France's power to harm British interests. His view was that the 'independence of Spain would be endangered, if not destroyed, by the marriage of a French Prince into the Royal Family of Spain'[4] (Doc. 39). On this occasion Aberdeen had the more realistic attitude. He never believed the French were innocent; he simply thought the question was 'not an adequate cause of national quarrel'.[5]

There can be little doubt that Palmerston sadly mismanaged matters in Spain itself. The Duke of Seville was quite unacceptable both to Queen Isabella and to her Government. His proposals,

[4] Henry Lytton Bulwer, *The Life of Henry John Temple, Viscount Palmerston* (London, 1874), iii. 273.
[5] Arthur Gordon, *Lord Aberdeen* (London, 1893), p. 195.

therefore, merely alienated the Spanish Government from British influence and drove them into the arms of France. On 29 August 1846 it was announced that the sisters would marry Cadiz and Montpensier and on 10 October the marriages took place simultaneously. Louis Philippe's triumph was short-lived. Isabella soon became dissatisfied with her husband and naturally blamed the French. Yet, somehow, she bore a son to frustrate their dynastic ambitions. Then, when revolution removed her from the scene in 1868, and Montpensier prepared to offer himself in her place, he hopelessly compromised his claim by killing the Duke of Seville in a duel. So the Orléans family failed to gain Spain; in the meantime they had also lost France. But Palmerston gained little from the French decline. After their apparent marriage triumph he tried hard to make his voice heard again in Madrid. His pressure culminated in March 1848 in a dispatch to his Minister in Madrid, full of haughty advice to the Spanish Government about adopting constitutional methods and more liberal policies (Doc. 50). Greville called this dispatch 'a choice specimen of Palmerston's spirit of domination'.[6] Worse still, it was a total failure. The Spanish Prime Minister considered it 'offensive to the dignity of a free and independent nation',[7] and handed his passports to the British Minister, Sir Henry Bulwer, who happened to be a particular friend and protégé of Palmerston's.

Palmerston's methods hardly had much more success in Portugal. Instead of bringing any real relief to that unhappy country, the final defeat of Miguel in 1834 had been followed by a period of chronic instability and insurrection, and instead of fulfilling Palmerston's hopes, Queen Maria increasingly tended to behave in a manner worthy of her reactionary uncle. Miguel had been defeated by the most rigorous use on Britain's part, not only of diplomatic intervention, but also of naval and military pressure. Military forces had been sent to aid Maria on several occasions and, still more important for its moral effect at least, a British naval force had been kept in the Tagus. The same weapons Palmerston now thought he could use to bring Maria to her senses. Much to Queen Victoria's disgust he lectured her Portuguese cousin in the bluntest language, and when this proved ineffective he revived in May 1847 the Quadruple Alliance of 1834 to bring pressure to bear in Portuguese affairs. 'A

---

[6] Charles C. F. Greville, *A Journal of the Reign of Queen Victoria from 1837 to 1852* (London, 1885), ii. 302.

[7] R. W. Seton-Watson, *Britain in Europe* (Cambridge, 1937), p. 254.

more glaring violation of the Whig principle of non-intervention',
Bulwer later confessed, 'could hardly be cited.' 'But', he went on,
'it was a useful one, and served to add to the many proofs . . . of the
absurdity of establishing general theoretic rules to be practically
applicable to every variety of case.'[8] Since Maria's new promises
once again turned out to be only so much paper, it is doubtful if
the intervention of 1847 was really 'useful'.

Palmerston's renewed co-operation with France and Spain in
Portugal, though at first sight surprising, probably did not signify
very much. The Quadruple Alliance was a handy tool for intervention,
more so since it appeared on this occasion to commit France and
Spain as much against Queen Maria as against the Miguelistas and
to ensure that they did not exploit Britain's unpopularity. In the
meantime the deterioration in Anglo-French relations was marked
by another unpleasant clash over missionary activity in Tahiti.
There was, too, a loud renewal of public concern about Britain's
defences. The military experts, including Wellington, had recently
discovered that steam had freed France's potential invasion fleets
from the restrictions of wind and tide and opened up new gaps in
Britain's defensive system. Palmerston had already taken up the
question while in opposition and he continued to press his colleagues
when the Whigs returned to power. But he had only limited success.
Metternich could therefore congratulate himself:

Abandoned by France and defeated on every diplomatic field, England
now finds herself alone and paralysed in face of the continental Powers.
All her resources are inadequate for the purposes of her government,
since she cannot make war for any of the ends which she pursues. She
did not dare do it when she had France at her side and could count upon
allies in every European country. To-day, if she threw down the gauntlet
to anyone, she would force France to take sides; and there is no doubt
as to which side France would take.[9]

Metternich clearly exaggerated, but in central and eastern Europe
it was no less clear that the *entente cordiale* of constitutional monarchies no longer operated to denounce and balance, if not to check, the
Eastern tyrannies.

After the settlement of 1815 and even after the abortive rebellion
of 1830–1, a free Poland had survived in the tiny Republic of Cracow.
Naturally enough, the republic served as a centre of Polish national-

---

[8] Bulwer, iii. 199.
[9] Herbert C. F. Bell, *Lord Palmerston* (London, 1936), i. 398.

ism and revolutionary propaganda. It was therefore occupied in 1836 and after risings in 1846, Russia and Prussia both pressed Austria to eliminate it. Metternich at length gave way, and on 6 November 1846 the republic was extinguished. This action was the first alteration in the Treaty of Vienna not to be put formally for approval to the Quadruple Alliance of 1815, and the reactions of the Western Powers were therefore of considerable significance. Metternich had been encouraged in the enterprise by the break-up of the Anglo-French *entente*, but the Eastern Powers still expected to receive 'a sheet of paper labelled protestation' from London and from Paris.[10] But Palmerston's quarrel with France made him spurn the suggestion of a joint protest and to tread carefully over affairs in eastern Europe, in the vain hope that he might get the Eastern autocracies to join him in prohibiting an Orléans succession in Spain. Although he heartily condemned the action in private and felt compelled to make some sort of public protest, that protest was only 'as strong as it is advisable to make any document which there is not any intention of following up by any action'.[11] 'Palmerston's protest is as moderate as it can be, and Cracow has not re-established the entente cordiale', rejoiced the Russian Chancellor Nesselrode. 'I confess this result surpasses my expectations'[12] (Doc. 40).

Cracow was too remote to expect that the result would have been anything very different if Britain and France had still been united. As it was the Eastern Powers' successful repudiation of the Vienna Settlement made it easier for Palmerston to defend the cause of liberalism against the system which Vienna had imposed upon Switzerland. Early in November 1847 civil war had broken out between the *Sonderbund* of Catholic cantons and the liberal majority over the latter's attempt to revise the constitution. France and Austria both wished the Powers to intervene in defence of order and the Treaty of Vienna. But, though he was now isolated, Palmerston demonstrated superbly his particular diplomatic skills. First he haggled and disputed until the liberal majority had won; and then he successfully resisted a conference on the grounds that the crisis was over.[13] No one doubted that there was more at stake in Switzer-

[10] Charles de Nesselrode, *Lettres et Papiers* (Paris, 1904–12), viii. 360.
[11] Greville, ii. 150.
[12] Nesselrode, viii. 360.
[13] Ann G. Imlah, *Britain and Switzerland 1845–60* (London, 1966), pp. 37–40, suggests that the delay was not deliberate and that its fortunate result was not a calculated one.

land than the success of a particular liberal movement. Nesselrode complained that Palmerston had preserved 'a permanent centre of revolution and communism'.[14] Later it was even claimed that it was here that 'the bankruptcy of the Metternich system took place'.[15] Palmerston professed to think that the most important aspect of the crisis was the possibility of armed intervention by the Powers. If the Powers had intervened, he believed, they would have been bound to quarrel and the peace of Europe would have collapsed (Doc. 45).

Such an unwelcome turn of events was all the more likely if France and Austria meddled in Italy. Switzerland was not an insignificant centre of liberal and revolutionary activity on the borders of France and Germany, but it was quite overshadowed by the consequences of the election of a supposedly liberal pope in 1846. Pius IX began with gestures which aroused the hopes of liberals everywhere, but he was met at once with the implacable opposition of Austria and the rumour of an Austro-French agreement to intervene against him in Rome. He therefore appealed to Great Britain for 'a public manifestation of good will'. Palmerston was not the man to neglect such an opportunity and in the autumn of 1847 he responded rather more vigorously than the Pope would have wished. He sent Admiral Parker with a squadron to the west coast of Italy and his friend and colleague, the Earl of Minto, on a mission to Rome, Turin, and Florence. Both measures were intended as a warning to Austria and France not to interfere in Italy, but Minto was also to impress upon the Italian princes the importance of averting revolution by granting constitutional reform in time (just as, on his way to Berne, he was to warn the Swiss liberals against giving France and Austria any new pretext for intervention) (Doc. 44). Whether or not Minto had any real effect in Italy is a matter of speculation. Certainly he did not succeed in averting revolution, and it was revolution rather than any advice of Minto's, which persuaded the rulers of Italy to experiment with constitutions.

The Italian revolutions of 1848 began with a rising in Sicily on 12 January. In the last week of February the people of Paris transformed the revolution from an Italian to a European movement by throwing out Louis Philippe. By the end of March Metternich had fallen and revolution and constitutional change had engulfed as

---

[14] Nesselrode, ix. 52–5.
[15] Count F. F. Beust, *Memoirs* (London, 1887), i. 44.

well the Austrian Empire, Prussia and the other German states, and virtually the whole of Europe. Only Russia and Russian Poland in the east, and Britain and Belgium in the west, maintained their systems. Russia and Britain, however, had some reason to fear for their own stability and still more for the peace of Europe. Both therefore were concerned to preserve the Balance of Power, and especially to contain revolutionary France.

Palmerston believed that 'large republics seem to be essentially and inherently aggressive'.[16] He was certainly worried that the Second French Republic, 'despotically governed by eight or nine men who are the mere subordinates of 40 or 50,000 of the scum of the faubourgs of Paris',[17] would repeat all the excesses of the First, with terror at home and war abroad. His very sensible view, however, was that the Powers should not stimulate republican aggression by taking too strong a line. He therefore urged upon them the recognition of the Government as 'the only security at present against anarchy' (Doc. 48). He was not alarmed when Lamartine published his circular on 4 March 1848 denouncing the moral validity of the Vienna Settlement. He accepted that the French Government had to make the gesture and he had Lamartine's assurances that that was all it was. But on the same day Charles Albert of Piedmont granted a constitution and committed himself to the Italian uprising against Austria's domination. By the end of the month he was at war with Austria. It was here, in Italy, that Palmerston believed there was a real danger from France.

As yet Palmerston had not taken up the cause of Italian nationalism with any particular vigour; it was barely mentioned in his instructions to Minto. What now most concerned him was not the fate of a national or even constitutional movement, but that, whether Austria won or lost, France would not stand aside, that she might seek to aggrandize herself in Italy, and thereby provoke a general European war (Doc. 47). To avert this possibility Palmerston tried hard to anticipate the end of the war by pressing a compromise settlement on Charles Albert, France, and Austria. His particular scheme was to allow Austria to save something for herself in Italy, to buy off Charles Albert, and to fend off French intervention—both now and in the future—by establishing a new buffer state in northern

[16] Evelyn Ashley, *The Life of Henry John Temple, Viscount Palmerston: 1846–1865* (London, 1877), i. 81.

[17] Bell, i. 424.

Italy (Doc. 51). By this means Piedmont was to be enlarged by the addition of Parma, Modena, Lombardy, and perhaps Venetia. But this plan was completely upset by the internal recovery of Austria and the defeat of Charles Albert in July 1848. Palmerston still tried to obtain something for Piedmont and to hold back France from direct intervention by pressing Anglo-French mediation on Austria. Austria accepted in September, but Charles Albert ruined everything by renewing his hopeless war in March 1849. After this reckless undertaking and after yet another military defeat for the Italians, Palmerston could only concentrate on trying to soften Austria's vengeance. Fortunately Charles Albert abdicated and the peace which the Austrians imposed upon his successor, Victor Emmanuel, was very moderate, allowing him to keep both his territory and the new constitution. The Italians gave Palmerston and Britain a good deal of the credit. There is no good reason to suppose the French did not deserve as much. In any case, the Austrians apparently appreciated the value of conciliating Victor Emmanuel and of trying to re-enlist the house of Savoy in the old alliance against liberal nationalism. With Victor Emmanuel's help, they hoped the constitution might be made a sham to check the contagion of revolution. France herself contributed to the irony of the Italian Question when her new President, Louis Napoleon, bid for the support of public opinion in April-July 1849, not by marching against Austria, but by intervening to oust Mazzini and Garibaldi from Rome and to restore the Pope, who had deserted the liberal camp and been overthrown.

Palmerston displayed even less enthusiasm for the revolution in Germany, where he believed it also threatened international order. He had always appreciated the possibility of a close alignment between Britain and the North German States: there seemed to be no great conflicting issue to divide them and they had an obvious common interest in opposing the expansionist aggressions of France and Russia. But he did not particularly like Prussia, whose exclusive customs union, the *Zollverein*, was particularly offensive to British Free Traders, and for the time being he preferred to see the centre of Europe still held by Austria (Doc. 43). He hoped that Metternich and his 'System' were both gone for good and he would have liked to see Austria substantially withdraw from the Italian peninsula. But these changes, he believed, would strengthen rather than weaken the Austrian Empire and her position in the Balance of Power. The

Hungarian revolt, on the other hand, he believed *was* a threat to the Empire, and he was not prepared to let any sympathies he might feel interfere with Britain's interest in maintaining the Balance of Power (Doc. 52). When the Austrians repudiated their concessions and the Hungarians answered force with a declaration of independence, Palmerston firmly refused them recognition. He may even have urged the Russians to intervene actively on the Austrian side.[18]

Only when the Hungarians had plainly lost did Palmerston indulge in public condemnations of Austrian and Russian brutality. In August 1849 the last Hungarian forces surrendered to the Russians and some of the Hungarian leaders, together with a large number of Polish volunteers, fled over the border into Turkey. Austria, and to a less extent Russia, put strong pressure on the Porte to give them up and the Turks found yet another admirable opportunity to play off the Eastern and Western Powers against each other. Palmerston did not let them down, though once again he acted not so much out of sentiment but to defend the Sultan and British interests in the Turkish Empire. He joined France in stiffening the Porte's resistance and sent a fleet to demonstrate just outside the Straits. Privately he made clear his firm intention if necessary to offer 'support by arms as well as by the pen'.[19] Nicholas soon decided that he had better drop the matter and the Austrian Emperor sulkily followed suit.

Palmerston's concern for the preservation of Austria in central Europe also led him to frown upon the experiments with German nationalism which were being indulged at Frankfurt and Berlin. He said that he wished to support 'without any direct or unfitting interference any plan which has for its object to consolidate Germany and give it more unity and political vigour'.[20] But evidently he did not hear of any plan which he thought fulfilled these qualifications. In reality he did not think that German unity was as yet a practical possibility. Rather, in 1848, it was still a 'phantom' and a 'plaything'.[21] He would have been in complete agreement with the historians who have almost universally seen as too idealistic and too academic the Frankfurt Assembly which was then trying to direct

[18] Seton-Watson, p. 266.

[19] C. Sproxton, *Palmerston and the Hungarian Revolution* (Cambridge, 1919), pp. 126–127.

[20] W. E. Mosse, *The Great Powers and the German Question, 1848–71* (Cambridge, 1958), p. 16.

[21] Bell, ii. 3.

the German revolution towards the construction of a united and constitutional Germany.

Any residue of sympathy which this attitude might have allowed was dissipated by Germany's inconvenient policy in the Schleswig-Holstein Question. Neither of these Duchies was fully incorporated in the Kingdom of Denmark, but both were ruled by the Danish King. Moreover while Schleswig's people were mostly Danish, Holstein was predominantly German and was formally part of the German Bund. By 1848 this complicated structure was creaking under the strain of growing nationalist sentiment in Denmark, in the Duchies, and in Germany. It became seriously disturbed when Frederick VII succeeded to the Danish throne and, under the influence of the Danish nationalists, set about pressing Schleswig into more complete union with Denmark. His particular concern was to ensure that his heir in Denmark would also be accepted in the Duchies, for strictly speaking the Salic Law, which applied in the Duchies but not in Denmark, would have excluded descent through the female line. But the nationalists in Holstein wished to lead Schleswig into Germany and to do this they supported the rival claim of the Duke of Augustenburg to inherit the Duchies. When Frederick tried to impose his rule by force the Duchies rose in revolt and the Prussian army, with the approval of the Frankfurt Assembly, crossed the border to drive back the Danes. Britain had an ancient interest in keeping Prussia's hands off the Baltic Straits, which had controlled access to the main sources of timber and supplies for her navy. But this had ceased to be a vital interest with the advance of naval technology. Palmerston, however, agreed with the Tsar that Prussia must not be allowed so easily to override the integrity of international frontiers. Denmark might not be of very much importance any more, but Prussia's move was a dangerous precedent. And as in the Italian Question, there was always the danger of foreign intervention—this time by Russia—and the spread of the war throughout Europe. Palmerston therefore took a line very similar to the one he followed in Italy—trying to warn off Prussia without encouraging too much obstinacy on Denmark's part. It was not an easy task. Frederick William of Prussia, who was not entirely happy about serving the cause of the Frankfurt Parliament and whose troops had not performed particularly well, concluded the separate armistice of Malmö in August 1848 and Frankfurt had reluctantly to agree. But the Danes denounced the armistice and the war resumed in March 1849. Peace was not finally concluded until July 1850, when further military setbacks and a separate quarrel with Austria forced Prussia to withdraw. The London Protocol of August 1850 settled the succession question in favour of the Danes and Britain, Russia, France, Prussia, Sweden, and Denmark confirmed that decision in the Treaty of London of May 1852. Unfortunately they neglected to obtain the consent of either the Duchies or of the German Confederation.

Although Palmerston had not hesitated on occasions to express both his approval of constitutions and his disapproval of violence and severity whether in revolution or in reaction, he was always careful in 1848–9 to put Britain's interests and the preservation of the Balance of Power first. To this extent the criticism from German liberals was as misplaced as the gratitude of the Italian patriots. At home opinion seems to have been mostly on his side. Lord John Russell, the Prime Minister, was not inclined to flatter or protect him, but still he felt that his Foreign Secretary had been on the right course. Public opinion in general was enthusiastically behind Palmerston. But in the Queen and her consort Palmerston had two very severe and powerful critics. They approved hardly anything he had done since the Swiss affair and the credit for that they were inclined to place elsewhere. They did not like him lecturing fellow monarchs in Spain and Portugal or his tampering with other monarchs' territorial possessions as seemed to be the case with his policy towards Austria in Italy. The Italian policy was indeed especially offensive to them. 'The establishment of an *entente cordiale with the French Republic*, for the purpose of driving the Austrians out of *their dominions* in Italy', the Queen complained to the Prime Minister, 'would be a *disgrace* to this country.'[22] At first Russell was able to fend off the Queen's pressure for Palmerston's removal by insisting that his policy was generally right, however wrong his style of diplomacy and his manner with the Queen might be, and that the Government could hardly survive without him. But Russell was always jealous of Palmerston and as Europe recovered from the shock of revolution and the danger of international war receded, Palmerston became more and more reckless and all too willing to play into the hands of his critics and of his jealous colleagues. In the Hungarian refugees' affair he had endangered good relations with

---

[22] *The Letters of Queen Victoria*, 1st series (London, 1907), ii. 221.

Russia while considerably worsening those with Austria. This was probably unavoidable. But he did go out of his way to irritate the Eastern Courts, and to snub his royal critics at home, by openly sympathizing with the popular demonstrations in England which on the one hand reviled the Austrian 'butcher', General Haynau, and on the other feted the Hungarian patriot, Kossuth. It was not possible, however, to force Palmerston out on such popular issues, as had already been discovered when he was attacked for his high-handed policy towards Greece.

After the establishment of the independent Kingdom of Greece in 1832 the Powers soon found that they had very little about which to congratulate themselves. Royal despotism vied with constitutional monarchy but there was nothing to choose between them in the way of misgovernment and corruption, or in the persistence of brigand-age and want. At Athens, moreover, the French and British Lega-tions found an admirable opportunity for petty rivalry. No wonder then that Palmerston, who called the Greek King 'the spoilt child of absolutism',[23] should at length lose patience with the affronts given to British interests and British citizens. There was undoubtedly a lot to complain of, but the specific complaints which Palmerston took up and the methods which he employed to back them up were open to serious objection. The main one concerned the pecuniary compensation of a certain Don Pacifico who had some claim to British citizenship but who certainly exaggerated his losses in a most outrageous manner. None the less the Foreign Secretary decided that the presence of the fleet in the eastern Mediterranean was too fortu-nate a coincidence to overlook. Russia and France, who were with Britain the co-guarantors of Greece, objected to such unilateral action. Palmerston reluctantly accepted the French mediation—but then allowed his Minister at Athens to continue as if nothing had changed. In this manner Palmerston threatened to alienate France and to complete Britain's isolation. He also provided his critics at home with an apparently excellent opportunity to launch a wholesale attack upon his foreign policy. The campaign began with a debate and an adverse vote in the House of Lords on 17 June 1850. But although the merit of the argument lay clearly with the critics, the Government had already committed themselves to supporting Palmerston's Greek policy and they had, however reluctantly, to come to his defence in the Commons. Palmerston himself helped

[23] Ashley, i. 191.

by making one of his few outstanding speeches and by appealing, in advance of a merciless analysis of his policy by Gladstone, to Britain's unthinking pride with his cry *Civis Romanus sum* (Docs. 53 and 54).

Palmerston's triumph, in the Commons and in the country at large, was great but it was also brief. The showdown with the Queen had merely been postponed and the accumulated uneasiness of his colleagues had not been dissipated. The final crisis came over a matter which the Queen had constantly complained about. This was his habit of sending out dispatches before she had had an opportunity of seeing and formally approving them. In the end, of course, she could not have overruled the Cabinet but this constitutional right did give her a useful opportunity to bring her views to bear, especially if the Cabinet itself was uncertain and divided about a particular aspect of foreign policy. Considering how much she disapproved of his policy it is not surprising that Palmerston should have done everything he could to get around this problem. But he undoubtedly went much too far in his anticipation of her 'approval' of dispatches, just as she went much too far in her intrigues to curb him. In August 1850 he had had to promise to behave (Docs. 55 and 56). But on 3 December 1851 he commented approvingly to the French Ambassador about Louis Napoleon's *coup* in Paris. Given his distrust of republics and his dread of an Orléanist restoration it is not surprising that Palmerston should have felt in this way. But he did not have the Cabinet's approval for such a comment and it was very awkward that the Ambassador in Paris should have to maintain an official reserve while Palmerston spoke so warmly in London. It was even doubtful whether it was possible for a Foreign Secretary to express a 'private' opinion at all. This time Russell overcame his doubts and curtly dismissed his old rival.

Palmerston's successor at the Foreign Office was the son of his former Ambassador in Paris, the young and inexperienced Earl Granville, whom the Queen and the Prime Minister both hoped to dominate. But Granville had little time to do more than calm the Queen down with a memorandum on the principles of British foreign policy (Doc. 57). In February 1852 Russell was brought down, appropriately on a motion proposed by Palmerston, and his place was taken by the Earl of Derby. The Earl of Malmesbury, who took over the Foreign Office, was older than Granville but he had even less experience of foreign affairs and not much more time to learn about them. In December 1852 the Derby Government also fell and it was replaced by a coalition under Aberdeen. Palmerston, whom everybody recognized as still indispensable after all, did come in, but at the Home, not the Foreign Office. That office went first to Russell and, when he found the burden too much, it was taken over in February 1853 by the Earl of Clarendon.

By this time the dominating factor in European diplomatic relations was the emergence of a new Bonapartist empire in France. Napoleon III was no doubt sincere in claiming that he preferred peace to war. But he did want change: the 1815 Settlement imposed after the defeat of the First Empire was not compatible with the pride or the pretensions of the Second. Perhaps he was naïve enough to think that he could work great changes through diplomacy. He certainly tried to substitute, and to some extent succeeded in substituting, Paris for Vienna or London as the centre of European diplomacy. But, however much he was personally reluctant to use it, he was prepared to resort to force when other Powers resisted the changes he sought to impose upon the international system or when they had rival schemes of their own. Within less than twenty years the Emperor had disavowed his claim, 'L'Empire, c'est la paix', in war with three of the Great Powers, Russia, Austria, and Prussia, and had come very near also to war with the fourth, Great Britain.

Although very well aware of the dangerous implications of the Bonapartist restoration, Palmerston had welcomed both Louis Napoleon's election as President of the Republic and his *coup* against the Republic. The Prince's progress was a check to Jacobinism and a victory for constitutional monarchy. Public opinion in general responded conventionally to the *coup* with a French invasion scare, but Palmerston's successors at the Foreign Office demonstrated that his approval of the *coup* was merely the occasion, and not the cause, of his dismissal. Malmesbury reflected Tory criticism by going out of his way to conciliate Austria; but at the same time he carefully encouraged Louis Napoleon's friendliness towards Great Britain. The other Powers also took the emergence of Louis Napoleon very coolly. In the aftermath of the 1848 revolutions they too welcomed his arrival as a victory for order in Europe. On the other hand Tsar Nicholas in particular was much less happy about the actual restoration of the Bonapartist Empire, and the presumptions implied in Louis Napoleon's taking the dynastic numeral III rather than II. The establishment of the Second Empire indeed signified that there was to be no return to the pre-1848 situation. In Austria, it is true, reaction surpassed even the best efforts of Metternich, with the bureaucratic absolutism of the Bach System, while Nicholas's régime in Russia reached the pinnacle of repression. But, at the same time, the Second Empire meant that liberalism was to be submerged in nationalism, that nationalism was now the dynamic force in European affairs, and that a new Napoleon was going to lead it. Just as had happened at the end of the eighteenth century, the price of internal order after revolution was to be international disorder. This was bound sooner or later to bring Napoleon III into conflict with the Eastern Powers and particularly with Russia, since, with Metternich gone and with his repression in Poland and Hungary behind him, Nicholas could well claim to be the policeman of Europe.

The circumstances in which the showdown with Russia took place had very little to do initially with the liberal-national movement. Quite probably this wider theme played little or no part in producing in mid-century the first great war between the Powers since 1815,[24] though it certainly developed during its course and flourished on its consequences. The Crimean War concerned rather the fate of Turkey and arose from the British and, to a less extent, the French determination that it should not be settled by Russia alone. This broad question was opened up by Napoleon's defence of Roman Catholic privileges in the Holy Places of Palestine against the inroads of Greek Orthodox monks supported by Russia. On the French side it reflected a clash between France's thirst for glory anywhere and Russia's traditional power policies in the Near East. Conveniently, too, it allowed Napoleon to gloss over the ambiguities of his régime in France by defending an illiberal pope at the same time as he attacked an illiberal tsar. On the British side it represented a wish to defend the position achieved by the Straits Convention of 1841 that the Eastern Question was a collective European concern.

By the beginning of 1853 Napoleon was having such success in extracting concessions from the Sultan, and Austria was having such success in bullying the Turks to call off a minor war against Montenegro, that Nicholas felt sure the independence of the Turkish Empire was fundamentally undermined and that the collapse he

---

[24] So Agatha Ramm argues in vol. x, p. 468, of *The New Cambridge Modern History*, ed. J. P. T. Bury (Cambridge, 1960).

had long expected was now at hand. He therefore prepared to protect Russia's interests by force. At the same time he had not abandoned the policy of reinsurance against Russian isolation and of friendly agreement upon partition among the Powers which he had adopted at the end of the Russo-Turkish War of 1828–9. This policy of co-operation, indeed, had been confirmed at Munchengrätz in 1833, but Nicholas was never able to persuade Metternich to discuss partition in detail. He thought, however, that he had got further with Great Britain. In December 1840 he had tried to follow up the Anglo-Russian *rapprochement* in the Mehemet Ali crisis by asking if Great Britain would 'object to record and establish by some act the alliance which ... happily existed between the four powers to serve as a security against any efforts that France might make to awaken revolutionary feelings in Europe, or against, perhaps, a revolutionary war'.[25] But Palmerston was too wily to get so involved and he cautiously, but firmly, declined on the grounds of constitutional difficulties (Doc. 27). With Aberdeen, however, Nicholas thought he had had rather more success. Early in June 1844 he made a brief state visit to England and found an opportunity to come to an agreement with Peel and Aberdeen that they should work together for the maintenance of the Turkish Empire, but that they would also concert their policy in the event of its collapse. This verbal agreement was later written up as a memorandum by the Russian Chancellor and, in January 1845, accepted as an accurate version of the conversation by Aberdeen (Doc. 32). It was, however, extremely vague both in content and in its legal quality. It said almost nothing about the future disposition of the Empire and, although it was explained to Palmerston and Russell on their resumption of office in June 1846, it was never considered binding in England. Aberdeen himself had endorsed the memorandum only as the record of a 'mutual expression of opinion'. But Nicholas always believed that for a time at least he had established the basis of an agreement, and in the circumstances of Napoleon's pressure on the Turkish Empire, he felt sure he could revive it.[26]

Nicholas first thought of raising the possibility of an imminent Turkish collapse and the need for an agreement on partition at the

[25] Quoted in F. S. Rodkey, 'Anglo-Russian Negotiations about a "Permanent" Quadruple Alliance, 1840–1841', *American Historical Review*, xxxvi (1930–1), 343.

[26] For the status of the 1844 exchanges and their connection with later conversations, see Gavin B. Henderson, 'The Seymour Conversations, 1853', in *Crimean War Diplomacy and Other Historical Essays* (Glasgow, 1947), pp. 1–14.

end of 1852. When he heard that Aberdeen had returned to office and, moreover, this time as Prime Minister, he was naturally much encouraged, and in January 1853, he made two approaches to the British Ambassador, Sir Hamilton Seymour. The response he got from the new Foreign Secretary was not discouraging. Russell firmly denied that the collapse was imminent, but he agreed that the two Powers should co-operate in the Near East. In passing, Russell also appeared to concede Russia's claim to a special protectorate over the Christians of the Turkish Empire (Doc. 58). Although Nicholas had not got all that he had wanted he was pleased enough with these replies. He thought that Britain was now committed to co-operation with Russia and that he also had Russell's support in the Holy Places dispute. In fact Nicholas misunderstood Russell's answer. The professions of co-operation, though sincerely intended by the Cabinet if not by the Foreign Secretary himself, were little more than politeness; the reference to the Russian protectorate signified how limited they thought that protectorate to be. The emphasis should rather have been placed upon the British insistence that they did not consider the collapse of the Turkish Empire to be imminent. Upon this false basis Nicholas now blundered towards war. He sent a very tough negotiator, Prince Menshikov, to counter the French successes in Constantinople, and Menshikov's mission culminated in a demand that the Sultan acknowledge Russia's general protection of his Christian subjects. When the Turks refused, Russia broke off relations and on 3 July Russian troops crossed the Pruth into the Danubian Principalities.

These moves shattered the illusion of an Anglo-Russian Concert. At first the British, both with Russell and then with Clarendon at the Foreign Office, had moved cautiously and with sympathy for Russia rather than for France. They had refused to send a fleet to the Dardanelles and had tried, however unsuccessfully, to dissuade the French from sending theirs to the Aegean. At the same time their Ambassador in Constantinople had succeeded in getting the Russian and French representatives to agree on a compromise settlement of the Holy Places dispute (4 May). But when Menshikov followed this up by pressing for the general protectorate, the British concluded that his success would be worse than the effects of Unkiar Skelessi and would spell the end of the Turkish Empire. Russia's move across the Pruth, moreover, was in the British view a betrayal of the exchanges about co-operation in January and February.

From the early summer of 1853, therefore, Britain was firmly ranged against Russia and gradually she took over the lead at Constantinople from France. In England itself anti-Russian opinion swung into gear, liberal dislike of the tyrant of Europe combining with traditional prejudices, though some of the radical leaders like Cobden desperately insisted that of the two Turkey's tyranny was the worse (Doc. 62). At Constantinople the greatest of British ambassadors, Stratford Canning, cousin of George and recently made Viscount Stratford de Redcliffe, encouraged the Turks to resist Russia's pressure. 'Lord Stratford fulfills his instructions to the letter', admitted Prince Albert, 'but he so contrives, that we are constantly getting deeper into a war policy.'[27] Whether the Ambassador really intrigued to prevent a conference and force a showdown with Russia is a matter of endless controversy. Possibly it was merely his presence which stiffened the Turks. Some recent studies of his later career suggest that he was far from being the master diplomat who could have managed everything so cleverly.[28] Perhaps, on the other hand, this merely emphasized how easy it was to manipulate his masters in London. The principal cause of the Crimean War was undoubtedly Nicholas's clumsy truculence. But he could have been stopped—and Stratford de Redcliffe too if he really was at fault—if only the Cabinet in London had taken a firm line before Nicholas's pride had become too committed to a collision course. But it was the fatal weakness of the Coalition Cabinet that its counsels were divided and that it was never strong enough, not so much to resist public opinion in England, but to make Nicholas stop[29] (Docs. 59, 60, and 61).

The Russo-Turkish rupture in May brought the British fleet into Besika Bay in the following month. It was Austria, however, who was most immediately concerned when the Russians crossed the Pruth. Nicholas seems simply to have trusted in Austrian gratitude for his help against Hungary and to have assumed that she would not now object. But Austria did object; the advance seemed to her a

---

[27] Theodore Martin, *The Life of His Royal Highness The Prince Consort* (fourth ed., London, 1877), ii. 532.

[28] W. E. Mosse, 'The Return of Reschid Pasha; an Incident in the Career of Lord Stratford de Redcliffe', *English Historical Review*, lxviii (1953), 546–73; Lynn M. Case, 'A Duel of Giants in Old Stamboul: Stratford versus Thouvenel', *Journal of Modern History*, xxv (1963), 262–73.

[29] A recent study is J. B. Conacher, *The Aberdeen Coalition 1852–55: a study in mid-nineteenth century party politics* (Cambridge, 1968).

direct threat to the security of the Danube. It was on her initiative, therefore, that a conference of Austrian, French, Prussian, and British representatives produced in the Vienna Note of 28 July a new compromise for the dispute between Russia and Turkey. Russia accepted, but on 20 August the Turks, possibly on the advice of Stratford de Redcliffe, rejected it. Then, on 7 September, Nicholas foolishly squandered the sympathy this might have earned him by putting on the Note the utterly unacceptable interpretation that it gave Russia a general right of intervention on behalf of the Orthodox Christians. A meeting between the Russian and Austrian Emperors produced another formula, the Buol Project, in which the Tsar withdrew this condition, but Britain had now lost all faith in Nicholas and, followed reluctantly by France, she rejected the new move. Then, on the pretext of disorders at Constantinople which might threaten the lives of foreigners, the British and French fleets were ordered up to the capital. It was now the Porte's turn to seize the initiative—but it was not an initiative for peace. On 10 October they demanded the evacuation of the Principalities or war within a fortnight. This time Stratford de Redcliffe certainly tried to avert war, and on his own initiative delayed the movement of the British fleet through the Dardanelles. But on 23 October fighting broke out on the Danube and in the Caucasus.

The only hope now of averting a general war was by the mediation of the Powers. This Russia accepted, but in England the Cabinet was quite uncertain how to proceed, with Aberdeen and Clarendon on the one hand inclined to put pressure on Turkey and with Palmerston and Russell on the other insisting that it was Russia who was the real menace. But all the while Russophobia had been rapidly increasing in Britain. Early in December it was brought to a climax by news of the destruction of the Turkish fleet at Sinope. Quite unfairly Nicholas's victory was considered in Britain to be a treacherous betrayal of his earlier undertakings to conduct a purely defensive war. At the same time Palmerston resigned from the Government, and though this was apparently over a parliamentary reform proposal, it gave an enormous filip to the Russophobes. Nor was their progress checked by his return to office two days later, since the day before the Cabinet had finally agreed to take decisive action in the east. On 4 January 1854 the British and French fleets moved into the Black Sea. On 20 January the Russians indignantly refused the Powers' proposal of a peace conference and the evacuation of the

Principalities. On 12 March Britain and France signed an alliance with Turkey and on 28 March they declared war.

The outburst of opinion which pushed a divided Cabinet into war has been represented as a dramatic triumph for Palmerston.[30] Perhaps it was, but there is no convincing evidence that he engineered it. One authority affirms that it was 'the nation', not Palmerston or any other man 'who really made the war'.[31] And another, who certainly has little regard for Palmerston, agrees: 'It is the classic disproof of the view that peoples are always pacific and only the statesmen or financiers warlike.'[32] In fact Palmerston agreed that the war was a mistake. He firmly believed that once Russia and Turkey had come to blows it was foolish to prejudice material British interests through any fastidiousness or sentimental distrust for an alliance with the Turks. But he also had no doubt whatever that the war could and should have been averted by earlier taking a firm line with Russia. Once the war was begun, moreover, it was equally important to press it to a satisfactory resolution, militarily and diplomatically. In both areas the British continued to make mistakes—thanks very largely to their inability to consolidate a firm alignment with Austria and France.

Unable on this occasion to reconcile her commitment to eastern autocracy with her defence of the Turkish Empire, Austria determined upon a policy of vigorous neutrality. In the short-run she was completely successful—though in the long-run it gained her the enmity of all the Powers and cost her her position in both Italy and Germany. Her immediate concern was the Russian threat to the Danube; and in July and August 1854 she forced the Russians to evacuate the Principalities and occupied them herself. This removed the only good reason she thought she had to take active part in the war against Russia. It also prevented the combatants from coming to blows in the Balkan peninsula and compelled the western allies to find some other field for glory. They chose the Crimea partly because it was within reach of the forces they had already assembled in the east, and partly in the hope of destroying Russian naval power in the Black Sea.

[30] B. Kingsley Martin, *The Triumph of Lord Palmerston* (London, 1963). It should be pointed out, however, that this is more a study of press and public opinion than of its eponymous villain.

[31] W. F. Reddaway in A. Ward and G. P. Gooch, eds., *The Cambridge History of British Foreign Policy* (Cambridge, 1923), ii. 381.

[32] Seton-Watson, p. 325.

This objective also figured prominently in the war aims which the allies formulated in July and which Austria supported diplomatically. The Four Points, as they were called, were the renunciation of Russia's special rights in Serbia and in the Principalities, and of her claim to a protectorate over the Orthodox Christians of the Empire; and, ominously for Russia's naval power, a revision of the 1841 Straits Convention 'in the interests of the Balance of Power'. Setbacks in the Crimea eventually persuaded the Russians to accept (28 November) but too late, for the same events also determined the British to raise their price and to work for the complete destruction of Russian naval power in the Black Sea. The subsequent shock of military incapacity and disaster in the Crimea, followed, in February 1855, by Palmerston's displacement of Aberdeen as Prime Minister, served only to reinforce that determination. After all, even before the war had begun, Palmerston's 'beau ideal', as he put it in March 1854, had been:

Aland and Finland restored to Sweden. Some of the German provinces of Russia on the Baltic ceded to Prussia. A substantive Kingdom of Poland reestablished as a barrier between Germany and Russia. Wallachia and Moldavia and the mouths of the Danube given to Austria. Lombardy and Venice set free of Austrian rule, and either made independent states or incorporated with Piedmont. The Crimea, Circassia, and Georgia wrested from Russia, the Crimea and Georgia given to Turkey, and Circassia either independent or connected with the Sultan as Suzerain.[33]

'We have the plan sketched out for a thirty years' war', Aberdeen complained.[34] Certainly these were pretty fanciful ideas, but on that account all the more likely to appeal to Napoleon. But although the French Emperor did take some of them up from time to time—especially in Poland and Italy—Austria's inevitable opposition and still more his own increasing weariness with a disappointing war gradually weakened his alliance with Great Britain rather than, as Clarendon had hoped at first, extending its effects throughout the world. The chances of peace and even of a Franco-Russian *rapprochement* increased considerably with the death of Nicholas on 2 March 1855. His successor, Alexander II, was not committed to personal enmity towards Louis Napoleon and was soon convinced that Russia could not bear the strain of war much longer. Negotia-

[33] G. P. Gooch, ed., *The Later Correspondence of Lord John Russell, 1840–1878* (London, 1925), ii. 160–1.

[34] Spencer Walpole, *The Life of Lord John Russell* (London, 1889), ii. 214.

tions on the Four Points were resumed at a conference in Vienna on 15 March, but finally collapsed in June through Russia's unwillingness to consider any alteration in the Straits Convention. From this point peace waited more upon the fate of Russia's Crimean fortress at Sebastopol than upon the almost exhausted diplomacy of the Powers. Both Britain and France wanted to end the war with a compensating military triumph. Both were nearly satisfied in September when, after the French had taken one key position (the Malakov Tower), the British took another (the Redan). But the British were driven out again and the surrender of the fortress three days later left them bitterly dissatisfied. Palmerston had already forecast that after the fall of Sebastopol 'our danger will then begin—a danger of peace, and not a danger of war'.[35] They were alone among the Powers, however, in wanting to prolong the war. On 28 December Austria presented Russia with an ultimatum to accept the Four Points with the addition of the neutralization of the Black Sea and the cession of Bessarabia. When they learned that Prussia too was supporting the demand the Russians gave way on 16 January 1856.

To compensate for their failure to secure a decisive victory on land or at sea (their naval operations on the Baltic were also disappointing), the British tried hard to get still better terms with Russia at the peace conference which opened at Paris on 25 February 1856. But thanks very largely to Napoleon's defence of Russia, Britain had only slight success. In particular she failed to do more than restore Turkey's position in the Caucasus or to push Russia back as far in Bessarabia as she would have liked. Still the peace terms were a considerable defeat for Russia. On the promise of improvements for its Christian population, the Turkish Empire was formally admitted to the European Concert, and its integrity and independence were jointly guaranteed. Russia had to give up her claim to special rights of interference in Serbia and the Danubian Principalities and on behalf of the Christians in general. Instead the Principalities were to have some sort of undefined 'independent and national' existence under Turkish suzerainty. The Danube was shielded from Russian encroachment by the cession of southern Bessarabia and by placing its navigation under the control of a European commission. Most irritating of all to Russia, she was to be allowed neither warships nor naval bases in the Black Sea. And just in case the Treaty of Paris of 30 March were not sufficient, Britain, France, and Austria also concluded a separate treaty of 15 April to guarantee Turkey's independence and integrity.

Although the French had leaned heavily towards Russia at the Congress of Paris and although the British were very disappointed with its result, the peace terms were far from lenient. They were a more than adequate measure of the military success of the allies, if not, as the British illogically preferred, of the wasted and costly efforts they had made in the Crimea. The Russians believed they had suffered a tremendous blow, and a major setback in their Near Eastern policy. Certainly there was no major crisis in the Near East for twenty years. The more serious criticism, however, is that this lengthy breathing space was wasted. The neglect of the Turks to put their own house in order was their own fault; but the Powers had had no reason to expect any better result. Indeed by making Turkey safe from external attack, they indirectly encouraged internal neglect and decay. The war and the peace, then, did nothing to solve the Near Eastern Question, but merely postponed the crisis—though in matters of diplomacy postponement is not a despicable achievement. Furthermore if the Powers had only been able to maintain their Concert and the system established by the Congress, they might have made some progress in the actual solution of the Near Eastern Question. What mainly undermined the Paris peace settlement was that in erecting a superficial Concert in the Near East, the Crimean War had upset the Balance of Power in Europe and tipped the scales in favour of wholesale territorial revision for the first time since 1814–15.

4

THE WATERSHED IN EUROPE
AND AMERICA, 1855–1874

The Crimean War introduced a new Palmerstonian era of British foreign policy. With the short break of the Derby Ministry of 1858–1859, Palmerston himself was Prime Minister from February 1855 until his death in October 1865. In his first Cabinet Clarendon stayed on as Foreign Secretary: after Palmerston's return in June 1859 that office was taken over by Russell. Palmerston had taken over in the heat of war and amid strong criticism of the weakness and failures of Aberdeen's leadership. It was expected that he would attempt to reinvigorate British policy everywhere and not merely in the Crimea. His 'foreign broils and propensities' appeared, as Sir James Graham complained, 'congenial to the temper and spirit of the nation'.[1] But, as in the Crimea, he had very mixed results, finding that while the war had revived popular nationalism in England, its doubtful origins and disappointing course and consequences had also strengthened the hands of his critics.

The striking instance of the uncertainties of the post-Crimean period was the political table turning over the new Chinese war. The First China War and the Treaty of Nanking (1842) had not satisfactorily resolved affairs in that quarter. The Chinese actively resented the concessions they had been forced to make; the foreign merchants pressed for more. But the immediate origin of the new clash lay in the distant communications and local conditions which deprived both the Chinese and the British governments of detailed information and effective authority. The outbreak of the Taiping rebellion in 1850 had greatly weakened the position of the Chinese, and when in 1856 a French missionary was tortured and executed on the orders of a Chinese official the French and British Governments

[1] Charles Stuart Parker, *Life and Letters of Sir James Graham, 2nd Baronet of Netherby* (London, 1907), ii. 298–9.

prepared to intervene. Then, in October, the Chinese authorities at Canton boarded a British registered vessel, the *Arrow*, to take off a pirate, and incidentally imprisoned a dozen of her crew. The *Arrow* was Chinese owned and it appeared that vessels like it—lorchas, as they were called—were frequently used for smuggling and piracy. Britain's legal position was technically weak: the ship's British registration had in fact lapsed. Nevertheless the affront was again used locally as an occasion for a showdown over China's continued refusal to respect foreign powers, and London did not hesitate to back it up (Doc. 63). The British Consul at Canton, Sir John Bowring, demanded and eventually obtained the release of the crew. But the Chinese refused to make a written apology and a British squadron proceeded to bombard the forts in the Canton river.

This action brought down a stream of bitter criticism from what Palmerston himself called an 'unprincipled combination' of all his opponents in the House of Commons. On 3 March 1857 Cobden successfully moved for a committee of enquiry and rather than meekly surrender office, Palmerston appealed to the electorate. Here he won a tremendous victory. Many of his opponents lost their seats, Cobden and Bright among them, and he returned to power with a majority of seventy.

Apparently reassured that he was still the darling of the British public Palmerston proceeded to follow up the initiative in China. In the summer he sent out Lord Elgin with a list of demands, including the right to establish a diplomatic mission at Peking. With him Elgin took a strong force of British and French troops, and the diplomatic backing of Russia and the United States. None the less his mission outlived both the Palmerston Administration and the Derby Government which took over from Palmerston in February 1858, and was not completed until some time after the beginning of Palmerston's second Administration. At the end of June 1858 the Chinese agreed to new treaties with the Powers (the Treaties of Tientsin), opening eleven more ports to trade, admitting Christian missionaries and traders into the interior, and giving diplomatic access to Peking itself. Special arrangements were also to be made for the better regulation of the Chinese tariffs and trade, including the opium trade which it was considered impossible, if not undesirable, to abolish. But the following year the envoys who were sent to exchange ratifications found their way to Peking effectively barred. Force again had to be used and after some twenty-one members of the Anglo-French truce party had been treacherously murdered, Peking was occupied in 1860, and the Emperor's beautiful winter palace nearby burned down as an act of penal vengeance and warning. This last act has been universally condemned; but perhaps there was something in the argument that no better means could be found of impressing the Emperor. He had fled to safety from Peking and only his miserable subjects would have suffered by way of increased taxation from any further indemnities imposed by the Powers.

Palmerston considered the combination against his China policy unprincipled because it comprised utterly irreconcilable elements of opposition. That did not by any means invalidate their criticism, but there was some justification in the charge. The critics agreed only in condemning the hasty belligerence with which they believed the Government had acted. The majority certainly did not endorse as a whole the ideas which had been put forward since the 1830s by the Radical leaders, Richard Cobden and John Bright. The Cobdenite attack on Palmerston was quite fundamental. Its idea was best summed up by Cobden himself as 'no foreign politics'.[2] According to Bright the Balance of Power was a 'foul idol', condemning Great Britain to expensive and ineffective intervention (Doc. 82), and providing in such things as the diplomatic service 'a gigantic system of out-door relief for the aristocracy'.[3] Great Britain would far better concentrate her wealth and her interest on improving the condition of her own people, notably in Ireland. 'England', declared Cobden, 'will never speak in vain when she has moral power to back her.'[4]

To most statesmen, and especially to Palmerston, against whom Cobden and Bright's arguments were directly levelled, these ideas were manifestly absurd. When, as in the aftermath of the Crimean War, it seemed expedient to endorse some of them, they got little more than paper approval. One of the suggestions Cobden and his associates had continually brought before parliament since 1849 was that of international arbitration treaties. They had little success in parliament and their efforts suffered a severe set-back with the outbreak of the Crimean War. But at the close of the war a group of British pacifists tried again to persuade the British Government

[2] Richard Cobden, *Political Writings* (London, 1868), i. 9.
[3] G. M. Trevelyan, *The Life of John Bright* (London, 1925), p. 274.
[4] W. H. Dawson, *Richard Cobden and Foreign Policy* (London, 1926), p. 107.

to take up the cause of international arbitration at the Congress in Paris.[5] Neither Palmerston nor Clarendon could see how any nation could agree to surrender control over its 'vital interests' and 'national honour'. Some sort of an agreement on mediation, however, was not impossible. 'As every Government must be the judge of what affected its honor or its interests', Clarendon wrote, 'it could never bind itself beforehand to submit to arbitration, but . . . no Government would compromise its honor or its interests by consenting to listen to the opinions of one or more friendly Powers before it actually engaged in war.' The French in particular were not willing to make any actual agreement, but at Clarendon's insistence the plenipotentiaries at Paris expressed in Protocol 23, 'in the name of their Governments the wish that States between which any serious misunderstandings may arise, should, before appealing to arms, have recourse as far as circumstances might allow, to the good offices of a friendly power'. The Protocol was warmly welcomed by the pacifists, but it was really very far from what they wanted. It was vague and not at all binding. It did not even live up to Clarendon's suggestion that it would 'oppose an obstacle, though it might not oppose a barrier, to the renewal of war'.[6] It met with no response when it was invoked on the eve of Bismarck's wars in 1864, 1866, and 1870, and its first application during a minor excitement over the Near Eastern Question in 1869 had only the most superficial success.[7]

Although of great importance, arbitration and mediation were not the principal elements in Cobden's ideas. Typically, for a Victorian factory owner, that place was reserved for trade. Here he and Palmerston never seemed so far apart, for Cobden conceded that in adopting Free Trade England had established a 'moral power to back her'. Free Trade conveniently suited the moral temper and the commercial supremacy of Great Britain in mid-century. Palmerston shared this point of view. Before going up to Cambridge as a young man, he had been sent to Edinburgh to study at the house of the leading exponent of Adam Smith's ideas,

[5] G. B. Henderson, 'The Pacifists of the Fifties', in *Crimean War Diplomacy and Other Historical Essays* (Glasgow, 1947), pp. 123–52; Maureen M. Robson, 'Liberals and "Vital Interests": the debate on international arbitration, 1815–72', *Bulletin of the Institute of Historical Research*, xxii (1959), 50.

[6] Robson, 'Liberals and "Vital Interests" ', pp. 50–1.

[7] Maureen M. Robson, 'Lord Clarendon and the Cretan Question, 1868–9', *Historical Journal*, iii (1960), 38–55.

and there he became convinced of their material benefit. 'Our adoption of the principles of free trade', he claimed for those who had followed Huskisson in the 1820s, 'was not a course which would render the country poor, and unable to bear expense, but a course which had been resolved upon from a conviction of its superior profitableness and expediency.'[8] In the debate on the Corn Laws he even stressed the contribution that Free Trade would make to international relations (Doc. 29). But he would never have conceded to it any superior efficiency over international diplomacy. This, however, was precisely what Cobden and Bright and their followers did claim for it (Doc. 38). 'Free Trade', Cobden said, 'is God's diplomacy, and there is no other certain way of uniting people in bonds of peace.'[9] Ironically enough it has been suggested that Free Trade policies even encouraged the aristocratic conditions of which Bright complained: 'noblemen, bored, dispirited, and inexperienced in matters of commerce and finance, found in *laissez-faire* exactly the rationalization they were looking for; they could avoid a distasteful contact with the persons and problems of traders and financiers merely by referring in perfect good faith, to the traditions of non-intervention, Free Trade, and open competition.'[10] As the Crimean War amply demonstrated, Cobden's remained a pious hope, not an active principle of foreign policy. After the abandonment of Protection in 1846, British governments also abandoned the negotiation of trade reciprocity treaties in the expectation that foreign countries, observing the benefits of Britain's Free Trade policy, would soon follow suit.

The international response to Free Trade was even more disappointing than it had been in the era of reciprocity treaties. The Great Powers, in particular, remained unrepentant. When, therefore, late in 1859 Napoleon III authorized an approach for a liberal reciprocity treaty, both Cobden and the Palmerston Government were happy to respond, even though a 'Free Trade Treaty' was a contradiction in terms and a return to reciprocity. The treaty (23 January 1860) brought substantial material gains; in reviving the system of reciprocity treaties, Britain and France also spread through Europe during the next few years what Britain alone had

[8] Herbert C. F. Bell, *Lord Palmerston* (London, 1936), i. 53.

[9] J. A. Hobson, *Richard Cobden, the International Man* (London, 1918), p. 224.

[10] D. C. M. Platt, *Finance, Trade, and Politics in British Foreign Policy 1815–1914* (Oxford, 1968), p. xxv.

failed to do before 1846. Cobden naturally expected large political benefits as well. Certainly the treaty slowed the rapid deterioration of Anglo-French relations at a dangerous moment of the Italian Question.[11] It may well have been partly for this purpose that Palmerston's Government had taken it up in the first place. But Palmerston himself had no intention of adopting generally a Cobdenite view of foreign policy. That would have been a complete denial of all that he had ever stood for. So far as he was concerned, 'God's diplomacy' belonged only in the Kingdom of Heaven. On earth he despised the political arguments of the 'Manchester Men' as weakness. Certainly Cobden, for all the wisdom of his questioning of expensive meddling, never seems to have understood the fundamental validity of Palmerston's political experience. The successful defence of the 'vital political interest' which Cobden spurned was the prerequisite of the international trade and communication which he equated with international peace. So long as British public opinion permitted—and no one could stimulate it so well—Palmerston had no intention of withdrawing Britain's voice from European affairs or of neglecting her vital interests. He continued, as he had always done, to press for increased expenditure on armaments and he continued to quarrel about this with his brilliant Chancellor, W. E. Gladstone.

The battle between Palmerston and his critics was an interesting and constructive debate in international morality and diplomatic method. It also had important consequences on the practical side of British foreign policy. But in the broader sense the tug-of-war was being made irrelevant by developments in Europe and America.

The principal issue in Anglo-American relations throughout the 1850s was the Central American Question. No administration was able to iron out the differences over the interpretation of the Clayton-Bulwer Treaty and to reconcile Britain's interests and honour with American demands and the conditions of local Latin-American politics. Friction between Britain and the United States rose almost to fever pitch during the Crimean War. In part this was due to the aggressive attitude of the new Administration in Washington. President Pierce's Government (1853-7), taking advantage of the distractions of the European Powers in the Near East, looked around actively for opportunities of extending American influence and

[11] See below, p. 102.

territory. In Cuba, Santo Domingo, and Hawaii they pressed on such sensitive points that Britain and France diverted some of their attention to frustrate American schemes to acquire naval bases. In Central America the Americans even resorted to violence in an effort to undermine the authority of the Mosquito Indians at Greytown, which was the eastern terminus of the favourite canal route and where the Royal Navy had forcibly asserted the Indian claim against Nicaragua in 1848. Britain's diplomatic position in Central America was not strong enough to make any really active resistance, but Aberdeen and Clarendon agreed that they should not negotiate a treaty during a time of weakness like the Crimean War. From the Home Office, however, Palmerston seems to have been relatively undeterred by the efforts required in the Crimea and to have been pressing for a showdown with the Americans. Possibly he believed in the myth of a Russian-American combination to counter the Crimean alliance, and perhaps he expected that the popular enthusiasm which the war had generated in England might enable a British government for once to stand up against the aggressiveness of the Americans. For a time after he had succeeded Aberdeen as Prime Minister in February 1855, he found things rather more difficult in the Near East than he had hoped. Meanwhile private American adventurers threatened to do what their Government was forbidden to do by the Clayton-Bulwer Treaty and to take over in Central America. In the summer of 1855 William Walker intervened in a revolution in Nicaragua and ended the year in almost absolute control of the whole country. Then, in September, Sebastopol fell at last and at about the same time the American Government presented Palmerston with what seemed an ideal opportunity for a showdown, since it directly concerned the war in the east rather than the Central American Question about which he knew it was difficult to stir up the British public.

Palmerston's opportunity was the Crampton Recruiting Question. Late in 1854 the Government's sense of desperation about their military effort in the Crimea had led them to consider recruiting in the United States. They had soon dropped this idea when they realized that the Americans might object, but probably through some misunderstanding, the Minister in Washington, John Crampton, or perhaps his agents alone, continued to act in a manner offensive to American neutrality law. Before long the Americans were threatening to expel the Minister and Palmerston was almost gleefully preparing to retaliate and even make ready for war. Unfortunately for him his Cabinet colleagues were not so certain either about Crampton's innocence or about getting the support of English public opinion. Almost at the last moment, on 14 June, they forced the Prime Minister to give up any idea of retaliating against the Americans. Soon afterwards, on 1 July 1856, Palmerston made a very able defence of his policy in the House of Commons and won a handsome majority. But he knew that his policy was in ruins not only over the Recruitment Question but also over Central America.[12] The crisis had finally aired the Central American Question in the Press and clarified at last the direction British policy ought to take. On 2 June *The Times* argued once again against that 'greatest of human calamities', a war with the United States. The next day it even averred that Britain should not oppose but support American expansion. As *The Economist* put it a fortnight later:

We could not hinder the ultimate absorption by the Anglo-Saxon republicans of the whole of Central America if we would. . . . we can have no interest in upholding the present wretched and feeble governments of Spanish-America. Our interest lies all the other way. We wish ourselves for no extension of territory on that continent. We are half inclined to regret that we hold any possession at all there south of the Union. Desiring no territory, we desire only prosperous, industrious, civilized and wealthy customers. . . . Central America peopled and exploited by Anglo-Saxons would be worth to us tenfold its present value.[13]

Such ideas as these were sheer heresy to Palmerston, but he knew when he was beaten. He had to admit, however reluctantly, that his policy was 'controlled by the Indifference of the Nation as to the Question discussed, and by its Strong commercial Interest in maintaining peace with the United States'. In the circumstances, and with men like William Walker threatening to circumvent restriction on American expansion, even the Clayton-Bulwer Treaty hardly seemed worth supporting (Doc. 65). However, as the British began to express their doubts about keeping it, the Americans automatically began to discover its advantages. The result of these second thoughts about the treaty and of Britain's sense of hopelessness in Central America, was a renewed attempt to compromise their differences over the interpretation of the treaty. What made compromise easier

[12] K. Bourne, 'Lord Palmerston's "Ginger-Beer" Triumph, 1 July 1856', in K. Bourne and D. C. Watt, *Studies in International History* (London, 1967), pp. 145–71.

[13] J. Fred Rippy, *The United States and Mexico* (New York, 1926), pp. 103–4.

at this stage was probably the growing awareness on both sides that there was no immediate prospect of any canal being built. Both Governments had found that in such schemes rogues abounded while finance and engineering skills were lacking. For the time being at least the Central American Question therefore lost much of its importance. The ill-health and ineptitude of British agents and the complexities of Latin-American politics managed still to hold things up for a while. But at length, in November 1859 and January 1860, arrangements were made for the transfer of the Mosquito Coast and the Bay Islands from British protection.

The resolution of the Central American Question marked the end of any idea of a direct confrontation with the United States on her own continent. Even Palmerston was quite certain about that. But this did not stop him from keeping a look-out for some indirect means of checking American strength. One way was to encourage some other power, like France, to try it. To have kept the American Continent relatively free from the interference of the other European Powers was possibly the greatest achievement of Pax Britannica. Certainly its claims were greater than those of the Monroe Doctrine. But that achievement had also left Great Britain exposed to bear the brunt of American expansion and she had proved unable to cope with it. This was certainly what Palmerston had in mind when he came to consider the question of French policy in Mexico in 1861. Ostensibly the expedition of British, French, and Spanish forces to Mexico in December 1861, was a strictly limited operation to enforce the payment of debts. But it was known from the beginning that Napoleon III had ulterior designs, notably to establish a European monarchy in Mexico. Russell, as Foreign Secretary, sought to frustrate this design or at least to dissociate Great Britain by strictly limiting the scope of intervention by the treaty of 31 October 1861. And when, after the expedition had landed, the French proceeded with their scheme by advancing on Mexico City the British and Spanish withdrew their forces in April 1862. But Palmerston at least was glad enough to see French troops diverted from Europe and administering a check to the Monroe Doctrine: 'the French would be bound to resist the application of the Monroe Doctrine to the prejudice of French aggrandisement', he said in June 1860.[14] If Russell was less favourable to the monarchical

[14] Kenneth Bourne, *Britain and the Balance of Power in North America, 1815–1908* (London, 1967), p. 255.

scheme than Palmerston, it was largely because he was very sceptical about its chances of success. The only thing which made the establishment of Maximilian as Emperor in Mexico feasible, and then only for a time, was the outbreak of the American Civil War.

Opinion in Great Britain as well as in America had long anticipated the collapse of the Union. Some, like Palmerston himself, had looked forward to it as a consolation for the failure of British opposition to American expansion.[15] Yet when the war finally came in 1861, the predominant sentiment in England seems to have been regret. British sympathies were certainly divided between the contestants, though precisely how is a matter of some doubt. These sympathies did affect British views both about the causes of the war and its course. Those who stressed slavery as a cause of the war tended to side with the North; but there were also those who blamed the economic domination of the North. Cutting right across these considerations, however, were the tendencies of some Radical leaders to favour the democracy of the North, while the conservative and aristocratic elements believed they had a natural affinity for the land-owning classes of the South. In such circumstances there could be no clear-cut expression of opinion in England along traditional political or even social lines. After all Palmerston, who certainly had no love for the Union, liked slavery even less; while Cobden, who was among the North's staunchest friends, had dedicated his whole life to the fight against economic protection. Economic interests were no surer guide to Britain's attitude. British merchants naturally did a thriving trade in war supplies, and their shipping benefited enormously from the destruction of the Americans' mercantile marine. Still more important, however, was the effect of the war on Britain's supply of cotton from the South. About one-fifth of the population of Great Britain lived directly or indirectly by the cotton industry, and the South in 1861 provided about eighty per cent of Great Britain's imports of raw cotton. It had long since become an article of faith among politicians in the South, therefore, that England could not tolerate the suspension of this supply by war and that she would soon be compelled to intervene to stop the contest. To hasten the process the Confederate Government had even gone out of its way at the beginning of the

    [15] R. W. Van Alstyne, 'Anglo-American Relations, 1853–1857; British Statesmen on the Clayton-Bulwer Treaty and American Expansion', *American Historical Review*, xliii (1936–7), 499.

war to stop supplies to Britain before the North's blockade could really take effect. But although by the end of 1862 unemployment reached a frightful level in Lancashire, the South had miscalculated. The reduction in supplies may even have saved some manufacturers who had earlier accumulated a fifty per cent over-supply of raw cotton and a considerable surplus in manufactured goods. By the end of the war in 1865, moreover, the supply of raw cotton had been made up from alternative, though very inferior, sources. So far as the workers were concerned, their distress was localized and whatever popular agitation there was against the North it made no real impact on British policy. Instead, their supposed democratic sympathies were strongly represented by Radical leaders like Cobden and Bright, to outweigh any material need to help the South. Possibly too, the Government would have had some doubts about upsetting the country's considerable imports of grain from the North.

The balance of Britain's material interests, therefore, as well as humanitarian sentiment urged upon her a policy of neutrality and peace, rather than one which accommodated the South or justified the suspicions of the North. Neutrality and peace, however, were not easy to preserve. As the war dragged on, with each side suffering terrible losses and with neither gaining a decisive victory, opinion not only in England but in Europe generally began to urge that the Powers should take some peace initiative. But to intervene in the war would have been extremely dangerous since it would have played into the hands of the Confederates and alienated the North. The key to the question of mediation was the military course of the war. To be successful mediation would have to offer terms which were appropriate to the fortunes of the war, and in the first year these did not seem to favour the North. The North had been unable to force the South back into the Union, while the Confederacy seemed, as Gladstone once put it, to have 'made a nation'. Any suggestion of mediation therefore implied the North giving up the cause for which she had undertaken war. Clearly it was not going to be easy, perhaps impossible, to put this to the North in a pacific manner. The French were all for going ahead in the summer and autumn of 1862; but the British decided instead to wait for a decisive Southern victory to bring the North to its senses (Docs. 73 and 74). Fortunately, the British Cabinet was never unanimously convinced that the South had won such a victory. At the end of

August 1862 the South did win the second battle of Bull Run and Russell and Gladstone both pressed for mediation. But Palmerston did not agree, and he was right. The next major battle in the east, at Antietam, though largely indecisive, was strategically a check to Lee's invasion across the Potomac, and as the war moved into 1863 its course, though still occasionally erratic, gradually swung decisively in favour of the North. The British therefore moved no less decisively away from the idea of mediation. Early in November 1862 Napoleon III's suggestion that Britain and Russia join France in pressing for an armistice was decisively defeated in the Cabinet; by 1863 Russell was at last able to envisage the possibility of total victory for the North.

By the collective wisdom of the Cabinet then, rather than by the consistent good sense of any individual member, England avoided the danger of actual intervention. Even so her neutrality was by no means assured. The policy of neutrality was a grave disappointment to the Confederacy, but the word even was offensive to the North. The British issued a proclamation of neutrality in May 1861, and immediately recognized the belligerency, but not the independence, of the South because they believed they had no option. To have neglected to do so would have been to overlook the fact of a great war which must involve British citizens. But this was precisely what the Northern Government required. It was essential to her that foreign governments should not concede even a state of belligerency to the South, on constitutional as well as practical grounds, since the American constitution gave to the Federal Government the clear right to coerce individuals as rebels, but not states. The British therefore began with a well-intentioned measure that earned the consistent hostility of the North and confirmed its traditional Anglophobia. In addition the American Secretary of State, W. H. Seward, was no friend of Britain's and was even suspected—correctly as it happened—of nurturing schemes to reconcile the North and South in a common struggle against England and other European enemies. Fortunately Seward was restrained by President Lincoln, but in all the circumstances it is not surprising that Anglo-American relations were threatened throughout the war by a series of dangerous incidents.

The area of gravest danger was at sea, where it was always difficult to avoid clashes between the greatest maritime belligerent and the greatest maritime neutral. Here the traditional roles of

Great Britain and the United States were reversed, and the British tried to exploit this change by encouraging the United States in her unaccustomed role to move closer to the position normally adopted by the British. These efforts were of little use in the long run, but they helped to keep Britain out of dangerous quarrels by softening some of her objections to the Union's policy and practices at sea. As the greatest maritime Power, it was Great Britain's most important interest to have accepted the widest possible interpretation of the rules of regular naval warfare so as to exploit the Royal Navy's superiority to the maximum effect. At the same time she wished to have restricted as much as possible the opportunities legally available to an inferior naval power to attack Britain's merchant shipping by irregular naval warfare. At the Congress of Paris in 1856 Great Britain had compromised, conceding that blockades—the weapon of the superior naval power and therefore pre-eminently *her* weapon —must be effective to be legal. In return the other Powers had agreed to abolish privateering, pre-eminently the weapon of the weaker naval power. But the United States refused to accede to this agreement and at the beginning of the Civil War the Confederates issued letters of marque to privateers, while the North declared a paper blockade of the Southern coastline. Russell did protest, but he none the less explicitly recognized the blockade as effective in February 1862, when it was still far from being so.

The British did not succeed, however, in avoiding all serious clashes with the North. In the autumn of 1862 tension over Lincoln's blockade and British contacts with the South came near to war when the Americans stopped a British packet steamer, *Trent*, and removed from it two Confederate agents, Mason and Slidell. With right for once clearly on their side, the British rushed troops into Canada and reinforced their naval squadrons with a view to attacking the Northern coastline. Fortunately war was averted by second thoughts on the part of the Americans and by able diplomacy on the part of the British Minister in Washington. But Russell soon made up for the American blunder by making an even worse one himself. This was his failure to prevent the Confederacy exploiting technical loopholes in England's neutrality law. The most famous instance was the construction in England of the commerce raider *Alabama*, which left Liverpool in July 1862, and succeeded in its short life in destroying an enormous amount of Northern shipping. The *Alabama* was built in England, supplied from England, and manned mainly by English volunteers. Russell had to admit that it contravened the spirit if not the letter of the neutrality laws. But he neglected to do anything about it until it was too late. He was negligent too in seeing that it did not happen again. Legal sanctions were applied to the next ship to be completed, the *Alexandria*, but only at the last moment, and the ship was prevented from taking any part in the war only through the extreme slowness of the legal processes in which Russell had succeeded in entangling her. The next major danger, that from some rams being built by Messrs Laird, the British Government managed to avert by purchasing the ships themselves.

British policy throughout the Civil War was marked by a considerable amount of uncertainty and disagreement, and not a little incompetence too. But it is difficult to accept that ill will played any significant part. The most that could be asserted is what Gladstone once wrote: 'Lord Palmerston desired the severance as a diminution of a dangerous Power, but prudently held his tongue.'[16] However, by the time the war ended opinion had moved much more definitely in favour of the North. When the news of Lincoln's assassination reached England there was a general atmosphere of sadness and regret to register that change. When the war ended, however, the general relief was mixed with considerable apprehension that the North did not reciprocate that good will. The cause was simply the accumulated anger of the North for what they considered to be suspect and damaging neutrality on the part of Great Britain. That anger was amply expressed when in April 1869, United States' Senators catalogued American complaints and suggested that the cession of Canada would just about be adequate compensation.[17] The obvious way out of this wretched quarrel was to have recourse to the old, if little used, Anglo-American tradition of arbitration. Russell, as Prime Minister after Palmerston's death in October 1865, continued to maintain the line that no foreign government could be allowed to decide whether or not an English foreign secretary had been negligent in his duties. But privately he admitted that it had indeed been his fault.[18] In any case age was overtaking him too, and at the end of 1867 he surrendered the leadership of the Liberals to Gladstone. Gladstone had long been convinced that arbitration was

[16] John Morley, *Life of Gladstone* (London, 1903), ii. 82.
[17] H. C. Allen, *Great Britain and the United States* (London, 1955), p. 510.
[18] Spencer Walpole, *The Life of Lord John Russell* (London, 1889), ii. 373.

the only possible course to take. The difficulty was to get agreement on its precise scope and form. That agreement was not finally reached until 8 May 1871, when the Treaty of Washington cleverly reconciled hitherto irreconcilable differences and submitted the claims on both sides to the decision of a tribunal to meet at Geneva. The work of papering over the cracks was much more neatly done than that of the Clayton-Bulwer Treaty in 1850. Even so, it nearly failed when, to the horror of the British, the Americans after all presented their claims for indirect damages for Britain's conduct supposedly having prolonged the war. Fortunately this was probably only a tactical move to avoid domestic American criticism and these claims were eventually excluded from consideration by the arbitrators. Even so, the British had to pay damages of $15,000,000 though, in a sense, there was some compensation in that the United States had to pay nearly $7,500,000, mostly to Canada.

In isolation Gladstone's actions over the *Alabama* did not signify more than the satisfactory conclusion of an annoying dispute between two Great Powers. The resort to arbitration had been held up, on the British side, only by Russell's personal involvement, and, on the American, by some unfortunate public outbursts. In fact the main step forward had already been taken by the Conservative Ministry which intervened between Russell's last and Gladstone's first Administrations. Gladstone moreover did not see himself as endorsing the pacifists' compulsory arbitration proposals. Rather he saw that Britain's vital interest on this occasion lay rather in a practical resort to arbitration than in prolonging the quarrel by abstract arguments about the undesirability of arbitration in such cases.[19] When, however, the arbitration is seen against the background of the general withdrawal of British garrisons from North America in 1871, the significance of the Civil War and its aftermath in Anglo-American relations becomes much clearer. Throughout the war the British had watched with great apprehension the fantastic growth of American naval and military strength. They were not reassured by their re-examination during the *Trent* and other crises of their defensive position in Canada or by their undoubted ability to damage the United States coastline.[20] The post-war retreats, on

[19] Robson, 'Liberals and "Vital Interests" ', pp. 51–4. See also Mrs. Robson's 'The *Alabama* and the Anglo-American Reconciliation, 1865–71', *Canadian Historical Review*, xlii (1961), 1–22.

[20] Bourne, *Britain and the Balance of Power*, pp. 206–312.

both the military and the diplomatic fronts, were therefore not merely coincidences. They were an explicit recognition that Great Britain could never again hope to challenge the will of the United States on the continent of North America. But this was realism, not friendship. Official British policy still had a long way to go before it moved into complete alignment with popular sentiment in England. In any event American policy and American sentiment were not yet ready to reciprocate. The Americans now became so preoccupied with internal reconstruction and progress that for a generation Anglo-American relations were quieter than they had ever been before. But in that period of quiet they were allowed to deteriorate by neglect. The British once again had to be reawakened in a later generation by a nasty crisis and unpleasant thoughts of war.

Britain's diplomatic and military retreat in America was not taken in isolation from European affairs. Far from it; it was yet another instance of the priority which European affairs assumed in British foreign policy. Gladstone's first Foreign Secretary, Clarendon, had complained in May 1869: 'it is the unfriendly state of our relations with America that to a great extent paralyses our action in Europe. There is not the slightest doubt that if we were engaged in a Continental quarrel we should immediately find ourselves at war with the United States.'[21] Lord Granville, who took over the Foreign Office on Clarendon's death in June 1870, endorsed the resort to arbitration in the *Alabama* dispute on the grounds of the dangerous situation in Europe.[22] The military withdrawal from North America was part of a general concentration of forces in the United Kingdom partly on grounds of Gladstonian economy but partly, too, because of the dangerous situation in Europe.

Britain's problem in Europe in the late 1850s and the 1860s was that she was in increasing danger not merely of being isolated, but of being ignored in the great changes which transformed Europe during those years. The consciousness of her military weakness and of her diplomatic ineffectiveness reached their climax in Bismarck's triumphs of the late 1860s. But they dated really from the decline of the Crimean alliance with France. Napoleon III's disenchantment with England and his tendency to support Russia continued in the tidying up which followed the signature of the Treaty of Paris in March 1856. He sided with Russia when the British tried to keep

---

[21] G. E. Buckle, ed., *The Letters of Queen Victoria*, 2nd series (London, 1926), i. 594–5.
[22] Robson, 'Liberals and "Vital Interests" ', p. 53.

the Russians out of some disputed islands in the mouth of the Danube, and, more important, vigorously supported the cause of Rumanian union against the ambiguous settlement which the treaty had provided for the Danubian Principalities. Austria, Turkey, and after some hesitation, Britain were all opposed to the union. Britain's differences with France were patched up during a visit Napoleon paid to the Queen at Osborne on 6–10 August 1857. But this vaguely provided only for a 'broad administrative union', and early in 1859 the Rumanians took matters into their own hands and in defiance of the Powers elected the same man to be Governor of both Principalities.

The Rumanians succeeded in their defiance of the Powers, not merely because those Powers were divided on this question, but also because war had in the meantime broken out between France and Austria over the Italian Question. That conflict, however, was also in large measure the result of the changes in the international system following the Crimean War. Russia's defeat and, still more, her resentment of the so-called penal clauses in the peace treaty worked a radical change in her international policy. She lost not only her power to be the gendarme of Europe, but also much of her interest in being so. Instead her interest now lay in recovering what she had lost by an attack upon the *status quo* and by joining the other revisionist force in Europe, the Second Empire. The immediate and natural victim of this revisionism was Austria. She was the only Great Power committed to the *status quo* and she had made no friends by her conduct during the Crimean War. The importance of these new factors could hardly be exaggerated, for they swung the balance decisively in favour of major changes in the political map of Europe. At the same time the French and the Russians were never quite able to cement a positive alignment. Russia's revisionist interests were centred firmly in the Near East, in regaining her naval power in the Black Sea and her lost territory in Southern Bessarabia. Napoleon was by no means unsympathetic to these objectives and the two Powers acted together with some success in helping the Christian principalities of Rumania, Serbia, and Montenegro against the Porte. But Napoleon was reluctant to go so far as would alienate Britain and, beyond vague promises, he refused to commit himself to a revision of the Treaty of Paris without some positive help from Russia in his schemes. Napoleon's main interest was not in the Near East, but in the Italian peninsula. Here he hoped to oust Austria and to establish French influence by helping the cause of the nationalists. The Russians, however, were revisionist by circumstance, not by choice, and they were never enthusiastic about revolutionary nationalism. This was especially the case after the Polish revolt of 1863 and the Tsar's disenchantment with his own internal reform programme. But, even before that, these differences prevented any wholesale and positive alignment between France and Russia. The most they could achieve in the way of explicit agreement was the secret treaty of 3 March 1859. In this, however, nothing whatever was said about the Treaty of Paris, and Russia on her part promised no more than benevolent neutrality in the event of a war between Austria and France. But it was enough to encourage Napoleon to go ahead with the plan he had concocted with the Piedmontese Prime Minister, Count Cavour, at Plombières in the previous year. Austria was to be forced into war and out of Italy. Piedmont would then annex Lombardy and Venetia and, with Naples and a new Kingdom of Central Italy, join a federation under the presidency of the Pope. France would receive Savoy, and perhaps Nice as well.

The British were no less suspicious and no less fearful of Napoleon's activities in Italy than they were of Russian revisionism in the Near East. Indeed the Italian Question produced some more great Anglo-French war scares. They were, however, by no means antagonistic to the Italian cause itself. Rather it had an especially favoured place in their affections for liberal-nationalist movements. Like the Greek cause earlier in the century it flourished on the ruling classes' classical education. Piedmont's ostentatious devotion to Free Trade also endeared Italian nationalism to the middle classes while its anti-papal implications appealed to the Protestant prejudices of the masses. Sympathy for the Italian cause had certainly grown since the fiasco of 1848–9, especially after the entry of Piedmont into the Crimean War. Clarendon had made a vocal attack upon Austrian policy in Italy at the Congress of Paris and shortly afterwards the British had joined with France in breaking off relations with the barbarous Government of Naples. But fear of French intrigue and of international violence, and a desire not to see Austria utterly destroyed prevented them from doing more. The Mazzinian extremists gained support, it would seem, only among the working classes in Britain. On the other hand the strength of British feeling against France rather than for Italy, could lead even Palmerston to miscalculate. On 14 January 1858, an Italian extremist, Felice Orsini, attempted to assassinate the French Emperor on his way to the opera. It was this event, and still more Orsini's defence at his trial, which at last stirred Louis Napoleon's conscience and launched him once again into Italy. At the same time, however, it was discovered that the plot had been hatched in London and the bombs manufactured in Birmingham. The French naturally regarded this as an abuse of the right of asylum which Great Britain had traditionally given to political refugees. Palmerston, who was by no means unsympathetic to this point of view, agreed therefore to strengthen English law against such conspiracies. But he had reckoned without the strength of British feeling and without the outbursts of the French patriots who stupidly fanned its fury. For once it was he who was accused of truckling to foreign tyrants, and the Government was defeated on 19 February.

It was not Palmerston and Clarendon, therefore, but Derby and Malmesbury who now had to face the growing threat of war between France and Piedmont on the one hand and Austria on the other. The Conservatives were not much less sympathetic to the Italian cause. But they were at least as suspicious of France, and, more important, shared to a considerable extent the Court's unwillingness to assist the dismantling of the Austrian Empire. Malmesbury therefore worked hard to avert an Austro-French war by offering mediation. He warned Austria that England would not support her if she provoked an attack, and at the same time hinted to France that England might not be able to remain neutral. Only to Prussia, with whom he hoped to co-operate, did he reveal that England's policy would be 'neutrality at all events and as long as possible' (Doc. 66). The draft of this dispatch was considered too secret even to be kept at the Foreign Office.[23] Italy's high-placed English friends, however, saw to it that Cavour was made aware that Malmesbury's warnings were merely bluff.[24] Meanwhile Malmesbury suggested only the barest minimum of change in Italy in order to buy off Napoleon. It is unlikely that this would have been enough; in any case his schemes were completely upset by a proposal from Russia for a congress to discuss the Italian problem. The purpose of a congress could only have been to question and jeopardize the whole

---

[23] Derek Beales, *England and Italy 1859–60* (London, 1961), pp. 39–40.

[24] Denis Mack Smith, 'Palmerston and Cavour: some English doubts about the Risorgimento, 1859–60', in C. P. Brand, K. Foster, and V. Limentani, eds., *Italian Studies presented to E. R. Vincent* (Cambridge, 1962), p. 245.

of Austria's position in Italy. The Austrians therefore first made difficult conditions and then, on 19 April 1852, presented Piedmont with an ultimatum to demobilize. Since Piedmont had just very reluctantly yielded to pressure from the Powers to disarm, the Austrian ultimatum was especially ill-timed and stupid. It played into the nationalists' hands and allowed them after all to force war in the certainty that France would join in. The ultimatum was therefore rejected and the Austrians felt obliged to invade on 29 April.

Now Malmesbury could only flounder, searching anxiously for some means of restoring the *status quo ante bellum*. He appealed in vain to Protocol 23 of the Treaty of Paris and then concentrated on localizing the war by advising the German states not to interfere and by warning off Russia. The only effective step would have been intervention by Great Britain, but the fear of becoming involved in war as the ally of France, if Austria were then unwilling to respond, was too great. Malmesbury still believed himself to be a friend of the Italian cause, but it was fear of French ambitions alone which determined his attitude and policy. 'France having always been a curse to Europe', he wrote, 'we look upon it as the will of God, and resign ourselves to the torment, but . . . that Europe should be deluged with blood for the personal ambitions of an Italian attorney and a tambour-major, like Cavour and his master, is intolerable.'[25]

Public opinion generally in the country seemed to have agreed in emphasizing the danger from France above all else. Rumours in April 1859 of a Franco-Russian alliance even inspired another invasion panic and the unwelcome beginning of the Volunteer Rifle Movement. The Liberal leaders, Palmerston and Russell, seem however to have believed that Austria's blunder might allow them to exploit pro-Italian sentiment in the general election in May. Here they miscalculated. Anti-Austrian feeling had merely checked any tendency to move against France. It did not determine the result of the election in which the Conservatives actually gained seats. But the Conservatives were still in a minority in the House of Commons and on 10 June they were defeated over a reform bill. This brought back into power therefore men who had openly committed themselves to the Italian cause. The Queen had to have Palmerston either as Prime Minister or as Foreign Secretary. She preferred him not to have the Foreign Office and this therefore passed to Russell. And a powerful pro-Italian triumvirate was completed by the addition of Gladstone as Chancellor. He had become passionately committed to the Italian cause after seeing at first hand on a visit to Naples in 1850 what he described as 'the negation of God erected into a system of government'. The Liberal leaders' open support of Italy now gave him justification for joining their Government.[26]

Although the new Government was therefore clearly disposed to help Italy, it was not by any means agreed among its members quite how it should do so, and the Queen was still able to exploit their differences in defence of Austria. Palmerston was quite sure that France would beat Austria and that it was therefore advisable to take the same line as he had done in 1848–9 and press for the strengthening of Piedmont as a check to French power in the future. His colleagues, however, were not so sure. Nevertheless he and his Foreign Secretary now conspired to circumvent these doubts and the opposition of the Queen by just the sort of devices for which Russell had once dismissed Palmerston. On 7 July Russell sent out to Berlin a dispatch which rejected mediation on the *status quo ante bellum* and asserted that Austria must expect to lose some territory. In its final form this dispatch had not been submitted for the Queen's approval; nor, apparently, was it quite in accordance with the Cabinet's wishes (Doc. 67).[27] Palmerston's and Russell's calculations, however, were then completely upset by the news that Napoleon had abandoned Piedmont at the Peace of Villafranca (11 July 1859) and had conceded terms which left Venetia to Austria and looked forward to the restoration of the rulers who had been turned out of the central duchies and to the formation of an Italian confederacy under the Pope. Quite how this was all to be arranged was left over for the decision of a further meeting between the belligerents. It was then intended that a European congress should be summoned to approve what had been arranged. Palmerston and Russell hoped to defeat the idea of a confederation and to promote the principle of non-intervention in Italian affairs by getting an assurance that force would not be used to restore the Italian princes. Indeed they and Gladstone wanted rather to press for the annexation of the Duchies to Piedmont and Russell prepared a rather strong dispatch on these lines. But this time the Queen was able to alert the rest of the Cabinet who preferred a less active role for Great Britain

[26] S. Gopal, 'Gladstone and the Italian Question', *History*, xli (1956), 113–21.
[27] Beales, p. 100.

(Doc. 68). But neither Palmerston nor Russell could consider such an attitude at all suited to the real interests they believed to be in danger in Italy. As it was clear that the Italians themselves would not peacefully accept the restoration of the central duchies, the likelihood was that Austria would intervene by force to impose the Villafranca agreement and that Louis Napoleon would then be compelled to come to the rescue of the Italians. This would mean throwing over the Villafranca settlement, as the British desired, but giving further opportunities for French ambition, which the British most certainly did not desire. The best way of avoiding such a result was clearly for Britain to join with France in putting pressure on Austria to make some accommodation with the Italians. The enthusiasts in the Cabinet therefore concentrated during the winter of 1859–60 on concerting a firm alignment with France which was designed to help Italy but at the same time to check the expansion of French power. Palmerston even raised the possibility of using force against Austria (Docs. 70 and 71).

Such a strategy was at once too positive and too devious for the majority of the Cabinet. It was totally unwelcome to the Queen. Louis Napoleon himself, however, was quite responsive. He had already decided to give up supporting the extreme demands of the Pope and also to abandon the idea of a European congress. He preferred now to permit the annexation of the Duchies to Piedmont and to take Savoy as his due reward. It suited him to cultivate England and to sweeten her disposition by making concessions in the commercial negotiations that had been going on with Cobden. And it was from France too that there came the suggestion which allowed the English Cabinet to overcome their differences of opinion. It was agreed that instead of flaunting an unpopular Anglo-French alliance, England should merely ask France and Austria not to interfere any more in Italian affairs. This had the merit of accommodating the non-interventionist sentiments of the majority of the Cabinet while ensuring what both Britain's interests and her sentiments required in Italy without appearing to go with France or against Austria.

From France too, however, came a scheme which at once upset this clever compromise. Early in March 1860, plebiscites in the Duchies happily confirmed their annexation to Piedmont; but there also came news that Piedmont had agreed to pass Nice and Savoy by the same method into the possession of France. Napoleon had already mentioned this idea to the British Cabinet during the exchanges about co-operation late in 1859. Palmerston certainly was neither surprised nor particularly worried about the cession in itself. He probably helped the Cobden Treaty along in order to counter the effects that such a scheme would have on British public opinion. But he was none the less upset at the Emperor's failure to continue to consult the British about it and particularly at the effects he knew it must have on the policy of co-operation with France that he and Russell had been contriving with some difficulty. There was no question whatever of war with France over this issue but it did mean the end of the contrived but none the less effective Anglo-French alignment in Italy and it brought Britain's fundamentally anti-French prejudices and purposes in Italy right out into the open. Palmerston consoled himself with the support he now got against Gladstone's resistance to his naval and fortification schemes designed to protect the United Kingdom against a French invasion. But England's Italian policy merely drifted along.

By this time the process of liberating the Italian people had been extended to the southern part of the peninsula. In April 1860 there were risings against the Neapolitan Bourbons in Sicily and early in May Garibaldi and his Red Shirts decided to go to their aid rather than attempt the defence of Nice against Napoleon. The British, who had not yet digested the fact that the unification of virtually all Italy was at hand, were not sure what view to take. They were committed to an open disapproval of the reactionary Kingdom of Naples; but their faith in Piedmont had been shaken by Cavour's tortuous behaviour over Nice and Savoy. Palmerston, for a moment, even talked about having to join Austria in resisting the schemes of Cavour and Napoleon in Italy.[28] But they were certain of one thing at least—that France must not be given more opportunities to compensate herself. They therefore rejected a French proposal that they should prevent Garibaldi crossing to the mainland in August. Garibaldi, indeed, received all sorts of unofficial help from the British, possibly including covert assistance from officers of the Royal Navy. On 7 September he entered Naples and announced his intention of marching on Rome. Cavour, who had no wish to be outbid by Garibaldi, preferred to bar the way by invading the Papal States with the Piedmontese army. Having seized the initiative Cavour now thought it best to announce a programme for the annexation of the

[28] Mack Smith, p. 252.

central and southern states of Italy. Garibaldi, for his part, yielded gracefully to Victor Emmanuel. In October and November Naples, Sicily, and the Papal States voted for union with the north, and on 17 March 1861 the new Kingdom of Italy was proclaimed. Venetia and the city of Rome alone remained outside.

Garibaldi's entry into Rome would have brought him face to face with the French garrison and would have almost certainly forced Napoleon to intervene; Victor Emmanuel's entry into the Papal States merely provoked the breaking off of diplomatic relations by France and the conservative Powers. The English were naturally delighted to see Cavour and Napoleon at odds, especially as there was no need for them to take any positive action in Italy. Some sort of spirited verbal expression would do and this Russell supplied in a dispatch on which the Russian Ambassador in London commented, 'it was not diplomacy, but an obscene joke'.[29] It announced that Britain would not follow the other Powers in breaking with Piedmont and, in rather extravagant language, declared Britain's belated conversion from doubt and hesitation to enthusiastic endorsement of the unification of Italy (Doc. 72).

Russell, it seems, would have liked to add a second dispatch making a positive contribution to Italian unity by urging the cession of Rome and Venice as well, but he was defeated by the Queen who judged the character of the Cabinet rather better.[30] As it was, the dispatch of 27 October remained a fitting climax to the course of British policy in the Italian Question. That policy had been concerned throughout mainly with fear of France. 'In reality England was not pursuing an Italian policy so much as a French policy.'[31] The reconciliation of anti-French interests with pro-Italian sentiment, however, was not by any means badly done, especially when Palmerston got his way. British policy therefore always tended to favour the Italian cause. But at the same time that policy usually lagged behind the progress of events in the peninsula. Palmerston and Russell, and Gladstone too, would have preferred a more active role, but even they under-estimated the speed with which affairs were developing in Italy. They did not disapprove of the unification of Italy; it was simply that they had not thought it a

[29] Charles Frederick Vitzthum von Eckstaedt, *St. Petersburg and London in the years 1852–1864* (London, 1887), ii. 130, n. 2.

[30] H. Hearder, 'Queen Victoria and foreign policy. Royal intervention in the Italian question, 1859–1860', in Bourne and Watt, pp. 172–88.

[31] Beales, p. 169.

practical possibility. The rapid progress towards it simply caught them by surprise and left their policy out of date. Russell's dispatch of 27 October gaily ignored this fact and brashly asserted Britain's moral leadership after the event. Britain's Italian policy in the final stages was therefore a supreme example of muddling along. None the less the British had got what they wanted, however late they were in making up their minds. In the circumstances Italy therefore appeared to be a shining example of the success of a policy of non-intervention. Palmerston himself admitted that this was a success 'of opinion, but opinion only'.[32] The result was by no means congenial to him; it was the triumph of isolation in the guise of non-intervention.

The proclamation of the Kingdom of Italy on 17 March 1861 marked the virtual completion of the first stage of the post-Crimean transformation of Europe. The second stage, which much more clearly showed up the decline of British influence, began with the Polish rising of 1863. This second rising, like that of 1830, tended to arouse the vocal sympathies of Britain and France, while drawing the Eastern Powers themselves together. At the beginning Palmerston was not inclined to interfere, expecting that the revolt would soon be put down and leaving Napoleon to take the initiative. But although the French did press conciliation on St. Petersburg, their main preoccupation seemed to be to join with England and Austria in persuading Prussia to abandon the Alvensleben Convention (8 February 1863) by which Russia was permitted to cross Prussian territory in pursuit of Polish insurgents. Russell was favourably inclined to this proposal, but Palmerston felt that Britain ought rather to concentrate her efforts on the 'real culprit', and in this he was supported by public opinion in Parliament and in the country. After a House of Commons debate towards the end of February therefore, the French proposal was turned down and on 2 March Russell sent instead a dispatch to St. Petersburg which urged an immediate amnesty for the rebels and the speedy re-establishment of the Kingdom of Poland (Doc. 75). Palmerston and his Government, therefore, were led to interfere in the Polish Question primarily by the pressure of opinion. There is no evidence that theirs was a deliberate attempt to break up the dreaded Franco-Russian alignment, to score a petty victory over the French

[32] Beales, p. 171.

Emperor, or to divert Russian attention from the Balkans.[33] These were the unexpected consequences, rather than the intention of the British decision.

Russell's next move, in direct line with the desire expressed in the House of Commons debate, was to invite the co-operation of the signatories to the Treaty of Vienna. In spite of being irritated by the failure of his own earlier initiative, the French Emperor soon agreed. But Austria was difficult. After all, the Austrian Minister in London explained, 'no one could expect that Austria would embark in an enterprise which in its ultimate result might deprive her of a rich and tranquil province. She could not be an accomplice in the work of dismembering her own Dominions.'[34] In the end England and France had to be content with very lukewarm support from Austria. It was enough to imperil once again Austria's relations with Russia, without gaining her the friendship of the Western Powers. In the meantime the French and English went ahead with their stronger, but still significantly different initiatives. The French definitely hinted at the possibility of war; but the English were very careful not to commit themselves to anything. As the revolt continued, Palmerston and Russell apparently convinced themselves that Russia was too weak to stand up to such diplomatic pressure. They were successful, moreover, in inducing Prussia to reject Russian feelers for an alliance. Unfortunately the Russians were determined, even in isolation, to risk the revival of the Crimean alliance and a new war. They therefore refused all the suggestions of the Powers. His bluff called, and with France unwilling to act alone, Palmerston could make only a confused defence of his policy in the House of Commons (Doc. 76).

Although ultimately unsuccessful, British policy in the Polish revolt was not so inept as it has usually been made out to be. It was, in the most recent view, a 'reconnaissance in force'[35] which did not commit the Government to any ill-advised action. It succeeded in separating Prussia from Russia and when Russia made it clear that she would still resist to the point of war, it was quite properly abandoned. Unfortunately Napoleon, who had been much less discreet, felt humiliated and therefore betrayed—a feeling that was not

[33] W. E. Mosse, 'England and the Polish Insurrection of 1863', *English Historical Review*, lxxi (1956), 33–4.
[34] Ibid., p. 35.
[35] Ibid., p. 53.

in the least assuaged by the reasoned yet curt rejection the English made in November of his proposal for a congress to regulate Poland and 'substitute for the treaties of 1815, now in decay, new stipulations apt to assure the peace of the world'[36] (Doc. 78). The Polish crisis therefore finally killed off both the Franco-Russian and the Anglo-French alignments. Russia, on the other hand, gained confidence from the affair. More important, her friendship with Prussia survived, for Alexander did not blame Frederick William for backing out under the pressure of the Western Powers. In this manner the Polish crisis created almost ideal conditions for the attack which Bismarck was about to make upon the existing distribution of power and territory in Europe.

The immediate contribution of the Polish crisis was to prevent any effective Anglo-French co-operation over a new and more important phase of the Schleswig-Holstein Question. In spite of the arrangements previously made by the Powers, the Schleswig-Holstein problem had continued to fester in the 1850s, with the Danish extremists maintaining their pressure to bring Schleswig to heel and so antagonizing the German nationalists. The British, who were at least as confused as anyone else about this complication, were uncertain what line to take. They did not really know whom to blame, as the treaty of 1852 had in any case neglected to specify the obligations which the signatory Powers might have undertaken for its enforcement. Nevertheless Palmerston made a speech in the House of Commons on 23 July 1863 which maintained that Britain still held to the 1852 view that the integrity of Denmark was a European interest and that Denmark would therefore not have to contend alone with the aggressive designs of German nationalism (Doc. 77). This firm line was quite incompatible with the nervous and uncertain state of British opinion generally, and above all ill-suited to the skill and determination with which Bismarck now developed his plans to exploit German nationalism and the ambitions of Russia and Austria. It was all the more unfortunate therefore that the effect of Palmerston's speech and of similar diplomatic warnings issued by Russell,[37] was to encourage Frederick VII of Denmark in his plans to incorporate Schleswig.

The death of Frederick VII on 15 November 1863, far from

---

[36] Quoted by R. W. Seton-Watson, *Britain in Europe 1789–1914* (Cambridge, 1937), p. 436.
[37] Seton-Watson, p. 442.

improving the situation, still further intensified the danger. In the first place Christian IX, as a new and untried monarch, could not afford to alienate the Danish nationalists by retreating from the extreme line of policy about the Duchies which he had inherited from his predecessor. At the same time his assumption of the throne necessarily precipitated the old succession problem. Bismarck was not at all anxious to support anyone else's claims and he skilfully avoided making such a commitment. At the same time he no less skilfully persuaded Austria that the solid interests of the two German Powers should not be obscured by the romantic enthusiasms of German nationalism and that they should therefore together seize the initiative. German forces had already occupied Holstein at the beginning of December 1863. On 16 January 1864 Prussia and Austria presented Christian with a joint ultimatum to withdraw his new constitution and, in spite of Denmark's offer of a conference in London, they invaded Schleswig on 1 February and Denmark proper a fortnight later. Russell now talked angrily about France marching her army to the Rhine and England sending her fleet to Copenhagen.[38] But there was not really any question of English intervention. Even Palmerston sometimes admitted it in private, writing at this point to warn Russell that he very much doubted 'whether the Cabinet or the country are as yet prepared for active interference. The truth is, that to enter into a military conflict with all Germany on continental ground would be a serious undertaking.' As usual he was also unhappy about any movement on the part of the French Army and the possibility that the position of the Low Countries would be endangered.[39]

Britain's Schleswig-Holstein policy therefore was pure bluff: the question for her Ministers to decide was not really one of peace or war, but how far they dared to go in an attempt to bluff Germany into an acceptable compromise. This policy was weakened from the first by Napoleon's refusal to co-operate. Clarendon reported him as saying: 'We had received a *gros soufflet* with respect to Poland from Russia, and ... to get another from Germany without resenting it was more than he could stand, as he would have fallen into contempt. He could not therefore join us in strong language to the German

[38] Seton-Watson, p. 445.
[39] Evelyn Ashley, *The Life of Henry John Temple, Viscount Palmerston: 1846–1865* (London, 1877), ii. 247.

powers, *not being prepared to go to war with them.*[40] What little chance of success remained was further eroded by the attitude taken by the Queen, who once again employed the indulgent Granville to exploit the divisions in the Cabinet in order to frustrate what she considered to be the anti-German policy of 'those two dreadful old men', Palmerston and Russell[41] (Doc. 79). Every move, every dispatch, every suggestion of naval demonstrations, collective notes, and armistice proposals was criticized and resisted as too risky, too favourable to Denmark, and not in accord with British interests. Given that, for different reasons, neither France nor Britain wished to initiate any active intervention by the Powers, it is no wonder that all of England's efforts were too feeble to have any useful effect. Her proposal of a conference in London was accepted, but quite unenthusiastically. Nor were either Denmark or the German Powers really willing to compromise. In these circumstances the London Conference was hardly likely to succeed. It opened on 25 April and, at length, secured a temporary armistice. But it failed to discover any solution of the Schleswig-Holstein Question and it broke up completely on 25 June. The next day hostilities were resumed. Meanwhile, behind the scenes, the discussions and intrigues among the Cabinet had continued. Russell tried to use against the Queen the very tactics which he and the Queen had accused Palmerston of using in 1850. But he was no match for the Queen and sometimes he so confused bluff with reality that he frightened even Palmerston. By the time Prussia resumed hostilities Russell knew his efforts were hopeless and on 6 July he publicly admitted that fact in the House of Lords.[42] On 1 August Denmark had to agree to cede Schleswig-Holstein jointly to Austria and Prussia.

Palmerston's policy of bluff was certainly always dangerous—and it was made more so by Russell's tendency to forget that it was bluff. Even so, with active intervention out of the question, it was the only policy which stood any chance of success. That it did not succeed was due primarily to Bismarck's shrewd assessment of realities. But even his nerve might possibly have failed, had not the Queen and her collaborators behaved as they did. As it was, Britain's

---

[40] Walpole, i. 390–1.

[41] *Letters of Queen Victoria*, 2nd series, i. 168. On this subject see W. E. Mosse, 'Queen Victoria and her Ministers in the Schleswig-Holstein Crisis 1863–1864', *English Historical Review*, lxxviii (1963), 263–83.

[42] Although he continued to be known as Lord John Russell, he had entered the House of Lords as Earl Russell in 1861.

policy in the Schleswig-Holstein Question was not really Palmer-stonian at all, but rather the feeble result of Palmerstonian and anti-Palmerstonian pressures within the Cabinet. And the Queen's triumph was a double one in that the failure was naturally, though mistakenly, seen as the final discrediting of Palmerstonian policies (Docs. 80, 81, and 82). Of this Cobden seems to have had no doubt. By November 1864 he was writing:

> ... there is one great change amounting to a revolution which has been accomplished in our foreign policy. After the fiasco last Session on the Danish question, our Foreign Office will never again attempt to involve us in any European entanglements for the Balance of Power, or for any dynastic purpose. Henceforth we shall observe an absolute abstention from continental politics. Non-intervention is the policy of all future governments in this country.[43]

The following year death removed both Cobden and Palmerston from the scene. In the meantime the American Civil War came to an end, but without completely relieving British anxieties in that part of the world. In any case neither Russell, who succeeded Palmerston as Prime Minister in October 1865, nor Clarendon, who once again took over the Foreign Office, had any intention of trying to reassert a sort of Palmerstonian influence in European affairs. It was just as well, for Bismarck was about to initiate the second stage of his violent pursuit of Prussian hegemony in Germany.

Early in March 1866 news arrived in England that Bismarck was apparently trying to provoke war with Austria over the Schleswig-Holstein Question. Austria had soon come to realize that she was serving only her ally's selfish interest by co-operating with Prussia in that affair. But now she had fallen into a second trap by with-drawing from that co-operation and giving Bismarck some excuse for serious complaint. The real issue between them was the mastery of Germany. Ostensibly, however, it was the disposal of the Duchies they had rescued from Denmark. The Convention of Gastein, of 14 August 1865, 'papered over the cracks' by giving Austria the administration of Holstein while Prussia took Schleswig. But Bis-marck was determined to have both for Prussia, and by the end of February 1866 the Prussian Government had agreed that if Austria would not yield there would have to be war.

[43] John Morley, *The Life of Richard Cobden* (London, 1903), ii. 450.

In Britain they were well aware that more was at stake than merely the division of the spoils of war. When she heard of Gastein the Queen had wanted to follow the example of France in making a formal protest against such greedy and unscrupulous behaviour. Palmerston, however, in one if his last letters, had stressed that from a practical point of view it was better for England that Prussia's position in central Europe should be strengthened as a check to Russia and France (Doc. 83). Instead of any direct protest therefore Britain's representatives abroad were supplied only with 'observations' deploring 'the disregard thus shown to the principles of public right'. These 'observations' were not to be communicated to foreign governments but were intended only to guide British representatives if an opportunity arose to express a point of view (Doc. 84). Such a convenient attitude, however, seemed less appropriate as Prussia and Austria came nearer to blows. Even so Clarendon was far from being inclined to take any active line. England had already burned her fingers once over Schleswig-Holstein, he thought, and ought to keep clear of it on this occasion. When therefore the Austrians appealed to Britain for some gesture of benevolence at the beginning of March 1866, he firmly declined. But like the Queen, Clarendon strongly disapproved of Prussia's conduct and, more important, feared that an exhausting war between the two German Powers must tend to make France the arbiter of Europe and encourage Napoleon in his reckless schemes of aggrandizement. Early in March therefore he privately commended to Bismarck Protocol 23 of the Treaty of Paris (Doc. 85). A little later he even offered the good offices of Great Britain. But, after only a moment's hesitation, Bismarck effectively checked these moves and Clarendon was very reluctant to entertain any new ones. Joint representations with France, such as the Queen now urged, he argued, would not be backed up by public opinion and Bismarck was not the man they ought to try to bluff (Docs. 86 and 87). The Foreign Secretary was not even keen to join with France in bribing Italy to abandon her alliance with Prussia with offers of Venetia. Apart from an unwillingness to put any real pressure on Austria to give up her Italian province, the British were far too distrustful of Napoleon's plans for European rearrangement—all the more so when he made a speech castigating the Vienna Settlement early in May. Clarendon was reluctant even to agree to Russia's suggestion of a conference in Paris. This was the last hope of avoiding war and it disappeared at the end of

May, when, after Prussia had grumpily accepted, the Austrians insisted that it must not discuss any territorial changes.

Bismarck forced the issue with Austria by ordering Prussian troops into Holstein on 7 June and, when Austria mobilized the German Diet against her, Prussia retaliated by breaking off diplomatic relations and declaring the German Confederation to be at an end. Clarendon showed signs that he was considering some reaction to this unilateral breach of the 1815 Settlement, but on 26 June the Ministry resigned after a defeat on parliamentary reform. His successor, as Foreign Secretary in the Derby Government, was the Prime Minister's son, Lord Stanley, later fifteenth Earl of Derby. Stanley was a gloomy and somewhat distant personality and the Queen in particular did not think he would make an effective Foreign Secretary. But to public and parliamentary opinion at large he was generally welcomed as almost ideally suited to the new mood of downright non-interventionism in British policy. So far as the German crisis was concerned the Prime Minister on 9 July confirmed these expectations of his son by announcing in the House of Lords that England's honour was 'in no degree' involved in the war, and her interests only 'very remotely, if at all' (Doc. 88). Stanley in fact was disinclined to action as much by nature as by political conviction. Much more consistently than Clarendon, therefore, he poured cold water on all suggestions for intervention by the neutrals. England would join in a congress if one were called, but he had 'not the slightest faith in Prussia being stopped by words', and England would certainly not fight. And so far as concerned arranging for an armistice or a congress, peace terms would be 'dictated by events, rather than by the choice of any of the neutral powers'.[44] The Russians, as well as the Austrians, were quite impatient with an attitude which seemed to them to pass over much too casually the facts that the Vienna Settlement was now being torn to shreds and that France was being made arbiter of Europe. But on this occasion Stanley could justify non-intervention on simple grounds of self-interest. Like Palmerston he insisted that the consolidation of a powerful Protestant state in north Germany must serve England's real interests. He too regretted the unscrupulous policies of Count Bismarck and the decline of the Austrian Empire. But he correctly divined that Napoleon had overreached himself in

[44] W. E. Mosse, *The European Powers and the German Question 1848–1871* (Cambridge, 1958), p. 241.

meddling in German affairs and that Prussia would replace Austria in the defence of Europe against the expansionist tendencies of Russia and France. When he expounded his view to parliament there was hardly a single dissentient voice (Doc. 89). In the end, therefore, Stanley firmly refused to make even a formal gesture of protest against Prussia's defiance of the 1815 Settlement. And while he settled on an attitude of passive non-intervention, France, and somewhat more hesitantly Russia, pretty well made up their minds that as the Concert of Europe had clearly lapsed, they must come to terms with the new *Realpolitik* of Bismarck's Prussia.

Meanwhile the Prussian Army disposed first of Austria's German allies, and then of Austria herself at Sadowa on 3 July. This was accomplished before Stanley had even taken over the Foreign Office, but Prussia was helped by his complaisant attitude to conclude a preliminary peace at Nikolsburg on 26 July and a final peace treaty at Prague on 23 August. The peace settlement excluded Austria from Germany and in Germany north of the River Main established a new German Confederation under Prussian control. This rearrangement finally destroyed the old Balance of Power, but it did so without introducing a comparable era of stability in Europe. Prussia's victory and French diplomacy together secured Venetia for Italy but she could not be satisfied without Rome. Austria was dreaming of futile schemes for reversing her defeat. Russia had still not obtained the revision of the Crimean settlement in the Black Sea. Above all, France awoke belatedly to the realization that the Balance of Power had shifted against her. The main issue in Europe now was that between France and Prussia.

The immediate question in this new situation was how the other European states would line up. Once again the recurrent Eastern Question exerted a strong influence. During the summer the Rumanians had exploited the diversions in central Europe to secure a Hohenzollern prince as their ruler. This was a real step towards consolidation and independence, but being disliked as much by Russia as Turkey it was passed over without provoking a crisis. Much more serious, largely because it strained to breaking point the relations between Greece and Turkey, was the revolt which broke out against the Sultan in Crete in the summer of 1866. At the same time the energetic and ambitious Prince Michael of Serbia worked not only to free himself from the last vestiges of Turkish control but also to concert an anti-Turkish policy by alliances with

Montenegro, Rumania, and Greece. The French were in no doubt that here there lay a great opportunity to regain the co-operation of Russia. Over Crete in particular they were therefore prepared to offer a great deal in return for Russian support in the West. But they were unable to specify exactly what they wanted in the West and the Russians were not willing to commit themselves to unlimited support. The Russians therefore decided to revert to their reliance on Prussia, while France looked instead to Austria. The interaction of the Western and Eastern Questions therefore tended to separate the Powers into two camps—the Austro-French and the Russo-Prussian. Italy, who was disappointed with the rewards of her alliance with Prussia, flirted with the Austrians and the French and if the Roman Question could have been resolved—the French still felt themselves committed to the defence of the Holy City—France might have bound Austria more firmly to her side. The support of England, the only other uncommitted Power, would have been no less important. In a sense England held the balance between the Austro-French and the Russo-Prussian groups. And although Stanley was determined on complete non-intervention, it was quite possible that the Eastern Question might force England into the French camp, or fear for the Low Countries drive her into the Prussian group against France.

In the East Stanley tried hard, and on the whole very successfully, to follow a line which would not lead him into this sort of trap. Having no illusions about Turkey's ability to reform herself, he was inclined to develop an alternative policy in the Balkans. Late in 1866 his Ambassador in Constantinople was instructed to 'suggest to the Porte that a frank and timely compliance on the part of the Sultan, while it would tend to conciliate the future good will of the Servian nation would exclude any pressure on the part of foreign Powers in support of them . . .'.[45] Stanley's object was clearly to relieve Turkey from the constant tensions on the frontier and to cultivate a more effective barrier to Russian ambitions. He therefore approved of the progress being made in the consolidation of Rumania and Montenegro, and he even took the initiative in persuading Turkey to withdraw the garrisons she still maintained in Serbia. All his hopes, however, seem to have evaporated by the beginning of 1868, as he

[45] Kenneth Bourne, 'T. W. Riker and British Near-Eastern Policy: the Turkish Evacuation of Belgrade, 1867', *The Slavonic and East European Review*, xxxvi (1957–8), 197.

got to know of Michael's alliance schemes and as the various principalities continued to press on Turkey's frontiers. Michael's schemes
were brought to an abrupt end by his assassination in June 1868. But
the Cretan revolt continued to trouble Stanley. He had never been
able to hit on any really satisfactory policy for this problem. Britain's
concern about the island was partly strategic, and this concern was
enhanced by the prospect of the Suez Canal which had been under
construction since 1859 and which was to be completed in 1869.
Britain had been notoriously opposed to the canal, but that opposition had never really been based on solid commercial or strategic
grounds. The vital link with her Indian Empire remained—and still
remains—that via the Cape of Good Hope. In any case the strategic
problem was certainly not vital so long as Britain retained her naval
supremacy. It was, rather, simple and traditional political opposition
to French influence in the Near East which had so agitated Palmerston and his colleagues (Doc. 69). But as their opposition was unrealistic so it was also ineffective; gradually, during the 1860s, they
had become reconciled to the construction of the canal by the
French.[46] It nevertheless increased the importance of Britain's naval
supremacy in the Mediterranean, and this, as a Foreign Office
memorandum of 1866 stressed, might be threatened if Crete fell into
hostile hands:

> From its situation it may be considered as one of the chain of sentries
> which, in connection with Gibraltar, Malta, and Cyprus, serve in friendly
> hands to keep open this important connection with our Eastern Empire.
> Candia [Crete] and Cyprus have more than once been described as the
> keys of Egypt, and there is no doubt that in the possession of a maritime
> power hostile to England, they might be a great menace for our route
> across the Isthmus.[47]

Nor could Stanley himself see how he could apply in this instance
the experiment in which he had indulged for the sake of the Balkan
principalities:

> I do not believe in the Turkish Empire: it seems to be worn out and
> unable to maintain itself: and if Greece were like Piedmont or Prussia, a
> well governed and civilized state, the solution of the problem would be
> simple. But Greece is the very reverse of this: bankrupt, anarchical,

[46] K. Bell, 'British Policy Towards the Construction of the Suez Canal, 1859–65',
Transactions of the Royal Historical Society, 5th Series, xv (1965), 121–43.

[47] Richard Millman, *British Foreign Policy and the Coming of the Franco-Prussian
War* (Oxford, 1965), pp. 59–60.

without an honest politician or class which can be trusted with power. I see no natural heir to the sick man.[48]

In any case he very much feared that the infection might spread to the other Christian populations of the Empire. Such evaluations of British interests of course made nonsense of any idealistic policy of non-intervention. Yet Stanley found in them justification for a policy of relative inaction. Agreeing fully with the advice of his Ambassador in Paris that his 'object must be to prevent isolated action, or what would be worse the joint action of France and Russia',[49] Stanley successfully stalled while France and Russia grew weary of it all. Whether this was masterly inactivity is doubtful. Certainly it did not solve the Cretan crisis of itself, and it left increasing chance of a collision between Turkey and Greece. Clarendon was also very reluctant to get further involved, but was not anything like so nervous of effective activity or so suspicious of France. Not long after returning to the Foreign Office in December 1868, therefore, he accepted Napoleon's suggestion of a conference. Far from intensifying the crisis, Greece's behaviour was used instead at the conference as a means of concerting the Powers against her and therefore in defence of the Turkish Empire.

Whatever the local effects of Stanley's policy in the East, it certainly did nothing to commit Britain to a partisan line in the West. If anything Stanley personally was even more inclined than most Englishmen to favour the consolidation of Prussian power in Germany and, however reluctantly, to accept Bismarck as the only man who could carry the task through. At the same time he and many of his colleagues sympathized with the French Emperor. In spite of their permanent suspicion of French designs they admitted that Napoleon ought to be compensated for the shift in the Balance of Power and not least in order that he might survive in France as a bastion against the advance of socialism. In July 1866 Stanley even let the French know that England would not oppose their claims to compensation provided Egypt, Constantinople, and Belgium were not affected.[50] This matter came to a head and dragged Stanley reluctantly into the middle of it when angry questions were asked in the German Parliament on 1 April 1867 about French designs on Luxemburg. The Grand Duchy was a personal possession of the

[48] Millman, p. 59.
[49] Ibid, p. 62.
[50] Ibid, p. 39.

King of Holland, who was anxious to sell it. But Luxemburg had been a member of the German Confederation and the Zollverein, and although the Treaty of Prague dissolved the Confederation, Prussia still maintained a garrison in Luxemburg by a treaty made with Holland in 1816.

The Grand Duchy had figured in French and Prussian discussions about compensation since the summer of 1866 and Bismarck had certainly not given the impression that he was utterly opposed to Napoleon having it. When German opinion suddenly took it up and stressed its historic role in the defence of the Rhine against French aggression therefore, Napoleon was both surprised and offended. Both sides now felt their honour to be involved and the attention of Europe became concentrated on the possibility of war. This time, even in Bismarck's opinion, England's attitude was important, perhaps decisive.[51] Bismarck had therefore already tried at the end of March to lead England into an anti-French position by associating Napoleon's desire for Luxemburg with England's traditional interest in the neutrality of the Low Countries. Quite probably, if Bismarck had indeed deliberately led Napoleon on, it was not to provoke war but with this intention of keeping Britain and France at odds. But the situation was undoubtedly very dangerous and it was much to the credit of Stanley's policy of non-intervention that he was not tempted by Bismarck's tricks and that he even said the French ought to have the Grand Duchy. He did warn France to respect Belgian neutrality but at the same time he urged Berlin to consent to the French Emperor's demand that Prussia should at least evacuate the fortress of Luxemburg as a salve to his pride. More than this, however, Stanley was very unwilling to do. 'There never was a time', he insisted, 'when the English public was more thoroughly bent on incurring no fresh responsibilities for Continental objects.'[52] Yet he had to admit that they should do everything in their power to preserve peace and he at length gave way to the pressure of European statesmen and of his colleagues and agreed to a conference taking place in London.

Stanley's particular objection was to the condition on which Prussia was insisting as the price for her evacuation—a European guarantee of the neutralization of Luxemburg. On this too, however, he found himself isolated at the conference which assembled in

[51] Mosse, *The European Powers and the German Question*, p. 263, n. 1.
[52] *The Letters of Queen Victoria*, 2nd series, i. 423.

5—F.P.V.E.

London on 7 May and he was forced to agree to a treaty on 11 May which provided for it. Two days later, however, the Prime Minister used in the House of Lords language which laid special stress on the collective character of the new guarantee:

> The guarantee is not a joint and separate guarantee, but is a collective guarantee, and does not impose upon this country any special and separate duty of enforcing its provisions.[53]

In a debate a month later Derby made it even more clear that the guarantee was therefore no guarantee at all:

> The only two Powers by which the neutrality of Luxemburg is likely to be infringed are two of the parties to the collective guarantee; &, therefore, if either of them violate the neutrality, the obligation on all others would not accrue.

Such an argument, as was pointed out in the debate, made nonsense of the guarantee (Doc. 90). Bismarck certainly felt cheated and even Stanley was so embarrassed that he had to plead to the Prussian Ambassador that his father might have been 'imperfectly reported'. None the less he stressed the impossibility of a parliamentary monarchy binding itself 'as to the course to be adopted at a future period, and under circumstances not now foreseen' (Doc. 91).

Stanley had from the first been determined not to give a 'pledge to take up arms'.[54] There was, indeed, some truth in his private excuse to the Queen that 'no great Power could without utter discredit violate a solemn compact lately made in the face of Europe'.[55] But this was a plain contradiction of one of the fundamental bases of his policy of non-intervention—that no policy could be effective which could not, if necessary, be backed by force. Stanley's supposedly simple idealism, in contrast to Palmerston's and Russell's supposedly amoral policy of 'meddle and muddle', was therefore not reflected in a rational and consistent policy. It was his character, rather, which led him to see affairs, not through rose-tinted spectacles, but in a dim fog which justified as little action as possible. In April 1868 the standing army's justification that it was needed for the maintenance of the Balance of Power in Europe was for the first time dropped from the annual Mutiny Bill. But this was merely a gesture; Stanley looked on the shifts of power in East and West

---

[53] *Hansard's Parliamentary Debates*, 3rd series, clxxxvii. 379.
[54] Millman, p. 82.
[55] *The Letters of Queen Victoria*, 2nd series, i. 448.

alike in quite familiar terms. Manner and style, however, were all-important in foreign policy. Given the self-doubts of mid-Victorian England, Stanley was undoubtedly right to move as cautiously as possible in European affairs. But he should not have shouted caution so loudly from the rooftops. 'I begged him', Clarendon said of the advice he had given Stanley on handing over the Foreign Office, '. . . not to proclaim our determined inaction on every opportunity that arises—the policy of not meddling is of course the right one but it is not necessary that all mankind sh[oul]d be let into the secret twice a day.'[56] At the end of 1866 the European Powers still thought England capable of exercising a strong and possibly decisive influence on the issue between France and Prussia. By the end of 1867 they were inclined to write off England, very largely because of Stanley's attitude. If Palmerston had squandered England's credit in foreign affairs, Stanley dissipated much of what remained.

Stanley himself did not have to see the Franco-Prussian issue through as Foreign Secretary. Disraeli had succeeded the ailing Derby as Prime Minister at the end of February 1868 but even he was unable to save the Conservatives from defeat at the hustings and, as Russell had now retired, December saw the formation of the first Gladstone Government with Clarendon once more at the Foreign Office. Gladstone and Clarendon were also impressed with the necessity of caution but with a view to avoiding commitments, not action of any kind (Docs. 92, 93, and 94). 'All that Lord Clarendon desires', he told the Queen, 'is to secure the most perfect freedom of action for Your Majesty's Government in any contingency that may arise.'[57] Better than Stanley he also appreciated that it was the object of diplomacy not merely to match interest with strength but to bridge the gap between interest and weakness. So far as the Franco-Prussian Question was concerned his views were not essentially different from his predecessor's but he was rather more inclined towards France. But any real co-operation with France was ruined almost at once by a rather inept French bid to take over the Belgian railways. This looked to the British, as Clarendon put it, like 'an audacious attempt on the part of the French gov[ernmen]t to incorporate Belgium'.[58] Nevertheless Clarendon managed to preserve a position in the Franco-Prussian contest which led Bismarck to say

[56] Millman, p. 32.
[57] Mosse, *The European Powers and the German Question*, p. 300.
[58] Millman, p. 128.

after the Foreign Secretary's death that had he lived he would have been able to prevent war coming out of the Hohenzollern candidature for the Spanish throne.[59]

The Spanish Government had been looking for a respectable candidate for their vacant throne ever since the expulsion of Queen Isabella in September 1868. The favourite was Prince Leopold of Hohenzollern, the son of the leading member of the Catholic branch of the family which ruled Prussia. Quite when and why Bismarck decided to press this proposal is still something of a mystery. Probably it was part of a manoeuvring for position to counter the alliance which Napoleon was trying to negotiate between France, Austria, and Italy at this time. Certainly, it was eventually useful in whipping up German nationalist feeling in the south against France. Clarendon undoubtedly tried to act the peacemaker between France and Prussia. This role was always undermined by lack of up-to-date information about what was going on, but the Hohenzollern family themselves acknowledged the importance of England's attitude by seeking advice there as early as March 1870. No doubt Bismarck exaggerated Clarendon's importance but there was certainly a marked decline in England's influence after Clarendon's death in June 1870 and the succession of the complaisant Granville. 'We are happy in being able to fill the office with a man who has the deep calm of L[or]d Aberdeen, a strong sense of justice, much foreign knowledge, and singular tact', commented the Prime Minister.[60] A lack of tact had certainly marred Clarendon's relations with the Queen; Granville, on the other hand, had always got on well with her. Tact was so strikingly present in Granville however, that his foreign policy always trailed behind events. When he took over the Foreign Office on 3 July, the Permanent Undersecretary told him that he had never known 'so great a lull in foreign affairs'. There was some truth in this, since the Hohenzollern Question had so far been only simmering in the background. But within a few hours the news had arrived in London that Leopold had accepted the Spanish throne and that France had protested. The Hohenzollern crisis had now reached an explosive phase, but Granville still persisted in treating it as though it were merely a personal matter between the Prince's family and the Spanish Government. But he did not really

[59] Herbert Maxwell, *The Life and Correspondence of George William Frederick Fourth Earl of Clarendon* (London, 1913), ii. 366.
[60] Millman, p. 178.

believe such nonsense and the pose only irritated the French. Instead the quarrel became the occasion for a war for which both France and Prussia were now actively working. If, as was by no means impossible, a firm warning from Britain could have brought Prussia or France to heel, Granville was certainly not the man to formulate it. As it was, his tentative moves were all rapidly outdated and finally thwarted by the Ems telegram affair, which if it did not really trick France into war by insulting her, certainly highlighted the determination there was on both sides for a showdown.[61]

The only move which might have induced the Gladstone Government to intervene effectively in the war which broke out on 19 July was an immediate threat to Belgium. Between 16 and 19 July France and Prussia both gave assurances that they would respect the neutrality of Belgium and Luxemburg. But on 19 July the Prussians had also revealed to Gladstone and Granville the draft treaty which Bismarck and Benedetti, the French Ambassador at Berlin, had worked out together in August 1866 and which referred to the possibility of France acquiring both Luxemburg and Belgium. The British were not really deceived by this obvious move on Bismarck's part, but they were worried, especially after the treaty had been leaked and published in *The Times* on 25 July. Consequently on 9 and 11 August they secured from Prussia and France new treaties promising not only to respect Belgium's neutrality but to defend it if she were attacked. As an indication of the limits of British complaisance, even this episode, however, is not convincing. In April 1867 Stanley had in private told Disraeli that he was 'ready to go as far as possible in support of Belgium, short of giving an absolute pledge to fight for its independence'.[62] And it would seem very likely that the request for the new treaty in 1870 was a direct consequence of the law advisers' opinion given a few days before, on 6 August, that an attack by one of the guaranteeing powers would not, as had been argued in the case of Luxemburg, release the others from their individual obligation to defend Belgian neutrality[63] (Doc. 95). Belgium's material and strategic importance to the defence of Great Britain had certainly declined since steam propulsion had released a would-be invader from the restrictions of

[61] See appendix B, 'British Policy and the Outbreak of the Franco-Prussian War', in Mosse, *The European Powers and the German Question*, pp. 382–8.

[62] Millman, pp. 120–1.

[63] Seton-Watson, p. 498.

wind and tide. No doubt the residue preserved Britain's tendency to make a somewhat mechanical response to any move against the Low Countries. But it has been suggested that what was mainly at work from the early 1860s was calculated self-esteem:

> . . . to have cast aside at this moment what Europe had long been led to believe was a vital interest would have resulted in an ignominy far worse than that courted in 1864. Most of whatever prestige Britain had retained was tied up with Belgium, and constant concern and anxiety about Belgium was in large part an English reaction to what was expected of her, and what she expected of herself.[64]

But the security of Belgium was not in any case the great issue of the day. That was the outcome of the Franco-Prussian War and its implications for the Balance of Power in Europe. In that Britain had as great an interest as ever, but no adequate policy with which to pursue it. Thus the same writer goes on to say that 'what action Granville and the Cabinet did take was calculated to solve a dispute over fishing rights, not a controversy between two European powers of which war was a distinctly possible if not a probable outcome'.[65] The absorption of English politicians in the question of parliamentary reform in the late 1860s may possibly have distracted every administration and dissuaded it from taking a strong partisan line in foreign affairs lest it alienate some element of support. There was too a great deal of sincere conviction in the non-interventionists' revulsion from Palmerstonian policies. But they too readily made their idealism a cloak for timidity and inaction.

[64] Millman, p. 122.
[65] Ibid., p. 197.

5

FROM ISOLATION TO ALLIANCE, 1874-1902

THE war of 1870–1 did not force any abrupt change in British policy on the continent of Europe. On balance the results of the war even seemed favourable to England's interests. The new Germany would plainly be a very dangerous power with whom to quarrel, but there seemed no reason why England should quarrel with a fellow Protestant state still dedicated to Free Trade, and under the leadership of a statesman who was bent on consolidation at home and, like English statesmen, on maintaining the external *status quo*. Bismarck's conservative foreign policy therefore underlined Germany's usefulness to England as a check to Russian and French aggression. Moreover, after such a defeat, France was no longer an immediate danger, while Italy and Austria remained as England's friends. Russia alone therefore presented an active threat to British interests.

In spite of all this, the feeling of utter disenchantment with the ineffective style and manner of British policy remained as strong as ever. One British diplomat, who in July 1870 had complained that 'The [Franco-Prussian] war could have been prevented if for twenty-four hours the British people could have been furnished with a backbone', still in October 1873 bewailed the old lion's 'strange mania for eating dirt'.[1] These were not, perhaps, utterly inappropriate accusations to make against Foreign Secretaries like Stanley or Granville. But the 1860s represented only a transient stage. Stanley and Granville still had some years of office ahead, but the new age was to be dominated by Disraeli and Gladstone. Neither of these statesmen had been a true non-interventionist. Both could more accurately be described as active idealists, frustrated by the cata-

[1] Mrs. Rosslyn Wemyss, *Memoirs and Letters of the Right Hon. Sir Robert Morier, G.C.B. from 1826 to 1876* (London, 1911), ii. 153 and 296.

clysm of Bismarck's wars, and, during the 1860s, largely biding their time while England reorganized her forces and her people recovered their nerve. While Stanley had talked of holding the European balance 'even', so that England could remain inactive, Disraeli hoped that it would make England's position decisive, and he therefore looked forward to the resumption of an effective intervention in European affairs.[2] Gladstone too was very impatient with a Foreign Secretary and with a Cabinet who insisted on a cautious policy of conserving British strength for a supposedly appropriate occasion. He believed that England had a positive obligation as a Great Power to maintain an active role in foreign affairs. His great distrust and dislike for Palmerston had been based, not on disapproval of interference as such, but on what he thought were Palmerston's fundamentally selfish motives and condescending manner. He did not simply follow Cobden's lead and sigh for the elimination of foreign politics altogether. Rather he wanted England to adopt a vigorous policy, but one with the moral purpose of promoting international co-operation: 'the pursuit of objects which are European by means which are European, in concert with the mind of the rest of Europe and supported by its authority.'[3] Gladstone, therefore, had not been by any means so willing as his colleagues to stand aloof in the Franco-Prussian conflict. He had wanted in particular to protest at Prussia's seizure of Alsace-Lorraine: '. . . this violent laceration and transfer is to lead us from bad to worse, and to be the beginning of a new series of European complications.' It was being decided 'without any reference whatever to the attachments of the people', and without regard for the 'considerations of legitimate interest to all the Powers of Europe'. 'It bore on the Belgian question in particular', and it was 'likely to be of great consequence in the eventual settlement of the Eastern Question.'[4]

The first effects of the Franco-Prussian War on the Eastern Question indeed threatened to justify Gladstone's fears. Russia's reward for her benevolent attitude towards Prussia's war policy was permission to make a unilateral declaration, received in London on 9 November 1870, that she would no longer be bound by the Black Sea clauses of the Treaty of Paris. Gladstone himself had

[2] Richard Millman, *British Foreign Policy and the Coming of the Franco-Prussian War* (Oxford, 1965), pp. 103–4.

[3] Quoted by Philip Magnus, *Gladstone : a Biography* (London, 1954), p. 175.

[4] R. W. Seton-Watson, *Britain in Europe 1789–1914* (Cambridge, 1937), p. 499.

always felt that this part of the 1856 settlement was quite wrong, and he strongly disapproved of the violent outburst with which the Russian declaration was greeted by the British Press. But equally he disliked such arbitrary defiance of the Concert of Europe. For once, however, Bismarck was bluffed into thinking that England might go to war, and so he persuaded the Russians to accept a conference in London (17 December 1870–13 March 1871) which preserved the semblance of the Concert by formally abrogating the offensive clauses of the Treaty of Paris.

Bismarck's successful pressure on Russia seemed to confirm the view that a strong Germany would serve England's interests, especially by checking Russia as well as France. Nevertheless, although the majority of English statesmen kept to this view, there was an increasing uneasiness in English opinion about the extent as well as the manner of Prussia's victory. Some felt that England benefited only incidentally and at Bismarck's convenience. He had put pressure on Russia over the Black Sea clauses only because he feared British action while Prussia's army was still preoccupied with the siege of Paris. And when the war was over the *entente* between Russia and Germany was confirmed and consolidated in the conservative Three Emperors' League of 1872–3. With Austria joining in and with France so completely defeated, this left neutral and liberal England in virtual isolation.

In such a condition of things Gladstone's pious hopes about the Concert of Europe hardly seemed to make much sense. It was Disraeli, more than any other British statesman, who recognized that Bismarck had made the old debate between Palmerston and Cobden irrelevant and that in an age of blood and iron something more in the way of Morier's demand for a policy of 'self-assertion' based on an 'Imperial sense in its highest and noblest form' was needed.[5] Morier feared that this sense was 'absolutely dead', but Disraeli announced its revival in two great speeches at Manchester and the Crystal Palace in April and June 1872 (Doc. 96). Disraeli got his chance to prove his words when he formed a government in February 1874 after the decisive defeat of the Liberals in the general election. The purchase of the Khedive of Egypt's Suez Canal shares in November 1875, though tinged with Disraeli's personal diplomacy, at the time was less a demonstration of any new imperialism than a defensive measure to prevent France from getting exclusive

[5] Wemyss, ii. 298–9.

control of the canal. The proclamation of the Queen as Empress of India in January 1877 was rather more striking. But Disraeli's flamboyant style was balanced by the presence at the Foreign Office of the phlegmatic Stanley, now Lord Derby, and any change in foreign policy was checked by the continued domination—under Disraeli as much as under Gladstone—of the traditional evaluation of traditional interests. The War in Sight crisis of May 1875, when France appealed to England and Russia for support against Bismarck's apparent threat of a preventive war, seemed to give Disraeli his chance to revive England's role on the Continent and, in particular, to break up the Three Emperors' League. But although England and Russia joined in checking Bismarck, the success in exposing the limitations of the *Dreikaiserbund* belonged to the Russian Chancellor, Gorchakov, rather than to the English Prime Minister. Gorchakov's triumph was really a personal one over Bismarck. Politically it was intended to impress upon Germany how much she still needed Russia's friendship; it was not intended to break up that friendship. Disraeli was soon made to feel how little England's position had improved when a new eastern crisis sprang up.

If the Turks had only been able to put them down quickly the risings in Bosnia-Herzegovina in July 1875 would almost certainly not have led to any great crisis among the Powers. 'This dreadful Herzegovina affair, wh[ich] had there been common energy, or perhaps pocket-money even, among the Turks, might have been settled in a week', Disraeli complained.[6] For the time being all the Powers, even Russia, were anxious to maintain the *status quo*. It was on such a basis, after all, that it had been possible to bring Russia and Austria together in the Three Emperors' League. Unfortunately the rising occurred at the same time as a general financial collapse in the Turkish Empire and it was followed by further risings and massacres in Bulgaria in March 1876. Altogether these events suggested that the *status quo* could not after all be maintained and this gave a chance to opportunists, in the semi-independent principalities on Turkey's frontiers and in Austria as well as in Russia, to develop their more aggressive plans. The first result of the erosion of the Eastern Powers' agreement to maintain the *status quo* was the proposal of the Austrian Foreign Minister, Count Julius Andrássy, on

[6] W. F. Monypenny and George Earle Buckle, *The Life of Benjamin Disraeli Earl of Beaconsfield* (London, 1910–20), vi. 13.

30 December 1875 for a programme of local reforms for Bosnia-Herzegovina, with a mixed Christian/Moslem commission to supervise them. This was immediately accepted by his eastern partners and then, very reluctantly, by Disraeli who felt that the best chance of checking the development of a really serious anti-Turkish policy among the Powers was by co-operating to ensure the success of this very limited step. Unfortunately, while Turkey accepted, the rebels did not.

Meanwhile the English had received the first of several approaches from Germany which served so often in the next two decades to confuse rather than clarify, let alone improve, their relations with that country. Possibly because he was worried that after the disastrous War in Sight crisis, Russia and Austria were showing how little they needed German friendship in patching up the Eastern Question between them, Bismarck opened tentative discussions with both England and Russia in January and February 1876. On the one hand he talked vaguely about the need to partition the Turkish Empire; on the other about co-operating with England to check an expansionist combination of Russia and Austria or to mediate in a conflict between them. Gorchakov, who was still preening himself on his War in Sight triumph and relying on the co-operation of Austria, haughtily rejected Bismarck's approach as that of 'the tempter on the mountain'. Disraeli—and the Queen—seem to have been distinctly interested (Doc. 98). But any positive response was checked by Derby who did little more than acknowledge Bismarck's first approach and exploited the vagueness of the second by replying in kind. His formal reply, made on 16 February, thanked Bismarck for his offer, but stated categorically that England could not lay down generalized principles when circumstances varied so much. It described England's policy as the maintenance of the *status quo*, and merely asked Bismarck to explain his plans in detail (Doc. 99).

Derby never got any answer to his enquiry. Plainly Bismarck had dropped the idea, whatever his motive had been. The Eastern Powers, however, could not stand idly by while the crisis continued. So they produced the Berlin Memorandum of 13 May 1876, which was based on the Andrássy reform proposals, but with the important addition of a hint at coercion by the Powers if the proposals were not accepted. All this was rather clumsily put to the other Powers; none the less only England refused to co-operate. Derby wanted to accept, but Disraeli argued that it must be rejected because it sanctioned 'putting a knife to the throat of Turkey', and because of the way in which England had been excluded from the deliberations of the Powers (Doc. 100). On 16 May the Cabinet unanimously agreed not to accept the Berlin Memorandum.

Although Bismarck's earlier approaches had come to nothing, they had evidently encouraged Disraeli to think that there was now some chance of breaking up the alignment of the three Eastern Courts. In fact Gorchakov did not manage to push Austria and Germany forward without England. They preferred to behave as if the Turks would give way in any case. Disraeli therefore had some justification for writing on 7 June:

> I look upon the tripartite confederacy to be at an end. It was an unnatural alliance, and never would have occurred had England maintained, of late years, her just position in public affairs.
>
> I think not only peace will be maintained, but that Her Majesty will be restored to her due and natural influence in the government of the world.[7]

He even thought that England might now be able to make an agreement with Russia on the basis of limited concessions to the Bosnian insurgents. Both Disraeli and Derby had conversations on these lines with the Russian Ambassador during July. But it was not Disraeli's skill so much as the extension of the eastern crisis itself which was straining the *Dreikaiserbund* to breaking point. And before long the deepening of the crisis abruptly upset the approaches to Russia and at the same time also made untenable the passive and obstructive attitude which the British had so far maintained. On 30 June, Serbia, followed a couple of days later by Montenegro, declared war on Turkey. Whatever fortune their military adventure might meet, it was bound to raise the temperature of the crisis and increase Russia's pressure for intervention. Worse still, news now began to arrive in England that an abortive rising against the Sultan in Bulgaria had been followed by large-scale massacres.

The Conservative Government was not completely ignorant of the Bulgarian atrocities, nor did it attempt deliberately to conceal what it knew. But the Foreign Office and the Prime Minister were inadequately informed and, still more important, quite insensitive to the serious implications of what they did hear. Thus while Disraeli's notorious description of the rumours as 'coffee house babble'

---

[7] Monypenny and Buckle, vi. 31.

was a literal reference to the source of some of his information, it also indicated his basically sceptical point of view. He simply did not want anything to deflect him from the course which he believed was determined by British interests. Although horrible massacres had been committed, Disraeli was right to insist that the reports were exaggerated and that such atrocities were endemic on both sides in the Eastern Question. Unfortunately for him his offhand and even flippant protests were ill-suited to the high moral tone of the mid-Victorian age. Gladstone's involvement, though belated, was even more important. Here, he thought, was a chance to re-establish a sort of moral rapport with the masses whose hearts and minds he thought he had lost in his defeat in 1874. So he now re-claimed the formal leadership of his party and pronounced his con-demnation of British policy.[8] With his help public opinion now exploded in moral indignation against the Turks.

Disraeli soon realised that England could not simply go on as if nothing had happened. On 3 September he had to admit that the atrocities had 'obliged [the Government] to work from a new point of departure, and dictate to Turkey, who has forfeited all sym-pathy . . .'.[9] The next day he wrote to Derby that partition was now the probable outcome and that England should make the best of it by taking the lead to end the crisis. On 6 September, however, there appeared Gladstone's famous pamphlet, *Bulgarian Horrors and the Question of the East*, calling for the end of Turkish administration in the Balkan provinces of Bosnia-Herzegovina and Bulgaria, but through careless phraseology, usually taken as demanding the ex-pulsion of Turkey from Europe 'bag and baggage'. The pamphlet marked Gladstone's total identification with the atrocities campaign. But its main contribution was to offend Disraeli, revive his determin-ation to work for the *status quo* in the East, and rally behind him a few doubters like the Queen. 'Vindictive and ill-written—that of course', he complained. 'Indeed in that respect of all the Bulgarian horrors, perhaps the greatest.'[10]

With Turkey stalling over reform and Serbia suffering defeat after defeat, the great danger now was that Russia would intervene and that the change of feeling in England would prevent the British

---

[8] For this interesting interpretation see R. T. Shannon, *Gladstone and the Bulgarian Agitation 1876* (London, 1963).
[9] Monypenny and Buckle, vi. 52.
[10] Ibid., vi. 60.

Government taking any action to counter a Russian occupation of Constantinople. In these circumstances, and without much help from his colleagues, Disraeli twisted and turned until Russia over-reached herself and turned public opinion against her once more. Disraeli correctly divined that while Turcophilism was dead, Russo-phobia was not. But he had to go more carefully. Thus, after con-siderable delay and an exchange of bellicose speeches between Dis-raeli and the Tsar, the British Government was obliged to take part in a conference at Constantinople (12 December 1876–20 January 1877). When the conference failed Disraeli turned for a moment to plans of partition; he even talked openly of the possibility of an agreement with Russia. But he placed his main hope on an approach to Austria. But here he was too late, for Vienna had been recently 'squared' by Russia. All that now emerged therefore was the in-nocuous London Protocol of 31 March 1877, which merely called upon the Porte to adopt reforms. And Disraeli ensured that England's participation in the Protocol would have minimal effect on the Porte by replacing one discredited pro-Turkish Ambassador at Constanti-nople by an even more violently pro-Turkish successor. It was not surprising therefore that this Protocol too was rejected by the Porte on 12 April. On 24 April Russia at last declared war on Turkey.

The Bulgarian atrocities agitation had prevented Disraeli from making any effective move to prevent the outbreak of a war which he dreaded. England, however, still had some interests in the Near East for which he believed she ought ultimately to fight. These interests were pretty clearly spelled out in a note which Derby addressed to Russia on 6 May. In effect it warned Russia against any military action which would threaten Britain's interests in the Persian Gulf, Egypt and the Suez Canal, and at Constantinople and the Straits (Doc. 101). Disraeli later called this note 'the charter of our policy'.[11] It remained to be seen, however, if this 'charter' would be supported as Russia advanced upon Constantinople and the Straits. In fact public opinion in general did not hamper Disraeli. The Bulgarian atrocity agitation had died down considerably before the end of 1876 and when Gladstone published a second pamphlet in January 1877, it sold only 7,000 compared with the 200,000 which the first had sold within a month of its appearance. It was the Cabinet which gave the Prime Minister his real trouble.

While the Russians debated among themselves how far they might

[11] Monypenny and Buckle, vi. 135.

dare to advance—whether to liberate Bulgaria south of the last strategic frontier of Turkey in Europe, the Balkan Mountains, and whether to occupy Constantinople as a guarantee of a satisfactory peace settlement—the English Cabinet quarrelled about the precautions they ought to take. Disraeli wanted to provide for the worst, for example by seizing the Dardanelles; Derby, supported usually by the Marquess of Salisbury, Secretary of State for India, and by the Earl of Carnarvon, the Secretary for War, opposed his suggestions as unnecessary and provocative. The Cabinet remained seriously divided on this issue throughout the war, with sometimes Disraeli and sometimes Derby winning the point with a threat of resignation, and rumours and corrections alternately exciting and soothing their passions. From July to December 1877, while the Turks held up the Russians at Plevna, tensions within the Cabinet were allowed to ease. But with new Russian successes in Asia Minor and the resumption of their advance towards Constantinople after Plevna had fallen on 10 December, the quarrel broke out again in earnest. Matters finally came to a head in the new year over the peace terms which Russia had imposed on the Sultan by the Treaty of San Stefano (3 March 1878). This provided for a number of things which the English were worried about, in particular a big Bulgaria, Russian acquisitions in Asia Minor, and, possibly, a settlement of the Straits Question directly between Russia and the Porte. Derby thought that the Government ought to be satisfied with the assurances Gorchakov gave that matters of European interest would be submitted to a European congress. But Disraeli did not think these assurances were explicit enough and he continued to insist that Russia must submit the whole of the peace treaty to the Powers' scrutiny. On 21 March his Government demanded a categorical acceptance of their terms and when no reply was forthcoming Disraeli persuaded the Cabinet on 27 March to call out the reserve and to have troops moved from India to Malta with the secret purpose of seizing a *place d'armes* in the eastern Mediterranean. Once again Derby offered his resignation and this time he did not withdraw it. It is difficult to understand how men of such different temperaments and such differing views managed to stay together so long. Certainly Derby had been getting increasingly uncomfortable in the Government and relations between him and the Prime Minister had recently taken a sharp turn for the worse when it was discovered that either he or Lady Derby had been passing on Cabinet secrets to the Russians, though this was done presumably in the interests of peace to counter the effects of Disraeli's warlike noises with revelations of the Cabinet's deep divisions.

Derby's successor at the Foreign Office was the Marquess of Salisbury. The succession was not as odd or as inconsistent as it seemed. Salisbury's Cabinet alignments with Derby had been occasioned only by the necessity, as they both saw it, of checking the Prime Minister's more extravagant proposals. Certainly Salisbury had not positively agreed with Derby's foreign policy, considering it to be quite ineffectual. 'English policy', he had written in March 1877, 'is to float lazily down stream, occasionally putting out a diplomatic boat-hook to avoid collisions.'[12] As Secretary of State for India he naturally had a special interest in Britain's relations with Russia and he had been pushed more deeply into the Eastern Question as the principal British delegate to the Constantinople Conference. Derby regarded him then as a compromise appointment, not pro-Turkish, but at the same time, through his Indian preoccupations, very conscious of Russia's threat to the British Empire. It was true that the Bulgarian agitation had convinced Salisbury that Turkey could no longer be maintained as an effective barrier to Russian expansion in Europe. 'It is clear enough that the traditional Palmerstonian policy is at an end', he had written to Disraeli in September 1876.[13] It was also true that, although by no means as impressed as some with Russia's supposed threat to India, he was concerned about the damage to England's prestige which might be done among her Moslem subjects by an unsuccessful Turkish policy. But what most worried him was that England was clinging to an outmoded policy, which would founder on Turkish obstinacy, isolate Britain among the Powers, and advance Russia's ambitions without securing any compensation. At Constantinople he had tried, with some success, to make an accommodation with Russia on the basis of the division of Bulgaria into two autonomous provinces, and when this was ruined by lack of support from his colleagues at Constantinople and in London and by the intransigence of the Porte, he had turned, like so many others, to thoughts of partition. It was natural enough, therefore, that he should agree with Derby in thinking that Turkey had brought the war with

[12] Lady Gwendolen Cecil, *Life of Robert Marquis of Salisbury* (London, 1921–32), ii. 130.

[13] Ibid., ii. 85.

Russia on herself and that there was no reason to discredit Russia's good faith. But if he often disapproved of Disraeli's warlike proposals, he was even more disturbed at what he called 'Derby's emasculate, purposeless vacillation'.[14] As he too began to suspect that Russia was after all aiming at the Straits, he moved nearer to the Prime Minister's point of view, though he was still inclined to think that Russia could be stopped by a positive diplomacy short of war, rather than by warlike measures themselves. Austria's co-operation with England, he felt, would be enough to deter Russia from going too far, and if she did occupy Constantinople, England's best course would be to balance it by 'securing the waterway to India—by the acquisition of Egypt or of Crete' (Docs. 102 and 103). But gradually Salisbury came to accept that after all had been said in the way of public warnings to Russia, war rather than partition might be the only practicable step. He remained very apprehensive of 'the danger of sliding insensibly into an alliance with the Turks', and he continued to resist any precipitate action or unnecessary preparation for war.[15] But the Russians' unwillingness to submit the whole of the Treaty of San Stefano to the consideration of the Powers at last brought him into line with Disraeli at the same time as it brought the Prime Minister and Derby to their final disagreement.

Salisbury himself later belittled the importance of his innovations as Foreign Secretary. 'I never wish', he said, 'for my foreign policy to be judged by my action in '78. I was only picking up the china that Derby had broken.'[16] But although he had no intention of returning to the outworn Palmerstonian tradition—he had written a series of pungent criticisms for the *Quarterly Review* on that subject in the early 1860s—Salisbury's assumption of the Foreign Office freed England from the sterile policies of Granville and Derby. The change was marked immediately in a famous circular dispatch of 1 April 1878, reasserting England's demands about the Treaty of San Stefano but at the same time holding out the prospect of negotiation (Doc. 105). This at last broke the deadlock, allowing an exhausted Russia to give ground without too much loss of face. On 30 May the two countries sketched out the main lines of an agreement regarding Bulgaria and Asia Minor, and, after this had been supplemented by Anglo-Austrian and Anglo-Turkish arrangements,

[14] Cecil, ii. 141.
[15] Ibid., ii. 168.
[16] Ibid., ii. 232.

the Powers assembled at last on 13 June for a great new congress at Berlin in order to wind up the eastern crisis.

Salisbury's purpose, in all this, was by no means merely to save what he could of the *status quo*. He was determined to build the foundations of a new and practical policy (Doc. 104). He believed Britain now had to undertake an active, positive role in European affairs. If she did not involve herself in these affairs she would be ignored in the great changes that were about to take place. But equally, as he had complained when attacking the inconsistencies of British policy in the 1860s, and as he put it when warning the Liberal Government in 1871, if they did not 'adapt their promises to their powers or their powers to their promises', he foresaw 'a time of terrible humiliation'.[17] What was needed in the Near East now was a policy that was both positive and realistic. Thus he wrote to the rather too pro-Turkish Ambassador at Constantinople: 'You have hitherto laboured to prevent Russian preponderance by sustaining the Turkish breakwater. But the breakwater is now shattered, I fear, beyond repair, and the flood is pouring over it. Another dyke may have to be established behind, which possibly must be constructed from the material of the first.'[18] What Salisbury had in mind was not one dyke, but a series of three. Dividing the problem into three areas—Turkey in Europe, Turkey in Asia, and Turkey in Africa—he proposed in each case to substitute for the outworn Palmerstonian policy of maintaining the independence and integrity of the Turkish Empire, a sort of European protectorate (Docs. 106 and 108).

Salisbury was least sanguine about the European area. It was useless to go on pretending that the Turks could defend themselves much longer. The best that could be done would be to secure the Balkan Mountains as the last barrier on the road to Constantinople, induce Turkey to make what arrangements she could with her rebellious Christian provinces, and above all, get Austria to guarantee the Empire against attack by Serbia, Montenegro, and, if possible, Bulgaria too. The division of Bulgaria, conceded by Russia in the 30 May agreement and confirmed by the Treaty of Berlin, secured the line of the Balkan Mountains for the Turks. But the Russians so delayed their evacuation from the territory to the south that even after British pressure in particular had forced them to withdraw in the autumn of 1879, the Turks were too frightened at the recep-

[17] *Hansard's Parliamentary Debates*, 3rd series, cciv. 1366–7.
[18] Cecil, ii. 264.

tion they would receive from a prepared and indoctrinated population to attempt even to reoccupy the Balkan passes. The Turks also ruined what little chance there was of getting any firm commitment out of Austria. The Austrians had wavered all along between an arrangement of their differences with Russia and an anti-Russian concert with England. Before making his accommodation with Russia at the end of May, Salisbury had first tried and failed with another approach to Vienna. At Berlin he thought he was on the verge of securing a definite commitment from Austria but the Porte refused to pay the price demanded—a convention regarding the right to occupy Bosnia-Herzegovina, which had also been Austria's price for a deal with Russia and which was written into the Treaty of Berlin.

Salisbury's main emphasis, however, was on Turkey in Asia. What worried him here were the advances Russia had made in the Caucasus. With Afghanistan so unreliable and with Persia so feeble, Russia's new acquisitions greatly strengthened her communications on the route to the frontiers of India and the Persian Gulf. Salisbury had been able to push the Russians back a little in the agreement of 30 May; but he had not been able to make them give up the potential naval base they had acquired in Batum. To protect Constantinople from this increased exposure to attack and to balance the better facilities the Russians now had for penetrating into the Mediterranean, Salisbury secured a convention from the Turks on 4 June which allowed Britain to occupy Cyprus. At the same time he guaranteed Asiatic Turkey against further Russian encroachments. A base in Cyprus might have enabled British forces in an emergency to beat the Russians to Constantinople, but it would have been of little use in itself against a Russian advance overland through Armenia to the Persian Gulf or the Mediterranean. And it was this Salisbury now saw as the main danger. When, therefore, he failed at Berlin to get any unequivocal assurance that the Russians, who had still not established a fleet in the Black Sea, would not turn Batum into a naval base, he countered on 11 July with a curious, unilateral statement about the Straits. The best answer, he thought, would have been to throw over the 1841 closure and have the Straits open to all, but the Sultan would not agree to this. He also failed to persuade his colleagues to authorize getting a secret agreement from Turkey not to oppose a forcible passage of the Straits should it become necessary. Instead they agreed he should make a unilateral declaration about the Straits Convention to the effect that Great Britain must be allowed to judge for herself in any future crisis whether the Sultan was really free enough from foreign control to give or withhold his consent to a British passage through the Straits (Doc. 107).

Salisbury hoped that this would make it easier for the Royal Navy to act in an emergency, not only to save Constantinople and the Straits from a Russian advance but also to strike at Russian sea power in the Black Sea and destroy her opportunity to advance into Asia Minor. Salisbury was encouraged in his plan to defend Turkey in Asia by his belief that the Moslem provinces did not present the same problem as the Christian populations did for Turkey in Europe, and that by wise reform they could be reconciled and consolidated under the Sultan's rule. In this scheme, too, Cyprus was to serve an important role, providing a show-place and a model for reform elsewhere. In his advice to the Turks Salisbury put all his emphasis on good administration. 'Good Government in Asia', he wrote to Constantinople, 'means Government by good men.'[19] What he had in mind was a system of resident British advisers. This proposal was kept out of his official dispatch on reform because Salisbury feared publication might be offensive to the Turks as well as to foreign Powers. In this apprehension he was absolutely right. As usual, the Sultan promised much but performed little. In fact he strongly resented and soon upset the system which Salisbury had forced upon him. To him European supervision, symbolized in Constantinople itself by the hectoring tone adopted by Layard, the British Ambassador, seemed, with Austria's occupation of Bosnia-Herzegovina, just another aspect of partition. His co-operation could probably have been bought, but the British had had enough of Turkish finances. As it was, Turkey's jealousy and resentment prevented any real progress whatsoever; instead Moslem conservatism flourished under the obstinate rule of Abdul Hamid. The Sultan was also upset, and confirmed in his suspicions about partition, by the policy which Salisbury seemed to be promoting in Turkey's provinces in Africa.

England could not afford at that time to quarrel with France over North Africa. But Salisbury hoped that he might be able to compromise Anglo-French differences and even secure France's co-

[19] Lillian Penson, 'The Foreign Policy of Lord Salisbury, 1878–80. The Problem of the Ottoman Empire', in A. Coville and H. W. V. Temperley, eds., *Studies in Anglo-French History* (Cambridge, 1935), p. 134.

operation in extending his policy of 'protection' to the strategic portions of the Turkish Empire in Africa. As quietly and discreetly as possible he let the French know that he would not oppose their ambitions in Tunis, at the same time offering more open collaboration in Egypt where the Khedive's mismanagement was involving the Powers more and more deeply whether they liked it or not. A bondholders' enquiry reported in August 1878 that the root cause of Egypt's bankruptcy was the personal despotism of the Khedive, Ismail. As a result, the French and English Governments compelled the Khedive to accept both financial advisers and a constitution. In September 1879 he countered with an even more democratic constitution in an effort to rid himself of foreign control. They therefore had him deposed and a successor appointed by the Sultan. At the same time the position of the European financial advisers was made more secure. By these actions England and France assumed the responsibility for the good government of Egypt. In Salisbury's mind at least, this was designed to avoid any necessity of taking over the country directly and permanently. But given the endemic problems of the country, it really committed them to an apparently unending involvement. Furthermore, England's fear of Russia was not strong enough to prevent the re-appearance of Anglo-French rivalry in Egypt.

Salisbury's policy of 'protection' for the Turkish Empire and limited co-operation with Austria and France for this purpose was already crumbling when the Disraeli Government was defeated in the elections of April 1880 and Gladstone came back with Granville as Foreign Secretary. In spite of all the noise that Gladstone had made over the Bulgarian horrors he did not, it would seem, differ so very much even from Disraeli about the substance of British interests in the Near East. In view of his loathing for the 'one great anti-human specimen of humanity', as he called the Turk, there can be little doubt that he would personally have preferred a more radical solution of the Eastern Question. But he knew that the country still believed the strategic security of Constantinople to be a fundamental necessity to British interests. In the course of his public declarations therefore, his call for the expulsion of the Turks 'bag and baggage' was defined as a demand only for the expulsion of Turkish officials from Bosnia-Herzegovina. Even in Bulgaria Gladstone admitted that he envisaged the Sultan would retain 'his titular sovereignty'. The emphasis which Gladstone developed in his famous Midlothian election campaign speeches of 1879–80 concerned rather the way in which he believed the Disraeli Government, by rejecting the Berlin Memorandum in 1876, had broken the Concert of Europe and allowed the Turks to resist genuine reform and force Russia into an unnecessary and dangerous war. His declared intention therefore was to re-establish the Concert of Europe, as one of six 'right principles of foreign policy'—the other five being good government at home to conserve the strength of the Empire; the preservation of peace among the Christian nations of the world; a sympathy with freedom; the avoidance of needless alliances; and the equality of national rights (Docs. 110 and 111).

Gladstone's ideas clearly implied the rejection of the policies developed by Salisbury as well as the vagaries of Disraeli. In the latter part of the Midlothian campaign Gladstone had gone out of his way to denounce Austria as the 'unflinching foe of freedom of every country in Europe'.[20] He had been stung into this denunciation by reports that he had been publicly criticized by Francis Joseph, and when he returned to power he dropped his anti-Austrian line. But Salisbury's policy of bilateral co-operative arrangements with individual Powers was quite incompatible in Gladstone's view with the restoration of the Concert. Gladstone preferred the symbolic unity of the Congress of Berlin, and in the later stages of applying its decisions in 1880–1 he endeavoured to renew the Concert by putting joint pressure on the Turks to make concessions to Montenegro and Greece. The Powers joined in forcing concessions out of the Turks, however, only because it suited them; not because they favoured Gladstone's Concert policy. The Austrians, who could not forgive him his harsh words in 1880, felt that he was working for the destruction of the Turkish Empire and to upset the *status quo* they wished to maintain. In October 1879, as Bismarck was signing the Dual Alliance, he had made approaches for an understanding with England, perhaps to consolidate a triple alignment against Russia, but more probably in order to demonstrate to Austria by the lukewarmness he anticipated from the English, that there was no such possibility. Salisbury certainly did not want an alliance, but some sort of understanding among the three was by no means unwelcome and he was not as cold as Bismarck would apparently have liked. Gladstone's troublesome

[20] Quoted in W. N. Medlicott, *Bismarck, Gladstone, and the Concert of Europe* (London, 1956), p. 30, note 33.

initiatives, however, helped Bismarck, by persuading Austria that English policy was no longer reliable and that she had better make an accommodation with Russia. It was Gladstone's policy which in a sense therefore made possible the signature of the Three Emperors' Alliance of June 1881,

Gladstone also succeeded in alienating France. He strongly disliked the French occupation of Tunis in 1881 and he marked his disapproval of the promises which Salisbury had made to France, by having them published. This merely added Italy, who was quarrelling with France over Tunis, to the number who resented England's North African policies. Gladstone also tried to resist the process of involvement in Egypt, while the French wished to regulate and consolidate it. But he freely admitted the responsibility which British and French actions in the past had incurred for the future. British policy consequently drifted from expedient to expedient and into increasing conflict with both Egyptian nationalists and French activists. In February 1882 the Khedive was forced to accept a nationalist ministry; in May the Ministry was forced to resign by pressure from England and France. At once, however, the Khedive was compelled by popular pressure to recall the nationalists led by Arabi Pasha and on 12 June some fifty Europeans were killed in riots at Alexandria. Gladstone and Granville were both anxious to avoid military intervention and they hoped that an ambassadorial conference at Constantinople might persuade the Sultan to exercise his authority to intervene. Gladstone's main hope was that any intervention might be so arranged as to induce the European Concert to take over responsibility in Egypt from the dual control of England and France (Doc. 112). But the French first objected to Turkish intervention and then, out of fear of Germany, faltered at the prospect of undertaking it in conjunction with England. In these circumstances Gladstone and Granville found themselves isolated in the Cabinet and they had reluctantly to agree first to the fleet's bombarding Alexandria on 11 July and then to the landing of an expedition to protect the Suez Canal. By the end of 1882 England was therefore committed to the military occupation of Egypt and Gladstone's reluctance to get equally involved in the Khedive's rebellious province of the Sudan led to the Gordon disaster in 1884–5.

In attempting to shed the burden of dual control in Egypt Gladstone found himself drawn inexorably into unilateral intervention by Great Britain. This not only alienated France; it also marked the final collapse of Gladstone's Concert of Europe policy. For both reasons it was warmly welcomed by Bismarck, who indeed had been pressing Great Britain to take Egypt constantly since 1876. Moreover, by relieving Bismarck from the necessity of cultivating hostility between England and France, it completed England's isolation. This is probably the main reason why Bismarck was soon quarrelling with England over colonial rivalry in Africa. Another reason was undoubtedly his strong personal dislike for Gladstone (and Gladstonian Liberalism's appeal to his political opponents at home). In addition Gladstone's Concert was quite incompatible with Bismarck's policy of ensuring German security by maintaining controlled tensions among all the Powers. Bismarck's objective now, as his son put it, was 'to squash Gladstone against the wall, so that he can yap no more'.[21]

Gladstone and Granville first felt the full force of Bismarck's hostility when his overtures to France blocked any chance of that Power accepting a compromise which would make a success of the conference called in June 1884 to settle the Egyptian financial problem. The centre of the new tension between England and Germany, however, lay in direct colonial rivalry in Africa and in the Pacific. The crisis began over the German settlement at Angra Pequena between Angola and the British Cape Colony. The Germans had been making enquiries about British intentions since 1883 but Granville was shaken to find in 1884 that both Germany and the Cape laid claim to Angra Pequena. The British retreated, but there followed swiftly further quarrels over New Guinea and Germany's proclamation of a protectorate over Togoland (5 July) and the Cameroons (14 July). One of the main complaints about Britain's policy in Africa was the recognition she had granted in February to Portuguese claims in the Congo. Portugal, it was thought, would frustrate the ambitions of Belgium and France. Germany and France, however, soon found that a common hostility against England was not a satisfactory basis of understanding, and the English that their interest in the Congo was not worth the sacrifice of Bismarck's support against French competition on the Niger. In return for that support, therefore, they acquiesced in the German claims in the Cameroons and New Guinea, and at the Berlin West Africa Conference, called to settle the fate of the Congo and Niger River basins,

---

[21] Norman Rich and M. H. Fisher, eds., *The Holstein Papers* (Cambridge, 1959–63), iii. 131.

they accepted Leopold of Belgium's International Association in the Congo, which was what Bismarck favoured and which they found their own traders preferred to Portuguese rule anyhow.

The collapse of the Franco-German front against England made it possible for a *modus vivendi* to be arranged over the Egyptian Question. Britain reaffirmed her intention to evacuate and undertook to guarantee free navigation of the Suez Canal in negotiation with the French. Then a conference in Paris in March 1885 reestablished a partial international control over Egyptian finances. The Congo agreement and the Egyptian agreement both stored up greater troubles for the future; in any case England's isolation had been clearly exposed and just at a time when she was about to face a new crisis with Russia.

The Penjdeh crisis of April 1885 was the climax of a long period of concern about the continuation of Russia's advance into Central Asia after the Crimean War. This was inspired largely by the frustration of Russia's ambitions in Europe and in the Black Sea area. But it was also a direct answer to British actions in Central Asia. In 1856 the Persians had finally taken Herat and obliged the British to intervene by occupying Bushire. The war ended with the Treaty of Paris (1857) by which Persia agreed to abandon her claims to Herat and to use England's mediation in any dispute with Afghanistan. This success, following upon that in the Crimea, naturally alarmed the Russians and made them redouble their efforts to consolidate their Caucasian frontier. By 1864 they had broken the Circassians and resumed their forward movement towards the Oxus. Tashkent and Bokhara were swallowed up in 1866; Khiva in 1873.

As this process brought Russia nearer and nearer to the borders of Afghanistan the British were increasingly worried. Whether or not a Russian invasion of India was possible was a matter of considerable dispute in India as well as in England. But in the aftermath of the Indian mutiny no one had any real doubt that the Russians could collaborate with some dissatisfied Indian prince to set the border alight. There was also considerable disagreement about the best course for England to pursue to counter this danger. The death of Dost Mohamed in 1863, however, had been followed by a war of succession among his sons and, remembering the disasters of 1838-9, the British thought it best to hold back from the adoption of any forward policy in Afghanistan by which they might counter the Russian influence. They preferred instead to swallow, though distrustfully, Gorchakov's assurance in 1864 that Russia was only seeking to establish a stable frontier among the troublesome Khanates, and in 1873 to reject approaches from both Persia and Afghanistan in favour of a direct understanding with Russia. By this arrangement the Oxus was recognized as the frontier of Afghanistan and the independence of that state was acknowledged as a guarantee that it would be a true buffer state rather than a sphere for a contest between England and Russia.

This policy was not restricted only to Liberal ministers like Clarendon and Granville. As Secretary of State for India, Salisbury's view had also been that England's policy in Central Asia must be basically defensive; it was partly for this reason that when he became Foreign Secretary later he emphasized the necessity, in the event of a Russian attack, of a British response through the Straits. But while he agreed that 'a Russian advance upon India is a chimera,'[22] he did believe that if the independence of Afghanistan were directly threatened England would have to fight to defend it. He wanted therefore to adopt a more active policy to establish British influence, if not in Kabul, at least in such key positions as Quetta, Kandahar, and Herat. It was with this in mind that Disraeli and Salisbury chose the Earl of Lytton as the new Viceroy for India in April 1876 (Doc. 97). Unfortunately they had chosen too energetic a personality. Lytton interpreted his instructions as a mandate to end the buffer state policy and to press forward English influence instead. Coming after a long period of British indifference to his approaches and accompanied as it was by operations on the frontier (which were really inspired by fear of war with Russia arising out of the Near Eastern crisis), this British pressure must have seemed to the Emir, Sher Ali, to be a threat to his own independence. For support he naturally turned to Russia and in June 1878 the Russians established a military mission in Kabul, and in August concluded with the Emir a treaty of mutual support. Disraeli and Salisbury now had no option but to support Lytton's demand for a British mission as well. And they were pushed still further down the slippery slope after Sher Ali brusquely turned the mission back from the frontier. Lytton had defied his instructions by ordering the mission to go forward without the Emir's permission, but it was felt intolerable to British prestige on the frontier to accept Sher Ali's snub. Lytton was therefore allowed to send an ultimatum and when this was ignored

[22] Cecil, ii. 72.

war followed (Doc. 109). The second Afghan War (1878–9) came dangerously close to repeating the disasters of the first. After a brilliantly successful campaign by General Roberts, Sher Ali fled and his son, Yakub, signed the Treaty of Gandamak (26 May 1879) by which he was to accept a British mission at Kabul and Britain was to occupy the Khyber Pass. But on 3 September the entire mission was murdered and Roberts had to undertake a new campaign which ended in the abdication of Yakub and the acceptance of Gandamak by his successor, Abdurrahman.

Russian and British actions in 1878–9 had apparently destroyed the concept of Afghanistan as a buffer state between them. Yet this had not been the intention of either. As conceived by Salisbury and Disraeli, though not by Lytton, Britain's forward policy had been initiated to strengthen Afghanistan's independence, not to threaten it. The Russian military mission had been inspired by events in the Near East rather than in Central Asia and was designed to put pressure on England at the height of the crisis over the Treaty of San Stefano. After the Congress of Berlin, therefore, the Russians did not retort to Roberts's invasion, but in December 1879 withdrew their mission and disavowed their treaty with Sher Ali. For the British the problem of extricating themselves was much more difficult. Faced with the virtual fact of Afghanistan's extinction, Salisbury even considered the possibility of partition, with Britain annexing Kandahar and Persia enlarging her role as a buffer by taking Herat. Consequently, a convention was made with the Shah of Persia in November 1879 to provide for the cession of Herat and for his help against any Russian advance into Central Asia. To Salisbury such a *volte-face* over Herat seemed the logical consequence of the collapse of Afghanistan as a buffer state. To his Cabinet colleagues, on the other hand, the Afghanistan fiasco suggested the utter unwisdom of attempting a similar policy in Persia. Hence they rejected the Herat convention.

The Disraeli Government's handling of the Central Asian Question, and the Afghan War in particular, played a large part in the attack which the Liberals made on the Government's foreign and imperial policy. Not unnaturally therefore, Granville soon made it clear that the Gladstone Ministry preferred not to compete with Russia for influence in Persia and this attitude simply drove the Shah into Russian arms. In Afghanistan a halt was also ordered to the forward policy by stopping the construction of the strategic railway to Quetta and ordering a withdrawal to Kandahar. But Britain's interests in Afghanistan were fortunately secured by the unexpected emergence of Abdurrahman as a strong ruler. For this, however, Britain did have a price to pay. The understanding on the frontier of Afghanistan which had been made with Russia in 1873 had overlooked the existence of considerable Afghan claims to the territory beyond the Oxus. When therefore Russia continued her advance towards Merv and Abdurrahman called upon the British to support him, they were naturally embarrassed. Eventually, however, the appearance of Russian duplicity dissipated their embarrassment about the 1873 undertaking and convinced them that they must resist Russia's unnecessary approach upon the route to India. In March 1881 the Russians had promised that they would not take Merv; but in February 1884 they announced its annexation. The Gladstone Government therefore reluctantly ordered that work be resumed on the strategic railway to Quetta in order to outflank the Russian advance upon Herat which seemed threatened by her possession of Merv. Then, after the Russians had given further reassurances, it was heard that their forces had advanced beyond Merv, and on 30 March 1885, clashed with the Afghans at Penjdeh. Even Gladstone recognized that a stand had to be made. He virtually gave up on Penjdeh itself, but he insisted that Russia must not have the approaches to Herat, and in particular the Zulficar Pass.

Although the Penjdeh crisis was only one of the many problems which led Gladstone to resign after a budget defeat on 8 June 1885, it must have saddened him enormously that after all his criticism of Disraeli's anti-Russian bias, his own Government should have come again to the brink of war with Russia. They had even ordered the seizure of a Korean port (Port Hamilton) as a precautionary measure. Salisbury, who had succeeded to the leadership of the Conservative party on Disraeli's death in April 1881, and who now assumed both the premiership and the Foreign Office, did not really think that war was likely. What most impressed him was that, without securing any *détente* with Russia, the Gladstone Government had succeeded in isolating Great Britain once again among the European Powers. 'They have at least achieved their long desired "Concert of Europe" ', he commented: 'They have succeeded in uniting the Continent of Europe—against England.'[23] Salisbury therefore determined to break out of this dangerous isolation by positive co-opera-

[23] Cecil, iii. 136.

tion with other Powers. In the summer of 1885 he made various approaches to Germany for her support in Central Asia and for her benevolent neutrality in Europe in case England should be obliged to go to war with Russia and be compelled to attack by the only effective means available to her—through the Straits. These moves culminated early in August 1885 in a special mission to Berlin by the Assistant Undersecretary at the Foreign Office, Sir Philip Currie. Currie asserted that in return for a joint guarantee of Persia's integrity and German mediation in the Zulficar Pass Question, Bismarck would 'secure . . . the lasting gratitude of England, and . . . would be laying the foundations of a closer and more intimate alliance between the two countries' (Doc. 113). Salisbury certainly did not intend to offer Germany a formal and permanent general alliance, and when he had written to Bismarck a month before he had used much less extravagant language than did Currie. He had written then only of restoring 'the good understanding between the two countries' and instead of offering any written agreement to maintain it through successive administrations he had remarked: 'I think that you may reasonably count on a continuity of policy in this matter.'[24] So far as specific agreements were concerned, then, Salisbury was looking only for a limited bargain. But in expressing his willingness to enter the Bismarckian system of deals and exchanges, he was taking a distinct step forward into Europe. And for the next ten years he and his successors looked for co-operation with the Triple Alliance in order to protect British interests in the Near East and in particular to maintain Turkish rule at Constantinople.

Initially, Salisbury's efforts in this direction were a complete failure. Bismarck, wrongly, simply could not believe that 'the continuity of policy' would survive Gladstone's return to office; more important he was unwilling to compromise his relations with Russia, especially so soon after the renewal of the Three Emperors' Alliance. Fortunately the Russians themselves decided that they were not yet ready for a showdown with Great Britain and on 10 September they signed an agreement yielding the Zulficar Pass. This agreement did not resolve all England's differences with Russia. The Russians had once again clearly emerged as England's principal enemy and it was necessary to keep carefully on guard in the buffer states of Central Asia. Hardly had the agreement been

[24] Cecil, iii. 224.

signed, moreover, than a new eastern crisis sprang up to reinforce the drive towards an understanding with the Triple Alliance. And England's opportunity was improved by the crisis also removing the principal obstacle to an understanding with the Central Powers, their continued association with Russia in the Three Emperors' Alliance.

The Bulgarian crisis of 1885–7 found England and Russia reversing their roles of 1878. In 1878 Russia had supported, and England had opposed, a united Bulgaria because it was assumed that it would become a satellite of Russia. But after his election as ruler of Bulgaria in 1879 Prince Alexander of Battenberg had stubbornly resisted Russia's bullying and his relations with the Tsar had soon reached a point of open enmity. When, therefore, a revolution in Eastern Roumelia in September 1885 declared for union under Prince Alexander, the Russians announced their opposition to it, and Berlin and Vienna supported Russia in what seemed like an attempt to uphold the Berlin settlement and the *status quo* in the Near East. At first the British took a similar view and supported Bismarck's idea of a conference of ambassadors at Constantinople to 'drown the question in ink'.[25] But by the time the conference met, early in November 1885, Russia's attitude and his own longstanding lack of confidence in Turkey had caused Salisbury to change his mind and to see in Bulgaria's self-determination a more effective barrier to Russia than the decisions of the Congress of Berlin. He therefore put forward the idea of a 'personal union' of Bulgaria and Eastern Roumelia under Prince Alexander (Doc. 114). The great danger in this line of thinking was that Serbian and Greek demands for 'compensation' would open up the prospect of a final partition of Turkey in Europe. In fact Serbia's declaration of war on Bulgaria and her crushing defeat in November helped Salisbury by consolidating Prince Alexander's position and by frightening the Eastern Emperors into accepting a compromise in 1886 on the lines of Salisbury's suggested solution, rather than allow the Serbo-Bulgarian Question to revive Austro-Russian rivalries in the Balkans and to break up their alliance. Meanwhile Austria had intervened to save Serbia from utter destruction and the Royal Navy participated in a blockade which forced the Greeks to disarm. Salisbury's Government had resigned in 1886 but the Foreign Secretary in Gladstone's new Ministry, Lord Rosebery, confirmed the truth

[25] Colin L. Smith, *The Embassy of Sir William White at Constantinople* (Oxford, 1957), p. 16.

of Salisbury's prediction to Bismarck that the Gladstonian experiment was ended and that there would now be a fundamental continuity in British foreign policy. In any case the success in the first round of the Bulgarian Question undoubtedly belonged to Salisbury. But it was only the first round. Hardly had Salisbury returned as Prime Minister in July 1886 (he did not resume the Foreign Secretaryship until Lord Iddesleigh was forced from that office in January 1887) than the Russians kidnapped Prince Alexander, forced him to abdicate, and set up a virtual dictatorship under the Russian Minister in Sofia.

Salisbury's situation in England was much too difficult for him to make any decisive moves. The military experts advised that they had no power, the Cabinet lacked united will, and the Government had no majority in parliament. But in Europe, where he knew his policy must depend on Germany and Austria, the situation was changing in his favour. At first Bismarck categorically refused to risk his relations with Russia for the sake of Bulgaria and Austria would not commit herself without Germany's backing. But the outbreak of the French revanchist movement associated with Boulanger and the sympathetic response it received from Russian opinion, induced Bismarck to prepare for a new war with France and for a breakdown of his good relations with Russia. This line, however, was essentially a contingency plan and all Bismarck's moves were very cautious and accomplished indirectly through the initiative of Italy. Italy's main concern was her rivalry with France in North Africa and over tariff barriers, and she hoped to get English support by associating France and Russia as common dangers to the *status quo* in the Mediterranean and by exploiting Anglo-French tensions over Egypt. In fact Salisbury always hoped he would be able to work out some arrangement of the Egyptian Question which would be acceptable to France. He had therefore sent Sir Henry Drummond Wolff to Constantinople to negotiate a plan for Britain's military withdrawal, and he was not willing to make too strong a commitment to Italy. On the other hand, the Italian approach did suggest a means of forging a link with the Triple Alliance. Thus the first Mediterranean Agreement, as the exchange of notes between England and Italy on 12 February 1887 was called, was followed by the adherence of Austria, Spain, and Germany. The agreements spoke only vaguely of co-operation against France in North Africa and in support of the *status quo* in the Mediterranean.

Bismarck therefore had been more successful in avoiding any commitment against Russia than Salisbury had in avoiding one against France. Salisbury could none the less defend the arrangements as the best available means of warding off a hostile combination against the British Empire (Doc. 115).

Salisbury did not want to tie himself too tightly to the Triple Alliance lest Great Britain should become merely the tool of Bismarck's anti-French policy. Nor did he wish unreservedly to underwrite the ramshackle Empire of the Sultan. But the pressure of events pushed this way. On 22 May Drummond Wolff managed to conclude a draft agreement with the Turks which provided for England's conditional evacuation of Egypt. Unfortunately the French decided to gamble on getting better terms which would explicitly recognize their interests and with Russia's backing they succeeded in bullying the Turk into rejecting the convention. But this did not drive Salisbury into Germany's arms. He was already very annoyed at having had to pay for Bismarck's support at Constantinople by agreeing to withdraw from Zanzibar the British Consul whom the Germans thought hostile to their ambitions. He was therefore still anxious to work for an agreement with France and there was some evidence that Paris regretted having upset the Drummond Wolff convention. In the autumn of 1887 England and France managed at least to conclude a convention for the regulation of the Suez Canal. But at the same time the Russians were again forcing the Bulgarian Question to a crisis by their determined opposition to the election of Prince Ferdinand of Coburg as Alexander's successor in Bulgaria. In October Italy and Austria therefore pressed Salisbury to make a new Mediterranean agreement more explicitly supporting the Sultan and directly aimed at Russia rather than France. Since Bismarck had to some extent retrieved his position with Russia by signing the secret Reinsurance Treaty in June, he was not ready this time to be an actual party to the agreements. But he was always willing to play his customary double game and he therefore pressed the agreement upon Salisbury. Salisbury was even more justified than he knew in his distrust of Bismarck (Doc. 116). But as he did not want Great Britain to be so isolated again, he had no option but to agree. He therefore professed to be satisfied with a highly ambiguous expression of Bismarck's 'moral approbation'. An exchange of notes between Britain, Italy, and Austria on 12 December, moreover, slightly sweetened England's involvement by extending the agreement to cover Asia Minor as well as Bulgaria and the Straits.

With Bismarck giving his unqualified support to no one, the Bulgarian crisis soon fizzled out. The Russians got the Sultan to declare Ferdinand's election illegal. But this was only a token success. Much more important was the collapse of the Three Emperors' Alliance during the crisis. Both Bismarck and Salisbury tried very hard to limit the effects of this diplomatic revolution. In 1887 Salisbury did not take the bogey of a Franco-Russian alliance very seriously and felt that he could afford to keep clear of an outright continental alliance. In 1888, when tension again increased between France and Italy, he still resisted German and Italian pressure for a firmer guarantee of support in the Mediterranean and instead gave only some more vague verbal assurances. In his Mediterranean alignments he had had it in mind that in the event of war with Russia England's strategy of attacking through the Straits would require, not only predominant influence at Constantinople, but also the co-operation of a continental power to dissuade France from making any threat in the rear of the Royal Navy. But in the Naval Defence Act of March 1889 Salisbury again underlined his preference for a free hand with a policy of naval expansion aimed at securing the Two-Power Standard—a margin of superiority over the next two largest naval powers combined. Such a programme would enable the British Empire to protect her world-wide commerce and to face any Franco-Russian combination in the Mediterranean without having to rely on a continental ally. Bismarck, of course, took the Franco-Russian bogey more seriously. But his counter was not an alliance with England but the Reinsurance Treaty with Russia. Thus the mysterious and abortive alliance feelers which he made to Salisbury early in 1889 can hardly have been serious. One explanation suggests that he hoped the refusal he anticipated from Salisbury would demonstrate to his new Emperor the futility of an alliance with Great Britain. William II had no patience with Bismarck's complicated system of checks and balances and limited commitments, and he was determined to pursue a less tortuous and more straightforward line of policy both in domestic and foreign affairs. When a quarrel over domestic policy finally forced Bismarck out of office in March 1890, his departure liberated the Emperor's whim to pursue a 'new course' in foreign policy too. This policy envisaged more straightforward backing for Austria and relied on ultimately drawing England into the alliance.

The immediate consequence of this change of tactics was that the Reinsurance Treaty was allowed to lapse in June 1890 and France and Russia necessarily moved much closer together. In July of the following year the French navy made a showy visit to Kronstadt and on 27 August 1891 the two Powers made a general political agreement. An exchange of notes in December 1893—January 1894 eventually provided for full military aid in the event of a German attack on either. On the other hand the British remained singularly unwilling to commit themselves to Germany, even when the Franco-Russian bogey took firmer shape. Anglo-German co-operation may have reached its climax in 1889–90, but this was not so much because of William II as in spite of England's dislike of him. His state visit to London in July 1891 was not a practical success, and effective Anglo-German co-operation was limited largely to Africa. Up to the mid 1880s the British had been very tolerant of German ambitions in East Africa, largely because their own interest in the area was slight enough to make it worth paying here for German support in Egypt. But by 1887 public excitement in England had been aroused by gold fever and by Rhodes's publicity. Fortunately the Germans agreed by the treaty of 1 July 1890 to give up large claims in East Africa in return for the island of Heligoland.

Salisbury defended the Heligoland Treaty before the criticisms of the Queen and his Cabinet colleagues, largely on the grounds that without it friction in East Africa would have prejudiced the tenuous alignment with Germany and left England isolated once more (Doc. 117). The Egyptian Question still made the only alternative—an alignment with France—out of the question. But Salisbury was anxious to avoid any quarrel with France and he was determined not to be dragged unnecessarily into one by his contacts with the Triple Alliance. In 1891 therefore he refused to commit himself to opposing French policy in Morocco. Italy's activities in Africa, indeed, were becoming more and more of a nuisance. Her pressure on the Sudan from Abyssinia threatened an area of vital importance to Egypt and one whose future recovery the British had very much in mind. Nor could England support Italy's ambitions in Tripoli without further alienating Turkey. And this, important Admiralty and War Office memoranda argued in March 1892, might lead the Porte to open the Straits to Russia in the event of war with England. Taken together with the threat which the French fleet at Toulon would pose to the Royal Navy already fully occupied in the eastern

Mediterranean, this suggested that the English fleet could no longer expect to force the Straits in order to strike at Russia (Doc. 118). It also implied that Salisbury's policy of limited alignment with the Central Powers would no longer be an adequate counter to French power in the Mediterranean. But for the time being Salisbury was still unwilling to accept that implication, and when his Government fell in August 1892 he went out urging his successor to continue the policy of limited alignment with the Central Powers (Doc. 119).

In spite of Gladstone's well-known desire to evacuate Egypt, his Foreign Secretary, Lord Rosebery, accepted the Salisbury line in foreign policy just as he had done in his previous period of office. He therefore went out of his way at once to reassure Germany and through Germany, Italy. 'Any government, even Gladstone's,' the German Ambassador reported him as saying, 'was bound to help Italy in the event of an attack.'[26]

Rosebery was no doubt encouraged in this attitude by the fact that a new crisis was developing on the frontier of India just as he took office. The Pamirs crisis began when British exploring expeditions, which had just reported that it would be perfectly possible for the Russians to invade Chitral from across the Hindu Kush, were forcibly expelled from an area claimed by the Russians. Rosebery dubbed this area the 'Gibraltar of the Hindu Kush',[27] but it was really quite impossible for Britain to compete on the spot for its possession. He therefore launched a diplomatic offensive designed to cut Russia off from the Hindu Kush by compelling her to recognize that the Afghan boundary extended as far as Chinese Turkestan. Unfortunately neither Afghanistan nor China would co-operate and the Russians looked like pressing their advantage. Eventually, however, the Tsar decided to compromise, probably because he was anxious not to push the British further into the arms of the Triple Alliance. The Russians got the line of frontier they wanted, but the British got the passes on the strategic slopes of the Hindu Kush.

The final settlement of the Pamirs Question was not achieved until October 1895; but the crisis had really passed by the summer of 1893 when both sides decided that they could not afford an actual military clash. At that time, however, the bogey of the Franco-Russian

---

[26] E. T. S. Dugdale, *German Diplomatic Documents 1871–1914* (London, 1928–31), ii. 169.

[27] G. J. Alder, *British India's Northern Frontier 1865–95: a Study in Imperial Policy* (London, 1963), pp. 226–7.

Alliance was really beginning to impress British opinion and it was emphasized in October 1893 by the Russian fleet's return visit to Toulon. Rosebery's answer to the problem of Britain's naval weakness in the Mediterranean was to propose another substantial increase in the naval building programme. Nothing could have been less congenial to the Prime Minister, 'bred', as *The Times* of 6 November put it, 'in financial purism, saturated with economical traditions, absorbed in domestic preoccupations, and never very sensitive to the larger responsibilities of a world-wide empire, and indisposed alike by temperament and by the habits of thought and feeling acquired during a long and brilliant financial career to recommend or even to sanction an increase in the national armament.'[28] But Gladstone's resistance this time succeeded only in uniting the Cabinet against him. On 3 March 1894 he resigned, specifically on the naval estimates but ostensibly on account of his undoubtedly failing health. Rosebery, the liberal imperialist, now took over the premiership, and Lord Kimberley (formerly the Colonial Secretary but, as Lord Wodehouse, Parliamentary Undersecretary for Foreign Affairs under both Aberdeen and Palmerston in the 1850s) took over the Foreign Office.

After Gladstone's departure the Government continued to walk the tight-rope path mapped out by Salisbury. Colonial questions— Samoa, the Congo, and the fate of Portuguese Mozambique—revived the irritations in relations with Germany, and Italy continued, though unsuccessfully, to try and interest England in a joint forward movement in East Africa. While African questions again threatened to undermine England's alignment with the Central Powers, a *détente* with France eluded Rosebery just as it had eluded Salisbury. French penetration of Indo-China threatened England's position in Burma, but in July 1893 the problem was largely, though not finally, settled by agreeing that Siam should be regarded as a buffer state. In Africa, however, France and England threatened once again to move towards a confrontation. In West Africa the competition for control of the Niger was awkward but not incapable of a compromise solution. The Egyptian Question once again proved the stumbling block. The French decided to force a British evacuation by occupying the valley of the Upper Nile as far as Fashoda. For their part the British were well aware that they would eventually have to re-

[28] Arthur J. Marder, *The Anatomy of British Sea Power: A History of British Naval Policy in the Pre-Dreadnought Era, 1880–1905* (London, 1940), p. 190.

conquer the Sudan from the Dervishes in order to ensure the security of Egypt from foreign threats, whether or not they themselves evacuated Egypt. They therefore tried to strengthen their grip on the Upper Nile by annexing Uganda (12 April 1894) and by recognizing Leopold of Belgium's claim to an area of territory which would cut off the French advance (Anglo-Congolese Treaty of 12 May 1894). Unfortunately Uganda was not much use without a railway communication and the Congo treaty so annoyed the Germans that a Cabinet revolt forced Rosebery to modify it in such a manner as to make it useless as a barrier against France. A renewed attempt at direct negotiations with France failed and the Government had to fall back on a House of Commons statement of 28 March 1895 in which the Parliamentary Undersecretary for Foreign Affairs, Sir Edward Grey, publicly warned off the French (Doc. 121).

The Rosebery Government was also disappointed in the attempts it made to follow up the solution of the Pamirs dispute and to co-operate with Russia in the new crises which had arisen in the Far and Near East. The position in the Far East was being transformed on the one hand by Russia's construction of the trans-Siberian railway and on the other by the emergence of Japan as a modern industrialized nation. Together these developments greatly weakened the ability of British naval power to preserve the Chinese Empire from partition by the Powers and introduced a new element of Great Power rivalry in the Far East. At length the Japanese decided that they must act before the Russians completed the trans-Siberian railway. Their particular anxiety was to obtain a foothold on the mainland and to cover themselves against Russian expansion by establishing Korea as an independent buffer state under their influence. After years of intrigue they intervened forcibly in the summer of 1894 to establish a puppet régime in Korea and, after several clashes between their respective forces, China and Japan went to war on 1 August.

All this placed the British in a very difficult position. They wanted to protect the territorial integrity of the Chinese Empire and of course they greatly regretted the damage that war would do to their trade. Even before the official opening of hostilities there, they had carefully considered the possibility of intervening. But they had decided against such an undertaking. In the first place it would be bound to alienate Japan, and Japan they saw would be a useful check to Russian power. In the second place Britain's naval power in the Far East was insufficient to make unilateral intervention safe, while co-operation with Russia would serve only to strengthen that Power's position (Doc. 120). General intervention on the part of all the Powers would avoid the worst of these dangers. So, after the war had begun and the British had taken the precaution of ordering out a substantial reinforcement of their China squadron, Kimberley approached Germany, France, Russia, and the United States on 6 October 1894. But Germany and the United States both refused to take part and the Japanese were left free to crush China's resistance. By the Treaty of Shimonoseki of 17 April 1895 the Japanese forced China to recognize Korea's independence and to cede to them Formosa, the Pescadores, and the Liaotang peninsula which included Port Arthur. Now it was Russia's turn to get alarmed, for Port Arthur would give to Japan the maritime key to Manchuria and northern China. It was she therefore who now proposed intervention by the Powers and in April the pressure of Russia, France, and Germany forced Japan to give up the Liaotang peninsula in exchange for a larger war indemnity. This time, however, it was Britain's turn to refuse her co-operation (Doc. 122). Pique probably had something to do with it; but the main reason was a reassessment of her material interests. The Sino-Japanese War had amply demonstrated the limitations of British naval power and the hopeless weakness of the Chinese Empire. On the other hand the Japanese had proved their strength and at the same time soothed Britain's main fears by including in the peace terms a treaty of commerce with China which, through the operation of Britain's most favoured nation rights, would open up another seven ports to her trade. After a very shaky start therefore, the foundations of a future collaboration between England and Japan were already being laid.

Whatever the long-term benefits of Britain's decision not to co-operate with the other Powers in the Far East, the immediate effect in Europe was certainly not to her advantage. Kimberley exaggerated when he warned that 'our separation from Russia in this matter must have a prejudicial effect on the understanding which had been established between the two countries'.[29] The relief generated by the passing of the Pamirs crisis hardly warranted the extravagant references to the state of Anglo-Russian relations in which his Prime Minister had been indulging during the latter part

[29] George Earle Buckle, ed., *The Letters of Queen Victoria*, 3rd series (London, 1930–1932), ii. 496.

of 1894. But there can be no doubt that England's refusal to co-operate with Russia in the Far East ruined what little chance there was of a concert between them in the Near East. Here a new crisis had been produced by Armenian nationalists who had been disappointed by the failure of the Powers to secure for them the reforms envisaged in the 1878 Treaty of Berlin. There had been constant disturbances among the Armenians ever since 1890 and in August 1894 these had culminated in a rising which the Turks put down with great ferocity. Opinion in England reacted to this affair in much the same way as it had done to the Bulgarian horrors in 1876, forcing the British Government to take part in a commission of enquiry and, when the commission's reform proposals of May 1895 were resisted by the Sultan, to step up the pressure on the Porte. Inconvenient though this was for Britain's traditional Near Eastern policy, Rosebery nevertheless hoped to prevent Russia gaining influence at Constantinople at Britain's expense and even to promote an Anglo-Russian understanding by enlisting Russia's full co-operation on behalf of the Armenians. Unfortunately his Government's policy in the Far East and, still more, apprehension about the example that would be set for their Armenian subjects led the Russians firmly to decline his offer.

When the Irish Question brought about the fall of Rosebery's Government in June 1895, therefore, his achievements in foreign affairs hardly looked impressive. His vigorous pursuit of *rapprochements* with all the European Powers in turn had promised much; but in the end he had worsened relations with Germany without improving those with either France or Russia. In the circumstances it is no wonder that opinion at home and abroad expected a great deal of Salisbury's return to office. Unfortunately, Salisbury, far from coming any nearer a solution of the Eastern Question, found that it was rapidly undermining his Mediterranean policy, and with it, the *raison d'être* of his inclination towards the Triple Alliance.

In the summer of 1895 Salisbury felt more pessimistic than ever about maintaining the Sultan in Constantinople. The Armenian massacres had destroyed his last hope that the Sultan's rule could at least be maintained in Asia if not among the Christian populations of Europe. At the same time his naval and military experts were insisting that it would no longer be possible in an emergency to strike through the Straits so as to forestall a Russian seizure of

Constantinople. These difficulties, however, certainly did not induce Salisbury to abandon his traditional policy; rather he continued to look about for some means of postponing any radical change
for as long as possible. Like Rosebery he looked first to co-operation
with Russia as a means of bringing pressure to bear on the Sultan
to make concessions to the Armenians. But the Russians bluntly
refused. In the meantime an exchange of opinions between Salisbury
and Count Paul von Hatzfeldt, the German Ambassador in London,
had led to a more startling development. According to Hatzfeldt,
Salisbury was talking to him in July and August of the possibility
that England might have to abandon her traditional policy in the
Near East and resort instead to partition through negotiations with
Russia or Germany. Quite who was most at fault, Salisbury in
dropping such hints or Hatzfeldt in taking them too seriously, it is
impossible to say. Certainly Salisbury found the German response
most embarrassing. The Germans were very anxious to avoid any
détente between Russia and England which would weaken their own
bargaining position in Europe. They were therefore all too willing
to interpret Salisbury's conversation as an invitation to produce some
great Anglo-German solution of the Eastern Question and as an
opportunity to consolidate a permanent understanding with Great
Britain. William II took the matter up on a visit to Cowes and Osborne in August and, in spite of rebuffs, made another attempt
after he had returned to Berlin. In the end Salisbury had to make
an evasive reply, saying that England's policy had not changed and
that his views had been misinterpreted.

It was not unusual for Salisbury to be rather casual in his conversations even with foreign diplomats but he may have had a
serious purpose on these occasions in hoping that something of what
he said would get to the ears of the Sultan and frighten him into a
more accommodating attitude. Certainly this was the object of the
public outburst he made in parliament on 15 August. 'If, generation
after generation, cries of misery come up from various parts of the
Turkish Empire', he said, 'I am sure the Sultan cannot blind himself to the probability that Europe will at some time or other
become weary of the appeals that are made to it and the fictitious
strength that is given to his Empire will fail it.'[30] But Abdul Hamid
continued to disappoint Salisbury and there were further massacres

[30] J. A. S. Grenville, *Lord Salisbury and Foreign Policy: the Close of the Nineteenth Century* (London, 1964), p. 44.

of the Armenians in Constantinople in October. The horrors committed this time on their doorsteps did at last induce the Ambassadors in Constantinople to bully the Sultan into appointing a 'reform' ministry. But Salisbury's pleas for the Powers to do something about the massacres which continued in Asia Minor and which so outraged English opinion met with no response. The Russians remained utterly immovable and when the Austrians made a move to respond they were sharply checked by Berlin. Worst of all, when Salisbury proposed that the Ambassadors at Constantinople should have the authority to call up the fleet in an emergency, the Cabinet refused to agree. What had been done in 1834, 1853, and 1878, the Admiralty's arguments had made it clear, had now been made impracticable by the Franco-Russian Alliance.

The vital implications of this decision were not lost on the Prime Minister (Doc. 128). But during the winter of 1895–6 there was a lull in the Armenian Question and attention shifted to Crete where a new revolt against the Sultan broke out in February 1896. Pressure from the Powers persuaded the Porte to restore a measure of self-government, but when Greek support for the rebels persisted, this pressure was turned instead against Athens. Anti-Turkish feeling in England frustrated a blockade proposal from Austria, but in August an ambassadorial conference arranged a new programme of reforms. Hardly had this been done, however, than there were further massacres of Armenians in Constantinople on 26 August.

Salisbury knew that the efforts of the Ambassadors would soon fade away again unless he could bring their Governments, and especially the Russian, to co-operate in keeping up the pressure on the Sultan. First he tried a direct appeal to the Tsar. In September Nicholas visited the Queen at Balmoral and Salisbury took the opportunity to propose that the Powers should intervene to depose the Sultan and themselves take over the task of reform. Once again Salisbury talked very carelessly about the ultimate collapse of the Empire, no doubt out of his growing sense of desperation. He did not enter into details about a possible 'arrangement'. He did suggest, however, that, while Russia must not anticipate the collapse of the Sultan's power, England might no longer be so opposed to Russia ultimately gaining control of the Straits, but would instead follow the lead of the other Powers (Doc. 124). But Russia was not prepared to leave the fate of Constantinople to the determination of the Powers. If she were not yet strong enough on her own to decide the issue, she preferred to leave control of the Straits for the time being in the Sultan's feeble hands. Nicholas therefore refused Salisbury's advances and the Prime Minister then made a rather more limited proposal directly to all the Powers on 20 October. This envisaged the assembly of an ambassadorial conference at Constantinople to draw up a programme of reforms which they should be prepared to force on the Sultan if necessary (Doc. 125). After some hesitation, the Russians eventually agreed. Their reply was a little ambiguous on the vital question of coercion, but by and large it seemed that Salisbury's persistence had at last paid off. In fact the Russians had it in mind to exploit any intervention by the Powers to seize the Bosphorus for themselves. Before the conference met the Tsar had had second thoughts and had abandoned that particular scheme. But the Armenian Question was not solved; it was merely shelved. The conference duly met and on 2 February 1897 reached agreement on a programme of reform. But before anything could be done about it, it was buried in a new crisis, for on the same day the revolt in Crete resumed. This time Salisbury joined the Powers in an occupation of the island, but he refused to co-operate in a blockade of Greece. After the Greeks had defied the Powers and had got severely beaten by the Turks for their impertinence, Salisbury did actively support the Powers' efforts to mediate between the belligerents, at the same time seeing to it that Turkey did not exploit her successes to the further discomfort of her Christian subjects. Instead the Turks were obliged to withdraw from the Greek territory which they had occupied. They were even prevented from resuming control in Crete when the Powers evacuated the island. In 1898 Crete was made an autonomous province under Prince George of Greece and it was eventually annexed to Greece after the Balkan Wars of 1912–13.

The Cretan affair was the last occasion on which Salisbury took a leading part in the Eastern Question. Even before 1897, however, it was clear that Britain's Near Eastern policy was undergoing some crucial changes. Salisbury tried desperately to cling to the vestiges of his policy in the East. After all, he pointed out to the First Lord of the Admiralty in December 1895, it was not easy to abandon such a long-standing policy, however much its material basis might have been eroded:

I am not at all a bigot to the policy of keeping Russia out of Constanti-nople. On the contrary I think that the English statesmen who brought on the Crimean War made a mistake. But the keeping of Constantinople out of Russian hands has now for near half a century, if not more, been made a vital article of our political creed: it has been proclaimed as such by all statesmen of all parties, at home and in the East: our fame and prestige are tied up with it: that when it fails the blow will be tremendous.[31]

But there was no disguising the fact that Salisbury's failure to enlist the co-operation of the Powers in the Armenian crisis had left England patently unable to act effectively in isolation. The Austrians in particular sensed that England's policy was changing; and the positively misleading information that they got from Germany about his talks with Hatzfeldt in July and August 1895 made them suspicious even about Salisbury himself. They therefore decided in January 1896 to force the issue by refusing to renew the Mediterranean Agreements and by demanding instead a more far-reaching arrangement which would bind Great Britain to the military defence of Constantinople. Salisbury himself was prepared to go a long way to meet the Austrians, but such a commitment was utterly incompatible with the gloomy analyses now being made of England's naval position at the Straits. Although his colleagues refused even to compromise, Salisbury persisted throughout 1896 in trying to preserve the essence of an alignment with Austria, and the Austrians on their part continued to press him for some firmer commitment. But nothing could now reverse the trend of the new strategic thinking. Russia's reconciliation with Bulgaria in February 1896 further underlined her advantage at the Straits; and, after the failure of Salisbury's talks with the Tsar during September, there followed a further damning review of the strategic aspect of the Straits Question in October (Doc. 126). When the Austrians approached him again in January 1897, therefore, Salisbury had no option but to make it clear how hopeless the situation was (Doc. 127). It was no wonder that the Austrian Foreign Minister became convinced that 'whatever might occur in the Turkish capital [Great Britain would] certainly neither move nor interfere. . . . Great Britain had practically renounced her traditional policy in the East of the Mediterranean.'[32] Austria therefore turned aside to make an opportunist agreement with Russia in May which put the Balkan situation 'on ice'.

[31] Grenville, *Salisbury*, p. 28.
[32] J. A. S. Grenville, 'Goluchowski, Salisbury, and the Mediterranean Agreements, 1895–1897', *Slavonic and East European Review*, xxxvi (1958), 366.

The failure to renew the Mediterranean Agreements in 1896 marked an important stage in the evolution of Britain's foreign policy. It marked the end in fact of Salisbury's policy of limited association with the Triple Alliance. It still took some time, however, for it to become apparent that this was to be the permanent result. The immediate consequence of the collapse of Britain's policy at Constantinople and the Straits was a renewed emphasis on the importance which Egypt had for Britain's imperial communications (Docs. 126 and 128). And this emphasis led, inevitably so it seemed, to a new clash over the Sudan with Germany's enemy, France.

It had always been recognized in England that the reconquest of the Sudan would be necessary sooner or later. But the initial decision to begin the forward movement against the Dervishes does not seem to have had anything do to with France's plans or even with the collapse of Salisbury's co-operation with the Triple Alliance. The decision to order General Kitchener's advance was in fact taken as early as March 1896 and was taken in response to an approach from one of Britain's Mediterranean partners. Britain had been asked to rescue the Italians from the consequences of their defeat at Adowa by putting new pressure on the Dervishes from the north. It was certainly not pure altruism which induced the British to agree. The Italian request, however, did provide a plausible occasion for taking a limited step into the Sudan and one which would tend to prevent the Dervishes from digging in too securely after the repulse of the Italians. Even after the French Government in June 1896 had ordered Captain Marchand to advance to Fashoda, Salisbury was unwilling to retaliate. As always he preferred diplomatic negotiation to precipitate action. But with the progressive collapse of his Mediterranean policy he became more and more concerned about Egypt and when they at last got an assurance that adequate finance would be forthcoming the Cabinet agreed in January 1898 that Kitchener's forces should march beyond Dongola to Khartoum.

The British expedition reached its triumphant climax at Omdurman on 2 September 1898. Two weeks later Kitchener confronted Marchand at Fashoda. In October and November Anglo-French relations appeared to be in a really critical state, with naval strategists and yellow journalists each making their peculiar contribution to the general excitement. But neither side really wanted a war. In June the French had already made a settlement favourable to Great Britain on the Niger. Delcassé, their Foreign Minister since June 1898, also appreciated the impossibility of resisting England in the Sudan, especially as the Russians were too preoccupied in the Far East to offer any support to France. Salisbury stood firm; but equally he was anxious not to make matters worse by humiliating the French. So Kitchener was ordered not to make things too difficult for Marchand and the French eventually withdrew him. For a while they tried in the subsequent negotiations to preserve some hold on the Nile, but Salisbury was adamant and finally got his way in the agreement of 21 March 1899. This left only Leopold's Congolese Empire with any pretensions in the Nile Valley and these were hardly a threat to British power in Egypt and the Sudan.

Omdurman and Fashoda were notable victories for the cool traditional diplomacy to which Salisbury obstinately adhered. But they were also an encouragement to the rash imperialist emotions of a growing number of the Prime Minister's critics in the Cabinet. Foremost among them was Gladstone's former Radical colleague, Joseph Chamberlain. To him in particular Salisbury's cautious methods and measured objectives seemed utterly unsatisfying. Certainly they were not very conducive to the ambitious plans which the Colonial Secretary had in mind for British interests in South Africa.

Although there were special groups and special interests working hard to promote exclusive British control of South Africa, the evidence suggests that the British Government merely drifted into collision with the Boer republics in October 1899. Certainly the history of British policy in South Africa was a very unhappy one, being usually incompetent and often unscrupulous. But the Boers themselves made very awkward and unco-operative neighbours. When the discovery of gold and diamonds on the Rand rapidly converted the Transvaal by 1890 into the most prosperous part of the African continent, Cape Town threatened to become a mere economic dependency of the Boer republics. The favourite British compromise proposal was federation; but this the Transvaal stubbornly opposed. Increasingly the notion took hold among Englishmen, in the mother country as well as in South Africa, that the whole of South Africa must one day be either Boer or British, and it was vital to them that the Cape route, which was ultimately more important than the Suez Canal, should remain under British control.

Chamberlain fully shared this view. But he seems to have thought it unnecessary to push too hard since he believed that immigration would soon overwhelm the Boers in their own lands. Unfortunately the Boers had come to the same conclusion and their policy of denying political equality to immigrant *Uitlanders* played right into the hands of the more aggressive British imperialists. Cecil Rhodes, the Prime Minister of the Cape, was therefore able to persuade Chamberlain that if Great Britain did not intervene the English element in the Cape as well as in the Transvaal would become demoralized and would eventually go over to the Boers. Rhodes and Chamberlain therefore worked up a clumsy scheme to promote a *Uitlander* revolution in Johannesburg which would give a pretext for British intervention. The revolution was planned for the night of 28 December 1895, but at the last moment the leaders thought better of it. Nevertheless, one of Rhodes's henchmen, Dr. Jameson, stupidly went ahead with a raid into the Transvaal. It was a complete fiasco. Jameson had to surrender to the Boers; the Kaiser ostentatiously congratulated President Kruger of the Transvaal; and Rhodes had to resign the Cape premiership. Unfortunately the whole affair raised the hopes of the Boers, without effectively checking the aspirations of British imperialists. Instead, the necessity of a forward policy was forcibly restated in a Colonial Office memorandum in March 1896 (Doc. 123) and Rhodes's militant role in South Africa was taken over by the British High Commissioner, Sir Alfred Milner. The British and Transvaal Governments were anxious to negotiate, but Milner ruthlessly exploited every opportunity presented by *Uitlander* discontent and by Boer extremism to frustrate any chance of compromise. The British Government, including Salisbury as well as Chamberlain, really ought to have brought the High Commissioner under control. Instead, during the next few years, they so allowed affairs to drift in the direction he desired that in the end they had no option but to adopt his policy as their own invention. On 6 September 1899 Chamberlain finally presented the issue to the Cabinet in terms of a fundamental crisis for British 'power and influence in our colonies and throughout the world' (Doc. 134), and over Salisbury's objections secured his colleagues' consent to what was virtually an ultimatum to the Boers. In the circumstances it was not surprising that Kruger decided to strike the first blow himself on 12 October.

Much to their astonishment the South African War went badly for the British from the very first. Their forces met with stunning reverses almost everywhere during the winter and not until the spring and summer of 1900 did sheer force of numbers drive the Boers back and take their towns from them. Even then the adoption of guerrilla tactics by the Boer leaders held up the end of the war until by the spring of 1902 the British had an army of over 300,000 facing at most some 75,000 Boers. Worse than the humiliations of the war were the weaknesses it exposed in Britain's military power and in her external relations. The one greatly increased British preoccupations with the material sanctions of foreign policy; the other strengthened the growing impatience in the Cabinet and in the country at large with Salisbury's supposedly old-fashioned attitudes.

Britain's biggest bogey in foreign affairs was not Africa but Russian activity in China and on the approaches to the frontiers of India. So far as India was concerned, a direct military threat from Russia now seemed much nearer than in the past. The collapse of Salisbury's Constantinople policy had completely upset the idea of retaliating by a flank attack on Russia through the Straits. For a time new plans had envisaged meeting the Russians on the frontiers of India. But the success of these plans depended on the remoteness of the Russian bases and their difficult lines of advance giving the British sufficient time to prepare. By 1899, however, Russia's railway communications had reached the frontiers of Afghanistan and plans were already in hand which would soon link this system with that of European Russia. The only answer to this, it seemed, would be for a comparable development of British railway communications on the frontier such as would allow Britain's forces in an emergency to forestall any Russian advance. Yet in Persia British neglect had given the Russians the advantage of influence over the Shah and in Afghanistan they were again threatening Britain's privileged position. Already, too, both France and Germany were looking to establish a position in the Persian Gulf.

The Indian Viceroy, Lord Curzon, pressed for a vigorous forward policy in Persia, but after the fiasco made of Salisbury's plans for reforming Turkey in Asia the Prime Minister was very sceptical about trying to prop up Persia against Russian penetration. The preoccupations of the Boer War made it still more unlikely that anything very strenuous could be undertaken. Not until after the end of the century, when Salisbury had given up the Foreign Office and the threat to the Gulf had intensified, did a tougher line emerge. In the meantime Salisbury found enough to do worrying about Russia's advance in the Far East. The scramble for China, which began just as Britain was successfully winding up the scramble for Africa, followed inexorably from the demonstration of China's weakness in the Sino-Japanese War of 1894–5. After the war all the Powers indulged themselves to some extent in extracting further concessions from the Chinese. But it was Germany's seizure of Kiaochow in November 1897 that initiated a really dangerous scramble for concessions. The British had been concerned for some time that they might not be able to hold on to their economic predominance in the Yangtse Valley. It was already being challenged by France from her bases in Indo-China and the concession which Russia had gained in 1896 for a railway through Manchuria promised that before long she too would enter the field. Since he did not expect any effective help from Germany or Japan, Salisbury had reconciled himself to the partition of China into spheres of influence, but he hoped that these would not take the form of actual political annexation. Thus China's existing treaty obligations to give English trade most favoured nation treatment would continue to apply and the Open Door be preserved in spite of the virtual partition of the Empire. These hopes, however, were threatened by Germany's obtaining a definite lease of Kiaochow early in March 1898. As Salisbury feared, the Russians, who had moved their fleet into Port Arthur less than a month after the Germans had entered Kiaochow, now followed quickly with a lease on Port Arthur. Salisbury had already been persuaded to make an unparalleled approach to the United States for co-operation but there was never the slightest hope that the Americans would agree. Instead, as France followed the examples of Germany and Russia, the Cabinet decided, while Salisbury was away ill, that Great Britain had better protect her interests by demanding the port of Weihaiwei and an extension of her base at Hong Kong (Doc. 129).

A real crisis in Anglo-Russian relations was averted after the Prime Minister's return in May by his determined preference for negotiations, no matter how difficult and prolonged. Eventually, in April 1899, England and Russia agreed not to interfere with each other's railway plans. In the meantime, however, Chamberlain had taken advantage of Salisbury's absence and the excited anti-Russian atmosphere of March 1898 to make an unauthorized approach to Germany for an alliance (Doc. 130). The Germans in fact were not interested in taking on any international commitment concerning the

Far East. Their seizure of Kiaochow had been a typical piece of adventurism and they had no wish to alienate Russia for England's sake. What they wanted was an English commitment in Europe and since, as they wrongly thought, Chamberlain seemed to be offering to join the Triple Alliance they miscalculated that they could bargain for some colonial reward. All this Salisbury sensed better than anyone else. He bluntly pointed out that the Germans were too grasping and that Great Britain had no interest in helping Germany keep Alsace-Lorraine and no power to defend Austria's interests at Constantinople (Doc. 131). 'You ask too much for your friendship', the German Ambassador reported him as saying.[33] Chamberlain, however, did not give up. Once again without consulting anyone, he made a sensational speech in Birmingham on 13 May denouncing Salisbury's so-called policy of isolation, and calling for an alliance. He did not specifically mention Germany—presumably because of Salisbury's stand—but he went one better and proposed an 'Anglo-Saxon' alliance with the United States (Doc. 132).

Chamberlain's talk of an alliance with the United States was sentimental nonsense; but his persistence did succeed in inducing the Cabinet to reject Salisbury's view that Germany's colonial demands were sheer blackmail and to make concessions in the hope of cultivating an alliance. The main colonial question was the fate of the Portuguese colonies. Portugal was going through a series of financial and political crises which might well lead to revolution at home and the collapse of her Empire overseas. In view of the growing crisis in South Africa England had a special interest in the Portuguese possession of Delagoa Bay, the only outlet from the Transvaal which was not in British hands (Doc. 123). In 1875 Disraeli had obtained the right to purchase it in the event of the Empire's collapse. In January 1897 the financial crisis in Portugal gave the British an opportunity to propose that they should have control of the port in return for a loan. But the negotiations dragged on until June 1898 when the Germans intervened to demand compensation. With the memory of the Kaiser's congratulatory telegram to Kruger after the failure of the Jameson raid so fresh, Salisbury naturally felt sure that William had no genuine interest in the Boers and was simply using the South African crisis to blackmail England into making colonial concessions. He was soon proved right. Germany's intervention easily frightened the Portuguese into breaking off the

[33] Grenville, *Salisbury*, p. 168.

negotiations for a loan. But instead of being satisfied that 'compensation' was no longer involved the Germans insisted on discussing the fate of the Portuguese Empire with England. Salisbury was sadly amused: 'I could not help telling His Excellency [the German Ambassador] that we were like two Jews in the bazaar at Constantinople bargaining over property which did not belong to either of them.'[34] But at Chamberlain's urging the Cabinet again overrode the Prime Minister's objections and during Salisbury's illness Balfour forced through an agreement with Germany in August 1898. This provided for a joint Anglo-German loan to Portugal, on security which implied the eventual division of her Empire into British and German spheres of influence. In addition a secret convention spelled out a scheme of partition in the event of the Empire's collapse.[35] Still the Kaiser's grasping opportunism was not sated. In 1889 England, Germany, and the United States had established a condominium over the Samoan Islands in order to save them from a worse fate which internal chaos and the rapacity of the Powers threatened. But this arrangement was upset by a domestic quarrel over the royal succession in 1898–9 and the Germans took advantage of the situation to intrigue for the acquisition of a naval base. The South African War here too gave them an ideal opportunity to increase the pressure on Great Britain and once again the Cabinet obliged them by overruling Salisbury's objections to blackmail. The Anglo-German agreement of 14 November 1899 arranged a partition and William got the naval base he wanted.

Given such concessions it is no wonder that by the end of 1899 William seemed to be moving in the direction so much desired by Chamberlain. The Kaiser made an unusually good-tempered visit to England in November and, with gracious condescension, even proferred some advice about how to defeat the Boers! There were inevitably some unpleasant maritime incidents arising out of the war, but the Germans kept up good relations in spite of them. In particular they not only resisted approaches from Russia for the

---

[34] Grenville, *Salisbury*, p. 190.

[35] In 1899 the British again got worried about Boer preparations for war and they renewed their pressure on Portugal to close Delagoa Bay to the import of arms by Kruger. On 14 October they secured an agreement that this would be done if war broke out. In return Britain reaffirmed her ancient alliance and promised to help defend Portugal's colonies. This did not conflict with the German agreement, since Britain had never undertaken to work for the collapse of the Portuguese Empire. But the Portuguese Government insisted on keeping the new agreement secret and this tended later to confirm German suspicions that they had been cheated.

formation of a continental league against England; they also exposed the plot to London. But still the Colonial Secretary got no positive response to his proposals for an alliance. Another extravagant speech at Leicester on 30 November embarrassed the Germans almost as much as it did the Americans.

In the meantime a new crisis in the Far East encouraged Chamberlain to maintain his pressure for an understanding with Germany. The Boxer rising in China in 1899 was a part popular and part politically inspired attack on foreign intruders. It culminated in June 1900 in the murder of the German Minister in Peking and the famous siege of the foreign Legations. Salisbury was worried that foreign intervention would inevitably lead to further spoliations by the Powers. Already in March 1900 he had commented on the British Minister's participating in a joint request for a naval demonstration: 'Stupid of him to do this without asking us. One of the demonstrating powers will take the opportunity of appropriating something nice—and we with our engagements in South Africa will have to give and look pleasant.'[36] When the Powers moved during the summer to intervene with a joint military expedition, therefore, Salisbury joined in only very reluctantly and belatedly.

Salisbury rather underestimated the danger from the Boxers. But he was quite right to suspect the Russians. The Russian Government did use the occasion to consolidate their position in China and while the Powers' representatives were meeting in Peking in the autumn of 1900 to bring the Chinese to terms, St. Petersburg was secretly negotiating to secure virtual control of Manchuria. When news of this leaked out the Japanese were particularly alarmed and approached both Germany and England for help to check the Russian advance. Germany and England signed an agreement on 16 October providing for the maintenance of China's territorial integrity and the Open Door. But the commitment to uphold the Open Door was subject to a strong reservation—'as far as they can exercise influence'—and so even Russia was able to adhere to it, though in ambiguous terms. The fact of the matter was that Germany was not particularly interested in checking Russia's penetration of Manchuria, but rather in securing an adequate share of the spoils. Certainly Germany had no interest in Manchuria worth risking

---

[36] Grenville, *Salisbury*, p. 306.

Russia's hostility on the frontiers of East Prussia. This Salisbury at least understood, though he exaggerated a good deal: 'She [Germany] is in mortal terror on account of that long undefended frontier of hers on the Russian side. She will therefore never stand by us against Russia; but is always rather inclined to curry favour with Russia by throwing us over. I have no wish to quarrel with her; but my faith in her is infinitesimal.'[37] But by this time Salisbury's ill-health and old age were making it increasingly difficult for him to carry on his double burden in the face of so much dissatisfaction among his colleagues. In November therefore he finally gave up the Foreign Office.

Salisbury's successor at the Foreign Office was the Marquess of Lansdowne, formerly Secretary of State for War. Although by no means so impetuous as Chamberlain and although severely chastened by his unfortunate tenure of the War Office, Lansdowne was certainly not content to follow the Salisbury line in foreign affairs. He had in fact previously tended to side with the Chamberlain wing in their dissatisfaction with what they thought of as the Prime Minister's dangerously outmoded policy of isolation. But while he was willing to make definite commitments he certainly did not believe that unlimited alliances were either desirable or possible. What he wanted was a concerted agreement on the Far East. The exchanges which he had with the Germans on this subject, however, led nowhere, and Lansdowne became desperate enough to try and force the issue by making a particularly bold offer. Early in March 1901 he proposed that his Government should offer an actual, and if necessary secret, alliance to Germany by which the two Powers would undertake to prevent a third intervening in a future war between Russia and Japan. Such a proposal was too strong for the Cabinet and they refused to approve it. In any case it would not have suited the Germans who still looked to England for a European commitment and colonial *douceurs*. On 18 March the German Embassy came up with an offer of a general defensive alliance. Lansdowne knew there was no chance of this. 'It would oblige us to adopt in all our foreign relations a policy which would no longer be British but Anglo-German', he wrote.[38] But the two Powers continued to grope for an understanding, until firmly checked by Salisbury. When in April the Germans revived their proposal by stating bluntly that they expected England to join the Triple Alliance, Lansdowne put the whole matter to his Cabinet colleagues. At least two of them wanted to accept, but Salisbury squashed the idea with a masterly memorandum on 29 May 1901. Public feeling in Germany, he pointed out, had hardly shown itself ready for such an alliance by its reactions to the petty irritations of the last few years. And what need did England have of an alliance? Personally he still relied on friendly collaboration with Germany; but an actual alliance commitment could and should still be avoided. Far from emphasizing the dangers of England's isolation, the Boer War had revealed how even at their most favourable moment the continental Powers were unable to combine against her (Doc. 136).

Although Salisbury's arguments for the moment effectively checked the approaches to Germany, he was not able to reverse the trend of accumulated dissatisfaction with his own policies. Here the arguments of the strategic experts were crucial. Salisbury himself never gave up his concern for the defence of India, and after five years at the War Office Lansdowne was completely convinced of the necessity for England to concentrate her military resources and to enlist the co-operation of the Powers against Russia. Still more important, probably, was the influence of the Earl of Selborne who had entered the Cabinet as First Lord of the Admiralty in November 1900 at the same time as Salisbury had relinquished the Foreign Office. During the last decade Britain's naval supremacy had been increasingly undermined, especially by the Franco-Russian Alliance in the Mediterranean and in the Far East. Even so, by prodigious efforts and expenditure, it had been possible to maintain the Two-Power Standard as formally established by the Naval Defence Act of 1889. By the beginning of the twentieth century, however, it was becoming clear that the ambitious programmes of construction embarked upon by Japan, Germany, and the United States would bring so many naval Powers into existence as to make the Two-Power Standard ineffective. But the increasing financial strain of naval competition also made it out of the question to try and equal the combined force of more than two Powers. Clearly, Selborne kept on pointing out, Great Britain could no longer afford, for the purposes of naval planning, to regard every Power as a potential enemy (Doc. 135).

Selborne proposed in particular to exclude the United States

Navy from all future calculations. This was a new departure from tradition, but one which had been implicit in British policy towards the United States since the time of the Civil War if not from 1814. The British had long since come to recognize that it would be impossible ultimately to oppose United States expansion on the American continent or to challenge the power of the United States on its own ground. But only in the last few years of the nineteenth century did Britain's strategists and statesmen stop brooding over this gloomy prospect and try positively to measure its implications. Even then the change was forced upon them by American pressure, though British public opinion in general, it would appear, was much less unwilling.

British policy towards the United States had been allowed to rest on the virtual withdrawal of military forces from the interior of Canada after the end of the Civil War, largely because the United States thenceforward concentrated on internal reconstruction and development and allowed their vast army to fade away and their navy to rust into oblivion. But by the 1890s a sort of new Manifest Destiny had taken hold of the American imagination and compelled the United States Government towards a more expansionist foreign policy and the construction of a powerful navy. As usual Great Britain seemed to be standing in the way.

The first major confrontation between England and the United States occurred over the disputed frontier of British Guiana. The Americans had been growing increasingly suspicious of British influence in South America during the 1880s. They simply could not believe that there was no political motive in the British Government's renewed financial and commercial interest in Latin America. An unscrupulous former American diplomat, then in the service of the Venezuelan Government, therefore had little difficulty in persuading President Cleveland and other politicians that Britain's main aim was to acquire control of the Orinoco River and with it a strategic grip on a vast hinterland of South American wealth. There followed on 20 July 1895, a sharp note from the American Secretary of State, forcefully reasserting the Monroe Doctrine and bluntly demanding that England submit to arbitration: 'today the United States is practically sovereign on this continent, and its fiat is law upon the subjects to which it confines its interposition.' This impertinence annoyed Chamberlain as much as Salisbury, but the Prime Minister made a courteous if cool reply. Unfortunately it did not arrive in Washington in time to dissuade the President from making another belligerent declaration in his Annual Message to Congress on 17 December. So this petty affair now assumed the proportions of a minor crisis, with popular passions aroused and with strategists on both sides of the Canadian frontier making tentative preparations for war. But there was never any likelihood of such a clash. The United States was totally unready, as the collapse of the stockmarket soon indicated. Equally the British were much too concerned with affairs elsewhere in the world—in the Far East and in Africa.

Salisbury therefore had good reason to expect that 'the American conflagration will fizzle away'.[39] But the majority of his colleagues did not agree that they ought therefore to maintain a stiff attitude. Their feeling was rather one of shock that there should be such ill-feeling in the United States. 'The hatred of England by Americans is to me quite unaccountable', complained one junior Minister. 'We expect the French to hate us and are quite prepared to reciprocate the compliment if necessary; but the Americans, No!'[40] At a meeting of the Cabinet on 11 January 1896, therefore, the majority overruled Salisbury and forced him to agree to the American demand for arbitration.

In some respects the Anglo-American difference over Venezuela was unimportant because it was due to a simple misunderstanding. The British boundary claims were based on strict legal rights. It is true that they had become rather more important after the discovery of gold in the area; but there was no plot to control the Orinoco. Pride apart therefore, there was no substantial obstacle to prevent Britain satisfying the United States on this point and if necessary by means of arbitration. Equally, once reassured in this respect, the United States lost interest in Venezuela and the final arbitration in October 1899 largely favoured Great Britain. But England had bowed before the American assertion of the Monroe Doctrine, as she had never avowedly done before. And the crisis did play a vital part in alerting British opinion and British statesmen to the dangers of clashing with the new-found enthusiasm of the United States.

This lesson had very soon to be applied. At the end of April 1898

[39] Arthur D. Elliot, *The Life of George Joachim Goschen, First Viscount Goschen 1831–1907* (London, 1911), ii. 204.

[40] R. A. Humphreys, 'Anglo-American Rivalries and the Venezuela Crisis of 1896', *Transactions of the Royal Historical Society*, 5th series, xvii (1967), 156.

American patience with the long and cruel civil war in Cuba finally ran out and the United States declared war on Spain. In the view of most European statesmen the Americans forced the war just when the Spanish Government seemed to be coming to its senses. Personal sympathies, moreover, usually lay with the Spanish Queen-Regent. The most that the European Powers might have done, would have been to put moral pressure on the United States and there was no question of that unless England played a leading part. Although Salisbury's sympathies also lay with Spain, like Palmerston he too had now learned his lesson and he henceforth approached relations with the United States with the greatest circumspection. He had, in fact, frankly declared his attitude on the Cuban Question to the American Ambassador in the summer of 1896. 'It's no affair of ours', he said; 'we are friendly to Spain and should be sorry to see her humiliated, but we do not consider that we have anything to say in the matter whatever may be the course the United States may decide to pursue.'[41] And Balfour, who was in charge of the Foreign Office during Salisbury's illness on the eve of the Spanish-American War, was equally firm. He sympathized with the Spanish pleas, but assured the Americans that Great Britain would not 'take any steps which would not be acceptable to the Government of the United States'.[42] Thus although the British Ambassador in Washington, Sir Julian Pauncefote, joined the other Powers' representatives in presenting the United States with a note on 7 April urging a peaceful solution, he did so only after checking with the American Secretary of State that it would not be considered objectionable. And when Pauncefote, having found that the American Government was really bent on war, proposed to take a leading part in a new protest, he was firmly checked by Balfour.

Once the war had begun the British Government continued to preserve a neutrality which was so circumspect that, against a background of rising popular support for the United States and when so often executed by sympathetic individuals, it appeared in practice to be positively benevolent. Thus when the British postponed taking up a lease on Mirs Bay near Hong Kong so that the United States Navy could go on using it during the war, this did reflect a good deal of local good-will, particularly in the navy. But so far as the Government was concerned such actions followed from the simple aware-

---

[41] Henry James, *Richard Olney and His Public Service* (Boston, 1923), p. 244.
[42] Grenville, *Salisbury*, p. 203.

ness that it was more dangerous to annoy the United States than Spain. Yet so friendly did British policy as well as the British Press appear to be that American opinion became convinced that the United States owed a good deal to Great Britain. Even when, some years later, the German Government published the truth about Pauncefote, no one believed it. The story even took hold that at the battle of Manila Bay the British manoeuvred their force so as to prevent a clash between the United States Navy and a jealous German fleet. The British were there in fact merely to observe the quality of American gunnery. On the other hand the Germans were present with an eye to staking a claim in the future disposition of the Spanish Empire. In this matter too, British policy became obscured in legend, the impression being that pressure from Britain was somehow responsible for the Americans taking the Philippines as well as Cuba and Puerto Rico. The British certainly hoped that a deeper United States commitment in the Far East would strengthen the Americans' determination to defend the Open Door. Thus Salisbury publicly remarked: 'No one can deny that their appearance among the factors of Asiatic at all events and possibly European diplomacy is a grave and serious event which may not conduce to the interests of peace though I think that in any event it is likely to conduce to the interests of Great Britain.'[43] Hence also the approach made just before the beginning of the war for a joint front in China. But this approach had not been made with much expectation of success, and the negative response confirmed the futility of such advances. Afterwards, it seems, the British never directly urged the Americans to take the Philippines, lest the other Powers accuse them of seeking some reward and the whole question be turned into a new scramble for concessions. They made it clear, however, that they preferred the United States to have them rather than that they should go to Germany.

Salisbury's cautious policy during the Spanish-American War therefore earned more gratitude than it deserved, thanks very largely to an irrational development of sentiment on both sides of the Atlantic. The notion of two Anglo-Saxon Empires defending a superior civilization against the jealousies of other European Powers, in particular helped to check the tendency in the United States to take a disapproving and even hostile view of British actions in South Africa. But on the American continent the pressure was nevertheless kept

[43] R. G. Neale, *Britain and American Imperialism 1898–1900* (Brisbane, 1965), p. 91.

up on Great Britain and it was clear that a considerable price still had to be paid to avoid regaining the hostility of the United States.

The Spanish-American War had given a dramatic boost to United States interest in building a canal across the Central American isthmus. Nothing could have better illustrated Alfred Mahan's condemnation of having to divide the battle fleet between two oceans than the two months it took the U.S.S. *Oregon* to join the Atlantic fleet from San Francisco. But in the new mood of American self-confidence and self-assertion the old bargain that had been made with Great Britain by the Clayton-Bulwer Treaty was regarded as an obstacle rather than an encouragement to the construction of a canal. The Americans had no intention now of allowing any other Power to share in its construction or control. Exchanges about the treaty had begun in the usual manner of Anglo-American relations, with the British getting annoyed at the intemperate language employed by some Americans. Britain's expert advisers in fact argued that the construction of a canal would be disadvantageous to her. Clearly it would be of enormous strategic and economic importance to a world political and commercial Power like Great Britain. But this would put a considerable new burden on British naval resources just when they were already being stretched to the limit. At the same time there was no hope of preventing the construction of the canal. The conclusion therefore was that Britain should negotiate the surrender of her rights under the Clayton-Bulwer Treaty, but negotiate in such a way as to get some compensation for agreeing to what might seriously damage her interests (Doc. 133). The particular bargain settled on was an American concession to Canada, especially over the disputed boundary of Alaska.

The early weeks of 1899 were spent in negotiations on these lines between Pauncefote and the American Secretary of State, John Hay. But the Americans stood firm over Alaska and as the war in South Africa was going very badly when the negotiations were revived in December, the British were forced to abandon all idea of a bargain. On 2 February 1900, therefore, Pauncefote was instructed to sign a draft treaty providing for American construction. But the canal was to be kept open in times of peace and war and to ensure this the other Powers were to be invited to adhere to the agreement. A treaty on these lines never had much chance of being accepted by the Senate. They resented the affront to the Monroe Doctrine implied by the invitation to other Powers, and they had no intention of allowing any potential enemy free use of the canal during a war with the United States. They insisted instead that the United States should be allowed to fortify the canal in the interests of the defence of the United States as well as of the canal itself, and that the invitation to other Powers be dropped.

If the canal were not to be neutralized, it would clearly require still greater naval efforts on Britain's part to protect her interests. And if other Powers were not to join the agreement, she would be placed at a unique disadvantage. This second objection led the British to reject the amendments in February 1901 and in November they were able to accept a version which partially met their objections on this point. But the Americans retained the right to fortify the canal. Lansdowne was responsible for overruling the Admiralty's objections on this account. These objections, he pointed out in a memorandum of 15 January 1901, were made irrelevant by the Admiralty's own admission that local naval superiority, not fortification, would control the canal.

The importance of the Hay-Pauncefote Treaty extended far beyond the immediate question of an inter-oceanic canal. It was an open recognition by Great Britain that she must now concede naval, as well as military, supremacy on the American continent to the United States. The process of withdrawal was therefore rapidly accelerated and extended from land forces to the Royal Navy. By 1906 only token British forces remained in American waters. Although Lansdowne did not specifically say so, the fundamental weakness of the Admiralty argument against American fortification was that it assumed the United States was a potential enemy at the same time as the Admiralty was insisting in other documents that England could no longer afford to do so. The Hay-Pauncefote Treaty was therefore a recognition that if Britain could no longer afford to count the United States among her potential enemies, she had better get out of harm's way as soon as possible.

Although an alliance remained a nebulous possibility, some thought that conciliating the United States could have a positively beneficial effect. Clearly naval withdrawal facilitated the policy of concentration in home waters. It was also possible to argue that American suspicion of the activity of other European Powers in American waters, even more than in the Far East, would make it safe to leave British interests in the Caribbean to the protection of the United States Navy. This, indeed, was the gist of the advice which Francis Bertie, the Assistant Undersecretary in the Foreign Office, gave in a memorandum of 27 October 1901 (Doc. 137). More relevant at the time, however, than his support for a tacit reliance on the United States, were his arguments against seeking an alliance with Germany. Selborne had thought that his repeated warnings about the increasing strain of naval competition pointed to the ultimate necessity of an alliance with that country. Bertie, however, appreciated far better than Selborne or Lansdowne that Germany would never join any Far Eastern alliance against Russia. His more positive contribution was to point out that England had no need of a formal understanding with Germany. If England clashed with the Franco-Russian Alliance, Germany's interests in maintaining the Balance of Power in Europe would oblige her to support England. More than this, an actual alliance would be positively harmful, since it would tend to obstruct any chance England had of negotiating a settlement with France or Russia.

Although Lansdowne by no means shared the anti-German animus that largely inspired Bertie and an increasingly influential group in the Foreign Office, he was not antagonistic to some of the ideas put forward. He certainly appreciated the desirability of negotiating with all the Powers in conflict with England and he had already opened tentative approaches to France and more actively to Russia about Persia. He was also getting disillusioned about the prospects of an alliance with Germany. In November he admitted that the objections to the sort of alliance the Germans wanted were 'virtually insuperable'. But he was determined to break away from the past: 'We may push too far the argument that, because we have in the past survived in spite of our isolation, we need have no misgivings as to the effect of that isolation in the future.' He therefore insisted, against the Prime Minister's opposition, on making proposals to Berlin for a declaration of mutual interests. He was not hopeful that they would be immediately successful, but, he thought, they would at least prevent the Germans from saying that England had 'treated them inconsiderately or brusquely rejected their overtures' (Doc. 138). Lansdowne was right about the Germans not being interested in the suggestion; their new Ambassador did not even bother to send it on to Berlin. But he was wrong to think that he could avoid recriminations. In effect, though certainly not by design, the offers of only limited understandings which Landsowne made called the Germans' bluff. And having banked so much on bullying England into an alliance on their own terms, their disappointment led easily to bitter resentment. It was 'inculcated into the minds of the last two German generations', explained Holstein, the *éminence grise* of German foreign policy, 'not only that ever since 1864 England either sympathised with or materially assisted our enemies, but also that English policy, while keeping itself free from any sort of engagement, is leaving no stone unturned to bring about a great continental war'.[44]

Lansdowne's approach to Russia also failed. All that he could do in the face of a complete rebuff was to issue a stern but ineffective warning to the Shah—and indirectly to Russia—that the balance between British and Russian influence must be preserved (Doc. 140). But the failure of his approaches to Russia and Germany helped Lansdowne gain support in the Cabinet for a move in quite another direction. On the same day (25 October 1901) that he had prepared a memorandum for his colleagues on the desirability of an approach to Russia, Lansdowne had addressed them another on the possibility of an alliance with Japan. The initiative for such an alliance had come from the Japanese themselves. As the military became more dominant in Japanese politics and as Russia continued to challenge Japan's influence in Korea, the conviction grew in Tokyo that a showdown would have to be forced with the Russians. Without England's support, however, this would be an extremely dangerous course to take. Probably the Japanese never made up their minds which alternative to pursue, a showdown or an accommodation with Russia. It was the respective attitudes of Russia and England which decided the issue for them. While Salisbury's influence prevailed England was politely but firmly unresponsive. Lansdowne was less blunt but he too was evasive in discussions he had with the Japanese Ambassador in and after March 1901. But with the failure of the approaches to Russia and Germany the idea of an alliance rapidly became more attractive to him. What mainly forced his hand, however, were rumours that the Japanese were seeking an accommodation with Russia. He therefore drew up a draft of alliance and at a meeting on 5 November secured the approval of the majority of the Cabinet. What were probably crucial in the defeat of the traditional attitude in the Cabinet were the recent rebuff from Russia and the arguments of the First Lord of the Admiralty. 'Such an

---

[44] G. P. Gooch and Harold Temperley, eds., *British Documents on the Origins of the War 1898-1914* (London, 1926-38), ii. 84.

agreement', Selborne had ended a long memorandum on the subject on 4 September, 'would, I believe, add materially to the naval strength of this country all over the world, and effectively diminish the probability of a naval war with France or Russia singly or in combination.'[45]

The fact that an alliance with Japan would reduce the danger from the Franco-Russian Alliance substantially removed any immediate need for an alliance with Germany. Balfour alone in the Cabinet seems to have expressed any real regret about that (Doc. 139). It may even have softened the blow for Salisbury. But it was not all that easy to reconcile English and Japanese objectives. Making an agreement for mutual aid in the event that either should be attacked by more than one Power in the Far East was not difficult. But the British wanted to preserve the *status quo* in China; the Japanese to advance their own interests. The British therefore objected to recognizing Korea as a Japanese sphere of influence and, still more, to leaving Japan complete freedom to take whatever steps she felt necessary to 'safeguard and promote' her interests there. Since it would limit their freedom to concentrate in Europe the British also disliked being required to maintain a naval force equal to that of any other Power in the Far East unless the Japanese extended the alliance to cover the defence of India. These difficulties gave Salisbury one last chance to make his misgivings felt. In what was to be his last important memorandum for the Cabinet he dissected the alliance proposal in detail and concluded with respect to the Korean provisions that they surrendered 'without reserve into the hands of another power the right of deciding whether we shall or shall not stake the resources of the Empire on the issue of a mighty conflict' (Doc. 141). But although the Cabinet, including Lansdowne, had serious doubts, they decided to go ahead. On 30 January 1902 the Anglo-Japanese Alliance was therefore signed and signed with only ambiguous changes on the lines of the objections raised by Salisbury. England had surrendered to a foreign Power what Salisbury and his predecessors had hitherto resisted as utterly unacceptable by a parliamentary democracy: the decision of peace or war.

[45] The memorandum is printed in C. J. Lowe, *The Reluctant Imperialists. British Foreign Policy 1878–1902* (London 1967) ii. 129–32.

6

EPILOGUE: THE DRIFT
INTO WAR, 1902–1914

THE Queen had died on 22 January 1901. But so far as foreign policy was concerned the Victorian Age came to an end with Salisbury's retirement in July 1902. With the relative decline in naval power which Britain faced throughout the world in the last years of the nineteenth century, Salisbury had himself been forced to modify the policy of the completely free hand. But while he remained it was possible to imagine that even the Anglo-Japanese Alliance had not completely overthrown the traditional line of non-commitment. There was a material commitment, it was true; but it was one that was strictly limited to the Far East. More important, it was probably the necessary condition for Britain being able to maintain the free hand in Europe. Certainly, as Lansdowne himself had pointed out, 'the area of entanglement' was 'much more restricted' than it would have been in the case of an alliance with Germany.[1] The readiness to limit freedom of action in the Far East therefore illustrated the continued priority of the Balance of Power in Europe rather than any increasing importance of extra-European affairs to Great Britain. As late as March 1902 Salisbury still felt able to say of Britain's various European treaty obligations, like the alliance with Portugal or the Belgian guarantee: 'Our treaty obligations will follow our national inclinations and will not precede them.'[2]

After Salisbury's departure, however, Britain's 'national inclinations' took a path which progressively restricted her statesmen's freedom of action in Europe as well as in America and the Far East. Lansdowne and his successor, Sir Edward Grey, both resisted the

[1] George Monger, *The End of Isolation. British Foreign Policy 1900–1907* (London, 1963), p. 66.
[2] Valerie Cromwell, 'Great Britain's Treaty Obligations in March 1902', *The Historical Journal*, vi (1963), 279.

tendency, believing, unlike Salisbury, that 'limited commitments' could be kept limited. The most important factor in this process was the state of Anglo-German relations. Public regard between the two countries fell into a rapid decline after the end of the South African War and all hope of restoring a special relationship with Germany disappeared. Even Chamberlain, once its most ardent advocate, publicly admitted the fact in a speech in Birmingham on 6 January 1902:

> We are people of a great empire. . . . We are the most hated nation of the world and also the best loved. . . . We have the feeling, unfortunately, that we have to count upon ourselves alone, and I say, therefore, it is the duty of British statesmen and it is the duty of the British people to count upon themselves alone, as their ancestors did. I say alone, yes in a splendid isolation, surrounded by our kinsfolk.[3]

So, while anti-German sentiment was introduced into the Foreign Office by men like Bertie, others stimulated it in public affairs. Chamberlain himself made a vigorous display of it in 1903 to check the Cabinet's inclination to conciliate Germany over her Baghdad railway project.

Following their rising economic interest in the Near East in the last decades of the nineteenth century the Germans had obtained concessions to build a railway from Constantinople to Ankara in 1888 and on to Baghdad in 1899. The British did not much like this threat to their virtual monopoly in the Persian Gulf, but they were usually too anxious for Germany's friendship to think of making any effective opposition. Some argued too that German activity in Persia would help check that of Russia. The best course in the end therefore seemed to be to try and avert the danger of a German naval base in the Gulf by getting the railway project internationalized or at least having Britain take a share in it. Russian hostility was the main obstacle to internationalization, but as the Germans wanted foreign capital there was every prospect of Britain being welcomed by Germany at least as a junior partner. But when Lansdowne proposed this course in April 1903 it met with a venomous opposition in the British Press. Chamberlain took up the anti-German cause in the Cabinet and Lansdowne had eventually to back down. All that the Foreign Secretary could do then was to issue a statement in the House of Lords on 5 May that 'we should

---

[3] J. A. S. Grenville, *Lord Salisbury and Foreign Policy* (London, 1964), p. 366.

regard the establishment of a naval base, or of a fortified port, in the
Persian Gulf by any other Power as a very grave menace to British
interests, and we should certainly resist it with all the means at our
disposal.'[4]

One of those in the Cabinet who shared Lansdowne's deep sense
of shock at this display of anti-German feeling was the First Lord
of the Admiralty, Selborne. 'It cannot in any way serve our interests
to make the cleavage between England and Germany greater', he
complained.[5] Yet he himself had already urged upon the attention
of the Cabinet the view that made the most important contribution
to the deterioration in Anglo-German relations. This was the
Admiralty's discovery by late 1902 that Germany's naval expansion
must be aimed at Great Britain (Doc. 142). In a sense the accusation
was correct. It was natural enough that Germany should want a
respectable navy, but not one of such a type and size as she insisted
on building. The basis of her construction programme was Tirpitz's
theory that the German Navy must be so strong that not even the
greatest naval Power would risk attacking Germany. The short
range envisaged for the battle fleet confirmed that it was designed
to operate in the North Sea and against Great Britain. It was designed, however, not for a war, but as a weapon of political blackmail. The Germans still believed that England's quarrels with
Russia were insoluble and would ultimately force her into an alliance on Germany's terms. So far England had hardly shown
sufficient respect for Germany; the German Navy would help bring
her to her senses. But this was a fatal mixture of blackmail and bluff.
England simply could not afford to give in, while pride and mis-
calculation committed Germany to going on.

The first major consequence of this new awareness of a supposed
threat from the German naval programme was that it made the
British Government and, as was of increasing importance, British
public opinion more responsive to approaches from France. For
France the alliance with Russia had been of no help in the Fashoda
crisis and with the signature of the Anglo-Japanese Alliance it
threatened to embroil her in a war with England in which she had
no great interest. One obvious step for France in these circumstances
was to resist as much as possible the inclinations of the Russian
Government to make some positive retort to the Anglo-Japanese

[4] Monger, p. 123.
[5] Ibid., p. 122.

7—F.P.V.E.

Alliance. Another was to try and avoid new clashes with England on her own account. The principal cause of direct political conflict between the two countries had been brought to an abrupt end by the French defeat at Fashoda. Thereafter the centre of France's African ambitions moved to Morocco. But here Britain also had the largest share of trade, and it was important for the French to avoid Morocco simply replacing Egypt as the element of friction in their relations with England. In August 1902, therefore, the French Foreign Minister proposed that Morocco should be partitioned between France and Spain and that in return for the British Government's consent, France would accommodate England in Egypt. At first the British took a stiff attitude, and as late as November 1902 the new Prime Minister, Balfour, warned the French that their Moroccan policy was a threat to peace. The main obstacle so far as the British were concerned, however, was their anxiety not to alienate Germany by excluding her from any settlement. But by the end of the year public disapproval of co-operation with Germany in an episode of gunboat diplomacy against Venezuela seemed to make that calculation pointless and Selborne's warnings about the German Navy to make an improvement of relations with France especially desirable. In December 1902 Lansdowne therefore openly embraced the idea of a settlement with France. The negotiations that followed were not easy, but the essential momentum was maintained by the breakdown of authority in Morocco itself and still more by the rapid approach of the expected war between Russia and Japan. On 8 February 1904 the Japanese attacked the Russian fleet in Port Arthur. From that point, according to Lansdowne, 'The French negotiations, after sticking in all sorts of ignoble ruts, suddenly began to travel at the rate of an express train',[6] and the Anglo-French *Entente* was concluded on 8 April. The agreement settled various irritating disputes about the world, in the fisheries off Newfoundland, in West Africa, Madagascar, Siam, and the New Hebrides, in addition to the bargain over Morocco and Egypt. That bargain in effect was a recognition of each other's privileged position; but it also looked forward to the exclusive control of Egypt and most of Morocco by England and France respectively.

The Anglo-French *Entente* was designed to eliminate an enemy rather than to make an ally. But the condition of European Great Power politics was too volatile for such comfortable assumptions.

[6] The Marquess of Zetland, *Lord Cromer* (London, 1932), p. 281.

Germany, in particular, could not accept this negative view. Although it had marked the defeat of her attempt to secure a European alliance on her own terms, she had not been disturbed by the signature of the Anglo-Japanese Alliance since it confirmed the hostility between Russia and England on which her calculations of policy relied. But the British understanding with Germany's old enemy, France (and a similar one made with France by Italy in June 1902) threatened to upset the Balance of Power in Europe, especially if it led France to promote a settlement of England's differences with Russia. William therefore took advantage of the outbreak of the war in the Far East, and the tension that it brought in Russia's relations with England, to approach the Russians in the autumn of 1904 and again in July 1905, with the offer of an alliance. Although it was not easy to define the area of mutual interest which the alliance was supposed to defend, the Russians were by no means unresponsive but they insisted on consulting the French. In December 1904 the Germans refused to permit this and the negotiations broke down. When they were revived in July the following year, a formula seemed to have been found in the Treaty of Björkö, which could be submitted to Paris. But by this time the Germans had hopelessly offended the French Government.

After the failure of his first approach to Russia William had launched a frontal attack upon the Anglo-French *Entente* by taking a stand at Tangier on 1 April 1905 in favour of Morocco's independence, and by demanding an international conference to maintain it. The German threat brought down the French Foreign Minister, Delcassé, whose determination to resist was thought too strong by his colleagues. But the French were not prepared to accept the German demands unconditionally and they were able to sustain this attitude through the support they received from England. Lansdowne would not have wanted to surrender his ultimate freedom of action. At the same time French public opinion had not so far been enthusiastic about the *Entente* and he could not afford to let the French Government down now. Quite what he promised the French is uncertain. But he did at least warn the German Ambassador at a meeting on 28 June that if France were attacked British public opinion might force his Government to go to her aid. Faced with this threat, and with the disapproval too of the American President, the Germans backed down, though they were able to do so under the guise of a face-saving compromise. France accepted a conference at

Algeciras, but Germany in effect agreed in advance not to challenge the arrangements France had already made with England and Spain. Whatever chance Germany might have had of bullying France into approving the Treaty of Björkö was ruined by the support the French Government got from London. Worse still, from Germany's point of view, her tactics turned the windmill at which she had tilted her lance into a much stronger alignment. The *Entente* became at once far more popular in both England and France and for both Governments good Anglo-French relations became more or less a convention of good policy. In December 1905 there was even an exchange of views between the French and British Army General Staffs, which were belatedly authorized in January the following year.[7] But perhaps the most striking and most famous evidence of the impression that Germany's Moroccan policy had made in England is Eyre Crowe's memorandum on relations with Germany and France, dated 1 January 1907. Here the Senior Clerk in the Foreign Office ranged magisterially over the past record of German foreign policy. He was not sure that Germany was aiming consciously at European or world hegemony; nor did he feel that England should oppose the legitimate expansion of Germany's interests or even of her navy. But England could not afford to take any risks, especially as 'the action of Germany towards this country since 1890 might be likened not inappropriately to that of a professional blackmailer, whose extortions are wrung from his victims by the threat of some vague and dreadful consequences in case of a refusal.' In this respect he thought that her Moroccan rebuff had 'had on the German Government the effect of an unexpected revelation' (Doc. 144).

In spite of its many reservations Crowe's memorandum was a very hostile interpretation of German foreign policy. This certainly reflected a powerful body of opinion in the Foreign Office, but that was not the only voice in policy-making. Lord Sanderson, who had recently retired as Permanent Undersecretary, replied for example with another memorandum in which he maintained that Crowe's version of history was very biased and that in any case sanity would ultimately prevail in German policy (Doc. 145). Sir Edward Grey,

---

[7] These exchanges are still veiled in mystery. The latest view is that Lansdowne was probably wrong in recalling that he had had anything to do with them, and that they were first given government blessing by his Liberal successor in January 1906. Only a few other Ministers, including the Prime Minister, knew of them; the rest of the Cabinet was not informed until 1911 (Monger, pp. 237–48).

who had become Foreign Secretary in the new Liberal Government of December 1905, stood somewhere in between. He certainly shared Crowe's tendency to analyse the international situation in terms of the Balance of Power and, although definitely not anti-German, he too feared what he saw, rightly or wrongly, as the militaristic element in German public life. At the time of the Moroccan crisis he had recognized that in the event of a showdown between France and Germany, England would have to join France. On 10 and 11 January 1906 he had therefore repeated Lansdowne's warnings to the German Ambassador. Soon afterwards he was also talking of the possibility of seeking a *rapprochement* with Russia. 'An *entente* between Russia, France and ourselves would be absolutely secure. If it is necessary to check Germany it could then be done' (Doc. 143). But he was by no means sure that it would be necessary to present Germany with some final and irreversible confrontation. Like Sanderson he hoped Germany would return to the paths of sanity and he proposed to help by continuing to negotiate with her. For the same reason it was important not to commit Great Britain too deeply to France. In any case the present requirements of the Balance of Power had to be prevented, so far as possible, from prejudicing Britain's freedom of action in the future, when the Balance of Power might well require a very different course. During the Moroccan crisis therefore he had refused to give any formal pledge to France and he had insisted that the staff talks were informal and not binding.

A British *rapprochement* with Russia was greatly assisted by the breakdown of William's alliance approaches in 1904 and 1905 and by the renewal of the Anglo-Japanese Alliance, even before the war in the Far East had ended, on 12 August 1905. This time the alliance was altered to provide for mutual aid in the event of attack by only one Power and was extended to cover the defence of India. In effect the Russians were therefore prevented from risking a war of revenge against Japan or a war of compensation against Britain. Talks between the Russians and the British had therefore begun before the end of 1905; the Moroccan crisis gave them another spurt. It took a long time to bring them to a conclusion, but on 31 August 1907 agreements were finally signed. The two Governments recognized China's sovereignty over Tibet and promised to respect its independence and territorial integrity. Russia accepted Afghanistan as a British sphere of influence, while Britain agreed not to alter its status or interfere in its domestic affairs. Persia was divided into three zones of influence: a British zone in the south-east on the frontier of India, a large Russian one in the north, and a neutral zone in the centre. By a separate note Russia also recognized Britain's predominant position in the Persian Gulf.

Like the Anglo-French *Entente*, the agreement with Russia was limited to 'colonial' disputes. In this respect it followed the new course of relieving the strain by eliminating or reducing areas of conflict overseas. It was this aspect in particular that made the whole arrangement acceptable to the Radical wing of the Government who loathed the tyranny of tsarist Russia. John Morley, the Secretary of State for India, for example, was probably made amenable to it by the relief it would bring to the problem of defending India. The sub-committee on 'the military needs of the Empire', of which he was chairman, had concluded in May 1907 that a war with Russia for the possession of India would require 'immense demands and vast sacrifices' and 'a military organization at home that would enable 100,000 men to be sent to India in the first year of war'. 'What a tremendous load of military charge and responsibility you have to carry if you won't come to terms diplomatically with Russia', he warned the obstinate Viceroy.[8] Yet, while all this was true, the new *Entente*, much more than the earlier understanding with France, *was* aimed at Germany. 'I am impatient to see Russia re-established as a factor in European politics', Grey had written as early as February 1906.[9] Some now talked even of encouraging Russia in Persia, in order to check Germany, rather than Germany to check Russia.

The pursuit of the Balance of Power was therefore driving Grey and his Government into a more positively anti-German association with France and Russia. But Grey was not aiming at the encirclement of Germany. During the negotiation of the *Entente* with Russia he had refused to give a promise of support for Russia's ambition to have the rule of the Straits changed in her favour. He knew that Britain had long since lost virtually all interest in opposing that ambition and certainly she had lost her power to frustrate it. But he did not want to involve himself in a Russian quarrel with the Central Powers. Moreover continued Anglo-Russian tensions helped preserve a strong element of flexibility in international relations. In the Far East Russia reconciled herself to Japan's victory and within a

[8] Monger, p. 285.
[9] Ibid., p. 281.

few years, especially after the revolution in China in 1911, she was
aligned with that Power in a secret agreement to divide large areas
of the Chinese Empire into spheres of special interest in opposition
to the Open Door policies of the other Powers. The major area of
direct Anglo-Russian quarrelling, however, was Persia. Here their
rivalry was brought to a head by the revolution which in 1909
overthrew the pro-Russian Shah. The Russians replied by trying
to conciliate Germany over the Baghdad railway so that England
might be frightened by the spectre of a Russo-German *rapprochement* into accommodating Russia's wishes in Persia. The attempt
failed; but it was leaked to the British Government who were
particularly annoyed in view of the fact that they had consistently
refused to negotiate with Germany on the railways question behind
Russia's back.

The *Entente* with Russia, unlike that with France, was far from
being a strong element in Britain's alignment against Germany. If
anything, Britain's difficult relations with Russia encouraged her to
persist in her attempts to negotiate with Germany. Not that the
Anglo-French *Entente* had any tendency to impede such negotiations.
In February 1909 the French themselves made a new agreement
with Germany concerning Morocco. Grey certainly was determined
to negotiate with Germany. The most urgent item to attend to was
naval rivalry. Concern about the German Navy had risen still further with the destruction of the Russian fleet at Port Arthur, though
this allowed, and the revised terms of the Anglo-Japanese Alliance in
1905 permitted, a reduction in British naval strength in the Far East
and made it easier for Britain to maintain her overall standards of
naval superiority. In 1906 she launched the *Dreadnought*, the first
all-big-gun ship. This at once rendered all navies, including her
own, out of date. Possibly this was a mistake. It meant an enormously expensive burden and it also initiated a new and intensified
round in the armaments race. But Britain could better afford that
race than anyone else and this fact gave her the strength to put up an
even stiffer resistance to German naval blackmail. If the British
Government therefore made a mistake, the Germans made a worse
one in taking up the challenge. In November 1907 the Germans
announced a large Dreadnought programme; and in the following
March the British responded with further increases in their naval
estimates. In March 1909 the revelation of a covert acceleration of
the German construction programme produced not only still

another increase in British naval expenditure but also the first real expression of public outrage and demand for an appropriate response: 'We want eight and we won't wait.' At the same time the German Foreign Secretary, Kiderlen-Wächter, revived the attempt to secure agreement with England. In April he offered not to undertake any further naval expansion, if England would sign a mutual undertaking not to join any hostile coalition and to preserve a benevolent neutrality in case of war. This could only confirm Grey's suspicion that Germany's real aim was to destroy the *Ententes*. 'An entente with Germany such as M. Kiderlen-Wächter sketches would serve to establish German hegemony in Europe and would not last long after it had served that purpose', he commented. 'It is in fact an invitation to help Germany to make a European combination which would be directed against us when it suited her so to use it.'[10] The negotiations dragged on with each side insisting on what the other would not give—an actual reduction of existing naval armaments by Germany and a political commitment from England—until they were rudely interrupted by a new international crisis in June 1911.

The crisis of 1911 was precipitated by the dispatch of the German gunboat *Panther* to Agadir in Morocco. German irritation about what was going on in Morocco was by no means unjustified. The French had not been very scrupulous about their interpretation of the agreement of 1909, prevaricating in particular about the economic equality it had given to Germany. When therefore France took advantage of further internal disturbances to occupy Fez the Germans were determined that although French control of Morocco was inevitable, they should have suitable compensation. There was nothing wrong in the warnings they sent to France; the sensational arrival of a gunboat on 1 July, however, was another matter, especially when it was followed by a demand for almost all of the French Congo. At first France was inclined to react as she had in the first Moroccan crisis of 1905 and to concede a great part of the German demands, but when she found how tough they were she turned again to England. Morocco, of course, involved the precise application of the *Entente* agreement of 1904. Even so Grey's desire to support the French was checked by the majority of the Cabinet. They rather believed that France ought to compromise. He was therefore allowed

[10] G. P. Gooch and Harold Temperley, eds., *British Documents on the Origins of the War 1898–1914* (London, 1926–38), vi. 266.

only to warn the German Ambassador that England would insist on being consulted about the settlement. To back up the warning Lloyd George, the Chancellor of the Exchequer, was authorized to make a public speech at the Mansion House on 21 July (Doc. 146).

Lloyd George's speech turned the crisis into an Anglo-German one. German public opinion exploded in indignation and in Britain preparations were made for war in which, for the first time, the Admiralty became involved in plans to move an expeditionary force to northern France. The Moroccan Question itself was settled by France's willingness to give adequate compensation to Germany for her protectorate over Morocco. But like the dispatch of the *Panther* the settlement itself, by Germany's acceptance of considerably less than she had originally demanded, confirmed the English impression that German policy was but a species of blackmail. None the less the crisis had hardly revealed a united front on the part of the Triple *Entente*; and by the end of the year the Russians were intervening by force in Persia to check the progress of the liberal revolution. In these circumstances, although he kept firmly to his resolve that in the event of aggression against France Britain must side with her, Grey embarked on a further attempt at a naval agreement with Germany. In February 1912 Viscount Haldane, the Secretary for War, went off to Berlin, prepared this time to waive the demand for a reduction in Germany's existing construction programme and to offer colonial concessions and even a political agreement. But in the wake of the public indignation aroused by Lloyd George's speech, the Germans demanded too much. They wanted a definite political commitment and Britain's agreement that a recent addition to the German naval programme, which had not yet been announced, be counted as part of the existing programme. Grey was prepared to declare that 'England will make no unprovoked attack upon Germany and pursue no aggressive policy towards her',[11] but he could not promise unconditional support and benevolent neutrality in all future circumstances. When the new German naval law was published late in March the main negotiations therefore came to an end.

Limited negotiations with Germany continued in spite of this setback. In June 1914 a draft settlement of the Baghdad railway question was at last approved and when the Archduke Francis Ferdinand was assassinated at Sarajevo the two Powers were on the verge of a new agreement concerning the Portuguese colonies. But

[11] Gooch and Temperley, vi. 713.

the failure to resolve the naval question could only bring England and the *Entente* Powers closer together. Grey still tried to restrain the process. In April 1912 the best assurance he could give was that 'although we cannot bind ourselves under all circumstances to go to war with France against Germany, we shall also certainly not bind ourselves to Germany not to assist France.'[12] But in the course of the year, the British decided that in answer to the threat from the German Navy they must not only expand their own construction programme but concentrate still further in home waters by withdrawing the bulk of their force in the Mediterranean. In turn the French moved their fleet from Brest to Toulon. These moves were undertaken separately and reflected a concentration on the area of most importance to each Power. But it was unrealistic to suppose that they were unconnected. In the autumn Grey and the French Ambassador agreed in an exchange of letters that:

Dans le cas où l'un ou l'autre des deux Gouvernements aurait des raisons d'appréhender un acte d'aggression de la part d'une tierce puissance ou des complications menaçantes pour la paix, ils se livreraient ensemble à une discussion sur la situation et rechercheraient les moyens d'assurer de concert le maintien de la paix et d'écarter toute tentative d'aggression.[13]

In this exchange in the autumn of 1912 the British insisted and the French explicitly acknowledged that neither in this agreement nor in the various staff talks had England given any pledge of support to France. 'Almost a platitude', was how the British Prime Minister described the wording of the 1912 formula.[14] Grey certainly tried, with considerable success, to maintain an independent line in the developing Near Eastern crisis. But it was the gravest element in this crisis that it was getting beyond the ability of any of the Powers to control it by diplomacy. The Austro-Russian agreement to keep the Balkans 'on ice' had been replaced in September 1908 by a plan for mutual support in pursuit of their respective interests in Bosnia and at the Straits. But the plan had gone wrong and the resulting Bosnian crisis of 1909 had left Russia with the smouldering resentment that she had been cheated of the Straits while Austria had gained Bosnia and Herzegovina. The two Governments eventually

---

[12] Gooch and Temperley, vi. 580.
[13] Ibid., x (2). 611.
[14] Ibid., x (2). 612.

found it expedient to revert to their policy of maintaining the *status quo*, but at the same time Russia's distrust led her to encourage the formation of a defensive alliance between Serbia, Bulgaria, and Greece against Austria's supposed ambitions. But this project too went badly wrong, with the allies letting loose their armies on Turkey instead. The smaller states were learning fast how to exploit the growing tensions between the Powers and they had also deduced from recent events that the final opportunity to partition the Sultan's dominions was at hand. The Agadir crisis had already encouraged Italy to proceed with her plans to seize Tripoli. She had exploited international tensions to secure in advance the reluctant consent of all the Powers except England, and after she had forced war with Turkey to get what she wanted in September 1911 she had successfully defied all their efforts at mediation. Before the war ended the Balkan allies also seized their chance. They took advantage of a rising in Albania to demand that the Porte grant reforms to the Macedonians and in spite of pressure from the Powers forced Turkey into war in October 1912. The Powers were equally unable to prevent the allies clawing large slices of territory from the Turks or from fighting a second war among themselves in 1913 for a redistribution of the spoils.

The worst aspect of the wars in the Balkans was that they helped bring Austria and Russia into final confrontation, with Serbia as the centre of their conflict. The Austrians had successfully insisted during the first Balkan War that Serbia must not gain access to the Adriatic, by getting independence for the Albanians. But they had not been able to prevent Serbia soothing her disappointment at the expense of her former ally, Bulgaria, in the second war. Serbia therefore emerged greatly strengthened from the wars in spite of Austria's opposition and this fact played into the hands of those elements in Austria-Hungary who insisted that the problem of the Empire's internal loyalties could be solved only by attacking her external enemy, Serbia. Clearly there was never going to be a better excuse than the assassination of the Austrian heir-apparent by a Serb at Sarajevo on 28 June 1914. But the Russians by that time had decided that they simply could not afford another Austrian victory in the Balkans. With the recollection of the defeat by Japan and the revolution of 1905 behind it the tsarist régime doubted if it could survive another humiliation. But what was probably decisive in Russia's determination to make a stand was the new and greater threat which she believed had been made to her interests and ambitions at the Straits.

Germany had sided with her ally in the Bosnian crisis and during the first Balkan War. But far from blindly supporting Austrian policy towards Serbia Germany in fact favoured a reconciliation with Serbia right down to June 1914. It was only a genuine sense of shock and anger at the Sarajevo murder that destroyed her illusions. Moreover the Germans were always anxious to avoid a real clash with Russia, and they did not want to be dragged into one by Austria. But ultimately they recognized that they would have to fight with Austria if they were ever forced to choose sides. Their policy therefore constantly wavered between restraining Austria's reckless disregard of Russia's vital interests and grudgingly giving her support for fear of breaking up the Dual Alliance. But they themselves had made a disastrous mistake in the Near East. After Turkey's defeats in 1911–12 the Germans could not resist an invitation from the new Turkish Government for General Liman von Sanders to rebuild her shattered armies. Since it was proposed that Liman von Sanders should have an actual command at Constantinople itself the Russians thought that their worst fear of a foreign control of the Straits was about to be realized and by a Power whom they had hardly suspected harboured such a plan. The affair was eventually compromised at the end of 1913, but it left a new antagonism between Russia and Germany centred on an area of absolutely vital concern to Russia. When a new crisis occurred in the Balkans therefore, Germany was much readier to support her ally and Russia to fear the worst from Germany.

By the time of the Sarajevo crisis in the summer of 1914, Russia was already convinced that she would have to face the firm alliance of Austria and Germany at the Straits. Her only hope of defending her vital interests was in concert with France and Britain. France, who was her ally, had stuck to her loyally during the Eastern crisis of 1912–13; but the support of England, with whom she had only an uneasy *entente*, was by no means assured. Grey had given partial support to Russia in the Bosnian crisis, but during the Balkan Wars he had easily taken the view that the Balkan states were in the wrong and so he had sympathized with Austria rather than Russia. At France's urging however, he made a gesture in Russia's direction by authorizing naval talks in the spring of 1914. But, as with the French, he insisted that these were not binding. In any case they had not been brought to a conclusion by the time of Sarajevo. That crisis therefore found it uncertain what line England would take. Grey himself was shocked both by the Serbian atrocity and by Austria's ruthless determination to have revenge. He therefore concentrated his efforts on trying to bring about some compromise arrangement between the Powers, at the same time refusing to guarantee England's neutrality to Germany or to promise her support to France and Russia. But with Austria bent on a war with Serbia and with Russia and Germany both convinced that they must take sides, these efforts were doomed. In any case they were overtaken by the pace of military decisions. On 28 July Austria declared war on Serbia; two days later the Russians replied with a general mobilization after they had found a partial mobilization against Austria alone impracticable. But in an era when most experts wrongly believed that modern wars would be decided by the first victories in the field, the German General Staff had long ago decided that in the event of war they must exploit their superior organization before Russia could assemble her massive but ponderous armies. They had also decided that since the greatest danger was a war on two fronts against Russia and France combined, they must anticipate that danger by knocking out France as soon as war began with Russia. The German Government therefore replied to Russia's mobilization order with an ultimatum on 31 July and when that was ignored with declarations of war against Russia and France on 1 and 3 August.

For Grey the German declaration of war against France was decisive. He had always maintained that in the event of an unprovoked attack on France, England would have to support her. This was a matter of interest, not of obligation. He admitted to the French that, while not binding, the various naval and military exchanges of past years had constituted something of an 'obligation of honour', but this led him, in view of the redistribution of the French fleet, to undertake on 2 August only that England would not permit the German Navy to operate against France in the Channel. What mattered to Grey was the overthrow of the Balance of Power which would follow from a French defeat (Doc. 147). Even so he might well not have been able to lead the Cabinet into war against Germany if that country had not insisted, in spite of Britain's warnings, on violating Belgian neutrality so as to carry out her lightning attack on France. This action on Germany's part confirmed the now well-established belief in the fundamentally aggressive methods and designs of German policy. It allowed Grey, rightly or wrongly, to persuade his colleagues that they were not helping France, let alone Russia, so much as saving Europe from German militarism and Germany's drive to European hegemony. The moment had finally arrived for which Foreign Secretary after Foreign Secretary had for a century kept England's hand free. The opinion of historians remains uncertain whether or not Germany was really making a bid for mastery in Europe. What is certain is that the means by which England had maintained her freedom from commitment since Salisbury's day inclined her fundamentally against Germany and towards France. To that extent the free hand in the twentieth century was an illusion.

Part II

NOTE

The documents which follow have been selected, not only from the dispatches which, with treaties, protocols, and notes, may be considered as the official 'record' of British foreign policy, but also from a variety of other sources, such as parliamentary debates and Foreign Office memoranda, illustrating some of the more important influences upon and criticisms of that policy. In particular it is hoped that something of the contemporary style and flavour of British foreign policy will have been conveyed.

Many of the documents, in whole or in part, have previously appeared in print. Wherever practicable these have been checked against the manuscript originals, or where these have not been found, against the manuscript draft or office copy. It would have been pedantic, however, to restore every idiosyncrasy of punctuation and every archaic spelling in such private letters as Palmerston's. It is impossible to believe that his indulgence in capital letters had any significance, and to have restored his all-purpose semi-colons would have made him very hard going for the reader.

In the heading to each document the manuscript source, if any, is followed by a reference to any version of the whole or a substantial extract that has appeared in print and in a context which may be helpful to the student. The absence of any reference to the manuscript source of a letter indicates that I have not been able to find it. Manuscript collections in the British Museum and the Public Record Office in London are shown simply by the initials B.M. and P.R.O. The Broadlands MSS. are the Palmerston family papers at present in the care of the Historical Manuscripts Commission in London; the Salisbury MSS. are those at Christ Church, Oxford.

SELECTED DOCUMENTS

---

1. Extract from Pitt's 'Official Communication made to the Russian Ambassador at London, . . . explanatory of the views which His Majesty and the Emperor of Russia formed for the deliverance and security of Europe', 19 January 1805. P.R.O., F.O. 65/60; C. K. Webster, ed., *British Diplomacy 1813–1815. Select Documents Dealing with the Reconstruction of Europe* (London, 1921), pp. 389–393, and Harold Temperley and Lillian M. Penson, *Foundations of British Foreign Policy, 1792–1902* (London, 1938), pp. 10–21.

. . . the first Step must be, to fix as precisely as possible, the distinct objects to which such a Concert is to be directed.

These, according to the explanation given of the Sentiments of the Emperor, in which His Majesty entirely concurs, appear to be three:—

1st To rescue from the Dominion of France those countries which it has subjugated since the beginning of the Revolution, and to reduce France within its former limits, as they stood before that time.

2ndly To make such an arrangement with respect to the territories recovered from France, as may provide for their Security and Happiness, and may at the same time constitute a more effectual barrier in future against Encroachments on the part of France.

3rdly To form, at the Restoration of Peace, a general Agreement and Guarantee for the mutual protection and Security of different Powers, and for re-establishing a general System of Public Law in Europe.

* * * *

Supposing the Efforts of the Allies to have been completely successful, . . . His Majesty would nevertheless consider this salutary work as still imperfect, if the Restoration of Peace were not accompanied by the most effectual measures for giving Solidity and Permanence to the System which shall thus have been established. Much will undoubtedly be effected for the future Repose of

Europe by these Territorial Arrangements, which will furnish a more effectual Barrier than has before existed against the Ambition of France. But in order to render this Security as complete as possible, it seems necessary, at the period of a general Pacification, to form a Treaty to which all the principal Powers of Europe should be Parties, by which their respective Rights and Possessions, as they shall then have been established, shall be fixed and recognized, and they should all bind themselves mutually to protect and support each other, against any attempt to infringe them. It should re-establish a general and comprehensive system of Public Law in Europe, and provide, as far as possible, for repressing future attempts to disturb the general Tranquillity, and above all, for restraining any projects of Aggrandizement and Ambition similar to those which have produced all the Calamities inflicted on Europe since the disastrous era of the French Revolution. This Treaty should be put under the special Guarantee of Great Britain and Russia, and the Two Powers should by a separate engagement, bind themselves to each other jointly to take an active part in preventing its being infringed. . . .

2. Extract from the 'Minute of the Cabinet' (commonly known as Castlereagh's State Paper) enclosed in Castlereagh's dispatch no. 27 to Lord Stewart (Ambassador in Vienna), 5 May 1820. P.R.O., F.O. 120/39; Temperley and Penson, pp. 48–63.

The Events which have occurred in Spain have, as might be expected, excited, in proportion as they have developed themselves, the utmost anxiety throughout Europe. . . .

The British Cabinet, upon this, as upon all other occasions, is ever ready to deliberate with those of the Allies, and will unreservedly explain itself upon this great question of Common Interest; but as to the form in which it may be prudent to conduct these Deliberations, they conceive they cannot too early recommend that course of deliberation which will excite the least attention or alarm, or which can least provoke Jealousy in the minds of the Spanish Nation or Government. In this view it appears to them advisable, studiously to avoid any reunion of the Sovereigns;—to abstain, at least in the present stage of the question, from charging any ostensible Conference with Commission to deliberate on the affairs of Spain:—They conceive it preferable that their intercourse should be limited to those confidential Communications between the Cabinets, which are in themselves best adapted to approximate ideas, and to lead, as far as may be, to the adoption of common principles, rather than to hazard a discussion in a Ministerial Conference which, from the necessarily limited Powers of the Individuals composing it, must ever be better fitted to execute a purpose already decided upon, than to frame a course of policy under delicate and difficult circumstances.

There seems the less motive for precipitating any step of this nature in the case immediately under consideration, as, from all the Information which reaches us, there exists in Spain no order of things upon which to deliberate, nor as yet any Governing Authority with which Foreign Powers can communicate.

. . . till some Central Authority shall establish itself in Spain, all notion of operating upon her Councils seems utterly impracticable, and calculated to lead to no other possible result than that of compromizing either the King or the Allies, or probably both.

* * * *

The present State of Spain no doubt seriously extends the range of political agitation in Europe, but it must nevertheless be admitted that there is no portion of Europe of equal magnitude in which such a Revolution could have happened, less likely to menace other States with that direct and imminent danger, which has always been regarded, at least in this Country, as alone constituting the case which would justify external interference. If the case is not such as to warrant such an interference; if we do not feel that we have at this moment either the Right or the Means to interfere with effect by force;—if the semblance of such an interference is more likely to irritate than to overawe, and if we have proved by experience how little a Spanish Government, whether of King or Cortes, is disposed to listen to advice from Foreign States, is it not prudent at least to pause, before we assume an attitude which would seem to pledge us in the eyes of Europe to some decisive proceeding? Before we embark in such a measure, is it not expedient at least to ascertain with some degree of precision what we really mean to do? This course of temperate and cautious Policy, so befitting the occasion and the critical Position in which the King is personally placed, will in no degree fetter our action, when, if ever, the case for acting shall arise. . . .

There can be no doubt of the general danger which menaces more or less the stability of all existing Governments from the principles which are afloat, and from the circumstance that so many States of Europe are now employed in the difficult task of casting anew their Governments upon the Representative Principle:— but the notion of revising, limiting, or regulating the course of such experiments, either by Foreign Council or by Foreign Force would be as dangerous to avow as it would be impossible to execute, and the illusion too prevalent on this subject should not be encouraged in our Intercourse with the Allies.

That circumstances might arise out of such experiments in any Country directly menacing to the safety of other States cannot be denied, and against such a danger, well ascertained, the Allies may justifiably, and must in all prudence be on their guard; but such is not the present case; fearful as is the example which is furnished, by Spain, of an Army in revolt, and a Monarch swearing to a constitution which contains in its frame hardly the semblance of a Monarchy, there is no ground for apprehension, that Europe is likely to be speedily endangered by Spanish Arms.

*   *   *   *

It remains to be considered what course can best be pursued by the Allies in the present critical state of Europe, in order to preserve in the utmost cordiality and vigor, the Bonds which at this day so happily unite the Great European Powers together, and to draw from their Alliance, should the moment of danger and contest arrive, the fullest extent of benefit, of which it is in it's nature susceptible.

In this Alliance as in all other human Arrangements, nothing is more likely to impair or even to destroy it's real utility, than any attempt to push it's Duties and it's obligations beyond the sphere which its original Conception and understood Principles will warrant:—It was an Union for the Re-conquest and liberation of a great proportion of the Continent of Europe from the Military Dominion of France, and having subdued the Conqueror, it took the state of Possession as established by the Peace under the Protection of the Alliance:— It never was however intended as an Union for the Government of the World, or for the superintendence of the internal Affairs of other States:—It provided specifically against an infraction on the part of France of the state of possession then created:—It provided against the return of the Usurper or of any of his Family to the Throne:—It further designated the Revolutionary Power, which had convulsed France, and desolated Europe, as an object of it's constant solicitude; but it was the Revolutionary Power more particularly in it's Military Character actual and existent within France against which it intended to take precautions, and not against the Democratick Principles, then as now, but too generally spread throughout Europe.

In thus attempting to limit the objects of the Alliance within their legitimate Boundary, it is not meant to discourage the utmost Frankness of Communication between the Allied Cabinets;—their Confidential Intercourse upon all matters, however foreign to the purposes of the Alliance, is in itself a valuable expedient for keeping the current of Sentiment in Europe as equable and as uniform as may be: It is not meant that in particular and definite Cases, the Alliance may not (and especially when invited to do so by the Parties interested) advantageously interpose, with Caution, in matters lying beyond the Boundaries of their immediate and particular Connection; but what is intended to be combated as forming any part of their duty as Allies, is, the notion, but too perceptibly prevalent, that whenever any great Political Event shall occur, as in Spain, pregnant perhaps with future danger, it is to be regarded almost as a matter of course, that it belongs to the Allies to charge themselves collectively with the responsibility of exercising some Jurisdiction concerning such possible eventual danger.—

One objection to this view of our duties, if there were no other, is, that unless we are prepared to support our interference with force, our judgement or advice is likely to be but rarely listened to, and would soon by frequent repetition fall into complete contempt:— so long as we keep to the great and simple conservative Principles of the Alliance, when the dangers therein contemplated shall be visibly realized, there is little risk of difference or of disunion amongst the Allies:—All will have a common interest but it is far otherwise when we attempt with the Alliance to embrace subordinate, remote, and speculative cases of danger; all the Powers may indeed have an interest in averting the assumed danger, but all have not by any means a common faculty of combating it in it's more speculative shapes, nor can they all, without embarrassing seriously the internal administration of their own Affairs, be prepared to shew themselves in jealous observation of Transactions which before they have assumed a practical Character, Public Opinion would not go along with them in counteracting.—

This principle is perfectly clear and intelligible in the case of Spain;—We may all agree that nothing can be more lamentable, or of more dangerous example than the late Revolt of the Spanish Army; We may all agree, that nothing can be more unlike a Monarchical Government, or less suited to the wants and true Interests of the Spanish Nation, than the Constitution of the year 1812;—We may also agree, with shades of difference, that the consequence of this state of things in Spain may eventually bring danger home to all our own Doors, but it does not follow, that we have therefore equal means of acting upon this opinion:—For instance the Emperor of Russia, from the nature of His authority, can have nothing to weigh, but physical or moral difficulties external to His own Government and Dominions which are in the way of His giving effect to His designs; If His Imperial Majesty's mind is satisfied upon these points, His action is free and His means are in His own hands.— The King of Great Britain, from the nature of our Constitution, has on the contrary, all His means to acquire through Parliament, and He must well know by experience, that if embarked in a War, which the voice of the Country does not support, the efforts of the strongest Administration which ever served the Crown would soon be unequal to the prosecution of the Contest:—

In Russia there is but little Public Sentiment with regard to Spain which can embarrass the decision of the Sovereign;—In Great Britain there is a great deal, and the Current of that Sentiment runs strongly against the late Policy of the King of Spain:— Besides the People of this Country would probably not recognize (unless Portugal were attacked) that our safety could be so far menaced by any state of things in Spain, as to warrant their Government in sending an army to that Country to meddle in it's internal Affairs:—We cannot conceal from ourselves how generally the acts of the King of Spain since His restoration have rendered His Government unpopular, and how impossible it would be to reconcile the People of England to the use of Force (if such a proceeding could for a moment be thought of by the British Government) for the purpose of replacing Power in His hands, however He might engage to qualify it. . . . The Interposition of our Good Offices, whether singly or in concert with the Allied Governments, if uncalled for by any authority within Spain, even by The King Himself, is by no means free from a like inconvenience so far as regards the Position of the British Government at home:—This Species of intervention especially when coming from 5 Great Powers, has more or less the air of dictation and of menace, and the possibility of it's being intended to be ultimately pushed to a forcible intervention is always assumed or imputed by an adverse Party:—The grounds of the intervention thus become unpopular, the intention of the Parties is misunderstood, the public Mind is agitated and perverted, and the general Political Situation of the Gov[ernmen]t is thereby essentially embarrassed.—

This Statement is only meant to prove, that we ought to see somewhat clearly to what purpose of real utility, our effort tends, before we embark in proceedings which can never be indifferent in their bearings upon the Government taking part in them.—In this Country at all times, but especially at the present Conjuncture, when the whole energy of the State is required to unite reasonable men in defence of our existing Institutions, and to put down the Spirit of Treason and disaffection which in certain of the Manufacturing Districts in particular, pervades the lower Orders, it is of the greatest moment, that the Public Sentiment should not be distracted or divided, by any unnecessary interference of the Government in events passing abroad, over which they can have none, or at best but very imperfect, means of Controul:— Nothing could be more injurious to the Continental Powers than to have their affairs made matter of daily discussion in our Parliament, which nevertheless must be the consequence of their precipitately mixing themselves in the affairs of other States, if we should consent to proceed *pari passu* with them in such interferences. It is not merely the temporary inconvenience produced to the British Gov[ernmen]t by being so committed, that is to be apprehended, but it is the exposing ourselves to have the Public Mind soured by the effects of a Meddling Policy,—when it can tend to nothing really effectual,— and pledged perhaps beforehand against any exertion whatever in Continental Affairs:—The fatal effects of such a false step might be irreparable when the moment at which we might be indispensably called upon by duty and interest to take a part, should arrive.

These considerations will suggest a doubt whether that extreme degree of unanimity and supposed concurrence upon all political subjects, would be either a practicable or a desirable Principle of action, among the Allied States, upon matters not essentially connected with the main purposes of the Alliance. . . .

. . . The fact is that we do not, and cannot feel alike upon all Subjects:—Our Position, our Institutions, the habits of thinking, and the prejudices of our People, render us essentially different;—We cannot in all matters reason or feel alike; We should lose the confidence of our respective Nations if we did, and the very affectation of such an impossibility would soon render the Alliance an object of odium, and distrust, whereas if we keep it within its *common sense* limits, the Representative Gov[ernmen]ts and those which are more purely Monarchical, may well find such a common Interest, and a common facility in discharging their duties under the Alliance, without creating an impression that they have made a surrender of the first principles upon which their respective Governments are founded.—Each Government will then retain it's due faculty of independent Action, always recollecting that they have all a common refuge in the Alliance, as well as a common duty to perform, whenever such a danger shall really exist, as that against which the Alliance was specially intended to provide.

There is at present very naturally a wide spread apprehension of the fatal consequences to the public tranquillity of Europe, that may be expected to flow from the dangerous Principles of the present day, at work more or less in every European State, Consequences which no human foresight can presume to estimate.

In all Dangers the first calculation of prudence is to consider what we should avoid, and on what we should endeavour to rely.—In considering Continental Europe as divided into two great Masses, the Western consisting of France and Spain, the Eastern of all the other Continental States still subsisting with some limited exceptions, under the form of their ancient Institutions;—the great question is, what system of general and defensive policy (subject of course to special exceptions as arising out of the circumstances of the particular case) ought the latter States to adopt, with a view of securing themselves against those dangers, which may directly or indirectly assail them from the former.

By the late proceedings at Vienna, which for all purposes of internal tranquillity bind up the various States of Germany into a single and undivided Power, a great degree of additional simplicity as well as strength has been given to this portion of Europe. By this expedient there is established on that side of Europe, instead of a multitude of dispersed States, two great Bodies, Russia and Germany, of the latter of which, Austria and Prussia may, for purposes of internal tranquillity be regarded as component parts. In addition to these there remain but few pieces on the board to complicate the game of Public safety.

In considering then, how the game can best be played, the first thing that occurs for our Consideration is, what good can these States hope to effect in France or Spain by their mere Councils? Perhaps it would not be far from the truth to say none whatever:— When the chances of error, jealousy and national sentiment are considered, the probability of mischief would be more truly assigned to the system of constant European interference upon these volcanic masses. . . .

. . . What could the Allied Powers look to effect by their Arms, if the supposition of an Armed interference in the internal concerns of another State could be admitted? Perhaps as little: because in supposing them finally triumphant, we have the Problem still to solve, how the Country in which such interference had been successful, was to provide for its self-government, after the Allied Armies shall have been withdrawn, without soon becoming an equal source of danger to the tranquillity of neighbouring States: but when we consider how much danger may arise to the internal safety of the rest of Europe, by the absence of those Armies which must be withdrawn to over-run the Country in which the supposed interference was to take place,—what may be the danger of these Armies being contaminated; what may be the incumbrances to be added by such renewed exertions to the already overwhelming Weight of the debts of the different States,—what the local irritation which must be occasioned by pouring forth such immense Armies, pressing severely as they must do upon the Resources of Countries already agitated and inflamed;—no rational Statesman surely would found his prospects of security on such a calculation; he would rather be of opinion that the only necessity which could in wisdom justify such an attempt is that, which, temperately considered, appears to leave to Europe no other option than that of either going to meet that danger which they cannot avoid, or having it poured in the full tide of Military Invasion upon their own States. The actual existence of such a danger may indeed be inferred from many circumstances short of the visible Preparations for Attack, but it is submitted that on this Basis the conclusion should always be examined.

If this Position is correctly laid down, it may be asserted that the case supposed not only does not at present exist, but the chances of such a danger have latterly rather declined, in proportion as both France and Spain are almost exclusively and deeply occupied by their own internal embarrassments:—The Military Power in France is at this day circumscribed within those limits which are not more than competent to the necessary Duties of the Interior;—That of Spain is upon even a more reduced scale, whilst the Military Establishments of all the other European States, and especially that of Russia, were never perhaps at any period of their History upon a footing of more formidable efficiency both in point of discipline and Numbers:—Surely then, if these States can preserve harmony amongst themselves, and exercise a proper degree of vigilance, with respect to their interior Police, there is nothing in this state of things which should prevent them from abiding with patience and with firmness, the result of the great political process to which Circumstances have given existence in the States to the westward of their Frontiers. They may surely permit these Nations to work out by their own means and by the lights of their own Councils, that Result which no doubt materially bears upon the general Interests of the World, but which is more especially to decide their own particular destinies, without being led to interfere with them, at least so long as their own immediate security is not directly menaced, or until some crisis shall arise which may call for some specific, intelligible, and practicable Interposition on their part.

The Principle of one State interfering by force in the internal affairs of another, in order to enforce obedience to the governing authority, is always a question of the greatest moral as well as political delicacy;—and it is not meant here to examine it.—It is only important on the present occasion to observe, that to generalize such a Principle, and to think of reducing it to a system, or to impose it as an obligation, is a scheme utterly impracticable and objectionable.—There is not only the physical impossibility of giving execution to such a system, but there is the moral impracticability arising from the inaptitude of particular States to recognize or to act upon it.—No Country having a Representative System of Government, could act upon it,—and the sooner such a doctrine shall be distinctly abjured, as forming in any Degree the Basis of our Alliance, the better;—in order that States, in calculating the means of their own security, may not suffer disappointment by expecting from the Allied Powers, a support which, under the special Circumstances of their National Institutions they cannot give:— Great Britain has perhaps equal Power with any other State to oppose Herself to a practical and intelligible danger, capable of being brought home to the national feeling:— When the Territorial Balance of Europe is disturbed, she can interfere with effect, but she is the last Government in Europe which can be expected, or can venture, to commit Herself on any question of an abstract character.

These observations are made to point attention to what is practicable and what is not: . . .

. . . But upon all such cases we must admit ourselves to be, and our Allies should in fairness understand that we are, a Power that must take our Principle of action, and our scale of acting, not merely from the Expediency of the Case, but from those Maxims which a System of Government strongly popular and national in it's Character, has irresistibly imposed upon us:—We shall be found in our place when actual Danger menaces the System of Europe, but this Country cannot and will not act upon abstract and speculative Principles of Precaution. The Alliance which exists had no such purpose in view in it's original formation:—It was never so explained to Parliament; if it had, most assuredly the Sanction of Parliament would never have been given to it, and it would now be a Breach of Faith were the Ministers of the Crown to acquiesce in a Construction being put upon it, or were they to suffer themselves to be betrayed into a Course of Measures, inconsistent with those Principles which they avowed at the time, [and] which they have since uniformly maintained both at Home and Abroad . . .

3. Extract from Canning's House of Commons Speech on Portugal, 12 December 1826. *Hansard's Parliamentary Debates*, new series, xvi. 367–9 and 395–8.

* * * *

Sir, I set out with saying, that there were reasons which entirely satisfied my judgment that nothing short of a point of national faith or national honour, would justify at the present moment, any voluntary approximation to the possibility of war. Let me be understood, however, distinctly, as not meaning to say that I dread war in a good cause (and in no other may it be the lot of this country ever to engage!), from a distrust of the strength of the country to commence it, or of her resources to maintain it. I dread it, indeed, but upon far other grounds; I dread it from an apprehension of the tremendous consequences which might arise from any hostilities in which we might now be engaged. Some years ago, in the discussion of the negotiations respecting the French war against Spain, I took the liberty of adverting to this topic. I then stated that the position of this country in the present state of the world was one of neutrality, not only between contending nations, but between conflicting principles; and that it was by neutrality alone that we could maintain that balance, the preservation of which, I believed to be essential to the welfare of mankind. I then said, that I feared that the next war which should be kindled in Europe, would be a war not so much of armies, as of opinions. Not four years have elapsed, and behold my apprehension realized! It is, to be sure, within narrow limits that this war of opinion is at present confined: but it is a war of opinion, that Spain (whether as government or as nation) is now waging against Portugal; it is a war which has commenced in hatred of the new institutions of Portugal. How long is it reasonable to expect that Portugal will abstain from retaliation? If into that war this country shall be compelled to enter, we shall enter into it with a sincere and anxious desire to mitigate rather than exasperate,—and to mingle only in the conflict of arms, not in the more fatal conflict of opinions. But I much fear that this country (however earnestly she may endeavour to avoid it), could not, in such case, avoid seeing ranked under her banners all the restless and dissatisfied of any nation with which she might come in conflict. It is the contemplation of this new power in any future war, which excites my most anxious apprehension. It is one thing to have a giant's strength, but it would be another to use it like a giant. The consciousness of such strength is, undoubtedly, a source of confidence and security; but in the situation in which this country stands, our business is not to seek opportunities of displaying it, but to content ourselves with letting the professors of violent and exaggerated doctrines on both sides feel, that it is not their interest to convert an umpire into an adversary. . . . The consequence of letting loose the passions, at present chained and confined, would be to produce a scene of desolation which no man can contemplate without horror; and I should not sleep easy on my couch, if I were conscious that I had contributed to precipitate it by a single moment.

. . . Let us fly to the aid of Portugal, by whomsoever attacked, because it is our duty to do so; and let us cease our interference where that duty ends. We go to Portugal, not to rule, not to dictate, not to prescribe constitutions, but to defend and to preserve the independence of an ally. We go to plant the standard of England on the well-known heights of Lisbon. Where that standard is planted, foreign dominion shall not come. . . .

. . . when, with reference to the larger question of a military occupation of Spain by France, it is averred, that by that occupation the relative situation of Great Britain and France is altered; that France is thereby exalted and Great Britain lowered, in the eyes of Europe;—I must beg leave to say, that I dissent from that averment. The House knows—the country knows—that when the French army was on the point of entering Spain, his majesty's government did all in their power to prevent it; that we resisted it by all means, short of war. I have just now stated some of the reasons why we did not think the entry of that army into Spain a sufficient ground for war; but there was, in addition to those which I have stated, this peculiar reason,—that whatever effect a war, commenced upon the mere ground of the entry of a French army into Spain, might have, it probably would not have had the effect of getting that army out of Spain. In a war against France at that time, as at any other, you might perhaps, have acquired military glory; you might, perhaps, have extended your colonial possessions; you might even have achieved, at great cost of blood and treasure, an honourable peace; but as to getting the French out of Spain, that would have been the one object which you almost certainly would not have accomplished. How seldom, in the whole history of the wars of Europe, has any war between two great powers ended, in the obtaining of the exact, the identical, object for which the war was begun!

* * * *

But then, Sir, the balance of power!—The entry of the French army into Spain disturbed that balance, and we ought to have gone to war to restore it! I have already said, that when the French army entered Spain, we might, if we chose, have resisted or resented that measure by war. But were there no other means than war for restoring the balance of Power?—Is the balance of power a fixed and unalterable standard? Or is it not a standard perpetually varying, as civilization advances and as new nations spring up, and take their place among established political communities? The balance of power a century and a half ago was to be adjusted between France and Spain, the Netherlands, Austria, and England. Some years afterwards, Russia assumed her high station in European politics. Some years after that again, Prussia became not only a substantive, but a preponderating monarchy. Thus, while the balance of power continued in principle the same, the means of adjusting it became more varied and enlarged. They became enlarged, in proportion to the increased number of considerable states,—in proportion, I may say, to the number of weights which might be shifted into the one or the other scale. To look to the policy of Europe, in the times of William and Anne, for the purpose of regulating the balance of power in Europe at the present day, is to disregard the progress of events, and to confuse dates and facts which throw a reciprocal light upon each other.

It would be disingenuous, indeed, not to admit that the entry of the French army into Spain, was in a certain sense, a disparagement—an affront to the pride—a blow to the feelings of England: and it can hardly be supposed that the government did not sympathize, on that occasion, with the feelings of the people. But I deny that, questionable or censurable as the act might be, it was one which necessarily called for our direct and hostile opposition. Was nothing then to be done? Was there no other mode of resistance, than by a direct attack upon France—or by a war to be undertaken on the soil of Spain? What, if the possession of Spain might be rendered harmless in rival hands—harmless as regarded us—and valueless to the possessors? Might not compensation for disparagement be obtained, and the policy of our ancestors vindicated, by means better adapted to the present time? If France occupied Spain, was it necessary, in order to avoid the consequences of that occupation—that we should blockade Cadiz? No. I looked another way—I sought materials of compensation in another hemisphere. Contemplating Spain, such as our ancestors had known her, I resolved that if France had Spain, it should not be Spain 'with the Indies.' I called the New World into existence, to redress the balance of the Old. . . .

4. Extract from Aberdeen's dispatch no. 22 to Lord Heytesbury (Ambassador in St. Petersburg), 31 October 1829. P.R.O., F.O. 181/78; *Parliamentary Papers*, (347), 1854, lxxii. 1–5.

. . . the Treaty [of Adrianople] . . . , certainly not in conformity with the expectations held out by preceding declarations and assurances, appears vitally to affect the interests, the strength, the dignity, the present safety, and future independence of the Ottoman Empire.

The modes of domination may be various, although all equally irresistible. The independence of a state may be overthrown, and its subjection effectually secured, without the presence of a hostile force, or the permanent occupation of its soil. Under the present Treaty the territorial acquisitions of Russia are small, it must be admitted, in extent, although most important in their character. They are commanding positions, far more valuable than the possession of barren provinces and depopulated towns, and better calculated to rivet the fetters by which the Sultan is bound.

The cession of the Asiatic fortresses, with their neighbouring districts, not only secures to Russia the uninterrupted occupation of the eastern coast of the Black Sea, but places her in a situation so commanding as to control at pleasure the destiny of Asia Minor.

Prominently advanced into the centre of Armenia, in the midst of a Christian population, Russia holds the keys both of the Persian and the Turkish provinces; and whether she may be disposed to extend her conquests to the East or to the West, to Teheran or to Constantinople, no serious obstacle can arrest her progress.

In Europe the Principalities of Wallachia and Moldavia are rendered virtually independent of the Porte. A tribute is indeed to be paid to the Sultan, which he has no means of enforcing except by the permission and even the assistance of Russia herself; and a Prince, elected for life, is to demand investiture which cannot be withheld. The Mussulman inhabitants are to be forcibly expelled from the territory. The ancient right of pre-emption is abolished; and the supplies indispensable for Constantinople, for the Turkish arsenals, and for the fortresses, are entirely cut off. The most important fortresses on the Danube are to be razed, and the frontier left exposed and unprotected against incursions which at any future time may be attempted.

It is sufficient to observe of the stipulations respecting the islands of the Danube, that their effect must be to place the control of the navigation and commerce of that river exclusively in the hands of Russia.

Servia, by the incorporation of the six districts referred to in the Treaty, is erected into an independent and powerful State; and when the allied Powers shall have finally decided upon the character of the Government, and the limits to be assigned to Greece, the circle will be completed of territories nominally dependent or tributary, but which must be animated with the most hostile spirit; and the recognition of which by the Powers of Europe is scarcely compatible with the security, perhaps not with the existence, of the Turkish Empire.

The commercial privileges and personal immunities which are secured by the Treaty to the subjects of Russia, appear to be at variance with any notion we are able to form of the authority of a sovereign and independent prince. It is true that by capitulations with the Porte, in consequence of the defective administration of justice by the Turkish Government, rights have been obtained by European nations, of such a description as would not have been conceded by the States of Christendom. These rights have not only been still further extended by the present Treaty, but the stipulations, so far from being drawn up in the spirit of peace, are to all appearance rather calculated to invite and justify the renewal of hostilities. What reasonable prospect of 'eternal peace, friendship, and good understanding,' can be afforded by an instrument which contains a special provision, making the calamities of war almost dependent upon the capricious extortion of a Turkish officer, or the unauthorized arrogance of a Russian trader.

His Majesty's Government are persuaded that it will be impossible for His Imperial Majesty to reflect upon the terms of Article VII. of the Treaty of Adrianople, without perceiving at once that they must be utterly subversive of the independence of the Ottoman power.

This Article stipulates that merchant vessels of all nations, without any restriction of size or tonnage, shall be admitted to pass freely through the Straits of the Dardanelles and the Bosphorus. The right of visit on the part of the Turkish Government is expressly excluded. This provision not only deprives the Porte of the exercise of a right in its own waters, inherent in the very nature of independent sovereignty, but it also destroys a necessary protection against the effects of foreign hostility or domestic treachery. The power of marching a Russian army, at any moment, through any part of the Turkish territory without the permission of the Government, could not be more degrading or more dangerous.

Such stipulations are not only destructive of the territorial rights of sovereignty, and threatening to the safety of the Porte, but their obvious tendency is to affect the condition and the interests of all maritime States in the Mediterranean, and may demand from those States the most serious consideration.

*   *   *   *

Is it too much to say that such stipulations are inconsistent with the desire of His Imperial Majesty to preserve the independence of the Turkish Empire?

*   *   *   *

Even if the Emperor were not thus to yield at once to the impulse of his own disposition, the same determination would still be recommended by considerations of prudence, as being essential to the success of objects which he has professed to have much at heart. His Imperial Majesty has declared that a regard for the true interests of Russia induced him to feel more desirous than any other European Power of maintaining the independent existence and integrity of the Ottoman Empire. He has also repeatedly avowed that the condition of the Christian subjects of the Porte demanded his constant solicitude, and that the obligations both of his own conscience and of public Treaties imposed upon him the special duty of consulting their welfare, and providing for their protection. These objects, at all times difficult to reconcile, would, under the strict execution of the Treaty, become altogether incompatible with each other. The real situation of the Turkish Power is too obvious to escape the most common observation. The Sultan is surrounded by independent States formed out of his own territories, and with the great mass of the European population of his Empire anxiously waiting for the moment when they may profit by this example, and shake off his dominion altogether. Defeated and reduced to the lowest degree of humiliation, he has retained his throne and political existence by the mercy of his conqueror. The disaffection of his Mahomedan subjects of all ranks, whether produced by repeated disgrace, or the effect of a gradual change long since in operation, has become general. In this condition, with a broken authority and exhausted resources, he is called upon to provide for the indemnity which is exacted from him. In what manner is the Sultan to relieve himself from this burthen, and by whom must the sacrifices principally be made? If the Turkish Government be still permitted to act at all as an independent Power, it is clear that the necessary sums must be raised by fresh impositions upon the people, and by such means as are authorised by the law and customs of the Empire. It is equally certain that the Christian subjects of the Porte must largely contribute to furnish these supplies. Compliance with the demands of the Government will be difficult, but the urgency of the case will justify severity. Resistance may be attempted: if successful, leading to general confusion and revolt; if otherwise, spoliation and oppression will follow. At all events, new scenes of calamity will be opened, calculated to frustrate the admitted objects of His Imperial Majesty, and fatally destructive both to the independence of the Porte and to the happiness and prosperity of the Christian subjects of the Empire.

There are other considerations which ought to have their due weight in the mind of His Imperial Majesty.

It cannot be doubted that the result of the war has been such as to change entirely the relative position of the belligerents towards each other, as well as towards the neighbouring States and the rest of Europe. This change, it may be admitted, is to a certain extent the natural consequence of an unequal contest; for at the termination of hostilities characterised on one side by the most signal success, and on the other by continued disaster, it would be unreasonable to suppose that the parties could in every respect resume their former relations. It is, therefore, not exclusively to the conditions of the peace, but also to the events of the war, that we are to ascribe the change which has taken place. In whatever manner it may have been accomplished, the fact is sufficient to justify some anxiety on the part of those Powers, who have always felt a deep interest in the preservation of the system of the European balance established by the Treaty of Paris and at the Congress of Vienna. This anxiety must be greatly increased when, in addition to the unavoidable weakness and prostration of the Turkish Power, it is found that fresh causes are brought into action which are obviously calculated to hasten and ensure its utter dissolution. The evils attending upon uncertainty, expectation, and alarm, must be universally felt throughout Europe. Encouragement will be afforded to projects the most adverse to the general tranquillity; and the different Powers, so far from disarming, will probably augment their warlike preparations, already too extensive for a state of peace.

It is only by a frank and cordial desire on the part of His Imperial Majesty to remove all reasonable grounds of suspicion and apprehension; it is only by a sincere endeavour in conjunction with his allies to confirm and perpetuate the repose which has hitherto been enjoyed; and by making this the main object of European policy, that we shall be enabled to avert the threatened dangers. In this salutary work His Imperial Majesty will assuredly call to mind the example of his illustrious predecessor; and he will recollect that whatever may have been the glories of his reign, the last ten years of his life, devoted exclusively to the preservation of peace, eminently entitled him to the gratitude of Europe.

* * * *

5. Extract from Wellington's Memorandum on the Revolution in France, 14 August 1830. Aberdeen MSS., B.M., Add. MS. 43059; *Despatches, Correspondence, and Memoranda of Field Marshal, Arthur, Duke of Wellington* (London, 1867–80), vii. 162–9.

... What has happened is the revolution acted over again by many of the same characters, the use of the same means, the same symbols, and the adoption of nearly the same measures. ... the measures and the course pursued are the same, and if persevered in, or rather if not changed, will certainly affect the interior of France ultimately in the same manner; or in the words of the Treaty [of Paris] will 'convulse France, and thereby endanger the repose of other States'. There will be a civil or a foreign war, possibly both, if the latter should precede the former, and all Europe will be more or less involved.

In the meantime the Liberal party in every country in Europe will be in operation against the Government and under the protection of France.

These are undoubtedly the dangers upon which it was the intention of that part of the second article of the Treaty of Paris, that the Allies should deliberate *among themselves* ...

But it must be observed that the distance between them is very great, and that much time must elapse before any real consultation or concert can take place; that the progress of events is most rapid, and that no man can calculate upon those which may occur in the six weeks, or even twice that time, which must elapse before there could be any real consultation and decision by the four Allied Courts.

In the existing state of the House of Bourbon, the Duc d'Orléans, whether as King or Regent, is the only person to whom the four Courts could look to conduct the government of France if the choice could rest with them. All may wish, and some might be disposed to stipulate that he had continued in his office of Lieutenant-General, or had assumed that of Regent, and guardian of the Duc de Bordeaux. But it cannot be denied that, whether in one office or the other, the Duc d'Orléans is the person under whose administration of the government the best hopes of continued peace are afforded under existing circumstances.

Nobody can believe that the revolutionary evils which I have above discussed would not be aggravated, the authority of the Duc d'Orléans injured, and the confidence of the country in him diminished, by any declaration of the four Allied Courts against him, and by any doubt or hesitation in recognising his authority, particularly by his Majesty and the government of this country.

The evil hanging over Europe as the consequence of the transactions of the last fortnight will come soon enough. I cannot hope that any step that we, or our Allies, can take will prevent it.

It is obvious that the only feeble hope we have of maintaining the peace of the world is in the moderation of the character of the Duc d'Orléans. He will endeavour to preserve peace, and he may succeed if he has strength to govern the country. But he can have strength only by the countenance, and the protection which that countenance can give him, of the great Powers of Europe.

It appears to me, then, that good policy requires that we should recognise the Duc d'Orléans as king at an early period after notification of his authority, allowing a reasonable period for deliberation.

I think that it is expected by the ambassadors of our Allies that we should take this course. We ought to consult with them, although we should persevere in taking the course proposed. I am convinced that none of them will object to it, and that our example will be followed by every Court in Europe. Indeed, we may be anticipated by some.

* * * *

6. Palmerston's private letter to Viscount Granville (Ambassador in Paris), 7 January 1831. Granville MSS., P.R.O. 30/29/404; Henry Lytton Bulwer, *The Life of Henry John Temple, Viscount Palmerston* (London, 1870), ii. 27–9.

In a conversation which I had a few days ago with Talleyrand, about the affairs of Belgium, I mentioned to him an idea which had occurred to me, as an arrangement which might possibly smooth some of our difficulties. The King of the Netherlands would wish his son to wear the crown of Belgium; the Belgians want much to have Luxembourg. Could not the King give up Luxembourg to his son, on condition of his being elected by the Belgians, and might not the Belgians choose the Prince of Orange, on condition that he should bring Luxembourg with him? Talleyrand looked very grave, and said he doubted whether such an arrangement could be agreed to in Paris. He thought his Government would not like to see Luxembourg united to Belgium. I asked why, inasmuch as it has been so united hitherto, and could not be more inconvenient to France when united to Belgium alone, than when united to Belgium joined with Holland. He said, the fact was that their frontier in that direction is very weak and exposed, and Luxembourg runs into an undefended part of France. I replied that a nation of 32 millions of whom every man is born a soldier need not be particular about frontiers, and that the true defence of their frontier must consist in men and not in bricks. He then said, Would there be no means of making an arrangement *by which Luxembourg might be given to France?* I confess I felt considerable surprise at a proposition so much at variance with all the language and professions which he and his Government have been holding. I said that such an arrangement appeared to me to be impossible, and that nobody could consent to it. I added that England had no selfish objects in view in the arrangements of Belgium, but that we wished Belgium to be really and substantially independent. That we were desirous of living upon good terms with France, but that any territorial acquisitions of France such as this which he contemplated would alter the relations of the two countries, and make it impossible for us to continue on good terms. I found since this conversation that he had been making similar propositions to Prussia about her Rhenish provinces, in the event of the possibility of moving the King of Saxony to Belgium and giving Saxony to Prussia. Today he proposed to me that France should get Philippeville and Marienburg by means of a line to be drawn from Givet to Beaumont, in consideration of France using her influence to procure the election of Leopold for Belgium. I do not like all this; it looks as if France was unchanged in her system of encroachment, and it diminishes the confidence in her sincerity and good faith which her conduct up to this time had inspired. I trust that these may be the spontaneous manoeuvres of Talleyrand himself and not the result of orders from his Court. But it may not be amiss for you to hint, upon any fitting occasion, that England considers the present state of possession of France to be a matter, in the permanence of which we have a deep interest, and though we are anxious to cultivate the best understanding with her, and to be upon the terms of the most intimate friendship with her, yet that is only upon the supposition that she contents herself with the finest territory in Europe and does not mean to open a new chapter of encroachment or conquest.

7. Extract from Palmerston's private letter to Granville, 11 March 1831. Granville MSS., P.R.O. 30/29/404; Bulwer, ii. 50–1.

I am sorry for the determination of Austria about Italy; it is wrong and foolish; and brings on at once a general war, which one had hoped might have been avoided. The inevitable consequence will be, the expulsion of the Austrians from Italy; and for that, one shall not be sorry, provided the French are not established there, in their stead. It is impossible for England to take part with Austria in a war entered into for the purpose of putting down freedom and maintaining despotism; neither can we side with France in a contest the result of which may be to extend her territories; we shall therefore keep out of the contest as long as we can.

*   *   *   *

8. Extract from Palmerston's private letter to Granville, 29 March 1831. Granville MSS., P.R.O. 30/29/404; Bulwer, ii. 61.

*   *   *   *

The Poles fight gallantly, and the Russians have suffered more than people supposed; but the Emperor must ultimately succeed. I have had conversations with Wielopolski and Walewski [the Polish spokesmen in London], and have told them both that we must stand upon our treaties; and while, on the one hand, we should remonstrate if Russia tried to depart from the Treaty of Vienna, on the other hand, we could not do so ourselves by helping to make Poland entirely independent.

9. Extract from Palmerston's private letter to Lord Holland (Chancellor of the Duchy of Lancaster), 9 April 1831. Holland House MSS., B.M., Add. MS. 51599.

... I entirely share your feelings about Poland and should like myself to see it restored to independence; but one scarcely sees how that can be accomplished without breaking the Treaty of Vienna which however objectionable in some of the details of its arrangements, is yet with its accessories of Paris and Aix-la-Chapelle, the great security of Europe against the inveterately enervating spirit of France.

10. Palmerston's private letter to Granville, 16 August 1831. Granville MSS., P.R.O. 30/29/404; Bulwer, ii. 108–10, following the imperfect copy in the Broadlands MSS., GC/GR no. 1341, misdates it.

The sky begins to darken and I fear the storm will soon break.

I like not your letter nor your despatches [reporting that the French would only evacuate Belgium after the fate of the frontier fortresses had been settled], nor those which Talleyrand read to me to-day by desire of Sebastiani [the French Foreign Minister].

The despatches which Talleyrand himself writes to Sebastiani are perfect, and evidently written that he may read them to me. What else he writes I cannot tell, but I am not so sure that what he reads to me is all he sends, and that the rest is in the same tone.

One thing is certain—the French must go out of Belgium or we have a general war, and war in a given number of days. But, say the French, we mean to go out, but we must choose our own time and our own terms. The time, however, they have agreed shall be settled by the conference, and it must be as early as is consistent with the objects for which they professed to go in.

They are to escort the Dutch to their own frontier and thus to have military possession of Belgium. This looks very like a juggle between them and the Dutch, but it must necessarily delay the evacuation. Now as to the terms. They came in at the invitation of an allied sovereign, whose neutrality and independence they have agreed to guarantee, and they marched for the accomplishment of the objects which the five Powers have all been aiming at. What terms then are they entitled to make as to their retreat? *None!* With regard to the fortresses, make them understand that their pretensions are utterly inadmissible. The very basis upon which we can agree to the demolition of any of these fortresses is the security derived from the guarantee of France and of the other Powers.

That guarantee, then, must be given in the fullest and most formal manner before we can stir a step; and to dismantle these fortresses while the French have them in possession would be a disgrace to all the five Powers; and as to making France a party to the treaty for their demolition, that is *impossible*. Nothing shall ever induce me to put my name to such a treaty, and I am quite sure the Cabinet never would sanction it.

We have had no Cabinet to-day upon your letters and your despatches, because we want to learn the result of my letter and Grey's of Saturday last. My own opinion is that we shall be at war in ten days and that Sebastiani and Soult [the French Minister of War] mean to drive us to it. They evidently want to pick a quarrel with all their neighbours, or to compel everybody to submit to their insolence and aggressions; witness the language about Spain.

They miscalculate their chances, however, I think; and they will find that a war with all the rest of the world, brought upon them by a violation of their word, will not turn to their advantage, nor redound to their honour. They will not be the better able to carry on the war on the Continent for losing all their commerce, and for being deprived of the revenue arising therefrom. The ruin of their seaports will create general distress throughout the country; the Chambers will soon be sick of barren glory if they succeed, or of defeats brought needlessly upon them if they fail; the ministry will be turned out, and the King may go with them. The Carlist party will make an effort, and with the Republicans may give much embarrassment. Austria and Prussia are well prepared for war and their first operation will be to assist the Russians in crushing the Poles, the better to be able to direct all their forces against France and the destruction of the Poles will thus be owing to the French.

The Belgians will not join the French and if they did they would equally run away.

On our side a naval war will be exceedingly popular because it will be eminently successful. Our commerce will resume its monopoly and any military effort we may have to make, being in Belgium, will be comparatively cheap.

11. Extract from Palmerston's private letter to Lady Cowper (later Lady Palmerston), 21 September 1831. Sir Charles Webster, *The Foreign Policy of Palmerston 1830–1841* (London, 1951), i. 47–8. (Webster says that the letter is in the Lieven MSS. in the British Museum, but these papers are at present being sorted and this letter has not yet been found.)

... The fact is that the only influence which my office possesses over the *Courier* or any other paper is *positive* not *negative*. I could get him [the Editor] to insert any article I wished today but I have no means or power of preventing him from inserting any other of quite a different kind tomorrow. I can compel but I cannot control. The only communication that takes place is that every now and then when we have any particular piece of news, it is given to the editor and he thereby gets a start of his competitors, and on the condition of receiving these occasional intimations he gives his support to the Government. But no editor would bring his daily article to a public office to be looked over before they [*sic*] are printed and no public officer who had any sense in his brains would undertake the responsibilities of such inspections ... Though they look to Government for news, they look to their readers for money, and they never can resist flying out upon popular topics when they think that by a flourish they shall gain a little éclat among Club and Coffee House politicians and have their paper talked of for four and twenty hours.

12. Extract from Palmerston's private letter to his brother, the Hon. William Temple, 6–7 October 1833. Broadlands MSS., GC/TE no. 216; Bulwer, ii. 169–71, misdates it 8 October. This extract was written on 7 October.

* * * *

What have been the subjects of discussion at ... Munchengrätz seems [*sic*] to be gradually getting out ... An eventual partition of Turkey between Austria and Russia is thought to be one of the topics; and this seems to me very probable. It is needless to say that England and France would oppose this to the utmost of their means, and I think we should be able, with the assistance of Mehemet Ali, to offer a strong barrier against the accomplishment of this project. I told Esterhazy [the Austrian Ambassador] of this report, and said it was very inconsistent with what Neumann [the Austrian Chargé d' Affaires] had been ordered to tell me six months ago by Metternich —that if Russia attempted to appropriate to herself one inch of Turkish territory, it would be war with Austria. Esterhazy said that Metternich had never gone quite so far with him, but had told him that Russia had frequently asked him to consider what should be substituted for the sultan and his empire, if they should fall; and that Metternich had always evaded the discussion, saying that his object was to maintain what exists, and that it was therefore needless for him to inquire what should be set up in its place. The Russians at Berlin affect to ridicule our protest at Constantinople but Ancillon and Nesselrode [the Prussian and Russian Foreign Ministers] do not like it. We shall repeat it at Petersburgh; and we have ordered the *Caledonia*, a three-decker, and one of the seventy-fours from the Tagus, together with an armed steamer, fully equal to a seventy-four, to join [Admiral] Malcolm off the Dardanelles. This will give him six sail of the line, a steamer, and two or three fifty-gun frigates, besides smaller vessels—a very respectable squadron, three of them three-deckers. We shall send an eighty-gun ship to the Tagus, to keep up our complement of three sail of the line there; and if things were to end well in that quarter, we should send another line-of-battle ship from thence to Malcolm.

I have not, however, yet authorized Malcolm to go up the Dardanelles. The Cabinet meet the 3rd November, and then we must consider this Eastern question, and give instructions about it. If all remains quiet, of course there is nothing to be done. But an insurrection is probable. If it produces civil war, the Sultan, at the head of one party, may call in the Russians to put down the other; and then comes the question, Shall we let them return, or can we prevent them from doing so? We hear from Odessa that their Black Sea fleet is not to be laid up in ordinary this year; but the Black Sea is difficult of navigation in the winter. Still they *might* come; and we should not find it easy to force the Dardanelles unless we had troops to land. Mehemet Ali, to be sure, could lend us plenty and would be ready enough to do so. Still this case is not very likely. The Sultan is so unpopular that if there is an insurrection he will probably be dethroned at once and his son set up immediately; and the most likely event is that a Government so erected may be threatened by Russia, and may invite the English and French squadrons to come up to Constantinople to defend the Bosphorus. My own opinion is, that in such case they ought to go up; but that would be almost

tantamount to a declaration of war against Russia unless she was wise
and declined coming in contact with the combined fleets; and I think
that when we have seven liners and the French six, the eleven or
twelve Russians will never venture to face us, with a host of trans-
ports besides in their train; indeed, the English fleet alone would be
enough to stop them.

They have laid down two sail-of-line at Archangel, to be sent
round to the Black Sea next summer; but we must have some explanation with the Turks about the passage of ships of war through
the straits, which, by the treaty of 1809 with us, is declared not
allowable.

Another and more likely subject of discussion between the three
sovereigns are the affairs of Germany; and this extra congress of
prime ministers, which is to take place next December or January,
will probably lead to some violent and foolish resolves about Germany, its press, the universities, and the legislative chambers.
These sort of measures are likely to recoil upon their authors, and
do them more harm than good.

If Portuguese and Spanish affairs were more within their reach,
they would have done something about them, but geography forbids.
As to Belgium, the three courts are seized with a sudden desire to
finish that matter, having probably at last discovered that this
question has been the means of bringing England and France into
closer contact.

*   *   *   *

13. Extract from Palmerston's private letter to W. Temple, 21
April 1834. Broadlands MSS., GC/TE no. 219; Bulwer, ii. 180–1.

I have been very busy ever since . . . the 4th of this month, working out my quadruple alliance between England, France, Spain, and
Portugal, for the expulsion of Carlos and Miguel from the Portuguese dominions. . . . I hope it will be signed to-morrow. I carried it
through the Cabinet by a *coup de main*, taking them by surprise, and
not leaving them time to make objections. I was not equally successful with old Talley[rand] and the French Government, for they have
made objections in plenty. But they were all as to the form in which I
had proposed to make them parties to the transaction, and not to the
thing itself. I have, however, at last satisfied their vanity by giving
them a proper place among us. My first plan was, a treaty between

the other three, to which they should be acceding parties. I reckon this to be a great stroke. In the first place, it will settle Portugal, and go some way to settle Spain also. But, what is of more permanent and extensive importance, it establishes a quadruple alliance among the constitutional states of the west, which will serve as a powerful counterpoise to the Holy Alliance of the east. I have, ever since Ferdinand's death [which on 29 September 1833 precipitated the contest for the Spanish throne between his daughter, Isabella, and his brother, Carlos], felt that morally this alliance must exist; but it was not till a fortnight ago that I saw the opportunity of giving it a substantive and practical form. The communications of Miraflores [the Spanish Minister in London], and his renewal of the Spanish wish that we should send troops to Portugal, suggested the idea to me, and I have found its execution easier than I should have imagined. Miraflores and Sarmento [the Portuguese Minister in London] are delighted; the former says the only thing he regrets is that he cannot himself be the bearer of the treaty to Madrid, to see the joy it will occasion. Those who will like it least, after the two Infants, are Pedro [Maria's father, formerly King of Portugal and Emperor of Brazil] and his ministers, who wish the civil war to go on, that they may continue to plunder and confiscate; but as soon as peace returns the Cortes must assemble, and these people will be removed. I mean the ministers, for there is nobody to make a Regent of but Pedro. I should like to see Metternich's face when he reads our treaty. Our naval co-operation is merely put in to save appearances, and to prove our goodwill, for there is nothing for us to do in that way . . .

14. Extract from Palmerston's dispatch no. 3 to Henry Ellis (Ambassador in Teheran), 25 July 1835. Draft in P.R.O., F.O. 60/36.

The King having determined to reestablish a direct Diplomatick Intercourse between Himself and the Schah of Persia, and His Majesty deeming it fit to commence his renewed Relations with the Court of Teheran by sending an Ambassador to convey His Majesty's Congratulations to the Schah upon his recent accession to the Throne of Persia, the King has been graciously pleased to appoint you His Ambassador for this purpose . . .

You will make known to the Schah the lively interest with which

His Majesty has learnt his successful establishment upon the Throne of Persia . . .

The Relations of Great Britain and Persia towards each other are such, that even if the King's personal Regard and Friendship for the Schah were less strong than they are, His Majesty would still feel an anxious desire that Persia should be powerful, tranquil, and independent. Great Britain, therefore, is an ally, in whom Persia may at all times place the most entire confidence; because our Friendship is founded upon a concurrence of natural Interests, and is not alloyed by any secret wish for aggrandizement, to be obtained at the expense of Persia.

The Dominions of His Majesty, both in Europe and in Asia, are separated by great distance from the Territories of the Schah; and the first and only wish of His Majesty's heart with respect to the Persian Monarchy must be, that its integrity should be preserved and its independence maintained.

But these great objects are best secured by the continuance of peace abroad, and by a well ordered system of Government at home. . . .

The points, therefore, which, in the spirit of friendship, without any appearance of dictation, you will press upon the consideration of the Schah and his advisers, are,—the preservation of peace with all neighbours; the cultivation of the most friendly relations with Turkey; the introduction of order and regularity into the internal administration of the Government; the improvement of the Revenue; and the creation of an efficient and regularly disciplined military force.

* * * *

You will of course find the influence of Russia strong at the Court of Teheran; and though Russia and England both concurred in supporting the claims of the present Schah to the Throne, yet the interest and policy of Russia, as regards Persia, are in almost all things not only different, but opposite to those of Great Britain.

The behaviour which you should pursue with respect to Russia and the Russian Mission, should therefore be regulated with circumspection and prudence. As England and Russia are for the moment acting in unison, you should be careful that your deportment towards the Russian Mission, should neither indicate unfriendly feelings, nor unnecessarily imply suspicion; but on the other hand you should not allow the Russian Minister to suppose that the British Government does not attach the greatest importance to the maintenance of the Independence and integrity of Persia; or that England is not firmly resolved to uphold that integrity and independence.

In your confidential intercourse with the Persian Government, you must not conceal the opinion entertained by His Majesty's Government, that however cautiously Russia may be acting at present, it is from her that the great danger to Persia must arise, and against her that the defensive arrangements of Persia should be directed.

You will warn the Persian Government against being made the tools of Russian policy, by allowing themselves to be pushed on to make war against the Affghans.

Russia has objects of her own to gain by exciting the Persian Government to quarrel with its Eastern neighbours. The attention of Persia is thus turned away from what is passing to the North and the West, and the intrigues by which Russia is paving her way to further encroachment upon Persia, have a better chance of being carried on unobserved. Whatever may be the result of such quarrels, Russia is sure to gain. Whether Persia is successful or not, her resources will be wasted in these wars, and her future means of defence against the attacks of Russia must be diminished.

15. Extract from Palmerston's private letter to Melbourne, 1 March 1836. Melbourne MSS., Royal Archives, box 16; Lloyd C. Sanders, ed., *Lord Melbourne's Papers* (London, 1890), pp. 337–40.

... My ... opinion has certainly not been shaken by the progress of events. Every day brings fresh proofs of the complete union of the three powers [Austria, Russia, and Prussia] on every question of European policy, and affords additional evidence that they are for the present what they told us three years ago they must be considered—namely, a unity. Here is Austria setting at defiance the keen sympathy which her Galician, Hungarian, and Transylvanian subjects have openly manifested for the Poles, and making herself the tool to execute a measure of Russian vengeance [the occupation of Cracow], in which she herself has no interest whatever, or, rather, with respect to which her interests are directly at variance with those of Russia. Her motive is obvious. She found Russia determined to execute the measure; she knew the consequences of a Russian occupation, and to avert that evil she chose rather to encounter the unpopularity of the act, and to perform it herself. But this is a fresh proof that in the present state of things we must not look to Metternich for any co-operation in measures destined to hold Russia in check. He will edge away to us and France, if we and France boldly take up our own ground; but he will not, and cannot join us in the first instance.

The answer then which Austria will infallibly make you will be, that we all wish the same thing, and that therefore we ought all to concert as to the best means of obtaining our common object. That for this purpose we must establish a conference at some central place, and Vienna will be proposed as best suited for speedy communication with Petersburg, Constantinople, Berlin, Paris, and London. Are we to accept such an offer or to decline it? If we accept it we enter into a labryinth of negotiations out of which I see no clue. England and France will be in the minority. We were so about Belgium; but in that case the negotiation was in London, and the weight of a government on the spot speaking through its plenipotentiary gave that plenipotentiary double authority; while also England and France being the two powers the closest to Belgium, had on that account the greatest means of action in the country which was the subject of negotiation. The reverse of all this would happen with respect to the Vienna conference, and we should be dragged along by the three against our opinions or else compelled to withdraw. But a conference broken up by disagreement does not leave the parties upon the same terms on which it found them at its commencement, and Europe would in such a case be still more divided into two camps than it is now.

But say that we should refuse the proposed conference. What reason could we assign for doing so that would not be offensive to some of the parties concerned? Why invite Austria, and decline to concert with Russia and Prussia? Is that not plainly declaring that we trust the former and distrust the latter? And is not such a declaration thus publicly made affronting to the two latter powers? If you had a fair chance of detaching Austria from them by the offer, well and good; but we may be quite sure we shall do no such thing. We should therefore needlessly and unprofitably offend Russia and Prussia; be represented as having been baffled and repulsed in an attempt to separate Austria from her allies; and then when England and France came to sign their treaty, *after* having failed in their overture to Austria, that treaty would bear the character of a proceeding arising out of an ascertained difference with the three powers; whereas if you begin with such a treaty and ask the others afterwards to accede to it, beginning with Austria, your proceeding bears the character only of a foundation upon which you hope to build a subsequent concert with other powers.

The division of Europe into two camps, as Ancillon [the Prussian Minister for Foreign Affairs] calls it, to which you so much object, is the result of events beyond our control, and is the consequence of the French Revolution of July. The three powers fancy their interests lie in a direction opposite to that in which we and France conceive ours to be placed. The separation is not one of words but of things; not the effect of caprice or of will, but produced by the force of occurrences. The three and the two think differently, and therefore they act differently, whether it be as to Belgium, or Portugal, or Spain. This separation cannot really cease till all the questions to which it applies are decided—just as it is impossible to make a coalition ministry while there are questions pending on which public men disagree. But when Ancillon and Metternich complain of this division of Europe into two camps, that which they really complain of is, not the existence of two camps, but the equality of the two camps. The plain English of it all is, that they want to have England on their side against France, that they may dictate to France as they did in 1814 and 1815; and they are provoked beyond measure at the steady protection which France has derived from us. But it is that protection which has preserved the peace of Europe. Without it there would long ago have been a general war.

16. Extract from Palmerston's private letter to T. Spring Rice (Chancellor of the Exchequer), 9 October 1837. Copy in Broadlands MSS., GC/MO no. 129; Kenneth Bourne, *Britain and the Balance of Power in North America 1815–1908* (London, 1967), pp. 77–8.

... We cannot pretend to exert much influence on the destiny of Texas; & have little to do, but to watch the course of events.

Mexico will not reconquer Texas; we must see whether the Band of outlaws who occupy Texas will be able to constitute themselves into such a community as it would be decent for us to make a Treaty with—At all events it would not do for us to make a Treaty with a self denominated State, till events had proved that such state could permanently maintain its independence.

Perhaps when the Texians no longer fear Mexico, their wish for admission into the Northern Union may diminish. That admission would be objected to by the Northern States who are not slave holders, & by the cotton growers of the southern states. The Latter Parties would view with jealousy the superior fertility of the Texas soil; & would fear that if that soil were brought into full cultivation the Price of Cotton would be lowered by the increased production of it; & that they should not make proper interest upon the Capital they have invested in their own cotton lands.

To us perhaps it does not very much signify what becomes of Texas, though in a Political view, it would be better that Texas should not be incorporated with the Union; commercially it would make little difference. But we may be pretty sure that if it should suit the Two States to unite their union would not be prevented by a Commercial Treaty between us & Texas. I told Iturbide the Mexican chargé d'affaires the other day when he wanted us to help Mexico against Texas, that the Mexicans behave so ill to us, & the North Americans so honestly that as far as our Commercial Interests are concerned we should have no objection to see the whole of Mexico belong to the United States. He laughed & said perhaps I was right.

17. Palmerston's private letter to Granville, 8 June 1838. Granville MSS., P.R.O. 30/29/423; Bulwer, ii. 267–9.

I have only time to write you a few lines about Egypt. The Cabinet yesterday agreed that it would not do to let Mehemet Ali declare himself independent, and separate Egypt and Syria from the Turkish Empire. They see that the consequence of such a declaration on his part must be either immediately or at no distant time conflict between him and the Sultan. That in such conflict the Turkish troops would probably be defeated; that then the Russians would fly to the aid of the Sultan, and a Russian garrison would occupy Constantinople and the Dardanelles; and once in possession of those points, the Russians would never quit them. We are, therefore, prepared to give naval aid to the Sultan against Mehemet, if necessary and demanded; and we intend to order our Mediterranean fleet immediately to Alexandria, in order to give Mehemet an outward and visible sign of our inward resolve. We should like the French squadron to go there too at the same time, if the French are willing so to send it. With respect to the mode of making our communications to Mehemet, much is to be said both ways. Separate declarations have the advantage which Molé [the French Prime Minister] mentions; a joint and collective declaration would give us some hold over Russia, if it was founded upon a previous and recorded agreement between the five Powers, giving to the five some determining authority over the conduct of each; but this would be a tedious matter to arrange, and would not be settled in time. What *I* should like, and what I *think* I could get the Cabinet to agree to would be a short convention between England and France on the one hand, and Turkey on the other, by which the two former should bind themselves for a limited time, say eight or ten years, to afford to the other naval assistance, in the event of his demanding it to protect his territory against attack; and the wording might be so framed as to include the case either of Russia or of Mehemet Ali.

This is in short my old scheme which was rejected when I proposed it some time ago, because then some of us placed reliance on Austria. I think all our eyes are now open to the utter impossibility of depending upon any active assistance from Austria against Russia, though we may confidently reckon upon her now aiding Russia in Turkish affairs at least against England and France. I am convinced that such a convention as I describe would save Turkey and preserve the peace of Europe, by its mere moral effect, and without our being called to act upon it. But it would have one important result immediately; it would entitle the Sultan to let our fleets up to Constantinople, and that of itself would be checkmate to Russia.

Now, all this I write to you on the supposition that France is honest and can be trusted—not in the execution of the treaty, because, at all events, she could not help executing such an engagement,—but I mean in the previous negotiation; and you will use your judgment as to the degree to which you will confidentially sound Molé on this matter. If the only use he were to make of your suggestion were to be to make it known to Russia, and then to decline the plan, he would do us harm, because then Russia might take immediate steps at Constantinople which would prevent us from getting the sultan to agree to such a convention with England alone, and my perfect conviction is that such a convention between England and Turkey without even the participation of France would accomplish the great object I have mentioned. But we had rather have France with us in it, because the union of the two Powers would of course carry more weight with it. If indeed I was Autocrat I do not know whether considering how France is hampered about Algiers, I should not almost prefer the single treaty. But on the other hand it must not be forgotten that one great danger to Europe is the possibility of a combination between France and Russia, which, though prevented at present by the personal feelings of the Emperor, may not always be as impossible as it is now; and it would be well to fix the policy of France in the right track with respect to affairs of the Levant while we have the power to do so.

*   *   *   *

18. Palmerston's private letter to Granville, 6 July 1838. Granville MSS., P.R.O. 30/29/423; Bulwer, ii. 270–2.

According to your account of what Molé said to you upon Egyptian affairs, it seems to me that Sebastiani must have rather imperfectly brought the matter before his Government; I wish, therefore, that you would explain the thing to Molé, and urge him to authorize Sebastiani to co-operate with me in endeavouring to effect a joint arrangement on the subject between the five Powers. The short state of the case seems to be this: if Mehemet Ali finds the least disunion between the great Powers of Europe, he will endeavour to make himself independent, and take his chance of the split which consequent events may produce among us. But if he does declare himself independent, and war ensues between him and the Sultan, and the Russians interfere, the chances are that some serious quarrel will ensue between France and England on the one hand, and Russia on the other; or else that England and France will be forced to remain passive spectators of things done by Russia, which could not be acquiesced in without discredit to the Governments of England and France. The question then is, which is the most likely way to prevent Mehemet Ali from taking the step; and if he should nevertheless take it, which is the best way to prevent the evil consequences which that step might produce?

Our opinion is, that for both these purposes a previous concert between the five would be most desirable. First, that if we could announce to Mehemet that such a concert is established, and that we are all prepared conjointly to help the Sultan against him, he would abandon his intentions, and remain quiet. But next, we think that if, in spite of this warning, he was to move, such a concert would afford the best security for bringing the matter to an end without any disturbance of the peace of Europe. We wish, and so does Sebastiani, that the representatives of the five Powers should be assembled in London; that we should lay the case before them, say that all have already expressed the same opinion upon the subject and have given or intend to give similar instructions to their consuls in Egypt. But that such language ought not to be held by Great Powers without their having seen their way to act up to it in case of need; and that we therefore propose to them a combined system of action; that the Porte may want aid by sea and by land; that we propose that the three maritime Powers should give aid by sea, and Austria assistance by land; that we do not disguise from our allies that the solitary interference of Russia, however she may think herself either justified or bound to exert it, would excite great jealousy in this part of the world; that in the general interest and harmony it seems desirable to avoid such jealousy if it can be done with honour to all parties, and without any sacrifice of important interests; that the military action of Austria would from the intimate union existing between Austria and Russia be perfectly compatible with the honour of Russia, while, on the other hand, from the geographical position of Austria, it would not be the source of the same jealousy to England and France; that in all probability the mere announcement of such an arrangement would keep Mehemet quiet, but if it did not, it would at least insure a result consistent with the maintenance of general peace.

Moreover it is to be observed that the concert of the five Powers on the affairs of Belgium has tended rather to disunite than to bring together, and that it might be useful with a view to the general interests of Europe upon many other questions, if this affair of the Levant which left to itself might be the cause of war, were by skilful management converted into an occasion for greater harmony.

*   *   *   *

19. Extract from Palmerston's private letter to Henry Lytton Bulwer (Secretary of the Embassy at Constantinople), 22 September 1838. Copy in Broadlands MSS., GC/BU no. 492; Bulwer, ii. 286–7.

. . . I am glad to hear your opinions respecting the future prospects of the Sultan with reference to Egypt and Syria, because it is always interesting to know how matters strike an intelligent mind observing events on the spot.

I own that I have myself considerable doubts on the subject; but the present bent of my mind is to think that our policy should be founded upon the basis of an endeavour to maintain the Sultan and to uphold the integrity of the Turkish empire. To frame a system of future policy in the East upon the accidental position of a man turned seventy would be to build on sand; and no man can tell what will come when Mehemet Ali goes. A little addition of order, organization, and force to the scale of the Sultan, and a little less of sagacity, vigour of intellect, and administrative capacity on the part of the usurping Government of Egypt, would place Syria again at the command of the Sultan. The distance of Syria or of Egypt from Constantinople would be no bar to the effectual administration of those provinces by the Porte. Many provinces of other empires are just as far from the seat of Government. There can be no doubt that it is for the interest of England that the Sultan should by strong; and it is evident that he would be stronger with Syria and Egypt than without them. I am, therefore, for continuing to aim at a maintenance of the integrity of the empire; on the principle of 'That I can do when all I have is gone', we can think of a confederation when unity shall have been proved to be impossible.

People go on talking of the inevitable and progressive decay of the Turkish empire, which they say is crumbling to pieces.

In the first place, no empire is likely to fall to pieces if left to itself, and if no kind neighbours forcibly tear it to pieces. In the next place, I much question that there is any process of decay going on in the Turkish empire; and I am inclined to suspect that those who say that the Turkish empire is rapidly going from bad to worse ought rather to say that the other countries of Europe are year by year becoming better acquainted with the manifest and manifold defects of the organization of Turkey. But I should be disposed to think that, for some years past, the foundations at least of improvement have been laid; and it is certain that the daily increasing intercourse between Turkey and the other countries of Europe must in a few years, if peace can be preserved, throw much light upon the defects and weaknesses of the Turkish system, and lead to various improvements therein.

I should therefore be rather unwilling to propose at present any arrangement between Mehemet Ali and the Sultan founded upon the basis of a permanent alteration in their present mutual relations of sovereign and subject.

* * * *

20. Extract from Palmerston's private letter to Bulwer (Secretary of the Embassy in Paris), 1 September 1839. Bulwer, ii. 296–9.

Your letter of the 28th gives a very clear and distinct view of the confused and indistinct thinkings of the French Government. It is evident that, either from their own notions of French interests, or from fear of the newspapers, the French Government will not willingly take the slightest step of coercion against Mehemet Ali, either for the purpose of getting back the Turkish fleet, or in order to enforce any arrangement which the five Powers may agree to propose to the two parties. My last communications to you will, however, bring the French to a point. They will see from those communications that, anxious as we are to continue to go on with them, we are not at all prepared to stand still with them. . . .

They must therefore take their choice between three courses—either to go forward with us, and honestly redeem the pledges they have given to us and to Europe; or to stand aloof and shrink from a fulfilment of their own spontaneous declarations; or, lastly, to go right about and league themselves with Mehemet Ali, and employ force to prevent us and those other Powers who may join us from doing that which France herself is bound by every principle of honour, and every enlightened consideration of her real interests, to assist us in doing, instead of preventing from being done. I can hardly think Louis Philippe equal to the third course. The second is that which he would wish to pursue. But perhaps if he shall find that England, Austria, and Russia are agreed as to the first course he will follow us, even against his own inclination. The more I reflect on these matters the more convinced I am that there is no possibility of a permanent settlement without making Mehemet withdraw into his original shell of Egypt . . .

As to the Turkish empire, if we can procure for it ten years of peace under the joint protection of the five Powers, and if those years are profitably employed in reorganizing the internal system of the empire, there is no reason whatever why it should not become again a respectable Power. Half the wrong conclusions at which mankind arrive are reached by the abuse of metaphors, and by mistaking general resemblance or imaginary similarity for real identity. Thus people compare an ancient monarchy with an old building, an old tree, or an old man, and because the building, tree, or man must from the nature of things crumble, or decay, or die, they imagine that the same thing holds good with a community, and that the same laws which govern inanimate matter, or vegetable and animal life, govern also nations and states. Than which there cannot be a greater or more utterly unphilosophical mistake. For besides all other points of difference, it is to be remembered that the component parts of the building, tree, or man remain the same, and are either decomposed by external causes, or are altered in their internal structure by the process of life, so as ultimately to be unfit for their original functions; while, on the contrary, the component parts of a community are undergoing daily the process of physical renovation and of moral improvement. Therefore all that we hear every day of the week about the decay of the Turkish empire, and its being a dead body or a sapless trunk, and so forth, is pure and unadulterated nonsense.

21. Extract from Palmerston's private letter to Bulwer, 24 September 1839. Copy in Broadlands MSS., GC/BU no. 493; Bulwer, ii. 299-303.

* * * *

Brunnow says that the Emperor will entirely agree to our views as to the affairs of Turkey and Egypt, and will join in whatever measures may be necessary to carry those views into effect; and that he will unite with us, Austria, and Prussia, either with France or without her; and that though, politically speaking, he sees the advantage of having France of the party, personally he would be better pleased that she should be left out; that if we trust him as he hopes we do, and feels he deserves we should, he hopes we will trust him entirely, and not appear to show jealousy where we feel none;

that consequently, if the measures of Mehemet should place Constantinople in danger, and render necessary any naval or military operation in the Bosphorus or Asia Minor, he hopes we will leave that to him, and that we will on our part undertake whatever is to be done in the Mediterranean and on the coasts of Syria and Egypt; that he is willing not only that anything which he may do with his fleet and army shall be held to be the result of concert, and not the resolve of Russia alone, but he is ready to begin by signing a convention which shall define our objects, determine our means of accomplishment, and assign to each his appropriate part; and that of course under such a convention the Russian force would withdraw as it came whenever the object should have been attained; and Brunnow further said, in confidence, that if such a course were followed there would be no renewal of the treaty of Unkiar Skelessi. I have told Sebastiani all this, except the preference of the Emperor to leave France out. I said that I had seen Esterhazy, who entirely agreed with me, individually, that it would for many weighty reasons be highly expedient to accept this offer, but that I could not say what the Cabinet may resolve upon a matter which it has not yet deliberated upon, and that Esterhazy could not say what his Government would determine upon an overture with which it had not yet been made acquainted.

Sebastiani seemed little pleased with the prospect which this step of Russia seems to open of an arrangement of the Turco-Egyptian question in entire accordance with the views of the British Government; but the only point on which he much dwelt was the objection which he urged against leaving to Russia the task of defending Constantinople, which he represented as confirming Russian influence and preponderance in Turkey. I said I did not see this, because if the parts assigned to each Power were to be determined by previous convention, each would act, not for herself, but for the whole, and exclusive influence no longer followed. Besides, I said, it seemed to me that there was no wise medium between confidence and distrust; and that if we tie up Russia by treaty we may trust her, and trusting her, we had better mix no evidence of suspicion with our confidence. He at last only contended for our having a ship or two anchored within the Dardanelles if the Russians should be called to Constantinople; but that would be childish. Throughout the conversation I treated the matter as if France would of course be a party to the proposed convention, and he discussed it upon that assumption. As to the arrangement itself, nothing can be more miserable than the shifts and changes in the opinions and schemes of the French Government; and it is evident that they have wishes and objects at bottom which they are ashamed of confessing. That, in short, their great and only aim is to do as much as they possibly can do for Mehemet Ali, without caring a pin for the Sultan, or having the least regard for their declarations and pledges. . . . I wish you to see Soult [French Prime Minister, May 1839–February 1840], and to ascertain from him what Sebastiani has written, and what the French Government mean to do, letting Soult understand, that although the Cabinet has not yet come to a decision, they will meet about this matter in a day or two; and that the probability is, that they will resolve to proceed in conjunction with the three Powers whether France joins or not; but that on every possible account we should deeply regret that France should not be a party to the proceeding; and you might observe that France has distinctly approved of our object, though from internal difficulties she may hesitate as to taking a share in the means of execution. If Soult should hint that France would oppose the four Powers, you might suggest that she could not do so consistently with her own spontaneous declarations, and that it could not be worth while for France to make war with the four Powers for the sake of endeavouring to give to Mehemet a few square miles and some hundred thousand people in southern Syria; that no French interest could be promoted thereby; while, on the contrary, the character of France as a country which adheres to her word would thereby be greatly affected.

22. Extract from a Memorandum forwarded to Palmerston by Clarendon (then Lord Privy Seal), 14 March 1840. Broadlands MSS., GC/CL no. 438; Herbert Maxwell, *The Life and Letters of George William Frederick Fourth Earl of Clarendon* (London, 1913), i. 186–93.

. . . I must however in the first place entirely disown the 'weakness' you impute to me for 'that aged *afrancesado* freebooter, Mehemet Ali.' I can have no predilection for the Pacha over the Sultan; on the contrary, my tendencies are naturally in favor of the Sovereign and against the Vassal; but I look upon Mehemet Ali as representing great power, which, however much its existence may be lamented, can neither be denied nor despised. I consequently think he commands consideration and that the treatment he receives from us should have reference to *his* position and *our* means of influencing him.

With respect to his being an *afrancesado*, I believe he is so contrary to his inclinations, because his interests would manifestly lead him to seek an alliance with us rather than with any other Power. Our maritime superiority, our Indian vicinage, and the annually increasing commercial relation of Egypt with England, must make our friendship more valuable to him than that of France, from whom he must fear encroachment. But a man in the position of Mehemet Ali has to seek support where he can find it, and if he meets repulse from us, we cannot wonder if he throws himself into the open arms of France.

The accusation against him, however, is of comparatively recent date, for the *fons et origo* of our antipathy to him was the idea that he was a devoted instrument of Russian ambition—an idea which probably never had any foundation, as Mehemet Ali is too acute not to know that the only Power which the Ottoman Empire, however ruled or however divided it may be, has to fear is Russia.

Then as regards Mehemet Ali being a freebooter—I believe he has merely exhibited the same propensities which power never fails to engender in us all. He waxed strong and became aggressive, and really, when we think of the partition of Poland, of Austria in Italy, of France in Africa, and of ourselves *passim*—north, south, east and west, Gibraltar, Malta, the Ionian islands, the Cape, and our 100 million of Indian subjects—I cannot but think that giving ugly names to those who, being strong, have oppressed the weak, and who, being able to extend their dominions, have done so, is not very unlike Peachum and Lockit, and the less said about it the better. We must not either judge Sultans or Pachas by our European standard of sovereignty and allegiance; we must not disregard Eastern history and practice, and they teach us, that it is the *custom* for Sultans and Pachas to be at war with each other—that immediately a Pacha becomes strong, the Sultan endeavours by force or by intrigue to crush him, and that he resists upon grounds of self-preservation. He has to choose between defying his sovereign and losing his head, and it is not wonderful, therefore, that Eastern history should abound with instances of the former selection. How many attempts has the Porte not made to destroy Mehemet Ali?

How often has he [Mehemet] not been compelled to employ in self defence the means which he had created; and can we, in common justice, throw upon him all the obloquy which in civilised countries, with regular governments, attaches to rebellion?

All this, however, is beside the question, and I only wish to affirm that I have no fancies about foreign nations or individuals, and that, in any opinion I may form upon our relations with other countries, I look only to what may be most for the honor and advantage of England, and to what offers the fairest prospect of extending her commercial relations and the sphere of her influence and power.

We wish to maintain the 'integrity' of Turkey, but the word is somewhat vague and the interpretation to be given to it not very easy. When we consider that at no period of this century can Turkey be said to have had undisturbed possession of Syria, that a large portion of it was held in defiance of the Sultan by the Pacha of Acre who, dying in 1804, named one of his Mamelukes as his successor, and that he was recognised by the Porte, while the Druses, and the Maronites, and other tribes kept the remainder of Syria in perpetual insurrection; when we consider that the Morea and the islands of the Archipelago are lost to Turkey, that the Powers of Europe have made an independent kingdom of Greece, that Bessarabia and the provinces of the Euxine are become Russian, that Servia has an independent Prince, that Wallachia and Moldavia are under the protectorate of Russia, that Bosnia and Albania are in a state of *de facto* independence, that Arabia was lost to the Wahabees, that Egypt has for more than thirty years been despotically governed by Mehemet Ali, that the Pachalik of Arabia has been given to his son, and that the Powers of Europe are prepared solemnly to invest his family with the Pachalik of Egypt, I must consider the term 'integrity' vague and, as the groundwork of a system, not easy to be interpreted.

The word, however, according to its present application means slicing off Egypt *from* the Porte, and annexing Syria and Arabia *to* the Porte, and by that form of 'integrity' the 'independence' of Turkey is to be secured, or in other words, Turkey will then be able to resist Russia, for that is after all the real question—the only one that really interests or affects us, and call it by what name we may, or Austria may—integrity, independence, raising up or consolidating the Ottoman Empire—fear of Russia and desire to keep her out of Constantinople is at the bottom of all, and most properly so.

Will Turkey, then, under the contemplated arrangement be more able to resist Russia than she is now? It is my humble opinion that she will not, and that it is a fallacy to consider accession of territory synonymous with accession of strength. I believe it would be injurious to the interests of Turkey to transfer to her remote and turbulent provinces which she cannot hold. For the last forty years the state of Syria has been a permanent cause of misfortune to the Porte and has engaged her in perpetual wars, with twelve millions of revenue and a disposable army of 120,000 men; and when the population of Turkey was upwards of 15,000,000 she could not hold peaceable possession of Syria and Arabia. How could she do so now, when her revenue is not four millions? when she has no army at all—when her population is reduced by one half? What chance of authority would the Porte have now in those countries, and how could she be fitter to resist the encroachments of Russia when she had weakened herself by disseminating the little force she has in endeavours to establish her dominion and to quell the insurrection that would everywhere break out upon those Provinces being restored to her nominal rule?

Admitting, however, to its fullest extent the desirableness of such transfer, can we procure its accomplishment? Have we any available means for the purpose? England cannot give a man nor a shilling towards it, nor will Austria, and neither Power will permit Russia (even if Russia were inclined to embark in such an undertaking) to do it single-handed, and France will not only not join in any measure of coercion, but would probably at once take part with Mehemet Ali if they were attempted. To attack Alexandria is impossible: to destroy the Pacha's fleet in the port would be at the same time to destroy the Sultan's, together with a large amount of European shipping and property: to blockade the coast would be of doubtful efficacy for its object and it would be most injurious to our trade and produce, consequently [causing] great outcry at home. It would be somewhat distasteful to Americans and other neutral Powers, and we should run great risk of collision with France, for French adventurers reckoning on the protection of their flag and the profit to be made under it, would soon swarm to the assistance of Mehemet Ali and the first chastisement inflicted upon any of them would raise a war whoop from one end of France to the other.

If France were acting cordially with us and Mehemet Ali were without the encouragement which her advice, promises, and general moral support give him, I have no doubt he would submit now, altho' without any intention of remaining quiet hereafter; but France is not, and will not be, with us; we must take things as they are and be prepared to sacrifice a portion of what we are aiming at in order to secure for England her first and most indispensable necessity—peace. The Whig government has now for ten years (contrary to all predictions and in defiance of circumstances the most calculated to bring about war) maintained the peace of the world, and it would indeed be lamentable if, for objects with which in reality we have little to do, the curse of war were entailed upon us at a moment when we are so ill able to bear it that it would almost amount to national ruin. If suspicion only of such a danger be excited here, public opinion would soon find the means of paralysing the course of the government.

Looking exclusively at our own interests, I cannot but think they lie more in the direction of Egypt than of Turkey. The overland communication with India is daily becoming more important; it can hardly yet be said to be established, because as yet it is not connected with steam navigation, as it ought to be and will be; still, what benefits we already derive from it, and how many more may be expected when this *discovery* becomes fully developed! By the policy however, which we are now pursuing, we shall drive Mehemet Ali to declare his independence, which France will as surely recognise as we shall *not*, and we shall then have France thwarting us in Egypt with all her jealousy and all her resources, and the hostility which this will create on our part towards Mehemet Ali will only make France the more necessary to him, and rivet him more securely in her grasp.

As regards the progress of civilisation, too, and the development of the commercial and agricultural resources of the East, I think we have much more to expect from the Pacha than from the Sultan. It is true his government has been bad, that he has pursued a most ill-advised system of monopoly, which, together with the conscription, have kept the people in extreme poverty; still however Egypt has made great strides towards improvement under his reign; the productive powers of the country have been stimulated in a manner unknown in modern times. To him [it] is owing that Egypt is a cotton-growing and corn-exporting country; he has established and extended commercial relations with all the world; he is the only Mussulman who has really shown a desire to turn to account the knowledge, and education and superiority of Christians, and if he has been able to effect vast improvements during a long period of war, when his energies and resources were mainly devoted to the creation of the army and the navy he now possesses, how much more might not be expected of him on the restoration of tranquillity, when his soldiers again became laborers and he [has] adopted the more enlightened system of government and commerce which he is prepared for, as he now acknowledges and repents the errors he formerly committed?

What Mehemet Ali has done has been the work of a few years; while the Turks for nearly four centuries have occupied an enormous empire, stretching from 34° to 48° north and upon the same parallels of latitude with France, Spain and all the best portion of the U[nited] States. The soil of many parts of Turkey is the finest in the world; mines of silver, copper and iron still exist; cotton, tobacco and silk might be made the staple exports of the country; the wines are excellent; every species of tree flourishes in Turkey, and the animal productions are not less valuable than those of vegetable life. Yet in this favored region the population has retrograded, whilst surrounded by abundance; its wealth and industry have been annihilated; manufactures are unknown; commerce is despised; and ignorance, barbarism and poverty prevail. Can we then expect that these evils, 400 years old, and the vices that a brutalising government have almost made inherent in Turkish nature, should be eradicated by a Hatti Sheriff [the Sultan's reform decree of 3 November 1839], the duration of which even Lord Ponsonby [the Ambassador at Constantinople], admits to depend upon Reschid Pacha's frail tenure of office [as Turkish Foreign Minister]? Should we not rather turn to where some vitality has been exhibited and where amelioration, tho[ugh] slow, has still been constantly progressing? If it is to the advance of civilisation and to administrative improvements, with all their consequences, that we look for the means of checking Russia, Mehemet Ali will surely (having tranquillity in his favor) present a more imposing barrier than will be produced by the Hatti Sheriff, which for many years will be a dead letter, if it ever is anything else.

* * * *

I would come to an understanding with Mehemet Ali. I would treat him as a reasonable and easily-to-be flattered man. I would negotiate for the Porte the best terms I could; I would endeavour to obtain Adana and such portions of Syria as are Turkish, and which the Sultan might fairly hope to keep possession of (say as far as Aleppo, for south of Aleppo, I believe, the Turkish language is not even spoken). Arabia he [Mehemet] would give up and Candia [Crete] likewise; but the former it would be unadvisable in my opinion for the Porte to accept. I would then confer upon him the hereditary Pachalik of the remainder. I would next make him party to a treaty by which the whole should be formally arranged. The Powers of Europe could of course not make a treaty with him, but he might make one with the Sultan which should be guaranteed by them. He should further stipulate the amount of tribute he is to pay; he should engage never on any pretext (unless called upon by the Sultan to do so) to pass the frontier of his Pachalik, nor under any plea whatever to attempt making himself independent of the Porte, and that, failing in any of these, he would subject himself to the collective displeasure of the Powers guaranteeing the treaty to the Sultan.

I do not think Mehemet Ali could refuse this, because, by so doing, he would give the lie to all the professions he is now making; besides, it would be his interest to conclude such a bargain. France could not well decline to be a party to it, and we should thereby secure her never recognising the independence of the Pacha; and so long as he abided by the agreement and kept within his own territories, Russia could have no pretence for interfering. No treaty of Unkiar Skelessi would be necessary: no *casus foederis* would arise; but if Mehemet Ali did violate his engagements and intervention became necessary, it would be by all the Powers combined (France could have no pretext for seceding) and not by Russia alone.

* * * *

23. Palmerston's private letter to Melbourne, 5 July 1840. Copy in Broadlands MSS., GC/ME no. 536; Bulwer, ii. 356–61.

The difference of opinion which seems to exist between myself and some members of the Cabinet upon the Turkish question, and the extreme importance which I attach to that question, have led me, upon full consideration, to the conviction that it is a duty which I owe to myself and to my colleagues to relieve you and others from the necessity of deciding between my views and those of other members of the Cabinet on these matters, by placing, as I now do, my office at your disposal.

I have, indeed, for some time past found myself in a difficult situation in regard to this affair.

The collective note of July last, the decision of the Cabinet held at Windsor in October, the course and tenour of my written communications with foreign Governments for several months past, sent round in circulation to the Cabinet; our verbal communications with the envoys and ministers of those Governments in this country, and with Brunnow in particular; the two drafts of convention, which, if I mistake not, I read some time ago to the Cabinet, the one drawn up by myself, the other by Brunnow and Neumann, were all founded upon one view of the question, namely, the expediency of maintaining the independence and integrity of the Turkish empire; and I have considered myself as negotiating with the knowledge and sanction of the Cabinet in furtherance of that view. On the other hand, other members of the Cabinet have, in their conversations with those very foreign ministers with whom I was thus negotiating, held language and opinions founded upon a different view of the matter; and I have been told from various quarters, that persons not belonging to the Government, but known to be in habits of intimacy with members of the Government, have studiously, both at home and abroad, inculcated the belief that my views were not those of the majority of my colleagues, and that consequently I was not in this matter to be considered as the organ of the sentiments of the British Government.

The particular and immediate object which I have been endeavouring for some months past to accomplish, in conjunction with the representatives of Austria, Russia, and Prussia, has been to persuade the French Government to come in to some plan of arrangement between the Sultan and Mehemet Ali, which the other four Powers could consider compatible with the integrity of the Turkish empire, and with the political independence of the Porte. In this I have ultimately failed. Perhaps the object was in any case unattainable in the present stage of the affair; but the circumstances to which I have adverted were certainly not calculated to diminish my difficulties.

The question which the British Government now has to decide is, whether the four Powers, having failed in persuading France to join them, will or will not proceed to accomplish their purpose without the assistance of France; but with the certainty, both from positive and repeated declarations of the French Government and from conclusive political considerations, that they will meet with no assistance from France in the execution of their measures.

My opinion upon this question is distinct and unqualified. I think that the object to be attained is of the utmost importance for the interests of England, for the preservation of the balance of power, and for the maintenance of peace in Europe. I find the three Powers entirely prepared to concur in the views which I entertain on this matter, if those views should be the views of the British Government. I can feel no doubt that the four Powers, acting in union with and in support of the Sultan, are perfectly able to carry those views into effect; and I think that the commercial and political interests of Great Britain, the honour and dignity of the country, good faith towards the Sultan, and sound views of European policy, all require that we should adopt such a course.

I think, on the other hand, that if we draw back, and shrink from a co-operation with Austria, Russia, and Prussia in this matter, because France stands aloof and will not join, we shall place this country in the degraded position of being held in leading-strings by France, and shall virtually acknowledge that, even when supported by the other three Powers of the Continent, we dare embark in no system of policy in opposition to the will of France, and consider her positive concurrence as a necessary condition for our action. Now this appears to me to be a principle of policy which is not suitable to the power and station of England, and which must frequently, as I think it would in the present instance, lead England to make herself subservient to the views of France for the accomplishment of purposes injurious to British interests.

The immediate result of our declining to go on with the three Powers because France does not join us will be, that Russia will withdraw her offers to unite herself with the other Powers for a settlement of the affairs of Turkey, and she will again resume her separate and isolated position with respect to those affairs; and you will have the treaty of Unkiar Skelessi renewed under some still more objectionable form. We shall thus lose the advantages on this point which it has required long-continued and complicated efforts on our part to gain, and England will, by her own voluntary and deliberate act, re-establish that separate protectorship of Russia over Turkey, the existence of which has long been the object of well-founded jealousy and apprehension to the other Powers of Europe.

The ultimate results of such a decision will be the practical division of the Turkish empire into two separate and independent states, whereof one will be the dependency of France, and the other a satellite of Russia; and in both of which our political influence will be annulled, and our commercial interests will be sacrificed; and this dismemberment will inevitably give rise to local struggles and conflicts which will involve the Powers of Europe in most serious disputes.

I have given to these matters for some years past my best and unremitting attention. I do not know that I ever had a stronger conviction upon any matter of equal importance; and I am very sure that, if my judgment is wrong on this matter, it can be of little value upon any other.

Twice my opinion on these affairs has been overruled by the Cabinet, and twice the policy which I recommended has been set aside. First, in 1833, when the Sultan sent to ask our aid before Mehemet Ali had made any material progress in Syria, and when Russia expressed her wish that we should assist the Sultan—saying, however, that if we did not, she would. Secondly in 1835, when France was ready to have united with us in a treaty with the Sultan for the maintenance of the integrity of his empire. Subsequent events in each instance showed that I had not overrated the imminence of the danger which I wanted to avert, nor the magnitude of the embarrassments which I wished to prevent.

We are now arrived at a third crisis, when the resolution of the British Cabinet will exercise a deciding influence upon future events; but this time the danger is more apparent and undisguised, and the remedy is more complete and within our reach.

The matter to be dealt with belongs to my own department, and I should be held in a peculiar degree personally responsible for the consequences of any course which I might undertake to conduct. I am sure, therefore, that you cannot wonder that I should decline to be the instrument for carrying out a policy which I disapprove, and that I should consequently take the step which I have stated in the beginning of this letter.

24. Minute of Cabinet Meeting of 8 July 1840. Royal Archives, GI/9; Harold Temperley, *England and the Near East : the Crimea* (London, 1936), pp. 487–8.

Present
Viscount Melbourne, Viscount Duncannon, Lord Cottenham, Lord Holland, The Marquess of Lansdowne, Viscount Morpeth, The Earl of Clarendon, Sir John Hobhouse, The Marquess of Normanby, Mr. Baring, The Earl of Minto, Mr. Labouchere, Lord John Russell, Mr. Macaulay, Viscount Palmerston.

Your Majesty's confidential Servants most humbly submit to Your Majesty, that after a Negotiation of several Months, the Governments of Great Britain, Austria, Prussia, and Russia, have been unable to prevail upon the Government of France to unite with the Four Powers above mentioned and with the Porte, in carrying into effect Such an arrangement of the Differences between The Sultan and Mehemet Ali, as, in the opinion of those Governments, would be consistent with the Principle upon which the Collective Note of the 27 July 1839 was founded, or with the Spirit of the Negotiations which have Since taken Place; and under these Circumstances, Your Majesty's Confidential Servants, with the Exception of the Earl of Clarendon and Lord Holland are humbly of opinion that it is expedient that Viscount Palmerston Should prepare for Consideration a Draft of a Convention between the Four Powers and the Porte, founded upon the Principle of the Collective Note, and in accordance with the Spirit of the Subsequent Negotiations.

The Earl of Clarendon and Lord Holland in fulfilment of those Duties which Your Majesty's Gracious appointment imposes upon every Confidential Servant of Your Crown, feel themselves painfully compelled to acknowledge that they cannot concur in the Minute which is this Day submitted to the Consideration of Your Majesty.

Your Majesty is therein advised to accede to a Treaty which has for it's [*sic*] object the Expulsion of Mehemet Ali from Syria and Candia, & of his Son from the Pachalick of Arabia conferred upon him by the late Sultan—Such Interference appears to Lord Clarendon and Lord Holland to be questionable in Policy, and neither necessary to the Honour of Your Majesty's Crown in satisfaction of the Obligations contracted in the Collective Note of July 1839, nor directly or obviously advantageous to Your Majesty's Subjects.

The means by which it is proposed that these Objects, in the event of Resistance, should be attained seem to them insufficient and yet onerous, and, above all, hazardous in the extreme.—Your Majesty in no remote or improbable Contingency may be required in virtue of the Stipulation of such a Treaty to wage War on the Coasts, and to sanction the Introduction of other Foreign and European Troops into the Asiatic Provinces of Turkey.

Such Operations, in themselves humiliating to the Mussulman Powers, and ominous of the dismemberment of the Sultan's Dominions, even if they should be eminently successful cannot in the actual State of those Provinces be expected to enlarge the Resources or to consolidate the Strength of the Ottoman Empire.—They must in the first instance interrupt the Commerce of Your Majesty's Subjects with Countries now occupied by Mehemet Ali or his Son. —They must also interrupt or suspend the convenient Intercourse recently established through Egypt with Your Majesty's Eastern Possessions.—These Sacrifices would in the Apprehension of Lord Clarendon and Lord Holland be of no inconsiderable Importance, but the more remote and indirect, tho' it is feared not less undeniable tendency of the Treaty and of the Measures of Coercion arising therefrom threatens Consequences far more extensive and disastrous.—They may lead to a disturbance of that System of Policy and Alliances in Europe which under the happy auspices of Your Majesty and Your Predecessor has succeeded in preserving the Peace of the World, and has redounded to the Glory of Your Majesty's Crown by increasing the Prosperity of Your People and enabling their Enterprize and Industry to extend the Intercourse and improve the condition of Mankind in every Quarter of the Globe.—

Apprehensive of Consequences so alarming should any Coercion be resorted to for effecting the Purposes of the Treaty, Lord Clarendon and Lord Holland could not but refrain from becoming the Advisers of such a Step; And although earnestly solicitous to prevent all appearance as well as reality of Difference in Your Majesty's Councils, they yet feel it incumbent upon them to explain without Reserve, but they trust without Impropriety, the fact and grounds of their withholding their Assent to the Advice this Day submitted to the Consideration of Your Majesty.

25. Extract from Earl Spencer's private letter to Lord Tavistock, 25 August 1840. (Tavistock was Lord John Russell's elder brother; Russell was shown the letter and was apparently persuaded by it to challenge Palmerston's policy in the Cabinet.) Russell MSS., P.R.O. 30/22/3D; Spencer Walpole, *The Life of Lord John Russell* (London, 1889), i. 347–8.

I am very glad you are pleased and satisfied with the state of our foreign affairs. It is a good deal more than I am. I have been and am fully prepared to support Melbourne's Government to any length short of absolute criminality, but I should consider myself atrociously criminal if I supported them in any war which was not strictly and absolutely necessary. Now no war for the purpose of driving the Egyptians out of Syria can be anything like necessary. I am glad however you are satisfied because I feel almost confident you would not be satisfied unless Palmerston had proved to you that there was no danger of war. Whether there is danger of immediate war or not however, still I cannot imagine what can have induced Palmerston to abandon the French Alliance by which we have hitherto preserved the peace of Europe, and to connect us with the Holy Alliance again. Baring [presumably Sir Francis Baring, later Lord Northbrook, Chancellor of the Exchequer, 1839–1841] in 1830 prophesied we should not remain at peace a twelve-month, and if I was inclined to be a prophet, I should make the same prophesy now, unless we immediately conciliate the French and back out of our convention with Russia as quickly as we can. I hope and trust the language I see in the *Globe* [see above p. 9] does not express the feeling of any one of the Ministers, but from what I know of that paper I am not very confident of this, for there I see the same tone employed about France which was the tone of the Pittite newspapers in the first French war. We used to hear then that France would not go to war, but then as now you have only to give France sufficient provocation, and it will not require a great deal, and she will show that she is as capable as ever to drive the Russians, Austrians, and Prussians flying before her. I am no advocate of truckling to France, but surely there is no truckling in keeping friends with the nation in Europe most fitted to be our friend by situation, institutions, and civilization. You see by what I have said that I am very far indeed from being satisfied or pleased with what appears to me to be the state of our foreign affairs. I wish that the circumstances of which I am necessarily ignorant may be such as would lead me to a different conclusion if I was aware of them. I form my judgement only on appearances. Since we have made a treaty and left out France I assume that this was not done in any way that would make it more offensive to France than the connecting ourselves with her natural enemies must necessarily be. I see also that France is making warlike preparations and I see a hostile tone taken on both sides. This is a most lamentable state of things and I cannot form a conception of any circumstances which can justify our Government for allowing matters to have got into this state, and to me personally this last is the most lamentable consideration of all.

*   *   *   *

26. Extract from Palmerston's private letter to Granville, 29 October 1840. Granville MSS., P.R.O. 30/29/425; Bulwer, ii. 347–9.

Louis Philippe seems to have held to you . . . that it is necessary, in order to assist the King to maintain peace and keep down the war party, that we should make to the entreaties of the King those concessions which we have refused to the threats of Thiers. But this is quite impossible, and you cannot too soon or too strongly explain it to all parties concerned. We have not acted as we have done out of spite against Thiers, nor from any personal feeling of good-will or ill-will towards any man; nor can such feelings be made the foundation of the political conduct of a Government in matters of great European importance. We withstood the threats of Thiers, because what he asked could not be granted without great injury to the interests of Europe; and we cannot expose those interests to injury out of complaisance to Louis Philippe or Guizot, any more than out of fear for Thiers; and, moreover, if we were to give way, the French nation would believe that we gave way to their menaces, and not to the entreaties of Louis Philippe. Besides, there would be an end of all things if the Powers of Europe were to be making sacrifices of their important interests to appease the organizers of *émeutes* in Paris or to silence the republican newspapers; and then into the bargain we are carrying all before us in Syria, and shall very soon have placed the whole of that country in the hands of the Sultan; and it would indeed be childish to hold our hands when nothing but a little perseverance is required in order to carry all our points. Then also if the French Government choose to publish every communication which is made to them upon pending matters they must take the consequences; and the publication of my despatch to Ponsonby renders it impossible for us to go one step beyond what is stated in that despatch. I can assure you that you would be most usefully supporting the interests of peace by holding a firm and stout language to the French Government and to Frenchmen.

Nothing is more unsound than the notion that anything is to be gained by trying to conciliate those who are trying to intimidate us; by conciliate I mean to conciliate by concession. It is quite right to be courteous in words, but the only possible way of keeping such persons in check is to make them clearly understand that one is not going to yield an inch, and that one is quite strong enough to repel force by force.

Some of our Whig friends and grandees have done great mischief by giving way to unfounded alarms and holding what is called conciliatory language. The knowledge of the existence of such feelings and language in many quarters, where more spirit and sagacity ought to have been shown, has, I know, very much encouraged the French in their attempts to bully.

My opinion is that we shall not have war now, but that we ought to make our minds up to have war with France before many years have passed. Now we are allied with and backed by all Europe and France is not mad enough to break her head against such a coalition. But I have for some time seen a spirit of bitter hostility towards England growing up among Frenchmen of all classes and of all parties; and sooner or later this must lead to conflict between the two nations. Broglie and Guizot pass for being Anglomanes, but be assured that neither of them are friendly to us in their hearts.

All Frenchmen want to encroach and extend their territorial possessions at the expense of other nations, and they all feel what the *National* has often said, that an alliance with England is a bar to such projects. I am not in the least surprised that the *doctrinaires* in Thiers' Government should have been the most warlike. I should rather have expected it to be so. I do not blame the French for disliking us. Their vanity prompts them to be the first nation in the world; and yet at every turn they find that we outstrip them in everything. It is a misfortune to Europe that the national character of a great and powerful people, placed in the centre of Europe, and capable of doing their neighbours much harm should be such as it is; but it is the business of other nations not to shut their eyes to the truth, and to shape their conduct by prudent precautions so as to prevent this nation from breaking loose as long as possible.

27. Palmerston's dispatch no. 6 to the Marquess of Clanricarde (Ambassador in St. Petersburg), 11 January 1841. P.R.O., F.O. 181/168; Temperley and Penson, pp. 135–8.

I have received Your Excellency's despatch No. 76 of the 22nd of December, marked 'Confidential', reporting the wish expressed to You by The Emperor of Russia that some engagement should be entered into between England and the other three Great Powers who are Parties to the Treaty of July, with the view of providing for the contingency of an attack by France upon the liberties of Europe: and I have to instruct Your Excellency thereupon to state to His Imperial Majesty that Her Majesty's Government are much gratified by the confidence which he reposes in the Government of England, and by the frank and open manner in which he has been pleased to communicate his views and opinions to Your Excellency. Her Majesty's Government will be equally open with the Emperor, and will state to His Imperial Majesty exactly their sentiments on the subject on which he has touched in his conversation with Your Excellency.

One of the general principles which Her Majesty's Government wish to observe as a guide for their conduct in dealing with the relations between England and other States, is, that changes which foreign Nations may chuse to make in their internal Constitution and form of Government, are to be looked upon as matters with which England has no business to interfere by force of arms, for the purpose of imposing upon such Nations a Form of Government which they do not wish to have, or for the purpose of preventing such Nations having Institutions which they desire. These things are considered in England to be matters of domestic concern, which every Nation ought to be allowed to settle as it likes.

But an attempt of one Nation to seize and to appropriate to itself territory which belongs to another Nation, is a different matter; because such an attempt leads to a derangement of the existing Balance of Power, and by altering the relative strength of States, may tend to create danger to other Powers; and such attempts therefore, the British Government holds itself at full liberty to resist, upon the universally acknowledged principle of self-defence.

Now, it is quite true, as stated by The Emperor, that any Country, such as France, for instance, may, under the plea and pretext of altering its own Institutions, seek to overthrow the existing Governments of other Countries, for the purpose of adding those Countries to its own Territories, or of associating them with its own aggressive system; and such proceedings would cease to be domestic changes of arrangement, and would assume the unquestionable character of external aggression.—Such attempts England has in former times on many occasions resisted; and it is highly probable that if a similar case were again to arise, England would again pursue a similar course.

But it is not usual for England to enter into engagements with reference to cases which have not actually arisen, or which are not immediately in prospect: and this for a plain reason. All formal engagements of the Crown, which involve the question of peace and war, must be submitted to Parliament; and Parliament might probably not approve of an engagement which should bind England prospectively to take up Arms in a contingency which might happen at an uncertain time, and under circumstances which could not as yet be foreseen.

It is true that His Imperial Majesty has spoken of an understanding which need not be recorded in any formal Instrument; but upon which He might rely if the Turn of Affairs should render it applicable to events. But this course would not be free from objections. For, in the first place, it would scarcely be consistent with the spirit of the British Constitution for the Crown to enter into a binding engagement of such a nature, without placing it formally upon record, so that Parliament might have an opportunity of expressing its opinion thereupon, and this could only be done by some written Instrument; and to such a course the objection which I have alluded to above, would apply. But if the engagement were merely verbal, though it would bind the Ministers who made it, it might be disavowed by their successors; and thus the Russian Government might be led to count upon a system of policy on the part of Great Britain, which might not eventually be pursued.

Under these circumstances, it seems to Her Majesty's Government that the Cabinet of St. Petersburgh should be satisfied to trust to the general tendency of the policy of Great Britain, which leads her to watch attentively, and to guard with care the maintenance of the Balance of Power: and Her Majesty's Government hope that His Imperial Majesty will not think that this policy is the less deeply rooted in the minds of Her Majesty's Government, if they should not think it expedient to enter at the present moment into engagements such as those mentioned by The Emperor.

28. Palmerston's private letter to H. S. Fox (Minister in Washington), 9 February 1841. Fox MSS., P.R.O., F.O. 97/19; Bulwer, iii. 48–50.

We most entirely approve the tone you have taken and the language you have held about the affair of Mr. McLeod, and so do the public in general. There never was a matter upon which all parties Tory, Whig, and Radical more entirely agreed; and if any harm should be done to McLeod the indignation and resentment of all England will be extreme. Mr. Van Buren [the American President] should understand this, and that the British nation will never permit a British subject to be dealt with as the people of New York propose to deal with McLeod, without taking a signal revenge upon the offenders. McLeod's execution would produce war; war immediate and frightful in its character, because it would be a war of retaliation and vengeance.

It is impossible that Mr. Forsyth [the American Secretary of State] can wish to bring upon the two countries such a calamity, and we can have no doubt that he will prevent it. He must have the means of doing so, or else the Federal Union exists but in name. But I presume that if we tell him that in the event of McLeod's execution we should make war upon the State of New York, he would reply that in such case we should *ipso facto* be at war with the rest of the Union. But if that is so, the rest of the Union must have the means of preventing the State of New York from doing a thing which would involve the whole Union in war with England. Forsyth's doctrine is pure nullification doctrine; but that is what he cannot intend to maintain.

I have spoken most seriously to Stevenson [United States Minister in London] on this matter, and I have told him, speaking not officially, but as a private friend that if McLeod is executed there must be war. He said he quite felt it; that he is aware that all parties have but one feeling on the subject, and he promised to write to the President privately as well as officially by to-day's post.

29. Extract from Palmerston's House of Commons Speech on the Corn Laws, 16 February 1842. *Hansard*, 3rd series, lx. 618–19.

. . . there are larger grounds on which this doctrine [of economic self-sufficiency] ought to be repudiated by this House. Why is the earth on which we live divided into zones and climates? Why, I ask, do different countries yield different productions to people experiencing similar wants? Why are they intersected with mighty rivers—the natural highways of nations? Why are lands the most distant from each other, brought almost into contact by the very ocean which seems to divide them? Why, Sir, it is that man may be dependent upon man. It is that the exchange of commodities may be accompanied by the extension and diffusion of knowledge— by the interchange of mutual benefits engendering mutual kind feelings—multiplying and confirming friendly relations. It is, that commerce may freely go forth, leading civilisation with one hand, and peace with the other, to render mankind happier, wiser, better.

30. Extract from Aberdeen's private letter to Ashburton, 26 September 1842. Copy in Aberdeen MSS., B.M., Add. MS. 43123; Wilbur Devereux Jones, *Lord Aberdeen and the Americas* (Athens, Georgia, 1958), p. 14.

* * * *

The Treaty was at first either well, or silently received; but under the inspiration of Palmerston, the *Chronicle* has opened a series of attacks, and the *Globe* has quite changed the language it had first employed. Other papers have joined in taking up the same views, and we must expect a fierce hostility. But I am well satisfied, and am not at all afraid. The more the whole subject shall be discussed, the more favourable I think the result will be; and I think that we ought to take care to let our feelings be known in the most unequivocal manner.

As throughout the whole of this affair I have written to you with perfect frankness, I will now say that the only part of the negotiation which causes me any regret is the abandonment of the upper part of the St. John, as the boundary. I think it might have been obtained by perseverance; and although in point of value the difference is unimportant, the effect here would have been considerable. I am not certain that, failing to obtain the whole line of the St. John, it might not have been preferable, for the sake of the impression to be produced, to have adhered without alteration to the Award of the King of the Netherlands in all its parts.

I have said however that I am perfectly satisfied; and this is really the case. It is only with the view of being enabled more effectually to resist a popular ground of attack that I would have wished for any change.

The good temper in which you have left them all, and the prospect of a continued peace, with I trust improved friendly relations, far outweigh in my mind the value of any additional extent of Pine Swamp.

31. Extract from Palmerston's private letter to Lord Monteagle (formerly T. Spring Rice), 28 October 1842. Copy in Broadlands MSS., GC/MO no. 131.

... The Conquests which have been made without Bloodshed have indeed been made by the United States, for they have gained & have wrested from us by the Pen districts which they never would have acquired by the Sword; but if Ashburton ought ... to be made a Duke for such conquests, his Dukedom should be conferred by the party which has gained the Victory, and not by that which has sustained the defeat. It is quite true however ... that the official & diplomatic Correspondence which led to the Treaty forms a new Era in Negotiations, for never was there exhibited such a display of imbecility as by our Negotiator on that occasion. ... I will venture to say that there is no lad, unless he be a natural born spoony, who has been a twelve month at any public School who would not have known how to treat for a Bargain, more shrewdly and successfully than Ashburton has done. It is quite true ... that Ld. Ashburton never would have been the rich man he is, if he had negotiated Loans for Baring & Brothers in the same way in which he negotiated this Treaty for the Country by which he was employed— I do not say for his own country, because in fact he is more American in feelings than English; as is shown by the great anxiety with which he pressed upon Webster arrangements to promote the Commercial Interests of the people of Maine.

But the real History of the conclusion of what is most decidedly a disgraceful Treaty on our part, and the real Reason why some of our most busy Friends are trying to defend it, [are these:] Many Men who were deluded to risk their Money in American Securities, have again been deluded into the belief that by giving up to the United States every Question of National Interest in regard to which the two Countries have been at Variance, the private Interest of these individuals would be saved harmless, and the American States be persuaded to pay their debts—This speculation will prove just as illusory as the former one but in the mean time, that which will not be illusory, is the loss of Character, of Moral Influence, and of military Security which will result to us from this needless and gratuitous surrender.

Many of our party run about, as you say, braying forth that Peace is so good a thing, that any Sacrifice is worth making to secure it; but the Question was not between Peace & War; for the Americans had neither intention Desire nor Means to make War, being Bankrupts in Finance and having no Navy that could put to Sea—not above 10 or 12 Sail of the Line altogether; Moreover even supposing, which is entirely a mistake, that the Question was between Peace & War, it is manifest from Ashburton's Correspondence that if the Negotiation had been conducted in a less Asinine Manner on our part we might have obtained much better Terms; and lastly if a nation once establishes & proclaims as its Rule of Conduct, that any Sacrifice of Interest is preferable to war, it had better at once abdicate its Independence & place itself under the Protection of some less Quakerlike state; For to that Condition of Subjection it must come at last and it is better to get to it decently and at once, than to arrive at it painfully, after successive Humiliations, and all the Losses and Sufferings resulting from repeated Spoliations.

I quite agree with you that the Surrender of more Square Miles of Territory, and of more Shiploads of Timber to the Americans would be of no great Consequence to us. But on the other Hand the United States might be thought to have already enough of both to last them for some years to come, and therefore it does not seem very likely that they would go to war with us, only to wrest from us a Tract of desert waste, less valuable in those Respects than the almost boundless Regions which they already possess, and which would for Two

Centuries to come be more than enough to receive all their redundant
Population. But the Question between the Two Countries was
essentially Military & Political, & not agricultural and commercial.
The United States wanted the disputed territory because it inter-
venes between New Brunswick & Canada; because it affords a Strong
Military Position for attack against us; because it is a stepping Stone
towards the object which they have long avowed as one of their fixed
aims, the Expulsion of British authority from the Continent of
America.

This Treaty is an act of weakness & of Pusillanimity, which both
morally & Physically helps them on towards that End; while at the
same Time it lowers the Position of England in the opinion of all
Foreign Nations, and is a Source of weakness to us in all our Dealings with every other Power.

32. Nesselrode's Memorandum of the Anglo-Russian Verbal
Agreement of June 1844. Official English translation from *Parliamentary Papers*, [1737], 1854, lxxi. 866–8; the manuscript office
copy is in P.R.O., F.O. 65/307. (The title employed in the published
version is inaccurate and apparently deliberately misleading. See
Gavin B. Henderson, *Crimean War Diplomacy and Other Historical
Essays* (Glasgow, 1947), pp. 1 and 13–14.)

Russia and England are mutually penetrated with the conviction
that it is for their common interest that the Ottoman Porte should
maintain itself in the state of independence and of territorial possession which at present constitutes that Empire, as that political
combination is the one which is most compatible with the general
interest of the maintenance of peace.

Being agreed on this principle, Russia and England have an equal
interest in uniting their efforts in order to keep up the existence of
the Ottoman Empire, and to avert all the dangers which can place
in jeopardy its safety.

With this object the essential point is to suffer the Porte to live in
repose, without needlessly disturbing it by diplomatic bickerings,
and without interfering without absolute necessity in its internal
affairs.

In order to carry out skilfully this system of forbearance, with a view to the well-understood interest of the Porte, two things must not be lost sight of. They are these:

In the first place, the Porte has a constant tendency to extricate itself from the engagements imposed upon it by the Treaties which it has concluded with other Powers. It hopes to do so with impunity, because it reckons on the mutual jealousy of the Cabinets. It thinks that if it fails in its engagements towards one of them, the rest will espouse its quarrel, and will screen it from all responsibility.

It is essential not to confirm the Porte in this delusion. Every time that it fails in its obligations towards one of the Great Powers, it is the interest of all the rest to make it sensible of its error, and seriously to exhort it to act rightly towards the Cabinet which demands just reparation.

As soon as the Porte shall perceive that it is not supported by the other Cabinets, it will give way, and the differences which have arisen will be arranged in a conciliatory manner, without any conflict resulting from them.

There is a second cause of complication which is inherent in the situation of the Porte; it is the difficulty which exists in reconciling the respect due to the sovereign authority of the Sultan, founded on the Mussulman law, with the forbearance required by the interests of the Christian population of that Empire.

This difficulty is real. In the present state of feeling in Europe the Cabinets cannot see with indifference the Christian populations in Turkey exposed to flagrant acts of oppression and religious intolerance.

It is necessary constantly to make the Ottoman Ministers sensible of this truth, and to persuade them that they can only reckon on the friendship and on the support of the Great Powers on the condition that they treat the Christian subjects of the Porte with toleration and with mildness.

While insisting on this truth it will be the duty of the foreign Representatives, on the other hand, to exert all their influence to maintain the Christian subjects of the Porte in submission to the sovereign authority.

It will be the duty of the foreign Representatives, guided by these principles, to act among themselves in a perfect spirit of agreement. If they address remonstrances to the Porte, those remonstrances must bear a real character of unanimity, though divested of one of exclusive dictation.

By persevering in this system with calmness and moderation, the Representatives of the great Cabinets of Europe will have the best chance of succeeding in the steps which they may take, without giving occasion for complications which might affect the tranquillity of the Ottoman Empire. If all the Great Powers frankly adopt this line of conduct, they will have a well-founded expectation of preserving the existence of Turkey.

However, they must not conceal from themselves how many elements of dissolution that Empire contains within itself. Unforeseen circumstances may hasten its fall, without its being in the power of the friendly Cabinets to prevent it.

As it is not given to human foresight to settle beforehand a plan of action for such or such unlooked-for case, it would be premature to discuss eventualities which may never be realized.

In the uncertainty which hovers over the future, a single fundamental idea seems to admit of a really practical application; it is that the danger which may result from a catastrophe in Turkey will be much diminished, if, in the event of its occurring, Russia and England have come to an understanding as to the course to be taken by them in common.

That understanding will be the more beneficial, inasmuch as it will have the full assent of Austria. Between her and Russia there exists already an entire conformity of principles in regard to the affairs of Turkey, in a common interest of conservatism and of peace.

In order to render their union more efficacious, there would remain nothing to be desired but that England should be seen to associate herself thereto with the same view.

The reason which recommends the establishment of this agreement is very simple.

On land Russia exercises in regard to Turkey a preponderant action.

On sea England occupies the same position.

Isolated, the action of these two Powers might do much mischief. United, it can produce a real benefit: thence, the advantage of coming to a previous understanding before having recourse to action.

This notion was in principle agreed upon during the Emperor's last residence in London. The result was the eventual engagement, that if anything unforeseen occurred in Turkey, Russia and England should previously concert together as to the course which they should pursue in common.

The object for which Russia and England will have to come to an understanding may be expressed in the following manner:

1. To seek to maintain the existence of the Ottoman Empire in its present state, so long as that political combination shall be possible.

2. If we foresee that it must crumble to pieces, to enter into previous concert as to everything relating to the establishment of a new order of things, intended to replace that which now exists, and in conjunction with each other to see that the change which may have occurred in the internal situation of that Empire shall not injuriously affect either the security of their own States and the rights which the Treaties assure to them respectively, or the maintenance of the balance of power in Europe.

For the purpose thus stated, the policy of Russia and of Austria, as we have already said, is closely united by the principle of perfect identity. If England, as the principal Maritime Power, acts in concert with them, it is to be supposed that France will find herself obliged to act in conformity with the course agreed upon between St. Petersburgh, London, and Vienna.

Conflict between the Great Powers being thus obviated, it is to be hoped that the peace of Europe will be maintained even in the midst of such serious circumstances. It is to secure this object of common interest, if the case occurs, that, as the Emperor agreed with Her Britannic Majesty's Ministers during his residence in England, the previous understanding which Russia and England shall establish between themselves must be directed.

33. Extract from Peel's secret private letter to Aberdeen, 23 February 1845. Aberdeen MSS., B.M., Add. MS. 43064; Jones, pp. 57–8.

* * * *

The Proceedings of the United States with respect to the Oregon are . . . the most important as immediately affecting the maintenance of amicable Relations with the United States. After what has passed in Congress, and after the refusal of arbitration we cannot plead *surprize*—whatever may hereafter take place. These occurrences render compromise and concession (difficult enough before considering what stands on record of past negotiations) ten times more difficult now. The point of Honour is now brought into the foreground. What shall we do, in order to be on our guard against infraction or palpable evasion of the Treaty—or some act implying insult and defiance? You seem confident that we have the upper hand on the banks of the Columbia, that the settlers connected with the Hudson's Bay Company are actually stronger than the settlers the subjects of the United States are at present. Have you carefully ascertained this fact? If our subjects are the strongest at this present time—may not their superiority be *speedily* weakened or destroyed by the accession of fresh strength to the Americans? I know the bill for the occupation of the territory has not yet the force of Law— but the passing of such a Bill by the house of representatives ought to operate as notice to us—and justify precautionary measures. We have as much right under the existing Treaty I apprehend, to occupy and to fortify as the Americans have. It appears to me that an additional frigate at the Mouth of the Columbia [River], and a small artillery force on shore, would aid most materially the resident British Settlers. What is the most expeditious mode of sending a small artillery force to the Oregon? Probably by sea. Might not a stout frigate be immediately sent from hence, with sealed orders, carrying some marines & artillerymen—professedly for the Cape of Good Hope, or New South Wales, or where you will—but really for the mouth of the Oregon, the destination not being known to anyone but ourselves at the time of sailing?

34. Extract from Aberdeen's House of Lords Statement on the Oregon Question, 4 April 1845. *Hansard*, 3rd series, lxxix. 123-4.

... I am accustomed almost daily to see myself characterized as pusillanimous, cowardly, mean, dastardly, truckling, and base. I hope I need not say that I view these appellations with indifference; I view them, indeed, really with satisfaction, because I know perfectly well what they mean, and how they ought to be and are translated. I feel perfectly satisfied that these vituperative terms are to be translated as applicable to conduct consistent with justice, reason, moderation, and with common sense; and I therefore feel, as I said before, really not indifferent, but positively satisfied, when I see such observations. I believe I may conscientiously say that no man ever filled the high situation which I have the honour unworthily to hold, who felt more ardently desirous than I do to preserve to the country the blessings of peace, or who would be disposed to make greater sacrifices, consistent with propriety, to maintain it. [*Cheers.*] My Lords, I consider war to be the greatest folly, if not the greatest crime, of which a country could be guilty, if lightly entered into; and I agree entirely with a moral writer who has said, that if a proof were wanted of the deep and thorough corruption of human nature, we should find it in the fact that war itself was sometimes justifiable. [*Cheers.*] It is the duty, and I am sure it is the inclination, of Her Majesty's Government to preserve peace: at the same time, there are limits which must not be passed; and I say that, without attaching too much weight to questions of national honour—for I think, fortunately for this country, that we need not be very sensitive on these matters—it is not for us, God knows, to 'seek the bubble reputation at the cannon's mouth,' or anywhere else; our power, our character and position, are such as to enable us to look with indifference on that of which other countries might be, perhaps, more jealous. [*Cheers.*] But our honour is a substantial property that we can certainly never neglect, and most assuredly we may owe it to ourselves and to our posterity to adopt a course contrary to all our desires—to all our inclinations. My Lords, from what I have said, your Lordships will perceive an earnest of the spirit of peace which shall pervade this matter, if I continue to conduct this negotiation; and I cannot bring myself to think that at this day any civilized Government would desire to see any other course pursued; and I hope, therefore, and fully believe, that we shall have the happiness of seeing this important question brought to a satisfactory because an amicable conclusion. [*Loud cheers.*] Should it be otherwise, I can only say that we possess rights which, in our opinion, are clear and unquestionable; and, by the blessing of God, and with your support, those rights we are fully prepared to maintain. [The noble Earl resumed his seat amidst loud and general applause.]

35. Extract from Wellington's private letter to Peel, 8 April 1845. Peel MSS., B.M., Add. MS. 40461; Bourne, *Britain and the Balance of Power in North America*, pp. 136–7.

We must expect however that a war with the United States will not be with that Power alone.

Unfortunately the Democratick Party throughout the World is inimical to this country. The reason is, that our system is essentially conservative; that the freedom of the subject is founded upon law and order; which provides at the same time for the conservation of person, property, privileges, honor and character; and the institutions of the country. The Democracy abroad looks for plunder: which cannot exist with our system.

Wherever a democratick influence or even a democratick Press exists, we must expect to find enemies. But besides the democratick influence, we must expect that the existing manufacturing and commercial spirit throughout Europe will excite many against us, if we should be involved in hostilities with the United States.

The old questions of the Period of the Armed Neutrality will be revived; the United States will of course open their ports to the commerce of all nations of the world; and will employ the ships of all nations each under the flag of its own nation in the carrying on of its commercial intercourse. Thence there will arise the question of free ships and free goods.

We must not expect therefore, that we shall have allies as in the last years of the late war.

* * * *

36. Extract from Aberdeen's private letter to Peel, 18 September 1845. Peel MSS., B.M., Add. MS. 40455; Arthur Gordon, *The Earl of Aberdeen* (London, 1893), pp. 174-6, wrongly dates it 28 September.

. . . [Sir James] Graham [the Home Secretary] has assured me that his own views, with respect to our relations with France, have recently undergone an entire change; and such, I perceive, is also the case with yourself. A policy of friendship and confidence has been converted into a policy of hostility and distrust.

This change will, of course, justify and call for a corresponding change in the character of the measures adopted by us; and although, from the prudence and caution with which you will act, it is possible that I may feel no great objection to these measures when proposed, I cannot too strongly express my dissent from the spirit and motives by which they will have been suggested. It is my deliberate and firm conviction that there is less reason to distrust the French Government, and to doubt the continuance of peace, at the present moment, than there was four years ago, when your administration was first formed; and I cannot perceive the slightest ground for any change in the policy which at that time it was thought wise to pursue. I fully admit that, in spite of all calculation, it is possible that war may suddenly, and when least expected, take place. It is also certain that, sooner or later, this calamity must fall upon us. Every reasonable degree of preparation, therefore, for such a contingency is justifiable, and even necessary; but the character of the measures adopted will, of course, depend upon the greater or less amount of apprehension under which we act, For my own part, I would never for an instant forget the possibility of war, and would make all reasonable provision accordingly; but I would continue to live under the conviction of the greater probability of peace.

* * * *

It seems to me that we are now acting under the influence of a panic, both with respect to the intentions of France and our own real condition, and that such a course of conduct has a direct tendency to produce the very evil which it is intended to avert.

* * * *

The preparation of our 'advanced ships' has not quite the same character; and I am informed that there has been more activity in this respect during the last six months than for the three preceding years. If it be true, as I have been told, that the ships have *actually got their water on board*, I should be disposed to regard it as the evidence of childish restlessness; but our neighbours may draw other inferences, and give us credit for more serious intentions than we probably entertain.

A suggestion has lately been made to me from the Admiralty respecting the recall of the *Penelope* and one or two other steamers from the coast of Africa. If it be intended to substitute other steam vessels of less size and more speed, there can be no objection; but you must be aware that I could not agree to interfere with the success of the great experiment which is now in progress in that part of the world, without a little more evidence of danger at home than I have hitherto been able to perceive.

I trust that you are perfectly safe from any captious opinions, or undue pertinacity on my part. My habitual deference, and long tried attachment make anything of the kind impossible; but a case may after all occur, in which a regard for my own honour, conscience, and understanding, will leave me no option. Indeed, when I recollect the strong opinions of the Duke [of Wellington], the difficulty of my position with respect to him is greatly increased, and is inexpressibly painful. He must necessarily consider me as the only obstacle to the adoption of measures which he sincerely believes to be indispensable for the welfare and safety of the country. So long as the Duke's apprehensions were regarded as merely chimerical, the matter was of less importance; but the case is now greatly altered, and he is no longer entirely in error in this respect.

I have said, however, that it is not very likely that measures should be proposed in which it would be impossible for me to concur; but whether this be the case or not, the spirit and feeling with respect to France are so different from mine, and everything is looked at in such a different point of view, that it is difficult not to anticipate some unpleasant consequences.

A trifling matter of recent occurrence will explain how extensively, and in what manner, this difference of feeling operates. The visit of the Prince de Joinville to examine the injuries sustained by the new floating breakwater at Brighton, and of which as a scientific work he spoke to me with much interest, appeared to me to be not only innocent but laudable. I find, however, that this visit is considered here as an event of political importance, and a serious offence on the part of the Prince!

Under all the circumstances to which I have referred, and the apprehensions I entertain, it is my belief that it will be the safest course for you to allow me now to retire from the Government. No difference as yet has taken place, and none whatever is expected. It is well known to my friends and connections that office is not only irksome to me, but that considerations of health have more than once pretty urgently called for this proceeding. No other motive will be assigned, and it will be the more easy to sanction this, as I have no wish ever to enter the House of Lords again.

I am very sensible that this change would expose you to some inconvenience; and I do not deny that at the present moment, from various causes, it is probable that there may be no person altogether so acceptable to the Great Powers of Europe as myself. But this is merely temporary, and I can contemplate more than one mode of arrangement which would leave you little reason to complain. At all events, the danger of any difference of opinion would be removed, which, if it should unfortunately occur, could scarcely fail to lead to the most serious mischief.

37. Extract from Peel's private letter to Aberdeen, 17 October 1845. Aberdeen MSS., B.M., Add. MS. 43065.

Guizot's letter to you left unchanged my impression that his desire is for Peace. I think his Policy as a Minister—and especially as the Minister of Louis Philippe—is a pacific Policy.

He says that he doubts the soundness of the axiom *Bellum para— pacem habebis* and you concur in his opinion. I think it is very difficult without reference to the circumstances to maintain or to deny the soundness of that axiom. I think it unwise, generally speaking to waste the Resources of a Country during peace in preparations for war. I think that if all Countries in Continental Europe would agree upon the reduction of their Military Establishments to the lowest point, consistent with the maintenance of internal order there would be wisdom in such a course. But I greatly doubt whether speaking of this Country, the *reverse* of the axiom is true. I do not believe that there would be security for peace, by our being in a state which would unfit us to repel attack without several months' preparation.

We ought in my opinion even in the midst of Peace, to be at ease upon *vital* points, to be enabled to assert our rights, to maintain a becoming Tone in the many instances of unavoidable collision which occur even during peace, without feelings of alarm and uneasiness in the Event of sudden and apparently improbable Rupture.

There is a medium which we ought to observe between preparation for war, and the defenceless state in which we might be content to remain, if we could have entire confidence in Peace.

As I have before said I have confidence in the disposition and intentions of Louis Philippe and Guizot, but is it possible to review the History of France and its Government for the last 50 years, and feel that confidence with regard to the disposition and intentions of those who may be the successors of Louis Philippe and Guizot, and whom so probable an event as the death of a man of 73 years of age may make their successors, within a month?

When I reflect on the Revolutions in Government which have taken place in France, on the military genius and recklessness and

want of principle of the people of that Country, the influence which
the Recollection of former successes and conquest and dominion,
the influence also which the Recollection of the Reverses of 1814 and
1815 must exercise, when I look at the tone of the French Press,
little less mischievous and exciting (I admit) than our own, when I
see the helplessness of the present Pacific Government, when I
see that by far the most powerful man who is likely to be at the head
of the Government of France, for the next fifty years—Louis Philippe—is unable to maintain subordination among his own military
and naval servants, ... looking at all these things I cannot feel
confidence in the maintenance of Peace. I cannot but feel that a
Government sincerely desirous to maintain peace may be overruled
by the predominance of national feeling, or by that same dictation
on the part of the military and naval authorities which now controls
the action of civil Government.

There is another consideration which diminishes my confidence
in the Continuance of Peace.

For the last twenty years the *Government of France* has I think
been disposed to maintain Peace with England. If the simple question had been Peace or War with England the answer of every Government (except possibly that of Thiers after the Treaty of July
[1840 concerning Mehemet Ali]) would have been, Peace.

But then I think these Governments commit acts which without
the intention on their part to endanger Peace, do endanger it. I need
only refer to the Terms in which you yourself have spoken of the
conduct of France in retaining Algiers after the engagements given
to us in 1830, and of the proceedings of the present Government of
France in swindling Queen Pomarée out of Tahiti, and provoking
gratuitously the absurd collision with England, to prove that acts
may be done by Governments sincerely deprecating hostilities with
England; which acts have a tendency to produce them.

Now as to Guizot himself. He may be perfectly sincere as an
individual in controverting the maxim, *Bellum para, pacem habebis*.
But as the Minister of France, speaking for France, for France not
of the month of September or October 1845, but of France even for
the last five years, can he point to her *Practice* as confirming his
Theory? . . .

. . . The continental position of France, the estrangement of foreign Sovereigns, the temper and spirit of the People, may justify,
may render unavoidable a state of military preparation such as that

to which I have referred. But can anyone doubt the existence of it? And is it not rather late in the day for a Minister of France . . . to exclaim: 'I reject and abominate the doctrine, *Bellum para, pacem habebis*'?

I am a strenuous advocate for Peace, for Peace with France especially, for a friendly understanding with France, for the exhibition by the Ministers of the two Countries of forbearance, of an earnest wish to control the senseless cry for war of vile newspapers and to prevent causes of misunderstanding by Conciliatory and honorable Compromises, but when I see the weakness of civil authority in France, the fruitful germs of war with France which will spring up in the Event of war with the United States, when I look back on the suddenness with which there have been within our short memory Revolutions in the Government of France, and forward to the events which *may* occur on the death of Louis Philippe, I cannot feel sanguine as to the future . . .

38. Extract from Cobden's Speech on Free Trade, Manchester, 15 January 1846. John Bright and James E. Thorold Rogers, *Speeches on Questions of Public Policy by Richard Cobden, M.P.* (London, 1870), i. 362–3.

. . . I believe that the physical gain will be the smallest gain to humanity from the success of this principle. I look farther; I see in the Free-trade principle that which shall act on the moral world as the principle of gravitation in the universe,—drawing men together, thrusting aside the antagonism of race, and creed, and language, and uniting us in the bonds of eternal peace. I have looked even farther. I have speculated, and probably dreamt, in the dim future— ay, a thousand years hence—I have speculated on what the effect of the triumph of this principle may be. I believe that the effect will be to change the face of the world, so as to introduce a system of government entirely distinct from that which now prevails. I believe that the desire and the motive for large and mighty empires; for gigantic armies and great navies—for those materials which are used for the destruction of life and the desolation of the rewards of labour—will die away; I believe that such things will cease to be necessary, or to be used when man becomes one family, and freely exchanges the fruits of his labour with his brother man. I believe that, if we could be allowed to reappear on this sublunary scene, we should see, at a far distant period, the governing system of this world revert to something like the municipal system; and I believe that the speculative philosopher of a thousand years hence will date the greatest revolution that ever happened in the world's history from the triumph of the principle which we have met here to advocate. . . .

39. Extract from Palmerston's private letter to the Queen, 12 September 1846. Royal Archives, J44/48; Brian Connell, *Regina v. Palmerston* (London, 1962), pp. 38–42.

. . . With respect to the Montpensier marriage the Count de Jarnac [Secretary of the French Embassy in London] stated that it had been understood with Lord Aberdeen that the British Government would not object to the Duke of Montpensier marrying the Infanta provided the marriage should be deferred till after the marriage of the Queen of Spain should have produced a successor to the Spanish Crown, but that in February last the French Government had stated that they should withdraw that limiting condition if the Prince Leopold should ever be put forward by the British Government as a candidate; that this Prince had been so put forward in Viscount Palmerston's first despatch to Mr. Bulwer, and that consequently the French Government felt themselves released from the restriction; that Queen Christina [the Queen Mother] had refused to consent to the marriage of Queen Isabella with the Duke of Cadiz unless the King of the French consented at the same time to the marriage of the Duke of Montpensier to the Infanta, and that for the reason above mentioned the French Government felt themselves at liberty to consent to that request.

Your Majesty will at once see the weakness and fallacy of this line of argument, and Viscount Palmerston did not fail to point it out to the Count de Jarnac. He said that with regard to the marriage of the Queen of Spain he found no trace in the Foreign Office of any such agreement as Count Jarnac had claimed between Lord Aberdeen and the French Government, nor did Lord Aberdeen, when he gave Viscount Palmerston an account of the state of affairs make any mention of it . . . That even if such a verbal agreement had been made by Lord Aberdeen, it was not binding upon your Majesty's present Government. But Viscount Palmerston added that such agreement even if it ever took place had not been infringed; that Prince Leopold has not been put forward by the British Government as a candidate for the Queen of Spain; that Viscount Palmerston had explicitly stated to Count Jarnac from first to last that Prince Leopold was not an English candidate; and that all the leading members of the British Government thought on the contrary that a Spanish Prince would be the fittest husband for the Queen of Spain; and that consequently unless the French Government believed Viscount Palmerston to be capable of deliberate deceit and wilful falsehood, they had no ground for suspecting that the British Government had departed from the understanding asserted to have been come to with Lord Aberdeen, although they were at perfect liberty to do so if they thought fit. That in point of fact not only had England not put forward Prince Leopold as a candidate but it was mainly owing to British influence and counsel that Prince Leopold had refrained from accepting the offers which the French Government well knew had been made to him; and that the French Government most assuredly knew the non-acceptance as well as they knew the offer. That England has therefore behaved towards the King of the French with the most scrupulous delicacy, and with the greatest regard for feelings on his part which they neither admitted to be just, nor acknowledged to be reasonable; and that the return which has been made by the French Government has been to *escamoter un mariage* which they well knew would be most offensive to England.

That whereas about the 27th August or some days sooner Count Jarnac said to Viscount Palmerston that the French Government would willingly co-operate with that of England in recommending Don Enrique, it now seems by M. Guizot's admission that in consequence of instructions which must have been sent some time previously from Paris, M. Bresson [the French Ambassador in Madrid] was on that very day settling the marriage of the Duke of Cadiz.

Viscount Palmerston said that with regard to the marriage of the Queen of Spain that was a matter as to which the British Government have no political objection to make. They deeply regret that a young Queen should have been compelled by moral force, and to serve the personal and political interests of other persons, to accept for husband a person whom she can neither like nor respect, and with whom her future life will certainly be unhappy at home, even if it should not be characterized by circumstances which would tend to lower her in the estimation of her people. But these are matters which concern the Queen and people of Spain more than the Government and people of England. But that the projected marriage of the Duke of Montpensier is a very different matter, and must have a political bearing that must exercise a most unfortunate effect upon the relations between England and France.

That even upon Count Jarnac's own statement the King of the French has departed from a condition of his own proposing, without the intervention of that releasing circumstance which Count Jarnac says had been specified in February, but of which Viscount Palmerston never heard before. That consequently the word and promise of the King of the French given to your Majesty has been broken, and in a secret and underhand manner. That not only has this promise been so broken but that the King of the French has virtually departed from a principle which he himself acknowledged to be just when he declined to allow one of his sons to become husband to the Queen of Spain; because by marrying one of his sons to the heiress presumptive to the throne, he placed that son in a situation by virtue of which he might at any time arrive indirectly at the very position which it was admitted he ought not directly to fill; and that your Majesty's Government have great reason to complain that such a step should have been taken without any previous communication with them.

That whatever may have passed between the French Government and Lord Aberdeen on this matter, your Majesty's present Ministers, being in no degree bound by such communications consider a marriage between a French Prince and the Infanta to be under any circumstances liable to the strongest and most just and well founded political objections on the part of Great Britain. That it betokens a revival of those ambitious designs of France over Spain which disturbed the peace of Europe in the beginning of the last century, when acted upon by Louis XIV, and which in the beginning of the present century, when again attempted by Napoleon Buonaparte, again made Spain the battlefield for England and France. That there is but too much reason to fear that a similar attempt on the part of the present dynasty of France will sooner or later lead to similarly deplorable results; but that the responsibility of such calamities, if they should happen must rest upon those who have chosen wantonly to become their cause.

That in the meantime Great Britain will cling as long as she can to peaceful and friendly relations with France, but that this marriage if it shall take place, will be so manifest a proof of divergent policy, if not of the contemplation of contingent hostility, on the part of France, and the whole of this transaction will so clearly show the absence of entente or cordiality on the side of France, that England must henceforward look to herself alone, and make her own interests the exclusive guide of her conduct; or that if she shall seek alliances and intimacy with foreign powers, that intimacy and those alliances must be calculated with the view of obtaining for Great Britain a counter-balance for the accession of political military and naval strength which it [is] the evident object of this projected marriage to secure to France on the side of Spain. That it is for the French Government to judge whether the friendship and confidence of England is of any and of what value to France; it is also for them to consider what, after all, the chances may be, that this marriage may fail in procuring for France all the advantages which she expects to derive from it.

Insurrections or disturbances in Spain may lead the Spanish Government to call for military assistance from France; that assistance, which without a family alliance would be declined, may in consequence of such alliance be granted. The scenes of 1808 may be revived; in addition to 100,000 men in Algiers, France may have to send 100,000 men to Spain. A national war may again be excited, British assistance may again be asked for and granted, and another Peninsular War may terminate in the loss of all the political advantages to secure which it was begun. That no doubt can be entertained of the advantage to England and to France of a cordial and confiding and good understanding between the Governments of the two countries; that it was for the French Government to judge whether it was expedient or not for France to sacrifice the certain advantage for the chance of the uncertain one, but that Viscount Palmerston begged Count Jarnac to impress upon M. Guizot that the sentiments which he had thus explained were not to be considered as those of the present Government, or of the present moment, but that they would be shared by any men who may hereafter become Ministers of the Crown, and are more likely to be increased than weakened by future events.

40. Palmerston's private letter to Lord Normanby (Ambassador in Paris), 19 November 1846. Bulwer, iii. 321–2.

I have just received your letter about Cracow. You will have received mine of Tuesday. I have prepared an answer, which I shall send off to Vienna without waiting for Guizot. Our answer is, that we dont admit the necessity of doing what the three Powers are going to do; and that we deny their competency to do it, and protest against it as a clear violation of the Treaty of Vienna. It comes very awkwardly at the present moment. Metternich has no doubt long intended it, and thinks the time propitious when England and France have differed, and when he thinks each would be willing to gain his support about Spain by being easy with him about Cracow.

Guizot will make a show of resistance, but the fact is that even if France and England had been on good terms, they have no means of action on the spot in question, and could only have prevented the thing by a threat of war, which, however, the three Powers would have known we should never utter for the sake of Cracow. The measure is an abominable shame, and executed by the most hollow pretences and the most groundless assertions.

I suspect that Prussia consents to it unwillingly; that Austria is urged on by her own covetousness and hatred of freedom and independence, even in name, and is pushed on by Russia, who wants to have an example set, which may hereafter be quoted by her as an excusing precedent when she swallows and assimilates the Kingdom of Poland.

41. Extract from Palmerston's private letter to Sir John Davis (Governor of Hong Kong), 9 January 1847. Bulwer, iii. 376–8.

We shall lose all the vantage ground which we have gained by our victories in China, if we take the low tone which seems to have been adopted of late by us at Canton. We have given the Chinese a most exemplary drubbing, and that brought them, not to their senses, because they never were deceived as to what we were; but it brought them to leave off the system of pretended contempt, under which they had so long concealed their fear. They will not forget that drubbing in a hurry, unless we set them the example of forgetting it ourselves; and we must take especial care not to descend from the relative position which we have acquired. If we maintain that position morally by the force of our intercourse, we shall not be obliged to recover it by forcible acts; but if we permit the Chinese, either at Canton or elsewhere, to resume, as they will, no doubt, be always endeavouring to do so, their former tone of affected superiority, we shall very soon be compelled to come to blows with them again.

Of course we ought—and, by we, I mean all the English in China —to abstain from giving the Chinese any ground of complaint and much more from anything like provocation or affront; but we must stop on the very threshold any attempt on their part to treat us otherwise than as their equals, and we must make them all clearly understand, though in the civilest terms, that our treaty rights must be respected, unless they choose to have their seaports knocked about their ears. Last time the Government was the aggressor, and we systematically spared the people; but if the people become the aggressors, they must pay the penalty of their offence; and when we bombard Canton and set it on fire, we shall not be able to prevent many from suffering who were not sharers in the offence. The Chinese must learn and be convinced that if they attack our people and our factories they will be shot; and that if they illtreat innocent Englishmen who are quietly exercising their treaty right of walking about the streets of Canton, they will be punished. So far from objecting to the armed association, I think it wise security against the necessity of using force. Depend upon it, that the best way of keeping any men quiet is to let them see that you are able and determined to repel force by force; and the Chinese are not in the least different in this respect from the rest of mankind.

42. Extract from Palmerston's private letter to Russell, 9 August 1847. Russell MSS., P.R.O. 30/22/6E; Evelyn Ashley, *The Life of Henry John Temple, Viscount Palmerston: 1846–1865* (London, 1877), i. 18–20.

With regard to the possible union of Spain with Portugal, or, rather, the incorporation of Portugal with Spain, it may be said that if Spain is not now by itself a great free state forming a counter-poise to France, and securing by that means Belgium and the Rhenish provinces, it is not because Spain is not large enough in territory, population, and natural resources; nor would the acquisition of Portugal give her, in this respect, any means the want of which cripples her at present, neither can it be said that by such incorporation Spain would be freed from controlling dangers in her rear which prevent her from facing France boldly to her front; because as long as Portugal is closely connected with England, Portugal would be a help and not a clog to Spain in the pursuit of such a policy. There seems no reason, therefore, to think that Spain, after having swallowed up Portugal, would be a bit more politically independent of France than she is or will be, without having so absorbed her neighbour, and, consequently, the probable result of such an annexation would be that some fine day England would not only find Spain become a satellite of France, but would lose all the counterbalancing resources which, in such a case, Portugal, as a separate state, would afford us. Those advantages are many, great, and obvious; commercial, political, military, and naval, and if we were thus to lose them, some of them would not be mere loss, but would become formidable weapons of attack against us in the hands of a hostile power. For instance, the naval position of the Tagus ought never to be in the hands of any power, whether French or Spanish, which might become hostile to England, and it is only by maintaining Portugal in its separate existence, and in its intimate and protected state of alliance with England, that we can be sure of having the Tagus as a friendly instead of its being a hostile naval station. Only fancy for a moment Portugal forming part of Spain, and Spain led away by France into war with England, and what would be our naval condition with all the ports from Calais to Marseilles hostile to us, St. Malo, Cherbourg, Brest, Rochefort, Corunna, Vigo, the Tagus, Cadiz, Carthagena, Port Mahon, Toulon, and with nothing between us and Malta but Gibraltar, the capture of which would be the bait which France would hold out to Spain to induce her to go to war with us. If, on the contrary, the Tagus were at our command, we should occupy an intermediate position greatly impeding the naval movements of France and Spain. Perhaps, if the scheme of an Iberian Republic could be realised, such a state might be more likely to remain independent of France than a Spanish Monarchy promises to be, but such a republic would soon fall back to be a monarchy, and could not be created without sweeping away two existing dynasties allied to us by treaty engagements, and for which France would certainly take the Field.

43. Extract from Palmerston's Memorandum on Relations with Germany, 16 September 1847. Royal Archives, I 1/43; T. Martin, *The Life of the Prince Consort* (London, 1877), i 447–8, and Frank Eyck, *The Prince Consort a Political Biography* (London, 1959), pp. 66–7.

There can be no doubt that it is greatly for the interest of England to cultivate a close political connection and alliance with Germany, as it is also the manifest interest of Germany to ally itself politically with England. The great interests of the two are the same. Germany & England are as regards the state of territorial possession in Europe the two great conservative powers. Geographical reasons prevent England, and ethnical reasons prevent Germany from aiming at territorial aggrandisement; neither therefore can wish to subjugate any neighbours but both have a common interest in preventing any neighbour from subjugating them. Both England & Germany are threatened by the same danger & from the same quarters. That danger is an attack from Russia or from France separately, or from Russia & from France united. The union of France & Russia for purposes of aggression is the great danger which might fall upon Europe; and France & Russia being both of them aggressive powers, essentially ambitious, and strongly coveting territorial acquisitions to be made at the expense of neighbouring nations such a union for aggressive purposes would be founded upon interests & passions common to both of those powers. While Nicholas reigns in Russia, & Louis Philippe in France personal feelings, and political opinions which are still stronger even than traditional policy will prevent such an alliance; but a state of things may easily be supposed, in which such an alliance would be the natural tendency of events.

The danger which might arise from such a combination is greater for Germany than for England. The insular position and the naval resources of England would enable her successfully and single handed to defy even such a combination. But England in such a case would be greatly assisted by the co-operation of Germany. To what extent Germany would succeed single handed in repelling such a double attack in front & in rear, it would be presumptuous for a person not a German to pretend to determine. The probability is that single handed Germany would defend herself with success; but the exertion would be great, the sacrifices of all kinds to be incurred would be severe; and her difficulties in such a struggle would be very much diminished if she had England for an active ally.

England & Germany therefore have mutually a direct interest in assisting each other to become rich united & strong, and there ought not to be in the mind of any enlightened man of either country any feeling of jealousy as to the progress made by the other country in civilisation & prosperity.

As far then as the Zollverein is to be viewed politically as uniting Germany by one common national feeling; as far as it is to [be] viewed commercially, as assisting the development of German industry, internal commerce & consequent wealth & prosperity, by the breaking down & the sweeping away of all those obstructing barriers which were opposed to trade by the frontier custom houses of the separate states, in both those respects every sensible Englishman must rejoice at the establishment of the Zollverein, and must wish to see it include the whole of Germany.

But unfortunately (such is the imperfection of human affairs) the good which the Zollverein was thus calculated to accomplish has been dashed & mixed up with evil; and while on the one hand the abolition of internal custom houses tended to give encouragement to trade, the imposition of high duties to be levied at the frontier circle on the importation of foreign commodities, more than counter-balanced this encouragement, & cramped, as it was specifically intended to do, the trade of other countries with Germany. England being perhaps the country which would naturally have the greatest trade with Germany, is on that account the country against which these high duties have been most pointedly levelled, and is also the country in which the establishment of those high Zollverein duties has created the greatest degree of irritation and resentment.

If that portion of Germany which is included within the Zollverein derived any real advantage from the system of protective duties which it has established against England, it might console itself for the ill will which it has created in the public mind in England as against Germany, by the consciousness of the advantages which it had reaped; and it might well enough set off the immediate gain, against any contingent & future political inconvenience which it might sustain from having weakened if not destroyed those feelings of cordiality in England which ought to exist between the two countries. But it may be demonstrated by arguments as conclusive as those which prove the truth of any proposition in Euclid, that protecting duties are more injurious to the country by which & in which, than to the country against which they are established. It can be demonstrated that protecting duties are not even as by some they are supposed to be, the gain of the few at the expense of the many; but that in fact even those few persons who carry on the protected trades & pursuits of industry are rendered indolent & careless by the protection on which they rely; and that the large sums which are raised for their benefit upon the rest of the community in the shape of monopoly prices for bad articles which might be got cheaper & better elsewhere, do not & cannot give to the persons engaged in these protected trades a higher rate of interest upon the capital which they employ than the ordinary rate of interest which is made upon other capital employed in the same country in other pursuits. . . .

Can it be surprising then that at a time when almost all men in England who are engaged in commercial & manufacturing pursuits are become familiar with these elementary truths, the British nation should see with displeasure a system of protective & prohibitory policy pursued in Germany, which without doing any good to Germany is intended to cripple, and to a certain degree does cripple the trade & manufactures of England; and as that system was introduced by the Zollverein, it is in the minds of men in general, identified with the Zollverein; and most men in England have no other notion of what the Zollverein is than that they understand it to be a league formed for the purpose of excluding by high duties the importation of British manufactures into Germany. The political bearing of the league is not understood; the free trade part of it is not attended to; the prohibitory part of it is all, by which it is generally known in England.

* * * *

It seems to follow from the foregoing observations, that as long as the Zollverein continues to act upon its protective system and imposes high duties on British commodities for the express reasons of either excluding them altogether, or of restricting the quantity of them to be imported, so long will the public in England look upon the Zollverein as a league founded in hostility to England; that as long as those high duties continue to be levied by the Zollverein, so long will it continue to be an advantage to British commerce that the states of northern Germany should not join it; because as long as those states do not belong to the Zollverein their own interests will lead them to persevere in a system of low duties on importation; and as long as their duties are low British goods landed in those states, and paying those low duties, will be sure to find their way upon easy terms to the consumers in the Zollverein states, and without paying the high Zollverein duties.

It also follows from the foregoing remarks that any English ministry would have been thought to have much neglected its duty and to have sacrificed the commercial interests of the country, if it did not make every proper effort within its power to persuade the states of northern Germany who have not joined the Zollverein to continue to refrain from doing so; but it is also manifest that those states have so strong an interest of their own to stand aloof from the Zollverein that a very little persuasion on the part of England can be requisite to induce them to remain as they are.

44. Extract from Palmerston's instructions to Minto, 18 September 1847. Draft in P.R.O., F.O. 44/1.

*   *   *   *

You will in the first place proceed to Berne & you will there enter into communication with the Federal Gov[ernmen]t of Swizzerland [*sic*].

You will say that although the relative geographical position of Great Britain & Switzerland is such, that Great Britain has not the same direct interest in Swiss affairs, which those States have, that are the most immediate neighbours of Switzerland, yet that Great Britain, as a contracting Party to the Treaty of Vienna, some of the stipulations of which have a direct & important bearing on the political conditions, & upon the International relations of Switzerland cannot remain an indifferent spectator of events which might tend to affect the arrangements which were established for Switzerland by that Treaty; & you will further say that the friendly feelings & the political sympathy which have ever existed between the Swiss & the British Nations, must necessarily lead the British Govt. to take a deep interest in any matter which may seriously affect the welfare of Swizzerland. That upon these grounds this Govt. have witnessed with great regret the progress among the different Cantons, of dissensions which in the opinion of some persons threaten in their course to lead to civil war. H.M.'s Govt. would view with the deepest concern such an interruption of the internal Peace of Swizzerland; & that concern would be much increased if civil war so begun between the different Cantons, should draw in other Powers to take part one way or the other in the Contest; & if the Integrity & Independence of the Swiss Territory should thus come to be violated.

H.M.'s Govt. therefore as a sincere friend to Swizzerland, & free from any selfish Interests in these matters, would most earnestly exhort all Parties in Swizzerland to act with the utmost moderation & forbearance in regard to the matters out of which their dissensions have arisen, & would strongly advise them to abate Pretensions however just they may be thought, & to yield somewhat of rights however valid they may be considered rather than to begin an appeal to arms, the consequences of which it would be easier to lament than to foresee.

H.M.'s Govt. purposely abstain from entering into an argumentative examination of the questions now in controversy between the different Cantons of which the Confederation is composed; but while on the one hand they hope that the majority will trust to reason & to persuasion rather than to any unnecessary employment of physical strength, for the attainment of objects which they may think themselves entitled to demand, on the other hand H.M.'s Govt. if their voice could reach the directing authorities of the minority of the Cantons, would earnestly intreat them not to push matters to extremity, on points in regard to which, whatever their own feelings & convictions may be, their differing fellow countrymen may have much to allege.

There is one matter however which H.M.'s Govt. cannot pass over in silence & upon which they deem it due to themselves that their opinion should not be withheld. The Diet is among other things about to take into consideration a revision of the Federal compact, & there may doubtless be many parts of that compact which may be susceptible of improvement. But an apprehension exists in some quarters that the intention of those who have proposed this revision is to endeavour to alter the fundamental basis of the political organization of Swizzerland; to sweep away the separate Sovereignty of the several Cantons; to blend the whole of Swizzerland into one single Republic.

H.M.'s Govt. do not believe that any such scheme is entertained by any Persons in Swizzerland whose political position can give authority & weight to their opinions, & H.M.'s Govt. moreover are convinced that such an extinction of antient & hereditary rights, & such a submission of Cantonal Independence to Central Power, could not be effected except by overwhelming force; & that such a scheme would imply the conquest & subjugation of one Part of the Country by the other & there can be little doubt that the smaller Cantons who might wish to maintain their present rights would in such a case apply for foreign aid to assist them, if they found their own resources insufficient for their defence. But the Brit. Govt. as a Party to the Treaty of Vienna, would remind the Swiss Govt. if any such Plan should be in contemplation that the fundamental Principle upon which the arrangements of the Treaty of Vienna in regard to Swizzerland repose, is the separate Sovereignty of the several Cantons.

When Yr. Lordship has communicated with such Persons in Swizzerland as you may be able readily to meet with, who on the one hand may be competent to inform you which are the real views of the leading men on both sides, & to whom on the other hand you may think it would be useful that the sentiments of H.M.'s Govt. should be made known, you will proceed to Turin & you will there place yourself in communication with the Govt. of His Sardinian Majesty. You will assure the Sardinian Govt. of the sincere friendship & cordial goodwill of the Govt. of Great Britain; you will say that Her Majesty never can forget that the Crown of Sardinia has been the faithful & steady ally of the Crown of Gt. Britain, through Periods of the greatest difficulty, through trials of extreme severity, through sacrifices the most painful & distressing & that His Sardinian Majesty may at all times & under all circumstances rely upon finding in Her Majesty a true & disinterested Friend.

You will say that H.M.'s Govt. have learnt with no less surprize than regret the official communication which has lately been made by the Austrian Minister at Turin to the Sardinian Govt. & which seems to imply a Threat that the Sardinian Territory would be entered by Austrian Troops, if the King of Sardinia should in the exercise of his Indisputable rights of Sovereignty make certain organic arrange[men]ts within His own Dominions which would be displeasing to the Govt. of Austria. H.M.'s Govt. cannot believe that the Govt. of Austria can seriously contemplate a proceeding which would be so flagrant a violation of international law, & for which no excuse of any kind could be alleged, but H.M.'s Govt. will of course be informed by the Govt. of Sardinia of anything further which may pass upon this matter . . .

The King of Sardinia will no doubt pursue in regard to these affairs that course which is befitting his dignity & rights; & while on the one hand he will not be deterred by such menaces from adopting any measures within his own dominions, which he may think useful & right, He will on the other hand not suffer any feelings of natural irritation which such com[munication] may have produced to impel him to any steps which might bear the appearance of unnecessary military defiance. You will say however that H.M.'s Govt. have learnt with much pleasure the assurances of friendly & defensive support, which His Sardinian Majesty has recently caused to be conveyed to the Pope, & which do Great honor to H.M. as a generous Prince & as an Italian Sovereign. From Turin Yr. Lordship will proceed to Florence where you will place yourself in commun[ication] with the Govt. of the Grand Duke.

The Relations of Gt. Britain with Tuscany have not been so intimate as those which have existed between Gt. Britain & Sardinia, & the connection of relationship between the Reigning Families of Tuscany & of Austria, may perhaps place the Tuscan Govt. in a somewhat different position in regard to Austria, from that in which stand the Govts. of other Italian States.

But the Tuscan Govt. seems of late to have been taking an independent line, & to have been shaping the course of its internal policy with a view to its own sense of the wants & interests of the Tuscan People, rather than with a view to doing that which might be agreable [*sic*] to any foreign Govt.

Such a course seems to be wise & judicious, & if followed up with Prudence & discretion, with an enlightened sagacity, & with a foresight preceding popular manifestations cannot fail to confer great benefits on the subjects of the Grand Duke, & to secure for H.M. their gratitude & attachment. Her Mj.'s Govt. will at all times receive with interest & attention any communication which the Tuscan Govt. may wish to make.

From Florence Yr. Lordship will proceed to Rome.

In the present state of the law of England Her Majesty cannot properly be advised to accredit you in any official capacity to the Court of Rome. At Rome therefore you will be not as Minister Plenipotentiary but as a Member of H.M.'s Govt. fully informed of the views, & sentiments, & opinions of that Govt. & entirely possessing the confidence of Your Sovereign & of yr. Colleagues.

The nature of your position at Rome will therefore guide you as to the character to be given to the commun[ication]s which you will have with the Members of the Roman Govt. You will be at Rome not as a Minister accredited to the Pope but as an authentic organ of the British Govt. enabled to explain its views & to declare its sentiments upon events which are now passing in Italy & which both from their local Importance & from their bearing on the general interests of Europe, H.M.'s Govt. are watching with great attention & anxiety.

H.M.'s Govt. are deeply impressed with the conviction that it is wise for Sovereigns & their Govts. to pursue in the administration of their affairs a system of progressive improvement; to apply remedies to such evils as upon examination they may find to exist; & to remodel from time to time the antient Institutions of their Country, so as to render them more suitable to the gradual growth of Intelligence, & to the increasing diffusion of political knowledge and H.M.'s Govt. consider it to be an undeniable truth that if the independent Sovereign in the exercise of his deliberate judgement shall think fit to make within his Dominions such Improvements in the Laws & Institutions of his country as he may think conducive to the welfare of his People no other Govt. can have any right to attempt to restrain or to interfere with such an employment of one of the inherent attributes of independent sovereignty.

The present Pope has begun to enter upon a system of administrative Improvement in his Dominion, & it appears to H.M.'s Govt. that His proceedings in these matters are upon general principles highly praiseworthy & deserving of all encouragement from all who take an interest in the welfare of the People of Italy. But in 1831 & 1832 a peculiar combination of political circumstances induced the Govts. of Austria, France, Great Britain, Prussia & Russia, most urgently to advise the then reigning Pope to make great changes & improvements, both administrative & organic in his Dominions, & the principle [*sic*] Improvements thus recommended were detailed in a Paper which was presented to the Roman Govt. by Ct. Lutzow the Austrian Ambassador at Rome, & by him in the name of the Five Powers strongly pressed upon the Papal Govts. Those recommendations however produced no result & were put by unattended to by the Govt. of the late Pope. H.M.'s Govt. have not learnt that as yet the reforms & Improvements effected or commenced by the present Pope, have reached the full extent of what was recommended in the Memorandum of 1831, & H.M.'s Govt. therefore conceive that all the Powers who were Parties to the framing of that Memorandum are bound to encourage & to assist the Pope as far as he may require encouragement or assistance from them in carrying out to their full extent the recommendations given by the Five Powers to His Predecessor. Such a course the Brit. Govt. at all events is prepared to pursue & you are authorized to give an assurance to this effect to the Roman Govt. & to say that H.M.'s Govt. would not see with indifference any aggression committed upon the Roman Territories with a view to prevent the Papal Govt. from carrying into effect those internal Improvements which it may think proper to adopt.

* * * *

45. Extract from Stratford Canning's Memorandum of a Conversation with Palmerston about Switzerland, 12 November 1847. (Canning had been British representative in Switzerland in 1814–19 and in December 1847 he was sent on a special mediation mission to Berne.) P.R.O., F.O. 100/54; Ann G. Imlah, *Britain and Switzerland, 1845–60* (London, 1966), pp. 181–5.

* * * *

The importance of Switzerland is not to be measured by the extent of its territory, the resources of its industry, or the amount of its population. Its position in the heart of civilized Europe, its command of the main channels of communications between Italy, France, and Germany, the hardy character of its inhabitants, and its capacity for defensive operations would alone make it an object of deep interest even if the features of the country were less remarkable, its institutions less free, and its early records less glorious and affecting. It cannot long suffer even by its own fault without enlisting the sympathies of every kindred state and generous mind. It cannot be enfeebled, convulsed, or mutilated without imparting a shock to the present system of peace,—without suggesting dangerous fears or guilty hopes to the great military monarchies which nearly surround it.

An immense boon was, no doubt, conferred upon Switzerland by the formal recognition of its neutrality. . . . But Europe also had a beneficial interest in these arrangements, and while the Swiss Cantons rejoiced in the prospect of maintaining their independence and neutrality without the burthen of a large military establishment, it was matter of general congratulation that the Alpine barriers were at the same time closed against the operations of war, and rendered emphatically subservient to the demands of peaceful intercourse. To the bordering states it must have been satisfactory to find the elements of disturbance & political contagion reduced to order along the line of an extensive frontier.

To withdraw that moral safeguard from the Swiss Cantons while they are plunged into war among themselves, is in effect to nullify their usefulness in the system of European policy, and to furnish very plausible pretexts for an intervention dangerous to their independence, and anything but european [*sic*] in its spirit and direction.

There is surely no power to which an issue of this character would be more distasteful and disparaging than to Great Britain. The nation would impatiently inquire by what fatality it had occurred, and the Government would find itself strangely embarrassed either to resist with effect, or to acquiesce with decency. Already in more than one instance the bulwarks erected at the close of the last general war by the united efforts of Europe against the encroachments of any one preponderant power have been violently overthrown, and if Switzerland be destined to draw a similar lot, there is no denying that a fatal shock will be given to what remains of the general settlement, and a new opening made for those continental struggles which England can never witness with indifference nor share without sacrifices of a perilous magnitude.

But however strong & numerous the motives which engage the British Government to join in the proposed mediation, as the only available chance of arresting civil war and preventing an armed intervention by France and Austria, it is most essential to provide for the consequences of failure, in case of the worst, for keeping all the parties to the mediation, if possible, under the control of a strictly European principle.

The mediation may fail in the outset by the refusal of one or both of the hostile parties. It may also fail from want of means to enforce the decision of the mediators, with the temporary advantage, however, of a postponement or suspension of hostilities. The difficulty consists in finding sufficient motives for the Swiss to consent, without violating their independence or playing the game of any interested power.

. . . it is manifest that the Five Powers would produce a most powerful impression by taking their stand on the principles consecrated in the settlement of 1815. They might declare to the Diet, with the proffer of their mediation, that while they are ready to assist in promoting an amicable revision of the Federal Compact with the view of establishing a more uniform system for mutual convenience, they would regard any *organic* change of that solemn instrument without the unanimous consent of the Cantons as a violent departure from the reciprocal engagements, of which their joint recognition of Swiss neutrality was a conditional part, and they might call simultaneously upon the seven Catholic Cantons to join with them in obtaining the arbitration of the Court of Rome as to the retirement of the Jesuits, their separate league terminating naturally with that question.

So far the pressure would be stronger upon the Diet than upon the Sonderbund. To adjust the balance it should be distinctly agreed that none of the Five Powers will under any circumstances directly or indirectly assist the contending parties, and that although the reference to Rome will be made on grounds of humanity in the name of all, the Courts of Paris and Vienna will specially pledge themselves to exert their utmost influence to overcome any obstacle to the recall of the Jesuits and the consequent dissolution of the League.

It remains to provide against the danger of a separate armed intervention in case of failure, without entirely losing the advantage of bringing that strongest object of apprehension to bear upon the Swiss Counsels. This, it would seem, could only be done by reserving the further determination of the Powers, under an agreement among themselves that no such measure shall be adopted without the consent of all, and a special recorded understanding as to the mode, the time, the object, the instruments and other leading points of the operation.

In this manner . . . Her Majesty's Government will have taken a position consistent alike with considerations of humanity and the best interests of Europe, reserving all their rights in case of disagreement, and combining, in that of acceptance, as much efficiency of action, and security from dangerous contingencies as the difficult nature of the question will allow.

46. Palmerston's Circular to British representatives abroad respecting debts due by foreign states to British subjects, 15 January 1848. Draft in P.R.O., F.O. 83/110; *Parliamentary Papers*, [1049], 1849, lvi. 1–4.

Her Majesty's Government have frequently had occasion to instruct Her Majesty's Representatives in various foreign States to make earnest and friendly, but not authoritative, representations in support of the unsatisfied claims of British subjects who are holders of public bonds and money securities of those States.

As some misconception appears to exist in some of those States with regard to the just right of Her Majesty's Government to interfere authoritatively, if it should think fit to do so, in support of such claims, I have to inform you, as the Representative of Her Majesty in one of the States against which British subjects have such claims, that it is for the British Government entirely a question of discretion and by no means a question of international right, whether they should or should not make this matter the subject of diplomatic negotiation. If the question is to be considered simply in its bearing upon international right, there can be no doubt whatever of the perfect right which the Government of every country possesses to take up, as a matter of diplomatic negotiation, any well-founded complaint which any of its subjects may prefer against the Government of another country, or any wrong which from such foreign Government those subjects may have sustained; and if the Government of one country is entitled to demand redress for any one individual among its subjects who may have a just but unsatisfied pecuniary claim upon the Government of another country, the right so to require redress cannot be diminished merely because the extent of the wrong is increased, and because, instead of there being one individual claiming a comparatively small sum, there are a great number of individuals to whom a very large amount is due.

It is therefore simply a question of discretion with the British Government whether this matter should or should not be taken up by diplomatic negotiation, and the decision of that question of discretion turns entirely upon British and domestic considerations.

It has hitherto been thought by the successive Governments of Great Britain undesirable that British subjects should invest their capital in loans to foreign Governments instead of employing it in profitable undertakings at home, and with a view to discourage hazardous loans to foreign Governments who may be either unable or unwilling to pay the stipulated interest thereupon, the British Government has hitherto thought it the best policy to abstain from taking up as international questions, the complaints made by British subjects against foreign Governments which have failed to make good their engagements in regard to such pecuniary transactions.

For the British Government has considered that the losses of imprudent men who have placed mistaken confidence in the good faith of foreign Governments would prove a salutary warning to others, and would prevent any other Foreign Loans from being raised in Great Britain except by Governments of known good faith and of ascertained solvency. But nevertheless, it might happen that the loss occasioned to British subjects by the non-payment of interest upon Loans made by them to Foreign Governments might become so great that it would be too high a price for the nation to pay for such a warning as to the future, and in such a state of things it might become the duty of the British Government to make these matters the subject of diplomatic negotiation.

In any conversation which you may hereafter hold with the— Ministers upon this subject, you will not fail to communicate to them the views which Her Majesty's Government entertain thereupon, as set forth in this despatch.

47. Extract from Palmerston's private letter to Lord Ponsonby (Ambassador in Vienna), 11 February 1848. Copy in Broadlands MSS., GC/PO no. 807; Ashley, i. 63–5.

I send you an important despatch to be communicated to Prince Metternich, and I wish you to recommend it to his most serious consideration. It is worded, I trust, in such a way as not to be liable to give offence; but it must be understood as meaning and implying more than it expresses. The real fact is, that upon Metternich's decision in regard to the affairs of Italy depends the question of peace or war in Europe. If he remains quiet, and does not meddle with matters beyond the Austrian frontiers, peace will be maintained, and all these Italian changes will be effected with as little disturbance as is consistent with the nature of things. If he takes upon himself the task of regulating by force of arms the internal affairs of the Italian States there will infallibly be war, and it will be a war of principles which, beginning in Italy, will spread over all Europe, and out of which the Austrian Empire will certainly not issue unchanged. In that war England and Austria will certainly not be on the same side; a circumstance which would occasion to every Englishman the deepest regret. In that war, whatever Louis Philippe and Guizot may promise, the principal champions contending against each other would be Austria and France; and I would wish Metternich well and maturely to consider what would be the effect on the internal condition of Germany which would be produced by a war between Austria and France, in which Austria was engaged in crushing and France in upholding constitutional liberty. It would be well for Prince Metternich to calculate beforehand, not merely what portion of the people of Germany he could count upon as allies in such a contest, but how many of the governments even would venture to take part with him in the struggle. If he wished to throw the greater part of Germany into close alliance with France, he could not take a better method of doing so.

He best knows the disposition of his own states; but I should greatly doubt his receiving any support in such a struggle from Hungary or Bohemia; and he would of course have all the Emperor's Italian subjects against him.

When one comes to reflect upon all the endless difficulties and embarrassments which such a course would involve, one cannot believe that a statesman so prudent and calculating, so long-sighted and so experienced, could fall into such an error; but the great accumulation of Austrian troops in the Lombard and Venetian provinces inspires one with apprehension. . . .

The recent debates in the French Chambers will have shown to Prince Metternich how little he can count upon the support or even the neutrality of France; and he may depend upon it, that in defence of constitutional liberty in Italy the French nation would rush to arms, and a French army would again water their horses in the Danube.

Pray exert all your persuasion with the Prince to induce him to authorize you to send us some tranquillising assurances on this matter. We set too great a value upon the maintenance of Austria as the pivot of the balance of power in Europe to be able to see without the deepest concern any course of action begun by her Government which would produce fatal consequences to her, and which would place us probably, against our will, in the adverse scale.

48. Extract from Palmerston's private letter to Lord Westmorland (Minister in Berlin), 29 February 1848. Copy in Broadlands MSS., GC/WE no. 189; Ashley, i. 83–4.

. . . I firmly believe Lamartine to mean peace and no aggression; it will be of importance, therefore, that the three Powers should not take any steps which might look like a threat of attacking France or an intention to interfere in her internal affairs. The only thing to do is to wait and watch, and be prepared. As for us, whenever there is a settled Government established, we shall, according to our usual custom, acknowledge it by sending fresh credentials to our ambassador. But we should like to do this in concert with the other Powers; only we should not be able perhaps to wait for them if they were disposed to hesitate or demur when the proper time may come; and we may not think it expedient to wait till after the constituent Assembly shall have met. . . . All men of mark of all parties, including the Legitimists, are supporting Lamartine's Government as the only security at present against anarchy, conflagration, and massacre. It must be owned that the prospect of a republic in France is far from agreeable; for such a Government would naturally be more likely to place peace in danger than a monarchy would be. But we must deal with things as they are, and not as we would wish to have them. These Paris events ought to serve, however, as a warning to the Prussian Government, and should induce them to set to work without delay to complete those constitutional institutions of which the King last year laid the foundations.

49. Extract from Palmerston's reply to his critics in the House of Commons, 1 March 1848. *Hansard*, 3rd series, xcvii. 121–3.

. . . I am conscious that, during the time for which I have had the honour to direct the foreign relations of this country, I have devoted to them all the energies which I possess. Other men might have acted, no doubt, with more ability—none could have acted with a more entire devotion both of their time and faculties. The principle on which I have thought the foreign affairs of this country ought to be conducted is, the principle of maintaining peace and friendly understanding with all nations, as long as it was possible to do so consistently with a due regard to the interests, the honour, and the dignity of this country. My endeavours have been to preserve peace. All the Governments of which I have had the honour to be a Member have succeeded in accomplishing that object. The main charges brought against me are, that I did not involve this country in perpetual quarrels from one end of the globe to the other. There is no country that has been named, from the United States to the empire of China, with respect to which part of the hon. Member's charge has not been, that we have refrained from taking steps that might have plunged us into conflict with one or more of these Powers. On these occasions we have been supported by the opinion and approbation of Parliament and the public. We have endeavoured to extend the commercial relations of the country, or to place them where extension was not required, on a firmer basis, and upon a footing of greater security. Surely in that respect we have not judged amiss, nor deserved the censure of the country; on the contrary, I think we have done good service. I hold with respect to alliances, that England is a Power sufficiently strong, sufficiently powerful, to steer her own course, and not to tie herself as an unnecessary appendage to the policy of any other Government. I hold that the real policy of England—apart from questions which involve her own particular interests, political or commercial—is to be the champion of justice and right; pursuing that course with moderation and prudence, not becoming the Quixote of the world, but giving the weight of her moral sanction and support wherever she thinks that justice is, and wherever she thinks that wrong has been done. Sir, in pursuing that course, and in pursuing the more limited direction of our own particular interests, my conviction is, that as long as England keeps herself in the right—as long as she wishes to permit no injustice—as long as she wishes to countenance no wrong—as long as she labours at legislative interests of her own—and as long as she sympathises with right and justice, she never will find herself altogether alone. She is sure to find some other State, of sufficient power, influence, and weight, to support and aid her in the course she may think fit to pursue. Therefore I say that it is a narrow

policy to suppose that this country or that is to be marked out as the
eternal ally or the perpetual enemy of England. We have no eternal
allies, and we have no perpetual enemies. Our interests are eternal
and perpetual, and those interests it is our duty to follow. When we
find other countries marching in the same course, and pursuing the
same objects as ourselves, we consider them as our friends, and we
think for the moment that we are on the most cordial footing; when
we find other countries that take a different view, and thwart us in
the object we pursue, it is our duty to make allowance for the
different manner in which they may follow out the same objects. It is
our duty not to pass too harsh a judgment upon others, because they
do not exactly see things in the same light as we see; and it is our
duty not lightly to engage this country in the frightful responsibilities of war, because from time to time we may find this or that
Power disinclined to concur with us in matters where their opinion
and ours may fairly differ. That has been, as far as my faculties have
allowed me to act upon it, the guiding principle of my conduct. And
if I might be allowed to express in one sentence the principle which I
think ought to guide an English Minister, I would adopt the expression of Canning, and say that with every British Minister the
interests of England ought to be the shibboleth of his policy.

50. Palmerston's confidential dispatch no. 28 to Bulwer, 16 March
1848. P.R.O., FO. 185/229; Bulwer, iii. 245–6.

I have to instruct you to recommend earnestly to the Spanish
Government and to the Queen-Mother, if you have an opportunity
of doing so, the adoption of a legal and constitutional course of
Government in Spain. The recent fall of the King of the French,
and of his whole family, and the expulsion of his Ministers, ought to
teach the Spanish Court and Government how great is the danger
of an attempt to govern a country in a manner at variance with the
feelings and opinions of the nation, and the catastrophe which has
happened in France must serve to show that even a large and well-
disciplined army becomes an ineffectual defence for the Crown,
when the course pursued by the Crown is at variance with the
general sentiments of the country.

It would then be wise for the Queen of Spain in the present
critical state of affairs to strengthen the executive government by

enlarging the basis upon which the Administration is founded and by calling to her councils some of those men who possess the confidence of the Liberal Party.

51. Palmerston's private letter to King Leopold of the Belgians, 15 June 1848. Copy in Broadlands MSS., RC/MM no. 115; Ashley, i. 96–9.

I was much obliged to Your Majesty for the letter which I had the honour of receiving from Your Majesty some little time ago; and I am happy to have the opportunity which is thus afforded me of congratulating Your Majesty upon the continued tranquillity and stability of your kingdom. It would seem as if the storms which have shaken everything else all over the continent of Europe had only served to consolidate more firmly the foundations of Your Majesty's throne. As to France, no man nowadays can venture to prophesy from week to week the turn affairs may take in that unfortunate country. For many years past the persons in authority in France have worked at the superstructure of Monarchy without taking care of the foundation. Education and religion have been neglected, and power has now passed into the hands of a mob ignorant of the principles of government, of morality, and of justice; and it is a most remarkable fact in the history of society that in a nation of thirty-five millions of men, who have now for more than half a century been in a state of political agitation, which, in general, forms and brings out able men, and who have during that time been governed by three dynasties, there is no public political man to whom the country looks up with confidence and respect, on account of his statesmanlike qualities and personal character combined; and there is no prince whom any large portion of the nation would make any considerable effort to place as sovereign on the throne. The principle of equality seems to have been fully carried out in one respect, and that is that all public men are equally without respect, and all candidates for royalty equally without following.

As to poor Austria, every person who attaches value to the maintenance of a balance of power in Europe must lament her present helpless condition; and every man gifted with ever so little foresight must have seen, for a long time past, that feebleness and decay were the inevitable consequences of Prince Metternich's system of government: though certainly no one could have expected that the rottenness within would so soon and so completely have shown itself without. Lord Bacon says that a man who aims at being the only figure among ciphers is the ruin of an age: and so it has been with Metternich. He has been jealous of anything like talent or attainment in individuals, and of anything like life in communities and nations. He succeeded for a time in damming up and arresting the stream of human progress. The wonder is, not that the accumulated pressure should at last have broke the barrier and have deluged the country, but that his artificial impediments should have produced stagnation so long.

I cannot regret the expulsion of the Austrians from Italy. I do not believe, Sire, that it will diminish the real strength nor impair the real security of Austria as a European Power. Her rule was hateful to the Italians, and has long been maintained only by an expenditure of money and an exertion of military effort which left Austria less able to maintain her interests elsewhere. Italy was to her the heel of Achilles, and not the shield of Ajax. The Alps are her natural barrier and her best defence. I should wish to see the whole of Northern Italy united into one kingdom, comprehending Piedmont, Genoa, Lombardy, Venice, Parma, and Modena; and Bologna would, in that case, sooner or later unite itself either to that State or to Tuscany. Such an arrangement of Northern Italy would be most conducive to the peace of Europe, by interposing between France and Austria a neutral State strong enough to make itself respected, and sympathising in its habits and character neither with France nor with Austria; while, with reference to the progress of civilisation, such a State would have great advantages, political, commercial, and intellectual. Such an arrangement is now, in my opinion, Sire, inevitable; and the sooner the Austrian Government makes up its mind to the necessity, the better conditions it will be able to obtain. If Austria waits till she be forcibly expelled—which she will soon be—she will get no conditions at all.

52. Extract from Palmerston's House of Commons Speech on Hungary, 21 July 1849. *Hansard*, 3rd series, cvii. 808–15.

. . . We have been allied with Austria in most important European transactions; and the remembrance of the alliance ought undoubtedly to create in the breast of every Englishman, who has a recollection of the history of his country, feelings of respect towards a Power with whom we have been in such alliance. It is perfectly true, that in the course of those repeated alliances, Austria, not from any fault of hers, but from the pressure of irresistible necessity, was repeatedly compelled to depart from the alliance, and to break the engagements by which she had bound herself to us. We did not reproach her with yielding to the necessity of the moment; and no generous mind would think that those circumstances ought in any degree to diminish or weaken the tie which former transactions must create between the Governments of the two countries. But there are higher and larger considerations, which ought to render the maintenance of the Austrian empire an object of solicitude to every English statesman. Austria is a most important element in the balance of European power. Austria stands in the centre of Europe, a barrier against encroachment on the one side, and against invasion on the other. The political independence and liberties of Europe are bound up, in my opinion, with the maintenance and integrity of Austria as a great European Power; and therefore anything which tends by direct, or even remote, contingency, to weaken and to cripple Austria, but still more to reduce her from the position of a first-rate Power to that of a secondary State, must be a great calamity to Europe, and one which every Englishman ought to deprecate, and to try to prevent. . . . I take the question that is now to be fought for on the plains of Hungary to be this—whether Hungary shall continue to maintain its separate nationality as a distinct kingdom, and with a constitution of its own; or whether it is to be incorporated more or less in the aggregate constitution that is to be given to the Austrian empire? It is a most painful sight to see such forces as are now arrayed against Hungary proceeding to a war fraught with such tremendous consequences on a question that it might have been hoped would be settled peacefully. It is of the utmost importance to Europe, that Austria should remain great and powerful; but it is impossible to disguise from ourselves that, if the war is to be fought out, Austria must thereby be weakened, because, on the one hand, if the Hungarians should be successful, and their success should end in the entire separation of Hungary from Austria, it will be impossible not to see that this will be such a dismemberment of the Austrian empire as will prevent Austria from continuing to occupy the great position she has hitherto held among European Powers. If, on the other hand, the war being fought out to the uttermost, Hungary should by superior forces be entirely crushed, Austria in that battle will have crushed her own right arm. Every field that is laid waste is an Austrian resource destroyed—every man that perishes upon the field among the Hungarian ranks, is an Austrian soldier deducted from the defensive forces of the empire. Laying aside those other most obvious considerations that have been touched upon as to the result of a successful war, the success of which is brought about by foreign aid—laying that wholly aside, it is obvious that even the success of Austria, if it is simply a success of force, will inflict a deep wound on the fabric and frame of the Austrian empire. It is therefore much to be desired, not simply on the principle of general humanity, but on the principle of sound European policy, and from the most friendly regard to the Austrian empire itself—it is, I say, devoutly to be wished that this great contest may be brought to a termination by some amicable arrangement between the contending parties, which shall on the one hand satisfy the national feelings of the Hungarians, and on the other hand not leave to Austria another and a larger Poland within her empire. ... It is most desirable that foreign nations should know that, on the one hand, England is sincerely desirous to preserve and maintain peace—that we entertain no feelings of hostility towards any nation in the world—that we wish to be on the most friendly footing with all—that we have a deep interest in the preservation of peace, because we are desirous to carry on with advantage those innocent and peaceful relations of commerce that we know must be injured by the interruption of our friendly relations with other countries: but, on the other hand, it is also essential for the attainment of that object, and even essential for the protection of that commerce to which we attach so much importance, that it should be known and well understood by every nation on the face of the earth, that we are not disposed to submit to wrong, and that the maintenance of peace on our part is subject to the indispensable condition that all countries shall respect our honour and our dignity, and shall not inflict any injury upon our interests. Sir, I do not think that the preservation of peace is in any degree endangered by the expression of opinion with regard to the transactions in Hungary or other countries. I agree with those who think—and I know there are many in this country who entertain the opinion—that there are two objects which England ought peculiarly to aim at. One is to maintain peace; the other is to count for something in the transactions of the world—that it is not fitting that a country occupying such a proud position as England—that a country having such various and extensive interests, should lock herself up in a simple regard to her own internal affairs, and should be a passive and mute spectator of everything that is going on around. It is quite true that it may be said, 'Your opinions are but opinions, and you express them against our opinions, who have at our command large armies to back them—what are opinions against armies?' Sir, my answer is, opinions are stronger than armies. Opinions, if they are founded in truth and justice, will in the end prevail against the bayonets of infantry, the fire of artillery, and the charges of cavalry. Therefore I say, that armed by opinion, if that opinion is pronounced with truth and justice, we are indeed strong, and in the end likely to make our opinions prevail; and I think that what is happening on the whole surface of the continent of Europe, is a proof that this expression of mine is a truth. Why, for a great many years the Governments of Europe imagined they could keep down opinion by force of arms, and that by obstructing progressive improvement they would prevent that extremity of revolution which was the object of their constant dread. We gave an opinion to the contrary effect, and we have been blamed for it. We have been accused of meddling with matters that did not concern us, and of affronting nations and Governments by giving our opinion as to what was likely to happen; but the result has proved, that if our opinions had been acted upon, great calamities would have been avoided. Those very Governments that used to say, 'The man we hate, the man we have to fear, is the moderate Reformer; we care not for your violent Radical, who proposes such violent extremes that nobody is likely to join him—the enemy we are most afraid of is the moderate Reformer, because he is such a plausible man that it is difficult to persuade people that his counsels would lead to extreme consequences—therefore let us keep off, of all men, the moderate Reformer, and let us prevent the first step of improvement, because that improvement might lead to extremities and innovation.' Those Governments, those Powers of Europe, have at last learned the truth of the opinions expressed by Mr. Canning, 'That those who have checked improvement, because it is innovation, will one day or other be compelled to accept innovation, when it has ceased to be improvement.' I say, then, that it is our duty not to remain passive spectators of events that in their immediate consequences affect other countries, but which in their remote and certain consequences are sure to come back with disastrous effect upon us; that, so far as the courtesies of international intercourse may permit us to do, it is our duty, especially when our opinion is asked, as it has been on many occasions on which we have been blamed for giving it, to state our opinions, founded on the experience of this country—an experience that might have been, and ought to have been, an example to less fortunate countries. At the same time, I am quite ready to admit that interference ought not to be carried to the extent of endangering our relations with other countries. There are cases like that which is now the subject of our discussion, of one Power having in the exercise of its own sovereign rights invited the assistance of another Power; and, however we may lament that circumstance, however we may be apprehensive that therefrom consequences of great danger and evil may flow, still we are not entitled to interpose in any manner that will commit this country to embark in those hostilities. All we can justly do is to take advantage of any opportunities that may present themselves in which the counsels of friendship and peace may be offered to the contending parties.... Sir, to suppose that any Government of England can wish to excite revolutionary movements in any part of the world—to suppose that any Government of England can have any other wish or desire than to confirm and maintain peace between nations, and tranquillity and harmony between Governments and subjects, shows really a degree of ignorance and folly which I never supposed any public man could have been guilty of, which may do very well for a newspaper article, but which it astonishes me to find is made the subject of a speech in Parliament.

53. Russell's private letter to Palmerston, 22 May 1850. Broadlands MSS., GC/RU no. 343; Walpole, ii. 60–1.

I saw the Queen on Monday, by her desire, and it is right I should inform you of the course which I stated to her I should pursue, and which she has been pleased to sanction. I first stated that all your colleagues were prepared to assume the responsibility of your conduct on the Greek question, and that if any change took place on that question it must be a change of the entire Ministry. The Queen deprecated the resignation of the Ministry, and desired me not to propose it. I then said that there were some questions pending in Parliament which might make that resignation necessary. I would not, however, anticipate votes, of which the bearing and the importance must be weighed at the time. But, supposing the Ministry to arrive at the end of the session, it was my duty to tell her Majesty that I thought the interests of the Crown and the country required that a change should take place in the Foreign Department; that, without imputing blame to you, I thought it must be confessed that, looking at the position of England, her readiness to acknowledge all forms of government, despotic and democratic, and her wish to respect the rights of all foreign nations, she was encountered by more hostile feelings in her course than was natural or necessary; that I thought, if you were to take some other department, we might continue the same line of foreign policy without giving the same offence; that I should object to any change which implied that we preferred the intimate alliance of Austria and Russia to those we had hitherto maintained; that, with respect to the particular arrangement to be made, I could not make any definitive proposal at the present time. The Queen assented entirely to all that I had stated, but declared her opinion that the change to be proposed should not take place later than the end of the present session. I will only add that I consulted Lord Lansdowne [Lord President of the Council] before and since my audience with the Queen. He has made a suggestion as to the proposed arrangements, which I shall be glad to communicate to you, as well as various details on this matter, when we have an opportunity of talking it over together.

[On this Palmerston made the following note, dated 30 January 1851:]

This scheme was afterwards abandoned. Towards the end of the session Ld. John again brought the subject forward & proposed to me a change of office. I replied that after what had passed in the House of Commons on Roebuck's motion [the Don Pacifico debate of 24–28 June 1850], and after the general and decided approbation of my policy & conduct which had been expressed from one end of the country to the other by all the Liberal Party it was quite impossible for me to consent to any such arrangement. To do so would be to pass condemnation on myself after I had received a public approval, and to say that I thought the House of Lords which had blamed me was in the right, and the House of Commons which had approved me was in the wrong. I said that I had not had my opinion of myself altered by the great numbers of demonstrations & expressions of approval public and private which I had received, but those expressions of opinion had at least satisfied me that public opinion was with me and I could not do anything that would appear to imply a doubt on that point. That if it was any convenience to the Government I was ready now as I had been after the vote in the Lords, to relieve my colleagues of all difficulty by retiring altogether, but that if I remained in the Govt. I would not give up the Foreign Office.

Ld. John said that he wished me to remain a member of the Govt., and he afterwards said that the Queen had consented thereto. I had given no answer written or verbal to his letter of May.

54. Extract from the House of Commons Debate on Don Pacifico and Greece, 24–28 June 1850. *Hansard*, 3rd series, cxii. 443–4, 575–6, and 582–90.

PALMERSTON [25 June]: . . . I do not complain of the conduct of those who have made these matters the means of attack upon Her Majesty's Ministers. The government of a great country like this, is undoubtedly an object of fair and legitimate ambition to men of all shades of opinion. It is a noble thing to be allowed to guide the policy and to influence the destinies of such a country; and, if ever it was an object of honourable ambition, more than ever must it be so at the moment at which I am speaking. For while we have seen . . . the political earthquake rocking Europe from side to side—while we have seen thrones shaken, shattered, levelled; institutions overthrown and destroyed—while in almost every country of Europe the conflict of civil war has deluged the land with blood, from the Atlantic to the Black Sea, from the Baltic to the Mediterranean; this country has presented a spectacle honourable to the people of England, and worthy of the admiration of mankind.

We have shown that liberty is compatible with order; that individual freedom is reconcilable with obedience to the law. We have shown the example of a nation, in which every class of society accepts with cheerfulness the lot which Providence has assigned to it; while at the same time every individual of each class is constantly striving to raise himself in the social scale—not by injustice and wrong, not by violence and illegality—but by persevering good conduct, and by the steady and energetic exertion of the moral and intellectual faculties with which his Creator has endowed him. To govern such a people as this, is indeed an object worthy of the ambition of the noblest man who lives in the land; and therefore I find no fault with those who may think any opportunity a fair one, for endeavouring to place themselves in so distinguished and honourable a position. But I contend that we have not in our foreign policy done anything to forfeit the confidence of the country. We may not, perhaps, in this matter or in that, have acted precisely up to the opinions of one person or of another—and hard indeed it is, as we all know by our individual and private experience, to find any number of men agreeing entirely in any matter, on which they may not be equally possessed of the details of the facts, and circumstances, and reasons, and conditions which led to action. But, making allowance for those differences of opinion which may fairly and honourably arise among those who concur in general views, I maintain that the principles which can be traced through all our foreign transactions, as the guiding rule and directing spirit of our proceedings, are such as deserve approbation. I therefore fearlessly challenge the verdict which this House, as representing a political, a commercial, a constitutional country, is to give on the question now brought before it; whether the principles on which the foreign policy of Her Majesty's Government has been conducted, and the sense of duty which has led us to think ourselves bound to afford protection to our fellow subjects abroad, are proper and fitting guides for those who are charged with the Government of England; and whether, as the Roman, in days of old, held himself free from indignity, when he could say *Civis Romanus sum;* so also a British subject, in whatever land he may be, shall feel confident that the watchful eye and the strong arm of England, will protect him against injustice and wrong.

GLADSTONE [27 June]: . . . I have thought it right in a case of this serious nature to make the charge against the noble Lord as clear, definite, and circumstantial as possible. I do not wish to insinuate anything; my desire is only to meet the noble Lord in open warfare; and if we, who are now in conflict with him, were capable of entertaining any different wish, I must say that the manner in which the noble Lord himself has fought his battle in this House, would have set us the example of the spirit and the temper in which we should proceed. I therefore thus sum up my complaints of the noble Lord in terms the most explicit: I affirm, first . . . that your demands, even if they had been just, were urged in a tone and manner wholly unjustifiable. I affirm, secondly, that you urged as just, and that upon a State both feeble in itself, and specially entitled to your regard as one of its protecting Powers, demands which bore upon the very face of them the abundant proofs of fraud, falsehood, and absurdity. I affirm, lastly, that instead of trusting and trying the tribunals of the country, and employing diplomatic agency simply as a supplemental resource, you have interposed . . . the authority of foreign power, in contravention both of the particular stipulations of the treaty in force between this country and Greece, and of the general principles of the law of nations; and have thus set the mischievous example of abandoning the methods of law and order, in order to repair to those of force.

. . . there is plainly a great question of principle at issue between us, to which I cannot hesitate to advert. This is a matter in which mere words and mere definitions convey little meaning; but the idea which I have in my mind is that commonly expressed by the word non-interference or non-intervention. Such a word, apart from all cavils as to exact definition, does convey a principle, a temper, a course of policy, which is practically understood and practically approved by the people of England. Sir, so strong is this House, with a strength founded both in its nature as a representative body and in its general conduct, that it can sometimes even afford to deviate a little from the true line of action; its credit with the people may suffer some deduction, and yet remain in great vigour. You may, I say, afford the loss, but certain I am that you will incur such a loss, if you pass any vote which shall seem to disparage that principle and policy which shall be calculated to impress the people with the belief that you are infected with a mania and an itch for managing the affairs of other nations, and that you are not contented with your own weighty and honourable charge. . . . what is the antagonistic principle which we advance? . . . it is the principle of non-intervention in the domestic affairs of other countries. . . . Greatly as I respect in general the courage, the energy, the undoubted patriotism of the noble Lord, I accuse him of this, that his policy is marked and characterised by what I must call a spirit of interference. I hold that this is a fundamental fault: a fault not to be excused. The noble

Lord tells us, indeed, that he does not go abroad to propagate extreme opinions in other countries; and that I do not for a moment doubt. I do not doubt that he has the feeling—which must, indeed, be the feeling of every Englishman, and especially of every Secretary of State in England for Foreign Affairs—which has been the feeling, I am convinced, of the various distinguished persons who have held that office since the Peace—of the Earl of Aberdeen, of Mr. Canning, and of the Marquess of Londonderry likewise; I mean a sincere desire that when a legitimate opportunity creates itself, and makes it our duty, in conformity with the principles of public law, to exercise a British influence in the regulation of the internal affairs of other countries, that influence should be exercised in the spirit which we derive from our own free and stable form of government, and in the sense of extending to such countries, as far as they are able and desirous to receive them institutions akin to those of which we know from experience the inestimable blessings. Upon this there can be no difference of opinion among us; no man who sits here can be the friend of absolute power any more than of licence and disorder. There can be no difference upon the proposition that, considering how the nations of Europe are associated together, and, in some sense, organised as a whole, such occasions will of necessity from time to time arise; but the difference among us arises upon this question: Are we, or are we not, to go abroad and make occasions for the propagation even of the political opinions which we consider to be sound? I say we are not. I complain of the noble Lord that he is disposed to make these occasions: nay, he boasts that he makes them. He refers back to his early policy in Spain and Portugal, and he says it was to us a matter of very small moment whether Portugal were ruled by Dom Miguel or Donna Maria; whether the Crown of Spain went to Don Carlos or to Donna Isabella; but then, he says, there were opportunities of propagating the political sentiments which we think sound, and therefore we did what otherwise it might not have been wise to do. This doctrine, Sir, of the noble Lord is, I admit, a most alluring doctrine. We are soothed and pleased with denunciations the most impartial alike of tyranny and of anarchy; and assured, I doubt not with truth, that the only part played by the noble Lord is that of the moderate reformer. Sir, I object to the propagandism even of moderate reform. In proportion as the representation is alluring, let us be on our guard. The noble Lord lays a snare for us, into which, as Englishmen, glorying in our country and its laws, we are but too likely to fall. We must remember that if we claim the right not only to accept, where they come spontaneously and by no act of ours, but to create and to catch at, opportunities for spreading in other countries the opinions of our own meridian, we must allow to every other nation, every other Government, a similar licence both of judgment and of action. What is to be the result? That if in every country the name of England is to be the symbol and the nucleus of a party, the name of France, of Russia, or of Austria, may and will be the same. And are you not, then, laying the foundation of a system hostile to the real interests of freedom, and destructive of the peace of the world?

Sir, we hear something in this debate of success as not being the true test of the excellence of public measures. And God forbid that I should say it is their true test, when you are in your own sphere, minding your own affairs. But when you think fit to go out of that sphere and to manage those of other people for them, then do I think success throws much light upon the examination of the question whether your intervention was wise and just. Interference in foreign countries, Sir, according to my mind, should be rare, deliberate, decisive in character, and effectual for its end. Success will usually show that you saw your way, and that the means you used were adapted and adequate to their purpose. Such, if I read them aright, were the acts done by Mr. Canning in the nature of intervention: they were few, and they were effectual—effectual whether when, in his own noble language, he 'called the new world into existence to redress the balance of the old', or when, founding himself on the obligations of public law, he despatched the troops of England to prevent the march of a Spanish force into Portugal. I do not find the same character in the interventions of the noble Lord opposite. I cannot look upon all that has taken place during the four years which are the subject-matter of this Motion, without seeing a rash desire, an habitual desire, of interference—a disposition to make the occasions of it, and, that which will always follow, a disposition, in making them, to look too slightly at the restraints imposed by the letter and spirit of the law of nations. . . .

Sir, I am well prepared, following the example of other and more distinguished men, to bear my share in the abuse which, I doubt not, may attend the part which we shall take on this occasion. I am prepared to hear it said that we are espousing the cause, as against England, of countries other than our own; that we cabal against the noble Lord because he is the protector of Englishmen domiciled abroad. Sir, I deny that he has truly protected Englishmen by the course he has pursued. I hold that no Minister in his place can really give to Englishmen resident in foreign lands either an effectual or a permanent protection, except by a careful observance of the principles that have been consecrated by the universal assent of mankind for governing the conduct of nation to nation. In vain do you talk to us of a knot of foreign conspirators: the only knot of foreign conspirators against the noble Lord, is the combined opinion of civilised Europe. In vain you talk of the two kinds of revolutionists— the revolutionists who will have too much reform for the noble Lord's taste, and the revolutionists who will have too little. These, he says, are the persons opposed to him and his moderate reforms, and all on grounds petty, paltry, narrow, and personal; but under his description there will, I fear, be found to fall nearly every party in nearly every country of Christendom.

Sir, great as is the influence and power of Britain, she cannot afford to follow, for any length of time, a self-isolating policy. It would be a contravention of the law of nature and of God, if it were possible for any single nation of Christendom to emancipate itself from the obligations which bind all other nations, and to arrogate, in the face of mankind, a position of peculiar privilege. And now I will grapple with the noble Lord on the ground which he selected for himself, in the most triumphant portion of his speech, by his reference to those emphatic words, *Civis Romanus sum*. He vaunted, amidst the cheers of his supporters, that under his administration an Englishman should be, throughout the world, what the citizen of Rome had been. What then, Sir, was a Roman citizen? He was the member of a privileged caste; he belonged to a conquering race, to a nation that held all others bound down by the strong arm of power. For him there was to be an exceptional system of law; for him principles were to be asserted, and by him rights were to be enjoyed, that were denied to the rest of the world. Is such, then the view of the noble Lord, as to the relation that is to subsist between England and other countries? Does he make the claim for us, that we are to be uplifted upon a platform high above the standing-ground of all other nations? It is, indeed, too clear, not only from the expressions, but from the whole spirit of the speech of the noble Viscount, that too much of this notion is lurking in his mind; that he adopts in part that vain conception, that we, forsooth, have a mission to be the censors of vice and folly, of abuse and imperfection, among the other countries of the world; that we are to be the universal schoolmasters; and that all those who hesitate to recognise our office, can be governed only by prejudice or personal animosity, and should have the blind war of diplomacy forthwith declared against them. And certainly if the business of a Foreign Secretary properly were to carry on such diplomatic wars, all must admit that the noble Lord is a master in the discharge of his functions. What, Sir, ought a Foreign Secretary to be? Is he to be like some gallant knight at a tournament of old, pricking forth into the lists, armed at all points, confiding in his sinews and his skill, challenging all comers for the sake of honour, and having no other duty than to lay as many as possible of his adversaries sprawling in the dust? If such is the idea of a good Foreign Secretary, I, for one, would vote to the noble Lord his present appointment for his life. But, Sir, I do not understand the duty of a Secretary for Foreign Affairs to be of such a character. I understand it to be his duty to conciliate peace with dignity. I think it to be the very first of all his duties studiously to observe, and to exalt in honour among mankind, that great code of principles which is termed the law of nations, which the hon. and learned Member for Sheffield has found, indeed, to be very vague in their nature, and greatly dependent on the discretion of each particular country; but in which I find, on the contrary, a great and noble monument of human wisdom, founded on the combined dictates of reason and experience—a precious inheritance bequeathed to us by the generations that have gone before us, and a firm foundation on which we must take care to build whatever it may be our part to add to their acquisitions, if, indeed, we wish to maintain and to consolidate the brotherhood of nations, and to promote the peace and welfare of the world.

Sir, the English people, whom we are here to represent, are indeed a great and noble people; but it adds nothing to their greatness or their nobleness, that when we assemble in this place we should trumpet forth our virtues in elaborate panegyrics, and designate those who may not be wholly of our mind as a knot of foreign conspirators. When, indeed, I heard the hon. and learned Gentleman the Member for Sheffield glorifying us, together with the rest of the people of this country, and announcing that we soared in unapproachable greatness, and the like, I confess I felt that eulogies such as those savoured somewhat of bombast; and thought it much to the honour of this House that the praises thus vented seemed to fall so flat; that the cookery of the hon. and learned Gentleman was evidently seasoned beyond the capacity and relish of our palates. It is this insular temper, and this self-glorifying tendency, which the policy of the noble Lord, and the doctrines of his supporters, tend so much to foment, and which has given to that policy the quarrelsome character that marks some of their speeches; for, indeed, it seems as if there lay upon the noble Lord an absolute necessity for quarrelling. No doubt it makes a difference, what may be the institutions of one country or another. If he can, he will quarrel with an absolute monarchy. If he cannot find an absolute monarchy for the purpose, he will quarrel with one which is limited. If he cannot find even that, yet, sooner than not quarrel at all, he will quarrel with a republic. . . .

Sir, I say the policy of the noble Lord tends to encourage and confirm in us that which is our besetting fault and weakness, both as a nation and as individuals. Let an Englishman travel where he will as a private person, he is found in general to be upright, high-minded, brave, liberal, and true; but with all this, foreigners are too often sensible of something that galls them in his presence, and I apprehend it is because he has too great a tendency to self-esteem— too little disposition to regard the feelings, the habits, and the ideas of others. Sir, I find this characteristic too plainly legible in the policy of the noble Lord. . . .

No, Sir, let it not be so: let us recognise, and recognise with frankness, the equality of the weak with the strong; the principles of brotherhood among nations, and of their sacred independence. When we are asking for the maintenance of the rights which belong to our fellow-subjects resident in Greece, let us do as we would be done by, and let us pay all the respect to a feeble State, and to the infancy of free institutions, which we should desire and should exact from others towards their maturity and their strength. Let us refrain from all gratuitous and arbitrary meddling in the internal concerns of other States, even as we should resent the same interference if it were attempted to be practised towards ourselves. If the noble Lord has indeed acted on these principles, let the Government to which he belongs have your verdict in its favour; but if he has departed from them, as I contend, and as I humbly think and urge upon you that it has been too amply proved, then the House of Commons must not shrink from the performance of its duty, under whatever expectations of momentary obloquy or reproach, because we shall have done what is right; we shall enjoy the peace of our own consciences, and receive, whether a little sooner or a little later, the approval of the public voice, for having entered our solemn protest against a system of policy which we believe, nay, which we know, whatever may be its first aspect, must of necessity in its final results be unfavourable even to the security of British subjects resident abroad, which it professes so much to study—unfavourable to the dignity of the country, which the Motion of the hon. and learned Member asserts that it preserves—and equally unfavourable to that other great and sacred object which also it suggests to our recollection, the maintenance of peace with the nations of the world.

55. The Queen's private letter to Russell, 12 August 1850. Draft in Royal Archives, A 79/44; *The Letters of Queen Victoria*, 1st series (London, 1907), ii. 315.

With reference to the conversation about Lord Palmerston which the Queen had with Lord John Russell the other day, and Lord Palmerston's disavowal that he ever intended any disrespect to her by the various neglects of which she has had so long and so often to complain, she thinks it right, in order *to prevent any mistake* for the *future*, shortly to explain *what it is she expects from the Foreign Secretary*. She requires: (1) That he will distinctly state what he proposes in a given case, in order that the Queen may know as distinctly to *what* she has given her Royal sanction; (2) Having *once given* her sanction to a measure, that it be not arbitrarily altered or modified by the Minister; such an act she must consider as failing in sincerity towards the Crown, and justly to be visited by the exercise of her Constitutional right of dismissing that Minister. She expects to be kept informed of what passes between him and the Foreign Ministers before important decisions are taken, based upon that intercourse; to receive the Foreign Despatches in good time, and to have the drafts for her approval sent to her in sufficient time to make herself acquainted with their contents before they must be sent off. The Queen thinks it best that Lord John Russell should show this letter to Lord Palmerston.

11—F.P.V.E.

56. Palmerston's private letter to Russell, 13 August 1850. Royal Archives, A 79/46; *The Letters of Queen Victoria*, 1st series, ii. 315–16.

I have taken a copy of this memorandum [no. 55] of the Queen, and will not fail to attend to the directions which it contains. With regard to the sending of despatches to the Queen, they have some-times been delayed longer than should have been the case, in con-sequence of my having been prevented by great pressure of business, and by the many interruptions of interviews, etc., to which I am liable, from reading and sending them back into the Office so soon as I could have wished. But I will give orders that the old practice shall be reverted to, of making copies of all important despatches as soon as they reach the Office, so that there may be no delay in sending the despatches to the Queen; this practice was gradually left off as the business of the Office increased, and if it shall require an additional clerk or two, you must be liberal and allow me that assistance.

57. Granville to Russell, 12 January 1852. Draft in Granville MSS., P.R.O. 30/29/18 part I; Temperley and Penson, pp. 183–6.

In obedience to Her Majesty's gracious Commands transmitted by you, I will endeavour to state, altho' very imperfectly, the views of Her Majesty's present Government with respect to the Foreign Policy of Great Britain. I will point out what I conceive to be the objects of that Policy, the principles of action, by which those objects are to be obtained, and the application of those principles to our relations with the principal countries of Europe.

In the opinion of the present Cabinet, it is the duty and the interest of this country, having possessions scattered over the whole globe, and priding itself on its advanced state of civilization, to encourage moral, intellectual and physical progress among all other nations.

For this purpose the Foreign Policy of Great Britain should be marked by justice, moderation, and self-respect, and this country should in her relations with other States do by others as it would be done by. While the Cabinet do not believe that all considerations of a higher character are to be sacrificed to the pushing our manufactures by any means into every possible corner of the globe, yet considering the great natural advantages of our Foreign Commerce, and the powerful means of civilization it affords, one of the first duties of a British Gov[ernmen]t must always be to obtain for our Foreign Trade that security which is essential to its success.

British subjects of all classes, engaged in innocent pursuits, are entitled abroad as well as at home to the protection of their Gov[ernmen]t. Where they have been treated with injustice, they have a right to expect that redress should be demanded in strong but dignified language, followed if necessary by corresponding measures; where they may, by their own wanton folly or misconduct, have got into difficulties in a Foreign Land, they have no right to expect assistance, and even where they unwittingly but imprudently subject themselves to the penal laws of the country in which they find themselves, they can only claim those good offices, the efficacy of which must depend upon the friendliness of our relations with the country in which the difficulty has arisen.

The Cabinet adhere to the principle of non-intervention in the internal affairs of other countries, as one tending most to maintain the dignity of the Crown, the security of the Country, and to strengthen the lasting influence of this Nation upon the opinion of the world.

They do not attach to the word 'non-intervention' the meaning implied by some who use it, viz. that Diplomacy is become obsolete, and that it is unnecessary for this country to know, or take a part in what passes in other countries. H.M.'s Gov[ernmen]t ought to be informed accurately and immediately, by their Agents, of every important event which may arise.

With regard to occurrences likely to have international consequences, no general rule can uniformly be applied. In each case, the Gov[ernmen]t must exercise its own discretion, whether it shall interfere at once, or remain aloof till its arbitration or good offices be required. The latter course may often be advisable when, as at present, opinion abroad is in extremes, and the Foreign Policy of England has obtained, whether justly or unjustly, the reputation of interfering too much. It will also often be found advisable to combine with other great Powers, when no sacrifice of principle is required, to settle the disputes which may arise between other nations.

With respect to those internal arrangements of other countries, such as the establishment of Liberal Institutions and the reduction of Tariffs, in which this country has an indirect interest, H.M.'s Representatives ought to be furnished with the views of H.M.'s Gov[ernmen]t on each subject, and the arguments best adapted to support those views, but they should at the same time be instructed to press these views only when fitting opportunities occur, and when their advice and assistance are required. The intrusion of advice which is suspected to be not wholly disinterested, never can have as much effect as opinions given at the request of the person who is to be influenced.

With reference to the support to be given to those Countries which have adopted Liberal Institutions similar in Liberality to our own, it will be the endeavour of H.M.'s Gov[ernmen]t to cultivate the most intimate relations with them.

It will be the duty of H.M.'s Gov[ernmen]t to inform them of all that may expose them to danger, and to give them, when required, frank and judicious advice. It will exert its influence to dissuade other Powers from encroaching on their territory, or attempting to subvert their institutions, and there may occur cases in which the honour and good faith of this country will require that it should support such Allies with more than friendly assurances.

H.M.'s Cabinet believe that every assistance, within the one competency of Gov[ernmen]t should be given to all those undertakings which tend to promote a more rapid interchange of knowledge and opinions among various countries; they believe that such increased intercourse will tend more than anything else to promote the Peace of the world.

The Cabinet is also of opinion that new measures should be taken to secure the efficiency of those who enter into the diplomatic career, and who are promoted in that profession—that a stricter discipline should be established among the members of each mission, and that those persons who combine those personal qualities which engage respect and popularity with activity in obtaining information, and zeal in executing their instructions, should be selected to represent Her Majesty, at the different Courts.

I will now endeavour to show how the principles which I have laid down as adopted by H.M.'s Gov[ernmen]t can be applied to our relations with the different European Nations and the United States; but it must be remembered that one unforeseen event may, like a move on a chessboard, necessitate perfectly different arrangements.

58. Russell's secret and confidential dispatch no. 38 to Sir G. Hamilton Seymour, 9 February 1853. Draft in P.R.O., F.O. 65/420; *Parliamentary Papers*, [1736], 1854, lxxi. 840–2.

I have received, and laid before the Queen, your secret and confidential despatch of the 22nd of January.

Her Majesty, upon this as upon former occasions, is happy to acknowledge the moderation, the frankness, and the friendly disposition of His Imperial Majesty.

Her Majesty has directed me to reply in the same spirit of temperate, candid, and amicable discussion.

The question raised by His Imperial Majesty is a very serious one. It is, supposing the contingency of the dissolution of the Turkish Empire to be probable, or even imminent, whether it is not better to be provided beforehand for a contingency, than to incur the chaos, confusion, and the certainty of an European war, all of which must attend the catastrophe if it should occur unexpectedly, and before some ulterior system has been sketched; this is the point, said His Imperial Majesty, to which I am desirous that you should call the attention of your Government.

In considering this grave question, the first reflection which occurs to Her Majesty's Government is that no actual crisis has occurred which renders necessary a solution of this vast European problem. Disputes have arisen respecting the Holy Places, but these are without the sphere of the internal government of Turkey, and concern Russia and France rather than the Sublime Porte. Some disturbance of the relations between Austria and the Porte has been caused by the Turkish attack on Montenegro; but this, again, relates rather to dangers affecting the frontier of Austria than the authority and safety of the Sultan; so that there is no sufficient cause for intimating to the Sultan that he cannot keep peace at home, or preserve friendly relations with his neighbours.

It occurs further to Her Majesty's Government to remark, that the event which is contemplated is not definitely fixed in point of time.

When William the Third and Louis the Fourteenth disposed, by treaty, of the succession of Charles the Second of Spain, they were providing for an event which could not be far off. The infirmities of the Sovereign of Spain, and the certain end of any human life, made the contingency in prospect both sure and near. The death of the Spanish King was in no way hastened by the Treaty of Partition.

The same thing may be said of the provision, made in the last century, for the disposal of Tuscany upon the decease of the last prince of the house of Medici. But the contingency of the dissolution of the Ottoman Empire is of another kind. It may happen twenty, fifty, or a hundred years hence.

In these circumstances it would hardly be consistent with the friendly feelings towards the Sultan which animate the Emperor of Russia, no less than the Queen of Great Britain, to dispose beforehand of the provinces under his dominion. Besides this consideration, however, it must be observed, that an agreement made in such a case tends very surely to hasten the contingency for which it is intended to provide. Austria and France could not, in fairness, be kept in ignorance of the transaction, nor would such concealment be consistent with the end of preventing an European war. Indeed, such concealment cannot be intended by His Imperial Majesty. It is to be inferred that, as soon as Great Britain and Russia should have agreed on the course to be pursued, and have determined to enforce it, they should communicate their intentions to the Great Powers of Europe. An agreement thus made, and thus communicated, would not be very long a secret; and while it would alarm and alienate the Sultan, the knowledge of its existence would stimulate all his enemies to increased violence and more obstinate conflict. They would fight with the conviction that they must ultimately triumph; while the Sultan's generals and troops would feel that no immediate success could save their cause from final overthrow. Thus would be produced and strengthened that very anarchy which is now feared, and the foresight of the friends of the patient would prove the cause of his death.

Her Majesty's Government need scarcely enlarge on the dangers attendant on the execution of any similar Convention. The example of the Succession War, is enough to show how little such agreements are respected when a pressing temptation urges their violation. The position of the Emperor of Russia as depositary, but not proprietor, of Constantinople, would be exposed to numberless hazards, both from the long-cherished ambition of his own nation, and the jealousies of Europe. The ultimate proprietor, whoever he might be, would hardly be satisfied with the inert, supine attitude of the heirs of Mahomet the Second. A great influence on the affairs of Europe seems naturally to belong to the Sovereign of Constantinople, holding the gates of the Mediterranean and the Black Sea.

That influence might be used in favour of Russia; it might be used to control and curb her power.

His Imperial Majesty has justly and wisely said: My country is so vast, so happily circumstanced in every way, that it would be unreasonable in me to desire more territory or more power than I possess. On the contrary, he observed, our great, perhaps our only danger, is that which would arise from an extension given to an Empire already too large. A vigorous and ambitious State, replacing the Sublime Porte, might, however, render war on the part of Russia a necessity for the Emperor or his successors.

Thus European conflict would arise from the very means taken to prevent it; for neither England nor France, nor probably Austria, would be content to see Constantinople permanently in the hands of Russia.

On the part of Great Britain, Her Majesty's Government at once declare that they renounce all intention or wish to hold Constantinople. His Imperial Majesty may be quite secure upon this head. They are likewise ready to give an assurance that they will enter into no agreement to provide for the contingency of the fall of Turkey without previous communication with the Emperor of Russia.

Upon the whole, then, Her Majesty's Government are persuaded that no course of policy can be adopted more wise, more disinterested, more beneficial to Europe than that which His Imperial Majesty has so long followed, and which will render his name more illustrious than that of the most famous Sovereigns who have sought immortality by unprovoked conquest and ephemeral glory.

With a view to the success of this policy it is desirable that the utmost forbearance should be manifested towards Turkey; that any demands which the Great Powers of Europe may have to make, should be made matter of friendly negotiation rather than of peremptory demand; that military and naval demonstrations to coerce the Sultan should as much as possible be avoided; that differences with respect to matters affecting Turkey, within the competence of the Sublime Porte, should be decided after mutual concert between the Great Powers, and not be forced upon the weakness of the Turkish Government.

To these cautions, Her Majesty's Government wish to add, that in their view it is essential that the Sultan should be advised to treat his Christian subjects in conformity with the principles of equity and religious freedom which prevail generally among the enlightened nations of Europe. The more the Turkish Government adopts the rules of impartial law and equal administration, the less will the Emperor of Russia find it necessary to apply that exceptional protection which His Imperial Majesty has found so burthensome and inconvenient, though no doubt prescribed by duty and sanctioned by Treaty.

You may read this despatch to Count Nesselrode, and, if it is desired, you may yourself place a copy of it in the hands of the Emperor. In that case you will accompany its presentation with those assurances of friendship and confidence on the part of Her Majesty the Queen, which the conduct of His Imperial Majesty was so sure to inspire.

59. Aberdeen's private letter to Russell, 15 February 1853. Copy in Aberdeen MSS., B.M., Add. MS. 43066; Walpole, ii. 178–9.

I think that it will be necessary to be very careful in preparing instructions for Lord Stratford, if, as I presume, we must consider his memorandum as giving an outline of what he would desire.

'The assurances of prompt and effective aid on the approach of danger', given by us to the Porte, would, in all probability, produce war. These barbarians hate us all, and would be delighted to take their chance, of some advantage, by embroiling us with the other powers of Christendom. It may be necessary to give them a moral support, and to endeavour to prolong their existence; but we ought to regard as the greatest misfortune any engagement which compelled us to take up arms for the Turks.

Lord Stratford is not very consistent in his descriptions of the Turkish Government. He refers to their present course of rashness, vacillation, and disorder; and speaks of their maladministration as hopeless. At the same time he looks to their power of carrying into effect a system of internal improvement—particularly in the essential branches of justice, revenue, roads, police, and military defence.

I do not believe that any power, at this time, entertains the intention of overthrowing the Turkish Empire, but it is certainly true that any quarrel might lead to this event; or, as Lord Stratford says, it might take place without such a deliberate intention on the part of any one of these powers.

We ought by all means to keep ourselves perfectly independent,

and free to act as circumstances may require. Above all, we ought not
to trust the disposal of the Mediterranean fleet—which is peace or
war—to the discretion of any man.

60. Russell's Memorandum on 'Russia and Turkey', 19 June 1853.
(Russell remained in the Cabinet after giving up the Foreign Office
in February 1853.) Russell MSS., P.R.O. 30/22/11A; G. P. Gooch,
ed., *The Later Correspondence of Lord John Russell* (London, 1925),
ii. 148–9, and Walpole, ii. 181–2.

The present position of Russia and Turkey must be viewed with
great uneasiness by all who have watched the progress of affairs
and the relative strength of these two Powers. If the existing dispute
can be arranged, matters may remain *in statu quo* for some time. I
do not propose to speak of any of those questions which in this
case must come before the Cabinet from day to day. But in the event
of the Emperor of Russia's persisting in his demands unmitigated,
and of the Sultan's refusal to accept them without modification,
serious events must occur. The 'status quo' and 'territorial cir-
cumscription of Europe,' on which the three Northern Powers have
so much insisted, is at once disturbed. No one can say what new
shapes this disturbance may assume. But without speculating on
contingent revolutions and wars, let us look at the immediate effect
of an attack by Russia on the provinces of Turkey, and even on
Constantinople itself. The Turkish army is of little avail against a
Russian army. No one doubts this fact. The population of the Turkish provinces three parts Christian would not fight for the Sultan,
and might very probably rise against him. The fleets of England
and France might destroy the Russian fleet in the Black Sea. But
they could not prevent the gradual, perhaps not even the speedy,
advance of the Russian army by land. Where then is their strength ? I
believe it to consist first in the unwillingness of Europe to see the
aggrandisement of Russia, secondly in the difficulty which Russia
would have in subduing the Greek Christians after she had favoured their insurrection, and thirdly in the apprehension of war
entertained by the Russian nobility whose revenues depend on the
sale of their raw produce. With respect to the first point, there can
be no doubt that Russia with Petersburg and Constantinople in the

same hands would be an object of just alarm to Europe, but especially to England and France and Austria. It is probable that Russia would seek to disguise her preponderance at Constantinople by placing some kind of Wallachian hospodar there. But she would never have so convenient a neighbour as the Sultan. So that in the end, to pacify Europe and avoid new complications, she might consent to restore Constantinople to the Porte. If she should not be willing to do this, but attempt to fix a Viceroy on the Bosphorus, the attempt must be resisted even by war on the part of England. Short of such an attempt Russia might be allowed to deprive the Sultan of his suzeraineté in the Principalities. It would be a cheaper concession for the Sultan to make than the signature of Prince Menshikoff's note. It would not introduce a Russian protectorate over all the Sultan's Christian subjects.

The second source of strength to the Allies, and of danger to Russia, consists in the ambition of the Greek Christians who have advanced too much in wealth and knowledge to be satisfied with a vassalage to the Czar of Russia. This point requires some further consideration. The war which was concluded in 1774 by the Treaty of Khainardji placed the Christian subjects of the Sultan in general terms under the protection of Russia. About the same time the armies of Russia began to assume an organization which made them very superior to the Turks. Thus both in spiritual sympathy and opinion of physical power, the Greek and Slavonic Christians were inclined to look to Petersburg. Of late years Lord Stratford has endeavoured to revive the power of Turkey, not by improving the Turkish race, but by making Turkish Government a shield and a security instead of a terror to its Christian subjects. It is obvious that if this plan were successful the ambition of Russia would be checked, and her plan of slowly waiting for the decease of her neighbour, in order to take out letters of administration to his property would be defeated, not for a time, but for ever. The heirs to the Mahometan Sultan would be vigorous, and intelligent Christian States. Russia has hitherto looked on smiling at the absurdity of this plan, while she quietly counteracted it. But it is evident she now thinks she can look on no longer. She must either grasp her prey at once, or lose it for ever. Nicolas is giving way to the Muscovite ambition.

The third obstacle in the way of Russia consists in the material interests of her nobility and merchants. But seeing the power of the Emperor, the strength of the military force, and the fanaticism of the people it would not be safe to calculate too much on this element of resistance.

On the whole, supposing peace not to be made during the Russian occupation of the Principalities, three separate stages of suspense and conflict appear to be approaching.

1. While Russia holds the Principalities, and persists in her present demand.

2. While Russia, having invaded Turkey, is marching on Constantinople.

3. When Russia, having taken Constantinople, is setting forth terms of peace, distinguished by 'moderation.'

Our policy in the first case is already decided on supposing that peace is not made.

In the second stage we must, I conceive, aid the Sultan in defending his capital and his throne.

In the third stage we must be prepared to make war on Russia herself. In that contest we ought to seek the alliance of France and Austria. France would willingly join; and England and France together might, if it were worth while, obtain the moral weight, if not the material assistance, of Austria in their favour. It is not necessary to point out how this might be done.

61. Memorandum by Palmerston, 20 June 1853. Russell MSS., P.R.O. 30/22/11A; Gooch, ii. 150–1.

I quite agree with Sir James Graham [First Lord of the Admiralty] that it is unwise to settle too long beforehand what course is to be pursued in regard to future and hypothetical events which may never happen at all, and with respect to which intervening circumstances and concomitant circumstances must, if they should come to pass, very materially determine the course to be pursued. But there are things so contrary to right and justice and so adverse to essential interests of this country and of Europe that the decision in regard to them cannot depend upon the course of any future events.

Of this kind of things I consider the appropriation by Russia of the Turkish Principalities on the Danube to be, and I cannot contemplate the acquiescence of England in such an appropriation. The invasion of those Provinces by Russia is an act of war against Turkey, and would justify the Sultan in sending an army to drive the Russians out if he was strong enough to do it. But he is not strong enough, and therefore he should be advised not to try it. The English and French squadrons cannot help him to do so; and it would not be advisable at present at least that England and France should make direct war upon Russia to compel her by pressure elsewhere to evacuate the Principalities. But nothing like acquiescence ought to be expressed or implied. The Sultan ought to remonstrate and protest in the face of Europe and the world against such an unjust aggression, and England and France ought to support him in denouncing the act as a violation of the rights of nations and of the peace of Europe; and the Emperor ought to be made plainly to understand that he is expected to go out again and that soon. On the other hand the Sultan cannot be advised to consent to the conditions demanded from him nor to agree to anything which would have the same effect upon his independence and authority.

My opinion is that if England and France stoutly support Turkey in this matter by negotiation, backing up their negotiation by adequate naval demonstration, they will ultimately succeed even if Austria and Prussia give them no assistance. But Austria and Prussia cannot see with indifference a hostile occupation of the Principalities by Russia, and whether they openly join us or not they will somehow or other assist us at Petersburgh. We may not succeed in weeks, it may take us months; but if England and France make the Russian government clearly understand that the Russian troops *must* go out, the Russian Government will somehow or other find the way to make them go out, and that without any infringement on the independence of the Sultan. I must say that I think any other result would be dishonourable to England and to France, and dangerous to the Balance of Power and to the security of the other States of Europe.

Beyond this question I cannot agree to look forward. I hold any further inroads by Russia upon the Turkish dominions at least in Europe to be out of the question the moment that England and France have declared themselves the allies of the Sultan and ready to assist him in defending his territories. I believe very great misapprehension to exist as to the offensive means of Russia on the one hand, and as to the defensive means of Turkey on the other. Russia is strong against invasion because of the vastness of her territory, and the scantiness of its supplies, and the scattered distribution of towns and villages; but the same causes make her weak for war beyond her frontier. Her armies never come into the field anything like what they appear on paper. They soon dwindle away in a campaign. Peculation misapplies the means destined for their maintenance; a bad commissariat leaves the men ill-fed; bad medical arrangements leave them to be disabled or to die from fatigue and disease. As the army advances, and the line of communication lengthens all these causes operate with increasing intensity. No successful invasion of Turkey with a view to getting south of the Balkans could be carried on by the Russians without free communication by sea with Odessa and Sebastopol. This would be cut off by the combined squadrons.

The Turkish army is much improved of late years. The men will fight as well as the Russians; England, France, and Poland would supply the officers wanted to make the army efficient. In point of numbers and of artillery it would be equal if not superior to the Russians. I greatly doubt any formidable rising of the population of any of the Christian provinces, but were that to be, it would have no material effect on the conflict between the two armies, and might be dealt with after the Russians were driven back. If the Sultan were to invite the Poles in Europe now in exile to join him the Poles in the Russian army could not be depended upon. And if Austria were to join Russia in such a war Hungarian exiles would flock to the scene of action, and Austria would not long remain quiet. Austria would from her own interest at all events be neutral.

The Russians have been waging an unsuccessful war in Circassia ever since 1849. Supplies of arms and ammunition thrown into Circassia when the combined fleets were masters of the Black Sea would turn the scale and give Schamyl [the Circassian rebel leader] possession of the country. Georgia would thus be cut off from southern Russia. This is always supposing England and France to act only locally and as auxiliaries in a defensive war. But the Russian nobles and merchants would look to the possibility of our going further; and more especially if fortune should not favour the Russian arms public opinion in Russia would exert an irresistible pressure on the Emperor, and prove that even autocrats are not always able to dispose as they will of the nation they govern. I do not therefore enter into a consideration of what is to be done with Turkey in the event of the overthrow of the present state of things because I am convinced that if England and France unite to maintain that state of things against Russia, it will be maintained; and I am of opinion that their honour and interest alike require them to do so.

62. Extract from the House of Commons Debate on 'Russia and the Porte', 16 August 1853. *Hansard*, 3rd series, cxxix. 1768, 1798–1810.

RUSSELL: . . . I can only add that, whilst I regret not to be able to state that the whole of these transactions are terminated, yet I do think that there is now a fair prospect that, without involving Europe in hostilities, the independence and integrity of Turkey, which from the beginning of the Session I have always stated to be the main object of the policy of Her Majesty's Government in reference to the affairs of the East, will be secured, and that in no very long period. I am sure this House will feel—I know that this country feels—that, if that object can be secured by negotiation, without involving Europe in the calamities of war, it will be a result which the whole world will value, and upon which we shall have reason to congratulate ourselves. I am quite sure that my noble Friend at the head of the Government may well console himself for any attacks that may have been made upon him in contemplating such a result, and that we have cause to appreciate highly the mixture of firmness and judgment by which he has been enabled to attain the end that is before us. Sir, I will only further say that this question of the maintenance of Turkey is one that must always require the attention—the vigilant attention—of any person entrusted with the conduct of the foreign affairs of this country; and further, that I think it can only be secured by a constant union subsisting between England and France, and by a thorough concert and cordial communication between those two Powers. . . .

COBDEN: I do not exactly see, Sir, that there is any difference of opinion on the question that is before us. I find everybody is agreed that Russia has acted in a manner that is treacherous, overbearing, and violent. I find that, in and out of this House, everybody entertains the opinion that the most fortunate result of the late proceedings in the East is, that it has brought about a firm alliance, not only between the people of England and France, but between the Governments of England and France, for I never can cease to separate the people, *de facto*, from their Government. Everybody wishes that Russia would evacuate the Principalities, and the noble Lord (Lord John Russell) has himself expressed his conviction that this object will be attained; and I believe everybody in this House, and out of it, would be willing to wait a few months longer, and have all those objects accomplished peaceably. I think that even in Birmingham itself, notwithstanding muskets are manufactured there, the people, if there was a meeting held in the Town Hall, would rather support the noble Lord in a pacific policy, than precipitate the country into a war to obtain the same objects a month or two earlier. But though evidently there is a great acquiescence of opinion amongst us all, there is still a great deal of uneasiness on the subject of Turkey. Is not the reason obvious, though we will not face it, and will rather deal with the superficies of the matter than deal with the interior of it? It is this: Because there is a growing conviction in our minds that what has been hitherto a current phrase, 'the independence of the Turkish Empire', has now become a mere empty phrase, and nothing more; because the fact is, that within the last twenty years there has been a growing conviction in the minds of people that the Turks in Europe are intruders—that it is not their domicile or their permanent home—that their home is in Asia, and that Mahomedan-ism cannot exist in Europe alongside of civilised States. The pro-gress of events has given a vast impetus to that opinion, which is grounded on the conviction that you cannot maintain Mahomedan-ism in Europe. Do what you will, that is your opinion—that is the embarrassment we feel—and that is, without doubt, the embarrass-ment of the Government in dealing with the subject. Disguise it as you will, we are not in earnest in the belief that we can preserve Mahomedanism in Europe. I have no wish to see the Russians in Constantinople; but I will not prevent them by our taking our stand for the preservation of Mahomedanism in Europe. If we or the Americans were the next neighbours of Turkey, judging by what they and we have done with regard to half a dozen Mahomedan dynasties in India, we would have swallowed them up long ago. The fact was, we could not maintain independence in a country if the people were not in a position to maintain it themselves, especially such a people as that of Turkey, numbering 20,000,000 or 30,000,000 in Europe and in Asia. There is another fact that has come up, and that is the existence of a large Christian population in Turkey in Europe. The fact is prominently before us, that the Christian element in Turkey in Europe is now the prominent one, and we cannot ignore it, because, for every one Turk in Turkey in Europe, there are three Christians in Turkey in Europe. The great majority of the people in Turkey in Europe are Christians, and the question is, what are the feelings of the Christian population towards their Mahomedan rulers. I believe that the feeling amongst the Christian population in the interior of Turkey is not favourable. I believe that in the large cities, in Smyrna and Constantinople, the Christians enjoy a certain portion of protection; but if you go into the interior of Turkey all the evidence goes to confirm me when I state that the Christian population in the interior of Turkey, in the small towns and villages, have a very hard lot indeed, and they are as much now under the rule and violent domination of an insolent caste and a barbarous people as ever they were. At this moment there is not a cadi, or pacha, or soldier that may not oppress the poor peasant in the interior almost as badly as they were oppressed two or three hundred years ago. These are facts that you cannot ignore in coming to a decision on the question of what is the feeling of the Christian population. The noble Lord (Lord D. Stuart) offered the opinion that they would prefer the rule of the Turks to that of the Russians. Well, that is possible. . . . I admit it is a matter of opinion, but still it is an open question whether they would not prefer the Russian to the Mahomedan rule. All I wish to urge is this, that that is a question which we must entertain. We are not taking the course which will ensure Turkish independence of other Powers, unless we carry the great bulk of the population in Turkey with us. It is obvious that we cannot consider their wishes at present. The question ought to be more discussed; it presses upon us all, and it will press upon us still more—it will hamper the Government in all their negotiations, especially on the question of resisting Russia by force. It may be possible for a time, if you will, to undertake to say how the eastern part of Europe shall be governed; but in the end we must go further, and from a consideration of the wishes of the people themselves we must undertake to say who shall permanently govern the Turkish Empire. . . . As to sending our fleet to the Bay of Besika, and keeping the Russians out of Constantinople—that you may do, no doubt. Russia has always avoided a collision with a maritime Power. She has avoided it with America—she has avoided it with England— because in such a collision all the illusion respecting her greatness would be dispelled at once. But in the meantime you are keeping

up an enormous armament, which does not tend to settle the question—you are inducing the Turkish Government to prepare for war,
which will bring ruin and bankruptcy on her finances—you are
thereby placing Turkey in a more feeble and prostrate condition
than she was in before. I have no doubt the Government will
prevent a war, but the question will not be settled; it will come up
again; and you must, therefore, address yourselves, as men of sense
and men of energy, to the question—what are you to do with the
Christian population? for Mahomedanism cannot be maintained;
and, what is more, I should be sorry to see this country fighting for
the maintenance of Mahomedanism. I never could get up any zeal
on behalf of the Mahomedans; they keep the plague—they keep
slavery—they have a bazaar for the sale of black and white slaves.
You may keep Turkey on the map of Europe; you may call the
country by the name of Turkey, if you like, but do not think you
can keep up the Mahomedan rule in that country. A great deal has
been said about the necessity of maintaining the independence of
Turkey on account of our commerce with her. Now, as a free trader,
I must once for all enter my protest against fighting for a market at
all. I never would consent to fight for a low tariff. In the first place, I
deny that you could do so. What has experience shown? You fought
for a tariff in Spain, and after spending between 200,000,000£ and
300,000,000£ of money in keeping Spain out of the hands of an
enemy who would have excluded your commerce, you accomplished
your object, and Spain and Portugal repaid your exertions by enact-
ing the most restrictive tariffs in Europe. You occupied Sicily during
the whole of the last war; and when you left it, what sort of tariff
was enacted for your manufactures? In the next place I have too
much faith in my principles to go to war for them. I believe that
free-trade principles will spread and make converts by means of
peace. We are making converts every day by the proofs we are
affording of the salutary and striking benefits of free trade. Therefore, do not talk of war as a means of removing restrictions, or of
opening markets. Besides, the noble Lord (Lord J. Russell) is under
a great delusion as to the accounts of our commerce with Turkey.
The returns which the noble Lord has given to the House, and on
which he relies, are the returns of exports to the Black Sea, which are
sent most of them to Austria, up the Danube. That is not Turkish
commerce. Constantinople is a mere depôt from whence our goods
are sent to Trebisond and elsewhere; there is very little consumption

of our commerce in the dominions of Turkey. Though I have no partiality for Russia—on the contrary, I am not sorry to see the great representative of the despotic principle humiliated and dishonoured by the mean plottings and contrivances which he has carried on through the whole of these transactions; yet, let us not delude ourselves with any idea of danger resulting to the commerce of this country from Russian ascendancy. I maintain that all the commerce we have on the Black Sea is owing to Russian invasion. We never had any commerce in the Black Sea until Russia took possession of the Crimea. . . . I therefore, discard the idea altogether that Russia will discourage our trade. What, on the other hand, is the prospect of our trade with Turkey? It is a country literally without a road. . . . Do not deceive yourselves, and pretend that we are the natural allies of such a country for the purposes of trade. I protest against the argument that it is for the interest of England, or that we are bound to maintain Turkey in possession of those rich and fertile territories. There may be other political reasons, but I object to facts being brought forward which have no foundation, in order to mislead the English people in regard to their true interests. These points must be developed—they must be reasoned upon—they must be dwelt on for the next few years. The present question may be settled—I do not expect that it will lead to war—I do not find any sensible people who ever did expect that. A great deal has been said about the power of Russia, and about the danger to England if Russia were allowed to occupy the countries of the Bosphorus. I never shared that opinion. . . . The country is poor and thinly populated—it is a mere series of villages; how could it injure England or France? It may possess Turkey, because Turkey is in state of decay, and when a country falls into decrepitude, its next neighbour will be sure to take it if he can. I repudiate the notion of Russia invading England. But what has been done, and by England, towards such of the Mahomedan Powers as we are neighbours to in India? We have not been a whit less unscrupulous in our diplomacy towards them than Russia has been to Turkey, and especially in the way that, within the last two years we have dealt with Burmah. But however Russia may deal with Turkey, I do not see what right we have to interfere with a matter so far removed from us. I believe that England would be ready to resist an attack from whatever quarter it might come, and that she would be ten times more powerful to resist than Russia to atttack.

All the resources that we have in our vast manufactures—all the appliances that we possess in our prodigious steam vessels, and in our mechanical skill, would be turned in six months—ay, in six days—to the contrivance of engines of destruction which would render us more powerful than any other nation on the face of the earth. All these are wanting in Russia; they must come here for their steam boats, or for the artisans to make them, and there is not a chance of their injuring us. . . . Let me tell my Friends the Members for the manufacturing towns, who talk so glibly of war, that while I agree with them that in a war to defend this kingdom, England would bring all her resources to bear, and would defend herself against all the world, yet I say that if England were to go further, and to engage in a continental war, you do not know what belligerents you might have in six months from its declaration. A war now would be attended with consequences of which the present generation little think, or they would not talk of it so glibly. In the first place, you would have the Americans, whose country was a mere infant in 1793, and to whom we could then say, 'You shall come to no part[port?] in Europe except by our permission,' and we could seize their ships and press their crews at our pleasure. Now, if war were to break out, what would be the first thing we should be called upon to do? Why, we should be called upon by the Americans to disavow the right of search. We could not refuse that, and that concession would place America at once as our rival in the carrying trade of Europe. And, remember, you have now repealed your navigation laws. In 1793 you could send out large fleets of merchant ships, under the convoy of ships of war, twice a year. You had the monopoly of the seas; and it did not matter to you when or how your ships sailed, because other countries must wait upon you for their supplies. But what would be the case now, if you were to go to war? If you were engaged in war with a maritime Power, they would issue letters of marque to fleets of steamers, who could take refuge when they pleased in Stockholm or other neutral ports. Your insurances for freights would rise at Lloyd's in proportion to the risk of capture. How would your manufacturers—how would your numerous and wealthy colonies, consent to bring over their freights in English bottoms, when Dutchmen, Hamburghers, and Frenchmen were not subject to the same risk? Remember that the repeal of the navigation laws has thrown you open to the competition of the whole world in shipping, as in everything else. . . . I think the Government

have done wisely in disregarding the cry of thoughtless men; they
have done wisely in not listening to the cry of the newspapers, some
of which profess the democratic principle, as if democracy ever
gained by war. The Government have done right, not only for the
interests of the country, but even for the interests of themselves; for
if they should plunge the country into war, the shallow men who
now cry for war would, in less than six weeks, call for the disgrace
and the removal of the very Ministers who began the war. I have
nothing to say to the Ministers. I do not blame them because they
have taken up a position to defend the Turkish empire. It is a traditional policy they have followed, which has been handed down to
them by previous governments, and unless they had public opinion
with them, no Government could avoid doing so. All I say is, that I
have no doubt they will soon get rid of the difficulties respecting
the Wallachian provinces; and I congratulate them on having been as
peaceable as the people would allow them to be.

PALMERSTON: . . . I cannot accept the praise which the hon. Gentleman has bestowed on the conduct of the Government at the conclusion of his speech on the ground on which he has been pleased to
place it. Nothing is so painful as to see a man of great ability labour-
ing to bring about a conviction which he knows to be contrary to
the opinions of the great majority of his fellow-countrymen, and
which, therefore, he is afraid—I will not use a stronger expression—
openly to express, but which he endeavours to conceal under every
specious device which human ingenuity could afford to the practised
orator. The hon. Gentleman, in the beginning, agreed with every
person and everything, and he ended in differing with every one on
all points. The hon. Gentleman began by assuming it to be a proper
maxim of policy to maintain the independence of Turkey, and to
prevent Russia from taking a portion of that territory which belonged
to the Turkish empire. But in the course of his speech, the hon.
Gentleman used every argument to show that Turkey was not worth
anything, and that it was not of much consequence if it fell to pieces.
If the hon. Gentleman stood forth as the advocate of the aggressive
and ambitious policy of Russia, as the advocate of that system of
policy which he pretended so lately to denounce and condemn, in
the present state of feeling in this House and the country, I know
not how he could dare to pursue a course more calculated to defend
and assist and facilitate the views which he pretended to oppose. I

confess, Sir, I never heard a speech in my life so full of contradictions. At one moment he tells us that Russia—not as formerly—could be crumpled up like a sheet of brown paper—but he tells us that Russia is so weak that she is perfectly incapable of resisting any serious efforts that might be made against her on the part of this country; at another moment, he declares that war with Russia would be ruin to England. How can he reconcile the two statements? At one time, Russia is a barbarous Power, with scattered territories, weak in the interior; and then he launches out into praises of the beauty of St. Petersburg, and, because that city is more beautiful than Constantinople, he thinks that Russia ought to be possessed of both. The hon. Gentleman is a free trader, and says free trade has made great progress throughout Europe. He has himself made a tour through Europe in that character, and because he has been received with the courtesy and civility to which his personal qualities entitled him, he thinks that he has persuaded all Europe to abandon their former systems and to become free traders. The hon. Gentleman says, that the efforts which this country has made in former times were in favour of low tariffs, and he asks what has been the result to this country? Why, Sir, we went to war for the liberties of Europe, and not for the purpose of gaining so much per cent on our exports. We went to war, not for the purpose of increasing the export of our commodities, but in defence of the liberty and independence of nations, and for the maintenance of that balance of power, which, however the hon. Gentleman may treat it with contempt and sneer at, because he does not understand it—everybody else considers to be a point deserving of assertion, and essential to the liberty and well-being of mankind. I admit that no man has done more in this country for the assertion and practical enforcement of the principle of free trade than the hon. Gentleman, and I am the last man to withhold the tribute of my acknowledgments to him for the great services he has rendered in that respect. But the hon. Gentleman seems entirely to forget his principle when he compares the commercial system of Turkey to that of Russia. Does the hon. Gentleman not know—and if he knows, why does he seek to withdraw the attention of the public from it?—that the commercial system of Russia is a restrictive and prohibitory one, while that of Turkey is the most liberal one that exists in any country with which we have commercial relations? The hon. Gentleman says that Turkey is immaterial in a commercial point of view, because, forsooth, we had no great commerce in the Black Sea till the time of the Empress Catherine. Why, Sir, I never heard an argument from the hon. Gentleman less calculated to support the conclusion which he wished to draw. But it is not true that the commerce of Turkey is immaterial to this country. It is material to this country. Her natural and internal products are as important as those that come to us from Russia, and as her natural and internal resources increase, her commerce will become more and more valuable. . . . Whether, therefore, we are to consider Turkey as a consumer, or as the channel through which our manufactures pass into Asia, in either point of view it is of great importance to the commercial interests of England that Turkey should remain independent, in order that a liberal system of commerce may exist. But the hon. Gentleman is a great advocate for non-interference. He says, 'Do not interfere at all in the internal affairs of other countries; do not dictate to other nations or people their form of government'; and then he says that the state and position of Turkey must be specially committed to the deliberation of the Government and Parliament of this country. He says that the question which we have to determine is, what we are to do with the Turkish Empire—that we have to dispose of the relative situation of Mahomedan and Greek, and that we are to decide who are to be the inhabitants of this part of the Turkish Empire. He says that you are now yielding to a vulgar prejudice; that Turkey is a rotten fabric that cannot last long; that the Turkish Empire must expire; that, as the Sultan, his army, and 2,000,000 or 3,000,000 of inhabitants are only encamped in Europe, it would be quite ridiculous and absurd to interfere for their preservation; and, that, on the contrary, we should consider how best to dispose of their territories, and relieve Europe of the blighting presence of the Moslem. That, Sir, is a strange doctrine from one who maintains the necessity of leaving foreign countries to decide on their own form of government. But, Sir, I do not admit to him that Turkey, as an Empire, is in that state of decay which he represents. I say that the maintenance of the integrity of Turkey is not only an object desirable, but one worth contending for, and capable of being carried out to a successful result. The hon. Gentleman has been greatly misinformed as to the state of Turkey for the last thirty years. I assert, without fear of contradiction from any one who knows anything on the subject, that, so far from having gone back, Turkey has made greater progress and improvement than any other country in the same period.

Compare Turkey now with what she was in the reign of Sultan Mahmou—take either her system of government or the prosperity of her inhabitants—take her army—take her navy—take her administration of justice—take the prosperity of her agriculture—take her improvements in such manufactures as she has—take her commercial system—take her religious toleration—I say, that in all these respects Turkey has made immense progress during the period which I have mentioned. So far from going with the hon. Gentleman in that sort of political slang which is the fashion of those who want to partition and divide Turkey—who say that Turkey is a dead body, or an expiring body, that cannot be kept alive, I am convinced that if you only keep out of it those who wish to get into it—if you only leave those who are now in it to deal with it as they now deal with it, so far is it from internal dissolution that I consider there are not many countries in Europe with whom it would not bear a favourable comparison. I think it as likely to increase in power and prosperity, if you only keep other people's hands off it, as some of those countries to which the hon. Gentleman has referred. Turkey, it must be remembered, has no Poland or Circassia to distract her. Sir, I am bound to say, that if ever I heard a speech which, while it ostensibly commended the course pursued by the Government, was calculated to damp the proper feeling of the country in support of that Government, it was the speech of the hon. Gentleman. But, I am happy to say, it is the only speech we have heard to-night in that tone; and I trust it will not mislead any one beyond the limits of this country, who might be deceived by it. I hope that such language will not excite abroad a feeling that might render it more difficult for Her Majesty's Government to bring about a settlement of the question satisfactorily to the honour of the country. I trust that the great preponderance of the proper feeling and sentiment on this subject will have shown all Europe the real sentiment of Parliament on this subject, and the determination of the British nation and the British Parliament to support the Government, and, that though there may be one man who wishes to see Russia extend her conquests over Turkey, that is not the wish of the British nation, and that the Government of England, ·supported by the people of England, are determined to maintain the independence of Turkey—an independence which we think it essential to maintain both for political and commercial purposes. I do not mean to go with the hon. Gentleman into a rearrangement of the Turkish Empire, or to dictate to the

Bulgarians, Slavonians, Greeks, or Mussulmans, who are to be their governors, or what their form of government is to be. But it has been the policy of this country to give advice to the Turkish Government, with a view to those internal improvements which we thought would add to the strength of Turkey, and to the happiness and prosperity of the people who are placed under the rule of the Sultan. Our suggestions have, I am happy to say, been attended with most beneficial consequences to Turkey. Our consular agents in the different provinces of Turkey inform us that tranquillity has increased, that justice is better administered, that oppression has ceased, and that those benefits have resulted, which it must be the anxious desire of England to promote in every country which considers its advice worthy of its attention. If that system is pursued; if England, united with France, determine that Turkey shall not belong to Russia or to any other Power, and if that doctrine is enforced in practice, I am convinced that if no foreign Power endeavour to destroy Turkey, our policy, so far from being ridiculous, as the hon. Gentleman endeavoured to represent it, will prove a sound policy—a policy which deserves the approbation of the country, and which it will be the duty of every future British Government to pursue.

63. Extract from an account of a Cabinet meeting on the *Arrow* incident, February 1857. George Douglas, Eighth Duke of Argyll, *Autobiography and Memoirs* (London, 1906), ii. 67–9.

At one of the early meetings of the Cabinet after the opening of Parliament, Palmerston told us that he understood that the naval proceedings in the Canton River were attracting more and more attention, and that an attack upon the Government was being prepared by the usual combination of malcontents. He added that it was to be founded on an accusation of having violated the principles of international law, and that the legal members of the House were shaking their heads very much about it. In case, therefore, of the Cabinet desiring to hear their opinion, he had asked the Attorney-General to be within reach, and suggested that he should be called in. . . .

When the mellifluences of the Attorney-General's voice and his precise syllabic utterances had come to an end, Palmerston thanked him for the assistance he had given to us, and he rolled gently out of the room, as he had rolled into it. We all thought it very evident that, were it not for his office, it would give him immense pleasure to take the part of leading counsel against us. But however struck I may have been by the obvious great abilities of our new law officer of the Crown, I was not equally impressed by the relevance of his argument. The whole of it was founded on the assumption that our representative officers on the Canton River were bound by the same highly complex rules of so-called international law which govern the relations of the civilized nations of the Christian world, and that assumption appeared to me to be absurd. Our relations with the Chinese at Canton were exclusively commercial, largely determined by local habits and usages, and liable to suffer the most serious injury from the local functionaries of a barbarous Government, whose conduct was apt to be arbitrary and violent.

I did not care to ask whether the conduct of Sir John Bowring had or had not been somewhat more high-handed than was absolutely necessary. It was enough for me to see that the disavowal of our Commissioner, when such serious action had been taken, would inflict a severe blow on all our officers who might succeed him, and throw into confusion the whole system on which our commerce rested in that part of the world. I was convinced that this common-sense view would be taken by the country and by the House of Commons. . . .

64. Extract from Palmerston's private letter to Clarendon, 1 March 1857. Clarendon MSS., Bodleian Library, MS. Clar. dep. c 69; Maxwell, ii. 300–1, and Ashley, ii. 125–6.

* * * *

As to the Emperor's schemes about Africa . . . It is very possible that many parts of the world would be better governed by England, France and Sardinia than they are now, and we need not go beyond Italy, Sicily and Spain for examples. But the alliance of England and France has derived its strength not merely from the military and naval power of the two States, but from the force of the moral principle upon which that union has been founded. Our union has for its foundation resistance to unjust aggression, the defence of the weak against the strong, and the maintenance of the existing balance of power. How then could we combine to become unprovoked aggressors, to imitate in Africa the partition of Poland, by the conquest of Morocco for France, of Tunis and some other State for Sardinia, and of Egypt for England, or more especially how could England and France who have guaranteed the integrity of the Turkish Empire turn round and wrest Egypt from the Sultan? A coalition for such purposes would revolt the moral feelings of mankind, and would certainly be fatal to any English government that became a party to it. Then as to the balance of power to be maintained by giving us Egypt. In the first place we don't want to have Egypt. What we wish about Egypt is that it should continue attached to the Turkish Empire, which is a security against its belonging to any European power. We want to trade with Egypt and to travel through Egypt but we do not want the burthen of governing Egypt, and its possession would not as a political, military and naval question be considered in this country a set-off against the possession of Morocco by France.

Let us try to improve all these countries by the general influence of our commerce but let us all abstain from a crusade of conquest which would call down upon us the condemnation of all the other civilized nations.

65. Palmerston's private letter to Clarendon, 31 December 1857. Clarendon MSS., Bodleian Library, MS. Clar. dep. c 69; Kenneth Bourne, 'The Clayton-Bulwer Treaty and the Decline of British Opposition to the Territorial Expansion of the United States, 1857–1860', *Journal of Modern History*, xxiii (1961), 290–1.

These Yankees are most disagreeable Fellows to have to do with about any American Question; They are on the Spot, strong, deeply interested in the matter, totally unscrupulous and dishonest and determined somehow or other to carry their Point; We are far away, weak from Distance, controuled by the Indifference of the Nation as to the Question discussed, and by its Strong commercial Interest in maintaining Peace with the United States. The Result of this State of Things has been that we have given way Step by Step to the North Americans on almost every disputed matter, and I fear that we shall have more or less to do so upon almost every other Question except the maintenance of our own Provinces and of our West Indian Islands. I have long felt inwardly convinced that the Anglo-Saxon Race will in Process of Time become Masters of the whole American Continent North and South, by Reason of their superior Qualities as compared with the degenerate Spanish and Portugueze Americans; But whatever may be the Effect of such a Result upon the Interests of England, it is not for us to assist such a Consummation, but on the contrary we ought to delay it as long as possible.

The Clayton Bulwer Treaty opposes a barrier to North American advance, by stopping the Yankees out of Central America, and therefore they all hate and detest the Treaty. It fetters them and makes them halt. If we were quite sure that the Treaty could be permanently kept in Existence, and that it would be honestly observed I should be inclined to say let us stick to it, even at the Sacrifice of those Points of Difference as to its Interpretation on which the United States insist. But the Yankees are such Rogues, and such ingenious Rogues that it is hardly possible to hope that even if the present Questions were settled to their liking by the abandonment of the Bay Islands and of Mosquitia and of part of our Honduras some new Cavils would not be found, or at least that by the indirect agency of such men as Walker & his followers some independent North American States would not be established in Central America, in alliance with the United States if not in Union with them, in short Texas all over again. If the Spanish Race in Central America had the slightest energy or courage, if they were like the English, the French, the Germans, or the Russians they would soon have Walker & his Followers with Bullets through their Heads, or dangling on the gallows, but small as Walker's Bands may be, they may possibly succeed, and they may have allies in Nicaragua. But even if Walker fails some other adventurer may have better Fortune, and New Orleans seems prepared to furnish sufficient means for success. Under these circumstances I am inclined to agree with you in thinking that our best Course would be to sound Buchanan as to what arrangement he would be prepared to substitute for the Clayton Bulwer Treaty, supposing that we were prepared to concur in its abrogation. He would thus be obliged to show his Hand, we should at all events gain Time, and we should not be bound to any particular course. Logically speaking we might require him first to answer our offer of Mediation, and that would be the Course which probably would embarrass him the most, as we may infer from his having said nothing about our offer in his speech (or message rather) and I am not sure that this would not be the most regular thing to do. He would decline arbitration and give his Reasons which would probably be bad ones, but his Refusal would be a ground-work on which we could directly found some other Proposal. Should we not appear to be in unseemly haste if without waiting for an answer to a firm offer of arbitration we at once hurried to the President with an Intimation that we were ready to consider the abrogation of the Treaty. I cannot conceive that the Senate would take so violent a Step as to vote the abrogation of the Treaty while a Communication was going on between the two Governments with a view to settle amicably the Points of Difference which have arisen out of its Interpretation. If arbitration is refused we may then make another Proposal. If it is accepted the award of the arbiter whether for or against us would give fresh Force to the Treaty.

66. Malmesbury's secret dispatch to Lord Bloomfield (Ambassador in Berlin), 'upon the supposed prospect of rupture between France and Austria', 7 January 1859. Copy of draft in Royal Archives, J 14/19.

Your secret despatch of the 20th Decbr., received by me on the 3rd inst., was of such importance that I could not reply to it until I had consulted with Lord Derby. I have now to instruct your Lordsp. to express the thanks and satisfaction of H.M.G. at the friendly proof of confidence which H.R.H. the Prince Regent has placed in them in thus making a timely communication of his opinions as to the present state of Europe, and H.M.G. will meet it with equal frankness.

Altho' H.M.G. do not share with that of Prussia the apprehension of an immediate war between France and Austria, they cannot be insensible to the precarious relations unfortunately existing between those two states.

On the one hand H.M.G. still believe it will only be when forced, or supposing himself to be forced, by circumstances involving his own political existence, that the Emperor Napoleon will abandon the wise and loyal course which he has hitherto followed towards Europe, and that no common accidents of temper or irritation displayed against H.I.M. will goad him into a new & less happy policy. From the best information which H.M.G. can obtain, it would also appear that the French Army & Materiel are not on a footing to predict campaigns of such magnitude to be impending this year.

On the other hand there is a peril to which H.M.G. cannot be blind—It is that, in the probable event of disturbances taking place in the Legations or other states of Central Italy, Austria should, without any previous concert with France, march troops into those countries. This would offer a '*casus belli*' to Count Cavour, who is doubtless most anxious to avail himself of any excuse to employ an army twice too large for the population and resources of Piedmont, but which he hopes will be hereafter compensated by additional territory. That territory can only be taken from Austria.

If such an eventuality shd. occur, H.M.G. apprehend that the Emperor Napoleon would not in the interest of his popularity remain neuter, & that he would side with Piedmont. The marriage about to take place in his family & that of Savoy, would be an additional inducement to act with the king, while the continued ill-humour prevailing between the ministers of France and Austria must inevitably aggravate the feeling of hostility towards the latter state, and add their weight against the balance of peace.

Such appears to H.M.G. to be the present aspect of the future respecting the relations of these great empires. The consequences of a breach between them are entirely understood by the P[russian] G[overnment]; & it is needless to linger on the effects of an event which would be an European disaster.

Yr. Lordshp.'s despatch, after contemplating the probability of such misfortunes, proceeds to ask, on the part of the P.G. what course England would follow should they occur.

H.M.G. entirely approve of your Lordshp.'s reply that 'no English Govt. would feel disposed to enter into any solemn engagement with a foreign power of a nature prospectively binding'. They cannot do so on this occasion, and they earnestly trust that Prussia will also continue to retain for herself an entire liberty of action.

In the event of a war begun, and engaged in, as I have contemplated, H.M.G. would preserve as long as possible a strict neutrality, but I cannot conceal from your Lordshp. and the P.G. that if Austria places herself in the wrong in her first move by armed intervention with other Italian states than her own, public sympathy in England will be on the side of France, or rather of Italy.

The duty and interest of the British and Prussian Govts. would at present appear to be evident.

First, it should be to encourage as much as possible the good feeling and amity of all the German powers with one another. In such a wise and just union and sympathy France must see a barrier to any ambitious views of territorial aggrandisement in which she may possibly indulge.

Secondly. To use our best endeavours to convince Count Buol [the Austrian Foreign Minister] of the paramount importance that he should keep in the right and make no military movement out of Austrian Italy without previous concert with France. He should be convinced by England and Prussia that any contrary course must inevitably alienate the hearts of two free states like ours, and eventually estrange their Govts.

But another policy should, in the opinion of H.M.G., be suggested both at Paris & Vienna by England and Prussia. It must be evident to the statesmen of the latter that the dominions of the Pope are the most grievous sore of Italy, & that from that central point arises the principal mass [?] of misery and just discontent. In the opinion of H.M.G. if that portion of Italy were well-governed and happy, we should hear far less of the general oppression of the Italian people, and of that long and vain dream of Italian unity.

H.M.G. believe that the good govt. of the Papal States is possible, but that it can be only effected by France & Austria to the eternal honor of the first, & to the great advantage of the latter, who would have peaceful neighbours, instead of a hive of enemies upon her frontier. H.M.G. believe that an amelioration of the state of central Italy can only be brought about by the two Catholic Empires I have named. H.M.G. are convinced that, if the Protestant Kingdoms of England and Prussia were to interfere actively, they would injure rather than benefit the cause, by the religious suspicions which their presence would engender. But, as parties to the territorial treaties of 1815 they might give all their moral support to Austria & France, and H.M.G. would not, under certain circumstances, which promised a stable and good govt. in Central Italy, be indisposed to consider the territorial redistribution of that part of the peninsula. The consent and aid of Prussia in such an important act would be indispensable & invaluable.

It is therefore with these views that H.M.G. would ask Prussia to press upon the courts of Paris & Vienna this line of Italian politics, as the one best adapted to give a reasonable hope of improving Italian government, by pacifying the Roman states & rendering them less dangerous to Austria who is often driven by these against her will, to measures of a coercive and apparently a tyrannical character towards her own subjects. H.M.G. see in this course the only probable means of averting an Austrian and French war in Italy.

I have said that H.M.G. would not be disinclined to a redistribution of Central Italy, if any new arrangement gave Europe a fair promise that such a one would be lasting and beneficial to the people. Yr. Lordsp. will add that H.M.G. do not contemplate any hostile movement against the spiritual authority of the Pope by such a policy. On the contrary such an authority exercised over a large portion of the Christian world would seem to be indispensable & cannot be interfered with. Yr. Lordsp. will also express to the P.G. that H.M.G. foresee no circumstances that, with this exception, would incline them to consent to any further change of the territorial arrangements established for Europe by the Treaties of 1815.

Whether perfect or faulty, they have undoubtedly been the main cause of the longest peace on record, and, in the opinion of H.M.G. they still answer their original purpose by maintaining an equitable balance of power. H.M.G. would therefore oppose any attempt, from any quarter, to infringe those Treaties, which the successive dynasties and sovereigns of France, including Napoleon III, have solemnly promised to maintain.

I will only remark in conclusion that Russia is at present far from able to undertake active military operations. The reduced state of her army and finances, her internal reforms, & the character of the Emperor Alexander all tend to relieve us from such an apprehension, but, if hostile to Austria, she might paralyse a large part of her army by a corps of observation on her northern frontier.

More than this I am unable to say at present to Yr. Lordsp. on the part of H.M.G., & in their opinion the P.G. would do unwisely were they to take any step more decided until we see these misfortunes fall upon Europe, which we shall have vainly tried to avert. It will then be, I trust, the inclination, as well as the interest of England & Prussia, bound as they are by ties of religion and political interest to concert together the best means of resisting the storm which they failed to confine.

67. Extract from Russell's dispatch no. 18 to Bloomfield, 7 July 1859. P.R.O., F.O. 244/161; *Parliamentary Papers*, [2550], 1859, session 2, xxxii. 567–9.

Count Bernstorff [the Prussian Minister in London] has read to me two despatches from Baron Schleinitz [the Prussian Foreign Minister], one marked 'very confidential,' upon the subject of the present aspect of affairs, and upon the policy which Prussia is desirous, in conjunction with England and Russia, to pursue with regard to the Italian war and its consequences.

Those despatches were dated respectively the 24th and the 27th of June.

Baron Schleinitz, in the former of these despatches, alludes to the state of affairs which has induced Prussia to mobilize part of her army. Not only, he says, has the agitation in Germany caused by the advance of the war towards her frontier rendered necessary armaments not disproportioned to those of her neighbours; but Prussia has considered it necessary at once to place herself in a position to control a course of events which might tend to modify the balance of power in Europe, by enfeebling an empire with which Prussia is confederated, and by affecting the bases of European rights laid down in acts to which Prussia was a party.

Baron Schleinitz observes, however, that the position adopted by Prussia does not prejudge the Italian question, although the interests of Prussia and Germany make it incumbent on the Prince Regent to use the influence which it is his duty to exert, and prevent his prematurely sanctioning, by a passive attitude, territorial modifications affecting a nation which forms an essential portion of the great European family.

But Prussia only wishes to act, as she has done before, in concert with England and Russia, in order to re-open negotiations in the cause of peace; and Count Bernstorff is accordingly instructed to concert with Her Majesty's Government as to the means of obtaining this result, and thereby putting an end to the effusion of blood, and of restoring to Europe that calm which her moral and material interests demand.

Baron Schleinitz then observes that, however much Prussia regretted the decision of Austria to proceed to extremities, neither Europe as a whole, nor Germany in particular, could view with indifference any step which should tend to enfeeble Austria.

He is far from misapprehending the difficulties created by the events of the war, and he thinks that considerable reform will be required in the administration of affairs in Northern and Central Italy, and that this will be a surer mode of peacefully governing those districts than by the employment of the military resources of Austria. He thinks also that the Treaties which bind Austria to exercise a sort of protectorate over certain Italian States may be replaced by a better system.

Thus while Prussia does not seek to restore a past state of things which may be looked upon as a present impossibility, she will eagerly seize any proposition having for its object an Italian reconstruction, which, while acknowledging the rights of Austria, shall by being founded on liberal principles, conciliate the legitimate wishes of the Italian population.

Prussia further thinks herself entitled to take note of the explicit declarations of the Emperor Napoleon that he neither covets conquest nor territorial aggrandizement, and this appears to Baron Schleinitz an earnest of the possibility of coming to a common understanding with England and Russia as to the course to be pursued.

Count Bernstorff is then desired to ask for the views of Her Majesty's Government upon this subject; and the despatch concludes by instructing him not to omit any opportunity of putting forward the idea of a mediation in common ('médiation commune').

* * * *

I stated to Count Bernstorff that this communication should receive the attentive consideration of Her Majesty's Government, but that I wished, in the first place, to ask him the full significance of the terms 'stop the effusion of blood' and a 'mediation in common,' namely, whether if England and Prussia together, or those Powers with Russia joined to them, found the proposals which they might make to the belligerents refused, it was meant that they should employ force.

His Excellency said that he had no explanations to offer on that head: that Prussia could not propose to Austria any alienation of territory, but only reforms and changes in modes of administration.

He wished, however, to obtain an immediate answer from me; and I said that, pending the decision of the Cabinet, I could only express my own opinion that the time had not arrived for making any proposition to the belligerents.

Such being the proposition of the Court of Prussia, I have in the first place to desire that you will express to Baron Schleinitz the thanks of Her Majesty's Government for the friendly tone and zeal for the welfare of the States of Europe which have inspired this overture. The efforts made by a Power so enlightened as Prussia to restore peace to the Continent of Europe will always be duly appreciated by Her Majesty. Her Majesty's Government are at once ready to declare that they would hail with joy the moment when any equitable proposal for an armistice or negotiation might be accepted. But Her Majesty's Government think themselves bound in fairness to go further, and meet the friendly proposition of Prussia with equal candour. It is their opinion that, in the present posture of affairs in Italy, no termination of this war can be expected without some cession of territory on the part of Austria. The Emperor of the French has not contented himself with repelling the Austrian invasion of the territory of his ally: he has declared it to be his purpose to liberate Italy from the Alps to the Adriatic. This Proclamation has been received with transport where, in Northern and Central Italy, Austrian troops do not exercise a power of compression. Milan and the whole of Lombardy, Parma, Modena, and Tuscany have eagerly proclaimed their adherence to the war to which they were thus invited.

It were an affront to the Emperor of the French to suppose that he would so far belie his declarations as to restore the dominion of Austria in Lombardy, and the other states in which at his summons that rule has been overthrown.

Yet, neither have we reason to suppose that the Emperor of Austria is at present prepared to yield his hereditary possessions to any other Sovereign. Such is the difficulty of the present European crisis.

The great and ancient monarchy of Austria may naturally be slow to acknowledge any defeat as irreparable, or to record by Treaty the success of any popular insurrection against her dominion.

Yet, after the events which have occurred since the declaration of war, it is not to be expected that any Treaty, procured by the whole force of Germany, which should restore Austrian supremacy in Italy, would have in it the elements of permanence and security.

The Prince Regent of Prussia looks with becoming anxiety to the maintenance of the balance of power in Europe. Let us examine this matter.

The balance of power in Europe means, in effect, the independence of its several States. The preponderance of any one Power threatens and destroys this independence.

But the Emperor Napoleon, by his Milan Proclamation, has declared, as Baron Schleinitz has justly noted, that in this war he seeks neither conquest nor territorial aggrandizement.

It might, perhaps, be premature to discuss whether the King of Sardinia should reign over Lombardy, Parma, Modena, and Tuscany, or whether several independent States in Northern Italy should be maintained or created.

Be their divisions and boundaries arranged as they may, it is the firm persuasion of Her Majesty's Government that an Italy in which the people should be 'free citizens of a great country' would strengthen and confirm the balance of power.

The independence of States is never so secure as when the sovereign authority is supported by the attachment of the people.

A Sovereign maintained wholly by the force of arms over a disaffected people, is a perpetual object of attack to her ambitious neighbours; and a balance of power founded on such discordant elements, gives only an unstable equilibrium.

If Italy could be ruled over by Sovereigns possessed of the affections of their people, that country, with its twenty-five millions of inhabitants, its natural wealth, and its ancient civilization, would, in the opinion of Her Majesty's Government, be a valuable member of the European family.

I must not omit to state that any settlement of Italy would, in the eyes of Her Majesty's Government, be incomplete, which did not effect a permanent reform in the administration of the States of the Church.

Every one knows that Rome and the Legations have been much worse governed by the Pope's Ministers than Lombardy by Austrian Archdukes, and that would be a partial and unsatisfactory arrangement which struck down the rule of the latter, and left the former in all its deformity.

Our views upon this subject have not been withheld from the Government of the Emperor of the French.

Such being the opinions of Her Majesty's Government on the present state of affairs, they are averse to any interposition which might either prove fruitless in the first instance, or which might lead to a partial and insecure settlement.

Her Majesty used her utmost efforts, consistent with peace, to maintain the faith of Treaties. At the last moment Austria, by an act of supreme imprudence, began the war and invaded Piedmont. From that time everything has been changed. Austria overstepped the frontier laid down in the Treaties of 1815. It could no longer be expected that those Treaties would be regarded as binding by France and Sardinia. Italy has been roused to war, and is taking her part in the struggle.

In these circumstances Her Majesty's Government are bound to take a larger view of the whole field of contest. They will be glad to consult Prussia on every occasion where either Power is of opinion that a step towards peace can be made with good effect. It gives them pleasure to find that the Cabinet of Berlin does not partake of the violent excitement which has lately arisen in some parts of Germany, and that in directing the efforts of the German Confederation, it is animated by an enlightened care for the best interests of European civilization.

68. Extract from Granville's private and confidential letter to Prince Albert, 29 August 1859. Royal Archives, J 22/81; *The Letters of Queen Victoria*, 1st series, iii. 467.

. . . in Italian matters, I believed the Cabinet was agreed. Our language to Italian Governments ought to show sympathy with Italy, and let them know that we were anxious that they should be left free to act and decide for themselves, that it should inform them in the clearest manner that in no case were they to obtain active assistance from us, and it ought to avoid giving any advice as to their conduct, which might make us responsible for the evil or danger which might accrue from following such advice. That our language to France and Austria ought to press upon them in every *judicious* manner the expediency of doing that which was likely to secure the permanent happiness of Italy, and to persuade them to abstain from forcing upon the Italians, persons and forms of Government to which they objected; nothing like a menace or a promise to be used.

*   *   *   *

69. Palmerston to J. T. Delane (editor of *The Times*), 16 December 1859. *The Times* Archives; Arthur Irwin Dasent, *John Thadeus Delane* (London, 1908), i. 326–8.

I was sorry to read *The Times* article to-day in favour of the Lesseps scheme of the Suez Canal, which has been truly described by Girardin [a prominent French journalist] as founded in political hostility to England. The attack on our interests is twofold—first as regards Egypt, next as regards India. It has been deemed by all English statesmen that the possession of Egypt by France would be injurious to England, and the like opinion has always been entertained by French rulers, from the First Napoleon to the Third. The French, therefore, have always tried to separate Egypt from Turkey, as a first step towards making it French. We, on the contrary, have always endeavoured to maintain the connection of Egypt with Turkey, in order to prevent Egypt from becoming French. The French have long laboured to place Egypt in a condition of independence of Turkey. The Mediterranean coast of Egypt has been industriously fortified according to plans framed in the War Department at Paris, executed by General Gallois (Gallois Bey), and partly paid for by French money in Louis Philippe's time. These works would mount from three to four hundred guns, and would make a landing very difficult. The road to Alexandria by Cairo from the Red Sea, by which some of our troops came from India in 1801, has been closed by a military work erected under the modest name of 'a barrage for agricultural purposes.' The road from Syria by the coast remains open, and one object of the Suez Canal, which would be accomplished even if the canal was as a passage impracticable, is to cut a deep and wide trench from the Mediterranean into the desert, to stop the march of an army from Syria. A canal three hundred feet wide and thirty feet deep, with batteries on the Egyptian side, would be an impassable barrier to a Turkish force coming to re-establish Turkish authority in Egypt, and if this cut were only carried far enough into the country to cut off all practicable route for an army, the Pasha of Egypt for the time being would only have to choose his own time for throwing off all connection with the Sultan. Then comes in French influence. Part of the scheme is an extensive grant of land in Egypt for Mr. Lesseps's company, a wide district on each side of the canal and a large district at right angles to the canal from the canal to the Nile—a French colony in the heart of Egypt. It requires no great sagacity to see how in many ways this would lead to constant interference by the French Government; and this consideration has opened the eyes of the Pasha and made him adverse to the scheme. All these evils to us would be completed even though the canal should prove physically impracticable.

But if the canal could be made, it would open to the French in the event of war a short cut to India, while we should be obliged to go round the Cape. The first thing the French would do would be to send a force from Toulon or Algeria to seize the canal. An expedition, naval and military, would steam away through the canal to India, sweep our commerce, take our colonies, and perhaps seize and materially injure some of our Indian seaports, long before our reinforcements, naval and military, could arrive by long sea voyage; and we might suffer in this way immense loss and damage. As to the commercial advantage of the canal if made, it would be next to nothing. The railway suffices for all purposes, or would do so if better managed. The Red Sea would not answer for sailing ships and for steamers; the navigation would be quite as expensive as round the Cape.

The wind blows down the Red Sea halfway to Bab-el-Mandeb during great part of the year; the sea is narrow for ships to beat up against a wind, and full of coral reefs.

Then again, Egypt would lose the profit made from passengers overland; and this also the Pasha sees and feels.

On the whole, the scheme is, as Emile Girardin declares, conceived in hostility to the interests and policy of England. If the canal cannot be made to carry sea-going ships the scheme will lay the foundation for the severance of Egypt from Turkey, and for its being converted into a dependency of France, in furtherance of the scheme of making the Mediterranean a French lake. If the canal can be made, it will pay no remunerative interest on the capital invested, but it will open to the French, whenever they want it, a short cut to the Indian Seas, to the Mauritius, to Ceylon, to Australia, to New Zealand, and possibly to Bombay, or even to Calcutta. For a long time the French Government promised not to interfere in the matter; their schemes of advance policy may now be more ripe, and they depart from their former assurances and give Mr. Lesseps open support. For a long time he was paid by the Pasha. Charles Murray [British Consul-General in Egypt, 1846–53] opened the eyes of the Pasha, and his money supplies ceased. The French Government thereupon seem to have thought that it was necessary for them to step in, and to take up a scheme which both the Porte and the Pasha opposed.

70. Extract from Gladstone's private letter to Russell, 3 January 1860. Russell MSS., P.R.O. 30/22/19; Derek Beales, 'Gladstone on the Italian Question January 1860', *Rassegna Storica del Risorgimento*, xli (1954), 99–104, is based on the draft in the Gladstone MSS., B.M., Add. MS. 44291.

I was not aware till we came into the Cabinet Room today how grave and difficult a question we were to discuss.

We have I think two things to desire—I mean within the limits of what is practicable—on behalf of Italy—

First that force should not be used from without to replace the governments overthrown in the Central States.

Secondly that the question of their condition, relatively to external intervention, should be brought to an early issue.

There may be those who say, why be impatient? Is not the *status quo* in your favour, and have you anything to wish beyond its indefinite continuance?

It is in our favour negatively, as it implies the absence of what we think should be absent. It has been in our favour positively, as it has given to the misunderstood population of Central Italy an opportunity of exhibiting their admirable qualities.

But how can any people endure for an indefinite or a very long time to have their entire fate hanging in the balance, and that balance liable at any moment to be decisively swayed by hands not their own and even entirely hostile to what they have thought and done? . . . There is therefore I think the utmost hazard attendant upon prolonged delay.

As respects the exclusion of foreign force from the settlement of the Central States, it need not be argued, for we are all agreed.

Under these circumstances you propose that we should prepare ourselves to give France an assurance that we will join her in resisting the imposition of a Government by force upon Central Italy. The two questions we have to ask ourselves are

1. Will this tend to render resort to force less probable—which is in other words, to preserve the peace of Europe.

2. Will it tend to an early settlement of the question of a government for Central Italy.

It is argued against your proposition

> That it is a threat of war—
> That we can place no reliance on the Emperor of the French.
> That we should not be supported in it by public opinion—
> That after having committed ourselves though France recede we must persevere—
> That the proper time for considering the question will be after the Congress has met and after some plan involving the use of force shall have been proposed—

Now, as to the first of these reasons, I think the term applied is a misnomer—we nominally threaten war only against those who shall already have *made* war. He only in reality threatens war who threatens first to take up arms, not he who says he will defend some body when attacked.

As respects reliance on the Emperor of the French generally, it may be true that we ought not to venture it, or that in refusing it we at any rate take the safe course. But as respects relying on him with regard to the English alliance,—and still more with respect to the English alliance where it may powerfully promote his views in Italy, in this sense, & for this purpose, it appears to me that he may be relied upon as well as other States or Princes—

I am rather conscious of prejudice against him than in his favour: but I think candour must admit that on the whole he has not given cause for complaint in the conduct of his relations with England—that in some cases where he might have found cause or plea of quarrel, he has not chosen to find it—that on some occasions where we were weak and assailable, he either has not desired or has not thought it convenient, to turn them to hostile account. At the same time he has shown real even if partial and inconsistent indications of a genuine feeling for the Italians—and far beyond this he has committed himself very considerably to the Italian cause in the face of the world.

When in reply to all this we fling in his face the Truce of Villafranca, he may reply, and the answer is not without force, that he stood single-handed in a cause when at any moment Europe might have stood combined against him. We gave him verbal sympathy and encouragement or at least criticism: no one else gave him anything at all. No doubt he showed there that he had undertaken a work to which his powers were unequal; but I do not think that when fairly judged he can be said to have given proof by that measure of insincerity or indifference.

Since the articles of Villafranca, he has been in a great degree on common ground with us—and every step he has taken, without I believe any exception, has been in the direction we have wished. Even down to the time when we agreed to enter the Congress, we were looking for stronger assurances from him of his disposition to stand by the Italians. Now he has passed us; and he says I am disposed to resist any attempt to force a Government upon them— how are *you* disposed?

If we were asked to commit ourselves in advance of him, we might reply that we could not be sure of his following us: but when the question simply is whether we shall agree to support in conjunction with him a principle which we have loudly and uniformly proclaimed, I must say that for one I cannot see reason to apprehend his abandoning it and us. Neither can I feel very fearful on the subject of public opinion in this country. No doubt it would be unlikely to follow us were we going to repeat the experiment of the war of last spring which was believed to be a war of aggression on the part of the France [*sic*].

But the public opinion of this country has during the last year moved rapidly and steadily in favour of the Italians. It is now on their side: and when the Englishman has taken his side he loves measures of decision. Even to this day it is a popular idea in England that the Government of 1853 might by a more pronounced course of action at an early stage that is by threatening Russia with armed resistance; have prevented the Crimean War. Yet such threats would have proceeded upon no such broad and intelligible principle as we should now have to rest upon; for the ideas and intentions which at this time menace Italian liberty would at a former period have been not less fatal to our own. I do not believe that England would approve of a crusade on behalf of freedom either in Italy or elsewhere. But, ever since the day when Malmesbury determined to settle the whole matter by himself and without Europe, our credit and influence, our duty and honour have been absolutely involved in the settlement. It can neither be well settled without our having much of the praise, nor ill without our taking a large share of the disgrace.

The Country has emphatically approved the principle . . . that we were opposed to forcing a Government upon Central Italy. I believe that if we take the measures most likely to give effect to that principle of action, we shall have its support. Yet I would add that even if this be uncertain, still, if your proposal be one favourable to peace and to liberty, we ought cheerfully to stake in so noble and great a cause the existence of an Administration. For we have at this moment a power in our hands to *pledge* the country, which will bind it to good, or keep it from evil, whether we are or are not the instruments through which the Government is to be administered.

Neither do I think there is any force in the argument that when once committed we cannot recede. For what we have in view is a matter of European right and order. But our obligations in that respect are certainly limited by our means. We objected when France in the last spring, took into her own hands the vindication by force of a cause which in the main we believed to be just. If we engage in this matter with France, it will be because we think that united with France we are strong enough to cause justice to be done. Our engagement to act in union with her will be conformable to this conviction. But to undertake singly the cause for which the two would not be more than sufficient, would be alike beyond the letter and the spirit of the engagement. We should be no more bound to it, than we should have been bound to invade the Crimea, if France had announced to us in July 1854 that she would not set her foot on Russian territory.

But lastly it is said the proper time for adopting your proposal would be when the Congress shall have met.

It is always agreeable to postpone a critical and highly responsible decision.

But the question surely is at what time we can oppose ourselves with the greatest prospect of success, and with the best hope of preventing a breach of the peace of Europe, to the disposition which we know exists to re-establish the expelled governments by force.

We know, for it is not mere surmise, that Austria desires this course to be pursued. We know that she has tolerable grounds for hoping that she may find a majority of votes in the Congress disposed to it.

It was most justly asked today by Sir Geo[rge] Lewis [the Home Secretary] what change has taken place within the last month, which should induce us to take so great a step in advance as the declaration that we are ready to join France in resisting by force the imposition of a Government upon Central Italy from without?

I think the change, or the manifestation, is threefold. Austria has shown what indeed could hardly be doubted, that she meant to feel her way, and to proceed as far as she could, in this direction. Russia and Prussia have shown, by their answers to our overtures, that they will give us no right to count on their co-operation in a direction adverse to that which their traditions dictate. Above all, the Pope has been brought into the field: and we have been taught that we have among ourselves a minority not inconsiderable who are ready, if they find the occasion, to maintain his temporal sovereignty and enforce it upon his subjects, for the supposed interests of their religion, even in derogation of their allegiance to the Crown of England. Little as I am disposed to stronghanded measures, I think that the spirit lately exhibited among the Roman Catholics of this country is one which we must resolutely confront, and which the nation will support us in confronting.

The real and main question I take it is this: can we reasonably expect to find *in* the Congress a better opportunity for declaring our principle and our intention, than that which is now offered before it meets?

A month ago we invited Russia and Prussia to join us in limiting the action of the Congress, by excluding from it *forcible* restoration of the expelled Governments. Just as France, and particularly as Austria, has limited it in other respects, each in accordance with its own views. For a Congress is a body without definite rights, and one to which each Power is entitled to aim at giving a direction according to its belief of what is just and politic. Russia and Prussia thought fit to decline giving us any clear indication. Is it not natural that we should seek in some other quarter for the strength in support of our principle which we had hoped to derive, but which we now find we cannot derive, from their avowed and positive concurrence?

There is no great European combination pledged to use force in Central Italy. Be it so. But there is one great temporal Power, and one great spiritual Power, secretly determined to strain every nerve in that direction. There are two secondary Powers, at the least, Spain and Naples, which sympathise with them. There are two

Great Powers of Europe, Russia and Prussia, who have heretofore been wont to act in the same sense. Here are the elements of a formidable conspiracy. Shall we by a bold act before they are combined endeavour to put the combination out of the question, or shall we wait till they are enabled to combine in a regular or in something of an authoritative form, and thus with France set ourselves up as a *minority* in opposition to their views?

Your argument is that the decision which you invite us to take, is likely to *prevent* any Resolution to interfere by force in Central Italy. You say France is now ready. She, whom we have been soliciting, now solicits us: and solicits us to act decisively in support of the principle which we first definitely proclaimed, and have uniformly maintained.

What is the answer to you?

It would be a powerful reply indeed could it be said this resolution, which we are prematurely asked to take, will probably *bring about* the very decision which it aims at averting. But this no one has said. And I take it to be clear that while your proposal, at the very least, *may* prevent the combination which we look upon as so dangerous, there is not the slightest idea on the other hand that it can invite or provoke such a combination.

There plainly exists, at least with Austria and the Pope, an intention towards Italy with which we must deal as we would deal with an enemy. The question in regard to an enemy is, how to take him at the best advantage. At present the elements of mischief lie before us, scattered and uncombined. In the Congress they will be clothed with authority and susceptible of organisation. You invite us to deal with them promptly in their state of weakness. It is disagreeable to be brought to so sharp an issue: but I must admit that delay really means giving advantage and strength to that which I want in the interest alike of peace and justice to resist and to baffle.

If the Congress cannot meet, I am sorry for it. The announcement that the project has been abortive, will be a shock to public confidence already too much shaken. But the Congress was after all chiefly valuable as a means to an end. Our chief motives for agreeing to enter it were that we might support and encourage France to assist the cause of justice, peace and European order—and might bring the questions now depending to a speedy issue. But the alliance with France is the true basis of peace in Europe, for England and France never will unite in any European purpose which is radically unjust. And it is far more important to confirm France in support of *our* principle with respect to Italy, than it is to go into any Congress, if indeed it be the case that the Congress stands on one side, and the invitations and policy of France on the other. Again as regards a speedy issue, I take it to be beyond doubt that if we unite with France in the resolution you propose, and if in consequence the Congress fails to meet, we shall at once proceed to make arrangements under which the States of Central Italy may proceed to establish a settled government for themselves.

Upon the whole I must conclude as follows. One great advantage of a peaceful and temperate foreign policy is that it reserves and husbands power to spend it upon great occasions. And this is a great occasion for with Italy as it has been since 1848 Europe never can be safe. Your invitation is an invitation to confront danger while it is small, to attack it in its beginnings: the strength now available against you, that of Austria and the Pope, is a strength with which you can cope, and France extends her own hand, and asks for yours. If we delay, then around Austria and the Pope, emboldened by our hesitation, may gather many other powers, some from secular and some from religious motives. While the force of the foe thus increases ours may dwindle. England can controul and carry the unruly elements within her—we are not too sure of France, and the Emperor who took alarm and flinched at Villa Franca, may take alarm and flinch again. It may be difficult to anticipate, and to preclude before discussion, a decision to which the Congress might come: it would be far more difficult as a receding minority to denounce and to resist by the strong hand one which it had adopted, even if the French Emperor were able to hold his ground so long and did not leave to us the honour of a barren protest. After reflecting on the conversation of today I firmly believe your proposal to be, like the decision in the Belgian case, prudent as well as bold, and for one I heartily adopt it: leaving open the question what the precise form should be, but hoping that it will be one that may involve closer union with France for what now clearly appears to be a common object, and a more distinct and developed affirmation of the principle we have adopted from the first that foreign force ought no longer to be used as the instrument of government in Central Italy.

PS. I have taken it for granted that the exclusion of foreign intervention means the exclusion of foreign Italian as well as foreign non-Italian Powers. I mean of Sardinia as well as of other States. Tuscany and the Duchies are of course one with the Romagna.

71. Palmerston's Memorandum for the Cabinet on the Italian Question, 5 January 1860. Broadlands MSS., MM/IT no. 38; Ashley, ii. 174–80.

The affairs of Italy are coming to a crisis, and it is indispensably necessary that the English Government should come without further delay to a decision as to the course which England is to pursue. But, in truth, that course has been already marked out. The English Government might have determined that, in regard to Italian affairs, England should abdicate its position as one of the great Powers of Europe. We might have said that we live in an is-land, and care not what may be done on the Continent; that we think only of making money, and of defending our own shores; and that we leave to others the task of settling as they like the affairs of the continent of Europe. But such has not been the policy of the wisest and greatest statesmen who have taken part in the govern-ment of this country. We might have deemed the present an ex-ceptional case; we might have said the Emperor Napoleon has got into a scrape about Italian affairs; let him get out of it as he can: it is not our business to help him. But we rightly considered that what is at issue is not the interests of the Emperor Napoleon, but the interests of the people of Italy, and, through them, the welfare and peace of Europe. Therefore when a proposal was made that a Congress should meet to consider how best the independence and welfare of Italy could be secured, and when England was invited to be a party to that Congress, we accepted the invitation.

But it would have been unworthy of the Government of a great Power like England to have accepted such an invitation without having decided upon the policy which we were to pursue when in the Congress. We had a policy, and we lost no time in making that policy known to the principal Powers invited to the Congress. That policy is in accordance with those principles which English states-men in our times have professed and acted upon, and which are the foundation of public opinion in England. We declared that in going into Congress we should take our stand upon the principle that no force should be employed for the purpose of imposing upon the people of Italy any form of government or constitution, that is to say, that the people of Italy, and especially of Central Italy, should be left free to determine their own condition of political existence. We shall therefore go into Congress, if Congress there is to be, not as jurymen go into their box, discarding preconceived opinions and bound to be determined by what we hear in Congress, but like statesmen with a well-matured and deliberately formed policy, and with the intention of endeavouring to make that policy prevail. What is the best way of accomplishing this purpose? Why, obviously to persuade those Powers to agree with us, who are most able to sway the course of events in Italy and to bring them to the result we wish for.

What are those Powers? Obviously France and Sardinia. Austria, the Pope, and the King of Naples have views directly opposite to ours; and the other states to be represented in Congress are too far off to have the same influence as France and Sardinia on Italian affairs.

It is demonstrable, therefore, that we ought to endeavour to come to an understanding with France and Sardinia, for the purpose of common and united action with them in regard to the matters to be treated of in Congress. We need take little trouble about Sardinia, because we know that her views tally with our own; we can have little doubt as to the inclination of the Emperor Napoleon, because he has declared over and over again in manifestoes, in speeches, in letters and other communications that his object is to free Italy from foreign domination, to make Italy free from the Alps to the Adriatic, and to 'rendre l'Italie à elle-même.' There can be no reasonable doubt, therefore, that both France and Sardinia would unite with England in maintaining the principle that the Italians should be secured against foreign compulsion, and should be left free to determine, according to their own will, what shall be their future political condition. But what is the best time for endeavouring to establish this understanding? Shall we take steps now, or shall we wait till the Congress is assembled, and till some proposal is made by Austria or by the Pope, or by some other Power, which would be at variance with our views? Common sense seems to point out that if such an understanding is to be aimed at, we ought to endeavour to establish it without delay, and not to allow France and Sardinia to go into Congress ignorant whether England would or would not support efficiently the principles which she has theoretically declared. To put off endeavouring to establish an understanding with France and Sardinia till after the Congress had met and had begun its discussions, would be the most unbusiness-like proceeding that could well be imagined, and would, in all probability expose us to deserved disappointment. Austria does not trust thus to the chapter of accidents, but has been actively employed in canvassing for support to her views.

But what is the understanding or agreement which we ought to establish with France and Sardinia? Clearly a joint determination to prevent any forcible interference by any foreign Power in the affairs of Italy. This, it is said, would be a league against Austria. No doubt it would be, as far as regards the interference of Austria by force of arms in the affairs of Italy; and such a triple league would better deserve the title of holy alliance than the league which bore that name.

But such an engagement might lead us into war. War with whom? War with Austria. Well, suppose it did, would that war be one of great effort and expense? Clearly not. France, Sardinia, and Central Italy would furnish troops more than enough to repel any attempt which Austria could make to coerce Sardinia or Central Italy. Our share in such a war would be chiefly, if not wholly, naval; and our squadron in the Adriatic would probably be the utmost of our contribution, unless we were asked to lend a couple of regiments to garrison some point on the Adriatic, which, however, we should probably not be asked to do, and if asked, we might not consent to do. We ought not to be frightened by words; we ought to examine things. But is such a war likely? On the contrary, it is in the highest degree probable that such an engagement between England, France, and Sardinia would be the most effectual means of preventing a renewal of war in Italy. As long as England keeps aloof, Austria may speculate upon our joining her in a war between her on the one hand, and France and Sardinia on the other. It is so natural that we should side with France and Italy, that our holding back from doing so would be looked upon by Austria as a proof that there was some strong undercurrent which prevented us from doing so; and the Austrian Government would not unnaturally reckon that when the war had broken out, that undercurrent would drive us to side with Austria against France; and this speculation would be a great encouragement to Austria to take a course leading to war. If, on the contrary, we make it publicly known that we engaged ourselves heartily on the side of France and Italy, it might be affirmed, as

confidently as anything can be affirmed as to a future event, that
there would be and could be no renewal of war in Italy, and the
triple alliance, while it would be honourable to England (I might say,
the only course that would be honourable to England), would secure
the continuance of peace in Italy, and thereby avert one danger to
the general peace of Europe.

But it is said we cannot trust the Emperor Napoleon, and when
we had entered into this triple alliance, he would throw us over and
make some arrangement of his own without consulting us. It is no
doubt true that such was the course pursued by Austria during the
war which ended in 1815. Austria took our subsidies, bound herself
by treaty not to make peace without our concurrence, sustained
signal defeat in battle, and precipitately made peace without our
concurrence. But on what occasion has the Emperor Napoleon so
acted? On none. He differed with us about certain conditions and
the interpretation of certain conditions of the treaty of peace with
Russia, but the points in dispute were settled substantially in conformity with our views. There is no ground for imputing to him
bad faith in his conduct towards us as allies. But it is said that he
has not steadiness of purpose, and the agreement of Villafranca is a
proof of this. That agreement was certainly much short of the
declarations of intention with which he began the war, but he had
great difficulties of many kinds to contend with in further carrying
on the war; and though we, as lookers on, may think, and perhaps
rightly, that if he had persevered those difficulties would have
faded away, yet there can be no doubt that he thought them at the
time real; and he is not the only instance of a sovereign or a general
who has at the end of a war or a campaign accepted conditions of
peace less full and complete than what he expected or demanded
when hostilities began.

But there is no ground for imputing to Napoleon unsteadiness of
purpose in regard to his views about Italy. I have, during the last
four or five years, had at different times opportunities of conversation with him upon many subjects, and, among others, upon the
affairs of Italy, and I always found him strongly entertaining the
same views and opinions which have filled his mind since January
of last year, in regard to forcing Italy from Austrian domination,
and curtailing the temporal sovereignty of the Pope. There seems,
therefore, no reason to apprehend that if we came to an understanding with France and Sardinia, for the purpose of maintaining

the principle that no force should be employed to coerce the free will of the Italians, the Emperor Napoleon should turn round and leave us in the lurch. There is every reason, on the contrary, to be confident that by such an agreement with France and Sardinia, we should without war complete a settlement of Italy highly honourable to the Powers who brought it about, and full of advantage, not to Italy alone, but to Europe in general.

There would however be another advantage that would flow from such a course. We should by such a concert with France remove indefinitely any danger of a rupture with our powerful neighbour, and at all events secure for ourselves a sufficient interval of peace, to enable us to complete those defensive arrangements and preparations which if once accomplished would put us comparatively at our ease as to future contingencies.

I have argued thus far on the supposition that the Congress will meet, and I think it most probable that it will meet. Austria and the Pope look to the Congress (mistakenly, I trust and believe, and mistakenly if the proposed concert with France and Sardinia is established) as the means by which the Archdukes are to be restored and Romagna brought back to obedience. These two Powers will not lightly let the Congress slip through their fingers. The Emperor Napoleon also wishes the Congress to meet, in order to relieve him from responsibility as to the settlement of Italy. The probability therefore, is that the difficulty arising out of the pamphlet [*Le Pape et le Congrès*, supposed to have been dictated by Napoleon III and advocating the reduction of the Pope's temporal power to the city of Rome. Austria insisted that the French disavow it.] will be got over, and that the Congress will meet. But if that difficulty should prove insurmountable, and the Congress should be given up, everything which I have said in this memorandum would equally apply; or rather I should say, the necessity of coming to an agreement with France and Sardinia would be stronger still. In that case matters would have to be settled by diplomatic negotiation or by force of arms and in either way an agreement between England, France, and Sardinia would carry into effect the objects which such an agreement might have in view.

It is not foreign to the purpose to remember the helpless condition of Austria at the present moment. Her forces are deplorably embarrassed, her provinces are all of them ready to boil over with discontent, and some parts of her territory like Hungary are only waiting for a renewal of war to break out into rebellion, her army dissatisfied with recent military arrangements, and her Emperor universally disliked and extensively despised. This is not the condition in which Austria would be likely to run her head against a coalition of England, France and Sardinia, for the purpose too of doing an act of violent injustice.

It is said, however, that although the course now recommended might in itself be right and proper, it would not be approved by the country nor by Parliament.

My deliberate opinion is that it would be highly approved by the country, upon the double ground of its own merits, and of its tendency to avert a rupture with France, and to secure the continuance of peace with our neighbour. I am equally of opinion that it would be approved by Parliament; but if, by any combination of parties, an adverse decision were come to, it would, in my opinion, be the duty of the Government to appeal from Parliament to the country. My belief is that such an appeal would be eminently successful but if it were not, I would far rather give up office for maintaining the principle on which the course which I recommend would be founded, than retain office by giving that principle up.

I have put my thoughts thus in writing for circulation among my colleagues because it is easier to state them at length in this way than in conversation at the Cabinet table, and I shall be much obliged to my colleagues if they will give this paper and its content such consideration as they may deem to desire before the meeting of the Cabinet on Tuesday next.

72. Extract from Russell's dispatch no. 195 to Sir James Hudson (Minister in Turin), 27 October 1860. P.R.O., F.O. 167/114; *Parliamentary Papers*, [2757], 1861, lxvii. 241–3.

... There appear to have been two motives which have induced the people of the Roman and Neapolitan States to have joined willingly in the subversion of their Governments. The first of these was that the Governments of the Pope and the King of the Two Sicilies provided so ill for the administration of justice, the protection of personal liberty, and the general welfare of their people, that their subjects looked forward to the overthrow of their rulers as a necessary preliminary to all improvement in their condition.

The second motive was that a conviction had spread since the year 1849 that the only manner in which the Italians could secure their independence of foreign control, was by forming one strong Government for the whole of Italy. . . .

Looking at the question in this view Her Majesty's Government must admit that the Italians themselves are the best judges of their own interests.

That eminent jurist Vattel when discussing the lawfulness of the assistance given by the United Provinces to the Prince of Orange when he invaded England and overturned the throne of James II, says, 'The authority of the Prince of Orange had doubtless an influence on the deliberations of the States General, but it did not lead them to the commission of an act of injustice; for, when a people from good reasons take up arms against an oppressor, it is but an act of justice and generosity to assist brave men in the defence of their liberties.'

Therefore, according to Vattel, the question resolves itself into this: Did the people of Naples and of the Roman States take up arms against their Governments for good reasons?

Upon this grave matter Her Majesty's Government hold that the people in question are themselves the best judges of their own affairs. Her Majesty's Government do not feel justified in declaring that the people of Southern Italy had not good reasons for throwing off their allegiance to their former Governments. Her Majesty's Government cannot therefore pretend to blame the King of Sardinia for assisting them. . . .

It must be admitted, undoubtedly, that the severance of the ties which bind together a sovereign and his subjects is in itself a misfortune. Notions of allegiance become confused; the succession of the throne is disputed; adverse parties threaten the peace of society; rights and pretensions are opposed to each other, and mar the harmony of the State. Yet it must be acknowledged, on the other hand, that the Italian revolution has been conducted with singular temper and forbearance. The subversion of existing power has not been followed, as is too often the case, by an outburst of popular vengeance. The extreme views of democrats have nowhere prevailed. Public opinion has checked the excesses of the public triumph. The venerated forms of constitutional monarchy have been associated with the name of a Prince who represents an ancient and glorious Dynasty.

Such having been the causes and the concomitant circumstances of the revolution of Italy, Her Majesty's Government can see no sufficient grounds for the severe censure with which Austria, France, Prussia, and Russia have visited the acts of the King of Sardinia. Her Majesty's Government will turn their eyes rather to the gratifying prospect of a people building up the edifice of their liberties, and consolidating the work of their independence, amid the sympathies and good wishes of Europe.

73. Extract from Granville's private letter to Russell, 29 September 1862. Russell MSS., P.R.O. 30/22/25; Edmond Fitzmaurice, *The Life of Granville George Leveson Gower Second Earl Granville K.G. 1815–1891* (London, 1905), i. 442–4, wrongly dates it 27 September.

... Meade has given me your message, viz. that the Cabinet is likely to be summoned to consider the present state of the American question—whether the time is not come to offer the mediation of H.M.'s Government, and in case of refusal to recognise the Southern Confederacy. When I last saw Lord Palmerston, he mentioned the subject to me, so that I have had time to think over it.

If we were asked to mediate, we could not refuse. The North hate us now; the Southern leaders did hate us, and may for all we know do so now or hereafter; and therefore we might selfishly argue that it was not politically disadvantageous to us that both parties should exhaust themselves a little more before they make peace. It would however be monstrous not to avail ourselves of a good opportunity to put an end to the crimes and calamities which are now desolating North America, and inflicting at the same time injury on our commerce and manufactures. But the difficulties of mediation are great. Public opinion in England is diametrically opposed to that of both Northern and Southern statesmen on slavery. The questions of boundary are of vital importance not only to the North and South, but to the West. The negotiations would have to be carried on in common with the French, who, although they want cotton, are partial to the North. I doubt whether any European Government really understands American politics, or the objects of the North and of the South, and of the different states once released from the hope of preserving the Great Union; or the views of the different important parties in the Republic.

I doubt whether in offering to mediate, we should do so with any *bonâ fide* expectation of its being accepted. If either or both parties wished for mediation, we should certainly have had some (more or less direct) intimation of it.

It is possible that one or both belligerents might accept the offer of mediation, not with a view of peace, or with the intention of making concessions mutually acceptable, but for the purpose of gaining time, intriguing politically and renewing their military resources. In that case we should be dupes; we should give false hopes of a supply of cotton, and destroy the stimulus which although painful at the moment is likely to be so beneficial for the future, by giving us supplies from our own possessions and other parts of the world.

The probability is that our offers would be refused by one or both belligerents, as such offers generally are when made before they are wanted. If the South refuse, which in consistency with their public declarations, repudiating all foreign interference, they ought to do, it would be hardly a reason for recognising them. If the North alone refused, the question would then naturally arise, whether we ought not then to recognise the South. Such a recognition, as has been explained several times to Parliament by the Government, would not by itself relieve the blockade, or supply us with cotton. It would give no physical strength to the South, but it would greatly stimulate the North and undoubtedly assist their Government in raising men and money. By the time you will receive this letter you will probably know more of the relative position of the combatants. At present we know that the Federals have been defeated in their attempt to conquer the South, but we also know that the two parties have changed parts in the great tragedy. The Southerners, instead of being invaded, are become the invaders. . . .

It would not be a good moment to recognise the South just before a great Federal success. If on the other hand, the Confederates continue victorious, as is to be hoped, we should stand better then than now in recognising them.

In any case I doubt, if the war continues long after our recognition of the South, whether it will be possible for us to avoid drifting into it. The expectation of an immediate supply of the best cotton will have been raised in this country. The dislike which now exists between us will be much increased. The North will become desperate, and even against their intentions will give us innumerable *casus belli*.

The result of such a war under present circumstances is not doubtful, but much valuable blood would be unnecessarily spilt, infinitely more treasure would be spent than is sufficient to maintain the cotton operatives during their temporary distress, and whether the French went with us or not, it is not unlikely that circumstances might arise which would enable the Emperor more freely to adopt any foreign policy either in Italy or elsewhere which might suit him.

I am afraid your message was not intended to produce such a long rigmarole, but you will see by it that I have come to the conclusion that it is premature to depart from the policy which has hitherto been adopted by you and Lord Palmerston, and which, notwithstanding the strong antipathy to the North, the strong sympathy with the South, and the passionate wish to have cotton, has met with such general approval from Parliament, the Press, and the public.

74. Extract from Palmerston's private letter to Russell, 2 October 1862. Russell MSS., P.R.O. 30/22/14D; Gooch, ii. 326–7, and Ephraim Douglass Adams, *Great Britain and the American Civil War* (New York, 1925), ii. 43–4.

I return you Granville's letter which contains much deserving of serious consideration. There is no doubt that the offer of Mediation upon the basis of Separation would be accepted by the South. Why should it not be accepted? It would give the South in principle the points for which they are fighting. The refusal, if refusal there was, would come from the North, who would be unwilling to give up the principle for which they have been fighting so long as they had a reasonable expectation that by going on fighting they could carry their point. The condition of things therefore which would be favourable to an offer of mediation would be great success of the South against the North. That state of things seemed ten days ago to be approaching. Its advance has been lately checked, but we do not yet know the real course of recent events, and still less can we foresee what is about to follow. Ten days or a fortnight more may throw a clearer light upon future prospects.

As regards possible resentment on the part of the Northerns following upon our acknowledgment of the Independence of the South, it is quite true that we should have less to care about that resentment in the spring when communication with Canada was open, and when our naval force could more easily operate upon the American coast, than in winter when we are cut off from Canada and the American coast is not so safe.

But if the acknowledgment were made at one and the same time by England, France and some other Powers, the Yankees would probably not seek a quarrel with us alone and would not like one against a European Confederation. Such a quarrel would render certain and permanent that Southern Independence the acknowledgment of which would have caused it.

The first communication to be made by England and France to the contending parties might be, not an absolute offer of mediation but a friendly suggestion whether the time was not come when it might be well for the two parties to consider whether the war, however long continued, could lead to any other result than separation; and whether it might not therefore be best to avoid the great evils which must necessarily flow from a prolongation of hostilities by at once coming to an agreement to treat upon that principle of separation which must apparently be the inevitable result of the contest, however long it may last.

The best thing would be that the two parties should settle details by direct negotiation with each other, though perhaps with the rancorous hatred now existing between them this might be difficult. But their quarrels in negotiation would do us no harm if they did not lead to a renewal of war. An armistice, if not accompanied by a cessation of blockades, would be all in favour of the North, especially if New Orleans remained in the hands of the North.

The whole matter is full of difficulty, and can only be cleared up by some more decided events between the contending armies.

*   *   *   *

75. Russell's dispatch no. 53 to Lord Napier (Ambassador in St. Petersburg), 2 March 1863. P.R.O., F.O. 181/410; *Parliamentary Papers*, [3150], 1863, lxxv. 90–1.

Her Majesty's Government view with the deepest concern the state of things now existing in the Kingdom of Poland. They see there, on the one side, a large mass of the population in open insurrection against the Government; and, on the other, a vast military force employed in putting that insurrection down. The natural and probable result of such a contest must be expected to be the success of the military forces. But that success, if it is to be achieved by a series of bloody conflicts, must be attended by a lamentable effusion of blood, by a deplorable sacrifice of life, by wide-spread desolation, and by impoverishment and ruin, which it would take a long course of years to repair.

Moreover, the acts of violence and destruction on both sides, which are sure to accompany such a struggle, must engender mutual hatreds and resentments, which will embitter, for generations to come, the relations between the Russian Government and the Polish race.

Yet, however much Her Majesty's Government might lament the existence of such a miserable state of things in a foreign country, they would not, perhaps, deem it expedient to give formal expression to their sentiments, were it not that there are peculiarities in the present state of things in Poland which take them out of the usual and ordinary condition of such affairs.

The Kingdom of Poland was constituted, and placed in connection with the Russian Empire by the Treaty of 1815, to which Great Britain was a Contracting Party. The present disastrous state of things is to be traced to the fact that Poland is not in the condition in which the stipulations of that Treaty require that it should be placed.

Neither is Poland in the condition in which it was placed by the Emperor Alexander I, by whom that Treaty was made.

During his reign a National Diet sat at Warsaw, and the Poles of the Kingdom of Poland enjoyed privileges fitted to secure their political welfare.

Since 1832, however, a state of uneasiness and discontent has been succeeded from time to time by violent commotion and a useless effusion of blood.

Her Majesty's Government are aware that the immediate cause of the present insurrection was the conscription lately enforced upon the Polish population; but that measure itself is understood to have been levelled at the deeply-rooted discontent prevailing among the Poles in consequence of the political condition of the Kingdom of Poland.

The proprietors of land and the middle classes in the towns bore that condition with impatience; and if the peasantry were not equally disaffected they gave little support or strength to the Russian Government.

Great Britain, therefore, as a party to the Treaty of 1815, and as a Power deeply interested in the tranquillity of Europe, deems itself entitled to express its opinion upon the events now taking place, and is anxious to do so in the most friendly spirit towards Russia, and with a sincere desire to promote the interest of all the parties concerned. Why should not His Imperial Majesty, whose benevolence is generally and cheerfully acknowledged, put an end at once to this bloody conflict by proclaiming mercifully an immediate and unconditional amnesty to his revolted Polish subjects, and at the same time announce his intention to replace without delay the Kingdom of Poland in possession of the political and civil privileges which were granted to it by the Emperor Alexander I, in execution of the stipulations of the Treaty of 1815?

If this were done, a National Diet and a National Administration would, in all probability, content the Poles, and satisfy European opinion.

You will read this despatch to Prince Gortchakoff, and give him a copy of it.

76. Extract from Palmerston's House of Commons Speech on Poland, 20 July 1863. *Hansard*, 3rd series, clxxii. 1130–3.

... I always thought ... that the power of public opinion is almost equal to that of arms, and no doubt public opinion is a powerful engine in its influence upon the conduct of men and Governments. That which has happened is indeed a striking proof of the power of this. In the discussions of 1831 and 1832 the Russian Government denied that we had any right to remonstrate with them upon the affairs of Poland, founding ourselves on the Treaty of 1815. They said that Russia had reconquered Poland after the revolution, and that this conquest annulled all the engagements of 1815. The Russian Government, therefore, argued that any interference in the affairs of Poland was an interference in the internal affairs of Russia, and that we had no right to meddle with that which concerned the Emperor of Russia alone. Now, the ground taken by Russia is entirely different. Yielding to the joint opinion of so many of the Powers of Europe, Russia is willing to enter into discussions in regard to Poland within the limits of the Treaty. That is a great step gained, and it affords a prospect of a better condition of things than the former ground taken by Russia entitled us to expect. . . . At the beginning of the year, the opinion of the House and the country, the opinion also of Europe, was loudly expressed in favour of some representation to be made to Russia. And I hold it to be quite at variance with the common transactions of human affairs to say that you are never to remonstrate or negotiate unless you are prepared immediately to have recourse to arms, if you do not obtain by diplomacy what you are endeavouring to accomplish. That would put an end to all intercourse between nations, and it is the rule neither of States nor of individuals. We all know that much is gained without a resort to that final arbitrament . . . Her Majesty's Government in this case did that which I think was required by the public opinion of the country and which was advocated in debates in this House. We also did that which we have a right to do—we invoked the Treaty of Vienna, and we obtained the concurrence of France, of Austria, of Spain, Portugal, Italy, Turkey, Belgium, and Sweden, all of which agreed with us in urging upon Russia a milder course towards the Poles. It has been said that it would be no satisfaction to the Poles if that result were gained. Sir, I cannot see that there is any just foundation for that opinion. The condition of the Poles would be very much improved if they were re-established in the position in which the Treaty of Vienna placed them. But then it is said that we suggested one thing which was perfectly impracticable —namely, an armistice. Well, can any man look at the cruelties committed—I fear by both sides—in this lamentable struggle, at the dreadful waste of human life, and the sacrifice of some of the most distinguished members of the Polish nation, and not wish to see these hostilities suspended, even for a time, if they cannot be entirely stopped? But if that war were suspended for a time, I cannot but think that negotiation would intervene and a final settlement prevent the recurrence of the contest. It is asked, 'How can that be done?' Well, I think that has been answered in the course of this debate. If the Russian Government were to assent—which I am sorry to say they do not—to a suspension of this unhappy strife, we have been told, from what one would suppose to be authority, that the Revolutionary Government in Poland has made it known that it would agree to a Conference, provided it was represented in that Conference. Well, who has authority to say that? Could not those who have access to this representation of Polish authority on that point obtain from the same authority—secret or whatever else it is—some assurance which, if the Russian Government declared itself ready to agree to suspend hostilities, might draw from the other side some corresponding engagement, so that between the two the object might be accomplished of putting an end to such a frightful sacrifice of life and effusion of blood? Sir, I think that is worth attempting, and that we should have been neglecting our duty if we had not included an armistice among our proposals. Upon Russia be the responsibility of having refused it—we have done our duty. . . .

77. Extract from Palmerston's House of Commons Speech on the Schleswig-Holstein Question, 23 July 1863. *Hansard*, 3rd series, clxxii. 1249–52.

. . . I will not enter into the long details of what is called the Schleswig-Holstein Question. It is involved in the greatest obscurity in former times. . . . Now, I entirely concur . . . that it is an important matter of British policy to maintain the independence and integrity of the Danish monarchy. That monarchy is not a large one, but it has its rights as well as larger States, and its geographical position renders the maintenance of its independence and integrity a matter of peculiar interest to this country. . . . The position that we have always held is that Holstein is unquestionably a member of the Germanic Confederation; and such being the case, that the Germanic Confederation have a right to have an opinion on the affairs of Holstein in the same degree and in the same way in which they have a right to look to the affairs of the other members of the Germanic Confederation; and that any arrangement made by the King of Denmark in regard to the Duchy of Holstein, if it were at variance with the fundamental rules and privileges of the Germanic Confederation, would be one that the King of Denmark would not be entitled to make. With regard, however, to Schleswig, we contend that the Germanic Confederation has no rights. Any question as to the Duchy of Schleswig is a matter of international law and of European concern; and the Germanic Confederation are no more entitled to prescribe what should be done with regard to Schleswig than with regard to Spain, Portugal, England, Russia, or any other independent State. But there is in Schleswig a very considerable German population, and therefore it is not unnatural—indeed, it is perfectly justifiable—that the Germanic Confederation should take an interest in the condition of the German population; and it is entitled to make representations to the King of Denmark requesting that the German population should be put on a fair and equal footing with regard to the Danish population of Schleswig. That, however, is a matter of explanation and discussion, and not a subject that would justify an appeal to force. . . . Now, precipitation is not the characteristic fault of the Germanic Confederation; and I am persuaded that their good sense and the soundness of their views on the peace of Europe will lead them not rashly to have recourse to a step, the consequences of which might be far different from those which are immediately contemplated. It is impossible for any man who looks at the map of Europe, and who knows the great interest which the Powers of Europe feel in the independence of the Danish monarchy, to shut his eyes to the fact that war begun about a petty quarrel concerning the institutions of Holstein would, in all probability, not end where it began, but might draw after it consequences which all the parties who began it would be exceedingly sorry to have caused. But if any one Power more than another would, upon grounds of general policy, be disinclined to set fire to the combustible elements of Europe, that one Power is, I think, Austria. . . . I am satisfied with all reasonable men in Europe, including those in France and Russia, in desiring that the independence, the integrity, and the rights of Denmark may be maintained. We are convinced—I am convinced at least—that if any violent attempt were made to overthrow those rights and interfere with that independence, those who made the attempt would find in the result, that it would not be Denmark alone with which they would have to contend. I trust, however, that these transactions will continue to be, as they have been, matters for negotiation, and not for an appeal to arms. . . . I can assure the House that every effort will be made by Her Majesty's Government to induce the disputing parties to confine the question within the limits of diplomatic intercourse; and all their influence, and, no doubt the influence of other Governments also, will be exerted to impress on the Diet a reasonable view of the matter, and to urge a settlement which may be consistent on the one hand with the rights of the Diet with regard to the internal organization of Holstein and consistent, on the other hand, with the rights, the independence, and the integrity of the Danish monarchy. I do not myself anticipate any immediate danger, or indeed any of that remote danger which the hon. Gentleman seems to think imperils the peace of Europe arising out of the Danish and Holstein question.

78. Extract from Palmerston's private letter to the King of the Belgians, 15 November 1863. Copy in Broadlands MSS., PM/J/1; Ashley, ii. 236–42.

. . . Our answer to the Emperor's proposal has been, in substance, that we do not admit that the Treaties of Vienna have ceased to be in force, inasmuch as, on the contrary, they are still the basis of the existing arrangements of Europe; that, with regard to the proposed Congress, before we can come to any decision about it, we should like to know what subjects it is to discuss, and what power it is to possess to give effect to its decisions.

* * * *

My own impression is that the Congress will never meet, and that the Emperor has no expectation that it should meet.

The truth is that the assembling of a Congress is not a measure applicable to the present state of Europe.

In 1815 a Congress was a necessity. France had overrun all Europe, had overthrown almost all the former territorial arrangements, and had established a new order of things. Then came the returning tide of the Allied Armies overturning everything which France had created, and establishing, for the moment, military occupation of the greater part of Europe. It was absolutely necessary to determine to whom, and in what portions, and on what conditions, the vast regions reconquered from France should be thenceforward possessed. The Powers whose armies had made this reconquest were the natural and indeed the only arbiters; and they had, by their armies, the means of carrying their decisions into effect.

Nothing of the kind exists in the present state of Europe. There are no doubts as to who is the owner of any piece of territory, and there are not even any boundary questions in dispute.

The functions of a Congress, if now to be assembled, might be twofold, and would bear either on the past or on the future, or on both. Drouyn [the French Foreign Minister] says that the Congress might take up the treaties of 1815, go through them article by article, strike out whatever has been repealed or set aside, and re-enact the remainder as the Treaty of 1863–64, the name of which would be less disagreeable to France than that of the Treaty of 1815, which brings to mind Waterloo and St. Helena. This may be a natural feeling for France; but it is no good reason why all the rest of Europe should meet round a table to please the French nation; and those who hold their estates under a good title, now nearly half a century old, might not be particularly desirous of having it brought under discussion with all the alterations which good-natured neighbours might wish in their boundaries.

No doubt there have been some not unimportant changes made in the territorial arrangements of Europe established by the Treaty of 1815; but some of these were made regularly by treaty at the time, and the others, not so made, some of the parties to the Congress might not like to sanction by treaty acknowledgment.

Chief among the first class is the separation of Belgium from Holland; but that was solemnly sanctioned by negotiations the length of which I cannot easily forget, and by a treaty between the five Powers and Holland and the German Diet. That transaction requires no confirmation. Chief among the second class was the absorption of Cracow by Austria without any treaty sanction; and to that transaction the British Government, which protested against it at the time, would not be greatly desirous of giving a retrospective sanction by treaty now. Then come the cession of Lombardy to Italy, and of Savoy and Nice to France. These were legally made by the rightful owners of the ceded territory, and no confirmation can be required. There was indeed, in the case of Savoy, an omission to attach to the territory as conveyed to France the condition of neutrality as to Chablais and Faucigny, subject to which the King of Sardinia held Savoy; but it may be doubted whether France would consent to undertake that condition; and its real value, either for Switzerland or Italy, might, after all, be trifling. Then comes the absorption into the Kingdom of Italy of Tuscany, Parma, Modena, Emilia, Naples, and Sicily. These were all violations of the Treaty of Vienna, done without treaty sanction; but they were the will of the people of those countries. Those transactions have been virtually sanctioned by all the Powers who have acknowledged the King of Italy; and if Victor Emmanuel is wise, he would be content with leaving those matters as they are, the more especially because if a new European treaty were to describe the kingdom of Italy as it now is, that treaty would be a virtual renunciation by the King of Italy to any claim to Venetia and Rome. On the other hand, Austria and the Pope would hardly be prepared to give their formal sanction to acquisitions made by the Italian kingdom.

As to the past, therefore, the functions of the Congress would either be unnecessary or barred by insurmountable difficulties.

But then as to the future? Would the Congress have to range over the wide and almost endless extent of proposed and possible changes, or would it have to confine itself to questions now practically pending? There are but two such questions: the one relating to Poland; the other to the difference between the German Confederation and Denmark about Holstein and Lauenburg and about Sleswig. As to Poland, would Russia be more likely to yield in a Congress than she has shown herself to be in a negotiation? I much doubt it. And as to the question between Germany and Denmark, a smaller machinery than a European Congress might surely be sufficient to solve that question.

But if the Congress were to enter upon the wide field of proposed and possible changes of territory, what squabbles and animosities would ensue! Russia would ask to get back all she lost by the Treaty of Paris; Italy would ask for Venetia and Rome; France would plead geography for the frontier of the Rhine; Austria would show how advantageous it would be to Turkey to transfer to Austria Bosnia or Moldo-Wallachia; Greece would have a word to say about Thessaly and Epirus; Spain would wonder how England could think of retaining Gibraltar; Denmark would say that Sleswig is geographically part of Jutland, and that, as Jutland is an integral part of Denmark, so ought Sleswig to be so too; Sweden would claim Finland; and some of the greater German states would strongly urge the expediency of mediatizing a score of the smaller Princes.

If the members of the Congress should be unanimous in agreeing to any of these proposals, of course there would be no difficulty in carrying a unanimous decision into effect; but if a majority were one way, and a minority, however small, the other way, that minority including the party by which a concession was to be made, is it intended that force should be used, or is the Congress to remain powerless to execute its own decrees?

In the face of all these difficulties, my humble opinion is that no Congress will meet; and I shall be glad to think that the Emperor will have mended his position at home by making the proposal, while its failure will have saved Europe from some danger and much embarrassment.

*   *   *   *

79. The Queen's 'most confidential' letter to Granville, 27 January 1864. Granville MSS., P.R.O. 30/29/31; Fitzmaurice, i. 456–7.

The Queen has seen the repeated answers to our proposals, respecting the concert with the non-German Powers and material aid to Denmark, from France, which is decidedly against any promise of material aid. The Emperor and M. Drouyn de l'Huys [the French Foreign Minister] say: 'We wish to maintain the treaty, but if the alternative is maintaining it or a conflagration in Europe, we prefer to modify or cancel it, rather than a conflagration:' to which the Queen must subscribe. Russia has also told Denmark not to resist, as she can expect no material aid from Russia. All this would show that we are safe from this perilous proposal; but Lord Russell, to whom the Queen observed this, said: 'There is Sweden, and she might join us.' These words alarmed the Queen, and she wishes to warn Lord Granville and the Cabinet of what may be proposed to which she could not consent. Lord Russell is evidently very uneasy and very sore at the failure of all the endless proposals on the part of this country. We have done too much, been too active, and done ourselves no good. We are, alas! detested in Germany.

The one really very serious feature in the whole affair is that everywhere the Governments have been outvoted, and that we, constitutional England, are asking them to act in an unconstitutional way!

The Queen asks the Cabinet to be firm and support her. Lord Russell is very fair, but Lord Palmerston alarms him and overrules him. The Cabinet must also insist on no violent declaration in the Speech which would force us to be partisans of one side, or of a determination to maintain the treaty at all hazards. Lord Palmerston should likewise be strongly urged to be very cautious in Parliament, for any encouragement to Denmark would be fatal.

Lord Granville, while not mentioning this communication, may use the Queen's name whenever he thinks it may be useful. If Lord Granville thinks it necessary, the Queen is ready to write anything to the above effect to Lord Russell.

80. Extract from Derby's House of Lords Speech, 4 February 1864. *Hansard*, 3rd series, clxxiii. 27–9.

. . . I think that at the commencement the foreign policy of the noble Earl opposite [Russell] might be summed up in the affirmation of the principle of non-intervention in the internal affairs of other countries, the extension of Liberal principles by the exercise of our moral interference, and, above all, the maintenance of uninterrupted and cordial relations with the Emperor of the French. We were told more than once that the present Government was the only one to maintain a good understanding with the Emperor of the French, or, at least, that its predecessor could not possibly have done so; and that if the country desired to preserve cordial relations between itself and France, Her Majesty's present advisers, and especially the noble Earl opposite, were the only persons qualified to secure that most desirable object. Now, my Lords, as to non-intervention in the internal affairs of other countries, when I look around me I fail to see what country there is in the internal affairs of which the noble Earl and Her Majesty's Government have not interfered. *Nihil intactum reliquit, nihil tetigit quod*—I cannot say *non ornavit*, but *non conturbavit.* Or the foreign policy of the noble Earl, as far as the principle of non-intervention is concerned, may be summed up in two short homely but expressive words—'meddle and muddle.' During the whole course of the noble Earl's diplomatic correspondence, wherever he has interfered—and he has interfered everywhere—he has been lecturing, scolding, blustering, and retreating. In fact, I cannot think of the foreign policy pursued by the noble Earl and his Colleagues without being reminded of another very distinguished body of actors commemorated, as your Lordships will recollect, in *A Midsummer Night's Dream*. Of that celebrated troupe the two chief ornaments were Bottom, the weaver, and Snug, the joiner. Now, it appears to me that the noble Earl opposite combines the qualities which are attributed to both these distinguished personages. Like Bottom, the weaver, he is ready to play every part, not even excepting that in which he most excels—namely, 'Moonshine.' But his favourite part is the part of the lion. 'Oh,' says the noble Earl, 'let me play the lion. I will roar so that it will do any man's heart good to hear me; I will roar so that I will make the Duke say, "Let him roar again; let him roar again".' The noble Earl, too, knows as well as anyone, how, like Bottom, to 'aggravate his voice,' so that he will 'roar you as gently as any sucking dove;' and, moreover, he has had recourse more than once to the ingenious and somewhat original device of letting half his face be seen through the lion's neck, as if to say, 'For all my roaring I am no lion at all, but only

Snug the joiner.' There is, however, one point of difference which I would have you observe, because it is rather important. Bottom, the weaver, and Snug, the joiner, were possessed by an earnest desire not to alarm the ladies too much, and consequently they gave due warning at the outset of their intentions that the audience might not be alarmed. On the other hand, the noble Earl's disclosure that though the roar was like that of a lion, the face was only that of the noble Lord himself, was not made betimes in order that the audience might not be frightened, but only because he found that all the roaring in the world would not frighten them. Seriously, my Lords, for though there may be something ludicrous about it, the matter is of too great importance to be treated only in a light and jocular manner—seriously, then, I cannot but feel as an Englishman that I am lowered and humiliated in my own estimation and in that of other nations by the result of the noble Earl's administration of foreign affairs. Thanks to the noble Earl and the present Government, we have at this moment not one single friend in Europe, but that this great England—this great country whose failing, if it was a failing, was that it went too direct and straightforward at what it aimed, which never gave a promise without the intention of performing, which never threatened without a full determination of striking, which never made a demand without being prepared to enforce it—this country is now in such a position that its menaces are disregarded, its magniloquent language is ridiculed, and its remonstrances are treated with contemptuous indifference by the small as well as by the great Powers of the Continent.

81. Extract from the House of Commons Debate on Disraeli's Motion of Censure on the Government's Policy towards Denmark and Germany, 4–8 July 1864. *Hansard*, 3rd series, clxxvi. 744–6, 828–9, 838, 841–2, 1280–1.

DISRAELI [4 July]: ... I have given you a narrative of the manner in which our affairs have been conducted, and now I ask you what is your opinion? Do you see in the management of those affairs that capacity, and especially that kind of capacity that is adequate to the occasion? Do you find in it that sagacity, that prudence, that dexterity, that quickness of perception, and those conciliatory moods which we are always taught to believe necessary in the transaction of our foreign affairs? Is there to be seen that knowledge of human nature, and especially that peculiar kind of science most necessary in these affairs—an acquaintance with the character of foreign countries and of the chief actors in the scene? Sir, for my part, I find all these qualities wanting; and, in consequence of the want of these qualities, I see that three results have accrued. The first is that the avowed policy of Her Majesty's Government has failed. The second is, that our just influence in the councils of Europe has been lowered. Thirdly, in consequence of our just influence in the councils of Europe being lowered, the securities for peace are diminished. These are three results which have followed in consequence of the want of the qualities to which I have alluded, and in consequence of the management of these affairs by the Government. Sir, I need not, I think, trouble the House with demonstrating that the Government have failed in their avowed policy of upholding the independence and integrity of Denmark. The first result may be thrown aside. I come, therefore, to the second. By the just influence of England in the councils of Europe I mean an influence contra-distinguished from that which is obtained by intrigue and secret understanding—I mean an influence that results from the conviction of foreign Powers that our resources are great and that our policy is moderate and steadfast. Since the settlement that followed the great revolutionary war England, who obtained at that time—as she deserved to do, for she bore the brunt of the struggle—who obtained at that time all the fair objects of her ambition, has on the whole followed a Conservative foreign policy. I do not mean by a Conservative foreign policy a foreign policy that would disapprove, still less oppose, the natural development of nations. I mean a foreign policy interested in the tranquillity and prosperity of the world, the normal condition of which is peace, and which does not ally itself with the revolutionary party of Europe. Other countries have their political systems and public objects, as England had, though they may not have attained them. She is not to look upon them with unreasonable jealousy. The position of England in the councils of Europe is essentially that of a moderating and mediatorial Power. Her interest and her policy are, when changes are inevitable and necessary, to assist so that these changes, if possible, may be accomplished without war; or, if war occurs, that its duration and its asperity may be lessened. That is what I mean by the just influence of England in the councils of Europe. It appears to me that just influence of

England in the councils of Europe has been lowered. Within twelve months we have been twice repulsed at St. Petersburg. Twice have we supplicated in vain at Paris. We have menaced Austria, and Austria has allowed our menaces to pass her like the idle wind. We have threatened Prussia, and Prussia has defied us. Our objurgations have rattled over the head of the German Diet, and the German Diet has treated them with contempt. . . .

COBDEN [5 July]: . . . whether we have been lowered, or are to be lowered in the councils of nations, will depend on our future conduct; for at the present moment I am constrained to admit that, as far as the conduct of our Foreign Office is concerned, we do not stand in a very satisfactory position. But with respect to the declaration that the course which has been taken will have the effect of diminishing the securities for peace, I join issue distinctly with the right hon. Gentleman. I am of opinion that what has happened—I mean the exposure of the utter futility of our foreign policy—the complete breakdown of our diplomacy—will have the effect of extracting these foreign questions from this time henceforth, from the dark recesses of the Foreign Office to the publicity of this House, and will therefore afford, probably, a better guarantee for peace than anything else that could have occurred. But while I say this, do not let it be understood that I am prepared to endorse or excuse the course which the Foreign Department took in the late negotiations. I consider it to have been deplorable—most unsatisfactory. I do not speak with censure or harshness of any attempt made by the Government to promote peace. I would not even quarrel with them for hawking about in every capital of Europe their useless importunities for peace. But what has struck me in reading these voluminous despatches is the great want of sagacity on the part of our Foreign Minister—that is to say, the want of knowledge and appreciation of the forces and motives, and even the passions, which were guiding and controlling foreign nations in these matters—motives and forces that appeared to me to be so transparent that even a child might perceive them. In the absence of that knowledge our Foreign Department has, I think, needlessly and perseveringly exposed itself to rejections and rebuffs, and, I must say, as far as that department is concerned, to humiliation from all parts of the world. So much for the question, which lies very much between the front bench on the other side of the House, and the front bench on this side. There are, however, matters which go much beyond the opposite interests of those in power and the aspirants for office, and if it were not so, I should not take part in the debate. There grows out of this debate a question of principle as affects our foreign policy. With this question of Denmark and Germany, two issues are brought clearly before us—I mean, the question as to the dynastic, secret, irresponsible, engagements of our Foreign Office, and also the question which is not ancient but new, and which must be taken into consideration in all our foreign policy from this time—the question of nationalities—by which I mean the instinct, now so powerful, leading communities to seek to live together, because they are of the same race, language, and religion. Now, what is the Treaty of 1852, of which we have heard so much, and which forms the pivot and basis of this discussion? Eight gentlemen met in London about the celebrated round table to settle the destinies of a million of people, who were never consulted on the matter at issue. Let us take note of this event. It is the last page in the long history of past diplomatic action. It will not be repeated again. I mean that there will never again, in all probability, be a Conference meeting together to dispose for dynastic purposes of a population whose wishes they do not take into account. Let it be borne in mind that it is on that policy of secret, irresponsible diplomacy, and on the question of nationalities that our debate turns, and that our troubles —so far as they are wound up in this affair are concerned. . . . Well, why do we trouble ourselves with these continental politics? We have no territorial interest on the continent. We gain nothing there by our diplomatic meddling. Our general excuse is—and it is a phrase that is stereotyped in the despatches of the noble Lord the Foreign Secretary—that we have a policy founded on what is called 'the balance of power'—a thing I never could understand; but I believe the present balance is a figment that was supposed to have grown out of what is termed the great settlement of Vienna, but which I term the great unsettlement of Vienna. But can we, in the face of these growing popular interests, any longer base our foreign policy on that Treaty of Vienna? . . . I maintain that we must have a change in the foreign relations of this country, or a change in our Foreign Office. The present system of diplomacy has broken down. Our Foreign Office has lost its credit with foreign countries. You cannot from this time approach a foreign country on any question of foreign politics, in which you will not be looked upon with want of consideration, and, indeed, with mistrust. And why? Because foreign countries feel that when they are dealing with the Foreign Office the Foreign Office is not, in fact, a power; the power is here; and foreign Governments more than suspect that your Foreign Minister is often playing a game with them from time to time merely to suit his policy and his prospects in this House. Such being the case, I maintain—and I know I have spoken outside of your party contest in a way, perhaps, that entitles you to my thanks for having listened to me so well—I maintain that it behoves us to adopt a different policy, to let it be known that it is our policy, and to let the Government feel that it is necessary they should act up to it. The present system cannot go on. It requires a change not only in the interest of this country, but in the interest of other countries allied to us by neighbourhood or commerce; nay, it requires a change on higher grounds—in the interest of peace, civilization, and humanity.

PALMERSTON [8 July]: . . . The right hon. Gentleman . . . proposes that the House should affirm that the influence of England is lowered in the eyes of Europe, and that thereby the security for peace is diminished. That is supported by a great number of gentlemen, who maintain that we ought never to interfere in anything beyond our own shores. What, then, is the use of our influence if we are not to interfere, and how is the peace of Europe endangered by the loss of our influence, if that influence is to be confined to influence within these walls? The Resolution of the right hon. Gentleman is an admission that the doctrine of many of those who support it is unsound in the existing circumstances of the world, and that the great interests connecting a country like ours with every part of the world render it impossible for her to be passive or indifferent as to what is passing among other nations, and that circumstances requiring vigilant watching must sometimes cause her to interfere in transactions in which we are not directly concerned. Then we are told that the balance of power is an exploded doctrine belonging to ancient times. Why, it is a doctrine founded on the nature of man. It means that it is to the interest of the community of nations that no nation should acquire such a preponderance as to endanger the security of the rest; and it is for the advantage of all that the smaller Powers should be respected in their independence and not swallowed up by their more powerful neighbours. That is the doctrine of the balance of power, and it is a doctrine worthy of being acted upon. We have done our best to rescue Denmark from the danger to which she was exposed, first by counselling her to put herself right when she was wrong, and next by endeavouring to induce her aggressors to refrain from continuing their aggression; and by inducing the neutral Powers to join us in adopting the same course. And what said the right hon. Gentleman in his opening speech on this subject? He said that if England and France were agreed upon the same policy, war would be difficult; but that if England, France, and Russia were agreed, war would be impossible. Well, we tried to make war impossible. But France and Russia would not combine with us, and therefore war became possible, and took place. The right hon. Gentleman has therefore pronounced a panegyric upon our policy, and he ought to vote against his own Resolution. We adopted the best means of rendering war impossible, and the failure was not our fault. . . .

. . . It is a libel on our country to record by a vote of the House what is not the fact—namely, that the influence and position of England have been lowered. Sir, the influence of a country depends upon other things than protocols and despatches. It depends on its power to defend itself, on its wealth and prosperity, on its intelligence and cultivation of mind, on the development of the arts and sciences, and on all those things which made a nation truly great and powerful. As long as England retains these conditions, so long shall I deny that her influence has been diminished. . . .

82. Extract from John Bright's speech at Birmingham, 18 January 1865. James E. Thorold Rogers, ed., *Speeches on Questions of Public Policy by John Bright* (London, 1869), pp. 331–2.

. . . I think I am not much mistaken in pronouncing the theory of the balance of power to be pretty nearly dead and buried. You cannot comprehend at a thought what is meant by that balance of power. If the record could be brought before you—but it is not possible to the eye of humanity to scan the scroll upon which are recorded the sufferings which the theory of the balance of power has entailed upon this country. It rises up before me when I think of it as a ghastly phantom which during one hundred and seventy years, whilst it has been worshipped in this country, has loaded the nation with debt and with taxes, has sacrificed the lives of hundreds of thousands of Englishmen, has desolated the homes of millions of families, and has left us, as the great result of the profligate expenditure which it has caused, a doubled peerage at one end of the social scale, and far more than a doubled pauperism at the other. I am very glad to be here tonight, amongst other things, to be able to say that we may rejoice that this foul idol—fouler than any heathen tribe ever worshipped—has at last been thrown down, and that there is one superstition less which has its hold upon the minds of English statesmen and of the English people.

*   *   *   *

83. Palmerston's private letter to Russell, 13 Sept. 1865. Russell MSS., P.R.O. 30/22/15E; Gooch, ii. 314–15, and Ashley, ii. 270–1.

I concur with you in agreeing with the Queen in condemning the conduct of Austria and Prussia towards the Duchies, as recorded and defined by the Treaty of Gastein; and all that Drouyn says about the Treaty is perfectly true, forming in that respect according to general opinion an exception to Drouyn's general practice as to veracity. But it seems to me rather late for the Queen and Drouyn to have opened their eyes as to the injustice of the proceedings of the two German Powers, and the falsity of the allegations in which they have guarded their proceedings. What they are doing now is quite of a piece with what they did in the beginning of their quarrel with the King of Denmark about the Duchies. It was the Wolf and the Lamb from the beginning, and no wonder that two wolves were too much for one lamb, however pugnacious that lamb showed himself, and the two wolves having got hold of what they wanted would hardly be expected to give up their prey out of a mere sense of what may be called posthumous justice. The fact is, as far as the Queen is concerned, that so long as the injustice committed appeared calculated to benefit Germany and the Germans it was all right and proper; but now that an example is about to be set of extinguishing petty states like Coburgh, her sense of right and wrong has become wonderfully keen, and her mind revolts at the idea of consequences which grow naturally from the proceedings she approved of. It is quite right that we should record our disapproval of the selfish and unprincipled conduct which Prussia has pursued and contemplates pursuing, and that we should express our sorrow at the participation of Austria in those proceedings. But there is a future as well as a present and a past, and it is one thing to condemn proceedings that have taken place or are intended, and which are dishonest and unjust, it is another thing to consider what effect those proceedings may have on the general interests of Europe.

It was dishonest and unjust to deprive Denmark of Schleswig and Holstein. It is another question how those two Duchies, when separated from Denmark, can be disposed of best for the interests of Europe. I should say that, with that view, it is better that they should go to increase the power of Prussia than that they should form another little state to be added to the cluster of small bodies politic which encumber Germany, and render it of less force than it ought to be in the general balance of power in the world. Prussia is too weak as she now is ever to be honest or independent in her action; and, with a view to the future, it is desirable that Germany, in the aggregate, should be strong, in order to control those two ambitious and aggressive powers, France and Russia, that press upon her west and east. As to France, we know how restless and aggressive she is, and how ready to break loose for Belgium, for the Rhine, for anything she would be likely to get without too great an exertion. As to Russia, she will, in due time, become a power almost as great as the old Roman Empire. She can become mistress of all Asia, except British India, whenever she chooses to take it; and when enlightened arrangements shall have made her revenue proportioned to her territory, and railways shall have abridged distances, her command of men will become enormous, her pecuniary means gigantic, and her power of transporting armies over great distances most formidable. Germany ought to be strong in order to resist Russian aggression, and a strong Prussia is essential to German strength. Therefore, though I heartily condemn the whole of the proceedings of Austria and Prussia about the Duchies, I own that I should rather see them incorporated with Prussia than converted into an additional asteroid in the system of Europe.

84. Russell's circular dispatch on the Convention of Gastein, 14 September 1865. P.R.O., F.O. 181/434 (no. 104); Edward Hertslet, *The Map of Europe by Treaty* (London, 1875), iii. 1645–6.

The Chargé d'Affaires of Prussia has communicated to me the substance of a despatch relating to the Convention of Gastein, and the newspapers of Berlin have since published the text of that Convention.

Upon the first communication to Her Majesty's Government of the Preliminaries of Peace signed at Vienna, I stated at Vienna and Berlin the views of Her Majesty's Government upon those Preliminaries.

The present Convention has only served to increase the regret Her Majesty's Government then expressed.

The Treaties of 1815 gave the King of Denmark a seat in the German Diet as Duke of Holstein.

The Treaty of 1852 recognized the right of succession to the whole Danish Monarchy which the late King had established in the person of the present King.

That Treaty has, in spite of the assurances given in the Despatches of 31st January, 1864, been completely set aside by Austria and Prussia, two of the Powers who had signed it.

It might have been expected that when Treaties were thus annulled, the popular feeling of Germany, the wishes of the Duchies themselves, and the opinions of the majority of the Diet so explicitly put forth by Austria and Prussia in the sittings of the Conference of London, would have been recognized in their place. In this manner if an order of rights had been overthown, another title derived from the assent of the people would have been set up, and that title might have been received with respect, and maintained with a prospect of permanence.

But all Rights, old and new, whether founded on the solemn compact of Sovereigns, or on the clear expression of the popular will, have been set at naught by the Convention of Gastein, and the dominion of force is the sole power acknowledged and regarded.

Violence and conquest are the bases upon which alone the partitioning Powers found their agreement.

Her Majesty's Government deeply lament the disregard thus shown to the principles of public right, and the legitimate claims of a people to be heard as to the disposal of their own destiny.

This instruction does not authorize you to address observations on this subject to the Court to which you are accredited, but is intended only to point out, when the opportunity shall present itself, what is the language you are expected to hold.

85. Clarendon's private letter to Lord Augustus Loftus (Ambassador in Berlin), 7 March 1866. Copy in Clarendon MSS., Bodleian Library, MS. Clar. dep. c 145; *The Diplomatic Reminiscences of Lord Augustus Loftus, 1862–1879* (London, 1894), 2nd series, i. 43–5.

You may easily suppose that the state of things between Prussia and Austria occupies men's minds, and creates the greatest uneasiness respecting the calamities which a *civil war* in Germany would entail upon Europe. Many people think that Prussia would not push matters to extremities, and that Austria will at the last moment yield, but I am not of the number, for I believe that Prussia (i.e. M. de Bismarck) will put a pressure upon Austria which she will resist whatever the consequences may be. The dispatches that Count Apponyi has read to me and the language he has been instructed to hold leave me little doubt that Austria will face war rather than the humiliation which Prussia seeks to inflict upon her, and in adopting that course I think she is perfectly right. A disastrous war is better than voluntary disgrace. But in the name of all that is rational, decent and humane what can be the justification of war on the part of Prussia? She cannot publickly plead her greed for territorial aggrandizement and she cannot with truth say that the administration of Holstein by the Austrian authorities has been of a kind to constitute a *casus belli*, although Bernstorff has just told me that the licence allowed in Holstein by General Gablenz and the hostile articles of newspapers under the inspiration of Austria have produced a state of things so intolerable to Prussia that it must be put an end to by war if no other means for the purpose can be devised or are assented to by Austria.

I wish you would take an opportunity of saying to M. de Bismarck that we purposely abstain from making any official communication upon the present state of affairs but that as we desire to preserve the most friendly relations with Prussia we earnestly beg of him to pause before he embarks in a war of which no man can foresee the results or the termination.

It is improbable that any *well-founded* complaints which Prussia may have against Austria should not be capable of being settled by negotiation, and if ever there was a case calling for the sort of arbitration or rather of reference to a friendly Power which, to the credit of humanity and the civilization of our age, was agreed upon at Paris in 1856, it is the case which has arisen between the two

German Powers. It would reflect great credit upon Prussia if before she went out in this duel with Austria she volunteered to place herself in the hands of seconds upon whose impartiality she could rely and with whom her honour would be in safe keeping.

I well know how properly tenacious the King is of the honour of Prussia and of his army, and if I thought that either would be affected by such a course of proceeding I would not suggest it or indeed, any other course which would be liable to objection and refusal. I know not upon what means of resistance Austria can reckon or what support she would find in Southern Germany, but I am sure that any grievous injury to her such as would destroy the present equilibrium of power would be a misfortune for the rest of Europe and as such would be resented—in fact the more the question is considered the more certain it seems that Prussia will array against her the public opinion of Europe as an aggressive and unreasonable Power, and we have no wish for that. Setting aside family ties Prussia is the great Protestant Power of Europe with which we naturally have kindred feelings, and it would be with deep regret that we should see her regarded as a common enemy, *because* a wilful disturber of the peace of Europe, and still more if in the course of events we found ourselves compelled to take any part against her.

Pray submit these various considerations to M. de Bismarck as friendly and confidential, and offered without intention to interfere with the Policy of Prussia, but not concealing, as a friend ought not to conceal, our opinion upon the disastrous consequences to ourselves as well as to others which may ensue from that Policy being carried beyond the limits of absolute necessity.

I should like to know by telegr[am] in what spirit M. de B[ismarck] receives the communication.

86. Extract from Russell's private letter to Clarendon, 30 March 1866. Only the first half of the letter survives in Clarendon MSS., Bodleian Library, MS. Clar. dep. c 93; Maxwell, ii. 311.

I send you by the Queen's direction a memorandum written at her desire. It proposes clearly an interference by force against Prussian designs in the Duchies. Agreeing fully in Her Majesty's view of the iniquity of a war undertaken by Prussia in the pretence of delivering the Duchies from Danish oppression, and converted into a forcible appropriation of the Duchies to aggrandise Prussia I cannot acquiesce in the proposed course.

1. Because our proper plan in any war would have been to defend Denmark against both Prussia and Austria. But the Gov[ernmen]t and Parliament decided against undertaking such a war.

2. Because England having acquiesced, tho' under protest in the treaty by which Austria and Prussia obtained possession of the Duchies it remains for Germany which invoked the war, and which is strong enough to assist Austria to do right, to settle the Duchies in the manner conformable to the wishes of the inhabitants.

3. Because it would be an injustice to the people of England to employ their military and pecuniary resources in a quarrel in which neither English honour nor English interests are involved. Austria and Prussia undertook the war against Denmark in violation of their treaty with England and against the remonstrances of England. England has spoken in defence of right; she cannot interfere in the division of the spoil.

Pray convey to the Queen your sentiments and make what use of this letter you please. The ministers who attended the cabinet yesterday seemed decidedly against interference. An amicable mediation, if asked for by both parties, might be agreed to in conjunction with France and Russia. . . .

87. Extract from Clarendon's private letter to the Queen, 31 March 1866. Royal Archives, I 43/154; *The Letters of Queen Victoria*, 2nd series, i. 314–15.

*   *   *   *

It is unnecessary for Lord Clarendon to say how entirely he concurs with your Majesty respecting the outrageous conduct of Prussia, or rather of M. de Bismarck, who is the sole author of all these impending troubles, but Lord Clarendon much fears that they cannot now be arrested by the course of proceeding, wise and humane though it is, that your Majesty suggests.

Lord Clarendon some time ago consulted Lord Cowley [Ambassador in Paris] as to the possibility of a joint representation being made by England and France against the unjust and high-handed proceedings of Prussia, and he was informed that the prospects of war in Germany were by no means displeasing to the Emperor, and in Lord Cowley's letter of yesterday he says that this war may divert public attention from the unsatisfactory state of things in France. No co-operation therefore is to be expected from France, but Lord Clarendon will write this evening to Lord Cowley and desire him to ask M. Drouyn whether England and France could justify it to themselves not to make an effort in favour of peace, and to prevent a war so groundless and unjustifiable.

It is quite clear that the good offices of England single-handed would not be accepted by Prussia; they have been offered indirectly and confidentially, and declined; if they were proposed officially we should receive an insolent refusal.

Lord Clarendon ventures to express the opinion, in which Lord Russell entirely concurs, that although we might join with France in mediation or the employment of good offices, yet that we could not, even in conjunction with France, use the language of menace which might entail the necessity of action, first, because the time for such action is gone by; we might have gone to the defence of Denmark when she was attacked by Austria and Prussia, but it was wisely determined that such a war ought not to be undertaken. Secondly, because, England having acquiesced, although under protest, in the Treaty by which Austria and Prussia obtained possession of the duchies, it is for Germany, which invoked the war and which is strong enough, to assist Austria in doing right and to settle the duchies in the manner conformable to the wishes of the inhabitants. Thirdly, the case is one in which neither English honour nor English interests are involved. We have spoken in defence of right; we cannot actively interfere with those who are quarrelling over the spoils; and in the present state of Ireland, and the menacing aspect of our relations with the United States, the military and pecuniary resources of England must be husbanded with the utmost care. The country would not tolerate any direct interference in a quarrel with which we had no concern; and all those Members of your Majesty's Government, who attended the Cabinet on Thursday last, expressed themselves in the strongest terms against it. . . .

88. Extract from Derby's Ministerial Statement in the House of Lords, 9 July 1866. *Hansard*, 3rd series, clxxxiv. 736–7.

. . . My Lords, it has been industriously reported that a Conservative Government is necessarily a warlike Government. Now, I believe there never was a rumour circulated which had so little foundation either in past facts or in the character, the motives, and the principles of the Conservative party. My Lords, the Conservative party consists, in a great measure, of men who have the greatest interest and the largest stake in the country; they are the men upon whom the consequences of a war would fall the most heavily; they are the persons who have the greatest interest in the peace and prosperity of the State; and, above all, they are the party who are the least likely to be carried away by that popular enthusiasm and those popular impulses which may hurry even a prudent Government into the adoption of courses—I might say, into the adoption of Quixotic enterprizes—inimical to the welfare of the country. Now, my Lords, if there be any one party more than another which is free at this moment from any disposition to encourage such projects, I say it is the Conservative party. My earnest desire, I can honestly say, is that the Foreign Office should contribute to the preservation of the peace of this country and of the world. Now, there are two modes of contributing to the preservation of peace, both of which are essential to the object in view. The one is the mode in which you deal with the affairs and policy of foreign countries; the other is the amount of your preparedness to resist any attack, from whatever quarter it may come. Now, with regard to the first my principle is this—that it is the duty of the Government of this country, placed as this country is with respect to geographical position, to keep itself upon terms of goodwill with all surrounding nations, but not to entangle itself with any single or monopolizing alliance with any one of them; above all to endeavour not to interfere needlessly and vexatiously with the internal affairs of any foreign country, nor to volunteer to them unasked advice with regard to the conduct of their affairs, looking at them from our own point of view, and not considering how different are the views and feelings of those whom we address. Above all, I hold that it is the duty of a Government to abstain from menace if they do not intend to follow that menace by action. I am told that we found fault with the noble Earl (Earl Russell) with regard to Denmark for not having taken a more active part in her favour. That, however, was not the ground of our complaint. The ground of our complaint—and I take it to be a warning for all future Ministries—was that the noble Earl had held language which was not to be justified except upon the supposition that he was going to act upon it, and when those with regard to whom he held that language relied upon the performance of the implied engagement, he felt himself compelled to withdraw from that engagement. My Lords, it would be the height of impertinence and of impolicy if I were to attempt to say a single word upon the state of affairs on the Continent of Europe. A short—I hope a short, but at all events a bloody war has been prevailing for the last few weeks—a war in the objects of which the honour of this country is in no degree involved and a war in which the interests of this country are very remotely, if at all, involved. With regard to that war individuals may have their sympathies with Prussia, with Austria, with Italy, with this or with that Power; but the sympathy of individuals has nothing to do with the conduct of the Government; and I hold that the conduct of the Government with regard to such a war as that now raging is studiously to maintain a strict and impartial neutrality between all the contending parties, only ready at any time to offer their good offices, if there should appear the slightest gleam of hope that, combined with those of other neutral Powers, such as France and Russia, they might lead to a termination of this bloody struggle and to the restoration of peace. Those good offices ought to be at the disposal at any time of other neutral Powers, and we ought willingly and gladly to co-operate with them for the purpose of using our influence to stay the horrors of war. And, my Lords, I believe that influence would not be less efficaciously exercised because it was attended by no menace and by no meddlesome desire to give unasked advice, because we could have no selfish policy and no desire of reaping any advantage for ourselves, except that one inestimable advantage of staying the effusion of blood and restoring to Europe the blessings of prosperity and peace. . . .

89. Extract from Stanley's House of Commons Speech on the Austro-Prussian War, 20 July 1866. *Hansard*, 3rd series, clxxxiv. 1256–7.

. . . I think there never was a great European war in which the direct national interests of England were less concerned. We all, I suppose, have our individual sympathies in the matter. The Italian question I look upon as not being very distant from a fair settlement;

and with regard to the other possible results of the war, and especially as to the establishment of a strong North German Power—of a strong, compact Empire, extending over North Germany—I cannot see that, if the war ends, as it very possibly may, in the establishment of such an Empire—I cannot see that the existence of such a Power would be to us any injury, any menace, or any detriment. It might be conceivable enough that the growth of such a Power might indeed awaken the jealousy of other Continental States, who may fear a rival in such a Power. That is a natural feeling in their position. That position, however, is not ours, and if North Germany is to become a single great Power, I do not see that any English interest is in the least degree affected. . . . there is no danger, as far as human foresight can go, of Continental complications involving this country in war. I think, in the next place, that if we do not intend to take an active part in the quarrel, we ought to be exceedingly cautious how we use menacing language or hold out illusory hopes. If our advice is solicited, and if there is any likelihood that that advice will be of practical use, I do not think we ought to hesitate to give the best advice in our power; but while giving it under a deep sense of moral responsibility, as being in our judgment the best, we ought carefully to avoid involving ourselves or the country in any responsibility for the results of following that advice in a matter where no English interest is concerned. I do not think we ought to put ourselves in such a position that any Power could say to us, 'We have acted upon your advice, and we have suffered for it. You have brought us into this difficulty, and therefore you are bound to get us out of it.' We ought not, I say, to place ourselves in a position of that kind. . . .

90. Extract from the House of Lords Debate on the Luxemburg Guarantee, 20 June 1867. *Hansard*, 3rd series, clxxxviii. 144–58.

RUSSELL: . . . There were two subjects which must have engaged the attention of Her Majesty's Government in connection with this question of Luxemburg. One was, whether it was so much for the interests of this country that the peace of Europe should be preserved as to induce Her Majesty's Government to interpose its diplomatic offices; and the other was, whether, to maintain peace in Europe, we might not have to pay a higher price than the product was worth. With regard to the first question it has always appeared to me that it is the peculiar and very great interest of this country to preserve the peace of Europe. In the first place, as a commercial country it is of the greatest possible interest to us that peace should prevail. Not only would our commerce be interrupted by the blockade of ports, but many difficult questions must necessarily arise relating to our ships and commerce, which might endanger our neutrality. Again, if war had broken out between France and Prussia, there was every probability that before any long time had elapsed other questions would have arisen in which our honour was so far pledged that it would have been impossible for us not to have intervened. For these reasons I think Her Majesty's Government were quite right in deeming it their duty to offer such advice as lay in their power, with a view of preserving the peace of Europe. . . . I cannot consider that we have entered into a treaty which is likely to be infringed, or that any great danger has been incurred by our entering into an additional guarantee. I do not consider that we have entered into any new guarantee which is likely to prove onerous. I believe there is every probability that the peace of Europe will be continued. But even if Prussia and France were at war I do not think that either of them would be disposed to violate the neutrality of Luxemburg, because they would have to consider that by doing so they would provoke the interposition and hostility of the great Powers who have consented to give this guarantee. I am therefore of opinion, and I venture to state that opinion to your Lordships—in the first place, that it was most desirable to maintain the peace of Europe; and next, that we have not made too great a sacrifice to maintain that peace, and have not entered into any guarantee involving probable danger, or into any engagements that can be blamed or found fault with. I will say, and I am most happy to say, that the ability, the judgment, and the temper with which the Secretary of State for Foreign Affairs has conducted this correspondence and the manner in which he behaved in the Conference will give to Parliament and to the country great confidence in his conduct of foreign affairs. In the next place I desire to express my satisfaction that the Government has not listened to theories which last year I was somewhat apprehensive that they might have entertained, under the name of a new foreign policy—that however great our interest might be, we were not to interfere in the affairs of foreign countries. . . .

DERBY: . . . A proposal having been made which was accepted as satisfactory to the honour of both parties, we felt that it was incumbent upon us not to shrink from any responsibility which might attach to an additional guarantee on our part if that would secure the final acceptance of the proposal—especially when we knew that if we had refused nothing could have prevented war. The collective guarantee of the neutral Powers was made a *sine quâ non*, and if England had refused to join, upon England would have rested the heavy responsibility of a European war. . . . I do not entirely agree with the noble Earl (Earl Russell) as to the extent of our responsibility, even supposing it to be of the character he has described. If it had been a continuance of the guarantee first given, I should think it a very serious matter, because the guarantee of the possession of Luxemburg to the King of Holland was a joint and several guarantee similar to that which was given with regard to the independence and neutrality of Belgium; it was binding individually and separately upon each of the Powers. That was the nature of the guarantee which was given with regard to Belgium and with regard to the possession of Luxemburg by the King-Duke. Now a guarantee of neutrality is very different from a guarantee of possession. If France and Prussia were to have a quarrel between themselves, and either were to violate the neutrality of Luxemburg by passing their troops through the duchy for the purpose of making war on the other, we might, if the guarantee had been individual as well as joint, have been under the necessity of preventing that violation, and the same obligation would have rested upon each guarantor; but as it is we are not exposed to so serious a contingency, because the guarantee is only collective—that is to say, it is binding only upon all the Powers in their collective capacity; they all agree to maintain the neutrality of Luxemburg, but not one of those Powers is bound to fulfil the obligation alone. That is a most important difference, because the only two Powers by which the neutrality of Luxemburg is likely to be infringed are two of the parties to the collective guarantee; and therefore, if either of them violate the neutrality, the obligation on all the others would not accrue. I thought it right to point out that we had not incurred so very serious a responsibility as some have supposed . . .

CLARENDON: . . . the apprehension which has been expressed with regard to these guarantees is, I think, a perfectly just one; because such obligations are naturally viewed with fear and mistrust by the people of this country. They are sometimes lightly undertaken and are generally intended to tide over a difficulty; while there is at the same time generally a mental reservation founded on the belief that no demand will ever be made for their performance. I hope, however, that the time is far distant when from motives of cynical indifference this country will hesitate to incur the smallest sacrifice which may be necessary for securing such great advantages, and I think my noble Friend was perfectly right in the course he took after weighing the infinitesimal risk which England would incur by the course which has been adopted against the certain injury which would be inflicted upon this country by war between France and Prussia.... With regard to the guarantee, I will go somewhat further than the noble Earl at the head of the Government, and say that if we had undertaken the same guarantee in the case of Luxemburg as we did in the case of Belgium, we should, in my opinion, have incurred an additional and very serious responsibility. I look upon our guarantee in the case of Belgium as an individual guarantee, and have always so regarded it; but this is a collective guarantee. No one of the Powers, therefore, can be called upon to take single action, even in the improbable case of any difficulty arising. I cannot help regarding this guarantee as a moral obligation, a point of honour—as an agreement which cannot be violated without dishonour by any of the signing Powers; and I believe that an agreement of that nature may be more binding than the precise terms in which a treaty is couched, for it is a characteristic of these times that when formal treaties are found inconvenient, they are disregarded. . . .

GRANVILLE: . . . If Her Majesty's Government instead of increasing our liabilities have actually diminished them, it appears to me, as it will appear to most people, that there has been the most complete mystification of some of the most distinguished diplomatists of Europe ever heard of. . . . after the statement of the noble Earl it appears to be so utterly free from danger, that it is difficult to understand the importance which Prussia attached to it. That she did attach that importance to it is certain, else why on earth should she regard it as a *sine quâ non* without which she was prepared to go to war with the greatest military nation in the world. . . .

ARGYLL: . . . it was of great importance, not only to England but to the Continent generally, that the interpretation put by the English Government upon the engagement entered into should be accurately known. . . . Prussia insisted upon an European guarantee and the British Foreign Office gave way, consenting to . . . a guarantee; but, if he rightly understood the observation of the noble Earl, the demand of Prussia had, after all, been successfully evaded, and England had taken no obligation upon her. It was obvious that, as all the great Powers were parties to the treaty, Luxemburg, if attacked at all, would be invaded by one of the guaranteeing Powers, and in that case none of the other guaranteeing Powers could be called upon to secure her neutrality. But this reduced the whole thing to a sham, and a farce; it was not a guarantee at all, and it ought to be clearly understood, both by England and by the Continent, that we did not consider ourselves bound to interfere with the military possession of Luxemburg unless it was attacked by some Power not a party to the treaty. . . .

DERBY: . . . It is quite true that, if France were to invade the territory of Luxemburg, the other Powers, though they might be called upon to resist the invasion, would not be bound to do so. They might or might not think it proper to defend the neutrality of Luxemburg, but no individual Power could be compelled, under the treaty, to render assistance.

RUSSELL: . . . I do not put the same interpretation upon the treaty as the noble Earl does. My belief is that if France were to violate the treaty and invade the territory of Luxemburg, the other Powers who are parties to the treaty would feel bound to call upon France to retire.

91. Extract from Stanley's dispatch no. 200 to Loftus, 25 June 1867. P.R.O., F.O. 244/218; Temperley and Penson, pp. 313–14.

. . . I told Count Bernstorff that discussions in the House of Lords were, from the difficulty of hearing, often imperfectly reported; and that I could not undertake to defend words attributed to Lord Derby, without knowing whether they had been really used or not; but that

I would explain to him my idea of the obligations involved in a Collective Guarantee.

I said that it was absurd to suppose that each of the Powers that had signed such a Guarantee could be made singly and separately responsible for its being enforced. Supposing (to take an extreme case) that France and Prussia came to an understanding involving a violation of the territory of Luxemburg—that the King Grand Duke appealed to the Guaranteeing Powers,—that Austria, Russia and Italy held aloof,—would it be contended that England, single-handed, was bound, on that account to go to war with France and Prussia combined? It seemed to me, I said, impossible to define with legal strictness the amount of obligation really incurred; but whatever that might be, I could not see that the binding force of the engagement which we had signed, was in any degree lessened by comments made in debate upon it, even by its authors. The construction to be placed upon an international document was to be inferred from the words employed, and from the general usage of Europe. Once it was signed, the individual opinion of the Minister signing was of no more weight than that of any other person. In a Country like ours, no absolutely valid engagement could be entered into as to the course to be adopted at a future period, and under circumstances not now foreseen. Questions of war or peace must be decided by the Parliament of the day.

I would however add, as I had stated in the House of Commons, that if I had regarded the Guarantee which we had given as purely illusory, neither I nor my colleagues would have had anything to do with it.

* * * *

92. Extract from Clarendon's private letter to the Queen, 16 April 1869. Royal Archives, B 25/26; *The Letters of Queen Victoria*, 2nd series, i. 589–91.

Lord Clarendon presents his humble duty to your Majesty, and humbly begs to acknowledge the receipt of your Majesty's gracious telegram of this morning, which has removed a weight from his mind, as your Majesty's letter of yesterday had been the cause of deep regret to Lord Clarendon, who feared that, in the opinion of your Majesty, the peace of Europe and the honour of England were endangered by the language or the acts for which Lord Clarendon, more than any of his colleagues, is responsible, although they have always received the sanction of the Cabinet.

Lord Clarendon, however, is rejoiced to infer from your Majesty's telegram that nothing detrimental to the position of England fell from him in the course of his conversation with Marshal Saldanha,[1] and he ventures to think that nothing injurious to the honour and good faith of England can be said with reference to the Belgian question.

The object of the Belgian and Portuguese Governments is to hold out as a menace to their real or supposed enemies that the whole material force of England is at their disposal; the object of Lord Clarendon is to preserve an entire freedom of action for your Majesty's Government to be used as circumstances may arise and the duties of Treaty obligations may impose.

It is easy for Lord A. Loftus to repeat the language that Lord Clarendon has over and over again heard from General Moltke and other Prussians whose object is to embroil us with France, and whose policy would then be to leave England in the lurch; but it is the duty, as Lord Clarendon humbly conceives, of your Majesty's Government to consider the interests of England, and not to disguise from themselves the many difficulties of our position and the exceeding delicacy of calling upon Parliament to give effect to Treaties which, if public opinion years ago had been what it now is, would not have been sanctioned. It seems to be the duty of your Majesty's Government to bear in mind how widely different are the circumstances of this country now to when those Treaties were concluded, and that, if their execution were to lead us into war in Europe, we should find ourselves immediately called upon to defend Canada from American invasion and our commerce from American privateers.

Accordingly it would seem more honourable and dignified on the part of England not to menace if she is not sure of being able to strike, and not to promise more than she may be able to perform; though at the same time neither saying nor doing anything to warrant the supposition that, on a real necessity arising, England would shrink from any obligation that she might be rightfully called upon to perform.

Lord Clarendon feels convinced that your Majesty's enlightened judgment upon all foreign questions will lead to the admission that in every quarrel there are at least two principals, and that we are

---

[1] The Portuguese minister in London had asked for a public statement by England that she would defend Portugal if attacked.

bound to consider not only the deterring effect which menace would have on one of them, but also the stimulating effect it would be at least as likely to produce on the other, and the disregard of the laws of prudence which might follow. Lord Clarendon does not hesitate to submit to your Majesty that by a course of proceeding totally distinct from that of menace, however qualified, your Majesty's Government largely contributed in bringing the Turco-Greek question to a happy instead of a disastrous conclusion, and in materially modifying the original intentions of the Emperor towards Belgium. Each of these questions, however, menaced the peace of Europe, and Lord Clarendon ventures to remind your Majesty that he has received the thanks of Ct. Bismarck and Ct. Beust for his friendly intervention, by which a stop was put to the press warfare which was daily rendering Austria and Prussia more hostile to each other.

* * * *

93. The Queen's private letter to Clarendon, 17 April 1869. Draft in Royal Archives, B 25/27; *The Letters of Queen Victoria*, 2nd series, i. 591–2.

The Queen thanks Lord Clarendon for his very clear explanation of his views on Foreign Policy, in the general principles of which she must agree. She quite admits the propriety of reserving to ourselves entire freedom of action, and the inexpediency of encouraging any Power, which may think itself entitled to support from England, to such a 'disregard of the laws of prudence' as might wantonly provoke the consequences we desire to avoid.

At the same time the Queen cannot but be alive to the fact, that there is a disposition on the Continent to believe that England is not to be moved, either by interest, or the obligation of Treaties, into giving more than *moral* support in any complications that may arise, and that the aggressive Power may dismiss all fears of finding 'England across its path.'

The Crimean War shows how dangerous such a belief is to the preservation of Peace; and all that the Queen has ever wished to press upon Lord Clarendon, as she did upon Lord Stanley, is that, with the same firm but friendly language with which he gave the French Government to understand that England was not likely to stand by and see Belgium unjustly attacked, and thus turned aside (if indeed it is turned aside) a great danger, he will let it be known, beyond the possibility of mistake, that, while she indulges in no threats, England will be prepared to maintain the obligation of Treaties, wherever her honour or her interest may call upon her to do so.

Lord Clarendon's language to Marshal Saldanha, as reported in his despatch, is all that could be desired. The Queen had certainly feared, from his previous letter, that his refusal of any promise of support, in certain contingencies, had been more decided and peremptory than she could have approved.

94. Extract from Gladstone's private letter to General Grey (the Queen's Private Secretary), 17 April 1869. Royal Archives, Q 3/115; John Morley, *The Life of William Ewart Gladstone* (London, 1903), ii. 316–18.

... Apart from this question of the moment, there is one more important as to the tone in which it is to be desired that, where matter of controversy has arisen on the continent of Europe, the diplomatic correspondence of this country should be carried on. This more important question may be the subject of differences in the country, but I observe with joy that her Majesty approves the general principle which Lord Clarendon sets forth in his letter of the 16th. I do not believe that England ever will or can be unfaithful to her great traditions, or can forswear her interest in the common transactions and the general interests of Europe. But her credit and her power form a fund, which in order that they may be made the most of, should be thriftily used.

The effect of the great revolutionary war was to place England in a position which was for the moment of surpassing splendour, but which was essentially a false position as between her and the several Powers of Europe, because it imposed upon her too great a responsibility, and produced in them too great a disposition to rely upon the aid of her resources. This was no matter of blame to either party; it was the result of a desperate struggle of over twenty years, in which every one else was down in his turn, but England was ever on her feet; in which it was found that there was no ascertained limit either to her means, or to her disposition to dispense them; in which, to use the language of Mr. Canning, her flag was always flying 'a

signal of rallying to the combatant, and of shelter to the fallen.'
The *habit* of appeal, and of reliance, thus engendered by peculiar
circumstances, requires to be altered by a quiet and substantial
though not a violent process. For though Europe never saw England
faint away, *we* know at what a cost of internal danger to the Union
[?] and to all the institutions of the country, she fought her way
to the perilous eminence on which she undoubtedly stood in 1815.

If there be a fear abroad that England has forever abjured a resort
to force other than moral force, is that fear justified by facts? In
1853, joining with France, we made ourselves the vindicators of
the peace of Europe; and ten years later, be it remembered, in the
case of Denmark we offered to perform the same office, but we could
get no one to join us. Is it desirable that we should go further?
Is England so uplifted in strength above every other nation, that
she can with prudence advertise herself as ready to undertake the
general redress of wrongs? Would not the consequence of such
professions and promises be either the premature exhaustion of
her means, or a collapse in the day of performance? Is *any* Power
at this time of day warranted in assuming this comprehensive obligation? Of course, the answer is, no. But do not on the other hand
allow it to be believed that England will never interfere. For the
eccentricities of other men's beliefs no one can answer: but for any
reasonable belief in such an abnegation on the part of England, there
is no ground whatever. As I understand Lord Clarendon's ideas,
they are fairly represented by his very important diplomatic communications since he has taken office. They proceed upon such
grounds as these:—That England should keep entire in her own
hands the means of estimating her own obligations upon the various
states of facts as they arise; that she should not foreclose and narrow
her own liberty of choice by declarations made to other Powers, in
their real or supposed interests, of which they would claim to be at
least joint interpreters; that it is dangerous for her to assume alone
an advanced, and therefore an isolated position, in regard to European controversies; that, come what may, it is better for her to
promise too little than too much; that she should not encourage
the weak by giving expectations of aid to resist the strong, but
should rather seek to deter the strong by firm but moderate language,
from aggressions on the weak; that she should seek to develop and
mature the action of a common, or public, or European opinion,
as the best standing bulwark against wrong, but should beware

of seeming to lay down the law of that opinion by her own authority, and thus running the risk of setting against her, and against right and justice, that general sentiment which ought to be, and generally would be, arrayed in their favour.

I am persuaded that at this juncture opinions of this colour being true and sound, are also the only opinions which the country is disposed to approve. But I do not believe that on that account it is one whit less disposed than it has been at any time, to cast in its lot upon any fitting occasion with the cause it believes to be right . . . I therefore hope, and feel assured, her Majesty will believe that Lord Clarendon really requires no intimation from me to ensure his steadily maintaining the tone which becomes the foreign minister of the Queen.

95. Extract from Gladstone's House of Commons Speech on Belgian Neutrality, 10 August 1870. *Hansard*, 3rd series, cciii. 1786–9.

. . . too much has been said . . . of the specially distinct, separate, and exclusive interest which this country has in the maintenance of the neutrality of Belgium. What is our interest in maintaining the neutrality of Belgium? It is the same as that of every great Power in Europe. It is contrary to the interest of Europe that there should be unmeasured aggrandizement. Our interest is no more involved in the aggrandizement supposed in this particular case than is the interest of the other Powers. . . . What is the immediate moral effect of . . . exaggerated statements of the separate interest of England? The immediate moral effect of them is this—that every effort we make on behalf of Belgium on other grounds than those of interest—as well as on grounds of interest, goes forth to the world as a separate and selfish scheme of ours; and that which we believe to be entitled to the dignity and credit of an effort on behalf of the general peace, stability, and interest of Europe actually contracts a taint of selfishness in the eyes of other nations because of the manner in which the subject of Belgian neutrality is too frequently treated in this House. If I may be allowed to speak of the motives which have actuated Her Majesty's Government in the matter, I would say that while we have recognized the interest of England, we have never looked upon it as the sole motive, or even as the greatest of those considerations which have urged us forward. There is, I admit, the obligation of the Treaty. It is not necessary, nor would time permit me, to enter into the complicated question of the nature of the obligations of that Treaty; but I am not able to subscribe to the doctrine of those who have held in this House what plainly amounts to an assertion, that the simple fact of the existence of a guarantee is binding on every party to it irrespectively altogether of the particular position in which it may find itself at the time when the occasion for acting on the guarantee arises. The great authorities upon foreign policy to whom I have been accustomed to listen—such as Lord Aberdeen and Lord Palmerston—never, to my knowledge, took that rigid and, if I may venture to say so, that impracticable view of a guarantee. The circumstance that there is already an existing guarantee in force is of necessity an important fact, and a weighty element in the case, to which we are bound to give full and ample consideration. There is also this further consideration, the force of which we must all feel most deeply, and that is the common interest against the unmeasured aggrandizement of any Power whatever. But there is one other motive, which I shall place at the head of all, that attaches peculiarly to the preservation of the independence of Belgium. What is that country? It is a country containing 4,000,000 or 5,000,000 of people, with much of an historic past, and imbued with a sentiment of nationality and a spirit of independence as warm and as genuine as that which beats in the hearts of the proudest and most powerful nations. By the regulation of its internal concerns, amid the shocks of revolution, Belgium, through all the crises of the age, has set to Europe an example of a good and stable government gracefully associated with the widest possible extension of the liberty of the people. Looking at a country such as that, is there any man who hears me who does not feel that if, in order to satisfy a greedy appetite for aggrandizement, coming whence it may, Belgium were absorbed, the day that witnessed that absorption would hear the knell of public right and public law in Europe? But we have an interest in the independence of Belgium which is wider than that—which is wider than that which we may have in the literal operation of the guarantee. It is found in the answer to the question whether, under the circumstances of the case, this country, endowed as it is with influence and power, would quietly stand by and witness the perpetration of the direst crime that ever stained the pages of history, and thus become participators in the sin? . . . What if both these Powers with whom we are making this Treaty should combine against the independence of Belgium? Well, all I can say is that we rely on the faith of these parties. But if there be danger of their combining against that independence now, unquestionably there was much more danger in the position of affairs that was revealed to our astonished eyes a fortnight ago, and before these later engagements were contracted. I do not undertake to define the character of that position which, as I have said, was more dangerous a fortnight ago. I feel confident that it would be hasty to suppose that these great States would, under any circumstances, have become parties to the actual contemplation and execution of a proposal such as that which was made the subject of communication between persons of great importance on behalf of their respective States. That was the state of facts with which we had to deal. It was the combination, and not the opposition, of the two Powers which we had to fear, and I contend—and we shall be ready on every proper occasion to argue—that there is no measure so well adapted to meet the peculiar character of such an occasion as that which we have proposed. It is said that the Treaty of 1839 would have sufficed, and that we ought to have announced our determination to abide by it. But if we were disposed at once to act upon the guarantee contained in that Treaty, what state of circumstances does it contemplate? It contemplates the invasion of the frontiers of Belgium and the violation of the neutrality of that country by some other Power. That is the only case in which we could have been called upon to act under the Treaty of 1839, and that is the only case in which we can be called upon to act under the Treaty now before the House. But in what, then, lies the difference between the two Treaties? It is in this—that, in accordance with our obligations, we should have had to act under the Treaty of 1839 without any stipulated assurance of being supported from any quarter whatever against any combination, however formidable; whereas by the Treaty now formally before Parliament, under the conditions laid down in it, we secure powerful support in the event of our having to act—a support with respect to which we may well say that it brings the object in view within the sphere of the practicable and attainable, instead of leaving it within the sphere of what might have been desirable, but which might have been most difficult, under all the circumstances, to have realized. . . .

96. Extract from Disraeli's Speech in the Free Trade Hall, Manchester, 3 April 1872. W. F. Monypenny and George Earle Buckle, *The Life of Benjamin Disraeli Earl of Beaconsfield* (London, 1910–20), v. 191–2.

* * * *

Don't suppose, because I counsel firmness and decision at the right moment, that I am of that school of statesmen who are favourable to a turbulent and aggressive diplomacy. I have resisted it during a great part of my life. I am not unaware that the relations of England to Europe have undergone a vast change during the century that has just elapsed. The relations of England to Europe are not the same as they were in the days of Lord Chatham or Frederick the Great. The Queen of England has become the Sovereign of the most powerful of Oriental States. On the other side of the globe there are new establishments belonging to her, teeming with wealth and population, which will, in due time, exercise their influence over the distribution of power. The old establishments of this country, now the United States of America, throw their lengthening shades over the Atlantic, which mix with European waters. These are vast and novel elements in the distribution of power. I acknowledge that the policy of England with respect to Europe should be a policy of reserve, but proud reserve; and in answer to those statesmen, those mistaken statesmen, who have intimated the decay of the power of England and the decline of her resources, I express here my confident conviction that there never was a moment in our history when the power of England was so great and her resources so vast and inexhaustible. And yet, gentlemen, it is not merely our fleets and armies, our powerful artillery, our accumulated capital, and our unlimited credit on which I so much depend, as upon that unbroken spirit of her people, which I believe was never prouder of the Imperial country to which they belong.

* * * *

97. Extract from Salisbury's private letter to Disraeli, 31 October 1875. Monypenny and Buckle, v. 434–5.

* * * *

Touching Central Asia: I should much like to talk the matter over with you: for the decision is one of great responsibility. The dilemma is simply this. It concerns us much to have an agent in Afghanistan. We want to guide the Ameer, and to watch; for there is the double danger that he may play us false, or, remaining true, may blunder into operations which will bring him into collision with Russia. It would also be a great security for peace, if we were able to keep the Czar, who wishes for peace, informed of the intrigues of his frontier officers, who do not. But on the other hand it is of great importance—I quite admit it—not to irritate the Ameer. But this is a sort of difficulty which the Indian Government has had constantly to meet. Diplomacy has been a real power in Indian history—because of the moral ascendancy which British officers have acquired over the Princes at whose Courts they were placed. I do not propose to send a mission to Afghanistan against the Ameer's wishes: but I propose to tell the Government of India to make the Ameer wish it. It cannot of course be done straight off—by return of post; but by the exercise of tact in the choice of the moment and the argument I feel sure that it can be done. The Ameer is genuinely frightened of the Russians: and every advance they make will make him more pliable, *until* their power on his frontier seems to him so great, and he is so convinced of our timidity, that he thinks safer to tie himself to them than to us. But on all this I should much like to talk to you.

*   *   *   *

She [the Queen] told me that you proposed to make Lord Powis Viceroy. The intelligence rather startled me: for he has no experience of affairs, and I have noted in him no trace of practical ability. Your own judgment must of course guide you: but I hope you will not decide hastily, as there is plenty of time. The post is terribly important: a feeble occupant might bring about a great disaster.

98. Extract from Disraeli's private letter to the Queen, 12 February 1876. Royal Archives, H 7/25; *The Letters of Queen Victoria,* 2nd series, ii. 444.

*   *   *   *

If this practical, good understanding with Germany be accomplished, it will place our external relations on a rock, and England will again exercise that influence which, of late years, has so painfully and mysteriously disappeared.

Mr. Disraeli has unceasingly impressed upon Lord Derby the absolute necessity of frankly and definitely co-operating with the offers and overtures of Prince Bismarck; but it is on your Majesty that Mr. Disraeli mainly relies for success in this endeavour. Lord Derby, though he often seems ungenial, not to say morose, is, Mr. Disraeli knows, much influenced by your Majesty's opinion on external affairs, and really appreciates both your Majesty's information and judgment.

* * * *

99. Extract from Derby's confidential dispatch no. 117 to Lord Odo Russell (Ambassador in Berlin), 16 February 1876. P.R.O., F.O. 244/295; Temperley and Penson, p. 356, and D. Harris, 'Bismarck's advance to England, January, 1876', *Journal of Modern History*, iii (1931), 451–2. (The latter wrongly dates it 12 February.)

* * * *

It is unnecessary to point out . . . that England desires no exclusive alliances, nor do the principles of English policy admit of such being contracted. The principal object of Her Majesty's Government is, and must be, the maintenance of European peace. This object may, in certain circumstances be materially promoted by a cordial understanding, and by concerted action between Germany and England, and the line of policy thus indicated would undoubtedly recommend itself to the sympathies as well as to the judgment of the English people. It is one, however, which, desirable as it may be in principle, cannot be definitively adopted without a clearer knowledge than we now possess of the motives which have led to Prince Bismark's [*sic*] recent overtures, and of the expectations which he, and the Government which he represents may have formed of the results of the understanding proposed by him. You will make it your duty to ascertain the truth on these points, and you will lose no opportunity of inviting from Prince Bismark the fullest and most unreserved disclosure of his intentions and ideas.

100. Disraeli's 'most confidential' Cabinet 'Memorandum on his Eastern Policy', enclosed in Disraeli to the Queen, 16 May 1876. P.R.O., Cab. 41/7 no. 10; Monypenny and Buckle, vi. 24–6.

Mr. Disraeli fears that we are being drawn step by step, into participating in a scheme, which must end very soon in the disintegration of Turkey.

Though we may not be able to resist the decision of the three

Military Empires, he does not think that we ought to sanction, or approve, their proposals.

It is almost a mockery for them to talk of a desire, that the Powers should 'act in concert' and then exclude France, Italy, and England from their deliberations, and ask us by telegraph to say yes or no to propositions, which we have never heard discussed.

Moreover it is asking us to sanction them in putting a knife to the throat of Turkey, whether we like it or not.

Although the three Northern Powers have acted in a somewhat similar way twice during the last eight months, we had upon those two occasions no great difficulty in joining them, as we were asked to do so by the Porte.

Can we expect Turkey to make us the same request now? Mr. Disraeli thinks not, and that it would be impolitic for us to agree if she did, and for these five principal reasons:

(1) He believes it is impossible for the Sultan to reconstruct the houses and churches of the insurgents, or to find food for the refugees.

(2) The distribution of relief by means of such a Commission as that proposed, would be a huge system of indiscriminate almsgiving, totally beyond the power of the Porte to effect, and utterly demoralising to any country.

(3) The concentration of troops in certain places would be delivering up the whole country to anarchy, particularly when the insurgents are to retain their arms.

(4) The 'consular supervision' would reduce the authority of the Sultan to a nullity; and, without a force to support it, supervision would be impossible.

(5) The hope of restoring tranquillity by these means being, in Mr. Disraeli's opinion, groundless, we should then be asked to 'join in taking more efficacious measures in the interests of peace,' which, it is supposed, means taking more efficacious measures to break up the Empire.

In Mr. Disraeli's opinion it would be far better for Turkey to give up Bosnia and Herzegovina altogether, as Austria gave up Italy, than to acquiesce in the new proposals, and it would also be better for us that she should do so, than adopt the alternative now offered.

He would say, if Turkey agrees, we are ready to recommend an armistice and a European Conference based upon the territorial *status quo.*

One word as to the first part of the project which was not even alluded to in the telegram from Berlin. He thinks that we ought to take care that neither we, nor any other Power, send ships of war to Constantinople on the pretence of protecting the Christians.

But above all it is taking a leap in the dark to act in this matter before we know what Turkey herself thinks of the new programme, and it would seem that we may fairly tell the three Northern Powers that a general concert cannot be attained by the course they are adopting.

101. Derby's dispatch to Count Shuvaloff (Russian Ambassador in London), 6 May 1877. Draft in P.R.O., F.O. 65/986; *Parliamentary Papers*, [C.1770], 1877, lxxxix. 135–6.

I have the honour to acknowledge the receipt of your Excellency's letter of the 6th instant, in which you inform me that you are about to proceed to Russia on a short leave of absence,

As your Excellency will then doubtless have an opportunity of personally conferring with your Government, I take this occasion of placing before them some considerations of importance to the future good understanding between Great Britain and Russia.

Her Majesty's Government do not propose again to enter on the question of the justice or necessity of the present war; they have already expressed their views with regard to it, and further discussion would be unavailing. They have accepted the obligations which a state of war imposed upon them, and have lost no time in issuing a Proclamation of Neutrality. They, from the first, warned the Porte that it must not look to them for assistance, and they are determined to carry impartially into effect the policy thus announced, so long as Turkish interests alone are involved.

At the same time, they think it right that there should be no misunderstanding as to their position and intentions. Should the war now in progress unfortunately spread, interests may be imperilled which they are equally bound and determined to defend, and it is desirable that they should make it clear, so far as at the outset of the war can be done, what the most prominent of those interests are.

Foremost among them is the necessity of keeping open, uninjured and uninterrupted, the communication between Europe and the East by the Suez Canal. An attempt to blockade or otherwise to interfere with the Canal or its approaches would be regarded by them as a menace to India, and as a grave injury to the commerce of the world. On both these grounds any such step—which they hope and fully believe there is no intention on the part of either belligerent to take—would be inconsistent with the maintenance by them of an attitude of passive neutrality.

The mercantile and financial interests of European nations are also so largely involved in Egypt that an attack on that country, or its occupation, even temporary, for purposes of war, could scarcely be regarded with unconcern by the neutral Powers, certainly not by England.

The vast importance of Constantinople, whether in a military, a political, or a commercial point of view, is too well understood to require explanation. It is, therefore, scarcely necessary to point out that Her Majesty's Government are not prepared to witness with indifference the passing into other hands than those of its present possessors, of a capital holding so peculiar and commanding a position.

The existing arrangements made under European sanction which regulate the navigation of the Bosphorus and Dardanelles appear to them wise and salutary, and there would be, in their judgment, serious objections to their alteration in any material particular.

Her Majesty's Government have thought it right thus frankly to indicate their views. The course of events might show that there were still other interests, as, for instance, on the Persian Gulf, which it would be their duty to protect; but they do not doubt that they will have sufficiently pointed out to your Excellency the limits within which they hope that the war may be confined, or at all events those within which they themselves would be prepared, so far as present circumstances allow of an opinion being formed, to maintain a policy of abstention and neutrality.

They feel confident that the Emperor of Russia will appreciate their desire to make their policy understood at the outset of the war, and thus to respond to the assurances given by His Imperial Majesty at Livadia, and published at your Excellency's request, when he pledged his word of honour that he had no intention of acquiring Constantinople, and that, if necessity should oblige him to occupy a portion of Bulgaria, it would only be provisionally, and until the peace and safety of the Christian population were secured.

Her Majesty's Government cannot better show their confidence in these declarations of His Imperial Majesty than by requesting your Excellency to be so good as to convey to the Emperor and the Russian Government the frank explanations of British policy which I have had the honour of thus offering to you.

102. Extract from Salisbury's private letter to Lord Lytton (Viceroy of India), 25 May 1877. Lytton MSS., India Office Library, MSS. Eur. E. 218/516/2 no. 19; Lady Gwendolen Cecil, *Life of Robert Marquis of Salisbury* (London, 1921–32), ii. 144–5.

* * * *

Your anticipations as to the results of the Russian war in Europe are I fear likely to prove correct. It is more probable to my mind, and always has been, that the Turks will become a vassal state to Russia than that they will be driven out of Europe. The causes which have brought us to this position will be a curious study to the historian. It is obvious it could have only been averted by a very decided policy in one direction or the other. If a State is so weak that it is likely to become the vassal of a neighbour the catastrophe can only be averted either by making it strong—or by destroying it. The former policy was barred by the state of feeling here—by the feebleness of Turkey—by the want of a military ally—by the certainty that the process could not be done once for all, but that Turkey would require to be kept upright by a constant and costly process of nursing. The other policy was practicable, though harsh—but it was not adopted.

The commonest error in politics is sticking to the carcasses of dead policies. When a mast falls overboard, you do not try to save a rope here and a spar there, in memory of their former utility: you cut away the hamper altogether. And it should be the same with a policy. But it is not so. We cling to the shred of an old policy after it has been torn to pieces: and to the shadow of the shred after the rag itself has been torn away.

And therefore it is that we are now in perplexity.

103. Extract from Salisbury's private letter to Lytton, 15 June 1877. Lytton MSS., India Office Library, MSS. Eur. E. 218/516/2 no. 22; Cecil, ii. 145–6.

*   *   *   *

As to our foreign policy—I hardly dare to open the subject with you. If I took your gloomy view, I should commence immediate enquiries as to the most painless form of suicide. But I think you listen too much to the soldiers. No lesson seems to be so deeply inculcated by the experience of life as that you never should trust in experts. If you believe the doctors nothing is wholesome: if you believe the theologians nothing is innocent: if you believe the soldiers nothing is safe. They all require to have their strong wine diluted by a very large admixture of insipid common sense. I do not mean to say that our foreign policy has been immaculate—far from it. It has lacked a bold initiative, and a settled plan. Too many different people have pulled successively at the strings. On your view that Turkey is sustainable, and that Russia is the real danger of the future, the old Crimean policy should have been clearly avowed and followed from the first. The view which after two years study of the subject commends itself as the true one to my mind, differs from this. The Russian power appears to me feeble: and I do not think any protection could have set the Turk upon his legs again. This may be wrong—but at least the resulting policy would have furnished a satisfactory solution of the question. I would have devoted my whole efforts to securing the water-way to India—by the acquisition of Egypt or of Crete: and would in no way have discouraged the obliteration of Turkey. But the worst of our policy has been that it has not been a consistent whole on either side. A bit of each train of thought has been embedded in it—surrounded by a thick mass of general inertia.

Nevertheless, things are not so bad as they seem to you in the savage solitudes of Simla. Russia will be enormously weakened in men and money for this war—even if she gains a few strategic positions: and the effect of modern changes is constantly to diminish the value of strategic positions—and to increase the value of pecuniary resources. There is nothing in the events of the present campaign to give an overweening idea of Russia's strength.

*   *   *   *

104. Salisbury's private letter to Disraeli, 21 March 1878. Disraeli MSS., Hughenden Manor, B/XX/Ce. no. 233; Cecil, ii. 213-14.

I see no difficulty about considering the Treaty on Saturday as you suggest. We ought to prepare ourselves, in case there is *no* Congress, to state which are the articles of the treaty to which we specially object.

Of course, we have a right to object to all, as all are contrary to existing Treaties. But it would be doubtful policy to do so, in view of English opinion. At all events I think we should put in the forefront of our objection:

1. Those articles which menace the balance of power in the Egean:
2. Those which threaten the Greek race in the Balkan Peninsula with extinction:

And that we should indicate the necessity of either cancelling, *or* meeting with compensatory provisions, the portions of the treaty which, by reducing Turkey to vassalage, threaten the free passage of the Straits, and also menace English interests in other places where the exercise of Turkish authority affects them.

I am, as you know, not a believer in the possibility of setting the Turkish Government on its legs again, as a genuine reliable Power: and unless you have a distinct belief the other way, I think you should be cautious about adopting any line of policy which may stake England's security in those seas on Turkish efficiency. I should be disposed to be satisfied with war or negotiations which ended in these results:

1. Driving back the Slav State to the Balkans—and substituting a Greek province; politically, but not adminstratively, under the Porte.
2. Effective securities for the free passage of the Straits at all times, as if they were open sea.
3. Two naval stations for England—say Lemnos and Cyprus, with an occupation, at least temporary, of some place like Scanderoon for the sake of moral effect.
4. Perhaps I would add reduction of indemnity to amount which there would be reasonable prospect of Turkey paying without pretext for fresh encroachments.

These are merely suggestions for your consideration—and require no answer.

105. Extract from Salisbury's circular dispatch, 1 April 1878. P.R.O., F.O. 244/314 (no. 190); *Parliamentary Papers*, [C. 1989], 1878, lxxxi. 765–72, and Temperley and Penson, pp. 373–80.

Objections may be urged individually against these various stipulations [of the Treaty of San Stefano]; and arguments, on the other hand, may possibly be advanced to show that they are not individually inconsistent with the attainment of the lasting peace and stability which it is the highest object of all present negotiations to establish in the provinces of European and Asiatic Turkey. But their separate and individual operation, whether defensible or not, is not that which should engage the most earnest attention of the Signatory Powers. Their combined effect, in addition to the results upon the Greek population and upon the balance of maritime power which have been already pointed out, is to depress, almost to the point of entire subjection, the political independence of the Government of Constantinople. The formal jurisdiction of that Government extends over geographical positions which must, under all circumstances, be of the deepest interest to Great Britain. It is in the power of the Ottoman Government to close or to open the Straits which form the natural highway of nations between the Aegean Sea and the Euxine. Its dominion is recognized at the head of the Persian Gulf, on the shores of the Levant, and in the immediate neighbourhood of the Suez Canal. It cannot be otherwise than a matter of extreme solicitude to this country that the Government to which this jurisdiction belongs should be so closely pressed by the political outposts of a greatly superior Power that its independent action, and even existence, is almost impossible. These results arise, not so much from the language of any single Article in the Treaty, as from the operation of the instrument as a whole. A discussion limited to Articles selected by one Power in the Congress would be an illusory remedy for the dangers to English interests and to the permanent peace of Europe, which would result from the state of things which the Treaty proposes to establish.

The object of Her Majesty's Government at the Constantinople Conference was to give effect to the policy of reforming Turkey under the Ottoman Government, removing well-grounded grievances, and thus preserving the Empire until the time when it might be able to dispense with protective guarantees. It was obvious that this could only be brought about by rendering the different populations so far contented with their position as to inspire them with a spirit of patriotism, and make them ready to defend the Ottoman Empire as loyal subjects of the Sultan.

This policy was frustrated by the unfortunate resistance of the Ottoman Government itself, and, under the altered circumstances of the present time, the same result cannot be attained to the same extent by the same means. Large changes may, and no doubt will, be requisite in the Treaties by which South-Eastern Europe has hitherto been ruled. But good government, assured peace, and freedom, for populations to whom those blessings have been strange, are still the objects which this country earnestly desires to secure.

In requiring a full consideration of the general interests which the new arrangements threaten to affect, Her Majesty's Government believe that they are taking the surest means of securing those objects. They would willingly have entered a Congress in which the stipulations in question could have been examined as a whole, in their relation to existing Treaties, to the acknowledged rights of Great Britain and of other Powers, and to the beneficent ends which the united action of Europe has always been directed to secure. But neither the interests which Her Majesty's Government are specially bound to guard, nor the well-being of the regions with which the Treaty deals, would be consulted by the assembling of a Congress whose deliberations were to be restricted by such reservations as those which have been laid down by Prince Gortchakow in his most recent communication.

*   *   *   *

106. Salisbury's private letter to Sir Henry Layard (Ambassador in Constantinople), 9 May 1878. Layard MSS., B.M., Add. MS. 39137; Temperley and Penson, pp. 384–5.

The great problem which the Turk will have to solve, as soon as he has got rid of the Russian army off his soil is—how to keep his Asiatic Empire together. Sooner or later the greater part of his European Empire *must* go. Bosnia and Bulgaria are as good as gone. We may with great efforts give him another lease of Thrace: and he may keep for a considerable time a hold on Macedonia and Albania and possible [*sic*] on Thessaly and Epirus. But he will not get soldiers from them: for the Mussulman population will tend more and more to recede: and it is from them alone that any effective army can be drawn. The European provinces may bring in money: and to some extent, and for some time they may have a strategic value. But if the Turk is to maintain himself at Constantinople it is mainly with Asiatic soldiers that he will do it. The question is how is he to maintain himself in Asia. With the Russians at Kars, the idea of coming change will be rife over all Asia Minor—over Mesopotamia and Syria. If he has his own strength alone to trust to, no one will believe in his power of resistance. He has been beaten too often. The Arabs, and the Asiatics generally will look to the Russian as the coming man. The Turks [*sic*] only chance is to obtain the alliance of a great Power: and the only Power available is England.

Is it possible for England to give that alliance? I cannot speak yet with confidence: but I think so. For England the question of Turkey in Asia is very different from that of Turkey in Europe. The only change possible for the Asiatic Christians would be to come directly under the Government of Russia. There is and can be no question of autonomy—of young and struggling nationalities, and the rest of it. Now the direct Government of Russia is pleasant for nobody: but to Christians of a different rite, it is the most oppressive Government conceivable. Even, therefore, for the sake of the Christians, my hand would not be restrained by any considerations of humanity from engaging to resist the further advance of the Russians. And the vast majority of the populations of Asiatic Turkey are Mohometans: to whom the Turkish Government is congenial and as good as any other Mahometans get except our own. And, while Russian influence over the provinces of European Turkey would be a comparatively distant and indirect evil, her influence over Syria and Mesopotamia would be a very serious embarrassment, and would certainly through the connection of Bagdad with Bombay, make our hold on India more difficult. I do not, therefore, despair of England coming to the conclusion that she can undertake such a defensive alliance. But for that purpose it is, as I said before, absolutely and indispensably necessary that she should be nearer at hand than Malta. I have had ample opportunity during the past year of observing how utterly impossible efficient and prompt military action is from a port that is four days [*sic*] sail from the scene of action. The first blows at least have always to be struck suddenly and secretly: and four days [*sic*] notice—if there is to be a landing at the end of it is almost fatal to military action

The messenger is waiting. I will not pursue this theme on which my mind dwells constantly. I will only say with respect to the suggested understanding between Greece and Turkey, that it would be far the wisest measure that Turkey could adopt: for it would raise an effective barrier to the Slav. But I fear it could only rest on some alienation of territory.

107. Salisbury's Memorandum for the Cabinet, Berlin, 26 June 1878. P.R.O., F.O. 78/2911.

The telegrams received last night make me fear that I did not fully explain the course which Lord Beaconsfield and I propose. I therefore submit the matter again to the consideration of the cabinet together with a draft of the terms in which the proposal would be made to Congress.[1]

The idea of any special agreement with Turkey on the subject may be put aside as it is no necessary part of the proposal and has been abandoned. Nor will any change in Treaty stipulations be necessary. The exact language of the Treaty of 1841 on the subject, which has been repeated in 1856 and 1871, is ambiguous, and does not necessarily imply a mutual engagement by the Powers. A declaration placed upon the Protocol will be sufficient to determine this ambiguity in the sense now suggested. The proposal is of considerable importance and is earnestly pressed on the consideration of the Cabinet for two reasons:

1. The threat of doing it may have a powerful effect in inducing Russia to come to terms about Batoum; and of course if the intention is stated publicly, that unless Russia yields upon Batoum this policy with respect to the Straits will be pursued, it will be impossible to take any other course if Russia should not yield.

2. But even if Russia should not yield, it will be the wisest course to pursue. It supplements the existing engagements exactly where they have been found wanting. It will prevent Russia from appropriating the discretionary power we reserve to the Sultan, by coercing the Sultan or the Sultan's Ministers. It will therefore make the control over the Straits a real control, to be exercised by the Turkish Government itself—and not by another Government standing behind it.

[1] This declaration is printed in Dwight E. Lee, *Great Britain and the Cyprus Convention Policy of 1878* (Cambridge, Mass., 1934), pp. 196–7.

The Sultan now, to defend himself, has to summon his allies formally, an act of defiance to Russia he may well be too panic-stricken to take. If the policy we propose be adopted, he will only have to utter the much easier and safer words: 'I am too weak to resist England.' We on the other hand, instead of being taunted in Parliament with having 'entered into forbidden waters, and having committed an act of war against Europe', shall simply be in the position of dispensing with the formal summons of a friend who is under duress. Moreover we shall make good the only weak place in our policy. As matters now stand we shall fully cover every ground of objection against the Treaty of San Stefano stated in the Circular of the 1st of April, with one exception. We can scarcely say that we have done much to counteract the disturbance in the balance of power in the Black Sea caused by the alienation of Varna, Bessarabia, and Batoum. We have it is true, recovered for Turkey the coast south of the Balkans including Burgas. If we reserve to ourselves the practical power of entering the Straits whenever the independence of Turkey is threatened, we shall have done enough—even if we are not able to recover Batoum.

108. Extract from Salisbury's private letter to Layard, 13 August 1878. Layard MSS., B.M., Add. MS. 39138; Lillian Penson, 'The Foreign Policy of Lord Salisbury, 1878–80. The Problem of the Ottoman Empire', in A Coville and H. W. V. Temperley, eds., *Studies in Anglo-French History* (Cambridge, 1935), pp. 128–9.

The Austrian Ch[argé] d'Affaires has been very pressing during the last few days, as you may have gathered from my telegrams. I have been in some doubt how to act. On the one hand I am deeply convinced of the unwisdom of the course the Porte is pursuing. Its policy is to make Austria its friend: and though I can quite understand the contention that Austria's friendship is not worth two provinces, at least when the two provinces are hopelessly gone it is worth while for the sake of the two provinces to accept the inevitable with grace and promptitude. The Porte, it is abundantly proved, is not strong enough to stand alone. It must be held up. We offer ourselves as supporters on the East, Austria on the West. If Austria can only be bound to prevent attack from Servia or Montenegro from attacking Turkey, the latter can defend itself against any other:

for Servia, held back herself will not allow Bulgaria to go in for loot alone: and Russia has no further bribes now to offer to Roumania. This convention of Guarantee, which we have earnestly urged both on Austria and Turkey, is, therefore, an integral link in the line of defence. That Greece must have a rectification I do not doubt. . . .

But all these considerations both with respect to Austria and Greece are subordinate in my mind to the dominant object of using British influence for British purposes, i.e. for purposes which under the [Cyprus] Convention have become British. We want besides our demands as to Cyprus —which by this time I trust are being satisfied —our reforms in Asia, and security for their being carried out. And assuming that the Sultan will listen the more to our demands if we do not come too often as solicitors for others, I have been chary of recommending to you any urgent action with respect to Greece, and till very lately of Austria. I only pressed strongly on account of Austria these last few days when it seemed likely that a serious renewal of disturbances in the whole peninsula might result from a continuance of the conflict.

*　*　*　*

109. Disraeli's secret letter to the Queen, 26 October 1878. P.R.O., Cab. 41/11 no. 18; Monypenny and Buckle, vi. 386–8.

Meeting of the Cabinet yesterday on the affairs of Affghanistan. Lord Beaconsfield after a few preliminary observations, the object of which was to prevent recurrence in the discussion to what was passed and inevitable, called upon Secretary [for India] Lord Cranbrook to lay before the Cabinet the present position of affairs, which he did, and concluded by recommending the Cabinet to adopt the proposals of Lord Lytton.

He was followed by the Lord Chancellor, who said that the projected proclamation, proposed by Lord Lytton, was a declaration of war; that Parliament must be called together, and the first question that would be asked would be, What was the *casus belli*? Lord Cairns saw none. The Lord Chancellor then analysed the papers before the Cabinet, and showed that the Emir had acted towards the Russians with the same reluctance to receive them as he had exhibited to the envoy of the Viceroy; that it was a fair inference from the papers, that the Emir, when he had got rid of the Russians, would have received the English; that inference would certainly be drawn by Parliament. He spoke with great power, earnestness, and acuteness, and was evidently highly displeased with the conduct of the Viceroy.

The Leader of the House of Commons followed the Lord Chancellor, and said he was about to ask the same question—What was the *casus belli*? As at present advised, he could find none, and was sure our party would not support us in the Commons. He spoke at length and very earnestly.

Mr. Secretary Cross entirely agreed with the Leader of the House of Commons. He saw no case.

The Marquis of Salisbury said that the Viceroy was 'forcing the hand of the Government,' and had been doing so from the very first; he thought only of India, and was dictating, by its means, the foreign policy of the Government in Europe and Turkey. He had twice disobeyed orders: first in acting on the Khyber Pass; 2nd, in sending the Mission contrary to the most express and repeated orders that he was not to do so, till we had received an expected despatch from Russia, and never without the precise instructions of the Ministry in England; that, even now, he was not prepared to act even if we permitted him to do so. He spoke with great bitterness of the conduct of the Viceroy, and said that, unless curbed, he would bring about some terrible disaster.

Lord Cranbrook spoke in answer to the preceding speakers, taking the strong Indian view of affairs, and said the *casus belli* was formed by an aggregate of hostile incidents on the part of the Emir.

In this critical state of affairs, there being now silence, Lord Beaconsfield gave his opinion. He said it would doubtless be dangerous to summon Parliament to sanction a war, if our *casus belli* was not unimpeachable; but he was of opinion that a demonstration of the power and determination of England was at this moment necessary; that instead of the proposed manifesto of the Viceroy, which the Lord Chancellor informed them was a declaration of war, he would propose that a strong column should pass the frontiers and occupy the Kurram Valley, all our preparations in other quarters simultaneously proceeding, and that the Viceroy should issue a note, declaring that this invasion was not intended as an hostile act, but as the taking of a 'material guarantee' that justice should be obtained for the English demand. The occupation of the Principalities by

Russia before the Crimean War was quoted as a precedent. It was shown such a step was in the nature of 'reprisals' which were sanctioned by public law, and not considered as active hostilities.

The Duke of Richmond strongly approved of these remarks. Lord Salisbury said such a course would content him, as demonstrating power, and not necessarily leading to any disaster. The Lord Chancellor and the House of Commons members, following him, murmured approbation, when suddenly Lord Cranbrook startled us all by saying, that he would not undertake the responsibility of such a course; that his own opinion was for war, immediate and complete; that he believed it inevitable sooner or later, and very soon; that the 'material guarantee' project was a half measure, and would be looked upon as an act of timidity etc. etc.; that he would prefer continuing our preparations and postponing the inevitable campaign, to any middle course, and the more so because he would frankly confess that he was not altogether satisfied with the military preparations of the Viceroy; that Lord Lytton was acting in opposition to the military members of his Council—first in not employing as they thought sufficient English troops, and secondly in refusing to retain the reliefs, which Lord Cranbrook on his own responsibility, and in opposition to the opinion of Lord Lytton, had ordered to remain.

After this extraordinary statement on the part of the Secretary of India, in addition to the fact that none of the forces had as yet arrived at their stations, and that all was matter of calculation and estimate, there seemed only one course to take. The military preparations were ordered to be continued and completed, and even on a greater scale, while, in order to strengthen our case for Parliament, it was agreed that another message to the Ameer, to be submitted, before transmission, to the Cabinet, should be prepared and sent.

This is not a complete, and perhaps a feeble, but a faithful, sketch of one of the most remarkable meetings of a Cabinet that Lord Beaconsfield well remembers. It is certainly unfortunate that the Affghan business should have been precipitated, which was quite unnecessary, for we have much on our hands at this moment, and the utmost energy and resources of the country may have to be appealed to by your Majesty's Government; but Lord Beaconsfield himself, tho' anxious, looks forward to the future without dismay, and Lord Salisbury is prepared to support Lord Beaconsfield in some steps, which, if necessary, will be of a very decided character.

110. Extract from Gladstone's First Midlothian Campaign Speech, 25 November 1879. *Political Speeches in Scotland, November and December 1879* (Edinburgh, 1879), pp. 22–3.

... Why did we quarrel with the present Government about Turkey? ... The point upon which we quarrelled was this: Whether coercion was under any circumstances to be applied to Turkey to bring about the better government of that country. ... The foundation of the policy of the present Government was that coercion was not to be applied to Turkey. ... coercion in the extreme case that had arisen was recommended by the Liberal party. Coercion was objected to on the highest grounds by the Tory party; ... But there is an important limitation. We had never given countenance to single-handed attempts to coerce Turkey. We felt that single-handed attempts to coerce Turkey would probably lead to immediate bloodshed and calamity, with great uncertainty as to the issue. The coercion we recommended was coercion by the united authority of Europe, and we always contended that in the case where the united authority of Europe was brought into action there was no fear of having to proceed to actual coercion. The Turk knew very well how to measure strength on one side and the other, and he would have yielded to that authority. ...

111. Extract from Gladstone's Third Midlothian Campaign Speech, 27 November 1879. *Political Speeches in Scotland*, pp. 54–6.

... I first give you, gentlemen, what I think the right principles of foreign policy. The first thing is to foster the strength of the Empire by just legislation and economy at home, thereby producing two of the great elements of national power—namely, wealth, which is a physical element, and union and contentment, which are moral elements—and to reserve the strength of the Empire, to reserve the expenditure of that strength for great and worthy occasions abroad. Here is my first principle of foreign policy: good government at home. My second principle of foreign policy is this—that its aim ought to be to preserve to the nations of the world—and especially were it but for shame, when we recollect the sacred name we bear as Christians, especially to the Christian nations of the world—the blessings of peace. That is my second principle. My third principle is this—Even, gentlemen, when you do a good thing, you may do it in so bad a way that you may entirely spoil the beneficial effect; and if we were to make ourselves the apostles of peace in the sense of conveying to the minds of other nations that we thought ourselves more entitled to an opinion on that subject than they are, or to deny their rights—well, very likely we should destroy the whole value of our doctrines. In my opinion the third sound principle is this—to strive to cultivate and maintain, ay, to the very uttermost, what is called the concert of Europe; to keep the Powers of Europe in union together. And why? Because by keeping all in union together you neutralize and fetter and bind up the selfish aims of each. I am not here to flatter either England or any of them. They have selfish aims, as, unfortunately, we in late years have too sadly shown that we too have had selfish aims; but their common action is fatal to selfish aims. Common action means common objects; and the only objects for which you can unite together the Powers of Europe are objects connected with the common good of them all. That, gentlemen, is my third principle of foreign policy. My fourth principle is that you should avoid needless and entangling engagements. You may boast about them, you may brag about them. You may say you are procuring consideration for the country. You may say that an Englishman can now hold up his head among the nations. You may say that he is now not in the hands of a Liberal Ministry, who thought of nothing but pounds, shillings, and pence. But what does all this come to, gentlemen? It comes to this, that you are increasing your engagements without increasing your strength; and if you increase engagements without increasing strength, you diminish strength, you abolish strength; you really reduce the Empire and do not increase it. You render it less capable of performing its duties; you render it an inheritance, less precious to hand on to future generations. My fifth principle is this, gentlemen, to acknowledge the equal rights of all nations. You may sympathize with one nation more than another. Nay, you must sympathize in certain circumstances with one nation more than another. You sympathize most with those nations, as a rule, with which you have the closest connection in language, in blood, and in religion, or whose circumstances at the time seem to give the strongest claim to sympathy. But in point of right all are equal, and you have no right to set up a system under which one of them is to be placed under moral suspicion or espionage, or to be made the constant subject of invective.

If you do that, but especially if you claim for yourself a superiority, a pharisaical superiority over the whole of them, then I say you may talk about your patriotism if you please, but you are a misjudging friend of your country, and in undermining the basis of the esteem and respect of other people for your country you are in reality inflicting the severest injury upon it. I have now given you, gentlemen, five principles of foreign policy. Let me give you a sixth, and then I have done. And that sixth is, that in my opinion foreign policy, subject to all the limitations that I have described, the foreign policy of England should always be inspired by the love of freedom. There should be a sympathy with freedom, a desire to give it scope, founded not upon visionary ideas, but upon the long experience of many generations within the shores of this happy isle, that in freedom you lay the firmest foundations both of loyalty and order; the firmest foundations for the development of individual character, and the best provision for the happiness of the nation at large. In the foreign policy of this country the name of Canning ever will be honoured. The name of Russell ever will be honoured. The name of Palmerston ever will be honoured by those who recollect the erection of the Kingdom of Belgium, and the union of the disjoined provinces of Italy. It is that sympathy, not a sympathy with disorder, but, on the contrary, founded upon the deepest and most profound love of order—it is that sympathy which, in my opinion, ought to be the very atmosphere, in which a Foreign Secretary of England ought to live and to move.

*   *   *   *

112. Gladstone's private letter to Granville, 21 June 1882. Granville MSS., P.R.O. 30/29/125; Agatha Ramm, ed., *The Political Correspondence of Mr. Gladstone and Lord Granville 1876–1886* (Oxford, 1962), i. 380.

1. The more I reflect the more I feel unprepared to take any *measure* with regard to the Suez Canal single handed, or in union with France, apart from any reference to the authority of Europe.

2. I do not include in the class of *measures* such a step of protection as we have already taken in sending one vessel I believe to Port Said, nor the further sending of an iron-clad which you spoke of yesterday; holding over for the moment any question as to an *army* force on board.

3. But without reference to my wider proposition it occurs to me that, while the Suez Canal question is not before the Conference [of Ambassadors at Constantinople] for discussion, yet *as a part of the Egyptian territory* it cannot be wholly excluded from notice. Whether the Conference accept Arabi or not, whether the Sultan send troops or not, certain matters surely must be included & provided for (according to our definition) in any arrangement which the Conference can accept. First of all among them must be security for the peace of the territory, and in the territory the Suez Canal is included. Part therefore of the field under their view embraces it *quoad* peace and order, & cannot so far as I see be withdrawn from it.

This if sound is important.

4. Should not Dufferin [British Ambassador in Constantinople] make *known* to his Colleagues (not as inviting any action from them) our intention to have reparation, & *may* it not be politic to put this question in the van, by formulating if we can what it may be right to ask in respect of the persons in the Queen's service who were killed or injured.

5. Ought not the reparation to *include* all charges of transport for those who have been driven from their homes by the inability of Arabi & Co to keep order.

I am sorry to trouble you with so long a note.

113. Extract from the 'Paper shown to C[oun]t Herbert Bismarck at Koenigstein' by Currie, 3 August 1885. Copy in Salisbury MSS., E (unlisted); Rose Louise Greaves, *Persia and the Defence of India 1884–1892* (London, 1959), pp. 239–41.

The Affghan boundary negot[iatio]ns have come to a deadlock on the question as to how much of Zulficar Pass is to be given to Afghanistan. The Russian Gov[ernment] undertook, before Lord Salisbury came into office, to exchange Zulficar for Penjdeh. The Ameer was formally promised that he would have the Zulficar Pass and agreed to a boundary traced on that basis.

. . . The Russians will only give the first portion of the pass . . . and object to ceding the remainder on the ground that it would interfere with the communications on their side of the frontier.

The position is critical and, if a settlement is not arrived at within the next few months, is very likely to lead to war. The Russian Commanders are enterprising and are eager for a dash at Herat. The Afghans are rash, and another Penjdeh affair may occur at any moment. Either of these contingencies would inevitably produce a rupture between England & Russia, which would lead to hostilities, not only in Central Asia, but in every part of the world where England could deal a blow at her antagonist. The point on which we should concentrate the greatest part of our energies would be the cutting of the communications between Russia and her Central Asian possessions. For this it would be an absolute necessity for us to obtain an entrance to the Black Sea for our ships, and this we should unquestionably do by some means or other, whatever view Europe might hold as to the localisation of the war.

In order to avert this calamity, the only plan seems to be to make an appeal to Prince Bismarck to mediate between the 2 Countries. The questions at issue being now reduced to the one point of Zulficar, all that would be required to bring about a settlement, would be that H[is] H[ighness] should adjudicate upon the interpretation of the words of M. de Giers's [the Russian Foreign Minister] Telegram of April 16 agreeing to cede Zulficar in exchange for Penjdeh. We could lay before him the evidence of our officers as to what is included in the Zulficar Pass. The Russians might do the same. Or if the Prince thought it necessary, he might send a German officer to the spot to decide the question. In making this appeal to the Prince, stress might be laid upon the unprecedented position which he occupies in Europe, which has made him practically the arbiter of the destinies of other nations. The constant & unswerving desire for the maintenance of Peace which he has shown, his moderation and justice towards other Countries, inspire confidence that his intervention (if he would give it) would be exercised with perfect fairness. The English people trust him and would be satisfied with his verdict. It is not likely that in Russia, where it is believed that (outside the ranks of the military party) a sincere desire exists for peace, his judgment would be questioned. The Prince would be adding lustre to his renown, and it would not be the least of his great achievements that his moderating & pacific influence should have secured peace between two of the great Powers of Europe, when all other hopes of agreement had failed.

If he were to effect this, he would secure for himself and his Country the lasting gratitude of England, and he would be laying the foundations of a closer and more intimate alliance between the two Countries.

The present Prime Minister of England is known to be favorable to such an alliance in the fullest sense of the terms, and once established, the English people, who have the strongest leaning towards their old Protestant ally, would not allow their Government (from whatever party it might be taken) to swerve from it. A close union between the greatest military power and the greatest naval power would produce a combination that would not only secure the peace of the world, but would also be in the highest degree advantageous to the interests of the two Countries. It would put Germany at ease as regards the safety of her Colonial possessions in the event of European complications, and it would leave England free to defend her interests in the event of unprovoked aggression on the part of Russia against her Indian Empire, without fear of hostile neutrality on the part of the European Powers.

114. Salisbury's private letter to Sir William White, 24 September 1885. White MSS., P.R.O., F.O. 364/8 Pt. 2; Colin L. Smith, *The Embassy of Sir William White at Constantinople 1886–1891* (Oxford, 1957), p. 162.

As far as your post is concerned, it seems as though all questions had settled themselves. If the Turks had had a spark of vitality left they would have marched in all the force at their command and stamped out this insurrection at once. I do not say they would have been successful. Very likely they would have roused the Russians and we should have had another war. But, still no state with any life left in it would have allowed a province to be snatched from under its eyes, and stretched out no hand to save it.

That Turkey has not done this, spontaneously, proves that Turkey is dead. But it was not a course for any of the powers to advise: for such advice would have amounted to a promise of some sort of help if the advice failed; and England, alone, has certainly no motive to undertake any such responsibility. Our language must be to condemn Alexander's enterprise, to adhere to the Treaty, and not to commit ourselves to the abandonment of any right or claim of the Sultan's. But at present it is an internal matter exclusively. The Sultan has a rebellious subject to settle with: and it is not for us to advise him how to do it. If others try to coerce him, it may then be our business to interfere. Or if Austria takes measures herself to prevent the conflagration spreading, we may take joint action with her. But until the question reaches one of those two phases we are not called upon for action: and our opinion must simply be a condemnation of those who have broken a great law of Europe.

I have not much hope myself that a big Bulgaria will be avoided. It is an evil, and a danger to Turkey. But there seems to me nowhere the will to stop it: and stopping it, would require measures of considerable stringency. The next best thing to hope for is a personal union of the two Bulgarias in Prince Alexander, each retaining otherwise its present institutions. The institutions of Bulgaria are detestable: it would be hard that E. Roumelia should be subjected to them. It is to be hoped that the conflagration will not spread. If it does, we are at the beginning of the end.

115. Extract from Salisbury's Cabinet report to the Queen, 10 February 1887. P.R.O., Cab. 41/20 no. 31; *The Letters of Queen Victoria*, 3rd series (London, 1930–2), i. 272–3.

Lord Salisbury ... encloses—in print—two documents which have been the result of the Cabinet Council held to-day. The first is the exchange of despatches which constitute the *entente* with the Italian Government. The English despatch, which, of course, is the only one binding on this country, is so drawn as to leave entirely unfettered the discretion of your Majesty's Government, as to whether, in any particular case, they will carry their support of Italy as far as 'material co-operation.' But, short of a pledge upon this subject, it undoubtedly carries very far the *relations plus intimes* which have been urged upon us. It is as close an alliance as the Parliamentary character of our institutions will permit. Your Majesty's advisers recommend it on the whole as necessary in order to avoid serious danger. If, in the present grouping of nations, which Prince Bismarck tells us is now taking place, England was left out in isolation, it might well happen that the adversaries, who are coming against each other on the Continent, might treat the English Empire as divisible booty, by which their differences might be adjusted; and, though England could defend herself, it would be at fearful risk, and cost. The interests of Italy are so closely parallel to our own that we can combine with her safely. The despatches are only drafts; and the English one will of course not be signed till it has your Majesty's approval.

The second paper is in a less forward stage. It consists of 'Suggestions' for the settlement of the Egyptian question; and is designed to furnish a basis of Sir H. Wolff's negotiations at Constantinople. It has become evident that a *permanent* occupation of Egypt will not only be against our pledges, and exceedingly costly; but it also means permanent disagreement with France and Turkey, which may at any moment take an acute form. On the other hand we are pledged not to leave Egypt to the danger either of internal anarchy, or of foreign invasion. The enclosed 'suggestions' are designed to reconcile these difficulties. England undertakes to leave Egypt in five years, if at the time there is no apprehension of internal or external disturbance; but she retains the power of entering again at any time if there shall be danger of invasion, or anarchy, or of Egypt not fulfilling her engagements.

It is very probable that France will not consent to these proposals, and that the negotiations may be protracted; but they will be acceptable to Turkey, which chiefly desires to see the flag of the infidel disappear; and they will exonerate your Majesty's Government from any charge of attempting to ignore their pledges.

*   *   *   *

116. Salisbury's private letter to White, 2 November 1887. Copy in Salisbury MSS., D/84 no. 29; Cecil, iv. 70–1.

The result of your meditations and consultations at Constantinople with your two colleagues has come to the birth. Germany, Austria and Italy have each communicated to us your eight bases with an earnest recommendation that we should accept them. They are all struck with the opportuneness of the moment for such an agreement, in view especially of the failings of their intended partners. Austria presses on us to take advantage of the Chancellor's ill-temper with Russia, which Kalnoky says is an *atout* [Trumpcard] in our game. Germany urges us not to let slip the happy moment when Italy promises active assistance and yet repudiates the idea of compensation. Italy is especially struck by the phenomenal courage and decision of Austria and I have no doubt some equally complimentary reason founded on England's present condition has been a powerful argument for mutual cooperation among the trio. We submit the matter to the Cabinet tomorrow and on so difficult a question I cannot forecast the result. My own impression is that we must join, but I say it with regret. I think the time inopportune and we are merely rescuing Bismarck's somewhat endangered chestnuts. If he can establish a South-Eastern raw, the Russian bear must perforce forget the Western raw on his huge carcase. If he can get up a nice little fight between Russia and the three Powers, he will have leisure to make France a harmless neighbour for some time to come. It goes against me to be one of the Powers in that unscrupulous game. But a thorough understanding with Austria and Italy is so important to us that I do not like the idea of breaking it up on account of risks which *may* turn out to be imaginary.

The Suez Canal Convention has had the effect for the moment of improving our relations with France. After the experience I got of the Chancellor's pretty ways during Wolff's negotiations, I do not wish to depend upon his good will, and therefore shall keep friends with France as far as we can do it without paying too dear for it. The threat of making us uneasy in Egypt through the action of France is the only weapon he has against us, and we are free of him in proportion as we can blunt it.

117. Salisbury's telegram to the Queen, 10 June 1890. P.R.O., Cab. 41/21 no. 44; *The Letters of Queen Victoria*, 3rd series, i. 613–14.

Lord Salisbury's humble duty. Your Majesty's telegram was duly read to the Cabinet. They are of opinion that in any agreement arrived at with Germany the rights of the people of Heligoland should be carefully reserved. That has been done: no actual subject of your Majesty living now will be subject to naval or military conscription. The existing customs tariff will be maintained for a period of years, and every person wishing to retain his British nationality will have the right to do so. The Cabinet thought it was impracticable to obtain the formal consent of the 2,000 people who live there: anything like a plebiscite would be very dangerous as admitting the right of the inhabitants of an imperial post to decide for themselves as to the political disposal of that post. It might be used by discontented persons in Gibraltar, Malta, Cyprus, and even India. But the information the Cabinet get is that the population, which is not British but Frisian, would readily come under the German Empire if protected from conscription. The Cabinet unanimously and earnestly recommend this arrangement to your Majesty under these conditions.

The equivalent for Heligoland will be the protectorate over the islands of Zanzibar and Pemba and 150 miles of coast near the Sultanate of Monastir Witu, and the islands of Manda and Patta, and the abandonment of all claim to the interior behind it by Germany. Under this arrangement the whole of the country outside the confines of Abyssinia and Gallaland will be under British influence up to Khan, so far as any European competition is concerned. On the other hand, we could not without this arrangement come to a favourable agreement as to the Stevenson road, and any indefinite postponement of a settlement in Africa would render it very difficult to maintain terms of amity with Germany, and would force us to change our systems of alliance in Europe. The alliance of France instead of the alliance of Germany must necessarily involve the early evacuation of Egypt under very unfavourable conditions.

On these grounds the Cabinet unanimously recommend the arrangement for your Majesty's sanction.

118. Salisbury's Memorandum for the Cabinet, 4 June 1892. P.R.O., Cab. 37/31 no. 10; C. J. Lowe, *The Reluctant Imperialists: British Foreign Policy 1878–1902* (London, 1967), ii. 85–8.

A Joint Report of the Director of Military Intelligence and the Director of Naval Intelligence [General E. F. Chapman and Captain C. A. G. Bridge, 18 March: also printed in Lowe, ii. 88–90] has just been placed in my hands by direction of the Lords of the Admiralty, who concur in it. It has reference to the possibility of a descent of Russia upon Constantinople, and upon the attitude which should be observed by this country in case of such an event.

I do not think it to be urgent, because, as far as it is possible to judge, a Russian descent is not imminent at present. They are not prepared for a general war, their fleet is not complete, their military armament is very imperfect, and their finance is in disorder.

I do not therefore advert to it as a matter requiring the immediate attention of Her Majesty's Government. But it is of the gravest possible moment, and the early attention of whoever is responsible for the conduct of public affairs cannot be withheld from it without public danger for very long.

For the upshot of this Report is, that the Foreign Office on the one side, and the defensive Departments on the other, have been proceeding on lines as far divergent as it is possible for lines of policy to diverge; and it is evident that if this difference is maintained until the moment for action arrives, nothing but the most serious disaster can be the result.

The protection of Constantinople from Russian conquest has been the turning point of the policy of this country for at least forty years, and to a certain extent for forty years before that. It has been constantly assumed, both in England and abroad, that this protection of Constantinople was the special interest of Great Britain. It is our principal, if not our only, interest in the Mediterranean Sea; for if Russia were mistress of Constantinople, and of the influence which Constantinople possesses in the Levant, the route to India through the Suez Canal would be so much exposed as not to be available except in times of the profoundest peace. I need not dwell upon the effect which the Russian possession of Constantinople would have upon the Oriental mind, and upon our position in India, which is so largely dependent on prestige. But the matter of present importance is its effect upon the Mediterranean; and I cannot see, if Constantinople were no longer defensible, that any other interest in the Mediterranean is left to defend. The value of Malta, our only possession inside that sea, would at all events be diminished to an indefinite degree.

It now appears from this Report that, in the opinion of General Chapman and Captain Bridge, it is not only not possible for us to protect Constantinople, but that any effort to do so is not permissible. Even supposing the fortifications in the Dardanelles could be silenced, even supposing the Sultan asked for our presence in the Bosphorus to defend him against a Russian attack, it would yet be, in the judgment of these two officers, a step of grave peril to employ any portion of the British Mediterranean fleet in protecting him. The peril would arise, not from any danger we might incur in meeting the Russian forces, not from the strength of any fortifications the fleet would have to pass, but from the fact that this is the extreme end of the Mediterranean and that so long as the French fleet exists at Toulon, the function of the English fleet must be to remain in such a position as to prevent the French fleet at Toulon from escaping into the Atlantic and the English Channel, where it would be a grave peril to this country. They conclude, therefore, that unless we had the concurrence of France, which is of course an absurd hypothesis, or unless we had first destroyed the French fleet at Toulon, which at all events must be a very distant contingency, it is not legitimate for us to employ our fleet at the eastern end of the Mediterranean. The presence of the French fleet therefore in the harbour of Toulon, without any declaration of hostile intention or any hostile act, has the power of entirely immobilizing, and therefore neutralizing, any force that we possess or could bring under existing circumstances into the Mediterranean.

Two very grave questions arise from this strategic declaration which it must be the task of Her Majesty's Government, before any long period has elapsed, definitively to answer.

In the first place, it is a question whether any advantage arises from keeping a fleet in the Mediterranean at all. The main object of our policy is declared to be entirely out of our reach, and it is laid down that even a movement to attain it would be full of danger. There is nothing else in the Mediterranean which is worth the maintenance of so large and costly a force. If its main duty is to protect the Atlantic and the Channel, it had better go there. If it is retained in Portsmouth Harbour it will, at least, be comparatively safe from any possible attack on the part of the fleet at Toulon, and a very considerable relief will be given to the Budget of the Chancellor of the Exchequer.

Secondly, the other consideration is that our foregn policy requires to be speedily and avowedly revised. At present, it is supposed that the fall of Constantinople will be a great defeat for England. That defeat appears to be not a matter of speculation, but of absolute certainty, according to the opinion of these two distinguished officers, because we may not stir a finger to prevent it. It would surely be wise, in the interest of our own reputation, to let it be known as quickly as possible that we do not pretend to defend Constantinople, and that the protection of it from Russian attack is not, in our eyes, worthy of the sacrifices or the risks which such an effort would involve. At present, if the two officers in question are correct in their views, our policy is a policy of false pretences. If persisted in, it will involve discomfiture to all who trust in us, and infinite discredit to ourselves.

I would merely say, in conclusion, that this momentous question is not one which either the Admiralty or the War Office can decide on their own responsibility. The Cabinet which undertakes to decide it (and the decision cannot be long delayed) must have at its command the opinion of all that England or India can furnish of naval or military strategic knowledge. We have been going on for long, evidently enormously overrating the utility of our fleet for any purpose except that of bare coast-defence at home. It is very important that the real facts, however disagreeable they may be, should be ascertained and presented in the clearest light to those who are responsible for the policy of the Empire.

119. Extract from Salisbury's 'Message to Lord Rosebery on leaving the F.O.,' 18 August 1892. Copy in Salisbury MSS., D/18 no. 36; Cecil, iv. 404–5.

* * * *

The key of the present situation in Europe is our position towards Italy, and through Italy to the Triple Alliance. Italy fears a war with France because her ports are exposed and her fleet is weak, and she is very anxious for our protection in such an event. We have always refused to give any assurance of material assistance. I have said that no English minister could do so, because the action of an English ministry must depend on the national feeling at the moment, and the national feeling would be decided by the nature of the *casus belli*. But while keeping clear of any assurance of material assistance, we have expressed the strongest concurrence in the Italian policy of maintaining the *status quo* in the Mediterranean, and in the seas belonging to it, and we have agreed to consult with them if any circumstances should arise by which the *status quo* should be threatened. I have always done my best to show friendliness to Italy, with a view to preventing her from thinking that she was deserted by us, or that there was no hope of assistance for her if she was wrongfully attacked.

In abstaining from any pledge of material assistance, I have gone as far in the direction of pure neutrality as I think I could safely go. If England were to become more cold to Italy than she has been, or were to give any indication of likelihood that she would give even a moral preference to France in the event of a conflict, I think very serious risks to European peace would be run, as well as to the interests of this country. Italy hard pressed by her financial necessities, might abandon the Triple Alliance and go over to France. In that case Austria and Germany would also feel themselves unequal to maintain a possible attack from Russia and from France. As Bismarck has repeatedly indicated, Germany would in that case offer herself to Russia, and it is well known that the alliance of Russia can be had at the price of acquiescing in her designs upon Constantinople. The grouping would then tend to take this form: Italy and France together, England say neutral, Germany Austria and Russia together, Russia receiving rights over Constantinople, Austria taking the rest of the Turkish Empire as far as Salonica. She probably would not care to have Albania, and might try to make separate peace terms with Italy at that price. I only speak of this grouping as a possible risk, and as indicating the nature of the danger that lies before us, and why I have thought and still think it expedient to be as friendly to Italy as we reasonably can, without of course pledging ourselves to any material succour. The position of Italy is the key of the present arrangement of Europe.

* * * *

120. Rosebery's Memorandum on the Eve of the Sino-Japanese War, 30 July 1894. Draft in Rosebery MSS., National Library of Scotland, Edinburgh, box 91.

My view of the Chinese-Japanese imbroglio is simple enough. What O'Conor [British Minister in Peking] wishes us to do is to make an armed demonstration in conjunction with Russia so as to prevent war between the two Powers. In the first place I would observe that we should not be joined apparently by any other Power and that while collective action is one thing joint action is a very different affair. Moreover I distrust all demonstrations unless you are prepared to go all lengths. It is of course necessary to have recourse to them sometimes, but there is always a fear of their either leading you further than you wish, or of their becoming ridiculous. If we thus interfere, we must be prepared to engage in naval action, and to justify that proceeding to Parliament. I think it very doubtful if we could so justify it. It seems to me that on the letter of the Agreement of 1885 the Japanese have not gone much beyond their right, certainly not so much as to give us a case for violent interference. Again I am quite sure that Japan is determined on war. If then we take action, it must be in reality against Japan. Would this be politic on our part? In my opinion it would not. We should weaken and alienate a Power of great magnitude in those seas, and which is a bulwark against Russia. It is quite true that China and Japan may weaken themselves by war, but that will not, I suspect, be a very violent process. The methods, at any rate, of China are too languid to admit of their being rapidly or seriously weakened. It seems to me then, dictating hastily as I am on the receipt of your [Kimberley's] box, that as I think we can prove that we have used our best exertions to maintain peace, we should not do more than we have done. The eventuality of a joint occupation of Corea with Russia is in itself enough to deter one from action. It would as a matter of certainty only redound to the advantage of Russia, while it might engage us in great complications.

121. Extract from Sir Edward Grey's Speech in the House of Commons, 28 March 1895. *Hansard*, 4th series, xxxii. 405–6.

... Towards Egypt this country stands in a special position of trust, as regards the maintenance of the interests of Egypt, and the claims of Egypt have not only been admitted by us, but they have been admitted and emphasized lately by the Government of France. I stated the other day that, in consequence of these claims of ours, and in consequence of the claims of Egypt in the Nile Valley, the British and Egyptian spheres of influence covered the whole of the Nile waterway. That is a statement following logically upon what has happened in past years, and of what has been in the knowledge of the world for the last two years. I am asked whether or not it is the case that a French expedition is coming from the West of Africa with the intention of entering the Nile Valley and occupying up to the Nile. I will ask the Committee to be careful in giving credence to the rumours of the movement of expeditions in Africa. Even places in Africa are apt to shift about, and it is sometimes found that some place supposed to occupy a particular position does not, in fact, occupy that position. Rumours have come with greater or less freedom with regard to the movements of expeditions in various parts of Africa, but at the Foreign Office we have no reason to suppose that any French Expedition has instructions to enter, or the intention of entering, the Nile Valley; and I will go further and say that, after all I have explained about the claims we consider we have under past Agreements, and the claims which we consider Egypt may have in the Nile Valley, and adding to that the fact that our claims and the view of the Government with regard to them are fully and clearly known to the French Government—I cannot think it is possible that these rumours deserve credence, because the advance of a French Expedition under secret instructions right from the other side of Africa, into a territory over which our claims have been known for so long, would be not merely an inconsistent and unexpected act, but it must be perfectly well known to the French Government that it would be an unfriendly act, and would be so viewed by England. . . .

122. Kimberley's Cabinet report to the Queen, 23 April 1895. Royal Archives, B 47/126; *The Letters of Queen Victoria*, 3rd series, ii. 496–7.

Lord Kimberley presents his humble duty to your Majesty, and has the honour to state that after the Cabinet today he saw M. de Staal [Russian Ambassador in London] and told him that it was impossible for your Majesty's Government to join in the proposed communication to Japan without knowing what ulterior measures would be taken in the event of the Japanese Government refusing to listen to the communication.

Lord Kimberley cannot conceal from himself that our separation from Russia in this matter must have a prejudicial effect on the understanding which had been established between the two countries. He greatly regrets this, but he is convinced that it would be a fatal mistake to deprive Japan of the fruit of her victories by compelling her to relinquish a portion of the advantages she has secured by her Treaty with China. More especially would it be contrary to sound policy to interfere with regard to the Liaotung peninsula.

This country has no special interest in that part of China, and although it would no doubt have been better if everything could have remained *in statu quo*, the events of the war have rendered this impossible.

What may [be] the ultimate result of the great changes which must follow in that part of the world cannot now be foreseen. The wisest policy will be to watch events, and it will be time enough to consider whether we should interfere, when we are convinced that British interests are really in danger.

The attitude of Germany is singular, and it is not clear why she is now so eager to join Russia in endeavouring to induce Japan to reduce her demands. It is the more surprising because it was Germany which prevented the joint representation by the Powers which your Majesty's Government proposed on the breaking out of the war. If that representation had been made, it would have probably been successful.

Lord Kimberley could not learn from M. de Staal whether measures are in contemplation by Russia to coerce Japan. With the help of the French and German squadrons the Russian fleet may be able to overcome Japanese resistance by sea, but it seems almost certain that the Japanese will refuse to yield, and Russia may yet pause before she commits herself to an armed conflict.

By land Russia is not strong in that part of the world.

123. Extract from a Colonial Office Memorandum, 'British African Dominion; Question of creating', 26 March 1896, initialled 'S' and thought to be by the Parliamentary Undersecretary, the Earl of Selborne. Salisbury MSS., A/92 no. 12; Ronald Robinson and John Gallagher, with Alice Denny, *Africa and the Victorians: the Official Mind of Imperialism* (London, 1961), pp. 434–7.

Are the British Possessions in South Africa more likely to become separated from the British Empire,

　　1. If they become confederated with the two Republics under the British flag as a British African Dominion, or
　　2. If they remain as now separate units under various forms of Government and continue to have as their neighbours two independent Republics?

In endeavouring to answer this question I take as my postulate the fact, as I believe it to be, that the key to the future of South Africa is in the Transvaal. It is the richest spot on earth. The only properly speaking populous spots in South Africa are already within it; and while the population of Cape Colony, of Natal, of Rhodesia etc. will increase but slowly and gradually, the population of the Transvaal has increased, and will continue to increase, by leaps and bounds, and in 50 years time will probably be reckoned in millions.

My postulate therefore is that the Transvaal is going to be by far the richest, by far the most populous part of South Africa, that it is going to be the natural capital State and centre of South African commercial, social and political life.

1. Now given that the Cape Colony, Natal, the Chartered Company's territories, and the various Imperial administrations, such as Basutoland, Zululand etc. have with the present Transvaal and Orange Free State Republics, been somehow welded into one British South African Dominion on the analogy of Canada, what will be the probable eventual result?

I admit to the full that such political combinations have by nature a centrifugal tendency—yet there are other forces which so far have in some very important instances counteracted that tendency—Canada and Australia are both examples . . .

Now I think that in the case of the supposed British South African Dominion there are three forces which would combine to counteract the centrifugal tendency.

A. External pressure

Germany is firmly planted on the West in Damaraland and Namaqualand, and France on the East in Madagascar.

As regards Germany it is notorious how much she covets Walfisch Bay which belongs to the Cape Colony. The next day after the United States of South Africa had declared their independence Germany would walk into Walfisch Bay.

Moreover Germany is anxious to connect her possessions on the West Coast of Africa with those on the East Coast by a strip running parallel to the Zambesi and then across to Lake Nyassa. This ambition she could probably realize, if she chose, against a United States of South Africa but not against the British Empire.

. . . Therefore the external pressure on a British South African Dominion would be very great. With Germany on the West and France on the North and East,—would not that Dominion feel the need of the protection of the Mother Country?

B. Internal rivalries

Dutch and English; English and Dutch. Most curiously though sprung from the same stock, the two races do not amalgamate. It shows what a lot of Celtic and Norman blood must be infused in us.

. . . The present Government of the Transvaal teaches the English what they would have to expect if the dominating influence in a

15—F.P.V.E.

United States of South Africa were Dutch. The Dutch on the other hand are strongly imbued with the idea that if the English element got the upper hand of them, and there was no moderating Imperial influence, they would receive but scanty consideration.

C.

[1.] There are material advantages and sentimental advantages in being part of the British Empire. There are corresponding material and sentimental disadvantages. I believe the former to outweigh the latter, and that the evidence of this fact (as I assume it to be) is in a continuous degree impressing itself on men's minds who find themselves within the Empire.

* * * *

2. But if the Cape Colony and Natal remain separate self-governing Colonies; if Rhodesia develops into a third self-governing Colony, and if the Transvaal and the Orange Free State remain independent Republics, What then? I think nothing can prevent the establishment of a United States of South Africa.

A. There being no centralised government of South Africa the external pressure will not be so clearly perceived; it will lose its cohesive effect in being diffused over a congeries of separate provincial Governments.

B. The racial rivalry will exist in a less generalised form. The preponderance of advantages over disadvantages in belonging to the British Empire will also exist, but again in a less concentrated form. But both these factors of attraction to the Empire will be outweighed and rendered nugatory by the immediate commercial interests of the British South African States. The Transvaal will be the market for South Africa: the market for the manufactures of Cape Colony and Natal: the market for the agricultural products of those Colonies and of Rhodesia. The commercial interest of the closest connexion with the Transvaal will outweigh all other considerations. These British Colonies will sue for closer commercial union. The Transvaal will reply that so long as these Colonies remain British they will not grant it; that they have no intention of becoming British, but that if these Colonies will unite with them in forming a United Republic of South Africa they will welcome them with open arms.

If the Transvaal were always going to remain a Dutch Republic, I admit that this danger would not be so imminent. Racial jealousies might temporarily postpone the effects of commercial interests. But . . . the Transvaal cannot permanently remain a Dutch Republic.

There has never been a census; but the best information obtainable gives a maximum of 25,000 male Boers and a minimum of 50,000 Uitlanders, of whom ¾ are British. Before Jameson's criminal blunder the Uitlanders were said to be pouring into the Transvaal at the rate of 500 males a week. Just think what would be the result of 10 or of 20 years of an immigration maintained at one-fifth or even one-tenth of this rate! Therefore according to all the experience of history, this country so powerful in its future wealth and population ... situated at the geographical centre of political South Africa would assuredly attract to itself all British Colonies in South Africa.

A great part in the working out of this problem will be played by the Delagoa Bay Railway. If we could secure the control over it we should effect two great results. We should, by holding the balance even between the South African railway systems give an immense assistance to the Cape Colony, to Natal, and to the Orange Free State to maintain their commercial and financial position against the Transvaal. We should also bring conviction at last to the Transvaal Government that their best interests lay in coming to a complete understanding with us. They would feel themselves irrevocably hemmed in. They would renounce their foreign intrigues as of no further practical utility, and they would come to terms with us. If on the other hand the control of the railway passed to the Transvaal, or to a Foreign Power working with the Transvaal against British interests, the results would be very serious. They could then secure a monopoly of all Transvaal trade for the Delagoa Bay Railway with the effect not only of supplanting British imports, by (say) German imports, and not only of inflicting grievous commercial injury on the trading classes of the Cape Colony and Natal, but they could also reduce the Governments of those two Colonies and that of the Orange Free State to the verge of financial bankruptcy, so dependent are they upon their railway revenue. It needs no words to prove what a powerful use could be made of this instrument in squeezing the British South African Colonies into joining in a United South African Republic.

I maintain, therefore, that it is a matter of vital importance to us to prevent the Delagoa Bay Railway passing into the control of any power whatever except the Portuguese or British Governments, nor would I like to see it under the control of the Cape Colony or Natal Governments. No one seems to believe that Portugal will be able to afford to retain the railway long after the Berne Award is given and doubtless the Portuguese Government would be afraid to sell direct to us. We ought, however, to have a private buyer ready, who will afterwards transfer [it] to us. I was greatly surprised the other day to hear a doubt expressed whether the House of Commons would be willing to find the money, say $2\frac{1}{2}$ millions, for the purchase. I feel simply positive myself that the majority of the House of Commons would hail the vote with acclamation. . . .

My opinion, therefore, is that

1. If we can succeed in uniting all South Africa into a Confederacy on the model of the Dominion of Canada and under the British Flag, the probability is that that confederacy will not become a United States of South Africa.
2. If South Africa remains as now a congeries of separate States, partly British Colonies and partly Republics, it will inevitably amalgamate itself into a United States of South Africa.
3. That we must secure the control of the Delagoa Bay Railway for the British Imperial Government if Portugal is not able to retain the control herself.

124. Extract from Salisbury's report on his Audience with the Tsar at Balmoral, 27 and 29 September 1896. Confidential print in P.R.O., Cab. 37/42 no. 35.

I saw the Emperor of Russia tonight between 7 and 8.30. He was, of course, purely Russian in his views, but, subject to that qualification, his language was conciliatory, straightforward, and honest. . . .

He was distinctly in favour of maintaining the present territorial *status quo* in Turkey. On this point he received my views approvingly, but did not pledge himself as to the immediate steps to be taken. He agreed that it was dangerous for any Power to attempt to coerce Turkey by occupying any portion of her territory, because to do so would be to awaken a jealousy among the Powers so keen that it might lead to war; but, on the other hand, he agreed that it was dangerous to leave matters as they are, for many causes, and chiefly financial pressure, might speedily bring the Ottoman Empire to anarchy, and then the isolated action of some Power or other— especially Austria—become probable, and would in all likelihood lead to European war. Therefore, something must be done. Our

procedure could not, for the reasons stated, be levelled against the
territory of the Empire; therefore, it must be directed against the
Sultan himself. . . . I thought the mere knowledge of his predecessor's fate would make the successor pay due regard to the advice of
the Powers, and that no other security was needed or be of much
use. . . .

Then he advanced his own view, on which he dwelt at considerable length, and was thoroughly in earnest. It was that the Straits
should be under Russian control. I suggested that he might without
difficulty procure that they should be opened to all nations; but
that arrangement he emphatically said that Russian opinion would
reject. The Straits were the door to the room in which he lived,
and he insisted he must have the key of that door. I said this view
implied that the Sultan had disappeared, for while he was there, it
was only he that could have the control of the Straits. To some
extent, he replied that was true; he said he was in favour of the
status quo. But, he added, he could conceive the Sultan remaining,
even though Russia had command of the Straits. Russia did not
want Constantinople, or any of the Turkish territory on either side.
She only wanted the door, and the power of fortifying it.

*   *   *   *

I expressed the opinion, which he shared, that there seemed no
cause of opposition between Russia and England except this question of the Straits. I thought that the interest of England in the
matter was not so large as that of others, and was purely maritime. I
admitted that the theory that Turkish rule at Constantinople was a
bulwark to our Indian Empire could not be maintained. But I did
not see how we could abandon the allies by whom we had stood so
long. The task of Russian and Austrian statesmen should be to
see whether there was no contrivance by which not only compensation, but security, could be given to Austria in the case of any such
change taking place on the disappearance of the Turkish Empire. I
thought that if Austria, France, and Italy were (in that event) in
favour of Russia having control of the Straits, England would not
maintain her objection alone, but would seek for some arrangement
by which it could be met.

*   *   *   *

[29 Sept.] I saw the Emperor again this evening. . . . Referring to
what he said about Russian control of the Straits, I gave my opinion
that it was not impossible that the claim should be admitted if

made after the Turkish Empire had disappeared; because the other Powers would all have demands to satisfy, and it might be made part of a general arrangement. But I said that the idea, at which he had hinted, that this control of the Straits should be given to Russia while the Sultan was still at Constantinople, would be exceedingly unacceptable to the other Powers, and would be strongly resisted. It would not be a *situation nette.* The Sultan with his Treaty rights and his religious influence would still be there; but he would really only be a mask for Russia. He assented, and said he quite understood my objection, and would prefer the other arrangement himself. He had only proposed the course to which I objected because he wanted to emphasize what he had said before, that Russia wanted *no* addition to her territory, not the smallest; she had enough to occupy her whole energies for a century; but he wanted access to his dominions.

In discussing these future matters, I said that I was giving him my candid opinion on the questions he raised; but that I had colleagues, and Her Majesty's Government had allies, and past traditions, and therefore he must not take any expression of opinion as a pledge. To that he quite assented.

125. Extract from Salisbury's confidential circular dispatch on Turkish Reform, 20 October 1896. Draft in P.R.O., F.O. 83/1453; *Parliamentary Papers,* [C. 8304], 1897, ci. 279–83.

The recent lamentable occurrences in Asiatic Turkey, succeeded by the massacre of Armenians in the streets of Constantinople, give evidence of a state of maladministration and insecurity in the Ottoman Empire which cannot fail to be a subject of great solicitude to the Powers who have joined in guaranteeing that Empire.

The successive periods of urgent peril through which the Ottoman Government has passed in consequence of its inability to provide the elementary conditions of good government for its Christian subjects have powerfully affected the political history of Europe during the present century. The European Powers have, in the interests of general peace, earnestly desired to maintain the fabric of the Ottoman Empire, at least in that extensive portion of it in which the mixed character of the population makes an autonomous Christian Government impossible. But they have sought with equal earnestness, by the constant exercise of their influence, and from time to time by the conclusion of special stipulations, to secure due protection in these regions to the Christian subjects of the Porte.

* * * *

The massacre of Armenians which took place in the district of Sasun in the summer of 1894 brought the subject once more into notice, and showed the urgent necessity of steps being taken to secure the fulfilment of the promises which had been made seventeen years before. The result of a prolonged negotiation was the acceptance by the Sultan of a scheme intended to assure to the provinces where Armenians formed a considerable proportion of the population such institutions as would afford to them the elements of equitable government. Unfortunately, a few days before the consent of the Sultan had been obtained to this arrangement, a demonstration in the streets of Constantinople led to a disturbance in which, whether by the fault or the neglect of the authorities, numbers of Armenians, who cannot be held to have been guilty of any serious offence, were murdered or brutally ill-treated. This occurrence was followed shortly by sanguinary attacks on the Armenians in various parts of Asia Minor, resulting in the loss of many thousands of lives, enormous destruction of property, and widespread distress among the survivors. These attacks may possibly in some cases have originated in disturbances commenced by Armenian agitators, but it is impossible not to hold the Turkish authorities, civil and military, mainly responsible for them and for their effects. They have been succeeded by a massacre at Constantinople, in which it is estimated that between 5,000 and 6,000 lives of innocent persons have been sacrificed, which has every appearance of having been in some way organized by authority, and which certainly might, either wholly or in great part, have been prevented by timely action on the part of the Turkish military forces.

In the meanwhile, though the consent of the Sultan was given twelve months ago to the plan of reforms for the Armenian vilayets, no real progress has been made towards putting them in execution beyond the appointment of a few Christian officials.

It is impossible, on a review of these events, not to feel how great is the insecurity of the lives and property of the Christian subjects of the Porte, and how oppressive the misgovernment under which Christians and Moslems are suffering alike. The whole population of the Asiatic provinces is in a state of discontent and unrest, the soldiers and gendarmerie are suffering from want of pay, which is in many cases several months in arrear, the officials are powerless to exercise control. It seems that at any moment the fanatical feelings of certain sections of the Mussulman population may be excited into savage attacks on those who differ from them in creed, and that no reliance can be placed on the energy or good-will of those whose duty it is to provide for the preservation of the public peace.

The indiscriminate and wide-reaching slaughter of which the Turkish officials, and a portion of the Moslem population under their guidance or with their connivance, have been guilty, has had for its nominal aim the maintenance of the Sultan's Government. But it has had the effect of bringing the stability of that Government into greater peril than it has yet encountered. It has resulted either in exterminating or in driving away a large portion of the classes by whom the industry and trade of the country was carried on, and has reduced to the utmost extremity the material resources of the Government. Financial collapse threatens the military strength by which the Empire is supported, while the atrocious cruelty of many of those by whom the Government is administered has roused among Christian nations a sympathy and an indignation of unexampled intensity; and there is little probability that the Christian subjects of the Porte will submit again quietly to the oppression under which they have hitherto suffered. It necessarily follows that the causes which threaten the stability of the Empire are constantly gaining in force, while the forces which sustain it are melting away.

It is the common object of the European Powers that the Turkish Empire should be sustained, because no arrangement to replace it can be suggested which would not carry with it a serious risk of European conflict. The predominant importance of this consideration has led the European Powers to protect the Turkish Empire from dissolution, under the hope that the many evils by which the Ottoman rule was accompanied would be removed or mitigated by the reforming efforts of the Government. Not only has this hope been entirely disappointed, but it has become evident that unless these great evils can be abated, the forbearance of the Powers of Europe will be unable to protract the existence of a dominion which by its own vices is crumbling into ruin. It is difficult to say with confidence that any change that can be made will now prevent the threatened danger; but so long as the possibility of averting it exists, the Powers will feel it to be a matter of duty as well as matter of prudence, after satisfying themselves as to the changes which are the most urgent and best calculated to have a salutary operation, to provide effectively for those changes being carried through. Great authorities have up to this time been strenuously opposed to any measures by which Europe should become in any sense responsible for the internal administration of the Turkish Empire. The arguments against such a policy undoubtedly are very cogent, and nothing but the urgency and the imminence of the dangers which attach to a purely negative policy would justify us in disregarding them. All the Powers of Europe are at one in desiring to maintain the territorial *status quo* of the Turkish Empire, and those Powers whose territories lie nearest to that Empire are most strongly impressed with this necessity. Their convictions upon this point may be sufficient to guarantee the Empire from any possible shock arising from external aggression, but they will not save it from the effect of misgovernment and internal decay.

The consultation of the Six Ambassadors at Constantinople appears to have been accompanied with a favourable result in dealing with the disorders of the Island of Crete. Their guidance is probably superior to any other that we can command, and I think we shall do wisely to commit to them the larger problem presented to us by the general condition of the Turkish Empire, and especially those portions of the Empire which are inhabited in considerable proportion by a Christian population. I propose that the Six Powers should instruct their Representatives to consider and report to their Governments what changes in the Government and administration of the Turkish Empire are, in their judgment, likely to be most effective in maintaining the stability of the Empire, and preventing the recurrence of the frightful cruelties by which the last two years have been lamentably distinguished. But before those instructions are given, Her Majesty's Government are of opinion that provision ought to be made that any resolution to which the Powers may, in consequence, unanimously come should be carried into operation. It is an object of primary importance that the concert of Europe should be maintained; and as long as any of the Powers, or any one Power, is not satisfied with the expediency of the recommendations that are put forward, no action in respect to them can be taken. But if any recommendations made by the Ambassadors should approve themselves to all the Powers as measures suitable for adoption, it must not be admitted, at the point which we have at present reached, that the objections of the Turkish Government can be an obstacle to their being carried into effect. I trust that the Powers will, in the first instance, come to a definite understanding, that their unanimous decision in these matters is to be final, and will be executed up to the measure of such force as the Powers have at their command. A preliminary agreement to this effect will greatly facilitate the deliberations of the Ambassadors, and will prevent much of the evasion and delay by which ameliorations in Turkish administration have on former occasions been obstructed.

* * * *

126. Extract from the Director of Naval Intelligence's confidential 'Memorandum on Naval Policy viewed under the existing conditions', 28 October 1896. P.R.O., Adm. 116/866B; Arthur J. Marder, *The Anatomy of British Sea Power: A History of British Naval Policy in the Pre-Dreadnought Era, 1880–1905* (New York, 1940), pp. 578–80.

. . . the new naval and military policy—or rather the policy of England—must be reconsidered from the point of view that the 'Certain Changes' have established new conditions.

These new conditions are

(1) The Sultan of Turkey is antagonistic to England and friendly to Russia—therefore the assistance of the Turks cannot now be counted upon by us against Russia.

(2) The established friendship of France and Russia puts it beyond doubt that in war with either we should have to reckon with both. This last probability has been foreseen and, so far as the Admiralty can do so, provided for by the Navy—but 1 and 2 taken together aggravate the danger to be met. I mean by that that—so far as can be judged by an outsider—the Russian Fleet can issue from the Dardanelles at any moment. We counted on this before, but then it would have been in defiance of the Sultan—now it would be with his tacit if not his full consent.

The Black Sea Fleet in the Mediterranean, unable to go back and with no base, was a danger—but the Black Sea Fleet free of the Straits is a much more serious matter. And more than this—in the present condition and temper of the other Mediterranean Powers—the Russians can seize and hold the Gallipoli Peninsula before any one can prevent it. Their way is clear, the distance known, no doubt

their plans are made! To prevent them a force would have to anticipate their arrival at least man for man as strong, for they could
reach the Boulair lines before any new arrivals were able to organize
their defence. All this supposes the Turk to be a passive spectator
of this race for possession. Again, the seizure of the Gallipoli
Peninsula and the holding of the Boulair lines depended on the
Fleet passing up the Dardanelles to Gallipoli and defending the
flank of the occupying force. That is no longer possible—the Black
Sea Fleet and all the mining and torpedo-boat resources of the
Turks and Russians stand in the way—the Fleet (Russian) must be
destroyed, the resources swept away, and the Straits from the Black
Sea held before a force can maintain itself at Boulair against a
direct land attack from the Russians. In this way the conditions are
so altered that there is no practical way, as long as France supports
Russia by force of arms, of preventing the latter from using the
Straits unless opposed by the Turks. There is no material advantage
to England in the Straits being opened to all alike unless the fortifications are entirely removed. There is but small advantage to England, as regards making Russia assailable by her, even should this
be done, and it is most important that no concession should be wrung
from England on the plea that she would be the gainer by such a
decision on the part of the Great Powers. The Black Sea would still
remain a Russian lake and the Russian Fleet would retreat to it in
safety.

Looking farther ahead, Asia Minor will in time become Russian
or at least entirely subject to Russian influence. Europe cannot
prevent this. When this is done Marmorice will be the naval base of
Russia in the Mediterranean. The time therefore for jealously
guarding the inviolability of the Dardanelles is passing away, and is
not worth any important sacrifice now. The idea that any permanent effect can be produced to check Russia's advance by holding
Lemnos or any point so advanced in closed waters and so far from
our base is illusory. It would soon have to be abandoned after costing
enormously. We cannot afford to be off the entrance of the Dardanelles if France is a party to the war. If the foregoing be true, we
must now provide permanently for meeting the power of Russia in
the Eastern Mediterranean. At present this can be done by having a
Fleet for the purpose. Later, that Fleet must have a base in those
waters.

At present in a war with France alone the Fleet, as intended for the Mediterranean, would effectually crush the French Fleet or hold it completely in check. If Russia joined, and the Black Sea Fleet came down, the supremacy would have to be fought for everywhere. That is, the division of the English forces would make the issue uncertain and contestable and the war might be prolonged and hard fought.

It is clear that in the problem of making a successful stand against France of the Atlantic, France of the West Mediterranean, and Russia of the East Mediterranean, England will require 3 fleets and 3 bases—Gibraltar, Malta and Alexandria. This brings me to the new naval and military policy of England in the Mediterranean.

If the course of time is to see Russia in Asia Minor with a naval base in the Eastern basin of the Mediterranean, France still in alliance with her, or herself established in Syria, there would be only one way in which England could not only maintain herself in the Mediterranean at all, but continue to hold India, and that is by holding Egypt against all comers and making Alexandria a naval base.

If England leaves Egypt she will not get back even now, and much less then, and notwithstanding what is said in these papers, the Suez Canal cannot be blocked unless it is guarded as well, nor can it be commanded by ships at the Suez end, unless Suez is held, but all this can be done, and Europe defied if Egypt is strongly held and Alexandria, Malta and Gibraltar are naval bases. This is England's policy of the future, to work for this end should be her aim—do nothing that can jeopardise it, but quietly mould events to accomplish it. The advance of Russia to the sea and her establishment as a first-class naval Power both in the Mediterranean and Far East appears to be certain. That her Asiatic expansion must be antagonistic to England's continued connexion with India and retention of her quick communication with all her Eastern possessions through Egypt is also certain, and that she will use all her influence and strength to close this route to England and throw her into the alternative route round the Cape of Good Hope seems to me the logical sequence of what may be called natural causes. The advantages of holding the Suez Canal are bound up in the question of Egypt and need not be specially dwelt upon—but it may be said that if there was no Suez Canal, it would not be long before there was no India.

* * * *

To summarize—Retard the advance of Russia to the Mediterranean shores by all legitimate means—and do not imagine that any lasting check can be put upon her by action connected with the Dardanelles. Bear in mind that the last stand will have to be made in Egypt and work for that end. Count, that as long as France and Russia act together, England must prepare to meet the Black Sea Fleet in the Mediterranean. Decide, that when a Russian naval base is commenced in Asia Minor, an English naval base must be created in the eastern basin of the Mediterranean, preferably Alexandria. Try to secure that Italy shall guard her own waters in a war between France and England, which is her only chance of ridding herself of the menace of the French Fleet for a long time to come. Try to secure the good will of Spain and maintain the status quo on the Morocco coast. In a war with France, take Tangier and hold it for Spain to secure her benevolent neutrality.

127. Salisbury's 'very confidential' dispatch no. 6 to Sir Horace Rumbold (Ambassador in Vienna), 20 January 1897. P.R.O., F.O. 120/730; G. P. Gooch and H. W. V. Temperley, eds., *British Documents on the Origins of the War, 1898–1914* (London, 1926–38), ix. pt. 1, 775–6.

The Austrian Ambassador today renewed a proposal which he had made to me in the spring of last year, with respect to the protection of the Straits of the Bosphorus and Dardanelles from any possible enterprise on the part of Russia. He stated, as he had stated on former occasions, that in the view of the Austrian Government it was England that was more interested than any other Power in preventing the acquisition of dominion over the Straits by Russia: and that therefore it should be England that should take the lead in defending them against any attempt to establish that dominion. If England would undertake the maritime portion of the task, and would send up a fleet into the Bosphorus to resist any such attack on the side of Russia, the Austrian Government would not refuse on its part to undertake the military measures which would be necessary for preventing Russia, with the help of any of the Balkan States, from establishing itself in a position to command the Straits.

I replied that I did not think that my answer to him on the present occasion could differ substantially from that which I had given to him twelve months ago. I admitted the interest of England in the case, though I could not admit that England had an interest more vital than that of Austria and France. But I said it was quite impossible for England to make any such engagement as that which he desired. The institutions under which we lived entirely prevented Her Majesty's Government from making any engagement with respect to the military or naval action of England upon contingencies which had not yet arisen. When these contingencies arose, they would be fully considered by the Parliament and public opinion of this country, and no influence of any Government, and probably no promise into which any Government might have entered, would in such case avail to prevent this country from acting upon its own views of what was right and expedient in such a matter.

There were three considerations which altered the conditions of the problem, and which therefore made it more difficult to predict beforehand the course which England would think it right to take.

In the first place, as His Excellency might have observed, the sympathies of England in respect to the Ottoman dominion had undergone an entire transformation from the complexion which they presented forty years ago. The process had been to a certain extent gradual, that is to say it was the result of a series of agitations produced by the ruthless and unpopular conduct of the Ottoman Government in various parts of its dominions. But the change was now complete. The antipathy to assisting the Sultan would be extreme, and I could not answer for it that considerations of a higher policy would be sufficiently clear or sufficiently powerful to induce the English People to make great sacrifices of blood and treasure in support of a Government which they so thoroughly detested.

The second consideration was that on all former occasions when the policy of England was spoken of as binding her to maintain the Sultan's independence in the Straits, it was assumed and followed naturally from the facts of the time that such efforts would be made with the sanction and support of the Sultan, and not in spite of him. Such a view of the case could not be confidently held now. By the elaborate fortification of the Dardanelles, and the utter neglect of the Bosphorus, the Sultan had stated as clearly as if it had been written down in a proclamation, that he preferred the probability of being invaded by the Russians to the chance of being assisted by the Western Powers. I knew no declaration of English policy which had ever pointed in the direction of assisting the Sultan to an independence which he did not desire, against an invader whom he had himself welcomed.

The third consideration depended very much upon the second, namely that the forcing of the Dardanelles had become in later years a much more arduous task than it was twenty, or even ten years ago. I could not form a judgment myself on a matter which is not within my competence, but I had told His Excellency last year that the balance of opinion among our nautical experts was strongly unfavourable to any attempt to force the Dardanelles by the action of the Fleet, without accompanying it with military measures against the forts by land. If this was true it seemed to me to dispose of the idea that England could alone force her way through the Dardanelles. At the same time I was careful, while pointing out to His Excellency that this statement had been made to him before, to guard myself from any kind of intimation that England renounced the right of taking those measures, if when the contingency arose, it was thought desirable. I made no kind of pledge either one way or the other. I merely reserved our full liberty of action.

His Excellency replied that in that case Austria must reserve her full liberty of action also, and that she could not come under any engagement, expressed or implied, with respect to the Straits. It was the strong belief of her Government that whatever policy France might nominally pursue the necessity of her position would drive her into alliance with Russia, even in such a contingency, and he further stated that unless Austria was backed by the naval force of Great Britain, she could not count, in any action that she might be disposed to take upon Russia, upon the cooperation of Germany.

I stated to His Excellency the apprehensions which I constantly entertained, and which I had mentioned to other Ambassadors, that our hands might be forced by some movement at Constantinople which might threaten the lives of our own nationals. It was very difficult to foresee to what extent we should be placed under compulsion to disregard all other considerations in providing for their security. I hoped that sufficient pressure might be put upon the Sultan to ensure his taking the precautions that were necessary against such an emergency. I did not however dwell upon these considerations, because the point of view from which I spoke was almost exactly that of the Austrian Foreign Minister in speaking to your Excellency about a fortnight ago.

128. Extract from Salisbury's private letter to Currie, 19 October 1897. Copy in Salisbury MSS., A/138 no. 43; Lowe, ii. 107–8.

. . . I confess that since, some two years back, the Cabinet refused me leave to take the fleet up the Dardanelles, because it was impracticable, I have regarded the Eastern question as having little serious interest for England. We have no other way of coercing the Turk. 'Blockades' are of no use since it has been ascertained that (without a declaration of war) neutral nations need not accept them; and that America was this year very much disinclined to do so. I used to believe that the occupation of Jeddah might be a possible alternative; but the costliness of Indian troops and the extreme unhealthiness of the locality make that idea impractical.

. . . We have really no hold on—and therefore no interest in—any of the Sultan's territories except Egypt. On the other hand our interest in Egypt is growing stronger. After the Sultan's victories, it is clear that if Egypt is given back at all, it must be to the Sultan and the Khedive. No one else has any legal right; the idea that the Turkish Empire is on the verge of dissolution has been dissipated; and the Concert of Europe has conclusively shown that it can never be trusted with even the slenderest portion of Executive authority. It follows that either Egypt must be given back to the Moslems— which no one except the Moslems would approve; or we must use for the purpose of maintaining peace and order there, the authority with which we have been invested by the victory of Tel-el-Kebir. This is the only policy which it seems to me is left to us by the Cabinet's decision to which I have referred—to strengthen our position on the Nile (to its source) and to withdraw as much as possible from all responsibilities at Constantinople. Of course this last can only be done gradually by reason of past engagements.

129. Decypher of Balfour's telegram to the Queen, 26 March 1898. P.R.O., Cab. 41/24 no. 34; *The Letters of Queen Victoria*, 3rd series, iii. 238.

Humble duty. Cabinet met yesterday and deliberated for more than three hours and a half until 7 p.m. The discussion was entirely confined to the policy to be pursued in the Far East; her Majesty's Ministers held the opinion, in which Mr. Balfour knows that Lord

Salisbury concurs, that it was not worth while to promote a war with Russia in order to keep her out of Port Arthur: her influence at Peking depends principally on her land position, and, though the possession of Port Arthur may augment it, the difference is not sufficient to justify hostilities. It was, however, thought desirable that Great Britain should maintain her position in the Gulf of Pechili, and in the neighbourhood of Peking, by closing with the Chinese offer of the reversion of Wei-hai-wei.

130. Extract from Chamberlain's Memorandum of his First Conversation with the German Ambassador, 29 March 1898. Joseph Chamberlain MSS., Birmingham University Library, JC 7/2/2A/3; J. L. Garvin, *Life of Joseph Chamberlain* (London, 1934), iii. 259-60.

Count Hatzfeldt, having expressed a desire to see me, we met at a private house and had a long conversation.

Count Hatzfeldt began by referring to questions between Germany and G[rea]t Britain and especially to the partition of the Neutral Zone [in West Africa] and the promotion of railways in Shantung in China . . .

This part of the conversation was in the nature of a skirmish and Count Hatzfeldt did not press the subject.

I said that, as far as I knew, there was no question between the two Governments which affected any important interest, and they were all absolutely trivial in comparison with the great issues involving our relations with other nations. It seemed to me that in these greater issues the interests of Germany were really identical with our own.

Count Hatzfeldt assented. He said that until a few years ago this was generally recognised, but the circumstances which had followed the Jameson Raid had aroused much feeling in England and the two countries had drifted apart. That, however, was past, and he did not see why a better understanding could not now be arrived at. There was a general impression on the Continent that the policy of the U[nited] K[ingdom] was to bring about a war between other Powers but to take no part in it herself. This produced irritation and distrust and, in the case of Germany, led her to doubt the possibility of any arrangement with us while it pushed her towards Russia.

I admitted that the policy of this country for many years had been a policy of isolation—or at least of non-entanglement in alliances. But, I said, in the same way the policy of the United States since the time of Washington has been a policy of non-interference in European questions and I asked if he believed that that would last. He said 'Certainly not. Before long it must be changed.' Then I said it is possible that the policy of the United Kingdom may be changed by circumstances which are too strong for us to resist.

He asked if I thought the Parl[iamen]t and people of this country would accept the idea of an alliance, even though it would be a guarantee of peace.

The conversation then became more definite and in the course of question and answer the following suggestion was evolved. That an alliance might be established by Treaty or Agreement between Germany and Great Britain for a term of years. But it should be of a defensive character based upon a mutual understanding as to policy in China and elsewhere.

It was agreed and clearly expressed throughout that each of us was speaking in his private and personal capacity and that the interview was entirely unofficial.

* * * *

131. Extract from Salisbury's secret dispatch no. 109a to Sir Frank Cavendish Lascelles (Ambassador in Berlin), 11 May 1898. P.R.O., F.O. 244/562; G. S. Papadopoulos, 'Lord Salisbury and the Projected Anglo-German Alliance of 1898', *Bulletin of the Institute of Historical Research*, xxvi (1953), 216–18.

* * * *

A peculiar interest attaches to this discussion [with the German Ambassador concerning railway concessions in China] in consequence of the general considerations on which Count Hatzfeldt took the opportunity of dwelling. He complained, in terms of great earnestness, of the large portions of the world which had come under our occupation and the little that was left for any other Power to obtain, and intimated that the friendship or alliance of his government could only be looked for if we would concede to the demands of Germany in the various parts of the world where our interests were at present apparently in collision. I understood from him that Delagoa Bay, the Portuguese possessions of Africa, the neutral zone in West Africa, and concessions which might be sought for in China, ought in his judgment not to be dealt with simply on their merits, but in view of the great political importance, as he thought it, to us, of securing the friendship of Germany. I of course declined to admit that there was any ground for the assertion that we had obtained an excessive share of the advantages which might be derived from the less civilized portions of the world, and I could not recognize that Germany had any claim that we should purchase her support by concessions to which, except for the consideration of that support, we should be averse. With respect to any general alliance with Germany, I observed that there might be much to be said for it so long as it dealt with general European interests, but I was bound to remind him that with respect to one subject, the maintenance of the Ottoman Empire, this country was not in a condition to enter upon any further engagements. He had himself seen sufficient to convince him that in respect to that question the public opinion of this country was very deeply divided. He replied that he did not think either Germany or Austria, with whose interests Germany in this matter was principally concerned, would desire any further engagement from us in regard to the Ottoman Empire than an undertaking to prevent its fragments, when it fell to pieces, falling into Russian hands. I did not contest the soundness of such a policy, but I observed that a negative condition so vague could hardly be the foundation of an agreement, and I never heard from him any suggestion of the disposal that was to be made of the fragments of the Ottoman Empire, in case it should fall to pieces. He would not enter into detail, but only remarked that an arrangement might easily be made upon that subject.

In the course of this conversation Count Hatzfeldt observed upon the attitude of Great Britain towards the United States in the present crisis [the Spanish-American War] and alluded to the suggestions which had been sustained by some authority that it was the intention of the United States, when they became masters of the Philippine Islands, to hand them over to Great Britain, or to some other Power. I said I had heard not one word that could justify me in believing that the United States had the slightest intention, if they succeeded in conquering the Philippine Islands, of offering them to Great Britain. I had heard rumours of a different kind, but I gave no credit to them, for I doubted whether the United States themselves had yet formulated their policy in regard to a contingency which had not arrived. I did not think however that the precedents of international usage or law would sanction the idea that they were at liberty to present any territory which they might conquer from Spain to any Power they might select. The right of possession consequent on conquest might perhaps not be open to question, but in any case it did not carry with it the right of transferring the conquered territory to another Power: and if such a proposal were made I imagined that the other Powers would have to consider how far their interests were affected by it.

132. Extract from Chamberlain's Speech in Birmingham, 13 May 1898. *The Times*, 14 May 1898.

*   *   *   *

Now the first point I want to impress on you is this. It is the crux of the situation. Since the Crimean War, nearly 50 years ago, the policy of this country has been a policy of strict isolation. We have had no allies. I am afraid we have had no friends. . . . As long as the other Great Powers of Europe were also working for their own hand, and were separately engaged, I think the policy we have pursued—consistently pursued—was undoubtedly the right policy for this country. It was better we should preserve our liberty of action than become mixed up with quarrels with which possibly we had no concern. But now in recent years a different complexion has been placed upon the matter. . . . All the powerful States of Europe have made alliances, and as long as we keep outside these alliances, as long as we are envied by all, and suspected by all, and as long as we have interests which at one time or another conflict with the interests of all, we are liable to be confronted at any moment with a combination of Great Powers. . . . We stand alone. . . . What is the first duty of a Government under these circumstances? . . . to draw all parts of the Empire closer together . . .

What is our next duty? It is to establish and to maintain bonds of permanent amity with our kinsmen across the Atlantic. They are a powerful and a generous nation. They speak our language, they are bred of our race. Their laws, their literature, their standpoint upon every question are the same as ours; their feeling, their interest in the cause of humanity and the peaceful development of the world are identical with ours. I do not know what the future has in store for us. I do not know what arrangements may be possible with us, but this I know and feel—that the closer, the more cordial, the fuller, and the more definite these arrangements are with the consent of both peoples, the better it will be for both and for the world. And I even go so far as to say that, terrible as war may be, even war itself would be cheaply purchased if in a great and noble cause the Stars and Stripes and the Union Jack should wave together over an Anglo-Saxon alliance. Now it is one of the most satisfactory results of Lord Salisbury's policy that at the present time these two great nations understand each other better than they have ever done since more than a century ago. . . .

I suppose that it is in regard to the East, and especially the Far East . . .

. . . As to the way in which Russia secured that occupation [of Port Arthur], as to the representations which were made and repudiated as soon as they were made, as to the promises which were given and broken a fortnight afterwards, I had better perhaps say nothing except that I have always thought it was a very wise proverb, 'Who sups with the devil must have a very long spoon'. . . .

. . . We might have declared war on Russia. . . . But . . . I hope I am sensible enough never to give my voice for war unless I can see . . . a fair probability that at the end of the war the object of the war will have been obtained. . . . It is impossible to overrate the gravity of the issue. . . . it is a question of the whole fate of the Chinese Empire. . . . One thing appears to me to be certain. If the policy of isolation, which has hitherto been the policy of this country, is to be maintained in the future, then the fate of the Chinese Empire may be, probably will be, hereafter decided without reference to our wishes and in defiance of our interests. If, on the other hand, we are determined to enforce the policy of the open door, to preserve an equal opportunity for trade with all our rivals, then we must not allow jingoes to drive us into a quarrel with all the world at the same time, and we must not reject the idea of an alliance with those Powers whose interests most nearly approximate to our own. . . .

133. Extract from the 'Memorandum respecting the Clayton-Bulwer Treaty', by the Director of Military Intelligence, Maj.-Gen. J. C. Ardagh, 9 December 1898. P.R.O., F.O. 55/392; Charles S. Campbell, Jr., *Anglo-American Understanding, 1898–1903* (Baltimore, 1957), pp. 353–6.

The acquisition by the United States, of Cuba, Porto Rico, Hawaii, and the Philippines—their intention to raise their regular army to the number of 100,000—and to make a very large addition to their navy—are alone sufficient to modify very materially the strategical position both naval and military, of Great Britain, in the Atlantic and Pacific, as well as in the Dominion of Canada, in the event of war with the United States.

The long land frontier of the Dominion will henceforth be exposed at the outbreak of such a war to an attack from regular forces drawn from a body four times as numerous as that hitherto maintained.

The Imperial fortresses and coaling stations of Halifax, Bermuda, St. Lucia, Jamaica, and Esquimalt; the Atlantic and Pacific ports of the Dominion; the West Indian Islands, the Australasian Colonies, Borneo, Singapore, Hong Kong, and Wei-Hai-Wei, will all be subjected to an increased risk proportioned to the development of the naval forces which may be employed to attack them:—and this latter risk will be affected in a high degree by the construction of a ship canal at Panama or Nicaragua, and by the nature of the control exercised over it.

The Clayton Bulwer Convention of the 19 April 1850, engages Great Britain and the United States not to occupy, fortify, colonize, or exercise dominion over Nicaragua, Costa Rica, the Mosquito Coast, or any part of Central America; to promote the construction of a canal, and the establishment of a free port at each end, and to protect the canal when completed; to invite other States to enter into similar stipulations; and to extend the same to all interoceanic communications whether by canal or railway across the isthmus.

From a commercial point of view, these conditions are excellent; but they have practically acted as an insuperable bar to the construction of a canal, for the following reasons:—

1st. It is extremely doubtful that a canal for purely commercial purposes would be a remunerative investment;

2nd. The American people are fully aware of the great strategical advantage which a ship canal under their exclusive control would confer upon their navy; and have recently had this brought home to them conspicuously by the necessity of their warships having to circumnavigate South America in order to pass from the Pacific to the Atlantic and *vice versá*; and they perceive what an intolerable restriction on their freedom of movement, might arise from the control of the canal being shared with this country, or with an international body, or with the Isthmian States.

3rd. Great Britain considers that the construction of a canal across the isthmus would impair her maritime supremacy, increase the responsibilities of her navy, and conduce to the development of rivals to her mercantile marine.

For many years there has been a growing desire in the United States for the abrogation of the Clayton Bulwer Convention, but it was felt that the terms were so reasonable and so unequivocal from an international point of view, that if such a claim were submitted to arbitration, the verdict would certainly be given for Great Britain. This conviction had probably no slight influence in the rejection of the Arbitration Convention, and it may, not unreasonably, be inferred that the Clayton Bulwer Convention was the rock upon which it foundered.

Both the President and the Senate have revived the canal scheme within the last few days, from the standpoint of United States control, and in view of the results of the war with Spain it is quite natural that Americans should regard the construction of this link between the Atlantic and the Pacific, as more important and more urgent than before. Commercial interests, which were formerly the chief factor in the discussion, have now been superseded by the obvious requirements of the new position acquired in the Pacific, and these may be expected to have a preponderating influence in favour of a guarantee by the United States Government, of the interest on the requisite capital, whether there be a prospect of the enterprise being a paying concern or not.

* * * *

In peace, a canal with moderate dues would attract a large custom, and confer a great and continuous benefit upon our merchant ships, and it would ordinarily be a material convenience to our ships of war.

But if we were engaged in hostilities with the United States, the advantage would certainly at the outset lie with them, so long as they held the canal.

This is a question for the Admiralty; but even a superficial consideration of it would seem to indicate that the mere existence of such a canal under American control would impose upon us the necessity of maintaining stronger squadrons than we have hitherto regarded as sufficient in these waters.

The practical question now before us is—the *quid pro quo* which would be adequate to induce us to consent to the abrogation of the

Clayton Bulwer Convention, or its modification in terms which would be acceptable to both parties.

The *sine quâ non* of the United States is—exclusive control, to the exclusion of joint or international control. Assuming this concession there still remain many clauses and conditions in the Convention, which are susceptible of retention.

Some of the joint declarations might become unipartite—some may admit of modification—and some may be inadmissible.

We on our part should expect a sound Arbitration Treaty, adhesion to the open-door policy, a benevolent settlement of outstanding questions in Canada and elsewhere, special consideration for the West India Islands, facilities on the Alaska coast, a re-adjustment of boundary in the San Juan Straits, and other matters of mutual interest—to receive a treatment calculated to cement the ties and promote the intercourse which should bind us together, and which it is now desirable more than ever to maintain on a secure basis.

Upon some such conditions, the commercial advantages which we shall enjoy during a peace of prolonged duration from the use of the canal, may more than counterbalance the distant risk to which exclusive American control will undoubtedly expose us in war with the United States.

* * * *

134. Extract from Chamberlain's confidential Cabinet Memorandum on 'The South African Situation', 6 September 1899. Confidential print in P.R.O., Cab. 37/50 no. 70; J. A. S. Grenville, *Lord Salisbury and Foreign Policy: the Close of the Nineteenth Century* (London, 1964), pp. 257–8.

Our relations with the Transvaal have now entered upon a critical stage. We have practically exhausted our efforts on the lines hitherto followed, and it is necessary that the Cabinet should come to a decision as to the policy to be henceforth pursued.

* * * *

What is now at stake is the position of Great Britain in South Africa—and with it the estimate formed of our power and influence in our Colonies and throughout the world.

... The contest for supremacy is between the Dutch and the English—the natives are interested spectators, with a preference for the English as their masters, but ready to take the side of the strongest.

The Dutch in South Africa desire, if it be possible to get rid altogether of the connection with Great Britain, which to them is not a motherland, and to substitute a United States of South Africa which, they hope, would be mainly under Dutch influence. This idea has always been present in their minds. . . . But it would probably have died out as a hopeless impossibility but for the evidence of successful resistance to British supremacy by the South African Republic. The existence of a pure Dutch Republic flouting, and flouting successfully, British control and interference, is answerable for all the racial animosities which have become so formidable a factor in the South African situation.

The suspense and tension of the last few years, and especially of the last few months, have immensely increased the bitterness of feeling which has always existed more or less since 1881. Every one, natives included, sees that issue has been joined, and that it depends upon the action of the British Government now whether the supremacy, which we have claimed so long and so seldom exerted, is to be finally established and recognized or for ever abandoned.

This is, I repeat, the real question at stake. It has been simmering for years, and has now been brought to boiling point by a fortuitous combination of circumstances.

* * * *

I think that the object of the Government should now be to formulate its demands in a form to which a categorical yes or no may fairly be demanded.

I think the time has fully come when the troops in South Africa should be largely reinforced . . .

135. Extract from Selborne's confidential Cabinet Memorandum, 'The Navy Estimates, 1901–1902. Memorandum on Ship-Building', 17 January 1901. Confidential print in P.R.O., Cab. 37/56 no. 8; George Monger, *The End of Isolation; British Foreign Policy 1900–1907* (London, 1963), p. 11.

* * * *

Hitherto, the policy of this country has been stated to be so to build battle-ships as to maintain an equality of numbers with the combined battle-ships of the two Powers possessing for the moment the largest fleets. It does not seem to me that this basis of calculation is one that will any longer serve, considering that within the last five years three new navies have sprung into existence—those of the United States, Germany, and Japan. It is certain that it would be a hopeless task to attempt to achieve an equality with the three largest navies; but I go further, and say that, if the United States continue their present naval policy and develop their navy as they are easily capable of developing it if they choose, it will be scarcely possible for us to raise our navy to a strength equal to that both of France and of the United States combined. I propose therefore to consider our position almost exclusively from its relative strength to that of France and Russia combined, and from that point of view it seems to me that what we should aim at is, not a numerical equality, but a strength drawn partly from numbers but largely also from superiority of ships armaments crews and training, such as will enable us to have a reasonable expectation of beating France and Russia, if ever unfortunately we should find ourselves engaged in a war with them.

*   *   *   *

136. Salisbury's confidential Cabinet Memorandum on 'Anglo-German Understanding', 29 May 1901. Confidential print in P.R.O., Cab. 37/57 no. 52; Gooch and Temperley, ii. 68–9.

This is a proposal for including England within the bounds of the Triple Alliance. I understand its practical effect to be:—

1. If England were attacked by two Powers—say France and Russia—Germany, Austria, and Italy would come to her assistance.
2. Conversely, if either Austria, Germany, or Italy were attacked by France and Russia, or, if Italy were attacked by France and Spain, England must come to the rescue.

Even assuming that the Powers concerned were all despotic, and could promise anything they pleased, with a full confidence that they would be able to perform the promise, I think it is open to much question whether the bargain would be for our advantage. The liability of having to defend the German and Austrian frontiers against Russia is heavier than that of having to defend the British Isles against France. Even, therefore, in its most naked aspect the bargain would be a bad one for this country. Count Hatzfeldt speaks of our 'isolation' as constituting a serious danger for us. Have we ever felt that danger practically? If we had succumbed in the revolutionary war, our fall would not have been due to our isolation. We had many allies, but they would not have saved us if the French Emperor had been able to command the Channel. Except during his reign we have never even been in danger; and, therefore, it is impossible for us to judge whether the 'isolation' under which we are supposed to suffer, does or does not contain in it any elements of peril. It would hardly be wise to incur novel and most onerous obligations, in order to guard against a danger in whose existence we have no historical reason for believing.

But though the proposed arrangement, even from this point of view, does not seem to me admissible, these are not by any means the weightiest objections that can be urged against it. The fatal circumstance is that neither we nor the Germans are competent to make the suggested promises. The British Government cannot undertake to declare war, for any purpose, unless it is a purpose of which the electors of this country would approve. If the Government promised to declare war for an object which did not commend itself to public opinion, the promise would be repudiated, and the Government would be turned out. I do not see how, in common honesty, we could invite nations to rely upon our aids in a struggle, which must be formidable and probably supreme, when we have no means whatever of knowing what may be the humour of our people in circumstances which cannot be foreseen. We might, to some extent, divest ourselves of the full responsibility of such a step, by laying our Agreement with the Triple Alliance before Parliament as soon as it is concluded. But there are very grave objections to such a course, and I do not understand it to be recommended by the German Ambassador.

The impropriety of attempting to determine by a secret contract the future conduct of a Representative Assembly upon an issue of peace or war would apply to German policy as much as to English, only that the German Parliament would probably pay more deference to the opinion of their Executive than would be done by the English Parliament. But a promise of defensive alliance with England would excite bitter murmurs in every rank of German society—

if we may trust the indications of German sentiment, which we have had an opportunity of witnessing during the last two years.

It would not be safe to stake any important national interest upon the fidelity with which, in case of national exigency, either country could be trusted to fulfil the obligations of the Alliance, if the Agreement had been concluded without the assent of its Parliament.

Several times during the last sixteen years Count Hatzfeldt has tried to elicit from me, in conversation, some opinion as to the probable conduct of England, if Germany or Italy were involved in war with France. I have always replied that no English Minister could venture on such a forecast. The course of the English Government in such a crisis must depend on the view taken by public opinion in this country, and public opinion would be largely, if not exclusively, governed by the nature of the *casus belli*.

137. Francis Bertie's 'private and secret' Memorandum, 27 October 1901. Confidential print in Royal Archives, W 42/42; Gooch and Temperley, ii. 73–6, date it 9 November and print a slightly different version which they say is in the Sanderson MSS. No copy of the Memorandum has been found in Sanderson's papers (P.R.O., F.O. 800/1 and 2).

The German Emperor and Government have for some time past urged His Majesty's Government to enter into a defensive alliance with Germany, and recently they have been more insistent in their advice that we should lose no more time in coming to terms with them, stating that otherwise we shall be too late as they have other offers.

The German Government lay stress on the danger to England of isolation and enlarge on the advantages to her to be secured by an alliance with Germany. They have constantly and for some years past made use of these threats and blandishments.

There may be some danger, but there are also advantages to us in isolation. It would, no doubt, be a great relief to be able to feel that we had secured a powerful and sure ally for the contingency of an attack on the British Empire by two Powers such as Russia and France combined, but in considering offers of alliance from Germany it is necessary to remember the history of Prussia as regards

alliances, and the conduct of the Bismarck Government in making
a Treaty with Russia concerning and behind the back of Austria,
the ally of Germany, and also to bear in mind the position of Germany in Europe as regards France and Russia, and her position in
other parts of the world as regards the British Empire.

Germany is in a dangerous situation in Europe. She is surrounded
by Governments who distrust her and peoples who dislike or at all
events do not like her. She is constantly in a state of Tariff war with
Russia. She has beaten and robbed Denmark, and for that purpose
she took as partner Austria and then turned round on her confederate and drove her out of Germany, eventually making her a rather
humble ally. She has beaten and taken money and territory from
France. She covets the seaboard of Holland and the Dutch know it,
and, as the Belgians are well aware, she has designs on the Belgian
Congo. The Pan-German agitation in the Austrian Empire and
commercial questions may before very long bring about complications between Germany and Austria, and the internal troubles of
the Austro-Hungarian Empire detract from its value to Germany
as an ally, while the state of Italy politically, militarily, and financially,
is not such as to inspire the German Government with much trust
in effective Italian support.

In these circumstances it is essential for the German Government
to endeavour to obtain the certainty of armed support from England
for the contingency of an attack on Germany by France and Russia
combined; for if England be not bound to Germany, and His
Majesty's Government come to a general understanding with France
and Russia, or either of them, the position of Germany in Europe
will become critical. These considerations have made it incumbent
on Germany to create and maintain distrust between the Powers
not in alliance with her, and particularly between England and
Russia and between England and France. She therefore does what
she can to keep open sores between France and England. She is
always ready with information for our consumption of Russian and
French intrigues, and probably she supplies the Russian and
French Governments with particulars of our sinister designs.

Numerous instances might be given of the tortuous policy of the
German Government, but for a good example of it we need go no
further back than last spring (March). They then informed the
Japanese Government that they disapproved the Russian proceedings in regard to Manchuria, and being, they said, aware of the vital

importance of the Manchurian question to Japan, they would observe a benevolent neutrality in the event of matters coming to a crisis, and this attitude would keep the French fleet in check while England would probably support Japan. On inquiry it turned out that 'benevolent' neutrality meant 'the strictest and most correct neutrality towards all parties.' The German Government could not answer for France, but they were strongly of opinion that France would follow the example of Germany. A month later (April) the German Emperor described His Majesty's Government as a set of 'unmitigated noodles' for having missed the opportunity afforded by the Manchurian question of asserting the position of England in the Far East, and—as he did not say—of falling into the arrangement designed for them by His Majesty, viz., that they should ease the situation for Germany in Europe by joining with Japan in a war against Russia in the Far East.

The Emperor further said that the Japanese were furious with England for not giving them active support; but of this we have not had any indication from Japan.

A formal understanding between England and Japan for the protection of their interests in the Far East by force of arms is of the utmost importance to both countries; but at the time when the German Government were urging His Majesty's Government to resist Russia, our military forces were fully occupied in South Africa, and the Japanese Government, though encouraged by Germany, did not show much inclination to rely on her advice and go to war without being assured of the neutrality of France as well as of that of Germany.

Whatever hope may be held out to England and Japan of support from Germany, no effective aid will be forthcoming from that quarter in opposition to Russia unless there be a general conflagration and Germany finds herself obliged from European considerations to take part in the war.

Her policy in the Far East—not a difficult one—is to foster ill-feeling between Russia on one side and England and Japan on the other, and to encourage both sides to persist in their respective claims, taking good care not to commit herself to either party.

Germany is for the open door in China in principle and relies on England, Japan, and the United States to keep it open; but she will never use force in support of such a policy when it may bring her into collision with Russia. Of this her interpretation of the Anglo-

German Agreement, which the German Government call the Yang-tze Agreement, is good proof.

Germany would naturally be glad to see an Agreement made between England and Japan to resist Russian and French designs in the Far East, and to maintain the *status quo* in China, as her commercial interests would be protected without the necessity for her to offend Russia or France by being a party to the understanding, the existence of which the German Government would take good care should be known to Russia and France.

Friendship with Turkey is important to Germany as a counterpoise to Russian pressure on the Austro-Hungarian Empire and the Balkan[s], and she derives commercial advantages from supporting the Sultan. In most questions in which His Majesty is concerned Germany sympathizes with him, supports him to a certain extent, and only mildly deprecates Turkish proceedings when they are too flagrant to be supported; she does nothing to put a stop to them.

When lately it seemed probable that France would proceed to extremities with Morocco, the German Government consulted to a certain extent with the other Powers interested in the independence and integrity of that Empire, and then drew back saying that she was not primarily interested, though in 1899 Count Hatzfeldt suggested to Lord Salisbury that it would be very desirable that there should be an exchange of views and ideas between the German and British Governments on the subject of Morocco.

If the recent proceedings of Germany with regard to Koweit, where she endeavoured to stir up not only Turkey, but Austria and Russia against us, and in regard to the Peking Conferences, where, whilst pretending to fall in with our views, she voted and even moved Resolutions against them, are to be looked upon as consistent with her assurances of friendship, what would her attitude towards this country be if she held England bound by a defensive alliance?

The interests of England and Germany are not everywhere identical. In some parts of the world they are irreconcilable. For instance, Germany, whose intention it is to become a great naval Power, requires coaling stations which she can fortify. Good ones on the highways of trade can only be got in the great seas by purchase from Spain; by force from Holland—for she would not sell;—by the spoliation of Portugal, which we should be bound to resist; from Siam, whose integrity within certain limits we have guaranteed; or from France, as the outcome of a successful war.

If Germany seek a station in the Mediterranean it must be obtained from Morocco, Spain, Greece, or Turkey, and to the detriment of our naval position.

I do not mention her ambitions in the American seas. They may safely be left to be dealt with by the United States.

In the Indian and Pacific Oceans our Colonies of Australasia have interests which they sometimes consider to be gravely affected by the proceedings of Germany and France. In view of the effective assistance given to us by the British Colonies in the South African war they will expect their desires to prevail in questions between His Majesty's Government and foreign Powers whenever colonial interests are concerned.

If we had a formal alliance with Germany we should either have to shape our conduct over a large extent of the globe in accordance with her views and subordinate our policy to hers, as is the case with Austria and Italy; or, if we acted independently, whenever we took measures necessary for the protection of our interests in some distant part of the world, we might be told by Germany that we were bringing about a situation which might lead to an attack on us by France and Russia, obliging Germany without sufficient cause to take up arms in our defence, or Germany might find some moment opportune for herself, but inconvenient for us, for bringing on a war on a question in which we might not have a great interest. Discussions on these questions would cause bickerings and differences, and might lead to estrangement and end in an open quarrel.

The best proof that isolation is not so dangerous as the German Government would have us believe is that during our two years of war, when we have had nearly a quarter of a million men locked up in South Africa, and we have had the opinion of the educated classes abroad, as expressed in the press, and the sentiment of the peoples of most countries against us, and when more than one Power would have been glad to put a humiliation on us, it has not been found possible to form a coalition to call upon us to desist from war or to accept arbitration.

If we had an alliance making it incumbent on each ally to come to the aid of his partner when attacked by two Powers, it might be difficult to decide whether, in some particular case, the *casus fœderis* had arisen, for the attacking parties are not necessarily the real aggressors. It would be much safer to have a declaration of policy, limited to Europe and the Mediterranean, defining the interests which we shall jointly defend, as we have with Italy and Austria, of which understanding I annex a summary. If once we bind ourselves by a formal defensive alliance, and practically join the Triplice, we shall never be on decent terms with France, our neighbour in Europe and in many parts of the world, or with Russia, whose frontiers and ours are conterminous, or nearly so, over a large portion of Asia.

In our present position we hold the balance of power between the Triple and Dual Alliances. There is but little chance of a combination between them against us. Our existence as a great and strong State is necessary to all in order to preserve the balance of power, and most of all to Germany, whose representations as to the disasters which await the British Empire if His Majesty's Government do not make an alliance with her have little or no real foundation.

Treaty or no Treaty, if ever there were danger of our destruction, or even defeat, by Russia and France, Germany would be bound, in order to avoid a like fate for herself, to come to our assistance. She might ask a high price for such aid, but could it be higher than what we should lose by the sacrifice of our liberty to pursue a British world policy, which would be the result of a formal defensive alliance with the German Empire?

138. Extract from Lansdowne's 'very secret' Memorandum, 11 November 1901. Gooch and Temperley, ii. 76–9. (Gooch and Temperley seem to have found this and other documents relating to the Anglo-German alliance negotiations of 1901 in an unnumbered Foreign Office file which cannot now be found.)

* * * *

I fully admit the force of the Prime Minister's observation [in his memorandum of 29 May], that this country has until now fared well in spite of its international isolation. I think, however, that we may push too far the argument that, because we have in the past survived in spite of our isolation, we need have no misgivings as to the effect of that isolation in the future.

* * * *

The Prime Minister contends that neither His Majesty's Government nor that of Germany are competent to enter into such an arrangement as that which was proposed.

I fully admit that it would be impossible for us to determine by

16—F.P.V.E.

a secret contract the future conduct of Parliament upon an issue of peace and war. It is, however, I think, quite clear that those who inspired these overtures contemplated an open alliance, which should be communicated to the Parliaments of both countries.

With regard to the effects which the Prime Minister anticipates for it upon German sentiment, and 'in every rank of German society,' would it not be true to say that the suspicion and dislike with which we are regarded in Germany are, to a great extent, the result of the 'aloofness' of our policy, and that an openly declared change in that policy would not be without effect upon German sentiment?

I make these observations in order to guard against possible misunderstandings. I am, however, bound to admit, and I did not conceal this from Count Hatzfeldt or Baron Eckardstein [chargé d'affaires in Hatzfeldt's absence], that I see great difficulties in the way of a full-blown defensive alliance with Germany such as that suggested by Count Hatzfeldt, difficulties which are, I should say at the present moment, virtually insuperable. I need only indicate some of them in the most general terms, *e.g.* :—

1. The impossibility of arriving at a definition of the *casus fœderis* which would not be either so rigid as to greatly hamper our freedom of action or so vague as to deprive the alliance of all practical value.
2. The certainty of alienating France and Russia.
3. Complications with the Colonies, which might not at all approve of the idea of hanging on to the skirts of the Triple Alliance.
4. The risk of entangling ourselves in a policy which might be hostile to America. With our knowledge of the German Emperor's views in regard to the United States, this is to my mind a formidable obstacle.
5. The difficulty of carrying Parliament with us at a moment when the Parliamentary situation is as little satisfactory as it is at present.

In these circumstances, and in the face of the decided views which the Prime Minister has expressed, I regard it as out of the question that we should entertain the German overture in the form in which it was presented by Count Hatzfeldt.

I would not, however, for these reasons refuse all further discussion of the question.

The objections to joining the Triple Alliance do not seem to me to apply to a much more limited understanding with Germany as to our policy in regard to certain matters of interest to both Powers.

* * * *

Some . . . exchange of declarations as to the objects which Great Britain and Germany have in common and the interests in regard to which they are prepared to afford one another support might be offered to the German Government, the form which such support should take being reserved for consideration when the necessity should arise.

The arrangement would, no doubt, fall far short of what was suggested to us, but as a tentative and provisional step it might not be without value, and the offer would, at any rate, place it out of the power of the German Government to say that we had treated them inconsiderately or brusquely rejected their overtures.

139. Balfour's private letter to Lansdowne, 12 December 1901. Dictated draft in Balfour MSS., B.M., Add. MS. 49727; George Monger, *The End of Isolation. British Foreign Policy 1900–1907* (London, 1963), p. 64.

In reference to our conversation of yesterday, the difficulties I see in the present position of the question of Foreign Alliances chiefly arise out of the perhaps rather hasty decision come to at the first of our Autumn Cabinets with regard to Japan. No papers were circulated to me on this subject before the Cabinet: nor was there any warning that it was likely to be discussed. I was a few minutes late, and found the brief debate already in full swing, and the Cabinet not very anxious to hear any views on the general aspects of a problem, which they were treating in the main as one confined to the Far East. I ought perhaps to have insisted on pressing my views, but was taken so much by surprise that I should probably have done them very little justice.

I do not think we ought ever to have offered to enter into an offensive and defensive alliance with Japan without considering how such a course affects our relations with Germany and the Triple Alliance. Hitherto we have always fought shy of any such engagements, and, whether we have been right or wrong, we could at least say that we were carrying out a traditional policy of isolation which had been proved successful in the past. We can say so no longer. The momentous step has been taken, and, if the Japanese accept our proposals, we may find ourselves fighting for our existence in every part of the globe against Russia and France, because France has joined forces with her ally over some obscure Russian-Japanese quarrel in Corea.

Two trains of thought are suggested by this new condition of affairs. The first relates to the comparative advantages which we should reap from a Japanese as compared with a German alliance: the other—and much less important one—relates to the diplomatic difficulty in which I fear you will find yourself placed with Germany, owing to your rejecting her advances at the very moment we are secretly making precisely similar advances to Japan.

As regards the first point: It is evident that *if* war should arise out of either a German or a Japanese alliance, the forces you have got to fight are exactly the same, namely, Russia and France; while our ally in the one case would be Japan, and in the other case the Triple Alliance. In other words, the Japanese Treaty, if it ends in war, brings us into collision with the same opponents as a German alliance, but with a much weaker partner.

It is unnecessary to emphasise the obvious fact that the theatre and character of the military operations would be precisely the same in both cases. The quarrel might relate to the Far East, but the theatre of war so far as we are concerned would be the Channel, the Mediterranean, the frontier of India, and our great lines of commercial communication. Are then the British interests to be protected by the Japanese alliance more important than those involved in a German alliance? I cannot think so. By the Japanese Treaty the only admitted causes of quarrel are confined to the Eastern seas. Our interests there (including our interest in preserving Japan) are of course important, but they are not vital; and while Japan will have a right, in certain contingencies, to call upon us to go to war with France and Russia in a matter which may though indifferent to us be a matter of life and death to her, we have, from the nature of the case, no corresponding privileges. I do not think this is the case with regard to a war in which the Triple Alliance were [*sic*] involved. It is a matter of supreme moment to us that Italy should not be crushed, that Austria should not be dismembered, and, as I think, that Germany should not be squeezed to death between the hammer of Russia and the anvil of France.

If, therefore, we had to fight for the Central European Powers, we should be fighting for our own interests, and for those of civilisation, to an extent which cannot be alleged with regard to Japan.

But take the other side of the compact. The weakest spot in the Empire is probably the Indian frontier. In a war with Russia our military resources would be strained to their utmost to protect it, and, while the progress of events strengthens the position of Russia for aggressive purposes in this part of the world, no corresponding gain is possible on the side of the defence. A quarrel with Russia anywhere, or about anything, means the invasion of India, and, if England were without allies, I doubt whether it would be possible for the French to resist joining in the fray. Our position would then be perilous.

The Japanese alliance, from its very terms, would in such a case be useless, and we should have no right to call upon anybody else. Not so if we joined the Triple Alliance. The very fact that they would be bound to join us would probably prevent France throwing in her lot with Russia. If not they would be efficient allies.

I conclude therefore that the dangers are less and the gains are greater from joining the Triple Alliance than would follow from pursuing a similar course with regard to Japan.

I turn to the smaller diplomatic difficulties which you will have to face when you discuss the Japanese Treaty with Germany.

Hitherto, we have, as I understand it, rejected Germany's advances mainly for two reasons, (i) that a policy of alliances was contrary to the traditions of this country, and (ii) that it was scarcely possible for a Ministry to engage that, in certain contingencies, the country should go to war, since war was impossible without the support of Parliament, and, when the critical moment came, that support might be withheld. Neither of these arguments can any longer be employed. We have offered, in favour of Japan, to abandon our traditional policy, and we have proved in our own persons that a Ministry can promise to go to war in remote contingencies and over quarrels at present unforeseen.

It appears to me therefore that the only arguments left us for rejecting Germany's advances are that the sentiments of the German and English peoples are at present so hostile as to make negotiations undesirable (an argument of transitory value); or else that we cannot trust the leaders of the Triple Alliance, an argument, which, even if it were true, is one which can hardly be used in public. As a matter of fact, I suppose none of us think that the Japanese are more to be relied upon than European Governments.

140. Extract from Lansdowne's dispatch no. 2 to Sir Arthur Hardinge (Minister in Teheran), 6 January 1902. P.R.O., F.O. 248/754; Gooch and Temperley, iv. 369–71.

* * * *

The policy of His Majesty's Government in regard to the various Persian questions which most interest this country has from time to time been clearly indicated on the occasions when those questions have come under discussion. . . .

The Persian Government must be well aware, from the experience of 100 years, that Great Britain has no designs upon the sovereignty of the Shah or the independence of his State. It has, on the contrary, been one of our principal objects to encourage and strengthen the States lying outside the frontier of our Indian Empire, with the hope that we should find in them an intervening zone sufficient to prevent direct contact between the dominions of Great Britain and those of other great military Powers. We could not, however, maintain this policy if in any particular instance we should find that one of these intervening States was being crushed out of national existence, and falling practically under the complete domination of another Power. It would be necessary in that case, before the intervening State had virtually disappeared, to consider what alternative course our interests might demand now that the object to which our efforts had hitherto been directed was no longer attainable.

Applying these principles to Persia, we have long recognized the superior interests of Russia in the northern portion of the Shah's dominions, which must naturally result from the long extent of her conterminous frontier. Whatever steps we may have taken to maintain our position in Northern Persia have therefore been taken as much in the interests of Persia herself and of her national independence as in our own, which are not directly threatened by Russian superiority in those regions, except in so far as it might affect the Persian capital and seat of Government.

In the south, on the other hand, for fully a century our efforts have been successfully devoted to building up a substantial and pre-eminent mercantile position, with the result that we have acquired an altogether exceptional interest in that part of Persia. Persia herself has benefited immensely by these labours. . . .

It cannot reasonably be supposed that Great Britain would abandon a position attained by so many years of constant effort, or would acquiesce in attempts on the part of other Powers to acquire political predominance in the south of Persia. Although, therefore, His Majesty's Government have no desire to obstruct in any way the efforts of Russia to find a commercial entrance for her trade in the Persian Gulf, or to oppose any obstacle to the passage of her commerce from the north for export from Persian ports, they could not admit that such commercial facilities should form the pretext for the occupation by Russia of points possessing strategical importance or for the establishment of such an ascendency in the south as she already enjoys in the north.

The Persian Government should therefore distinctly understand and bear in mind that Great Britain could not consent to the acquisition by Russia of a military or naval station in the Persian Gulf, for the reason that such a station must be regarded as a challenge to Great Britain and a menace to her Indian Empire.

If the Persian Government were at any time to make such a concession to Russia, it would be necessary for His Majesty's Government to take in the Persian Gulf such measures as they might consider necessary for the protection of British interests: measures which, in view of their naval strength in those waters, would be attended with no serious difficulty.

Nor, again, could His Majesty's Government acquiesce in the concession to Russia of any preferential political rights or advantages, or any commercial monopoly or exclusive privilege in the southern or south-eastern districts of Persia, including Seistan. British interests must inevitably suffer by such concessions, and the Persian Government have themselves recognized and acquiesced in this view on more than one occasion. . . .

As regards railways, I may remind you that in March 1889 the late Shah of Persia gave a distinct promise in writing that Great Britain should have priority in the construction of a southern railway to Tehran; that if concessions for railways were given to others in the north a similar concession should be granted to an English Company in the south; and that no southern railway concession should be granted to any foreign Company without consultation with the British Government. This pledge was brought to the notice of the present Shah in April 1900, and was acknowledged by His Majesty to be of continued and binding validity.

As regards Seistan, I have quite recently, in my despatch of the 9th July, 1901, directed you to call the attention of the Persian Government to the interest which this district has for Great Britain on account of its proximity to India and its position on an important trade route between India and Persia, and to state that we regard it as of the utmost importance that it should remain free from the intrusion of foreign authority in any shape.

In all these matters, His Majesty's Government have consistently sought to maintain the continued national existence and the territorial integrity of Persia, and to develop her resources. Their policy in this respect is in strict accordance with the understanding arrived at between Great Britain and Russia in 1834, which was reaffirmed by an exchange of assurances in 1888, pledging the two Governments to respect and promote the integrity and independence of Persia. So long as the Persian Government will work with us cordially upon the lines indicated in this despatch, they will find His Majesty's Government ready to support them in the promotion and protection of what are, in fact, common objects, to the advantage of both countries alike.

If, on the other hand, in the face of our warnings, the Persian Government should elect to encourage the advance of Russian political influence and intervention in these regions in any of the forms which I have indicated above, His Majesty's Government would necessarily have to reconsider their policy; and they would regard themselves as justified in taking such measures as might appear to them best calculated to protect the interests so endangered, even though in the adoption of such measures it might no longer be possible to make the integrity and independence of Persia their first object as hitherto.

* * * *

141. Extract from Salisbury's Cabinet Memorandum, 7 January 1902. Cabinet print in P.R.O., Cab. 37/60 no. 3; Lowe, ii. 133–4.

* * * *

'Japan will, in my belief, never accept a stipulation that she is not to be allowed to take without our permission measures which we might regard as provocative but which she would defend upon the ground that they were forced upon her by the conduct of Russia. If we were to tell her that should she become involved in a quarrel with Russia in such circumstances without our concurrence, the *casus fœderis* would not be held by us to have arisen, she will, I am convinced, tell us that it is impossible for her to accept our terms.'

This extract is from the Minute circulated to the Cabinet by Lord Lansdowne on New Year's day. From the expressions used, I infer that it represents, not what the Japanese have actually said, but what Lord Lansdowne concludes from the language of their negotiations they would say if any such proposal were made to them.

But, if that is their last word, the prospect held out by the Agreement in that form is somewhat disquieting. It involves a pledge on our part to defend Japanese action in Corea and in all China against France and Russia, no matter what the *casus belli* may be. There is no limit: and no escape. We are pledged to war, though the conduct of our ally may have been followed in spite of our strongest remonstrances, and may be avowedly regarded by us with clear disapprobation. I feel sure that such a pledge will not be sanctioned by Parliament, and I think that in the interests of the Empire it ought not to be taken.

The suggestion that 'if Japan would be in a position to get us into scrapes by a too forward policy in Corea, we should equally be in a position to involve them by our action in the Yang-tsze Valley' does not seem to me to offer any solid comfort. If the Treaty imposes on us the liability of being committed against our will to a dangerous policy in Corea, it will be no consolation that Japan is committed against her will to a dangerous policy in the Yang-tsze. Japan offers us 'a formal declaration of non-aggressive policy;' but that will give us no security. It is a sentiment; not a stipulation.

Nor can I attach great importance to the plea of Japan that troubles are apt to break out on short notice, and that in case they should occur Japan may be compelled to adopt a line of policy without having time to consult us on the matter. The necessity for a decision so sudden that the telegraph will not be able to cope with the emergency is not a very probable contingency, and certainly does not furnish a justification for surrendering without reserve into the hands of another Power the right of deciding whether we shall or shall not stake the resources of the Empire on the issue of a mighty conflict.

We cannot rely on the goodwill, or the prudence, or the wise policy of the present Government of Japan, however conspicuous at present those qualities may be. Japan is, like ourselves, a Parliamentary country; and, like ourselves, is liable to have the policy of the Empire, on the most vital questions, reversed by the issue of a night's division. I do not think it will be wise to give to Japan the right of committing us to a war, unless the policy which Japan is pursuing has been approved by the British Government.

But, as I said, I do not gather from the papers that Japan has actually taken up the position which I apprehend. There is room for negotiation. I cannot think that Japan will definitively refuse us some discretion on the question whether the *casus belli* on which she is joining issue with France and Russia is one on which we can properly draw the sword.

142. Extract from Selborne's Cabinet Memorandum on 'Naval Estimates, 1903–1904', 10 October 1902. Cabinet print in P.R.O., Cab. 37/63 no. 142.

The basis of the naval policy which I have endeavoured to expound to the Cabinet in various Memoranda has been the attainment by a given date (the 31st December, 1907) of a definite margin of battleships over the next two naval Powers. This policy may be shortly described as equality plus a margin. France and Russia have, up to now, been the next two naval Powers. . . .

Since I wrote the two Memoranda for the Cabinet last autumn I have studied the naval policy of Germany more closely than I had previously done. The result of my study is that I am convinced that the new German navy is being carefully built up from the point of view of a war with us. This is also the opinion of Sir Frank Lascelles, and he has authorised me to say so. The more the composition of the new German fleet is examined the clearer it becomes that it is designed for a possible conflict with the British fleet. It cannot be designed for the purpose of playing a leading part in a future war between Germany and France and Russia. The issue of such a war can only be decided by armies and on land, and the great naval expenditure on which Germany has embarked involves a deliberate diminution of the military strength which Germany might otherwise have attained in relation to France and Russia.

*   *   *   *

Sir F. Lascelles does not believe that the German Emperor or Government are really unfriendly to this country, and he is convinced that the true interests of Germany lie in maintaining friendly relations with us; but he is equally convinced that in deciding on a naval policy we cannot safely ignore the malignant hatred of the German people or the manifest design of the German Navy.

143. Grey's Memorandum on Morocco, 20 February 1906. Grey MSS., P.R.O., F.O. 800/92; Gooch and Temperley, iii. 266–7.

The German Ambassador asked to see me yesterday for the purpose of telling me that his Government had met the last proposal of the French about police in Morocco with a point blank refusal.

If the Conference breaks up without result the situation will be very dangerous. Germany will endeavour to establish her influence in Morocco at the expense of France. France to counteract this or even simply to protect herself as a neighbour from the state of disturbance, which is now chronic in Morocco, will be driven to take action in Morocco, which Germany may make a *casus belli*.

If there is war between France and Germany it will be very difficult for us to keep out of it. The *entente* and still more the constant and emphatic demonstrations of affection (official, naval, political, commercial, Municipal and in the Press), have created in France a belief that we should support her in war. The last report from our naval attaché at Toulon said that all the French officers took this for granted, if the war was between France and Germany about Morocco. If this expectation is disappointed the French will never forgive us.

There would also I think be a general feeling in every country that we had behaved meanly and left France in the lurch. The United States would despise us, Russia would not think it worth while to make a friendly arrangement with us about Asia, Japan would prepare to re-insure herself elsewhere, we should be left without a friend and without the power of making a friend and Germany would take some pleasure, after what has passed, in exploiting the whole situation to our disadvantage, very likely by stirring up trouble through the Sultan of Turkey in Egypt. As a minor matter the position of any Foreign Secretary here, who had made it an object to maintain the *entente* with France, would become intolerable.

On the other hand the prospect of a European War and of our being involved in it is horrible.

I propose therefore, if unpleasant symptoms develop after the Conference is over, to tell the French Ambassador that a great effort and if need be some sacrifice should in our opinion be made to avoid war. To do this we should have to find out what compensation Germany would ask or accept as the price of her recognition of the French claims in Morocco. There is also a point about Egypt, which might be worked in on our behalf. I should myself be in favour of allowing Germany a port or coaling station, if that would ensure peace; but it would be necessary to consult the Admiralty about this, and to find out whether the French would entertain the idea, and if so what port?

The real objection to the course proposed is that the French may think it pusillanimous and a poor result of the *Entente*. I should have to risk this. I hope the French would recognise that in a war with Germany our liabilities would be much less than theirs. We should risk little or nothing on land, and at sea we might shut the German fleet up in Kiel and keep it there without losing a ship or a man or even firing a shot. The French would have a life and death struggle and vast expenditure of blood and treasure with a doubtful issue. They ought therefore not to think it pusillanimous on our part to wish to avoid a war in which our danger was so much less than theirs.

I have also a further point in view. The door is being kept open by us for a *rapprochement* with Russia; there is at least a prospect that when Russia is re-established we shall find ourselves on good terms with her. An *entente* between Russia, France and ourselves would be absolutely secure. If it is necessary to check Germany it could then be done. The present is the most unfavourable moment for attempting to check her. Is it not a grave mistake, if there must be a quarrel with Germany for France or ourselves to let Germany choose the moment, which best suits her.

There is a possibility that war may come before these suggestions of mine can be developed in diplomacy. If so it will only be because Germany has made up her mind that she wants war and intends to have it anyhow, which I do not believe is the case. But I think we ought in our own minds to face the question now, whether we can keep out of war, if war breaks out between France and Germany. The more I review the situation the more it appears to me that we cannot, without losing our good name and our friends and wrecking our policy and position in the world.

144. Extract from the secret 'Memorandum on the present State of British Relations with France and Germany', by Eyre Crowe (Senior Clerk in the Foreign Office), 1 January 1907. Confidential print in P.R.O., Cab. 37/86 no. 1 and F.O. 371/257; Gooch and Temperley, iii. 397–420.

* * * *

When the signature of the Algeciras Act brought to a close the first chapter of the conflict respecting Morocco, the Anglo-French *entente* had acquired a different significance from that which it had at the moment of its inception. Then there had been but a friendly settlement of particular outstanding differences, giving hope for future harmonious relations between two neighbouring countries that had got into the habit of looking at one another askance; now there had emerged an element of common resistance to outside dictation and aggression, a unity of special interests tending to develop into active co-operation against a third Power. It is essential to bear in mind that this new feature of the *entente* was the direct effect produced by Germany's effort to break it up, and that, failing the active or threatening hostility of Germany, such anti-German bias as the *entente* must be admitted to have at one time assumed, would certainly not exist at present, nor probably survive in the future. But whether the antagonism to Germany into which England had on this occasion been led without her wish or intention was but an ephemeral incident, or a symptomatic revelation of some deep-seated natural opposition between the policies and interests of the two countries, is a question which it clearly behoves British statesmen not to leave in any obscurity. To this point, then, inquiry must be directed.

The general character of England's foreign policy is determined by the immutable conditions of her geographical situation on the ocean flank of Europe as an island State with vast oversea colonies and dependencies, whose existence and survival as an independent community are inseparably bound up with the possession of pre-

ponderant sea power. The tremendous influence of such preponderance has been described in the classical pages of Captain Mahan.
No one now disputes it. Sea power is more potent than land power,
because it is as pervading as the element in which it moves and has its
being. Its formidable character makes itself felt the more directly
that a maritime State is, in the literal sense of the word, the neighbour of every country accessible by sea. It would, therefore, be but
natural that the power of a State supreme at sea should inspire
universal jealousy and fear, and be ever exposed to the danger of
being overthrown by a general combination of the world. Against
such a combination no single nation could in the long run stand,
least of all a small island kingdom not possessed of the military
strength of a people trained to arms, and dependent for its food
supply on oversea commerce. The danger can in practice only be
averted—and history shows that it has been so averted—on condition that the national policy of the insular and naval State is so
directed as to harmonize with the general desires and ideals common
to all mankind, and more particularly that it is closely identified
with the primary and vital interests of a majority, or as many as
possible, of the other nations. Now, the first interest of all countries
is the preservation of national independence. It follows that England,
more than any other non-insular Power, has a direct and positive
interest in the maintenance of the independence of nations, and
therefore must be the natural enemy of any country threatening the
independence of others, and the natural protector of the weaker
communities.

Second only to the ideal of independence, nations have always
cherished the right of free intercourse and trade in the world's
markets, and in proportion as England champions the principle of
the largest measure of general freedom of commerce, she undoubtedly strengthens her hold on the interested friendship of other nations,
at least to the extent of making them feel less apprehensive of naval
supremacy in the hands of a free trade England than they would in
the face of a predominant protectionist Power. This is an aspect of
the free trade question which is apt to be overlooked. It has been
well said that every country, if it had the option, would, of course,
prefer itself to hold the power of supremacy at sea, but that, this
choice being excluded, it would rather see England hold that power
than any other State.

History shows that the danger threatening the independence of this or that nation has generally arisen, at least in part, out of the momentary predominance of a neighbouring State at once militarily powerful, economically efficient, and ambitious to extend its frontiers or spread its influence, the danger being directly proportionate to the degree of its power and efficiency, and to the spontaneity or 'inevitableness' of its ambitions. The only check on the abuse of political predominance derived from such a position has always consisted in the opposition of an equally formidable rival, or of a combination of several countries forming leagues of defence. The equilibrium established by such a grouping of forces is technically known as the balance of power, and it has become almost an historical truism to identify England's secular policy with the maintenance of this balance by throwing her weight now in this scale and now in that, but ever on the side opposed to the political dictatorship of the strongest single State or group at a given time.

If this view of British policy is correct, the opposition into which England must inevitably be driven to any country aspiring to such a dictatorship assumes almost the form of a law of nature . . .

By applying this general law to a particular case, the attempt might be made to ascertain whether, at a given time, some powerful and ambitious State is or is not in a position of natural and necessary enmity towards England; and the present position of Germany might, perhaps, be so tested. Any such investigation must take the shape of an inquiry as to whether Germany is, in fact, aiming at a political hegemony with the object of promoting purely German schemes of expansion, and establishing a German primacy in the world of international politics at the cost and to the detriment of other nations.

*   *   *   *

. . . With 'blood and iron' Prussia had forged her position in the councils of the Great Powers of Europe In due course it came to pass that, with the impetus given to every branch of national activity by the newly-won unity, and more especially by the growing development of oversea trade flowing in ever-increasing volume through the now Imperial ports of the formerly 'independent' but politically insignificant Hanse Towns, the young empire found opened to its energy a whole world outside Europe, of which it had previously hardly had the opportunity to become more than dimly conscious. Sailing across the ocean in German ships, German merchants began for the first time to divine the true position of countries such as England, the United States, France, and even the Netherlands, whose political influence extends to distant seas and continents. The colonies and foreign possessions of England more especially were seen to give to that country a recognized and enviable status in a world where the name of Germany, if mentioned at all, excited no particular interest. The effect of this discovery upon the German mind was curious and instructive. . . . Here was distinct inequality, with a heavy bias in favour of the maritime and colonizing Powers.

Such a state of things was not welcome to German patriotic pride. Germany had won her place as one of the leading, if not, in fact, the foremost Power on the European continent. But over and beyond the European Great Powers there seemed to stand the 'World Powers.' It was at once clear that Germany must become a 'World Power.' . . .

So long . . . as Germany competes for an intellectual and moral leadership of the world in reliance on her own national advantages and energies England can but admire, applaud, and join in the race. If, on the other hand, Germany believes that greater relative preponderance of material power, wider extent of territory, inviolable frontiers, and supremacy at sea are the necessary and preliminary possessions without which any aspirations to such leadership must end in failure, then England must expect that Germany will surely seek to diminish the power of any rivals, to enhance her own by extending her dominion, to hinder the co-operation of other States, and ultimately to break up and supplant the British Empire.

Now, it is quite possible that Germany does not, nor ever will, consciously cherish any schemes of so subversive a nature. Her statesmen have openly repudiated them with indignation. . . .

But this is not a matter in which England can safely run any risks. . . . The aspect of German policy in the past . . . would warrant a belief that a further development on the same general lines would not constitute a break with former traditions, and must be considered as at least possible. In the presence of such a possibility it may well be asked whether it would be right, or even prudent, for England to incur any sacrifices or see other, friendly, nations sacrificed merely in order to assist Germany in building up step by step the fabric of a universal preponderance, in the blind confidence that in the exercise of such preponderance Germany will confer unmixed benefits on the world at large, and promote the welfare and happiness of all other peoples without doing injury to any one. There are, as a matter of fact, weighty reasons which make it particularly difficult for England to entertain that confidence. These will have to be set out in their place.

Meanwhile it is important to make it quite clear that a recognition of the dangers of the situation need not and does not imply any hostility to Germany. England herself would be the last to expect any other nation to associate itself with her in the active support of purely British interests . . . All that England on her part asks—and that is more than she has been in the habit of getting—is that, in the pursuit of political schemes which in no way affect injuriously the interests of third parties, such, for instance, as the introduction of reforms in Egypt for the sole benefit of the native population, England shall not be wantonly hampered by factious opposition. . . .

It has been so often declared, as to have become almost a diplomatic platitude, that between England and Germany, as there has never been any real clashing of material interests, so there are no unsettled controversies over outstanding questions. Yet for the last twenty years, as the archives of our Foreign Office show, German Governments have never ceased reproaching British Cabinets with want of friendliness and with persistent opposition to German political plans. A review of British relations during the same period with France, with Russia, and with the United States reveals ancient and real sources of conflict, springing from imperfectly patched-up differences of past centuries, the inelastic stipulations of antiquated treaties, or the troubles incidental to unsettled colonial frontiers. Although with these countries England has fortunately managed to continue to live in peace, there always remained sufficient elements of divergence to make the preservation of good, not to say cordial, relations an anxious problem requiring constant alertness, care, moderation, good temper, and conciliatory disposition. When particular causes of friction became too acute, special arrangements entered into succeeded as a rule in avoiding an open rupture without, however, solving the difficulties, but rather leaving the seed of further irritation behind. This was eminently the case with France until and right up to the conclusion of the Agreement of the 8th April, 1904.

A very different picture is presented by the succession of incidents which punctuate the record of contemporary Anglo-German relations. From 1884 onward, when Bismarck first launched his country into colonial and maritime enterprise, numerous quarrels arose between the two countries. They all have in common this feature—that they were opened by acts of direct and unmistakable hostility to England on the part of the German Government, and that this hostility was displayed with a disregard of the elementary rules of straightforward and honourable dealing, which was deeply resented by successive British Secretaries of State for Foreign Affairs. But perhaps even more remarkable is this other feature, also common to all these quarrels, that the British Ministers, in spite of the genuine indignation felt at the treatment to which they were subjected, in each case readily agreed to make concessions or accept compromises which not only appeared to satisfy all German demands, but were by the avowal of both parties calculated and designed to re-establish, if possible, on a firmer basis the fabric of Anglo-German friendship. To all outward appearance absolute harmony was restored on each occasion after these separate settlements, and in the intervals of fresh outbreaks it seemed true, and was persistently reiterated, that there could be no further occasion for disagreement.

. . . The immediate object of the present inquiry was to ascertain whether there is any real and natural ground for opposition between England and Germany. . . . such opposition has, in fact, existed in an ample measure for a long period, but . . . it has been caused by an entirely one-sided aggressiveness, and . . . on the part of England the most conciliatory disposition has been coupled with never-failing readiness to purchase the resumption of friendly relations by concession after concession.

It might be deduced that the antagonism is too deeply rooted in the relative position of the two countries to allow of its being bridged over by the kind of temporary expedients to which England has so long and so patiently resorted. On this view of the case it would have to be assumed that Germany is deliberately following a policy which is essentially opposed to vital British interests, and that an armed conflict cannot in the long run be averted, except by England either sacrificing those interests, with the result that she would lose her position as an independent Great Power, or making herself too strong to give Germany the chance of succeeding in a war. This is the opinion of those who see in the whole trend of Germany's policy conclusive evidence that she is consciously aiming at the establishment of a German hegemony, at first in Europe, and eventually in the world.

After all that has been said in the preceding paragraphs, it would be idle to deny that this may be the correct interpretation of the facts. There is this further seemingly corroborative evidence that such a conception of world-policy offers perhaps the only quite consistent explanation of the tenacity with which Germany pursues the construction of a powerful navy with the avowed object of creating slowly, but surely, a weapon fit to overawe any possible enemy, however formidable at sea.

There is, however, one obvious flaw in the argument. If the German design were so far-reaching and deeply thought out as this view implies, then it ought to be clear to the meanest German understanding that its success must depend very materially on England's remaining blind to it, and being kept in good humour until the moment arrived for striking the blow fatal to her power. It would be not merely worth Germany's while, it would be her imperative duty, pending the development of her forces, to win and retain England's friendship by every means in her power. No candid critic could say that this elementary strategical rule had been even remotely followed hitherto by the German Government.

. . . It might be suggested that the great German design is in reality no more than the expression of a vague, confused, and unpractical statesmanship, not fully realizing its own drift. A charitable critic might add, by way of explanation, that the well-known qualities of mind and temperament distinguishing for good or for evil the present Ruler of Germany may not improbably be largely responsible for the erratic, domineering, and often frankly aggressive spirit which is recognizable at present in every branch of German public life, not merely in the region of foreign policy; and that this spirit has called forth those manifestations of discontent and alarm both at home and abroad with which the world is becoming familiar; that, in fact, Germany does not really know what she is driving at, and that all her excursions and alarums, all her underhand intrigues do not contribute to the steady working out of a well conceived and relentlessly followed system of policy, because they do not really form part of any such system. . . .

If, merely by way of analogy and illustration, a comparison not intended to be either literally exact or disrespectful be permitted, the action of Germany towards this country since 1890 might be likened not inappropriately to that of a professional blackmailer, whose extortions are wrung from his victims by the threat of some vague and dreadful consequences in case of a refusal. To give way to the blackmailer's menaces enriches him, but it has long been proved by uniform experience that, although this may secure for the victim temporary peace, it is certain to lead to renewed molestation and higher demands after ever-shortening periods of amicable forbearance. The blackmailer's trade is generally ruined by the first resolute stand made against his exactions and the determination rather to face all risks of a possibly disagreeable situation than to continue in the path of endless concessions. But, failing such determination, it is more than probable that the relations between the two parties will grow steadily worse.

If it be possible, in this perhaps not very flattering way, to account for the German Government's persistently aggressive demeanour towards England, and the resulting state of almost perpetual friction, notwithstanding the pretence of friendship, the generally restless, explosive, and disconcerting activity of Germany in relation to all other States would find its explanation partly in the same attitude towards them and partly in the suggested want of definite political aims and purposes. A wise German statesman would recognise the limits within which any world-policy that is not to provoke a hostile combination of all the nations in arms must confine itself. He would realize that the edifice of Pan-Germanism, with its outlying bastions in the Netherlands, in the Scandinavian countries, in Switzerland, in the German provinces of Austria, and on the Adriatic, could never be built up on any other foundation than the wreckage of the liberties of Europe. A German maritime supremacy must be acknowledged to be incompatible with the existence of the British Empire, and even if that Empire disappeared, the union of the greatest military with the greatest naval Power in one State would compel the world to combine for the riddance of such an incubus. The acquisition of colonies fit for German settlement in South America cannot be reconciled with the Monroe doctrine, which is a fundamental principle of the political faith of the United States. The creation of a German India in Asia Minor must in the end stand or fall with either a German command of the sea or a German conquest of Constantinople and the countries intervening between Germany's present south-eastern frontiers and the Bosphorus. Whilst each of these grandiose schemes seems incapable of fulfilment under anything like the present conditions of the world, it looks as if Germany were playing with them all together simultaneously, and thereby wilfully concentrating in her own path all the obstacles and opposi-tions of a world set at defiance. That she should do this helps to prove how little of logical and consistent design and of unrelenting purpose lies behind the impetuous mobility, the bewildering sur-prises, and the heedless disregard of the susceptibilities of other people that have been so characteristic of recent manifestations of German policy.

If it be considered necessary to formulate and accept a theory that will fit all the ascertained facts of German policy, the choice must lie between the two hypotheses here presented:—

Either Germany is definitely aiming at a general political hege-mony and maritime ascendency, threatening the independence of her neighbours and ultimately the existence of England;

Or Germany, free from any such clear-cut ambition, and thinking for the present merely of using her legitimate position and influence as one of the leading Powers in the council of nations, is seeking to promote her foreign commerce, spread the benefits of German culture, extend the scope of her national energies, and create fresh German interests all over the world wherever and whenever a peace-ful opportunity offers, leaving it to an uncertain future to decide whether the occurrence of great changes in the world may not some day assign to Germany a larger share of direct political action over regions not now a part of her dominions, without that violation of the established rights of other countries which would be involved in any such action under existing political conditions.

In either case Germany would clearly be wise to build as powerful a navy as she can afford.

The above alternatives seem to exhaust the possibilities of explain-ing the given facts. The choice offered is a narrow one, nor easy to make with any close approach to certainty. It will, however, be seen, on reflection, that there is no actual necessity for a British Government to determine definitely which of the two theories of German policy it will accept. For it is clear that the second scheme (of semi-independent evolution, not entirely unaided by statecraft) may at any stage merge into the first, or conscious-design scheme. Moreover, if ever the evolution scheme should come to be realized, the position thereby accruing to Germany would obviously con-stitute as formidable a menace to the rest of the world, as would be presented by any deliberate conquest of a similar position by 'malice aforethought.'

It appears, then, that the element of danger present as a visible factor in one case, also enters, though under some disguise, into the second; and against such danger, whether actual or contingent, the same general line of conduct seems prescribed. It should not be difficult briefly to indicate that line in such a way as to command the assent of all persons competent to form a judgment in this matter.

So long as England remains faithful to the general principle of the preservation of the balance of power, her interests would not be served by Germany being reduced to the rank of a weak Power, as this might easily lead to a Franco-Russian predominance equally, if not more, formidable to the British Empire. There are no existing German rights, territorial or other, which this country could wish to see diminished. Therefore, so long as Germany's action does not overstep the line of legitimate protection of existing rights she can always count upon the sympathy and good-will, and even the moral support, of England.

Further, it would be neither just nor politic to ignore the claims to a healthy expansion which a vigorous and growing country like Germany has a natural right to assert in the field of legitimate endeavour. . . . It cannot be good policy for England to thwart such a process of development where it does not directly conflict either with British interests or with those of other nations to which England is bound by solemn treaty obligations. If Germany, within the limits imposed by these two conditions, finds the means peacefully and honourably to increase her trade and shipping, to gain coaling stations or other harbours, to acquire landing rights for cables, or to secure concessions for the employment of German capital or industries, she should never find England in her way.

Nor is it for British Governments to oppose Germany's building as large a fleet as she may consider necessary or desirable for the defence of her national interests. It is the mark of an independent State that it decides such matters for itself, free from any outside interference, and it would ill become England with her large fleets to dictate to another State what is good for it in matters of supreme national concern. Apart from the question of right and wrong, it may also be urged that nothing would be more likely than any attempt at such dictation, to impel Germany to persevere with her ship-building programmes. And also, it may be said in parenthesis, nothing is more likely to produce in Germany the impression of the practical hopelessness of a never-ending succession of costly naval programmes than the conviction, based on ocular demonstration, that for every Germany ship England will inevitably lay down two, so maintaining the present relative British preponderance.

It would be of real advantage if the determination not to bar Germany's legitimate and peaceful expansion, nor her schemes of naval development, were made as patent and pronounced as authoritatively as possible, provided care were taken at the same time to make it quite clear that this benevolent attitude will give way to determined opposition at the first sign of British or allied interests being adversely affected. This alone would probably do more to bring about lastingly satisfactory relations with Germany than any other course.

It is not unlikely that Germany will before long again ask, as she has so often done hitherto, for a 'close understanding' with England. To meet this contingency, the first thing to consider is what exactly is meant by the request. The Anglo-French *entente* had a very material basis and tangible object—namely, the adjustment of a number of actually-existing serious differences. The efforts now being made by England to arrive at an understanding with Russia are justified by a very similar situation. But for an Anglo-German understanding on the same lines there is no room, since none could be built up on the same foundation. . . . Into offensive or defensive alliances with Germany there is, under the prevailing political conditions, no occasion for England to enter, and it would hardly be honest at present to treat such a possibility as an open question. British assent to any other form of co-operation or system of non-interference must depend absolutely on circumstances, on the particular features, and on the merits of any proposals that may be made. All such proposals England will be as ready as she always has been to weigh and discuss from the point of view of how British interests will be affected. Germany must be content in this respect to receive exactly the same treatment as every other Power.

There is no suggestion more untrue or more unjust than that England has on any recent occasion shown, or is likely to show in future, a *parti pris* against Germany or German proposals as such, or displayed any unfairness in dealing strictly on their own merits with any question having a bearing on her relations with Germany. This accusation has been freely made. It is the stock-in-trade of all the inspired tirades against the British Government which emanate directly or indirectly from the Berlin Press Bureau. But no one has ever been able to bring forward a tittle of evidence in its support that will bear examination. The fact, of course, is that, as Mr. Balfour felt impelled to remark to the German Ambassador on a certain occasion, German communications to the British Government have not generally been of a very agreeable character, and, unless that character is a good deal modified, it is more than likely that such communications will in future receive unpalatable answers. For there is one road which, if past experience is any guide to the future, will most certainly not lead to any permanent improvement of relations with any Power, least of all Germany, and which must therefore be abandoned: that is the road paved with graceful British concessions—concessions made without any conviction either of their justice or of their being set off by equivalent counter-services. The vain hopes that in this manner Germany can be 'conciliated' and made more friendly must be definitely given up. It may be that such hopes are still honestly cherished by irresponsible people, ignorant, perhaps necessarily ignorant, of the history of Anglo-German relations during the last twenty years, which cannot be better described than as the history of a systematic policy of gratuitous concessions, a policy which has led to the highly disappointing result disclosed by the almost perpetual state of tension existing between the two countries. Men in responsible positions, whose business it is to inform themselves and to see things as they really are, cannot conscientiously retain any illusions on this subject.

Here, again, however, it would be wrong to suppose that any discrimination is intended to Germany's disadvantage. On the contrary, the same rule will naturally impose itself in the case of all other Powers. . . .

Although Germany has not been exposed to such a rebuff as France encountered in 1898, the events connected with the Algeciras Conference appear to have had on the German Government the effect of an unexpected revelation, clearly showing indications of a new spirit in which England proposes to regulate her own conduct towards France on the one hand and to Germany on the other. That the result was a very serious disappointment to Germany has been made abundantly manifest by the turmoil which the signature of the Algeciras Act has created in the country, the official, semi-official, and unofficial classes vying with each other in giving expression to their astonished discontent. The time which has since elapsed has, no doubt, been short. But during that time it may be observed that our relations with Germany, if not exactly cordial, have at least been practically free from all symptoms of direct friction, and there is an impression that Germany will think twice before she now gives rise to any fresh disagreement. In this attitude she will be encouraged if she meets on England's part with unvarying courtesy and consideration in all matters of common concern, but also with a prompt and firm refusal to enter into any one-sided bargains or arrangements, and the most unbending determination to uphold British rights and interests in every part of the globe. There will be no surer or quicker way to win the respect of the German Government and of the German nation.

145. Extract from the secret 'Observations' of Lord Sanderson (formerly Permanent Undersecretary in the Foreign Office) on Eyre Crowe's Memorandum, 21 February 1907. Grey MSS., P.R.O., F.O. 800/92 (there is a printed version in F.O. 371/257); Gooch and Temperley, iii. 421–31.

. . . the history of German policy towards this Country is not the unchequered record of black deeds which the Memorandum seems to portray. There have been many occasions on which we have worked comfortably in accord with Germany, and not a few cases in which her support has been serviceable to us. There have been others in which she has been extremely aggravating, sometimes unconsciously so, sometimes with intention. The Germans are very tight bargainers, they have earned the nickname of '*les Juifs de la diplomatie.*' The German Foreign Office hold to a traditional view of negotiation that one of the most effective methods of gaining your point is to show how intensely disagreeable you can make yourself if you do not. They are surprised that the recollection of these methods should rankle, and speaking generally the North Germans combine intense susceptibility as regards themselves with a singular inability to appreciate the susceptibilities of others.

On the other hand it is undeniable that we have at times been compelled to maintain an attitude in defence of British interests which has been very inconvenient to German ambitions. And of late

years while the British Gov[ernmen]t has remained calm and conciliatory, the press and public opinion here have interfered seriously
with our working so much together as would otherwise have been
desirable. It is not at all unnatural that the German Ambassador,
who has seen better days, should feel this rather keenly.

In considering the tendencies and methods of German policy, we
have to remember that the Empire took its present place among
the Great Powers of Europe only 35 years ago, after some 50 years of
helpless longings for united national existence. It was inevitable
that a nation flushed with success, which had been obtained at the
cost of great sacrifices, should be somewhat arrogant and over-
eager, impatient to realise various long-suppressed aspirations, and
to claim full recognition of its new position. The Government was
at the same time suffering from the constant feeling of insecurity
caused by the presence on the East and West of two powerful, jealous, and discontented neighbours. It is not surprising that with the
traditions of the Prussian monarchy behind it, it should have shown
itself restless and scheming, and have had frequent recourse to
tortuous methods, which have not proved wholly successful.

It is not, I think, to be expected that Germany will renounce her
ambition for oversea possessions, which shall assist and support
the development of her commerce, and afford openings for her surplus population. But, as time goes on, her manner of pursuing
these objects will probably be less open to exception, and popular
opinion, which in Germany is on the whole sound and prudent,
will exercise an increasing amount of wholesome restraint. If the
mere acquisition of territory were in itself immoral, I conceive that
the sins of Germany since 1871 are light in comparison to ours, and
it must be remembered that, from an outside point of view, a Country which looks to each change as a possible chance of self aggrandisement is not much more open to criticism than one which sees
in every such change a menace to its interests, existing or potential,
and founds on this theory continued claims to interference or
compensation. It has sometimes seemed to me that to a foreigner
reading our press the British Empire must appear in the light of some
huge giant sprawling over the globe, with gouty fingers and toes
stretching in every direction, which cannot be approached without
eliciting a scream. . . .

The moral which I should draw from the events of recent years
is that Germany is a helpful, though somewhat exacting, friend, that

she is a tight and tenacious bargainer, and a most disagreeable antagonist. She is oversensitive about being consulted on all questions on which she can claim a voice, either as a Great Power, or on account of special interests, and it is never prudent to neglect her on such occasions. Her diplomacy is, to put it mildly, always watchful, and any suspicion of being ignored rouses an amount of wrath disproportionate to the offence. However tiresome such discussions may be, it is, as a general rule, less inconvenient to take her at once into counsel, and to state frankly within what limits you can accept her views, than to have a claim for interference suddenly launched on you at some critical moment. It would of course be absurd to make to her any concessions of importance except as a matter of bargain and in return for value received. Her motto has always been 'Nothing for nothing in this world, and very little for sixpence.' But I do not think it can be justly said that she is ungrateful for friendly support. It is at all events unwise to meet her with an attitude of pure obstruction, such as is advocated by part of our press. A great and growing nation cannot be repressed. It is altogether contrary to reason that Germany should wish to quarrel with us though she may wish to be in a position to face a quarrel with more chances of success, than she can be said now to have. But it would be a misfortune that she should be led to believe that in whatever direction she seeks to expand, she will find the British lion in her path. There must be places in which German enterprise can find a field without injury to any important British interests, and it would seem wise that in any policy of development which takes due account of those interests she should be allowed to expect our good will.

146. Extract from Lloyd George's Mansion House Speech, 21 July 1911. *The Times*, 22 July 1911.

* * * *

But I am also bound to say this—that I believe it is essential in the highest interests, not merely of this country, but of the world, that Britain should at all hazards maintain her place and her prestige amongst the Great Powers of the world. (Cheers.) Her potent influence has many a time been in the past, and may yet be in the future, invaluable to the cause of human liberty. It has more than once in the past redeemed Continental nations, who are sometimes too apt to forget that service, from overwhelming disaster and even from national extinction. I would make great sacrifices to preserve peace. I conceive that nothing would justify a disturbance of international good will except questions of the gravest national moment. But if a situation were to be forced upon us in which peace could only be preserved by the surrender of the great and beneficent position Britain has won by centuries of heroism and achievement, by allowing Britain to be treated where her interests were vitally affected as if she were of no account in the Cabinet of nations, then I say emphatically that peace at that price would be a humiliation intolerable for a great country like ours to endure. (Cheers.) National honour is no party question. (Cheers.) The security of our great international trade is no party question; the peace of the world is much more likely to be secured if all nations realize fairly what the conditions of peace must be. And it is because I have the conviction that nations are beginning to understand each other better, to appreciate each other's points of view more thoroughly, to be more ready to discuss calmly and dispassionately their differences, that I feel assured that nothing will happen between now and next year which will render it difficult for the Chancellor of the Exchequer in this place to respond to the toast proposed by you, my Lord Mayor, of the continued prosperity of the public purse. (Cheers.)

147. Extract from Grey's House of Commons Speech on the Eve of War, 3 August 1914. *Hansard*, 5th series, lxv. 1810–27.

*   *   *   *

In the present crisis, it has not been possible to secure the peace of Europe; because there has been little time, and there has been a disposition—at any rate in some quarters on which I will not dwell—to force things rapidly to an issue, at any rate, to the great risk of peace, and, as we now know, the result of that is that the policy of peace, as far as the Great Powers generally are concerned, is in danger. I do not want to dwell on that, and to comment on it, and to say where the blame seems to us to lie, which Powers were most in favour of peace, which were most disposed to risk or endanger peace, because I would like the House to approach this crisis in which we are now, from the point of view of British interests, British honour, and British obligations, free from all passion as to why peace has not been preserved.

*   *   *   *

I come first, now, to the question of British obligations. I have assured the House—and the Prime Minster has assured the House more than once—that if any crisis such as this arose, we should come before the House of Commons and be able to say to the House that it was free to decide what the British attitude should be, that we would have no secret engagement which we should spring upon the House, and tell the House that, because we had entered into that engagement, there was an obligation of honour upon the country. I will deal with that point to clear the ground first.

There has [*sic*] been in Europe two diplomatic groups, the Triple Alliance and what came to be called the 'Triple Entente', for some years past. The Triple Entente was not an Alliance—it was a Diplomatic group. . . .

In this present crisis, up till yesterday, we have . . . given no promise of anything more than diplomatic support—up till yesterday no promise of more than diplomatic support. Now I must make this question of obligation clear to the House. I must go back to the first Moroccan crisis of 1906. That was the time of the Algeciras Conference, and it came at a time of very great difficulty to His Majesty's Government when a General Election was in progress, and Ministers were scattered over the country, and I—spending three days a week in my constituency and three days at the Foreign Office—was asked the question whether if that crisis developed into war between France and Germany we would give armed support. I said then that I could promise nothing to any foreign Power unless it was subsequently to receive the whole-hearted support of public opinion here if the occasion arose. I said, in my opinion, if war was forced upon France then on the question of Morocco—a question which had just been the subject of agreement between this country and France, an agreement exceedingly popular on both sides—that if out of that agreement war was forced on France at that time, in my view public opinion in this country would have rallied to the material support of France.

I gave no promise, but I expressed that opinion during the crisis, as far as I remember, almost in the same words, to the French Ambassador and the German Ambassador at the time. I made no promise, and I used no threats; but I expressed that opinion. That position was accepted by the French Government, but they said to me at the time—and I think very reasonably—'If you think it possible that the public opinion of Great Britain might, should a

sudden crisis arise, justify you in giving to France the armed support
which you cannot promise in advance, you will not be able to give
that support, even if you wish to give it, when the time comes,
unless some conversations have already taken place between naval
and military experts.' There was force in that. I agreed to it, and
authorised those conversations to take place, but on the distinct
understanding that nothing which passed between military or naval
experts should bind either Government or restrict in any way their
freedom to make a decision as to whether or not they would give that
support when the time arose.

As I have told the House, upon that occasion a General Election
was in prospect. I had to take the responsibility of doing that without
the Cabinet. It could not be summoned. An answer had to be given.
I consulted Sir Henry Campbell-Bannerman, the Prime Minister;
I consulted, I remember, Lord Haldane, who was then Secretary of
State for War, and the present Prime Minister, who was then
Chancellor of the Exchequer. That was the most I could do, and
they authorised that on the distinct understanding that it left the
hands of the Government free whenever the crisis arose. The fact
that conversations between military and naval experts took place was
later on—I think much later on, because that crisis passed, and the
thing ceased to be of importance—but later on it was brought to the
knowledge of the Cabinet.

The Agadir crisis came—another Morocco crisis—and throughout
that I took precisely the same line that had been taken in 1906. But
subsequently, in 1912, after discussion and consideration in the
Cabinet it was decided that we ought to have a definite understanding in writing, which was to be only in the form of an unofficial
letter, . . . on the 22nd of November, 1912, . . . to the French
Ambassador . . . that, whatever took place between military and
naval experts, they were not binding engagements upon the Government . . .

I think [it] is obvious from the letter . . . that we do not construe
anything which has previously taken place in our diplomatic relations with other Powers in this matter as restricting the freedom
of the Government to decide what attitude they should take now,
or restrict the freedom of the House of Commons to decide what
their attitude should be.

Well, Sir, I will go further, and I will say this: The situation in
the present crisis is not precisely the same as it was in the Morocco

question. In the Morocco question it was primarily a dispute which concerned France—a dispute which concerned France and France primarily—a dispute, as it seemed to us, affecting France, out of an agreement subsisting between us and France, and published to the whole world, in which we engaged to give France diplomatic support. No doubt we were pledged to give nothing but diplomatic support; we were, at any rate, pledged by a definite public agreement to stand with France diplomatically in that question.

The present crisis has originated differently. It has not originated with regard to Morocco. It has not originated as regards anything with which we had a special agreement with France; it has not originated with anything which primarily concerned France. It has originated in a dispute between Austria and Servia. I can say this with the most absolute confidence—no Government and no country has less desire to be involved in war over a dispute with Austria and Servia than the Government and the country of France. They are involved in it because of their obligation of honour under a definite alliance with Russia. Well, it is only fair to say to the House that that obligation of honour cannot apply in the same way to us. We are not parties to the Franco-Russian Alliance. We do not even know the terms of that Alliance. So far I have, I think, faithfully and completely cleared the ground with regard to the question of obligation.

I now come to what we think the situation requires of us. For many years we have had a long-standing friendship with France. [An Hon. Member: 'And with Germany!'] I remember well the feeling in the House—and my own feeling—for I spoke on the subject, I think, when the late Government made their agreement with France—the warm and cordial feeling resulting from the fact that these two nations, who had had perpetual differences in the past, had cleared these differences away. I remember saying, I think, that it seemed to me that some benign influence had been at work to produce the cordial atmosphere that had made that possible. But how far that friendship entails obligation—it has been a friendship between the nations and ratified by the nations—how far that entails an obligation let every man look into his own heart, and his own feelings, and construe the extent of the obligation for himself. I construe it myself as I feel it, but I do not wish to urge upon anyone else more than their feelings dictate as to what they should feel about the obligation. The House, individually and collectively may judge for itself. I speak my personal view, and I have given the House my own feeling in the matter.

The French Fleet is now in the Mediterranean, and the Northern and Western coasts of France are absolutely undefended. The French Fleet being concentrated in the Mediterranean the situation is very different from what it used to be, because the friendship which has grown up between the two countries has given them a sense of security that there was nothing to be feared from us. The French coasts are absolutely undefended. The French Fleet is in the Mediterranean, and has for some years been concentrated there because of the feeling of confidence and friendship which has existed between the two countries. My own feeling is that if a foreign fleet engaged in a war which France had not sought, and in which she had not been the aggressor, came down the English Channel and bombarded and battered the undefended coasts of France, we could not stand aside and see this going on practically within sight of our eyes, with our arms folded, looking on dispassionately, doing nothing! I believe that would be the feeling of this country. There are times when one feels that if these circumstances actually did arise, it would be a feeling which would spread with irresistible force throughout the land.

But I also want to look at the matter without sentiment, and from the point of view of British interests, and it is on that that I am going to base and justify what I am presently going to say to the House. If we say nothing at this moment, what is France to do with her Fleet in the Mediterranean? If she leaves it there, with no statement from us as to what we will do, she leaves her Northern and Western coasts absolutely undefended, at the mercy of a German fleet coming down the Channel, to do as it pleases in a war which is a war of life and death between them. If we say nothing, it may be that the French Fleet is withdrawn from the Mediterranean. We are in the presence of a European conflagration; can anybody set limits to the consequences that may arise out of it. Let us assume that to-day we stand aside in an attitude of neutrality, saying, 'No, we cannot undertake and engage to help either party in this conflict.' Let us suppose the French Fleet is withdrawn from the Mediterranean; and let us assume that the consequences—which are already tremendous in what has happened in Europe even to countries which are at peace—in fact, equally whether countries are at peace or at war—let us assume that out of that come consequences unforeseen, which make it necessary at a sudden moment that, in defence of vital British interests, we should go to war: and let us assume—which is quite possible—that Italy, who is now neutral—[Hon. Members: 'Hear, hear!']—because, as I understand, she considers that this war is an aggressive war, and the Triple Alliance being a defensive alliance her obligation did not arise—let us assume that consequences which are not yet foreseen—and which perfectly legitimately consulting her own interests—make Italy depart from her attitude of neutrality at a time when we are forced in defence of vital British interests ourselves to fight, what then will be the position in the Mediterranean? It might be that at some critical moment those consequences would be forced upon us because our trade routes in the Mediterranean might be vital to this country?

Nobody can say that in the course of the next few weeks there is any particular trade route the keeping open of which may not be vital to this country. What will be our position then? We have not kept a fleet in the Mediterranean which is equal to dealing alone with a combination of other fleets in the Mediterranean. It would be the very moment when we could not detach more ships to the Mediterranean, and we might have exposed this country from our negative attitude at the present moment to the most appalling risk. I say that from the point of view of British interests. We feel strongly that France was entitled to know—and to know at once!—whether or not in the event of attack upon her unprotected Northern and Western Coasts she could depend upon British support. In that emergency, and in these compelling circumstances, yesterday afternoon I gave to the French Ambassador the following statement:

'I am authorised to give an assurance that if the German Fleet comes into the Channel or through the North Sea to undertake hostile operations against the French coasts or shipping, the British Fleet will give all the protection in its power. This assurance is, of course, subject to the policy of His Majesty's Government receiving the support of Parliament, and must not be taken as binding His Majesty's Government to take any action until the above contingency of action by the German Fleet takes place.'

I read that to the House, not as a declaration of war on our part, not as entailing immediate action on our part, but as binding us to take aggressive action should that contingency arise. Things move very hurriedly from hour to hour. Fresh news comes in, and I cannot give this in any very formal way; but I understand that the

17—F.P.V.E.

German Government would be prepared, if we would pledge our-selves to neutrality, to agree that its Fleet would not attack the Northern coast of France. I have only heard that shortly before I came to the House, but it is far too narrow an engagement for us. And, Sir, there is the more serious consideration—becoming more serious every hour—there is the question of the neutrality of Belgium.

I shall have to put before the House at some length what is our position in regard to Belgium. The governing factor is the Treaty of 1839, but this is a Treaty with a history—a history accumulated since. . . .

. . . It is one of those Treaties which are founded, not only on consideration for Belgium, which benefits under the Treaty, but in the interests of those who guarantee the neutrality of Belgium. The honour and interests are, at least, as strong to-day as in 1870, and we cannot take a more narrow view or a less serious view of our obligations, and of the importance of those obligations than was taken by Mr. Gladstone's Government in 1870.

I will read to the House what took place last week on this subject. When mobilisation was beginning, I knew that this question must be a most important element in our policy—a most important subject for the House of Commons. I telegraphed at the same time in similar terms to both Paris and Berlin to say that it was essential for us to know whether the French and German Governments respectively were prepared to undertake an engagement to respect the neutrality of Belgium. . . .

It now appears from the news I have received to-day . . . that an ultimatum has been given to Belgium by Germany, the object of which was to offer Belgium friendly relations with Germany on condition that she would facilitate the passage of German troops through Belgium. . . . We were sounded in the course of last week as to whether if a guarantee were given that, after the war, Belgium [*sic*] integrity would be preserved that would content us. We replied that we could not bargain away whatever interests or obligations we had in Belgian neutrality.

Shortly before I reached the House I was informed that the following telegram had been received from the King of the Belgians by our King—King George:—

'Remembering the numerous proofs of your Majesty's friendship and that of your predecessors, and the friendly attitude of England in 1870, and the proof of friendship she has just given us again, I make a supreme appeal to the Diplomatic intervention of your Majesty's Government to safeguard the integrity of Belgium.'

Diplomatic intervention took place last week on our part. What can diplomatic intervention do now? We have great and vital interests in the independence—and integrity is the least part—of Belgium. If Belgium is compelled to submit to allow her neutrality to be violated, of course the situation is clear. Even if by agreement she admitted the violation of her neutrality, it is clear she could only do so under duress. The smaller States in that region of Europe ask but one thing. Their one desire is that they should be left alone and independent. The one thing they fear is, I think, not so much that their integrity but that their independence should be interfered with. If in this war which is before Europe the neutrality of one of those countries is violated, if the troops of one of the combatants violate its neutrality and no action be taken to resent it, at the end of the war, whatever the integrity may be, the independence will be gone.

* * * *

No, Sir, if it be the case that there has been anything in the nature of an ultimatum to Belgium, asking her to compromise or violate her neutrality, whatever may have been offered to her in return, her independence is gone if that holds. If her independence goes, the independence of Holland will follow. I ask the House from the point of view of British interests, to consider what may be at stake. If France is beaten in a struggle of life and death, beaten to her knees, loses her position as a great Power, becomes subordinate to the will and power of one greater than herself—consequences which I do not anticipate, because I am sure that France has the power to defend herself with all the energy and ability and patriotism which she has shown so often—still, if that were to happen, and if Belgium fell under the same dominating influence, and then Holland, and then Denmark, then would not Mr. Gladstone's words come true, that just opposite to us there would be a common interest against the unmeasured aggrandisement of any Power?

It may be said, I suppose, that we might stand aside, husband our strength, and that whatever happened in the course of this war at the end of it intervene with effect to put things right, and to adjust them to our own point of view. If, in a crisis like this, we run away from those obligations of honour and interest as regards the Belgian Treaty, I doubt whether, whatever material force we might have at the end, it would be of very much value in face of the respect that we should have lost. And do not believe, whether a great Power stands outside this war or not, it is going to be in a position at the end of it to exert its superior strength. For us, with a powerful Fleet, which we believe able to protect our commerce, to protect our shores and to protect our interests, if we are engaged in war, we shall suffer but little more than we shall suffer even if we stand aside.

We are going to suffer, I am afraid, terribly in this war whether we are in it or whether we stand aside. Foreign trade is going to stop, not because the trade routes are closed, but because there is no trade at the other end. Continental nations engaged in war—all their populations, all their energies, all their wealth, engaged in a desperate struggle—they cannot carry on the trade with us that they are carrying on in times of peace, whether we are parties to the war or whether we are not. I do not believe for a moment, that at the end of this war, even if we stood aside and remained aside, we should be in a position, a material position to use our force decisively to undo what had happened in the course of the war, to prevent the whole of the West of Europe opposite to us—if that has been the result of the war—falling under the domination of a single Power, and I am quite sure that our moral position would be such as to have lost us all respect. . . .

What other policy is there before the House? There is but one way in which the Government could make certain at the present moment of keeping outside this war, and that would be that it should immediately issue a proclamation of unconditional neutrality. We cannot do that. We have made the commitment to France that I have read to the House which prevents us from doing that. We have got the consideration of Belgium which prevents us also from any unconditional neutrality, and, without those conditions absolutely satisfied and satisfactory, we are bound not to shrink from proceeding to the use of all the forces in our power. If we did take that line by saying, 'We will have nothing whatever to do with this matter' under no conditions—the Belgian Treaty obligations, the possible position in the Mediterranean, with damage to British interests, and what may happen to France from our failure to support France —if we were to say that all those things mattered nothing, were as nothing, and to say we would stand aside, we should, I believe, sacrifice our respect and good name and reputation before the world, and should not escape the most serious and grave economic consequences.

* * * *

NOTES ON FURTHER READING

For the European context, the best work in English, unfortunately covering only the period after 1848, is A. J. P. Taylor, *The Struggle For Mastery
in Europe 1848–1918* (Oxford, 1954). There is no satisfactory general
history of British foreign policy. The *Cambridge History of British Foreign
Policy*, edited by A. Ward and G. P. Gooch (3 vols., Cambridge, 1923),
is largely out of date, though still useful in parts. R. W. Seton-Watson,
Britain in Europe 1789–1914. A Survey of Foreign Policy (Cambridge,
1937), is better but rather biased in places and not very reliable for the
period after 1870. C. J. Lowe, *The Reluctant Imperialists. British Foreign
Policy 1878–1902* (2 vols., London, 1967), is therefore essential; it also
has a volume of useful documents.

There is an enormous quantity of printed material, particularly in the
series of *Parliamentary Papers* and in the volumes of *State Papers* edited
by E. Hertslet. Hertslet's *The Map of Europe by Treaty* (4 vols., London,
1875–91) contains the most important documents, but is still very unwieldy. Harold Temperley and Lillian M. Penson, *A Century of Diplomatic Blue Books 1814–1914* (Cambridge, 1938), is an essential guide to
the Parliamentary Papers, but see the warnings in Sheila Lambert's
review article on the reissue of this work (*Historical Journal*, x (1967),
125–31). Temperley and Penson's *Foundations of British Foreign Policy
from Pitt (1792) to Salisbury (1902)* (Cambridge, 1938) is a useful
collection of documents.

For the influence of the Crown there is Frank Hardie, *The Political
Influence of Queen Victoria 1861–1901* (Oxford, 1935), and this should be
supplemented by H. Hearder, 'Queen Victoria and Foreign Policy.
Royal Intervention in the Italian Question, 1859–1860', in K. Bourne and
D. C. Watt, eds., *Studies in International History. Essays Presented to
W. Norton Medlicott* (London, 1967), and by Frank Eyck, *The Prince
Consort* (London, 1959). But the Foreign Office still awaits its historian
and there is very little of a general kind on the influence of press, public
opinion, and parliament. But there are: the charming *Recollections of the
Old Foreign Office* (London, 1901) by its Librarian, Sir Edward Hertslet;
the chapter on 'The Foreign Office' by Algernon Cecil in volume III of
the *Cambridge History of British Foreign Policy*; S. T. Bindoff, 'The

Unreformed Diplomatic Service, 1812–1860', *Transactions of the Royal Historical Society*, 4th series, xviii (1935), 143–72; and Zara S. Steiner, *The Foreign Office and Foreign Policy, 1898–1914* (Cambridge, 1969). A. Aspinall's *Politics and The Press c. 1780–1850* (London, 1949) contains a good deal about foreign affairs. On parliament there are: Valerie Cromwell, 'The Private Member of the House of Commons and Foreign Policy in the Nineteenth Century', in *Liber Memorialis Sir Maurice Powicke. Studies Presented to the International Commission for the History of Representative and Parliamentary Institutions* (Dublin, 1963), and Peter Godfrey Richards, *Parliament and Foreign Affairs* (London, 1967). Much more will be found on these matters, however, in studies of individual Foreign Secretaries.

The classic works on Castlereagh and Canning are Sir Charles Webster, *The Foreign Policy of Castlereagh 1815–1822* (2nd ed., London, 1934), and Harold Temperley, *The Foreign Policy of Canning 1822–1827* (2nd ed., London, 1925). For Palmerston there is no really satisfactory general study. The best modern biography is Herbert C. F. Bell, *Lord Palmerston* (2 vols., London, 1936). Sir Charles Webster's *The Foreign Policy of Palmerston 1830–1841* (2 vols., London, 1951) is the definitive work within its chosen limits but it deals only with European affairs. Donald Southgate, *'The Most English Minister . . .'. The Policies and Politics of Palmerston* (London, 1966), is a rather awkward but none the less useful survey based on the published sources. No modern studies of the general policies of Aberdeen, Russell, Clarendon, Malmesbury, or Granville have been published, though there are biographies of a kind for all of them. There is a good deal about the Fifteenth Earl of Derby in A. A. W. Ramsay, *Idealism and Foreign Policy* (London, 1925), and in the biographies of Disraeli by W. F. Monypenny and George Earle Buckle, *The Life of Benjamin Disraeli Earl of Beaconsfield* (6 vols., London, 1910–20), and by Robert Blake, *Disraeli* (London, 1967). P. Knaplund, *The Foreign Policy of Mr. Gladstone* (New York, 1935), needs to be supplemented by R. T. Shannon, *Gladstone and the Bulgarian Agitation, 1876* (London, 1963), and W. N. Medlicott, *Bismarck, Gladstone, and the Concert of Europe* (London, 1956). For Salisbury, Lady Gwendolen Cecil's unfinished *Life of Robert Marquis of Salisbury* (4 vols., London, 1921–32) is still essential. To it should be added the very important articles by Lillian M. Penson: 'The Foreign Policy of Lord Salisbury, 1878–80. The Problem of the Ottoman Empire', in A. Coville and H. W. V. Temperley, eds., *Studies in Anglo-French History* (Cambridge, 1935); 'The Principles and Methods of Salisbury's Foreign Policy', *Cambridge Historical Journal*, v (1935–7), 87–106; 'The New Course in British Foreign Policy, 1892–1902', *Transactions of the Royal Historical Society*, 4th series, xxv (1943), 121–38; and *Foreign Affairs under the Third Marquis of Salisbury* (Creighton Lecture, London, 1962). Essential also are C. J. Lowe, *Salisbury and the Mediterranean 1886–1896* (London, 1965), and, above all, J. A. S. Grenville, *Lord Salisbury and Foreign Policy. The Close of the Nineteenth Century* (London, 1964). There is also an interesting recent essay on a subject of abiding misunderstanding, Christopher Howard, *Splendid Isolation. A study of ideas concerning Britain's international position and foreign policy during the later years of the third Marquis of Salisbury* (London, 1967). For the remaining Foreign Secretaries the material has only recently become available which will lead to important new studies. On Kimberley there is at present nothing; for Rosebery there is only Robert Rhodes James's *Rosebery: a Biography of Archibald Philip, Fifth Earl of Rosebery* (London, 1963); Lord, Newton's *Lord Lansdowne. A Biography* (London, 1929) and the inadequate memoirs and biographical studies of Grey need to be supplemented by G. W. Monger, *The End of Isolation. British Foreign Policy 1900–1907* (London, 1963), and Zara S. Steiner, *The Foreign Office and Foreign Policy, 1898–1914* (Cambridge, 1969).

There is a vast number of biographies and collections of letters of diplomatists. Only a few of the most important can be mentioned here: S. Lane-Poole, *Life of Stratford Canning, Lord Stratford de Redcliffe* (2 vols., London, 1888); Lord Newton, *Life of Lord Lyons* (2 vols., London, 1913); Mrs. Rosslyn Wemyss, *Memoirs and Letters of Sir Robert Morier* (2 vols., London, 1911); and R. B. Mowat, *The Life of Lord Pauncefote* (London, 1929). There are also a few works of interest on critics of foreign policy: W. H. Dawson, *Richard Cobden and Foreign Policy* (London, 1926); A. A. W. Ramsay, *Idealism and Foreign Policy* (London, 1925), for the 'sixties; A. J. P. Taylor, *The Trouble Makers. Dissent over Foreign Policy 1792–1939* (London, 1957); and A. C. F. Beales, *The History of Peace: a Short Account of the Organized Movements for International Peace* (New York, 1931).

For economic and commercial influences on foreign policy there is an important recent book: D. C. M. Platt, *Finance, Trade, and Politics in British Foreign Policy 1815–1914* (Oxford, 1968). Also useful are: Leland H. Jenks, *The Migration of British Capital to 1875* (London 1927); Albert H. Imlah, *Economic Elements in the Pax Britannica* (Cambridge, Mass., 1958); and Herbert Feis, *Europe, the World's Banker, 1870–1914* (New York, 1930).

Naval and military factors have only recently been getting the attention they deserve. There is still nothing of much importance on the army but the navy has: C. J. Bartlett, *Great Britain and Sea Power 1815–1853* (Oxford, 1963); G. S. Graham, *The Politics of Naval Supremacy* (Cambridge, 1965); and Arthur J. Marder's *The Anatomy of British Sea Power.*

A History of British Naval Policy in the Pre-Dreadnought Era, 1880–1905 (New York, 1964) and *From the Dreadnought to Scapa Flow. The Royal Navy in the Fisher Era, 1904–1919* (3 vols., London, 1961–6).

Among problems of special interest to England the Near Eastern Question figures persistently and prominently. There is no detailed history of British policy but there is, fortunately, M. S. Anderson, *The Eastern Question 1774–1923* (London, 1966). The following are the most useful among the many monographs in English. C. W. Crawley, *The Question of Greek Independence, 1821–1833* (Cambridge, 1930), and V. J. Puryear, *International Economics and Diplomacy in the Near East, 1834–1853* (Stanford, 1935). For the Crimean War: Puryear's controversial *England, Russia, and the Straits Question, 1844–1856* (Berkeley, 1931); H. W. V. Temperley, *England and the Near East: the Crimea* (London, 1936); G. B. Henderson, *Crimean War Diplomacy and Other Historical Essays* (Glasgow, 1947); J. B. Conacher, *The Aberdeen Coalition 1852–1855* (Cambridge, 1968); and B. K. Martin, *The Triumph of Lord Palmerston* (London, 1924). For post-Crimean developments: T. W. Riker, *The Making of Rumania: a study of an International Problem, 1856–1866* (Oxford, 1931); and W. E. Mosse, *The Rise and Fall of the Crimean System 1855–71* (Cambridge, 1963). For the great crisis of 1875–8 and its aftermath: B. H. Sumner, *Russia and the Balkans 1870–1880* (Oxford, 1937); Mihailo D. Stojanović, *The Great Powers and the Balkans 1875–1878* (Cambridge, 1931); D. Harris, *A Diplomatic History of the Balkan Crisis of 1875–1878: the First Year* (Stanford, 1936); R. W. Seton-Watson, *Disraeli, Gladstone and the Eastern Question* (London, 1933); W. N. Medlicott, *The Congress of Berlin and After* (2nd ed., London, 1963), 'Bismarck and Beaconsfield', in *Studies in Diplomatic History and Historiography in Honour of G. P. Gooch*, ed. by A. O. Sarkissian (London, 1961), and *Bismarck, Gladstone, and the Concert of Europe* (London, 1956); and R. T. Shannon, *Gladstone and the Bulgarian Agitation, 1876* (London, 1963). To the works already mentioned on the Salisbury period should be added: Dwight E. Lee, *Great Britain and the Cyprus Convention Policy of 1878* (Cambridge, Mass., 1934); Colin L. Smith, *The Embassy of Sir William White at Constantinople 1886–1891* (Oxford, 1957); W. N. Medlicott, 'The powers and the unification of the two Bulgarias, 1885', *English Historical Review*, liv (1939), 67–82 and 263–84, and 'The Mediterranean Agreements of 1887', *Slavonic and East European Review*, v (1926), 60–88; F. H. Hinsley, 'Bismarck, Salisbury and the Mediterranean Agreements of 1887', *Historical Journal*, i (1958), 76–81; Margaret M. Jefferson, 'Lord Salisbury and the Eastern Question, 1890–1898', *Slavonic and East European Review*, xxxix (1960–1), 44–60; and J. A. S. Grenville, 'Goluchowski, Salisbury and the Mediterranean Agreements, 1895–1897', ibid., xxxvi (1957–8), 340–69.

For Africa the best general work is R. Robinson and J. Gallagher, *Africa and the Victorians* (London, 1961). On Morocco there are F. R. Flournoy, *British Policy towards Morocco in the Age of Palmerston, 1830–1865* (London, 1935), and A. J. P. Taylor, 'British Policy in Morocco, 1886–1902', *English Historical Review*, lxvi (1951), 342–74.

On Central Africa there is R. T. Anstey, *Britain and the Congo in the Nineteenth Century* (Oxford, 1962). On West Africa there is J. D. Hargreaves, *Prelude to the Partition of West Africa* (London, 1963). But see also the dispute in D. R. Gillard, 'Salisbury's African Policy and the Heligoland Offer of 1890', *English Historical Review*, lxxv (1960), 631–53, Sanderson, 'The Anglo-German Agreement of 1890 and the Upper Nile', ibid., lxviii (1963), 49–72, and Gillard, 'Salisbury's Heligoland Offer: The Case against the "Witu Thesis" ', ibid., lxxx (1965), 538–52.

The most important recent contribution on Africa is G. N. Sanderson, *England, Europe & the Upper Nile, 1882–1899* (Edinburgh, 1965). The standard work on the Suez Canal is C. W. Hallberg, *The Suez Canal: its History and Diplomatic Importance* (New York, 1931). Douglas Antony Farnie, *East and West of Suez: the Suez Canal in History, 1854–1956* (Oxford, 1969), is encyclopaedic rather than enlightening. To these should be added K. Bell, 'British Policy towards the Construction of the Suez Canal, 1859–65', in *Transactions of the Royal Historical Society*, 5th series, xv (1965), 121–43, and H. L. Hoskins, *British Routes to India* (New York, 1928).

Persian and Central Asian Questions are unevenly covered. Several very useful articles on these subjects are reprinted in A. P. Thornton, *For the File on Empire* (London, 1968). Other important monographs are: J. A. Norris, *The First Afghan War, 1838–1842* (Cambridge, 1967); John Barrett Kelly, *Britain and the Persian Gulf, 1795–1880* (Oxford, 1968); Firuz Kazemzadeh, *Russia and Britain in Persia, 1864–1914: a study in imperialism* (New Haven, 1968); Briton Cooper Busch, *Britain and the Persian Gulf, 1894–1914* (Berkeley and Los Angeles, 1967); Rose Louise Greaves, *Persia and the Defence of India 1884–1892* (London, 1959), and the same author's 'British Policy in Persia, 1892–1903', *Bulletin of the School of Oriental and African Studies*, xxviii (1965), 34–60 and 284–307. There is a useful essay by D. R. Gillard on 'Salisbury and the Indian Defence Problem, 1885–1902', in Bourne and Watt, *Studies in International History*. There is also G. J. Alder, *British India's Northern Frontier 1865–1895* (London, 1963).

On the Far East a good detailed chronological coverage is provided for China by: W. C. Costin, *Great Britain and China, 1833–1860* (Oxford, 1937); John King Fairbank, *Trade and Diplomacy on the China Coast,*

1842–1854 (Cambridge, Mass., 1964); J. S. Gregory, *Great Britain and the Taipings* (London, 1969); and E. V. G. Kiernan, *British Diplomacy in China, 1880–1885* (London, 1939). For Japan there are W. G. Beasley, *Great Britain and the Opening of Japan, 1834–1858* (London, 1951), Grace Fox, *Britain and Japan 1858–1883* (Oxford, 1969), and *The Anglo-Japanese Alliance. The Diplomacy of Two Island Empires 1894–1907*, by Ian H. Nish (London, 1966).

So far as the Americas are concerned there is not a great deal of major interest on direct relations with Latin American countries. Old but still the only work of its kind is J. Fred Rippy, *Latin America in World Politics* (New York, 1928). Other books worth noting are H. S. Ferns, *Britain and Argentina in the Nineteenth Century* (Oxford, 1960); J. F. Cady, *Foreign Intervention in the Rio de la Plata, 1835–50* (Philadelphia, 1929); and on the intervention in Mexico the unwieldy Carl H. Bock, *Prelude to Tragedy. The Negotiation and Breakdown of the Tripartite Convention of London, October 31, 1861* (Philadelphia, 1966). There is both an important collection of documents and a very useful introductory essay in C. K. Webster, ed., *Britain and the Independence of Latin America, 1810–1830* (2 vols., London, 1938). But Latin American questions have received most attention in the context of Anglo-American relations.

H. C. Allen, *Great Britain and the United States. A History of Anglo-American Relations (1783–1952)* (London, 1954), is the essential standard work. Kenneth Bourne, *Britain and the Balance of Power in North America 1815–1908* (London, 1967), makes a detailed examination of the naval and military aspects of British policy. Still of great importance are Dexter Perkins's three volumes, covering respectively the years 1823–6, 1826–67, and 1867–1902, on *The Monroe Doctrine* (Cambridge, Mass., 1927, and Baltimore, 1933 and 1937). The period of the 1812 War is examined in Bradford Perkins, *Castlereagh and Adams. England and the United States 1812–1823* (Berkeley and Los Angeles, 1964). Some aspects of the Canadian boundary questions and other disputes in the 1840s are covered in Wilbur Devereux Jones, *Lord Aberdeen and the Americas* (Athens, Georgia, 1958), and Frederick Merk, *The Oregon Question* (Cambridge, Mass., 1967). R. A. Humphreys's 'Anglo-American Rivalries in Central America', *Transactions of the Royal Historical Society*, 5th series, xviii (1968), 174–208, provides an excellent introduction to the scattered and uneven literature on this complicated subject. Ephraim Douglass Adams, *Great Britain and the American Civil War* (2 vols., London, 1925), is still the standard work. But Lionel Gelber, *The Rise of Anglo-American Friendship. A Study in World Politics 1898–1906* (Oxford, 1938), has been substantially revised by the work done since the opening of private and official British archives for the period it concerns. There are important revisions in: A. E. Campbell, *Great Britain and the United States 1895–1903* (London, 1960); Charles S. Campbell, Jr., *Anglo-American Understanding, 1898–1903* (Baltimore, 1957); R. G. Neale, *Britain and American Imperialism 1898–1900* (Brisbane, 1965); and J. A. S. Grenville, 'Great Britain and the Isthmian Canal', *American Historical Review*, lxi (1955–6), 48–69. Also useful is R. A. Humphreys, 'Anglo-American Rivalries and the Venezuela Crisis of 1895', *Transactions of the Royal Historical Society*, 5th series, xvii (1967), 131–64.

For European questions there is much in the works on the Eastern Question and, for the early period in particular, in the studies of Castlereagh, Canning, and Palmerston already mentioned. In addition there are on earlier Anglo-French relations: J. Hall, *England and the Orléans Monarchy* (London, 1912); E. Jones-Parry, *The Spanish Marriages, 1841–1876* (London, 1936); and A. B. Cunningham, 'Peel, Aberdeen and the *Entente Cordiale*', *Bulletin of the Institute of Historical Research*, xxx (1957), 189–206. On the period of the 1848 revolutions there are: Charles Sproxton, *Palmerston and the Hungarian Revolution* (Cambridge, 1919); Ann G. Imlah, *Britain and Switzerland 1845–60* (London, 1966); W. Carr, *Schleswig-Holstein 1815–1848* (Manchester, 1963), and Holger Hjelholt, *British Mediation in the Danish-German Conflict 1848–1850* (2 parts, Copenhagen, 1965–6); and A. J. P. Taylor, *The Italian Problem in European Diplomacy, 1847–1849* (Manchester, 1934). For the climax of the Italian Question there is Derek Beales, *England and Italy 1859–60* (London, 1961). *Germany and England. Background of Conflict 1848–1894*, by Raymond James Sontag (New York, 1938), is still useful. But to it should be added: W. E. Mosse, *The European Powers and the German Question 1848–71* (Cambridge, 1958); the same author's 'Queen Victoria and her Ministers in the Schleswig-Holstein Crisis 1863–1864', *English Historical Review*, lxxviii (1963), 263–83, and 'The Crown and Foreign Policy. Queen Victoria and the Austro-Prussian Conflict, March-May, 1866', *Cambridge Historical Journal*, x (1950–2), 205–23; and Richard Millman, *British Policy and the Coming of the Franco-Prussian War* (Oxford, 1965). Also important is W. E. Mosse's 'England and the Polish Insurrection of 1863', *English Historical Review*, lxxi (1956), 28–55.

The 1870s and 1880s are again dominated by the Eastern Question, but William L. Langer's *European Alliances and Alignments 1871–1890* (2nd ed., New York, 1950) is a magnificent general work and A. F. Pribram's lectures on *England and the International Policy of the European Great Powers 1871–1914* (Oxford, 1931) are still a useful introduction to the period. For the turn of the century Z. S. Steiner, 'The Last Years of the Old Foreign Office, 1898–1905', *Historical Journal*, vi (1963), 59–90, is interesting, but British policy is only incidentally covered in Christopher

Andrew, *Théophile Delcassé and the Making of the Entente Cordiale. A Reappraisal of French Foreign Policy 1898–1905* (London, 1968). Paul Jacques Victor Rolo, *Entente Cordiale: the Origins and Negotiations of the Anglo-French Agreements of 8 April, 1904* (London, 1969), adds nothing new. But there is a solid monograph, based on newly available sources, in G. W. Monger, *The End of Isolation. British Foreign Policy 1900–1907* (London, 1963). The sources are now available for the story to be continued but nothing on a similar scale for the period down to 1914 has yet appeared. Zara S. Steiner, *The Foreign Office and Foreign Policy, 1898–1914* (Cambridge, 1969), is useful but deals mainly with administrative history. In the meantime we must rely on the massive Luigi Albertini, *The Origins of the War of 1914* (3 vols., London, 1952–7). But special mention should, however, be made of E. L. Woodward's *Great Britain and the German Navy* (Oxford, 1935) and Herbert Feis, *Europe, the World's Banker, 1870–1914: An Account of European Foreign Investment and the Connection of World Finance with Diplomacy before the War* (New York, 1930).

INDEX

Abdul Hamid II (Sultan of Turkey, 1876–1909), 135, 136, 156

Abdurrahman (Emir of Afghanistan, 1880–1901), 143, 144

Aberdeen, George Hamilton Gordon, 4th Earl of (1784–1860: Foreign Secretary, 1828–30, 1841–6; Prime Minister, 1852–5), 81, 87, 120, 152, 304; and boundaries of Greece, 23; on Treaty of Adrianople, 34, 210–15; Foreign Secretary under Peel, 47; condemns Palmerston, 47; concludes peace with China, 47; and Afghan War, 47–8; and the *entente* with France, 48, 53–5, 264–7; and U.S.A., 50–6, 255–6, 261, 262–3; threatens to resign over war preparations, 55, 264–7; and Spanish Marriages, 58–9, 270–2; forms coalition, 71; his 1844 agreement with Russia, 73, 258–61; and Turkish crisis of 1852–4, 74, 76, 78, 316–17; resigns premiership, 78; and Central American Question, 87; and Belgian guarantee, 401

Abyssinia, 38, 150, 429

Acre, 27, 43, 239

Adams, John Quincy, 15–16

Adana, 243

Aden, 38

Adowa, 160

Adrianople, Treaty of (1829), 23–4, 34, 210–15

Adriatic, 191, 488

Aegean, 74, 411, 412

Afghanistan, Anglo-Russian competition in, 34–7, 42, 135, 141–4, 151, 163, 185–6, 226, 404, 423–5; first British war with, 35, 36–7, 47–8; second war with, 142–4, 417–19

Africa, 265; part of Britain's 'informal empire', 5; French expansion in, 24, 53, 54, 136–7, 139, 140, 333–4; Anglo-German relations in, 140, 150, 152, 429, 453–4; Italy and, 147; in Mediterranean Agreements, 147–8; Fashoda crisis, 152–3, 434–5; in 1904 *entente*,

182; *see also*, Algeria, Egypt, Morocco, South Africa, etc.

Agadir, 188, 191, 498

Aix-la-Chapelle, Congress of (1818), 219

Akkerman, Convention of (1826), 21, 22

Alabama, Anglo-American dispute concerning, 93–5, 387, 396

Aland, 78

Alaska, 174, 460

Albania, 191, 239, 413, 433

Albert, Prince Consort, 58, 344; attitude to Palmerston, 48, 59, 68; criticizes Stratford de Redcliffe's policy at Constantinople, 75

Aleppo, 243

Alexander I (Tsar of Russia, 1801–25), and Greece, 13, 19–20; and Spain, 13; peace plans agreed with Pitt, 197–8; and maintenance of Turkish Empire, 213; and Poland, 365–6; death, 20

Alexander II (Tsar of Russia, 1855–81), ends Crimean War, 78–80; opposed to revolutionary nationalism, 98; and Polish revolt, 107, 366; and Bulgarian crisis, 130, 408–9

Alexander of Battenberg (Prince of Bulgaria, 1879–86), 146, 147, 148, 425–6

Alexandria, 139, 230, 240, 345, 448, 449

Alexandria, 94

Algeciras Conference (1906), 183–4, 479–80, 481, 492, 497

Algeria, 24, 54, 231, 268, 273, 346

Alsace-Lorraine, 124, 165

Alvensleben Convention (1863), 105

America, *see* British North America, Central America, Latin America, United States

Ancillon, John Peter Frederick, 222, 228

Ancona, 32–3

Andrássy, Count Julius, 126–7

Angola, 140

Angra Pequena, 140

Ankara, 180